INDIVIDUALS AND GROUPS

UNDERSTANDING SOCIAL BEHAVIOR

CORE BOOKS IN PSYCHOLOGY SERIES

Edward L. Walker, Editor

Personality: Effective and Ineffective
David G. Martin, The University of Manitoba

Environmental Psychology
Norman W. Heimstra, The University of South Dakota
Leslie H. McFarling, The University of South Dakota

Environments: Notes and Selections on Objects, Spaces, and Behavior
Stephen Friedman, Montclair State College
Joseph B. Juhasz, University of Colorado, Boulder

Human Socialization
Elton B. McNeil, The University of Michigan

Abnormal Psychology: Foundations, Issues, Disorders, Therapies
Anthony J. Marsella, University of Hawaii

Individuals and Groups: Understanding Social Behavior
Albert A. Harrison, The University of California at Davis

The Scope of Motivation: Environmental, Physiological, Mental, and Social
Wilson McTeer, Wayne State University

Psychological Theories and Human Learning: Kongor's Report
Guy R. Lefrancois, The University of Alberta

Behavior Modification: Theory and Practice
A. Robert Sherman, The University of California, Santa Barbara

Operant Learning: Procedures for Changing Behavior
Jon L. Williams, Kenyon College

An Introduction to Cognitive Psychology
Melvin Manis, The University of Michigan

An Invitation to Cognitive Psychology
W. Lambert Gardiner

Motivation: Theories and Issues
Fred P. Valle, University of British Columbia

Comparative Animal Behavior
Richard A. Maier, Loyola University, Chicago
Barbara M. Maier

Readings in Ethology and Comparative Psychology
Michael W. Fox, Washington University

Experimental Contributions to Clinical Psychology
Erasmus L. Hoch, The University of Michigan

INDIVIDUALS AND GROUPS

UNDERSTANDING SOCIAL BEHAVIOR

Albert A. Harrison

The University of California at Davis

Brooks/Cole Publishing Company

Monterey, California

A Division of Wadsworth Publishing Company, Inc.

Cartoons by Bill Bates, Carmel, California

ISBN: 0-8185-0176-6
L.C. Catalog Card No.: 75-25147
Printed in the United States of America

10 9 8 7 6 5 4 3 2

Production Editor: *Micky Lawler*
Interior & Cover Design: *John Edeen*
Cover Photograph: *Jim Pinckney*
Technical Illustrations: *Reed Sanger*
Typesetting: *Typothetae, Inc., Palo Alto, California*
Printing & Binding: *R. R. Donnelley & Sons Co., Crawfordsville, Indiana*

To Mary Ann and to Kathy

Preface

An introductory course in social psychology can be a cooperative venture involving the student, the instructor, and the author of a text. Ideally, all parties in this venture would meet to discuss hopes, demands, and expectations, but the limitations of the printed page prevent the full realization of this ideal. Here, however, I can briefly describe what I think this text has to offer a partnership. Because different parties are likely to have somewhat different concerns, I will address separate remarks to the student and to the instructor.

A Few Words for the Student

Perhaps you are taking this course because you are interested in becoming a social psychologist or a professional in a related field, or perhaps you are taking it for an entirely different reason, such as because it is the least obnoxious way to satisfy an annoying college requirement. But whatever your motives for reading these words, you have probably asked yourself questions about people and their impact on one another. If you have, then you should find that this book will both further arouse and help satisfy your curiosity.

This text discusses what social psychologists have had to say about individuals, about groups, and about the interrelationships among individuals and groups. Some of the questions that social psychologists have asked about people may be strikingly similar to those that you have asked, and the answers they have proposed may coincide with what you have found through firsthand experience. In other cases you are likely to find that social psychologists have asked questions that have not yet occurred to you or have proposed answers that conflict with your intuition or common sense. To help you weigh and assess social psychologists' claims, I will describe in detail the evidence on which they are based.

Because you are an individual who takes part in many groups, you will find that much of the material we will consider is relevant to an understanding of yourself and the people around you. Throughout this text you will be alerted to the ways in which you openly or subtly influence others and the ways in which others are likely to influence you in return. In our exploration of social psychology, we will consider such issues as how we form impressions of others, how we learn from and teach others, how our attitudes are formed and under what conditions they are likely to be changed, why we associate with other people, why we find some people more attractive than others, and what happens when we participate in groups of different sizes. We will also deal with violence, prejudice, warfare, social change, and many other topics that are major concerns for society as a whole.

Since 1960, when I took my first course in the field, social psychologists have made tremendous inroads into traditional topics and have extended their efforts into many challenging new areas as well. I have done my best to capture the fascination and the excitement of contemporary social psychology in this text. To help spur your interest, I have included a number of anecdotes, some of which are rather unusual. In these pages you will discover, for example, the one printed word that would have kept Charles Fane from a lengthy illness, the activity that kept Georges Boulanger from accepting the dictatorship of France, and Carl Panzram's plan for touching off a war between England and the United States. I hope that you will find this book provocative and enjoyable as well as educational.

Shop Talk for the Instructor

As a quick glance at the table of contents or index should suggest, this text covers most, if not all, of the topics expected in a social-psychology text today. As a quick glance at the references should suggest, I have made every effort to be recent and up to date. Although I have ignored neither classical contributions nor originators of ideas, approximately half of the 1200 or so references cited have appeared since 1970, and a sizable proportion are from 1974 or later. But tradition and recent developments within a field are not the only determinants of a book's content; the author's prejudices and biases will have a powerful influence as well.

Four biases will be apparent in this text. First, although I am not committed to a narrow range of procedures, I definitely favor the experimental approach (broadly defined to include both the laboratory and the field). For reasons explained in Chapter 2, recent critics of the scientific experiment have done little to shake my fundamental belief that experimentation is still our most forceful tool for unraveling cause and effect.

Second, I am biased in favor of extensive coverage of the group. A number of recent experimentally oriented texts devote very little space to small-group and organizational phenomena. In my estimation, a continuation of the trend toward individualization will eventually rob social psychology of its most distinctive and potentially valuable historical characteristic: a simultaneous concern with the individual and the group. My third bias is against self-conscious efforts to *prove* the relevance of social psychology, since the field is by its very nature relevant. You will not find separate chapters on such "hot" topics as sex, sex typing, encounter groups, and prejudice. Instead, these subjects are presented as a natural part of social psychology and as continuous with other, more "traditional," topics. For example, sex is discussed in the chapter on interpersonal attraction, sex typing in the chapter on social learning, encounter groups in the chapter on group dynamics, and prejudice in the chapters on attitudes, attraction, and intergroup relations. Finally, my most pronounced bias is that I *like* social psychology, and I want the student to like the field too.

I have done my best to make this book appeal to students of widely differing backgrounds and interests. On the one hand, it should not insult the intelligence of the dedicated student. A large number of ideas are introduced, many studies are discussed in more depth than is currently the vogue, and controversies are raised and highlighted rather than ignored or glossed over. On the other hand, this book should also prove of value for students who have only a passing interest in social psychology. I have not assumed that the reader has a prior acquaintanceship with either psychology or sociology, although students who have had an introductory course in one of those fields may find the text a bit easier than students who have not. Chapter-opening outlines and midchapter summaries are intended to help the student organize the material and master it in fairly small doses. Major terms are introduced in boldface, and the complete glossary will help compensate for an incomplete memory. I have tried to choose examples, anecdotes, and cartoons that will both maintain the student's interest and clarify and underscore major points. Finally, to further encourage unflagging interest, I have kept the writing style informal throughout.

Silent Partners

When a textbook author enters into an educational partnership, a number of silent partners are brought in as well. Several reviewers commented on the technical accuracy and educational value of successive drafts. I am indebted to Philip Brickman of Northwestern University, John Brigham of Florida State University, Earl Carlson of California State

University, Long Beach, Joel Goldstein of the National Institute of Mental Health, Chester Insko of the University of North Carolina, Charles G. McClintock of the University of California, Santa Barbara, Daniel Perlman of the University of Manitoba, John Reich of Arizona State University, Warren Street of Central Washington State College, and Robert Suchner of Northern Illinois University. The suggestions offered by these reviewers and by Brooks/Cole's indefatigable consulting editors, Ed Walker and Larry Wrightsman, were based on years of expertise and hours of toil. All suggestions were treated seriously, but not all could be incorporated, and I admit sole responsibility for all remaining flaws.

I am also indebted to the many people and organizations that kindly granted me permission to reproduce their material. I extend my appreciation to Bill Bates, who with a magical flick of the hand produced the cartoons that adorn these pages, and to all the people at Brooks/Cole Publishing Company who helped me develop this project. Of special note are Field Representatives Ken Hickey and Randy Cade, Girl Friday Vena Dyer, Permissions Editor Jamie Brooks, Art Director John Edeen, and Production Manager Konrad Kerst. Of very special note are Editor Bill Hicks, who helped nurse me through this project from start to finish, and Managing Production Editor Micky Lawler, who untangled some rather convoluted passages, sought out and destroyed my unconscious sexist biases, and checked every spelling and punctuation mark (no small task, since I inexpertly typed the manuscript myself). Finally, I am indebted to my wife, Mary Ann, and my stepdaughter, Kathy Shirley, who not only offered me continual encouragement but also, despite their own busy schedules, assumed some of my cooking, dishwashing, and vacuuming responsibilities and thereby freed my time for work on the manuscript.

Albert A. Harrison

Contents

1

An Orientation to the Field   1

The Scope of Social Psychology   3
Social Psychology as a Science   20

2

Guidelines for Inquiry   35

Observing Social Behavior   38
Correlational Studies: The Prediction of Social Behavior   53
Experimental Studies: Unraveling Cause and Effect   63

3

Social Perception   85

The Perceiver   89
The Situation   107
The Target   116

4

Social Learning   137

Observational Learning   140
Social Reinforcement   162
Observational Learning, Social Reinforcement, and Sex-Role
    Behavior   178

5

Attitude Formation and Change   189

Cognitive-Consistency Theories   195
Functional Theories   220
Persuasive Communications   228

6

Attraction to Others   243

Affiliation   246
Liking   261
Love   275

7

Harmful and Helpful Behavior   293

Aggression   295
Helping Behavior   319

8

Interaction in the Dyad   337

Communication   340
Cooperation in the Dyad   359
Influence in the Dyad   373

9

Interaction in Small Groups   387

Communication and Influence within the Small Group   390
Conformity   399
Encounter Groups   425

10

Performance in Small Groups   437

Individual versus Group   439
Group Properties and Group Performance   462

11

Behavior in Organizations   479

Three Perspectives on Organizations   484
Motivation, Satisfaction, and Performance in Organizations   492
Leadership in the Organizational Setting   508
Organizational Adaptation and Change   521

12

Intergroup Relations   535

Harmony and Conflict in Intergroup Relations   538
Conflicts within Society   551
Conflict between Societies   567

Glossary   581
References   609
Name Index   657
Subject Index   668

1

An Orientation to the Field

THE SCOPE OF SOCIAL PSYCHOLOGY

CORE CONCERNS

The Effects of Other People on the Individual
The Consequences of These Effects, for the Individual
  and for the Group
Behavior within Groups
Relations among Groups

DISPOSITION, SITUATION, AND BEHAVIOR

Dispositional and Situational Variables as Interactive

THE SOCIAL FRAMEWORK FOR INDIVIDUAL BEHAVIOR

Characteristics of Groups
Positions and Roles
Individuals in Groups

PART SUMMARY

SOCIAL PSYCHOLOGY AS A SCIENCE

ASSUMPTIONS AND GOALS OF SCIENCE

Physical, Natural, and Social Sciences
Social Psychology, Common Sense, and the Obvious

SOCIAL PSYCHOLOGY AS HISTORY

THE RISE OF SCIENTIFIC SOCIAL PSYCHOLOGY

Comte and the Science of Social Behavior
The Early Years
The Rise of Group Dynamics
The Spotlight on the Individual and the Eclipse of the Group

SOCIAL PSYCHOLOGY AND SOCIAL RELEVANCE

PART SUMMARY

Students completing questionnaires for researchers Bibb Latané and John Darley (1968) at Columbia University were confronted by some unexpected and potentially frightening circumstances. Shortly after the students had been ushered into the laboratory, smoke began wafting in through a ventilator opening. Most of the individuals who were alone in this situation reacted quite sensibly: After carefully inspecting the ventilator opening and sniffing at the smoke, they promptly left the room and reported the emergency. Students who were in the company of two companions, however, tended to respond quite differently: Even when the smoke billowed forth in gigantic, stinging clouds, they proceeded doggedly with the questionnaire. Thus students reacted quite differently when other people were present than when they were alone.

People's behavior is social, in that it is affected by the presence and actions of others. Borrowing from Gordon Allport (1954a) and others, we'll define **social psychology** as the discipline that seeks to understand the ways in which the thoughts, feelings, and actions of one person (or group of people) are affected by the actual, imagined, or implied presence or actions of another person (or group of people). In a sense, anyone who has ever questioned people's impact on one another can be considered a a social psychologist. Like most other people, the social psychologists whose work is discussed in this book have asked such questions as: Who is likely to make a good impression? What causes one person to be friends with another? When is a person likely to grant another's request? How can prejudice, warfare, and other forms of intergroup conflict be eliminated? Unlike most other people, the social psychologists whose work is discussed in this book have sought answers to such questions by proceeding carefully within the framework of science.

THE SCOPE OF SOCIAL PSYCHOLOGY

Contemporary social psychology is an enormous field that represents a diversity of interests. As we shall see, social psychologists have something to say about everything from the manufacture of ashtrays to the construction of the Grand Coulee Dam, from the vilest and most brutal acts of aggression to the most noble acts of self-sacrifice, and from relationships between roommates to relationships among nations. The staggering breadth of contemporary social psychology is only hinted at by noting that the five-volume "bible" of social psychologists, *The Handbook of Social Psychology* (Lindzey & Aronson, 1968–1969), contains more than 4000 pages of highly concentrated material and cites approximately 7000 books and articles. Furthermore, given the tremendous rate of growth of scientific knowledge (Eisner, 1974), the glut of information implied by these numbers has probably *doubled* since the *Handbook* appeared in 1969.

But despite such foreboding figures, most of this material reflects a limited number of interests or themes. To understand these themes, it is necessary to briefly consider the intellectual parentage of social psychology.

Contemporary social psychology has been strongly influenced by two different disciplines. One discipline, **psychology,** literally means "the study of the mind" but is more typically regarded as "the study of behavior," since the mind has proven to be quite elusive. The second discipline, **sociology,** is typically regarded as the study of the origin, development, and functioning of the group or society.

Both psychology and sociology have characteristically asked questions about people and their interrelationships, but each field has followed different, early established, traditions. Psychology has always focused on the individual. Interest in the individual is retained even when the psychologist asks questions about individuals' relationships with one another. For example, the psychologist may ask how a certain type of person will react when other people try to induce him or her to conform, what personal needs of one person might mesh with the personal needs of another with the result that the pair falls in love, and what early social experiences have given Archie Bunker his unique personality.

Sociology has traditionally focused on the group. It has not emphasized the unique individual but has instead stressed interpersonal relationships that are not dependent on the personalities of the individuals involved. Thus the sociologist may ask about the effects of group properties such as morale on conformity, the ways in which our society encourages some romances but discourages others, and the reasons why our society has produced a large number of people who are not distinct personalities but blurred carbon copies of Archie Bunker. Given this background, it is not too surprising that social psychologists are interested in individuals, in groups, and in the interrelationships between individuals and groups.

CORE CONCERNS

From the intermingling of psychological and sociological thought, four recurrent interests or *core concerns* have emerged that provide the main themes of contemporary social psychology. These are: (1) the effects "other people" have on the individual; (2) the consequences of these effects, for the individual and for the group; (3) behavior within groups; and (4) relations among groups. To help stake out social psychology's territory, let's consider four brief examples that illustrate each of these core concerns. Each topic will be discussed again; the purpose of touching on each one right now is to convey the scope of social psychology and, I hope, to whet your appetite for more.

The Effects of Other People on the Individual

Perhaps the least complex theme is that dealing with the ways in which the behavior of one person, *A,* is a cause or occasion for an *immediate* change in the behavior of a second person, *B*—ignoring the enduring or long-term effects that *A* has on *B* or any reciprocal effects that *B* has on *A*. Zajonc (1966, p. 1) has coined the term **behavioral dependence** to refer to "a relation among the behaviors of a number of individuals, such that a given behavior of one or more individuals is a cause or an occasion for change in the behavior of one or more other individuals."

A simple illustration of immediate and unidirectional social influence comes from Ellsworth, Carlsmith, and Henson (1972), who had someone pull up to a stoplight, riding a rather beat-up motor scooter. The rider took the inside lane, to be near the driver's side of adjacent automobiles. He then stared directly at the stopped driver's face from a distance of between 4 and 5 feet. Compared with drivers who were not stared at, these drivers raced across the intersection as soon as the light turned green. As we shall see in later chapters, under other conditions eye contact is associated with friendship, intimacy, and romance. Being stared at by a stranger in a public place, however, may be taken as indicative of hostile intent and thus may motivate evasion or escape from the relationship.

The Consequences of These Effects, for the Individual and for the Group

The consequences of social influence form the second core concern of contemporary social psychology. Humans are not mere creatures of reflex; they change as a result of their experiences. As a result of experience, they learn new habits, they form, change, or abandon attitudes, and they develop a unique personality. Many, if not most, of these formative experiences involve other people. Since one person's behavior can cause or occasion a permanent or semipermanent alteration in the behavior of another, social psychologists' interests thus include socially learned habits, attitudes, and personality. These are the **personal consequences** of our responsiveness to others. Habits, attitudes, and personality in turn have implications for the group or society. These are the **social consequences** of behavioral dependence.

An illustration of both personal and social consequences comes from research aimed at identifying the conditions under which a person will come to the aid of another. As we shall see in Chapter 7, many factors affect helping behavior, including the character of the person in need, the specific plight of this needy person, and the number of bystanders present. Here we'll focus on the personality of the helper. The origins of personality are often sought in parent-child relationships, which are *social* relationships.

Rosenhan (1970) compared two groups of "helpers" who were assisting with civil-rights work. One group consisted of workers who were only partially committed to the cause. Their efforts were an on-again/off-again sort of affair: performance of an unselfish act required a certain amount of encouragement from others. The other group consisted of workers who were totally dedicated to the civil-rights cause. Their efforts were not conditional on approval from others. Rosenhan found that both groups of workers reported that they had parents who tried to encourage unselfish activity. However, whereas the parents of the only partially committed workers tended to preach altruism more than they practiced it, the parents of the totally committed workers both preached and practiced unselfish activity. Furthermore, whereas the parents of the partially committed workers maintained cool, aloof, or even hostile relationships with their children, the parents of the fully committed workers maintained warm and friendly relationships with their children. Subsequent research has supported the general idea that parents who show hypocrisy and who maintain poor relations with their children tend to inhibit the children's helping behavior, but parents who show "Good Samaritanism" in word and deed and who establish warm and friendly relations with their children tend to encourage the children to help others (Grusec, 1972; Hoffman, 1975).

Rosenhan thus linked the parents' behavior during the workers' childhood to the workers' behavior during early adulthood. Parental behavior had an impact that transcended the immediate situation in which it occurred. The workers' behavior, in turn, has implications for a particular kind of large group (our society), in that it could result in the lessening of some widespread and traditional discriminatory practices. By instilling in their children some degree of willingness to help others, the parents' behavior had personal consequences for the child and, ultimately, social consequences for the group.

Behavior within Groups

The mutual and reciprocal effects that two or more people have on each other is the third core concern of contemporary social psychology.

Social interaction refers to a two-way influence process whereby two or more people affect each other's behavior. Often the influence is sequential, in that each person takes turns stimulating and responding to the other. For example, if we observe two people together, we are likely to discover that a comment from the first person serves as a stimulus that elicits a response from the second. If the second person's response in turn elicits a response from the first person, we have the simplest instance of social interaction.

An example of mutual and reciprocal influence is found in the antecedents of **self-disclosure,** or the extent to which a person is willing to reveal intimate or personal information to someone else. Standards of self-disclosure have been provided by Taylor and Altman (1966), who had a number of judges rate a large variety of conversational topics in terms of intimacy. In a discussion of sex, for example, a critique of a salacious movie is far less intimate than an in-depth opinion of premarital and extramarital affairs; in a discussion of families, revealing the number of cousins or the ages of brothers or sisters is less intimate than harping on Dad's troubles with the law or Mom's reactions while under the influence of alcohol.

In the course of a conversation, self-disclosure is usually a slow, reciprocal process. Superficial information is most likely to be traded first, and, if interaction continues, the discussion shifts toward increasingly personal topics. Altman and Taylor (1973) suggest that the recipient of a disclosure feels liked and trusted by the discloser; hence, hearing others' revelations is pleasurable. If a person's disclosure is reciprocated—that is, followed by a self-disclosure from the listener—the discloser is rewarded and further disclosures are likely. If a person's disclosure is not reciprocated, further disclosures become unlikely.

To demonstrate this process, Taylor (1973) arranged a discussion session between an unsuspecting individual and a secret accomplice of the experimenter's. This accomplice was coached to follow one of four procedures: (1) reciprocation of self-disclosure throughout the session, (2) nonreciprocation during the first half of the session but reciprocation during the second half, (3) reciprocation during the first half but nonreciprocation during the second half, or (4) nonreciprocation throughout the entire session. It was found that continuous reciprocation led to more self-disclosure than did nonreciprocation, and there were thoroughly predictable shifts in self-disclosure when the accomplice began or ceased disclosing in return. Most intriguing was the finding of more self-disclosure of highly intimate material when the accomplice was initially unresponsive and then opened up than when the accomplice reciprocated throughout. Altman suggests that, when an initially uncommunicative partner suddenly begins disclosing, there is a sharp contrast in perception that leads to greater openness and attraction. Much more will be said about self-disclosure and the development of intimate relationships in Chapter 8.

Relations among Groups

Relations among groups of many different sizes constitute the fourth core concern of social psychology. Relations among small groups (such as bridge teams), big groups (such as nations), and small and big groups (such as a small department and its parent organization) have all received close scrutiny. A major, guiding interest has been the attempt to understand intergroup tensions and conflicts.

One of the most important studies of this type was conducted by Muzafer Sherif and his associates (Sherif, Harvey, White, Hood, & Sherif, 1961). Their study, which involved preadolescent boys at a summer camp, had three phases. During the first phase the investigators created conditions to form two collections of previously unacquainted boys into close-knit groups. During the second phase they created conditions that sparked conflict between the two groups. During the third phase they created conditions that led to a reduction of this conflict.

After two collections of boys had arrived at the camp at locations sufficiently far apart that each was unaware of the other's existence, the first phase began. Close-knit groups were formed by allowing the boys to engage in such fun activities as cooking out and going on excursions that required a high degree of coordination of efforts for successful completion. Coordination of efforts to reach mutual goals is called **cooperation.** Intragroup, or within-the-group, cooperation united each collection of strangers into a spirited, closely knit group.

In the second phase the two groups were brought together under conditions whereby each group was striving for goals that only one group could attain. **Competition** refers to striving for gains at another's expense. Competitive conditions were established by arranging a series of games and contests and awarding the winner of each contest points that the ultimately winning group could redeem for handsome prizes. Although it began as a friendly tournament, this intergroup, or between-groups, competition generated tension and conflict. Among other things, there was name calling, garbage hurling, and raiding of each other's headquarters.

During the third phase, conflict was reduced by making it in each group's interests to cooperate with the other. For example, restoration of the camp water supply required that both groups help search for a breakdown in the water main. A series of such cooperative activities diminished tensions. Friendships formed between members of the two groups, and each group began to take pride in doing favors for the other.

Sherif and his associates found, then, that intragroup cooperation could bind a collection of strangers together into a close-knit group, that intergroup competition leads to tension and conflict, and that intergroup cooperation leads to reduced tension and even cordial intergroup relationships. We will return to this study of preadolescent boys in Chapter 12 and see that it has implications for labor-management relations, race relations, and even international affairs.

In sum, social psychology's heritage in psychology and sociology is reflected in attempts to understand (1) the effects that other people have on the individual, (2) the consequences of these effects, for the individual and for the group, (3) behavior within groups, and (4) relations among groups. Whether one treats social psychology as a subdiscipline of psychology because of its concern with the individual, as a subdiscipline of sociology because of its interest in social interaction and in groups, or as a special hybrid discipline representing the best of both worlds, the distinctive feature of social psychology is a *simultaneous concern* with both the individual and the individual's relationships with others. Social psychologists thus believe that understanding human thoughts, feelings, and actions requires understanding the individual, understanding the group, and understanding the individual's relationship to the group.

DISPOSITION, SITUATION, AND BEHAVIOR

A **variable** is anything that can vary or change. People are complex in that their thoughts, feelings, and actions depend on a multitude of variables. For example, striking out during a softball game could be a result of limitations in the biological apparatus of the organism; a failure to learn the skills and develop the interests conducive to good performance; the present condition of the player, including needs, moods, and expectancies; or a wide array of factors present in the immediate situation, such as the nature of the opposing team, the number and type of spectators present, and the condition of the field and equipment. Some of these forces come from within the person. These **dispositional variables** include biological states, habits, attitudes, personality, and all other contributors to people's thoughts, feelings, and actions that at the time of analysis operate from within the skin. Other forces come from outside the individual. These **situational variables** include the nature of the setting, the number, type, and arrangement of objects or "props" within the setting, the other people present in the setting, and the relationship of these other people to the individual. Taken together, dispositional and situational variables help explain consistencies and inconsistencies in the behavior of a given individual, as well as similarities and differences in the behavior of different individuals.

Dispositional variables explain why the same person acts in similar ways in different situations. On the "inside," each person has a core of consistency, and this core will to some extent show in every situation. Thus a true pessimist may weep both at losing a job *and* at winning an automobile—in the latter case because "every silver lining hides a cloud." Dispositional variables also explain why different people act in different ways in the same situation. Because they have unique personalities, they respond differently when confronted with identical conditions. Thus, although one person may be unmoved by the prospect of surgery, another may be reduced to a "nervous wreck."

Situational variables explain why the same person acts in different ways in different situations. Although the person may remain "the same," the conditions confronting him or her change, and these changing conditions are likely to trigger different reactions. Thus a normally forceful and aggressive motorist may drive slowly and carefully when followed by a police officer. Situational variables also explain why different people act in similar ways in the same situation. Although they are unique persons, they are responding to identical environmental conditions. Thus an entire audience may laugh at an unusually adept comedian, even though the members of the audience come from different backgrounds and have, in many ways, different interests and tastes. As you may have guessed, through judicious selection of situational and dispositional variables, it becomes possible to give some sort of accounting of any consistencies or inconsistencies in people's behavior.

Dispositional and Situational Variables as Interactive

Over the years many psychologists have proceeded in one of two wishful traditions. One such tradition suggested that, if we only knew enough about the person, it would be possible to predict how he or she would act in almost any given situation. The other wishful tradition suggested that, if we only knew enough about a given situation, it would be possible to predict how almost anyone would respond to it. Each tradition was wishful in that it presented an oversimplified view of the causes of people's behavior. In actuality, dispositional and situational variables combine or *interact* to determine what people think, feel, and do. That is, if we know something about the person and something about the situation, we can make better guesses about the person's behavior than if we know about either of these two factors alone.

Psychologists have erred in both directions, but, for purposes of illustration, let's trace certain developments in the field of "personality." Although there are many definitions of personality, most agree that it is something inside the person, that it accounts for consistencies in the person's behavior over time, that it accounts for individuality, and that it both contributes to and results from the person's unique adjustment to his or her environment. For our purposes, **personality** may be defined as "the sum and total of those dispositional variables that provide individuality and consistency in a given person's behavior."

For many years there was unwarranted optimism that a given personality variable could predict individual behavior in many different situations. The term **trait** is usually used to designate an inferred, relatively enduring characteristic or attribute of an individual that hypothetically shows itself in a variety of situations under differing conditions. Thousands of everyday terms, such as *honesty, aggressiveness, sociability, altruism,* and *dependency,* are used to designate traits (G. W. Allport & Odbert, 1936). On the basis of observing someone return a lost wallet, or on the basis of someone's responses to a paper-and-pencil personality test, a psychologist might infer that the person is "honest" and then predict that he or she would be honest in other situations, such as by not cheating on an exam when given the opportunity or by returning the extra money when given too much change.

Almost half a century of trying to identify traits and use them to predict behavior in different situations led to the disappointing conclusion that there was far less consistency or generality in individual conduct than psychologists had hoped (Mischel, 1968, 1973). That is, a person who reported a lost wallet might or might not cheat on an exam and might or might not return excess change—it depended largely on the situation.

Although psychologists had long given lip service to the idea that "behavior is a function of the person and the environment," and although findings showing variability in a given individual's conduct had been around since the 1920s (Hartshorne & May, 1928), crystallization of the difficulties with the traditional trait approach did not occur until forceful arguments were presented by Mischel in the late 1960s (Mischel, 1968). Of course, ignoring traits and personality factors would be as grievous as ignoring the situation (Bowers, 1973; Mischel, 1973; Ekehammar, 1974). People are neither unbending slaves to inner drives nor fragile reeds that bend to every external pressure.

An illustration of the way in which personality and situation combine has been provided by Gergen, Gergen, and Meter (1972), who studied people's willingness to help other people. In this study, Swarthmore students first completed a battery of personality tests. They were then given an appeal to volunteer to help in five different situations, which were: (1) counseling male high school students, (2) counseling female high school students, (3) helping with a research project on thinking, (4) helping with a research project on consciousness, and (5) collating papers. Personality-test results could be used to predict volunteering, but only in specific situations. For example, males scoring high on a measure of nurturance were likely to offer to counsel high school males but were not likely to offer to help out in other situations. Females who scored high in need for deference were willing to counsel high school girls but were particularly unwilling to help out with the secretarial task. No personality score predicted volunteering in all five situations, and only a few predicted volunteering in more than one situation. For a given situation the same personality variables associated with men's volunteering were not necessarily associated with women's volunteering.

Stating the abstract formula "Person X in situation Y will react in fashion Z" is not at all difficult; making such a formula work after plugging in real people, real situations, and real behaviors is very difficult. Applying this general formula requires coming to grips with the fact that there are *many different* dispositional variables and *many different* situational variables that will cause a given action. Dispositional variables and situational variables are *sets* of variables, and, in theory, any single variable from either set can augment, reduce, or negate the impact of any other single variable. Acknowledging that any action or reaction can represent an interplay of many different causes has three major implications.

First, there is always a fair chance that a prediction about any specific individual will be wrong. There may be an unknown or nonunderstood part of the person's history, or the person may perceive the situation that confronts him or her differently than we do. For example, many children seem delighted by midgets and dwarfs. Will Esmeralda be delighted by midgets and dwarfs? Maybe. And maybe not. Danish psychoanalyst Olaf Brüel (1938) described the case of a 15-year-old girl who fled in terror whenever a dwarf appeared. He traced her fear back to having watched the movie *The Hunchback of Notre Dame*. Watching the fate that befell another girl led to a pathological fear, and harmless dwarfs were seen as dangerous and hostile.

Second, there are few simple answers to questions about individuals or groups. Whereas some people enjoy demonstrating their ability for intricate, convoluted explanations, most of us want straight answers. However, because the effects of one variable can be enhanced, neutralized, or reversed by the effects of another variable, social psychologists are usually compelled to *qualify* answers—that is, to state the limiting conditions. Is this person likely to conform? It depends on the situation. Is this situation likely to produce conformity? It depends on the people. The student who asks the question may come away feeling that the social psychologist has hedged, and the answer sought may be obscured behind an intricate web of qualifications. Yet such qualifications are necessary to reflect the complexity of individuals and groups.

The third implication of acknowledging a multiplicity of variables is that the psychologist is forced to use expensive and time-consuming research procedures. The fact that different variables combine to produce a given effect does not pose a problem if we are willing to settle for understanding the *typical* effects of a given variable. This, however, requires the difficult procedure of comparing the average or typical behavior of different groups of people. In the next chapter I'll explain why the effects of a given variable are more clearly evident in the typical or average response of a group of individuals than in the behavior of any single individual.

In sum, individual thoughts, feelings, and actions can be understood only through consideration of both dispositional variables and situational variables. Acknowledging that human behavior reflects a complex interplay of variables is an admission that understanding people is a challenging task that promises few simple answers. Part of the complexity comes from people's involvement in groups.

THE SOCIAL FRAMEWORK FOR INDIVIDUAL BEHAVIOR

Each individual is influenced by social groups of many different sizes. At one extreme, the individual is affected by the two-person group, which consists of himself or herself and one other person. At the other extreme the individual is affected by society, which involves himself or herself and hundreds of millions of others. Each group that the person is born into (family, nationality), forced into (school, possibly the military), or elects to join (fraternity or sorority, a business concern) raises the likelihood of some behaviors and lowers the likelihood of others.

Characteristics of Groups

Since the term **group** is commonly used to designate anything from a dating couple to a society of hundreds of millions, a thoroughly satisfactory formal definition of a group is very difficult to provide. Most social psychologists feel, however, that, to dignify a collection of people with the title of "group," something more than bodies is needed (Cartwright & Zander, 1968). Riffling through a stack of proposed definitions, you'd find that reference to *social interaction* is common; that is, it is often suggested that people who are interacting with one another form a group, whereas those who do not interact are not part of the group. Also popular is the idea that people who work together for a *common goal* (which may merely involve having a good time) qualify as a group. A third recurring theme is *shared standards;* people who observe the same customs, traditions, and rules of etiquette would thus constitute a group. Finally, *self-definition* is sometimes proposed. That is, it may be useful to define as a group any collection of people who consider themselves to form a group. Obviously, what constitutes a group by one definition does not necessarily constitute a group by another definition. However, what the proponents of each definition share is a conviction that a group is not just a collection of individuals.

Different labels have been devised to designate groups of different sizes. The smallest groups, which are usually characterized by the highest degree of interdependence and interaction, are **dyads,** or two-person groups. **Small groups** include the dyad and are limited at the upper end by the restriction that each member must be able to interact with every other member on a person-to-person basis. "Small group" usually designates from four to eight people, but it is easy to envision circumstances in which 20 or so people could qualify as a small group. Processes within small groups (and the study of these processes) are called **group dynamics.**

Falling between the small group and the society is the organization. For now, we may define **organizations** as large, complex groups that are oriented toward the attainment of formally specified goals. The Catholic Church, the U.S. Marines, and American Telephone and Telegraph Company are examples of organizations.

A **society** is a very special kind of large, complex social unit that coordinates all the individuals, groups, and organizations that it comprises. Usually, but not invariably, a society is demarcated by national boundaries.

Variations in size, even within the limits of the small group, have many repercussions (Thomas & Fink, 1965; Lindsay, 1972). As the number of people in the group increases, the opportunity for face-to-face interaction with every other member decreases. At some point the group becomes unwieldy, and subgroups appear. Consider what usually happens at a party: as people trickle in, they sit in a circle in the living room; however, after a certain point the guests are likely to form small clusters in different parts of the house or apartment. In a large group, such as an organization, some of these subgroups may work at cross-purposes (Chapter 11). As groups become larger, they tend to become less homogeneous in composition, and consensus becomes more difficult to attain. A large group such as an organization or a society must incorporate enough flexibility in its rules to allow for the different needs of its members but nonetheless maintain enough inflexibility to prevent excessive intragroup conflict and possible disintegration. The size variable, then, is a very important one, partly in its own right and partly because variations in the number of members in a group (a quantitative variable) can have profound qualitative effects.

A fairly common practice, as we shall see, is to generalize from social behavior in small groups, or the **microcosm,** to social behavior in organizations, societies, and other large groups, or the **macrocosm.** The belief that the microcosm reflects the macrocosm is a convenient one, for, although it is easy to assemble four people and study the microcosm, it is far less easy to grasp the macrocosm. Thus social psychologists have generalized from cooperation within the dyad to cooperation between nations, or from the development of social standards in the small group to the development of social standards in society. In some cases it can be demonstrated that such generalizations are justified, but in other cases such generalizations are open to doubt. Uncritically generalizing from the goings-on in a group of one size to the goings-on in a group of another size can be a risky proposition—a point that must be continually borne in mind.

Positions and Roles

Anyone who has seen an organizational chart (or a pictorial representation of a "family tree," for that matter) realizes that groups may be represented graphically, or "mapped." For example, to begin mapping Intergalactic Business Machines, we might draw a circle at the top of a page to represent the president and chairman of the board. Below this circle we might draw a horizontal row of other circles to represent the organization's numerous vice-presidents. Below these come still other and longer rows to represent the offices held by increasingly less influential members of the organization. Such representations show that groups of people may be conceptualized as social networks—grids of people bound together by communication, power and influence, rights and obligations, and a mutual awareness. Each person represented on the grid may be said to hold an office or occupy a position that specifies his or her relationship to others on the grid. Thousands of everyday words are used to describe such positions in hundreds of everyday groups. For example, in an airplane flight crew, one could occupy the position of pilot, copilot, flight engineer, or flight attendant. Other positions in other groups include president, mother, apprentice seaman, immigrant, and student.

Occupying a given position within a given group often forces the occupant to behave in a prescribed fashion. For example, a pilot, no matter how sociable, is not supposed to serve drinks to passengers; a flight attendant, no matter how cool and levelheaded, is not allowed to make critical decisions during an emergency. The term **role** is used to refer to (1) a set of expectations concerning what a person in a given position must, must not, or may do, and (2) the actual behavior of the person who occupies the position. A central idea is that any person occupying a position and filling a role behaves similarly to anyone else who could be in that position.

Thomas and Biddle (1965) draw a strong analogy between the behavior of an actor filling a role in a play and the behavior of any one of us filling a role in a natural group. On stage, they note, an actor's behavior is determined by the script, the director's instructions, cue lines delivered by the other players, and the audience's reactions. In other settings the script allows a little more improvisation. The "director" is likely to be a parent, teacher, or sergeant, and the audience consists of the people who happen to be in the setting. Shakespeare's contention that "All the world's a stage/ And all the men and women merely players . . . " is developed in entertaining ways by Goffman (1959) and Berne (1964).

Role concepts have at least three major uses. First, they help us to understand similarities in the behavior of different people occupying a given position within a group. Second, they help explain why a given person behaves differently as he or she moves from one position in society to another. Third, role concepts are useful for dealing with recurrent patterns of interaction between two or more people who occupy adjacent positions in the social network. For example, we need not be prophets or soothsayers to predict in general terms the interaction among a bride, a groom, and a member of the clergy.

Among others, D. R. Miller (1963) and Thomas and Biddle (1965) have stressed that fulfilling a social role does not eliminate all individuality in the role player's behavior. There are at least two reasons why different people will fulfill the same role in different ways. First, prescriptions for filling a role are not always precise. Although some behavior may be mandatory and other behavior prohibited, still other behavior is likely to be elective. For example, although parents must feed and care for their children and cannot physically abuse them, they are allowed latitude in terms of the extent to which they are permissive, show warmth and acceptance, espouse spiritual or materialistic values, and so forth. Second, people vary in their perceptions of a role and in the degree to which they have learned the prescriptions and proscriptions associated with it. For example, soon after he assumed the Presidency, Lyndon Johnson horrified people by wheeling his hot-rod Lincoln around at breakneck speed, seemingly unaware that his new role required more caution concerning physical risk.

Although it may be possible to identify a role for any position in any group, there's no getting around the fact that in some groups we seem to have greater freedom to "be ourselves" than in other groups. In this regard a distinction has traditionally been made between primary groups and secondary groups.

The defining characteristic of a **primary group** is that, in the course of interaction within the group, each person recognizes the others' individuality. Each member responds to the others as distinct persons with unique strengths, weaknesses, and needs. Primary groups tend to be informal, enduring, tolerant of spontaneity, and composed of people with highly similar backgrounds, interests, and tastes. In our society, families, groups of good friends, and pairs of sweethearts constitute primary groups. Many other groups, such as work groups, dorm mates, and hobby and special-interest groups, may also qualify as primary groups.

The defining characteristic of a **secondary group** is that, in the course of interaction within the group, each person tends to ignore the unique strengths, weaknesses, and needs of the other people and treats them instead in accordance with general, impersonal social rules. The interaction is, in a sense, "preprogrammed," or governed by social roles. These businesslike groups tend to be formal, fleeting, and heterogeneous in composition. Work teams assembled of strangers, the U.S. Senate, the crew of an aircraft carrier, and college students and staff on registration day would most likely qualify as secondary groups.

The distinction between groups in which members treat one another as unique personalities and those in which members deal with one another as occupants of interlocking roles has been around for quite some time. Perhaps refinement is needed. First, as Kinch (1973) has noted, it may be more proper to speak of primary and secondary *relationships*. For example, in some families, spontaneity and intimacy are discouraged; in some usually business-oriented settings such as the military, close friendships develop. Second, only rarely do we relate to others on a completely personal or a completely impersonal basis. Thus we might do better to think of a continuum reflecting various *degrees* of involvement with one another as unique persons.

Individuals in Groups

As we progress through this text, we will find that societies, organizations, and small groups affect individual behavior by applying pressures to conform and by maintaining standards that the individual uses for evaluating his or her own and other people's behavior. In some cases the standards of these different-sized groups conflict, as when society sponsors a war that a religious organization rejects, or as when an adolescent gang encourages delinquent behavior that the society rejects. In many other cases, however, as we move from the society at the top of the scale through the organization and to the small group at the bottom of the scale, we are likely to find an increasing number of constraints on the individual's alternatives and options. That is, society sets limits for organizations, organizations set limits for small groups, and small groups set limits for individual conduct. For example, society requires that people wear clothes in public. A business or other organization may require that women wear stockings and dresses and that men wear coats and ties. A small group within the organization (such as a college English department) may develop an informal but usually obeyed code that specifies low heels for women, tweeds for both men and women, and checkered shirts and black knit ties for men.

We'll find that many social psychologists stress small groups when discussing the effects of groups on individual behavior. There are at least two reasons for this emphasis. First, people seem to have their most dramatic impact on one another when they come together in face-to-face situations. Second, small groups often serve as important intermediaries between the individual on the one hand and organizations and societies on the other. A person's views of a large group (such as an organization) and its impact on him or her are likely to be based on face-to-face contact with only a small percentage of the people who belong to the group. For example, two workers from different departments might be able to give a fairly complete description of what Intergalactic Business Machines "is like," but the worker who has a considerate supervisor may give a very different description than will the worker whose supervisor does not take principles of good human relations into account. Similarly, your interpretation and evaluation of our political system may depend very much on the political attitudes of your family and friends. In effect, small groups serve as filters or lenses that give the individual a selective and sometimes distorted view of larger groups such as organizations or societies.

PART SUMMARY

People's behavior is social, in that it is affected by the presence and actions of others. Social psychology represents an attempt to understand this social-influence process and its consequences. From the intermingling of psychological and sociological thought have come four core concerns characterizing contemporary social psychology: (1) the effects that "other people" have on the individual, (2) the consequences of these effects, for the individual and for the group, (3) behavior within groups, and (4) relations among groups.

People's behavior is complex, in that at any point in time it is influenced by a wide array of variables. A distinction may be made between dispositional variables, which are a part of the person, and situational variables, which are apart from the person. Individual behavior represents a combination of many different dispositional and situational variables; as a result, it is difficult to make predictions about any specific person, there are few simple answers to questions about human behavior, and expensive and time-consuming research procedures are made necessary.

Groups must be distinguished from mere collections of people. Groups of different sizes include dyads, small groups, organizations, and societies. In some cases it is justifiable to generalize from behavior in the small group (or microcosm) to behavior in the large group (or macrocosm), but in other cases it is not. Groups can be visualized as grids of people bound together by communication, influence, and mutual awareness. Associated with each position on the grid are certain ways of behaving. Expectations and behaviors associated with a given position are called roles. Role concepts help to explain the similarities in behavior of different people who occupy similar positions in a group, changes in behavior as the individual moves from group to group, and recurrent patterns of interaction that characterize people who occupy interlocking positions within a group.

Society, organizations, and small groups all affect individual behavior. The organization is embedded in the society, the small group is embedded in the organization, and the individual is embedded in the small group. As we proceed from the society at the top of the ladder to the small group toward the bottom, there is likely to be an increasing number of limits and constraints placed on individual conduct. Most social psychologists emphasize the small group because of its dramatic and immediate impact on the individual and because it serves as an intermediary between the individual and larger social groupings.

SOCIAL PSYCHOLOGY AS A SCIENCE

Confronted with a problem that can be approached from a number of different angles and that requires complicated procedures for solution, people tend to obstruct one another in their search for answers. Each person is trying to follow a complex series of steps, and his or her intricate chain of reasoning is likely to become confused when someone else interjects different ideas (Kelley & Thibaut, 1969). The riddle of the individual and his or her relationship to others is one such problem, and, as tens of thousands of publications each year attest, there seems no end of people who are eager to interject different ideas. To help reduce the confusion, most social psychologists adhere to a particular set of standardized rules.

Those who follow these rules understand one another's assumptions and, to some extent, one another's chains of reasoning. The consistency of approach to a problem imparted by a set of mutually agreed upon rules means that people working on the problem can profit from one another's efforts. **Science** represents a set of rules of inquiry for understanding regularities in the world about us. The rules of science are not the only set of rules devised with such considerations in mind, and not everyone believes that the rules of science provide the best guidelines for gaining insights about people. Senator William Proxmire, for example, has suggested that, to understand love, we must abandon science and turn instead to such experts as Elizabeth Barrett Browning and Irving Berlin (*Sacramento Bee*, March 12, 1975, p. A12). Nonetheless, the rules of science have been widely accepted and have done much to shape present-day social psychology.

ASSUMPTIONS AND GOALS OF SCIENCE

Social psychologists and other scientists share certain assumptions and certain goals. These assumptions reflect both impressively named philosophical positions and some very practical considerations. The major assumptions of science are: (1) that a real world exists independent of our experience of it, (2) that there are relationships in this world between cause and effect, and (3) that knowledge of this real world can be discovered by one individual and then verified by others. These assumptions can be neither proven nor disproven.

The goals of science are description, prediction, control, and understanding. **Description** refers to telling what has already happened; **prediction** involves telling what is likely to happen; **control** means varying conditions so that the course of future events is altered or changed. The assumption that there are regularities between cause and effect makes the goals of prediction and control possible. That is, if things happened in haphazard or willy-nilly fashion, it would not be possible to predict or alter the future. **Understanding,** of course, refers to providing a plausible and convincing account or explanation of what we can describe, predict, or control.

Physical, Natural, and Social Sciences

Physical, natural, and social scientists are alike in that they attempt to identify and explain regularities in the universe. The physical scientist looks for regularities in nonliving things. The natural scientist looks for systematic regularities in living things. The social psychologist and other social scientists also look for regularities in living things, but their emphasis is on how these regularities are caused by and affect other, similar living things.

Although scientists from all disciplines share assumptions and goals, the social scientist (and to some extent the natural scientist) is sometimes the target of criticism and hostility that is not directed toward the physicist or chemist. The central problem, apparently, is that, compared with other sciences, the social sciences seem thus far to have offered little in the way of undisputed truth. There are three factors that make social science the victim of invidious comparison: a misunderstanding of the physical sciences (McCain & Segal, 1973), the complexity of social behavior (Myrdal, 1972), and people's stake in their own behavior (McCain & Segal, 1973).

First, a common misconception is that some sciences (such as physics and chemistry) are "exact," whereas others (such as social psychology) are inexact. However, *no* science is exact; all sciences offer probabilistic statements. Even in the case of a falling weight, repeated measures taken under conditions that are as identical as possible yield different results (McCain & Segal, 1973).

Second, in certain ways the problems that social scientists are trying to solve are more difficult than those confronted by physical scientists (Myrdal, 1972). This does not mean that physical sciences are especially simple; it means that social sciences are especially complex. The physicist or chemist can begin with a relatively simple substance (for example, water) and can study it under carefully regulated conditions (for example, at 100° centigrade and at sea level). The social psychologist must begin with a relatively complex substance (for example, a married couple) and cannot approximate the carefully regulated laboratory conditions available to the physicist. Consider how exact laws about falling bodies would be if they had to be based on observations of lopsided boulders tumbling down steep hills in the course of a storm.

Third, as McCain and Segal note, because of its subject matter, social science invites dispute. People have a vested interest in human behavior and in social policy. Social-scientific findings may conflict with intuition or challenge long-held traditions and beliefs. Describe the properties of the element lithium, and few will dispute you; describe the properties of love, and you may have half the audience and a Congressional committee on your neck. People have not had much experience with the lightest of metals, but they have had a great deal of experience with love. If careful, systematic observations yield results that conflict with personal experience or with intuition, then those observations are likely to be dismissed. As we shall see, however, personal experience and intuition are not always the most trustworthy sources of knowledge.

Social Psychology, Common Sense, and the Obvious

Social psychologists study formally what many people study informally. In some cases the results of careful, painstaking scientific research seem disappointingly obvious. That is, it sometimes seems that years of

training, months of effort, and bundles of money are wasted on finding out something that everyone knew in the first place. Yet to many social psychologists a finding that seems to be "common sense" or "obvious" can be as informative as a finding that disconfirms all intuition or has never before been noted. Let's consider the reasons why we should be reluctant to accept commonsense explanations of behavior and should treat with caution the claim that a finding is "obvious."

Commonsense principles of behavior abound. However, there are three difficulties associated with relying upon them. First, they are often violated by human behavior. Consider, for example, the principle that "opposites attract." When we turn to a discussion of friendship, we will find that people who like each other tend to come from similar backgrounds and to have similar personalities, tastes, and attitudes. Second, commonsense principles tend to conflict. Compare, for instance, the ideas "Two heads are better than one" and "Too many cooks spoil the soup." Third, although commonsense principles may provide plausible "after the fact" explanations, they do not provide useful guidelines for predict-ing the future. Consider, for example, how common sense might explain two lovers rushing into each other's arms following a month's separation. "Absence makes the heart grow fonder!" However, suppose the month's separation led to a cooling off of the relationship. This result would leave the commonsense theorist undaunted, for, after all, "Out of sight, out of mind!" Commonsense principles may be used to make specific predic-tions, but they are more often used like this to account for something that has already happened. Certainly there are some conditions under which commonsense principles of behavior hold true. But commonsense princi-ples are worthless unless we can specify the conditions under which they apply. Once this is done, we begin moving away from the realm of com-mon sense and toward the realm of science.

Now let's consider the difficulty of labeling a finding "obvious." Here are some examples of some "obvious" findings:

1. In an emergency situation, bystanders are more likely to come to the immediate aid of a person who is covered with blood than they are to come to the aid of someone who is not so visibly injured.
2. In a comparison of members of a dull sex-discussion group, it was found that women who had undergone an embarrassing initiation liked the group and its members less than did women who had not undergone such humiliation.
3. Blacks and whites feel uncomfortable in each other's presence, and interracial contact usually leads to an exaggeration of differences and conflicts.

The problem with these particular findings is that, although they may seem obvious, they are also fictitious. That is, what was really found was that bystanders were less likely to help the bloodied victim (Chapter 7), that the women who had undergone the rough initiation were more attracted to the group (Chapter 10), and that interracial contact often leads to a reduction of prejudice and hostility (Chapter 12). If these true findings had been cited, they also would have seemed obvious. Because the range and variety of human behavior are so great, it is usually possible to find an example that supports any claim. The task confronting social psychol-ogy is to discover and explain what is *most likely* to occur under various conditions.

SOCIAL PSYCHOLOGY AS HISTORY

Social psychologist Kenneth Gergen (1973) has challenged social psychology's status as a science. The scientific goals of prediction and control require a certain amount of stability or repeatability of events.

For example, the tides can be predicted fairly accurately. But present formulas work only because the moon's wanderings have been quite repetitive over the centuries. On a topsy-turvy planet where some days there was no moon, some days one moon, and some days two or more moons following erratic orbits, it would not be possible to predict the tides. Gergen argues that the conditions surrounding human social behavior are nonrepetitive; the resulting fluctuation of conditions in the social arena precludes the formulation of general rules that would allow prediction and control of the future. Thus social psychologists must be content to be historians, recounting the past.

Gergen offers two arguments to support his thesis. The first is that economic, technological, and other historical or cultural changes make it unlikely that today's principles will work tomorrow. For example, the propaganda techniques of World War I that whipped up fear and hostility by portraying the enemy as totally inhuman would more likely whip up laughter and derision in these days when the media typically portray combatants from both sides as partly good and partly bad. Gergen's second argument is that the publicity accorded social-psychological findings may produce reactions among the public that serve to render the findings no longer applicable. There are at least three ways in which this might come about. First, although social-psychological findings are ostensibly nonevaluative, neutral descriptions, they often have clear overtones concerning what constitutes socially desirable or "good" attitudes and behavior. In a discussion of helping behavior, for example, it is usually pretty clear that altruism is "good"; having read that city slickers may be less likely than country folk to help a person in distress (Chapter 7), a city slicker may go out of his or her way to be a Good Samaritan (and thus invalidate the rule). Second, learning a psychological principle may liberate a person from its behavioral implications. (This is a variation of the old theme that, if a person with emotional problems is given "insight," these problems will disappear.) For example, a person may read that being insulted instigates aggression; provided with this insight into human nature, he or she may then take tremendous abuse and then turn the other cheek. Third, as we shall see in Chapter 8, people like to see themselves as free and in command of their behavior. After reading that under such and such conditions they are likely to conform, they may nonconform when these conditions arise—simply for the sake of retaining a sense of individual freedom. This "boomerang" effect would also invalidate a publicized finding.

Schlenker (1974) has severely criticized Gergen's thesis, arguing that it is neither novel nor valid. Schlenker notes that social psychologists have found general principles that apply in different cultures and at different times—for example, the principle that familiarity leads to liking (Chapters 3 and 6), the principle that an action on the part of one person is likely to elicit a similar action on the part of an observer (Chapter 4), and the principle that the presence of others aids or facilitates the performance of an already learned response but impairs the acquisition or learning of a new response (Chapter 10). According to Schlenker, cases in which there have been failures to predict social behavior "have more to say about our ability to understand than about the phenomena in question." Surface dissimilarities that appear when we compare different cultures or different times may mask underlying regularities. The apparent capriciousness of social behavior will disappear as new concepts are discovered that abstract regularities and constancies (Zajonc, 1972; Schlenker, 1974).

For social psychologists to accept Gergen's arguments, it would be necessary to abandon the central assumption of science that there are underlying regularities governing the course of events. This a number of social psychologists (myself included) are unwilling to do. Rather than abandon these assumptions, it is possible to add new factors to the equation—factors that adjust for the effects of economic, technological, and other historical or cultural changes. As for the argument that mass-media dissemination of knowledge invalidates social-psychological findings, we shall see at various points people's *predictable* reactions to claims about their behavior. In any event, Gergen may have overestimated psychology's impact through the mass media; after all, at least 200 million Americans do *not* subscribe to *Psychology Today*.

THE RISE OF SCIENTIFIC SOCIAL PSYCHOLOGY

The basic phenomenon of social psychology—behavior in response to the behavior of other people—has been with us throughout the memory of mankind. The simplest picture writing dates back about 10,000 years. It tells stories of group hunting activity and of military expeditions that met with varying degrees of success. In all probability, people had a rich and intricate social life before they evolved to their present form, *Homo sapiens*, many hundreds of thousands of years ago (Howell, 1965). Yet scientific observations, and to some extent the theories that constitute present-day social psychology, are less than a century old. To place this development in perspective, if the amount of time people have been on earth is likened to one year, social psychology as a scientific enterprise did not tiptoe onto the scene until the morning of December 31.

Comte and the Science of Social Behavior

Philosophers have long speculated on the nature of the individual and his or her relations to others, but it was not until the mid-19th century that August Comte argued that people could be studied scientifically (G. W. Allport, 1954a). At the time, people were startled by Comte's view that relations among people were as amenable to scientific analysis as was a falling apple. After thus becoming the "father" of modern sociology, Comte began grappling with a new science, a science of the individual. Although we now call this new science "psychology," Comte avoided this term because it was rooted in religion and myth.

Why is scientific social psychology of such recent advent? At least two reasons have been identified. First, as Zajonc (1966) has noted, prior to the Industrial Revolution social conduct was closely regulated by the feudal system and by the Church, and a knowledge of law, custom, and etiquette was sufficient for survival. The Industrial Revolution, which freed much of people's time, the breakdown of the feudal system, and the decline in the power of the Church brought new variability to social behavior and rendered traditional "explanations" inadequate. Second, during Comte's era, science and technology were reaching ever-higher levels. For the first time, one could ride on a self-propelled steamboat or a railroad train, or even have a technically perfect (if colorless) "light portrait" speedily made by means of the mysterious photographic process. Given tremendous advances in astronomy, physics, chemistry, and biology, it is not too surprising that science provided a model for answering questions about individuals and groups.

The Early Years

Application of the tools of science to human social behavior did not occur until many years after Comte's death. The first scientific study of the interrelationships among people is usually attributed to Durkheim (1897), who counted the number of suicides in different countries, and honors for the first experimentation are usually conferred upon Triplett (1897), who sought to discover if competition caused people to perform more energetically. In 1908 the first two social-psychology textbooks appeared, one by sociologist E. A. Ross (1908) and the other by psychologist William McDougall (1908). McDougall's text is more memorable, for he made the controversial suggestion that human social behavior was regulated by **instincts.** He defined an instinct as:

> . . . an inherited or innate psycho-physical disposition which determines its possessor to perceive, and to pay attention to, objects of a certain class, to experience an emotional excitement of a particular quality upon perceiving such an object, and to act in regard to it in a particular manner, or, at least, to experience an impulse to such action [McDougall, 1923 edition, p. 30].

Like other instinct theorists, McDougall described instincts as inherited or innate, based in neuroanatomy, and universal within a species. Although he also recognized that complex mental processes and experience contribute to behavior, he developed his arguments discussing "parental" instincts, the instinct of "pugnacity," the "gregarious" instinct, and others.

Over the years McDougall was shouted down. "Nature" explanations of behavior, which point to instincts or other inborn tendencies as causes of behavior, have enjoyed little popularity in social psychology. First, people's social behavior is characterized by a degree of variability and diversity not easily explained by the concept of instincts. Second, it is usually not possible to eliminate alternative explanations of human social behavior that are based on environmental factors. Third, instinct theories seem to offer little in the way of explanation, since they involve little more than the attachment of labels. Finally, instinct explanations are downbeat and pessimistic in that they don't offer much in the way of hope for the immediate future. On the brink of a world war, it would be little comfort to think that selective breeding might prevent another world war 2000 years hence.

A controversial issue during social psychology's early years was whether groups had a "reality" of their own (Cartwright & Zander, 1968). On the one side were sociology, anthropology, and other disciplines concerned with social entities such as small groups, organizations, and societies. These partisans considered groups to have a reality that was independent of the individual members involved. It was noted, for example, that a group continues to exist even after there has been a complete change of membership. To illustrate: every three years or so there is likely to be a complete turnover of members of a Girl Scout troop; yet today we might expect to find in any given troop many of the ideals, values, and goals that were prevalent in the troop 10 or 20 years ago. The ultimate expression of the "reality of groups" thesis was the argument for the existence of a "group mind" that was more than the sum of the minds of the individuals who constituted the group.

On the other side of the controversy was psychology, with its interest in the individual. F. H. Allport (1924), for example, argued that group members' common ways of thinking, feeling, and acting reflected nothing more than similarities among individuals. As for the "group mind," no self-respecting behavioristic psychologist of that day would even consider using the term.

The controversy seems to have lost much of its edge. Few contemporary social psychologists would argue that the social glue binding people together is real in the same sense as the neurons connecting the two hemispheres of the brain. Yet, although nobody talks about the group mind, many modern writers talk about "shared ideas," "shared values," and the like, implying that there is something to share (G. W. Allport, 1954a). Also, we will repeatedly encounter arguments that the interaction of individual minds produces attitudes and actions that are different from those sponsored by single minds or by a collection of individual minds in isolation. The simple truth is that it has often been very convenient to talk about groups and group properties *as if* they had an existence of their own.

The Rise of Group Dynamics

A highly significant development in the late 1930s was the rise of group dynamics. Cartwright and Zander (1968) see three major conditions as responsible for the emergence of small-group research in its own right at this time. First, as the conviction grew that such research might solve practical problems and contribute to social progress, society became willing to provide the resources required. Second, at about that time there was rapid growth and development within four professions, each of which stood to gain from a systematic understanding of small groups. Professionals in group social work, group psychotherapy, education, and business administration routinely saw the impact of the small group on the individual and helped create a favorable atmosphere for small-group research. Third, the social sciences had by this time developed to a great extent; assumptions and procedures had been clarified, and professionals within the field were gaining insights into how these might be applicable to the understanding of the small group. The birth of group dynamics thus awaited a supportive society, developed professions, and the emergence of new procedures in social science.

Several studies conducted on the eve of World War II showed important elements that became associated with subsequent group-dynamics research (Cartwright & Zander, 1968). Sherif (1936) showed that group phenomena could be studied experimentally in the laboratory. Newcomb (1943) studied individuals in their natural setting and showed that group membership affects individual attitudes. Roethlisberger and Dickson (1939) studied a small work group within a large industrial setting and found that, although the overall goals of the organization fostered productivity, informal standards within the work group tended to limit it. This study and a study by Whyte (1943) are important because they consider the interrelationships of the individual, the small group, and larger social systems. Finally, Lewin, Lippitt, and White (1939; Lippitt, 1940) studied the effects of three leadership "climates"—democratic, autocratic, and laissez-faire—on group members' satisfaction and productivity. This research represented the direct application of scientific methods to an issue of immediate social relevance. (The procedures and findings of each of these studies will be discussed later.)

The Spotlight on the Individual and the Eclipse of the Group

World War II spurred further developments in social psychology. Many practical questions were raised about leadership, group morale, and group performance (Chapters 9–11). Extensive in-depth surveys were conducted to understand the American soldier and the effects of mass bombings on civilian populations. Programs were undertaken to assess and change attitudes toward the war and wartime restrictions, such as food rationing. Following World War II, social psychology underwent a period of dramatic growth, and perhaps 95% of all social-psychological research has been conducted since that time.

Although the study of both individuals and groups had been prospering for some time, by the late 1950s more and more attention was focused on the individual and less and less attention was focused on the group (Steiner, 1974). By the late 1960s, the great majority of the papers published in the most widely read social-psychological journals dealt almost exclusively with the individual. Although the papers discussed such topics as attraction (which requires two people) and conformity (which involves two or more people influencing a third), research procedures were such that true interaction was typically not involved. For example, to study attraction, the researchers might have one person rate another on the basis of a written description; to assess the effects of a "discussion," a researcher might have the person passively listen to a tape recording.

Steiner (1974) has discussed several factors that may have led to the eclipse of the group. First, there is the practical consideration that studying interaction in small groups is much more difficult and time consuming than studying the individual. Second, although many exciting theories had developed that deal with the individual, few new theories were developed to nourish group dynamics. Third, conditions in society may have diverted attention from the small group. Steiner argues that, when society is serene and its tranquility is marred only by a few individuals, attention is directed toward sociological questions about the society and toward psychological questions about individual deviants. There is a time lag between societal conditions and research interests, so the focus of the 1960s most likely represented national tranquility during the 1950s.

The study of groups is still a difficult task, but there are reasons to expect that the small group is likely to come out of its eclipse. First, theoretical nourishment may be forthcoming from the area of organizational psychology (Chapter 11). Second, the serenity of the 1950s (which led to the eclipse of the group in the 1960s) was replaced by national turmoil in the middle and late 1960s. During this period many segments of society vied with one another and drew attention back to relatively small groups. These conditions, suggests Steiner, are likely to prompt a return to the study of the small group in the middle 1970s.

SOCIAL PSYCHOLOGY AND SOCIAL RELEVANCE

Kurt Lewin, an early and extremely influential social psychologist, envisioned a discipline that would not only provide an understanding of people but also contribute to their welfare. According to Kenneth Ring (1967), over the years many social psychologists have seemed to lose sight of the second of these goals. He suggested that much social-psychological research has had a "fun-and-games" quality to it that made it useless for bettering the human condition. Since the mid-1960s, a major issue has

been the extent to which social-psychological theory and research are "relevant," in the sense that they have real implications for real people living in a real world (Ring, 1967; McGuire, 1967; Elms, 1972; Caplan &

Nelson, 1973; Braginsky & Braginsky, 1974). Ghetto uprisings, campus riots, political assassinations, and slaughters in Vietnam led to some second thoughts about the value of research projects that involved pushing buttons and watching lights, assembling toy ashtrays, and sticking pins into balloons.

Getting social psychologists to admit some responsibility for understanding real people in a real world is one thing; getting them to agree on the best way to shoulder this responsibility is something else. According to what we might call the "traditionalist" position, careful laboratory experimentation, complete with buttons, lights, and popping balloons, can contribute heavily toward the development of theories that will have very practical applications. (The rationale underlying the traditionalists' methods is fully explained in Chapter 2.) According to what we might call the "activist" position, research should be action oriented and of immediate applicability. Leaning too far in the former direction can result in scientific rigor without social relevance; leaning too far in the latter direction can result in social relevance without scientific rigor.

There is a growing recognition that scientific rigor and social relevance are not incompatible goals. Rigorous methods can be applied to relevant problems, and the study of social issues can contribute to the development of no-nonsense theory. Blending rigor and relevance is not easy; it requires a breadth of perspective, a degree of creativity, and a willingness to use procedures not yet commonly accepted within the field (McGuire, 1973). Hopefully, the interplay among rigor, relevance, and theory will be made apparent at many points throughout this text.

PART SUMMARY

Contemporary social psychology is a scientific enterprise. The assumptions of this science are that a real world exists, that occurrences in this real world are lawfully related, and that these relationships can be uncovered by careful research. The goals of this science are description, prediction, control, and understanding. Physical and natural sciences share these assumptions and goals with social psychology and the other social sciences. However, the physical and natural sciences have been spared certain criticisms that have been leveled at the social sciences. These criticisms are typically based on the false assumption that nonsocial sciences are "exact," on a failure to appreciate the complexity of social behavior, or on an inability to lay aside strong personal prejudices concerning human behavior. One critic has suggested that, because of cultural changes and the publicity accorded social-psychological findings, there is insufficient stability in social behavior for the goals of prediction and control to be realized. However, social psychologists have identified some principles that work in different cultures and at different times. Social behavior that is unpredictable or uncontrollable is so because of present shortcomings in our ability to understand.

Scientific social psychology is a relatively recent enterprise. The Reformation and the development of the physical sciences made the mid-1800s ripe for the suggestion that the tools of science could be applied to the understanding of human social behavior. The first experiments and texts appeared around the beginning of the 20th century. The 1930s saw the rise of group dynamics. More than 90% of the growth of the field has occurred since World War II. To some extent the 1950s and 1960s were characterized by a diversion of attention from the small group to the individual, although there is reason to believe that the small group will again assume a major role in the field of social psychology.

The problems addressed by social psychologists represent a combination of scientific curiosity and human values. A recent debate has centered on increasing the "relevance" of social psychology to real people living in a real world. Both rigor without relevance and relevance without rigor leave much to be desired. There is a growing recognition that scientific rigor, social relevance, and solid theory are compatible goals.

2
Guidelines
for Inquiry

OBSERVING SOCIAL BEHAVIOR

NAÏVE AND SOPHISTICATED EMPIRICISM

TOOLS OF THE TRADE

Self-Report Measures
Coding Systems
Behavioral Tests

QUALITIES OF GOOD MEASURES

Reliability
Validity

OBSERVATION AND THEORY

Criteria for Evaluation

PART SUMMARY

CORRELATIONAL STUDIES: THE PREDICTION OF SOCIAL BEHAVIOR

RELATING VARIABLES

Contingency Tables
Correlation Coefficients
Correlational Findings and Predicting the Future

HARD TIMES AND CHURCH MEMBERSHIP: AN ILLUSTRATIVE CORRELATIONAL STUDY

CORRELATION, CAUSE, AND EFFECT

PART SUMMARY

EXPERIMENTAL STUDIES: UNRAVELING CAUSE AND EFFECT

THE LOGIC OF THE EXPERIMENTAL METHOD

The Use of Groups
When Does a Difference Make a Difference?

LABORATORY EXPERIMENTATION

Fear and Conformity: An Illustrative Study

DIFFICULTIES ASSOCIATED WITH LABORATORY EXPERIMENTS

Contrived Situations and Tasks
Unrepresentative Subjects
Demand Characteristics
Experimenter Bias
A Personal Opinion

FIELD EXPERIMENTATION

Initial Selling Price and Subsequent Sales:
  An Illustrative Study

DIFFICULTIES ASSOCIATED WITH FIELD EXPERIMENTS

Practical Concerns
Difficulties of Control
Rewards and Costs

THE NEED FOR MULTIPLE METHODS

RESEARCH AND ETHICS

Ethical Concerns
Ethical Guidelines

PART SUMMARY

What might you see if you were to take a guided tour of a social-psychology research facility? Peering into the first lab, you might see a nervous-looking woman being addressed by a man in a white lab coat. As he talks about "oral stimulation" he holds up baby-bottle nipples, pacifiers, lollipops, and other suckables. In the next lab you might find two people sitting at a table, separated by a partition. Lights flash, buttons are pushed, relays click, more lights flash—and then a woman takes some money from one person and gives some money to the other. In the third room you might find five people sitting around a table. They are furiously passing notes—but only to the person on their immediate left.

At about this time you might be feeling perplexed. This obviously costly nonsense seems to have no correspondence to the kinds of things that probably drew you to social psychology: issues such as why people associate with one another, why people cooperate, and what makes for good working conditions. But if you were to ask your guide, you might discover that in the first laboratory they are studying why people associate with one another, in the second, why people cooperate, and in the third, what factors affect worker satisfaction and productivity!

Certainly not all the research projects that we will discuss will seem somehow removed from the underlying issues. But enough research projects use artificial situations and contrived tasks that the underlying rationale for them needs some explanation. In this chapter we will consider the scientific guidelines that govern social-psychological research. More extended discussions can be found in Crano and Brewer (1973), Hendrick and Jones (1972), and Neale and Liebert (1973).

OBSERVING SOCIAL BEHAVIOR

Empiricism is a philosophical doctrine stating that the gateway to knowledge is through the evidence confronting our senses. An **empirical observation** is one that is made through using the senses. Thus, to discover the percentage of students who cut a 12:00 class, an empiricist would go to the class, count the number of students present, and compare this figure with the number enrolled.

Using the eyes, ears, and other sense organs to gain knowledge has a very practical advantage. Information gained in this way has the potential of being verified by others. For example, two people might have very different estimates concerning attendance at a 12:00 class. One person might argue that the percentage attending should be high, since by 12:00 everyone has had ample time to wake up and arrive on campus. A second person might reason that the percentage attending the class should be low, since at noon people are more interested in the pleasures of eats than in the poetry of Keats. If these two people go to the class, count the number of students present, and compare this figure with the total number of students enrolled, they will be able to reach agreement on the percentage of "cuts" that day. We probably learn very early in life that empirical evidence is both the most vivid type of evidence for ourselves and the most convincing type of evidence when trying to win an argument with others. Empirical observation is a mainstay of science.

NAÏVE AND SOPHISTICATED EMPIRICISM

For centuries people have set forth, on stone tablets, papyrus, and erasable bond, descriptions of what they have learned through their senses. In many cases two or more careful descriptions of the same event have differed, even though both observers used their eyes and ears and fervently believed that they were sticking to the facts. In these cases the observers were naïve.

Naïve empiricism, or the unaided use of the senses, is not terribly reliable. As we shall see in Chapter 3, an observer's expectations and motives are likely to affect his or her perception of "the facts." Of course, observations with a strong subjective coloring may be rewarding and useful to the individual observer. Chapters 3, 5, and 7 will show that people sometimes make sense out of the world and gain a sense of comfort through distorted perceptions and a misjudgment of evidence. Furthermore, observations with a strong subjective element can contribute to science by providing individuals with hunches or insights, which can later be confirmed or disconfirmed through careful study. However, because they so often exist only in the eye of the beholder, firsthand impressions are not invariably useful to other people. Therefore they cannot be relied upon to always contribute in a helpful way to the group enterprise of science.

Sophisticated empiricism refers to the use of procedures that check and extend unaided observations and provide some safeguards against the problems of subjective observation. An empirical observation is sophisticated when the observer carefully specifies the procedures that were used for making the observation. For example, suppose that I tell you that I have observed that Kent is a very popular person. On the basis of conversing with Kent and observing him interact with others, you may or may not draw the same conclusion. However, if I explain that I asked everyone in Kent's dorm to list the three people in the dorm whom they liked best and then discovered that Kent was listed more often than was anyone else, you would be able to use the same procedure and reach the same conclusion. Although specification of procedures raises the likelihood that agreement will be reached, this does not invariably work. I could tell you, for example, that two glasses of wine on an empty stomach will make everyone seem jolly and lovable, but, no matter how carefully you follow these instructions, you may fail to get the same result. For the most part, however, careful specification of procedures allows people to replicate one another's observations.

TOOLS OF THE TRADE

Many procedures have been used for checking and extending unaided observations so that agreement can be reached. Most of these techniques involve using measurement or assessment devices that are *external* to the observer. In the physical sciences, rulers, scales, and meters of all descriptions provide external measures. In social psychology, rating scales, questionnaires, and contraptions of all sorts serve this purpose. Because they are external, they are public; that is, the measures they provide can be obtained by anyone competent enough to use them.

Suppose we want to know if watching tightrope walkers and flagpole sitters reduces people's fear of heights. If we interview the fearful people before and after they observe such fearless performers, we might find all sorts of seemingly relevant evidence. They might state concerns about hot-air ballooning and skydiving, discuss the appearance of precipices and precarious platforms in nightmares, speak eloquently in defense of surface transportation, and so forth. Two interviewers who talked to them both before and after they watched the fearless performers might draw different conclusions concerning the results if they asked different questions or assigned different weights to the statements. But if the investigators followed a set series of questions, the likelihood of disagreement would be reduced. If they assessed people's fear of heights by counting the number of rungs of a ladder the people were willing to climb before and after watching fearless acrobats, there might be no disagreement at all. The questionnaire and the ladder are external measures. They provide objective yardsticks that anyone can use to gauge people's behavior.

Self-report measures, coding systems, and contrived behavioral tests are three popular measures for assessing individuals and groups. **Self-report measures** include rating scales and questionnaires that respondents use to express their feelings or beliefs. **Coding systems** are sets of rules that two or more observers use for classifying or categorizing what they observe. **Behavioral tests** consist of specific tasks or situations set up in such a way as to allow easy observation and recording of overt responses. Each type of measure, by itself, can provide useful information about individuals and groups. When used in combinations, the measures complement and supplement one another and can provide evidence far stronger than that yielded by any single measure alone. Later we will consider the advantages of using a variety of techniques to "triangulate" on a given problem.

Self-Report Measures

Questionnaires and rating scales take us beyond naïve empiricism by providing us with a standard set of items that can be used by any researcher. In the case of an **open-ended measure,** the question is simply asked, and the respondent is allowed to answer in his or her own words. This means that the answers can very faithfully reflect the respondent's feelings or beliefs, even if they are totally unanticipated by the researcher. In the case of **closed-ended measures,** the respondent is not allowed to answer in his or her own words but most choose one of a number of responses provided by the researcher. For example, the respondent may be asked to indicate whether a statement is true or false, or to check one of seven spaces arranged along a line running from "like" to "dislike." Limiting options in this way offers the decided advantage that the answers are easy to score and categorize and hence easy to agree upon. If the respondent were allowed to answer freely, there would be hundreds of possible answers, and any given answer might be interpreted in different ways by different people. On the other hand, if an answer contains only the alternatives "agree" and "disagree," then everyone inspecting the questionnaire can classify it in the same way. A multiple-choice format offers the two additional advantages that it makes quantification easy (an asset when one wants to compare different responses or scores) and that it makes machine or computer scoring easy (a major consideration, since a large research project may involve hundreds of thousands of scores).

There are several problems associated with self-report methods. These methods are based on the assumption that the respondent (1) understands the question; (2) is aware of and can express his or her feelings or beliefs; (3) is willing to give an honest answer; and (4) in the case of a closed-ended measure, finds an accurate alternative among the multiple-choice options. These assumptions may not always be warranted.

Another problem with self-report measures is that people have biases toward giving certain types of answers. Tendencies to respond in a certain way regardless of the content of the question are called **response sets** (Cronbach, 1969; Fiske, 1971). One response set is **acquiescence,** or a tendency to agree with an item no matter what it is. The opposite response set is **nay-saying,** or a tendency to disagree with an item independent of its content. A third response set is **social desirability,** or a tendency to choose answers that present oneself in a favorable light. Various procedures can help minimize the problems posed by response sets. For example, acquiescence and nay-saying may be combated by devising a test on which half the questions should be answered "yes" and the other half "no" to achieve a high score, and social desirability may be combated by forcing the respondent to choose between two answers of equal desirability.

Faking—that is, a deliberate attempt at misrepresentation—is a particularly thorny problem. For example, a person might believe that cripples should be kept off the streets. Yet the knowledge that other people would react with horror to this idea might inhibit honest self-expression and lead him or her to indicate favorable attitudes toward cripples.

A number of techniques have been tried to ensure that a respondent will give an honest or "straight" answer. One common procedure is to appear sympathetic and understanding and to convince the respondents that anything they might say will be met with a reaction of friendly acceptance. A second common procedure is to guarantee anonymity. Under this condition people feel a bit freer to express themselves, because they know that whatever they say cannot be held against them.

A recent and controversial procedure for coping with faking is the **bogus pipeline** (Jones & Sigall, 1971, 1973). The person who is being interviewed is seated before a steering wheel, which is connected to a pointer. The pointer can be moved along a seven-point scale by turning the steering wheel, and it is in this way that the interviewee makes his or her feelings known. Meanwhile, a formidable but fake electronic contraption called an "electromyograph," or EMG, is hooked up to the respondent. Through an elaborate set of procedures, the respondent is convinced that the EMG can measure minute muscle potentials and in this way reveal one's true, inner feelings when a question is presented. Thus the EMG bears a seeming similarity to a lie detector.

In effect, then, the respondent is led to believe that the device provides a "pipeline" that will lay bare his or her private feelings. Under these conditions respondents seem more willing to express negative, usually inhibited, attitudes (for example, negative attitudes toward minorities or toward the physically handicapped). One reason why the bogus pipeline seems to work may be that people don't like the idea of being second-guessed by a machine; another is that they may feel it better to let the interviewer know their true attitudes than to let him or her discover that, not only do they have reprehensible attitudes, but they are trying to be liars as well. Critics of the pipeline argue that it does not greatly increase the likelihood of an honest response and that the complicated procedures involved are not justified by the extra information gained (Ostrom, 1973; Brigham, Bloom, Gunn, & Torok, 1974). Furthermore, there is an ethical issue. When the pipeline is used, a dishonest interviewer (who lies about the EMG) is substituted for a dishonest subject (who would like to lie about his or her attitudes).

Coding Systems

A coding system is a set of rules that provides a common reference point for all users. It takes us beyond naïve empiricism by providing a set of external standards for classifying and categorizing observations.

Let's consider as an example a coding system that is presently being developed by one of my colleagues, Richard Coss, and his students (Coss,

Jacobs, & Allerton, 1975). These researchers have been interested in how people sitting alone in a public place such as a lounge or a lobby will react when an intruder sits down next to them. They expect that such an act of intrusion will induce a certain amount of stress or arousal. Earlier research by Coss (1973) and others had suggested that seemingly irrelevant activities, such as scratching, tugging one's ear, or tapping one's finger, serve to modulate (raise or lower) arousal. That is, engaging in these acts would seem to reduce arousal under conditions of stress but raise arousal when the person is underaroused or bored. On the basis of this earlier research, the present investigators expect that the arrival of an intruder would cause an increase in the number and rate of seemingly irrelevant acts. They are thus concerned with the development of a system to study such acts.

To begin with, the team simply jotted down the kinds of things people did when they were sitting alone in lounges or in lobbies. This informal observation yielded a list of 39 activities. On the basis of surface similarities, these activities were clustered into the six categories that presently constitute the coding system (see Table 2-1). To use this system, the observer is stationed in a place that is inconspicuous but allows a clear view of the person to be studied. Underneath a coat or a magazine, on the experimenter's lap, is a keyboard with six pushbuttons, one for each category. Each time a button is pressed, a tone is fed into a tape recorder hidden in a purse or a briefcase. Later the number and sequence of events can be reconstructed from playing the tape.

At this point you may be wondering "Why bother with six categories? Why not have just one button to record all acts?" The reason for breaking down acts into categories is twofold. First, some acts may be more common responses to intrusion than others, or more common among certain kinds of people (for example, men) than among others (for example, women). Second, some of these activities are likely to serve functions in addition to or instead of moderating arousal. For example, patting one's hair into place could represent an attempt to become attractive to a cute (or handsome) intruder. By attempting to separate activities into categories, it becomes possible for discoveries to be made that would not be possible otherwise.

There are three major problems associated with developing and applying coding systems. First, it is usually difficult to establish mutually exclusive and exhaustive coding categories. Second, it is difficult to establish an optimal number of categories. A scheme with few categories is easy to use but lacks precision; a scheme with many categories is precise but unwieldy and difficult to use. Third, training observers to use the system can be time consuming and difficult. Nonetheless, in many cases, coding systems have proven useful for reducing the complexity of social behavior to manageable proportions.

Table 2-1. A classification system for seemingly irrelevant (motoric) acts

Category	Behaviors
1. Scratching and rubbing	Rub eyes; scratch ears; scratch chin; tug eyelashes or eyebrows; rub moustache or upper lip; scratch cheek; move tongue in mouth; scratch side of nose; wipe mouth or nose with hand; scratch back of head; scratch thigh; scratch knee; scratch shoulder
2. Object fiddling	Chew gum violently; rub arm of chair; fiddle with some object such as pen or purse
3. Hand/leg movement	Rotate foot; tap foot; swing legs; play with thumb and forefinger
4. Grooming	Pat hair behind ear; run hand through hair or forehead
5. Object adjustment	Readjust pants; readjust something on lap; look at watch; adjust neckline of clothing
6. Change of position	Cover mouth with hand; stretch neck; put fingers in mouth; turn head to side; put hand on forehead; flex foot; twist ankle; readjust feet; change leg position; interlace fingers; twist in chair; shift shoulders; readjust weight in chair

Used by permission of Richard Coss.

Behavioral Tests

Contrived situations and tasks also aid the observational process. They provide a uniform set of conditions that can be easily understood, that make meaningful comparisons possible, and that can be replicated by other researchers at future points in time. For example, suppose we want to assess the effects of close supervision on the speed with which people work. We could monitor a housewife carefully while she mowed the lawn and then leave her completely alone while she tuned up her car. It might appear that, when she was supervised while doing lawn work, she became resentful and dragged her heels, whereas when she was left alone while working on the car she performed happily and efficiently. Yet it would be difficult to feel confident about this conclusion, for it involves a comparison of two different things—of apples and pears, so to speak. Furthermore, later researchers could not restore the original testing conditions of the lawn and the car and hence could not duplicate the comparison. If, on the other hand, we use some sort of standardized task, such as the folding of towels, it would be easier to evaluate her performance. This would simply involve counting the number of towels folded under each condition. Furthermore, subsequent researchers could duplicate our procedures, since they could readily obtain unfolded towels of the specified dimensions.

A useful distinction can be made between tasks that are contrived and tasks that are artificial. A **contrived task** is one that is deliberately set up by a researcher. An **artificial task** is one that is recognizable as having been set up by a researcher. A contrived task is not necessarily artificial. For example, to test the honesty of a job applicant, a personnel supervisor might put some loose change in the chair in which the applicant is likely to sit, show the applicant into the room, but then immediately excuse himself or herself for a couple of minutes. The job may hinge on whether or not the change is turned in. Although this is a contrived test of behavior, it is not artificial if the applicant reasons that the change probably slid out of the pocket or purse of a previous interviewee and can be kept without fear of detection. On the other hand, many tasks used by social psychologists are artificial, although it may not be possible for the person being assessed to correctly identify all the contrived aspects of the situation.

In a sense, social psychologists who test people by having them engage in artificial tasks and solve trumped-up problems can be compared to foreign-language examiners, who also test people with artificial measures. During a language exam, the passages selected for translation are likely to be contrived, since the instructor wants selections that involve complex grammar rules and a large vocabulary. From using these contrived passages, the examiner obtains a score that he or she believes *reflects* or *represents* the person's level of proficiency outside the testing situation. Similarly, the social psychologist examines behavior believed to *reflect* behavior outside the testing situation. Both a foreign-language examiner and a social psychologist can make mistakes; the pride of Chinese 1 may starve in Peking because of an inability to read Chinese menus, and the conditions that produce the world's best towel folder in the lab might spell the end of a thriving commercial laundry. However, if the language examiner and the social psychologist carefully develop and repeatedly check their tests, they are unlikely to go too far astray. Later in this chapter, and within the context of a specific experiment, we will further consider the rationale that underlies the use of artificial situations and tasks.

QUALITIES OF GOOD MEASURES

Some measures of individuals and groups are considered better than others, in that they are believed to more faithfully capture some aspect of reality. The chief criteria for evaluating measures are reliability and validity.

Reliability

Reliability refers to the extent to which an observation holds true for different people and on different occasions. A reliable measure is one that produces consistent, repeatable results. There are two major forms of reliability. **Test-retest stability** refers to the extent to which a measure produces similar results on different occasions. For example, an intelligence test implying that a person is a genius one day but an idiot the next would not have test-retest stability. **Internal consistency** refers to the extent to which an instrument measures one thing in a consistent way rather than two or more things in a haphazard way. For example, if we have a ten-item test of sociability, internal consistency might be examined by comparing people's answers to the first and the second halves of the test. If the scores obtained by a given person on the two subparts were closely interrelated, this would suggest that both halves of the test measured the same quality or attribute. If the scores on the two subparts were unrelated, the test would seem to measure two or more things in a haphazard way. To the extent that the scores on the subparts approximate each other, then, the test or measure would be internally consistent. This is a highly simplified example; the procedures for establishing internal consistency are for the most part quite complicated (Ghiselli, 1964; Cronbach, 1969; Fiske, 1971).

Procedures that are **precise**—in the sense that they allow careful quantification—are likely to yield more reliable observations than will procedures that are sloppy or imprecise. Consider the hypothetical example of two people using their wristwatches to judge which of two swimmers wins a race. One judge announces that Mark took 12 seconds and Ivan took 11. The other judge announces that Mark took 11 seconds and Ivan took 12. Who's right? The truth is somewhere between 11 and 12 seconds, and the disagreement exists because the observers rounded off in different directions. A more precise instrument (such as a stopwatch) that indicated tenths of a second might have revealed that Mark won by four-tenths of a second. With precise measures, gross errors due to "rounding off" are unlikely.

Validity

Validity refers to the extent to which an observation is "truthful" or is "an instance of that which it is supposed to be." Thus to the extent to which a test of intelligence measures a person's ability to understand the environment, to reason, and to identify or improvise solutions to problems, that test would be a valid measure of intelligence. To the extent that the test measured something other than a person's intellectual ability (such as classroom performance, middle-class attitudes, or motivation to do well on tests), that test would be an invalid measure of intelligence.

Observations and measures can be evaluated in terms of several forms of validity. **Face validity** refers to the extent to which a measure appears to assess that which it is intended to assess. For example, to measure people's honesty, we might devise a test that asks them to respond to a number of hypothetical situations. They might be asked such things as what they would do if they found a wallet containing money, what they would do if they saw their best friend cheating on an examination, and how they would react if the college registrar made a mistake and an undeserved "A" miraculously appeared on their transcript. Because responses to the test (in this case, hypothetical temptations) seem to resemble responses in the situations of interest (what the respondents might do when confronted with real temptations), it is easy to assume that the test is valid. That which a test appears to measure and that which it does measure often do coincide, but assuming such a correspondence is not always warranted. For example, our "honesty test" may measure not honesty but a desire to avoid being identified as dishonest by a too inquisitive researcher. Because of problems like this, a superficial resemblance between responses to a measure or test and responses in a situation of interest is not enough.

Criterion measures, which are accepted indicators of the behavior or attributes in question, are often used to establish validity. The scores obtained with the measure to be evaluated are related to the scores obtained with the criterion measure. A close relationship between the two suggests validity. For example, a test might be developed to indicate interest in the opposite sex. The criterion measure might be the number of times per week that the person goes on dates. If people who score high on the test date a lot and people who score low on the test do not date much, then the test is considered valid. If there is little or no relationship between test scores and criterion measures, then the test is considered invalid. Showing that a measure relates to a criterion measure is the most common way of demonstrating validity.

The next form of validity is more complicated and involves validation of an idea. A **hypothetical construct** is an inference used to tie together a number of different observations. For example, in some groups members like one another, like the group, appear promptly for meetings, and are reluctant to leave when the meeting is over. In other groups members are indifferent toward one another, indifferent toward the group, tardy for those few meetings that they do attend, and quick to leave as soon as circumstances permit. **Cohesiveness** has been offered as a construct, or inferred property, underlying these different indicators of interest and involvement (Chapter 10). **Construct validity** results from assembling enough evidence to infer a meaningful construct, using the construct to derive new propositions (for example, the proposition that cohesive groups will endure over a longer time span than will noncohesive groups), and then attempting to check or verify these propositions. The process of construct validation is a difficult exercise that requires the careful assembly of evidence from many different sources (Cronbach & Meehl, 1955).

A final type of validity is **content validity,** which refers to the extent to which the questions or items contained on a questionnaire or other measure faithfully reflect all the possible items that could be included. For example, there are innumerable items that might be included on a self-report measure of prejudice. How would you feel about having this kind of person as a supervisor? Do you feel that this kind of person is intelligent? Moral? How would you feel if this kind of person married your brother? The very difficult problem of content validation is to somehow select for the measure a set of questions that is representative of all the questions that could assess prejudice, as compared to an unrepresentative set of questions that taps some aspects of prejudice but leaves other facets totally unassessed. The reason why this is difficult or impossible is that we can never specify all the questions that could be asked.

Perhaps the idea of content validity is best conveyed by discussing a kind of measure that is probably all too familiar to you: a comprehensive final exam of 100 multiple-choice questions. The instructor has, let us say, a huge pool of 1000 questions that, taken together, cover everything presented in the course. If the final exam consisted of 100 items carefully drawn from all lectures and readings, the exam would be content valid. If the 100 items for the "comprehensive final" all came from the same lecture or from one or two chapters in the text, the exam would not be content valid. As you can see, content validity is seen as important for establishing a fair, overall picture.

OBSERVATION AND THEORY

In the preceding discussion we considered *how* observations are made. But *what* should be observed? The tools of the trade are not used aimlessly; their application typically awaits some sort of "hunch" about social behavior. Such hunches may be based on informal, impressionistic observations, or they may be derived from social-psychological theories. A **theory** is a set of statements intended to logically and convincingly capture or express some aspect of reality. Observation and theory are closely interrelated. A theory is usually prompted by something that the theorist has observed, and, in the course of testing out a theory, new observations are made.

Theories serve several useful and important functions in social psychology (Shaw & Costanzo, 1970; McCain & Segal, 1973). First, theories impose order and meaningfulness on observations that might otherwise seem chaotic. Like numbers, they provide summary statements about things and events in the world around us. Second, theories serve to stimulate and guide future research. Although they are based on a relatively limited number of observations, they can, if successful, generate many new propositions about the relationships among variables. An expected or tentatively identified relationship is called a **hypothesis,** and theories give rise to many new hypotheses. Third, theories tell what should be expected under conditions that have not yet occurred. Armed with a good theory, one can predict the future. Fourth, theories take us into the realm of understanding, since a good theory provides a plausible accounting or explanation of a phenomenon or situation. According to F. H. Allport, a theory:

> should provide more in the nature of an accounting than a mere analogy. There should be a feeling of inevitability once its postulates have been accepted and its rationale understood, and the explanations given should be sufficiently clear and detailed to be convincing [1955, p. 9].

As an example, consider Zajonc's (1965) theory about the effects of an audience on individual performance. For years it had been known that the presence of an audience had a sometimes beneficial and sometimes detrimental effect on behavior, but there was no convincing explanation for this inconsistency. A careful inspection of the research in this area led Zajonc to conclude that it was when the person was performing a simple or well-learned response that the audience had a beneficial effect, and when the individual was trying to learn a new response that the audience had a detrimental effect. Zajonc suggested that in both cases the presence of an audience leads to more forceful or energetic performances of a response. In cases in which the "right" response has already been learned and hence is being performed, this strengthening is of course beneficial. But in cases in which the "right" response has not already been learned and a "wrong" response is being performed, this "wrong" response is strengthened, which makes the learning of a "right" response more difficult. Zajonc's simple theory thus imposed order on some seemingly chaotic observations and made it possible to predict the conditions under which an audience would have a beneficial rather than a detrimental effect. His theory has also stimulated a great deal of subsequent research, which will be considered in greater detail in Chapter 10.

Criteria for Evaluation

In many cases there are two or more theories that attempt to account for the same aspect of reality. Although dealing with the same social behavior, they use different concepts and involve different arguments. When we have to choose between two or more competing social-psychological theories, how do we know which to pick?

Several criteria have been proposed for judging the merit of theories. Some of these criteria are *essential*, in that a theory must have them to survive. Others are *desirable*, in that theories that meet them have an edge over theories that don't (Shaw & Costanzo, 1970).

There are three qualities that Shaw and Costanzo consider essential for a theory. If any of these qualities is lacking, a theory must be revised or abandoned.

First, a good theory must have logical consistency; that is, it must start with its terms defined sufficiently clearly that different people will interpret them in the same way. It must proceed in a logical and consistent fashion to explain the relationships among these terms and to anchor these terms to observables.

Second, a good theory must be testable. It must generate hypotheses that are capable of proof or disproof. Although a theory can never really be proven (this would require observation of all possible cases—a clear impossibility), one unequivocal disconfirmation is sufficient to cast doubt on the theory in its existing form. Of course, it is sometimes difficult to gain agreement concerning what constitutes an "unequivocal disconfirmation," and a revision of the theory is always a convenient possibility.

Third, a good theory must agree with the relevant observations, some of which are collected after the theory is formulated. It is relatively easy to explain history, but it is not so easy to predict the future. Agreement with known facts and prediction of the future are both requirements for acceptability.

According to Shaw and Costanzo, the four *desirable* qualities for a theory are parsimony, generality, consistency with related theories, and usefulness. Of two or more theories with all the essential qualities, preference is given to the one with the most desirable qualities.

First, "parsimony," or simplicity in terms of definitions, propositions, and hypotheses, is considered desirable. Given two otherwise equally desirable theories, the less cumbersome of the two would be preferred. However, it should be emphasized that simplicity should not be bought at the expense of agreement with the facts. At one stage, social psychology was characterized by **simple sovereign theories,** which offered a single principle or concept, such as "sympathy" or "imitation," as a key to understanding all social behavior (G. W. Allport, 1954a). Although simple sovereign theories had the attractive feature of imparting to social psychology an overall coherence, they failed miserably because social behavior results from a multiplicity of variables operating in combination.

Second, favor is given to the theory that is more general, in the sense that it accounts for the wider range of behavior. Unfortunately, generality and precision are often negatively related, so that a theory general enough to "explain" anything predicts nothing. Most social-psychological theories today are **midrange theories,** which are general enough to provide some scope but restricted enough to offer some specific predictions.

Third, it is considered a virtue for a theory not to conflict with other theories already shown to have a high probability of being true. Shaw and Costanzo point out that, although a theory that is inconsistent with other, related, and generally correct theories is not necessarily invalid, it is likely to start out with a handicap. The prudent theorist profits from the wisdom offered by people who have worked on that problem earlier.

Finally, the nod should go to theories that are useful. Usefulness may be defined in terms of science's needs and purposes (Shaw & Costanzo, 1970) or, in accordance with our discussion of social psychology and social relevance (Chapter 1), in terms of society's needs and purposes. Thus I'm suggesting that a theory that leads to the prediction and control of international conflict is more useful than a theory that leads to the prediction and control of mating behavior among South American sloths.

We will encounter many different theories in our discussion of social psychology. When we compare two or more different theories that attempt to explain the same events, we will reconsider these various criteria.

PART SUMMARY

Empiricism, the doctrine that we learn about the universe through our senses, is a mainstay of science. Empirical observations have the best potential for being verified by others. Since individual observers have frailties, empirical observations are particularly likely to be verified when they have been gained with the aid of procedures that provide safeguards and checks. Checks are provided when the observer carefully specifies the procedures that were used to make the observation. Specification and replication of procedures is facilitated when the procedures involve devices that are somehow external to the observer. Because they are external, they are public and can be used by any competent person. Three of the most common tools for checking and extending unaided observation are self-report measures, coding systems, and behavioral tests.

Self-report measures consist of rating scales and questionnaires that provide a standardized set of items. Usually the questions are presented in a multiple-choice format. For self-report measures to be successful, the person must understand the questions and be able to give honest answers. The value of self-report measures is undermined by response sets and by attempts at deliberate falsification.

A coding system is a set of rules for classification that can be referred to by different observers. Coding systems provide impersonal umpires that render verdicts on behavior. A successful system requires establishing an optimal number of mutually exclusive and exhaustive coding categories and training people how to use it. Although these conditions are difficult to fulfill, such systems have served a useful role in social psychology.

Behavioral measures provide a fourth way for assessing individuals and groups. These involve situations and tasks that are uniform and repeatable and that make meaningful comparisons possible. Although fulfilling these requirements may involve artificial or contrived tasks, the accepted belief is that performance at such tasks reflects behavior that occurs outside the testing situation.

Several criteria exist for evaluating the adequacy of scientific observations and the measurement devices used to obtain them. Reliability refers to the extent to which an observation is repeatable and consistent. Test-retest stability and internal consistency are forms of reliability. Validity refers to the extent to which an observation is "truthful," in the sense that it is an instance of that which it is supposed to be. Forms of validity include face validity, criterion validity, construct validity, and content validity.

Observations and theories are closely interrelated. Theories attempt to capture and express some aspect of reality. They serve to impose order and meaningfulness on observations, provide a basis for predictions, and stimulate further research. Theories also provide us with an explanation of the world around us. A good theory is one that meets certain criteria. It is considered essential for a theory to be logically consistent, testable, and in agreement with the facts. It is considered desirable for a theory to be parsimonious, consistent with related theories, and useful.

CORRELATIONAL STUDIES: THE PREDICTION OF SOCIAL BEHAVIOR

We have considered in general terms some of the techniques social psychologists use for obtaining accurate descriptions of social behavior. But, as we have noted, science attempts to go beyond the present and to forecast or predict the future. To do so, it is necessary to study relationships among variables. Prediction requires some sort of systematic variation in two variables, such that fluctuations in the value or magnitude of one variable are associated with fluctuations in the value or magnitude of the other. Once a rule has been uncovered that expresses an association or relationship, it is possible to make an educated guess concerning the value of one variable if the value of the other variable is known.

RELATING VARIABLES

Correlational studies involve discovering the extent to which two (or more) variables naturally covary. These studies have the advantage that the phenomenon in question remains undefiled by the researcher. Correlational findings are commonly expressed in terms of *contingency tables* and *correlation coefficients*.

Contingency Tables

Schachter (1968, 1971) has stated some interesting ideas about overeating. According to him, internal bodily conditions determine whether a person of normal weight feels hungry and eats. When a normal person's stomach is full, that person will not feel hungry and will not eat; but when a normal person's stomach is empty, he or she will feel hungry and will eat. Less commonsensical is the additional argument that external, food-related cues will determine whether an overweight person will feel hungry and eat. According to Schachter, obese persons' reports of hunger and eating behavior depend not on whether they have eaten recently but on such things as the sight and aroma of tasty food. Obese persons are obese because food cues are abundant in our affluent society. In an impoverished society, in which food cues are rare, most obese people would probably be exceptionally underweight.

Schachter and his associates have completed a great deal of research on this theory. They have found, for example, that, although conditions that reduce gastric motility (stomach contractions) reduce a normal person's appetite, they do not have much effect on the fat person's appetite. Compared with normal people, obese people are more likely to feel hungry and eat simply on the basis of seeing other people eat, or because the clock indicates that it's dinnertime. The more recent findings (Schachter, 1971) suggest that the obese person's sensitivity to prominent external cues is a general phenomenon that occurs in different situations and contexts, not just in those somehow involving food.

Now let's shift from fact to fiction. Suppose one fall day as you are walking to the bank, you happen to notice that the bank's huge outside thermometer reads 92°. Mentioning this seeming overestimation to the teller, you are informed that the thermometer is broken and that the temperature is actually a comfortable 72°. As you leave, you notice a very heavy man walking by. As he glances at the thermometer, he draws a handkerchief out of his pocket, mops his brow, and proceeds to remove his jacket.

Remembering Schachter's findings, you have a brilliant idea. You get some paper and a pencil and sit down on a bench across from the bank. You then begin to keep track of how many people wearing coats approach the bank, whether or not they are overweight (I'm assuming that you are good at such estimates), and, as they approach the external

cue of the broken thermometer, whether or not they take off their coats. Your hypothetical findings could be expressed in a table such as Table 2-2.

Table 2-2. Hypothetical relationship between weight and removal of coat

	Fat person	*Thin person*	*Total*
Removed coat	8	2	10
Did not remove coat	2	8	10
Total	10	10	

This very simple two-by-two table is a convenient way of showing how such observations can be categorized into two categories (such as fat and thin) on each of two dimensions (weight and coat removal). Our table shows a strong hypothetical relationship between weight and apparent responsiveness to the external cue of the thermometer. This and any other similar table can be thought of as an "if-then" table: *if* the person is overweight, *then* he or she is likely to take off the coat. More categories and dimensions are possible for dealing with more complex problems or with finer measurements. Thus a **contingency table** may be defined as a multi-dimensional tabular presentation of frequencies by categories (Wilkening, 1973). Its function is to give some idea of how closely two variables are related.

Correlation Coefficients

Let's consider a more troublesome but potentially more interesting way in which you might have conducted your obesity study. Suppose that, along with your pencil and paper, you brought a bathroom scale (a good one), a tape measure for ascertaining height, and some rating sheets that people could use to express their feelings about the weather. Instead of merely classifying individuals as fat or thin, you could thus establish the percentage that they were overweight (by referring to insurance-company charts), and instead of merely categorizing them as coat wearers or coat removers, you classify them according to *how much* they found the "heat" oppressive. The hypothetical results for 20 people are presented graphically in Figure 2-1 and in tabular form in Table 2-3.

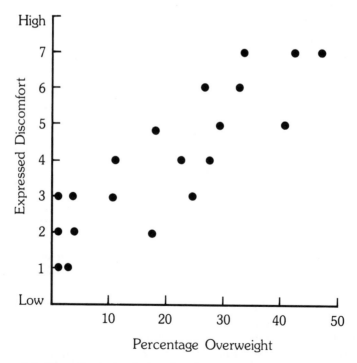

Figure 2-1. Hypothetical relationship between degree of obesity and expressed discomfort in the presence of a broken thermometer

Table 2-3. Hypothetical relationship between degree of obesity and expressed discomfort in the presence of a broken thermometer

Case	Percentage Overweight	Expressed Discomfort*
1	1	1
2	1	2
3	1	3
4	2	1
5	3	3
6	5	2
7	11	3
8	12	4
9	17	2
10	19	5
11	23	4
12	24	3
13	27	4
14	27	6
15	29	5
16	32	6
17	33	7
18	41	5
19	43	7
20	47	7

*High numbers indicate greater expressed discomfort.

These illustrations show a moderate degree of correspondence between obesity and expressed discomfort. Now it is possible to estimate the *degree* of discomfort from the *degree* of obesity. In a sense, a graph is a fancy contingency table; it just has many more categories along each dimension.

A handy way of describing a linear, or straight-line, relationship such as is expressed in Figure 2-1 is through a numerical summary statement known as a **coefficient of correlation** or, more conveniently, a **correlation**. These numerical statements range from -1.00 through 0 to $+1.00$. The plus and minus signs indicate the direction of the relationship, and the numerical value indicates the extent or degree of the relationship.

A **positive correlation** $(+)$ refers to a *direct* relationship such that an increase in the magnitude of one variable is associated with an increase in the magnitude of the other. In our hypothetical example, obesity and expressed discomfort are positively correlated. As obesity increases, reported discomfort increases; as obesity decreases, discomfort also decreases.

A **negative correlation** ($-$) refers to a relationship such that an increase in the magnitude of one variable is associated with a decrease in the magnitude of the other. For example, the more classes that are cut, the less impressive one's grades; or, the more unpopular positions a politician publicly adopts, the less likely his or her re-election. A negative correlation of a given value expresses the same degree of relationship as does a positive correlation of the same value. A negative correlation is therefore not to be confused with *no* correlation, which indicates a total lack of linear relationship between the variables.

The absolute numerical value (that is, the numerical value disregarding the plus or minus sign) expresses the degree or extent of the relationship between the two variables. A value of 0.00 would indicate no relationship at all. A value of $\pm$ 1.00 would indicate a perfect relationship such that, as one variable changes, there are exactly proportional changes in the other. The more a correlation deviates from 0.00, the more systematic and consequential the relationship and the better the job we can do with prediction. The more a correlation approaches 0.00, the more random, haphazard, and inconsequential the relationship and the poorer the job we can do with prediction. Although a correlation coefficient does not provide all the necessary bearings for making useful predictions (for example, a correlation coefficient would indicate nothing about the arms or axes in Figure 2-1), various formulas known as **regression equations** make it possible to anchor predictions with respect to reference points such as pounds and inches (Ferguson, 1971). The correlation expressing the data in Table 2-3 and Figure 2-1 is $+.86$.

Correlational Findings and Predicting the Future

Correlational findings are often useful because they can support or cast doubt upon various theories. For example, if they were real, the hypothetical results reported in the contingency table and in the graph would provide Schachter with reason to rejoice. As indicated earlier, correlational findings are also useful because they provide a basis for predicting the future. However, accurately predicting the future requires that two conditions be met.

First, the degree of association between the two variables must be of considerable magnitude. Most of the correlations we will be dealing with in this text fall somewhere in the .30 to .70 range and might thus be considered "low" or "moderate." Perfect predictions are not possible given such imperfect relationships. Fortunately, however, formulas exist for estimating the likelihood that a prediction will be accurate. When we know the chances that a prediction will come true, we know how much confidence to put into it.

Second, even if there is a very strong relationship between two variables, the operation of a third variable may render a prediction invalid. For example, there is a strong positive correlation between the extent to which people have similar attitudes and the extent to which they like one another (Chapter 6). However, a prediction that two people with highly similar attitudes will like each other might not be substantiated if it turned out that each of them was competing for the affection of the same third party. This third variable—competing for the affection of another—was not taken into account when attitudinal similarity and friendship were correlated.

What all this means is that, as scientists, we have to exercise caution when predicting the future. In daily life we are also likely to proceed with caution. For example, approaching an intersection where you have the right of way, you may be "reasonably confident" that an onrushing vehicle will yield. However, you may still pause and wait, fully aware that this prediction can sometimes go wrong.

HARD TIMES AND CHURCH MEMBERSHIP: AN ILLUSTRATIVE CORRELATIONAL STUDY

As an example of an actual, rather than fictitious, correlational study, let's consider an investigation bearing on Karl Marx' famous contention "Religion is the opiate of the masses." In this study by Sales (1972), economic conditions are correlated with conversion rates to various churches.

The concept of **authoritarianism** is central to an understanding of Sales' study. This term is used to designate individuals who might remind you of Archie Bunker. Authoritarians tend to emphasize power and toughness in social relationships, voicing law-and-order and get-tough-with-the-Commies views. They tend to be deferent toward social superiors but intolerant of social inferiors. There is a tendency toward prejudice. Authoritarians generally adhere to conventional morality. You will not find them using nonalcoholic mind expanders or living in sin. As Elms (1972) notes, a fair description of such people was provided by Plato, although it was not until the late 1940s that a scale was developed to measure authoritarianism (Adorno, Frenkel-Brunswik, Levinson, & Sanford, 1950).

The original research on authoritarianism suggested that harsh, threatening discipline in childhood leads to adult authoritarianism. Later findings suggested that threatening circumstances in adulthood could also raise the individual's level of authoritarianism. To study the relationship between threat and the authoritarianism of a wide spectrum of people, Sales defined threat in terms of economic insecurity and level of authoritarianism in terms of the rate at which people joined "authoritarian" and "nonauthoritarian" religious denominations. He expected that during economic "hard times," the "authoritarian" denominations would attract new members, whereas during prosperity, nonauthoritarian denominations would gain in popularity.

Four authoritarian and four nonauthoritarian churches were selected. Authoritarian churches were characterized as those in which (1) members were highly submissive to the dictates of church authorities, (2) intolerance toward other denominations was preached, (3) superstitious ritual was a major part of the worship services, (4) there was an overconcern with sexuality, (5) there was a pronounced holier-than-thou attitude, and (6) there was a preoccupation with toughness, strength, and power.

Sales' first study involved ascertaining the per capita income for each of the years from 1920 to 1939 and then correlating these figures with the church conversion rates for the same years. The correlations between these 20 pairs of observations for the four authoritarian churches were $-.87$, $-.46$, $-.46$, and $-.19$. Thus, for three of the four authoritarian churches, there was a reliable negative relationship between prosperity and conversion. The correlations for the nonauthoritarian churches were .53, .50, .41, and .31. For each of the four nonauthoritarian churches, then, there was a reliable relationship between prosperity and conversion. The two hypotheses were thus confirmed.

Sales' second study (1973) drew on statistics from Seattle, Washington. A "one-industry" (aerospace) city, Seattle's economy has ranged from vigorous to depressed, depending on the ever-changing fate of "aerospace." Correlating income and conversion rates for a recent ten-year period, Sales again found that authoritarian churches attracted more new members during hard times, whereas nonauthoritarian churches fared better during prosperity.

As noted earlier, Karl Marx described religion as the "opiate of the masses." He suggested that, when prosperity wanes, people flock to church to deaden the pain. Sales points out that this idea is not entirely correct, since only some churches (authoritarian) seem to provide comfort during times of recession or depression. Considering both kinds of churches obscures the relationship between economic threat and religion. On the basis of these results, one can cautiously predict that hard times will be accompanied by an increase in membership in authoritarian churches.

CORRELATION, CAUSE, AND EFFECT

Knowing what leads to what is a precondition for altering the future. Before we can infer a cause-effect relationship, three conditions must be satisfied.

First, the suspected cause and the suspected effect must covary so that changes in one are accompanied by changes in the other. By definition, correlational studies satisfy this condition.

Second, the suspected cause must precede the suspected effect. Correlational studies can satisfy this condition of showing a temporal sequence of events (Neale & Liebert, 1973). For example, McClelland (1961) pored through 1925-vintage children's readers from 23 different countries. He analyzed these stories in terms of **achievement imagery—** that is, the extent to which the central characters endorsed standards of excellence and strove to do tasks well. He then related this information to later measures of entrepreneurship and economic growth, such as the number of patents issued, the size of national income, and the amount of electricity produced. There was a correlation of .53 between achievement imagery in 1925 and growth in national output as indicated by increases in the amount of electricity generated between 1929 and 1950. But, although achievement imagery in the fairy tales of 1925 was positively correlated with economic output in the 1950s, achievement imagery in the fairy tales of 1950 was not correlated with economic output in the 1920s. It is thus more plausible that achievement imagery led to a vigorous economy than that the vigorous economy led to more achievement-oriented fairy tales. Presumably, as children, members of high-achievement societies were taught to value productivity and excellence.

Third, to demonstrate a cause-effect relationship, it is necessary to rule out alternative explanations of the effect. Unfortunately, correlational studies cannot satisfy this third condition for inferring causality. In McClelland's study, other variables (such as the presence of foreign advisers from I. T. & T. or Coca-Cola) could have caused variations in *both* achievement imagery and economic output. Additional correlations can eliminate these alternatives, one at a time. For example, if the presence of foreign advisers is found to be uncorrelated with achievement imagery and economic indices, this factor can be ruled out as an alternative. However, the process of elimination would be endless, and, whereas suspected alternatives could be eliminated one at a time, it would be impossible to cope with unsuspected alternatives. Careful correlational studies that relate measures taken at different points in time can be highly suggestive, and it is clear that sophisticated correlational techniques made possible through advancing computer technology offer tremendous potential that has yet to be exploited by social psychologists (McGuire, 1973). But many social psychologists do not accept correlational findings, however suggestive, as proof of causation. Only the experimental method, which combines manipulation and control, can eliminate large numbers of alternative explanations of an effect in one fell swoop.

PART SUMMARY

Correlational studies involve establishing the extent to which two or more variables naturally covary. Obtained relationships are usually expressed in terms of contingency tables or correlation coefficients. A contingency table expresses the relative frequency with which observations fall into two or more categories that represent two or more dimensions. A correlation is a numerical summary statement expressing the direction and extent of the relationship between two variables. Positive correlations indicate that, as the magnitude or value of one variable increases, the magnitude or value of the associated variable increases. Negative correlations indicate that, as the magnitude of one variable increases, the magnitude of the associated variable decreases.

Correlational findings can be used to support or deny a theory and to help predict the future. Reasonably accurate predictions require that the correlations must be of appreciable magnitude and that extraneous variables do not interfere. Since obtained correlations are often low, and since the world is characterized by flux and change, all predictions must be made with caution.

Sales' investigation of economic threat and conversion rates to authoritarian groups can be used as an illustration of a correlational study. Under conditions of economic threat people tend to join authoritarian churches, whereas under conditions of prosperity they tend to join nonauthoritarian churches. Marx' contention "Religion is the opiate of the masses" is only partially correct, since only some churches gain in membership during times of economic stress.

To unravel cause and effect, three conditions must be met. These are covariation, cause before effect, and the elimination of alternative causes. Correlational studies, by definition, satisfy the requirements of covariation and, when measures are obtained at different points in time, can satisfy the requirement of cause before effect. Sophisticated correlational studies can also eliminate, one by one, competing explanations of an obtained relationship. However, correlational studies are best taken as suggesting, rather than proving, cause-effect relationships.

EXPERIMENTAL STUDIES: UNRAVELING CAUSE AND EFFECT

The experimental method, with its combination of manipulation and control, is unequivocally the most logical procedure for inferring a cause-and-effect relationship. For this reason it has gained widespread acceptance in social psychology.

THE LOGIC OF THE EXPERIMENTAL METHOD

In the **experiment,** an attempt is made to arrange a sequence of events in order to see what led to what. The experimenter manipulates a suspected cause, or **independent variable,** and measures the consequences of this manipulation on the suspected effect, or **dependent variable.** Yet manipulation is only half the story; the other half is **control,** or somehow ensuring that variables other than the manipulated variable did not exert a systematic influence on the dependent variable. Manipulation and control are the defining characteristics of the experimental method (Katz, 1972).

Suppose a social-psychology student notes that, when people enter the school library and sit at an already occupied small table, earlier occupants are likely to get up and leave. As this observation is discussed in class, someone suggests a way to put the observation on a scientific footing: right after class as many students as possible should march over to the library, sit down at occupied tables, and record how quickly earlier occupants depart. The student is thus proposing manipulation—an activity aimed at altering the course of events.

During the next class meeting it is excitedly noted that, after a member of the class joined a table at the library, 80% of the occupants who were already there got up and left within five minutes. This finding seems like strong support for the hypothesis that people find invasion aversive. However, a woman sitting in the third row offers an interesting item of information. While all the other students were preoccupied with trying to crowd people out, she was busy discovering that as many non-crowded students as crowded students got up and left. Thus something other than invasion by the class must have accounted for the library users' hasty departure. Perhaps they were reacting to clocks and watches indicating that it was time to move on to class!

Although the membership of the class performed a manipulation, they did not satisfy the requirement of control. If all other conditions had been held constant, the class findings would have shown that invasion does cause retreat. (We will return to this kind of study in Chapter 8.) However, all other conditions were not held constant, and time was marching on. The world is characterized by variability, some of which is unavoidable. Thus, although experimenters strive to hold constant all variables except those that are consciously and willfully manipulated, they can never feel confident that all nonmanipulated variables have remained constant throughout the experiment. However, it is possible to discover if these other variables had a systematic effect on the dependent measure. The woman studying the noncrowded library students fulfilled this function with her observations.

Experimental findings take the form of a comparative statement. The comparison is between what happened under **experimental conditions,** during which a treatment or manipulation is present, and what happened under an alternative set of **control conditions,** which are equivalent except that the treatment or manipulation is absent. The control conditions provide a yardstick or measure with which to gauge the effects of the experimental manipulation. If the dependent variable is affected in the experimental but not in the control conditions, it is reasonable to conclude that the manipulation was responsible for the observed effect. If comparisons show no difference between experimental and control conditions, then any observed effects in the experimental conditions must be due to something other than the experimental manipulation.

The Use of Groups

Through experimental and control conditions, we can measure the effects of extraneous situational variables on observed behavior. However, as repeatedly noted, people's behavior reflects both situational and dispositional forces. This makes it difficult to say that a difference between any individual experimental subject and any individual control subject is due to the manipulation. It could be due to a dispositional difference instead. For example, a crowded person who gets up and leaves the library could be responding to a need to grab a snack or to some other internal motive that is not at that time affecting the noncrowded control person. The experimental subject's departure would thus be only coincidental with the appearance of the intruder.

The possibility that experimental subjects are responding to internal forces rather than to the manipulation can never be eliminated, but it can be shown to be unlikely. To begin with, individuals must be *randomly assigned* to the various conditions. That is, it must be arranged that each person is as likely to be in any one condition as in any other. Procedurally, in the present case, this assignment might be accomplished by the flip of a coin: heads, the man with the red beard is in the experimental condition and the man with the glasses in the control condition; tails, the man with the red beard is in the control condition and the man with the glasses in the experimental condition. However, if one of these two men is about ready for a snack, there is still a 50-50 chance that the hungry one will end up in the experimental condition; thus the hasty departure of an "experimental" subject would still have a 50-50 chance of having nothing to do with crowding by the experimenter.

On the other hand, it is to be expected that, in a comparison of groups to which individuals have been randomly assigned, individual differences in terms of personality, needs, bladder pressures, stomach contractions, and so forth will be random and will cancel one another out. If a crowded individual leaves and an uncrowded individual stays, it is plausible that the crowded person was responding to hunger or to some other personal need. If 20 crowded individuals leave and 20 uncrowded individuals stay, it may still be possible that the former all became hungry simultaneously whereas the latter did not, but the likelihood of this is exceedingly small. Thus, to help minimize the contributions of individual differences to results, experimenters typically compare *groups* of randomly assigned subjects.

When Does a Difference Make a Difference?

Whenever an experimenter obtains a difference between experimental and control conditions, he or she must choose between two explanations of that difference. One explanation is that the difference is due to the manipulation, and the other is that it reflects nothing more than randomness or chance.

In some cases, chance provides a plausible and intuitively compelling explanation of an occurrence. For example, suppose I tell you that I have ESP powers. To prove it, I propose to don a blindfold and, as you draw cards from a deck, call out the suits. We do so, and I call the cards right about 25% of the time. Although I claim that this proves my ESP powers, you probably wouldn't believe me, for it is quite plausible that chance alone accounted for my spotty successes.

In other cases, chance is not a plausible explanation of an event. Suppose I pull a fully functioning typewriter out of a washing machine. I then tell you that years ago I placed all the typewriter's parts into the washing machine and left the washer running until, due to chance alone, all the parts jiggled back into place to form a perfectly functioning typewriter (although the ribbon really needs replacement). You probably wouldn't believe me, for you would suspect that something other than chance accounted for the assembly of the typewriter. Yet the correct calling of suits of cards *could* reflect psychic powers, and the fully functioning typewriter *could* have been assembled by chance. One can never be sure.

Any result must be considered in light of the possibility that it is due to chance, since this alternative can never be completely ruled out. However, it is possible to calculate the likelihood of this alternative. If it seems that a result is due to chance, the result must be discounted, for it tells us nothing. This situation is exemplified in the case of the ESP demonstration, because it is very likely that chance alone would produce 25% correct calls given that there are four suits. By convention, when the likelihood that a result or difference is due to chance alone is 1 in 20 or less (such as 1 in 100), chance is ruled out as an explanation. Results meeting such criteria are called **statistically significant.**

Thus, in one sense, a difference makes a difference when it is not easily explained away by chance. In another sense, not all statistically significant results make a difference, for one can find manipulations that have statistically significant effects but that are at the same time of little practical value. If the groups compared were large enough, the finding that 51% of the experimental subjects and 49% of the control subjects got up and left the library after the experimenter's invasion would be statistically significant. However, with such a small difference, invasion would not be a very efficient way of getting people out of the library.

LABORATORY EXPERIMENTATION

Most experimentation within social psychology has taken place within the confines of the laboratory. Laboratory experimentation has some very staunch advocates—and some very tough critics. Because of the salience of laboratory research, let's consider in detail a representative example. This experiment, conducted by John Darley (1966), has been chosen as an illustration because it is straightforward and carefully done and because it offers some interesting results. It also incorporates certain kinds of features that have become targets for criticism.

Fear and Conformity: An Illustrative Study

Earlier research led Darley (1966) to reason that people who are made fearful will seek support and encouragement from others. To obtain this support and approval from a group, they will be likely to conform. He also reasoned that, if the other members of the group were also fearful, a frightened person would feel a strong sense of kinship with the group. This feeling of closeness to people in a similar plight should also raise the level of conformity. Thus Darley's two hypotheses were that threatening people will cause them to conform and that conformity will be further increased if the other members of the group are facing a similar threat. Testing these hypotheses required comparing all combinations of fearful individuals and fearful groups. The four conditions representing these combinations were (1) *Individual Threatened and Group Threatened;* (2) *Individual Threatened, Group Not Threatened;* (3) *Individual Not Threatened, Group Threatened;* (4) *Individual Not Threatened, Group Not Threatened.*

Darley then had to choose his **operations**—that is, set of procedures to define and manipulate the independent variable (in this case, fear) and to measure or assess the dependent variable (in this case, conformity). Individual fear was raised in the two *Individual Threatened* conditions by leading subjects to anticipate that they would be given strong electric shocks. This procedure had earlier proven useful for inducing fear in subjects similar to Darley's (Schachter, 1959). The apparent fate of the group was varied by leading subjects in the two *Group Threatened* conditions to believe that all the other members of the group would also receive strong shocks.

Forty-eight female college students participated in the study. Subjects of this type are easy to obtain. Because the experimenter already knows something about them and their likely reactions, he or she does not have to be a field anthropologist to devise some procedures that might affect them (Gerard & Conolley, 1972). With a homogeneous group of people such as this (that is, a group of people who are similar to one another in many ways), individual differences are less likely to obscure the effects of the experimental manipulation.

The women were randomly assigned, 12 each, to the four conditions. After they had undergone the appropriate threat manipulations, Darley administered a questionnaire to see if the threat of shock did affect reported fear. A manipulation check, or verification of procedures such as this, is important to make sure that the subjects perceived the conditions as intended by the experimenter. In this experiment, *Individual Threatened* subjects reported being more nervous and afraid than did *Individual Not Threatened* subjects.

Next came the conformity measure. To operationalize conformity, Darley asked his subjects to estimate the number of metronome clicks in rapid bursts of sound. It had been contrived that on some trials the other girls in the group would unanimously offer a wrong estimate. Conformity was defined in terms of the extent to which the subject agreed with these false or bogus estimates.

Finally, Darley applied statistical analyses. Although sometimes a nuisance, such analyses are crucial for two reasons. First, as indicated earlier, we are interested in what *typically happens* under various conditions, and statistics are necessary to reveal average performance. Second, as also indicated earlier, statistical analyses are required to evaluate the likelihood that any obtained results can be dismissed as reflecting chance alone. In this experiment, significant results supported both hypotheses: *Individual Threatened* women were more conforming than *Individual Not Threatened* women, and, considering only the two *Individual Threatened* conditions, conformity was greater when the group was threatened too (see Table 2-4).

Table 2-4. Median conformity responses of the four experimental groups*

		Individual	
		Threatened	Not Threatened
Group	*Threatened*	8.50	2.00
	Not Threatened	6.00	2.00

*The median is the middle case when scores are arranged from the largest to the smallest. The median is one indicator of average or typical performance and in most cases approximates the mean. Adapted from Darley (1966) with permission of the author and the American Psychological Association.

If significant results had not been obtained, either the hypotheses or the procedures for testing them would be wrong. Since there is no way to choose between these alternatives, studies lacking significant results are often considered too uninformative for publication in scientific journals.

At this point it should be cautioned that the results from one single experiment cannot be taken as an ultimate or final proof. Any results will reflect, in part, characteristics of the particular subjects and subtleties of the particular procedures used. If the same pattern of results can be obtained by different experimenters using different subjects and different procedures, our confidence in a set of findings is bolstered. For this reason it is desirable when someone duplicates or replicates an experiment to see if similar results emerge. Replications may be exact or conceptual. An **exact replication** is one that follows the original procedures as closely as possible. A **conceptual replication** involves retesting the hypotheses using different operations and, perhaps, a different type of subject as well. Of the two, conceptual replications are the more valuable; not only can they validate the original observations, but they can also extend them by showing that they hold for other procedures and subjects as well.

DIFFICULTIES ASSOCIATED WITH LABORATORY EXPERIMENTS

The laboratory experiment as exemplified by Darley's study is justified, according to Gerard and Conolley (1972, p. 242), by "the basic faith that human beings are human beings and that social influence phenomena occurring anywhere and at any time can be interpreted within the same basic framework." In the past decade or so, some of this basic faith has been shaken.

Laboratory experiments typically have **internal validity,** in that they affect the subjects' behavior within the experiment. But do they also have **external validity,** in that the procedures and results can be extended beyond the laboratory to representative people acting and interacting in representative, real-life settings? Severe critics of the laboratory experiment have argued that many such experiments are so lacking in external validity that they are likely to be uninformative or even downright misleading (Orne, 1962; Rosenthal, 1966; Rosenthal & Rosnow, 1969; Rosnow & Rosenthal, 1970; Adair, 1973).

Four major criticisms against laboratory experiments have been advanced: (1) that the artificial situations and tasks encountered in the laboratory are so dissimilar to the situations and tasks encountered in daily life that generalization is not possible; (2) that experimenters often fail to choose subjects who are representative of the population at large;

(3) that characteristics of the experiment may cause the subject to behave in ways that disguise or mask the activities the experimenter is trying to study; and (4) that the experimenter may bias findings, either by influencing subjects to behave in certain ways or by misperceiving the subjects as behaving in ways consistent with the hypotheses. Each of these criticisms will be discussed in detail. Not all of these charges are limited to the laboratory experiment, but they have generated the most spirited discussion in this context.

Contrived Situations and Tasks

The first criticism of laboratory experiments is that they usually use situations and tasks that are so artificial and contrived as to be meaningless. Darley threatened his subjects with electric shocks and found that this raised the likelihood that they would agree with false judgments concerning numbers of metronome clicks. It is unlikely that these women will ever again be threatened with shocks—or asked to estimate metronome clicks. So have we really learned anything about behavior?

The important relationship in Darley's experiment was not that between threat of shock and performance at a gimmicked metronome task but that between the conceptual variables, fear and conformity. **Conceptual variables** are abstract classes or categories that tie together or denote a number of different elements. Consider the concept of fear. Many stimulus conditions can produce fear (being threatened with a pistol, learning that expulsion from school is imminent, hearing one's zipper snap), and many responses are seen as symptomatic of fear (trembling hands, a tightness in the throat and stomach, high-pitched speaking, and so on). If we accept threat of shock as one instigator of fear and performance at the metronome task as one indicator of conformity, then the experiment is informative: knowing that fear leads to conformity is useful.

If the operations were inappropriate for the conceptual variables, however, we would have learned little. Suppose the subjects in the so-called fear and conformity experiment were masochists. The operations thought to produce "fear" might have produced titillating feelings of anticipation. What we would have found (without knowing it) was that arousal leads to conformity! Faulty operations are always possible. Most experimenters, however, choose their operations with great care and take pains to demonstrate their validity. In the case of Darley's experiment, the manipulation check reassures us that he was indeed manipulating fear.

In daily life, people are unlikely to be threatened with electric shocks, but fear may be induced by illness, natural disaster, military attack, the threat of losing a job, abortion, a close shave of one kind or another, or thousands of other possibilities. In daily life, people will not be confronted with the metronome task, but conformity may be expressed in choice of political candidates, clothing, music, hobbies, and countless other things. The sheer number of possibilities is a major factor encouraging laboratory procedures (Gerard & Conolley, 1972). It is impossible to catalog all the real-world conditions that could cause different individuals, different groups, and different cultures at different times to become fearful. It is also impossible to catalog all actions that reflect conformity. What *is* possible is to find a set of operations that induce fear in a given type of subject and to relate these factors to operational measures of conformity.

Unrepresentative Subjects

The second criticism of laboratory experimentation is that subjects are not likely to be representative of the population at large. Most laboratory studies use college sophomores. Not only do sophomore subjects fail to represent the many different groups that make up society (lawyers, designers, gardeners, flight attendants, retired librarians, and so forth), but they often fail to represent college sophomores. This happens because experimenters often restrict their subject pool to one sex. Males appear as subjects about twice as often as females (Holmes & Jorgensen, 1971).

A related problem has to do with the use of volunteers. Obvious legal and ethical concerns make it impossible to strong-arm people into participating in experiments. You cannot jab a gun into someone's ribs and demand "Your attitudes or your life." As a result, most experiments involve volunteers. It has been found that, compared with nonvolunteers, volunteers are likely to be more intelligent and educated, have a higher occupational status, score lower on measures of authoritarianism, and have a higher need for approval from others (Rosenthal & Rosnow, 1969; Rosnow & Rosenthal, 1970). Furthermore, it has been found that volunteers are more open about themselves than nonvolunteers—in some cases, perhaps, because they are somewhat troubled people who are seeking psychotherapeutic interactions with experimenters (Hood & Back, 1971).

Critics of the experiment argue that any or all of these variables could seriously undermine external validity. Proponents of the laboratory experiment counter that volunteers are not different from nonvolunteers in many important ways, and that the arguments of the critics are simply unsupported by the data (Kruglanski, 1973). Furthermore, even if volunteers do differ from nonvolunteers, it does not automatically follow that experimental results are conditional upon the subjects' special "volunteer" status (Kruglanski, 1973).

Although it is always risky to generalize from one group of subjects to another, generalizability depends in part on the phenomena under investigation. For example, certain performances involving effort expenditure seem to be generalizable not only across a wide spectrum of human subjects but across species as well, whereas activities that are highly influenced by intelligence, educational level, social class, and specialized interests hold for only a narrow sliver of the population pie. As far as I know, no one disputes the idea that laboratory experiments might be more informative if it were possible to use subjects who are more representative of the population at large. However, implementation of this principle in any specific case involves weighing potential gains (which can be small) against likely costs (which can be large).

Demand Characteristics

A third criticism of the laboratory experiment is that people's behavior is modified by virtue of the fact that they are in an experiment, thus making it almost impossible to draw correct conclusions about their typical, natural-habitat behavior (Orne, 1962, 1969; Weber & Cook, 1972; Adair, 1973). It has been suggested that the laboratory contains explicit and implicit cues, called **demand characteristics,** which activate behavior that masks or obscures the behavior of interest (Orne, 1962, 1969).

One major demand characteristic is to be a "good subject"—to do what the experimenter wants and to help out science. For example, Orne (1962) showed that, in the name of science, people would perform noxious, meaningless, and boring tasks that they would never consider performing outside the laboratory. In one case a person was told to start working through 2000 sheets of paper, each of which presented 224 addition problems. Five and a half hours into the task, the experimenter gave up! Other people have continued this task in the name of science, even when they were instructed to tear up and discard each sheet of completed additions.

Part of being a good subject, notes Orne, is to confirm the experimenter's hypotheses. If the experimenter makes it possible for the subject to guess the hypothesis, the subject is likely to lend it support. When this happens, the "finding" will have no useful application at all.

Another problem is that behavior in the laboratory may be misleading because subjects strive to look good in the eyes of the experimenter. Sigall, Aronson, and VanHoose (1970) had subjects engage in a repetitive clerical task. After establishing the rate at which the subjects worked, the experimenters told some subjects nothing, some subjects that an increased pace of performance was expected, and some subjects that a decreased pace of performance was expected. Of the latter group, some were left believing that a decrease would reflect poorly on their ability and motivation, whereas others were led to believe that a decrease would prove they did not have the "obsessive-compulsive" characteristic of working hard at trivial, boring, repetitive tasks.

Compared with the controls, subjects who believed the experimenter expected increased performance worked more briskly. Of the subjects who were led to believe that decreased output was expected, only those who thought that slack performance would free them of the label "obsessive-compulsive" slowed down. Subjects who thought that the anticipated slow rate of performance would lead to an unfavorable evaluation flaunted the experimenters' expectations and sped up. In other words, subjects tried to live up to the experimenters' expectations, but *only* if this behavior allowed them to look good. Although this and a subsequent study (Rosnow, Goodstadt, Suls, & Gitter, 1973) suggest that subjects will behave in ways that present a favorable image, a conflict between "looking good" and confirming the experimenter's hypothesis will not always be resolved by presenting a good image. If the experimenter's hypothesis and expectations are made extremely clear to a subject, the subject may conform even though he or she is presented in an unfavorable light (Adair & Schachter, 1972).

Experiments showing that one can deliberately create demand characteristics do not imply that all previous researchers have inadvertently produced such characteristics. Nonetheless, demand characteristics pose a potential threat, and it is certainly worth taking steps to try to minimize their effects. To counteract demand characteristics, an experimenter must try to assure the subject freedom of action, use every means possible to obtain conscientious performance, and make the situation inscrutable. Finally, the experimenter should consider careful interviews after the session to discover if the subject "psyched out" the hypothesis or acted in a misleading fashion.

Experimenter Bias

Finally, laboratory experiments have been criticized on the grounds that their findings reflect **experimenter bias** (that is, the experimenter's prejudices and expectations) more than anything else. A charge of deliberate falsification of data is, among scientists, more devastating than a charge of rape, murder, or arson (McCain & Segal, 1973), and, as far as we know, the major sin of deliberate falsification of data is rare. However, *unintentional* biasing may be more common.

Any experimenter hopes that his or her hypotheses will prove true. Consequently, he or she may unwittingly influence subjects to behave in the desired way or may misperceive the subjects' behavior as in line with expectations. Perhaps the most famous illustration of experimenter-bias effects is that of Rosenthal and Fode (1963), who gave psychology students rats to maze-train. In some cases the students were led to believe that the rats were very bright, and in other cases that the rats were very dull. In truth, the "bright" and "dull" rats were of equivalent bred-in intelligence. Nevertheless, presumably because of the experimenters' biases, the "bright" rats learned the maze faster.

Like the other criticisms of present-day laboratory research, the problem of experimenter bias seems to have been overstated (Barber & Silver, 1968). However, it is again advantageous if the experimenter can build in safeguards against this potential hazard. One possibility would be to conduct every experiment with two sets of experimenters, who have opposite biases. Another possibility is to automate the experiment. Instructions recorded by someone who knew nothing about the rationale underlying the experiment would be unlikely to subtly influence subjects, and responses recorded by a computer would not be misperceived as in accordance with the hypotheses when they were not. Still another possibility is to use procedures that keep the person who obtains the dependent measure from knowing the treatment accorded the subject prior to the measurement. For example, if the study dealt with the effects on subsequent play of watching an aggressive film, one experimenter could show the aggressive or control film while another rated the child's play without knowing which film had been shown.

A Personal Opinion

There have always been critics of the laboratory experiment. In the 1960s some of these critics became vocal and, since they began using experimental methods to demonstrate flaws in experiments, began to gain widespread attention. In my opinion, the issues raised are important and not to be neglected. Safeguards against unrepresentative subjects, demand characteristics, and experimenter bias will never hurt and may do some good. However, I think that the criticisms were initially overstated. Showing that it is possible to intentionally bias results through demand characteristics or through experimenter expectancies does not mean that researchers have unintentionally biased results. Also, research subsequent to the initial attacks suggests that the problems aired have been neither so severe nor so widespread as the critics originally supposed. There is not sufficient evidence to invalidate research that predated these issues.

FIELD EXPERIMENTATION

The **field** refers to people's natural settings: the home, the highway, the park, the drugstore, the football stadium—anywhere but the psychologist's laboratory. In the nonmanipulative **field study** the investigator examines conditions as they are found. In the **field experiment** the researcher creates the conditions of interest in people's natural environment. The field experimenter carefully stages natural-appearing incidences and compares people's reactions to them with the reactions of people confronted with alternative, control conditions. As we shall see throughout this text, social psychologists are recording the flow of people, bicycles, and automobiles; eavesdropping on conversations; observing reactions to faked mishaps and emergencies; and engaging in dozens of similar activities.

Although field experimentation has been with us throughout social psychology's history, interest was spurred by the criticisms leveled at laboratory research. The field setting seemed promising for circumventing many of the problems associated with the laboratory. First, the question of whether the results extend to the "real world" is avoided, since the results are obtained *in* the real world. Second, in the field, subjects are likely to be of different ages, interests, backgrounds, and abilities and thus more likely to reflect the population at large. Finally, the problem of demand characteristics is minimized, since field researchers can capitalize on **nonreactive measures**—that is, measures that leave subjects unaware that their behavior is under scrutiny. Examples of taking nonreactive measures would include assessing the attractiveness of different exhibits by measuring the amount of linoleum or number of tiles that have to be replaced in front of each exhibit, assessing the dreadfulness of television commercials by measuring drops in water pressure in the city where the commercial is aired (such drops caused by viewers leaving the TV to fetch glasses of water and use water-operated appliances), and assessing the scariness of a ghost-story session by noting the shrinking diameter of the circle of children seated around the campfire (Webb, Campbell, Schwartz, & Sechrest, 1966).

Initial Selling Price and Subsequent Sales: An Illustrative Study

As an example of how theoretically relevant research can be conducted in the field setting, let's consider a study by Doob, Carlsmith,

Freedman, Landauer, and Tom (1969), who related the initial selling price of an article to its subsequent sales. A common practice among marketing specialists is to offer items at "low introductory prices." The rationale is that the low price makes the article attractive to people who might otherwise not buy it. The idea is that, having tried it, they'll like it and show brand loyalty, even after the price is raised.

A contrasting analysis was offered by Doob and his associates. The theory on which this analysis was based—cognitive-dissonance theory—will be presented in detail in Chapter 5. A crucial aspect of dissonance theory is that people tend to perceive the world as orderly and consistent with their expectations, even when such is not the case. Relevant here is the idea that experience usually teaches us that the good things in life are hard to come by; we therefore expect inexpensive items to be of lower quality and worth less than expensive items. To prevent this expectation from being disconfirmed, we may persuade ourselves that an inexpensive but high-quality item "isn't really that great." Alternatively, we may convince ourselves that an expensive but low-quality item is really "terrific." The dissonance analysis states that, if the quality of the item is held constant, a person's evaluation of it should be positively correlated with the amount that has been paid for it.

According to this line of reasoning, although a low introductory price may initially attract a flock of customers, to avoid disconfirmation of their expectations, these purchasers would, on reflection, underrate the product and find themselves tempted to switch to another, "better" brand. A high introductory price might not attract as many customers initially, but, to maintain their expectations, these purchasers should, on reflection, give the product a high rating and develop brand loyalty. In sum, dissonance theory suggests that, the more people pay, the harder they'll try to convince themselves that the purchase was wise and the harder they'll fight before switching.

To test these ideas, five separate experiments were conducted at a chain of discount houses. The products were house brands that were, for the most part, equivalent in quality to nationally advertised brands. The first step was to match stores within the chain on the basis of gross sales. One store of each matched pair was then assigned to the experimental condition and the other to the control condition. In the experimental stores, items were introduced at a special low price that was later raised. In the control stores, items were introduced at the higher price. For example, in one experiment seven experimental stores sold aluminum foil for 59¢ a roll for three weeks and then raised the price to 64¢ a roll; in seven control stores the foil was sold for 64¢ a roll throughout the experiment. Figure 2-2 shows the effects of initial selling price of aluminum foil on subsequent sales. Although the low price initially attracted many cus-

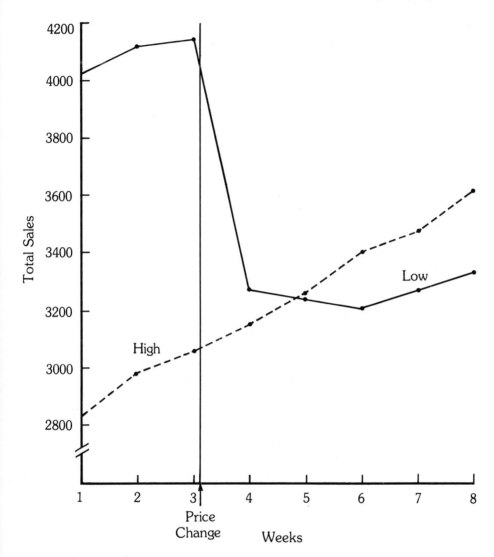

Figure 2-2. The effects of initial selling price on subsequent sales of aluminum foil. (From "The Effects of Initial Selling Price on Subsequent Sales," by A. Doob, J. Carlsmith, J. Freedman, T. Landauer, and S. Tom, *Journal of Personality and Social Psychology,* 1969, *11,* 347. Copyright 1969 by the American Psychological Association. Reprinted by permission.)

tomers, sales dropped off dramatically as soon as the price was raised. Foil introduced at the higher price did not show an initial spurt of sales, but sales increased over time. Generally similar results were found in marketing mouthwash, toothpaste, cookies, and light bulbs.

Taken together, the experiments showed that introducing products at a special low price had an adverse effect on final sales. Profits from the initial spurt of sales in the experimental conditions did not equal the profits coming from a higher profit margin and increasing sales under control conditions. The results are thus consistent with the dissonance analysis. The study of the effects of initial selling price on subsequent sales shows that powerful analytical tools of manipulation and control can be brought to bear on theoretically relevant behaviors in a real-life setting. In an experiment such as this, there seems to be little or no question about the applicability of results.

DIFFICULTIES ASSOCIATED WITH FIELD EXPERIMENTS

Despite some spectacular successes in the field, the laboratory experiment still overwhelmingly predominates in contemporary social-psychological research (Fried, Gumpper, & Allen, 1973). Although some people may suspect that laboratory experimenters are so burdened by tradition that they are unwilling to abandon the ways of the past, the laboratory experimenters might reply that the disadvantages of the field setting outweigh the advantages. The three major disadvantages of conducting field experiments are: (1) that there are practical concerns about implementing such projects, (2) that there are difficulties in establishing adequate controls, and (3) that the amount of information gained from field experimentation may provide insufficient justification for the extra trouble and expense.

Practical Concerns

First, the Doob team was quite fortunate in that it included a member who had access to a chain of department stores. In many cases it is not possible to manipulate conditions in the field, whereas it is possible to create analogous conditions in the laboratory. For example, a field test of the determinants of war could be a dangerous proposition. In addition, the field setting makes it difficult to implement some of the American Psychological Association's (1973) ethical guidelines (discussed later in this chapter), which state that participants in experiments should give their informed consent. People in the laboratory usually know that they are participating in an experiment, but people in the field usually do not.

Difficulties of Control

Second, studying representative subjects in representative situations often makes it difficult to provide rigorous controls. For example, in the field, random assignment of subjects to conditions is often not possible. Results may thus reflect a self-selection factor on the part of the subjects, rather than the experimental manipulation itself. To the extent that conditions are uncontrolled, the experimental method loses its force, since uncontrolled variables could produce any of the observed effects or mask other nonobserved effects. When this happens, the experiment is no longer fulfilling its intended purpose of ruling out alternative causes of the observed event. Lack of controls in the field setting could thus lead to false and erroneous conclusions.

Rewards and Costs

Finally, there is some question about whether the extra difficulties imposed by the field setting are justified in terms of additional information gained. In the Doob et al. experiment we see an interesting application of dissonance theory to shoppers' behavior. But the finding that the hardest-to-obtain grapes are the sweetest has been found repeatedly in the laboratory (Chapter 5). Thus it could be argued that field experiments are more likely to bolster our confidence in what we already know from the lab than to provide "all-new" information. On the whole, field experiments are methodologically innovative, but they have only infrequently dealt with new, previously untested theoretical relationships. Some people feel that, if field experimentation is to continue in this fashion, the extra trouble and expense hardly seem justified.

THE NEED FOR MULTIPLE METHODS

Correlational studies, laboratory experiments, and field experiments all have particular strengths and weaknesses. Correlational studies make it possible to study the natural flow of events without contamination from a manipulative experimenter. Yet this procedure does not provide the best vehicle for unraveling cause and effect. The laboratory experiment provides the ideal setting for manipulation and control. Yet findings may be difficult to generalize to people and tasks in the "real-world" setting. The field experiment studies representative people and tasks—but in settings that are difficult to manipulate and control. Each approach has advantages and disadvantages. To some extent, which method is best will depend on whom you ask.

In truth, there is a need for all these approaches, and the strengths of one method can compensate for the weaknesses of another. Evidence resting on only one method is always suspect, for the data may depend more on the method than on the phenomena. Evidence coming from a number of different methods generates more confidence, for the data cannot be method-contingent. Thus principles like "Fear leads to conformity" or "The hardest-gained goals are the best" are most trustworthy when supported by several strands of evidence, not just one. Individual researchers may find one approach more enjoyable than another. However, for the group enterprise of social psychology to proceed, there must not be universal commitment to any one narrow set of procedures (McGuire, 1973).

RESEARCH AND ETHICS

Social psychologists observe, and often manipulate, other human beings. Such activities, whether undertaken by peeping Toms, encyclopedia salespersons, or social psychologists, have always raised questions of ethics. To conclude our discussion of research methods, let's consider the kinds of moral issues involved in social-psychological research, and look at a set of guidelines that has been proposed for dealing with them.

Ethical Concerns

It is possible to compose a very long list of complaints about the activities of social psychologists. For example, I have heard studies of international relations attacked because they might "undermine Western democracies" and "play into the hands of the Commies"; studies of love and marriage have been criticized because they "squander the taxpayers' dollars"; studies of pornography are criticized because they "wallow the subjects in smut." From such a lengthy list, however, three ethical issues would stand out for their persistence and their pervasiveness. These are: (1) invasion of privacy, (2) the use of subterfuge and deception, and (3) possible harmful consequences of experimental manipulations.

First, whenever we study people, we infringe on their privacy. The extent of this infringement will depend, of course, on the study. At one extreme there is observation of the behavior of anonymous strangers in public places, such as cafeterias, libraries, shopping malls, and so forth. Invasion of privacy seems minimal when an observer counts the number of people standing in a line, records seating arrangements in a library, or takes notes in a crowded gambling casino. At the other extreme are studies that involve soliciting private and sensitive information about

identifiable individuals. Confidential files may be examined, or people may be asked highly personal and potentially embarrassing questions in the course of an interview. Admittedly, in the search to understand human beings, some of the most sensitive material is also some of the most important material. But under what conditions can such prying be condoned?

Second, although subjects in an experiment are sometimes asked to engage in straightforward tasks, more often the experiments involve deception. Researchers have been known to promise money that they will not pay, present one person as another, falsely claim that one person is liked or disliked by another, and lie and cheat in countless ways. Deception often seems necessary to create conditions to test the hypotheses. Yet should professional researchers be given special dispensation to lie and to cheat?

Third, there is concern about the potentially dangerous consequences of experimental manipulations. Most experimental procedures are innocuous. Yet in some experiments people have been insulted, told they are incompetent, made to feel responsible for damage of one type or another, threatened with shock, and sent away with the knowledge that they had agreed to inflict harm on others. They could thus leave the experiment burdened with feelings of inadequacy, inferiority, or guilt, which are all hazardous to mental health. The world is not an unending sea of bliss, and, to understand people and their relationships with others (and perhaps to build a better society), it may be necessary to discover how people respond to unpleasant conditions. Research reports suggest that, at worst, subjects suffer only temporary discomfort. But such temporary discomfort can be intense, and there is no way of determining if participation has, for example, contributed to a nervous breakdown after contact with the experimenter has been terminated. Granted, subjecting people to stress may be necessary to reach the goal of understanding. Yet is a researcher ever justified in subjecting others to humiliating or painful circumstances? Perhaps you should consider your own answers to these questions before you read on.

Ethical Guidelines

Psychology's leading professional organization, the American Psychological Association (APA), maintains a continuing interest in ethical issues and periodically offers a set of standards for future research. The most recent guidelines (APA, 1973) suggest ten practices:

1. Ethical acceptability must be given high priority when research is planned. Particular care must be taken if scientific and humane values might conflict.
2. Responsibility for planning and conducting an ethically acceptable study rests firmly on the shoulders of the individual investigator.
3. Investigators must inform participants of all the features of the project that might affect the subject's willingness to participate.
4. Openness and honesty should characterize the relationship between researcher and participant. If concealment or deception is involved, the participant must be made to understand the reasons for the deception.
5. The participant must have the right to refuse to take part in a study, or to terminate participation at any point in time.
6. The researcher and participant must agree upon each one's responsibility to the other. Any promise made by a researcher must be kept.
7. Safeguards must be used to protect participants from discomfort or harm. If there is the possibility of discomfort or harm, participants must be warned in advance.
8. After the participant has taken part in the study, the researcher must debrief the participant by explaining the study in detail and by removing any misconceptions that might have arisen.
9. The researcher must take corrective measures if the study results in any undesirable consequences for the participant.
10. All data obtained in the course of a study are to be treated as strictly confidential.

Not all the studies reported in this book meet all of these stringent standards. For example, although it may be desirable that "openness and honesty" characterize the relationship between researcher and participant, researchers often lie to participants (Menges, 1973) and subjects have been known to lie in return (Newberry, 1973).

Ethical questions have no easy answers. For the most part, psychologists do not advocate banning all research on the grounds that someone might be temporarily inconvenienced; neither do they advocate brutal or inhumane research in the name of science. The problem is a large gray area in between these two extremes. Typically, psychologists make a careful appraisal of the potential damage that could be done by an experiment and weigh this factor against the expected value or usefulness of results. The resulting appraisal is a value judgment—a matter of individual conscience. In a sense, the ultimate evaluation of social psychologists' ethical practices is up to you to make.

PART SUMMARY

The experimental method is the most reliable technique for untangling cause and effect. The distinguishing characteristic of the experimental method is active manipulation coupled with control observations. Control observations make it possible to eliminate alternative explanations of the phenomenon under investigation. Experimental findings take the form of a statement about differences in performance between experimental and control conditions. For such a difference to be theoretically relevant, it must be statistically significant. Statistical significance does not invariably imply practical significance.

Most social-psychological research is conducted in the laboratory. Darley's study of fear and conformity was described to illustrate the rationale underlying the laboratory experiment. Criticisms of laboratory experimentation are that it typically involves contrived situations and tasks, that it uses unrepresentative subjects, that it contains elements that cause people to act in atypical ways, and that experimenters are likely to bias their observations. Defenders of the laboratory experiment argue that the results are of general applicability and that the dangers of demand characteristics and experimenter bias have been grossly overstated.

A modest proportion of experiments take place in the field, or natural habitat. Doob et al.'s study of the effects of initial selling price on subsequent sales provided us with an example of a field experiment. Criticisms of the field experiment are that practical concerns make the field inappropriate for testing many hypotheses, that the field may make rigorous controls impossible, and that field experiments have for the most part done little more than verify laboratory results. Correlational studies, laboratory experiments, and field experiments are all useful for under-standing individuals and groups, since each method offers some strengths that compensate for the weaknesses of the others.

Ethical issues confront the responsible social psychologist. These concerns center around the invasion of privacy, the use of subterfuge and deception, and possible unpleasant consequences of experimental manipulations. The American Psychological Association has offered a set of guidelines intended to minimize these problems. In the final analysis, ethical standards represent personal values.

3

Social Perception

THE PERCEIVER

EXPECTANCY AND FAMILIARITY

Familiarity and Discriminability
Familiarity and Attention
Familiarity and Liking

MOTIVATION AND PERCEPTION

Values and Thresholds
The Perceptual-Accentuation Hypothesis
The Perceptual-Defense Hypothesis

ACCURACY IN PERCEIVING OTHERS

Judgmental Skills
Correlates of Accuracy
The Curious Effect of Special Training

PART SUMMARY

THE SITUATION

THE PHYSICAL SETTING AS A SOURCE OF CUES

The Setting and Judgments of Emotion
Informative and Noninformative Settings

THE SITUATION AS EXPRESSING A RELATIONSHIP BETWEEN TWO OR MORE TARGETS

Expressions in Context
Contrast and Assimilation

THE SITUATION AS DEFINING THE RELATIONSHIP BETWEEN PERCEIVER AND TARGET

Anticipated Interaction Distance
Situation-Appropriate and Situation-Inappropriate
    Target Behavior
Situation, Task, and Cognitive Tuning

PART SUMMARY

THE TARGET

IMPRESSION FORMATION

Positive and Negative Information
Central and Peripheral Traits
Implicit Theories of Personality
Summation and Averaging Models

ATTRIBUTION THEORY

Inferring Dispositions
Attribution of Abilities
Attribution of Motives and Intents
Biases, Errors, and Illusions
Attribution of One's Own Characteristics

PART SUMMARY

Watching a referee render a verdict against your favorite football team, you may have wondered how a person who is so incompetent or unfair could ever have gained a position of such importance. But, before acting on the impulse to commit violence, you would do well to consider a game played a long time ago. The opponents were Dartmouth and Princeton, and the year was 1951. Each team had a good record, and the stakes were considered high.

The game was a particularly rough one. A Princeton player who had attained national prominence was retired from the field with a broken nose; each team was heavily penalized by overworked referees. The game—which Princeton won—prompted heated discussion. Princeton's student newspaper noted on November 27, 1951: "This observer has never seen quite such a disgusting exhibition of so-called sport. Both teams were guilty, but the blame must be laid primarily on Dartmouth's doorstep."

The accounting in the Dartmouth newspaper expressed resentment at Princeton's "unjustifiable accusations" and proclaimed that, although Dartmouth may have received more penalties of the "illegal use of the hand" variety, Princeton received more for the more serious infraction of "roughing." This dispute prompted a classic study by Hastorf and Cantril (1954).

Two procedures were used. First, samples of undergraduates from each college were given questionnaires about the game. Second, samples from each college were shown a motion picture of the game and asked to note the number and extent of each side's infractions.

Survey results indicated that 86% of the Princeton students thought Dartmouth had started the rough play, but only 36% of the Dartmouth students saw the blame as theirs. Similarly, 35% of the Princeton students thought that Dartmouth had been unnecessarily rough, but only 8% of the Dartmouth sample agreed with this accusation.

During the movie, Princeton students saw Dartmouth make more than twice as many infractions of the rules as they saw their own team make. Dartmouth students saw each side as responsible for about an equal number of infractions—but they saw their own team make only about half the infractions that the Princeton students saw them make. Furthermore, the Princeton students rated Dartmouth's infractions "flagrant," whereas the Dartmouth students labeled their own infractions as "minor."

Both procedures thus revealed that each side was quick to see unsporting behavior on the part of the other side's team yet reluctant to recognize this behavior in their own team. Hastorf and Cantril conclude that the same game thus gave rise to very different experiences in different people and that "each version of the events that transpired was just as 'real' to a particular person as other versions were to other people." What you see and what a referee sees could thus be very different events.

Perception refers to the processes through which the individual receives, structures, and interprets information from the environment. **Social perception** refers to these processes when other people are somehow involved. Other people are peripherally involved when they contribute to expectations, motives, and personality characteristics that affect the perception of both social and nonsocial objects. Other people are directly involved when they are the focus or **target** of perceptual activity.

There are many similarities between the perception of nonsocial targets and the perception of social targets. For example, both types of perception begin with changes in physical energy impinging on the sensitive nerve endings called receptors (such as the rods and the cones in the eye). Both involve a remarkable chain of events that patterns or organizes this raw input into something with structure and meaning. In both cases also, the study of perception is mostly a *study of judgments.* We can neither hear through another's ears nor see through another's eyes, but we can ask people to judge the relative pitch of two tones or the relative attractiveness of two political candidates.

However, there are also some important differences between the perception of things and the perception of people. Heider (1958, p. 21) notes that, unlike objects, people are:

usually perceived as action centers and as such can do something to us. They can benefit or harm us intentionally, and we can benefit or harm them.

Persons have abilities, wishes, and sentiments; they can act purposefully, and can perceive or watch us. They are systems having an awareness of their surroundings and their conduct refers to this environment and that sometimes includes ourselves.

Unlike objects, then, people are *sources of deliberate action* and have *motives and intentions* that will enter into our perception of them. For example, a modest upturning of the corners of another person's mouth might be perceived as a friendly smile if he or she has just granted our request but as a sadistic smirk if the request has just been refused. Because people's motives and intents are so relevant to the impressions we have of them, studies of social perception often deal not with judged physical properties of stimuli but with judged psychological properties.

Perception is always the result of the interaction of three sets of variables: those associated with the *perceiver*, those associated with the *situation* or *context*, and those associated with the stimulus person or *target*. In some ways these distinctions are arbitrary, for at some point we must always come back to the psychological workings of the perceiver. However, this breakdown of variables offers a convenient way of organizing the rather loosely related studies typically classified as "social perception."

THE PERCEIVER

Although it cannot be demonstrated that any two people have ever experienced the same stimulus in exactly the same way, it has been demonstrated that there are differences in different people's perceptions of the same thing or event. Differences exist because, in addition to being influenced by public stimuli that originate outside the perceiver, perceptions are influenced by private stimuli, such as moods and expectations, that originate within the perceiver. Different people in any given situation may have access to the same public stimuli, but they do not have access to the same private stimuli; for this reason their perceptions will vary. Dartmouth and Princeton fans with different expectations and moods thus saw different games. Let's refer to the private determinants of perception as **perceiver variables.**

Considering all perceptions as the product of both public and private events helps explain the common observation that perceptions differ in terms of their **veridicality,** or the extent to which they seem to represent what is "really out there." One can, of course, get hopelessly entangled in the issue of what (if anything) is "really out there." However, most of us consider a perception veridical if it is verified by different people. If everyone agrees that the sky is blue, then it is blue; if everyone agrees that the sky is gray, then it is gray. To the extent that publicly available stimuli (such as the color of the sky) contribute to a perception, it will be veridical, and to the extent that private determinants (such as heavily tinted contact lenses) contribute, it will lack veridicality.

Our discussion of the perceiver will be organized around two types of perceiver variables. First, there are those that affect the subjective likelihood of occurrence of a stimulus. These variables include *expectancy* and *familiarity*. The second type consists of personal requirements of the organism. Thus *needs* and *motives* enter into perception.

EXPECTANCY AND FAMILIARITY

People see what they *expect* to see. Such expectations can be formed in a number of ways. First, having just seen something, we may anticipate its recurrence. This was shown in an early study by Bruner and Postman (1949). By skillfully applying poster paints, these experimenters prepared a number of "trick" playing cards on which the color did not match the suit (for example, a *black* four of hearts and a *red* two of spades). Next, these and conventional cards were presented by means of a **tachistoscope,** a device that presents visual stimuli very briefly under conditions of controlled illumination. One object was to determine the **recognition threshold**—that is, the minimum stimulation under which the stimulus could be more or less consistently identified. Although due to strong expectations the conventional cards required on the average only 28 milliseconds (thousandths of a second) to identify, proper identification of an unexpected "trick" card required on the average 114 milliseconds—and in some cases was not forthcoming even after the card had been shown for a full second. (Remarked one frustrated subject after having been shown the card for a full second, "I don't know what the hell it is now—not even if it's a playing card!") Furthermore, due to strong expectations the color was often misperceived as the correct one for the suit, or the suit as the correct one for the color. However, after realizing that some trick cards were being used, the subjects formed new expectancies that made it easier to identify subsequent trick cards. Whereas it required on the average 390 milliseconds to properly identify the first trick card slipped into the deck, it took only 230 milliseconds to identify the second trick card and less than 85 milliseconds to identify subsequent trick cards. Immediately preceding experiences created expectancies that made subsequent identifications easier.

A second way in which we form expectations is through other people's suggestions. Some of the items used on standardized tests of hypnotizability are based on the assumption that people perceive things in certain ways because of suggestion. Following the suggestion of the examiner, "hypnotizables" may smell nonexistent odors wafting from a small vial of water. In a later discussion of small groups (Chapter 9), we will consider abundant evidence that conformity pressures modify the way in which the individual perceives the world.

Third, expectancies can be built up on the basis of a long learning history. To the extent that a stimulus has been encountered in the past, it is familiar. In addition to Bruner and Postman's findings that familiar, conventional cards are easier to identify than trick cards, studies involving very different procedures have shown that familiar stimuli are more easily detected or recognized than are unfamiliar stimuli.

For example, Thorndike and Lorge (1944) estimated the relative frequency with which words appeared in print in the English language. Howes and Solomon (1951), presenting words of different frequencies tachistoscopically in order to determine recognition thresholds, found that high-frequency or common words, which presumably had become more familiar over the years, were easier to recognize than were low-frequency or uncommon words. A slightly different approach was taken by Zajonc and Sales (1966), who presented made-up or **nonsense words** varying numbers of times. They then flashed on a screen ambiguous stimuli that bore a vague resemblance to all of the nonsense words. Subjects tended to identify the vague stimuli as the more familiar nonsense words.

Different people have different pasts. What is familiar and easily perceived by me is not necessarily easily perceived by you. Ingenious demonstrations of this effect have been presented by Toch and Schulte (1961) and by Bagby (1957). Each experiment involved the **binocular rivalry** technique, which consists of simultaneously presenting two different pictures, one to each eye. Under such circumstances there tends to be neither fusion nor confusion; instead, people generally see one picture but not the other.

Advanced and beginning police-administration trainees and beginning psychology students participated in the Toch and Schulte experiment. Fifteen pairs of pictures were presented. One picture of each pair depicted crime or violence (such as murder, suicide, or an act of theft), and the other depicted a mundane, nonviolent scene. The advanced police-administration subjects reported more violent scenes (an average of 9.47) than did the beginning police-administration students (4.69) or the introductory psychology students (4.00). The negligible difference between beginning police-administration and introductory psychology students suggests that the greater readiness to detect violence on the part of the advanced police-administration trainees is attributable to their training rather than to possible personality factors.

Bagby's study showed that a lifetime of differential exposure affects perception. Subjects were 12 Americans and 12 Mexicans. They were shown ten pairs of pictures consisting of one American scene (such as a baseball game) and one Mexican scene (such as a bullfight). Subjects reported seeing the scenes common to their culture. These biases were so pronounced that the Mexican reporting the *most* American scenes reported fewer than the American reporting the *fewest* American scenes.

Do expectancies have a beneficial or a detrimental effect on perceptual accuracy? If a child at Christmastime expects to see Santa Claus, the briefest glimpse of a man dressed in red might lead to the instant identification of Santa Claus. On the other hand, the child may be so ready to see Santa Claus that he or she mistakenly identifies as such the Devil or a Communist dressed in red BVDs. If the man is Santa Claus, expectancies have proven to be a help; if he is not Santa Claus, expectancies have proven to be a hindrance.

If I had to venture a guess, it would be that expectancies more often result in veridical than in distorted perceptions. For an expectation to have a beneficial effect, the strength of that expectation should match the conditional probability (likelihood under stated conditions) of the real-world events. Since expectations often seem to be based on firsthand experience with objective conditions, they are likely to bear the necessary correspondence to objective probability. For example, chances are very good that a small orange sphere on the breakfast table is in fact a piece of fruit and that a small orange sphere by a croquet set is in fact a wooden ball. Although someone could trick you (such as by putting a croquet ball in the fruitbowl), you will be far more often right than wrong if your expectations lead you to see an orange on the table and a croquet ball on the lawn. The strength of these two expectancies corresponds closely with the probabilities of real-world events.

As the foregoing discussion shows, familiarity with a stimulus thus has a very clear effect on the ease with which that stimulus is detected. Familiarity has also been related to (1) discriminability, (2) attention, and (3) the affective, or emotional, response of liking (or disliking).

Familiarity and Discriminability

Discrimination refers to the process of distinguishing one stimulus from another. If stimuli are similar in many ways (such as two bottles of the same type of wine produced in two different years), familiarity makes it easier to tell them apart. Thus, although a child might not be able to tell apart a doorman and the Head of the Joint Chiefs of Staff, an experienced soldier could easily make the fine discrimination between a major (gold oak leaves) and a lieutenant colonel (silver oak leaves).

It is sometimes said that all Orientals (or Negroes, or Indians, or Caucasians) look alike. This statement may simply reflect a lack of familiarity with Orientals as individuals. Since people have more familiarity with individuals from their own race, they may be better able to discriminate among them than among people from other races.

In a study by Malpass and Kravitz (1969), blacks and whites attempted to discriminate among photos of blacks and among photos of whites. Subjects did a better job of telling apart people of their own color, which probably reflects greater amounts of experience and familiarity with individuals of their own color. It was also found that blacks did a better job of discriminating among whites than whites did of discriminating among blacks. The authors suggest that this latter finding does not conflict with the hypothesis that increased familiarity leads to sharper discriminatory powers. In our society, blacks are forced to become familiar with whites. They are likely to have white teachers and employers, to buy from white merchants, and to confront white bureaucrats and white officials. Whites, however, can go through life with only minimal contact with blacks.

Familiarity and Attention

Familiarity is also related to attention. All the evidence suggests that novel, infrequent, *unfamiliar* stimuli attract attention. For example, Berlyne (1958) presented pairs of slides, side by side. One slide was presented repeatedly, but the other was continually changed. There was an overall tendency to fixate on the infrequent slide, and this tendency increased over time. In another study, Patricia Hines and I presented nonsense words varying numbers of times and then allowed subjects brief glimpses of the words (Harrison & Hines, 1970). As Figure 3-1 shows, subjects became increasingly interested in viewing the less frequently presented words.

Familiarity and Liking

In 1967 a speech class at Oregon State University was the scene of a mystery. During each meeting, someone appeared enveloped in a big black bag and sat on a table near the back of the class. There were no clues as to the identity of the bag's occupant. Initially, the students' reactions to the bag were hostile. Later, hostility gave way to curiosity, and

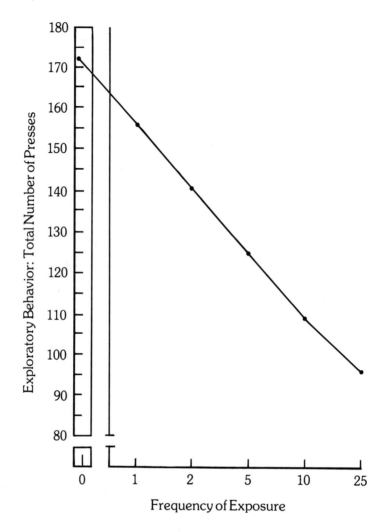

Figure 3-1. Familiarity and exploratory behavior. After being shown nonsense words 1, 2, 5, 10, or 25 times, subjects were allowed to push a lever for a $\frac{1}{10}$-second glimpse of each word. As this figure shows, subjects expressed greater interest in the novel words than in the familiar words. (From "Effects of Frequency of Exposure at Three Short Exposure Times on Affective Ratings and Exploratory Behavior," by A. A. Harrison and P. Hines, *Proceedings of the 78th Annual Convention of the American Psychological Association,* 1970, p. 392. Copyright 1970 by the American Psychological Association. Reprinted by permission.)

finally to an attitude of friendship and liking. The person in the bag did not dispense money, love, approval, or free tickets to the local theater. He or she did not deliver a stirring speech about his or her own virtues. There was no dramatic announcement that the person in the bag was a local leader, folk hero, or well-loved public figure. The bag just sat there, and over time the students grew to like it. One possibility is that familiarity led to fondness.

From the beginning of the 20th century, many investigators have reported a relationship between familiarity and liking. Meyer (1903) composed a piano melody and found that people liked it more following 15 performances than they did following only one performance. Gilliland and Moore (1924) found that repeated playing of phonograph records led to greater liking for three out of four selections. Krugman (1943) reported a correlation of .91 between the number of times phonograph records were played and the favorability ratings accorded them. Mull (1957) found that repeated playing led to greater liking not only for a given selection but also for specific passages within it. Cross, Halcomb, and Matter (1967) played classical music to rats for hours on end. The rats were then placed in a contraption in which they could trigger either the familiar or an alternate selection. Although one experimental group showed no clear preference, the other showed a preference for the familiar strains of Mozart. More recently, Heingartner and Hall (1974) used an exposure manipulation to make a group of Americans like Pakistani music.

Such findings as these led Zajonc (1968a, p. 1) to formulate the hypothesis that the mere repeated exposure of an individual to a stimulus is a sufficient condition for enhancing his or her attitude toward that stimulus. In his monograph, Zajonc reported a series of his own correlational and experimental studies supporting this **mere-exposure hypothesis.**

The correlational studies showed that things or events with a high probability of occurrence in the environment were more favorably judged than things or events with a low probability of occurrence. In these studies, familiarity was estimated by referring to the Thorndike-Lorge (1944) word count. High positive correlations were found using such different stimuli as foreign countries, U.S. cities, trees, fruits, vegetables, and flowers (see Table 3-1). In all cases the correlations were greater than .80. The experimental studies showed that manipulating familiarity affected liking. In these studies, Zajonc (1968a) presented stimuli 1, 2, 5, 10, or 25 times and then obtained likability ratings. Stimuli used included nonsense words, Chinese ideographs (picture writing), and photographs of men. In each case, increasing familiarity enhanced ratings of goodness or liking. Although this result may at first appear to conflict with the finding that people pay attention to low-frequency or novel stimuli, let's remember that looking at a stimulus does not necessarily signify liking

Table 3-1. Preference ratings of trees, fruits, vegetables, and flowers and their corresponding frequencies

Trees	f	APR	Fruits	f	APR	Vegetables	f	APR	Flowers	f	APR
pine	172	4.79	apple	220	5.13	corn	227	4.17	rose	801	5.55
walnut	75	4.42	cherry	167	5.00	potato	384	4.13	lily	164	4.79
oak	125	4.00	strawberry	121	4.83	lettuce	142	4.00	violet	109	4.58
rosewood	8	3.96	pear	62	4.38	carrot	96	3.57	geranium	27	3.83
birch	34	3.83	grapefruit	33	4.00	radish	43	3.13	daisy	62	3.79
fir	14	3.75	cantaloupe	1.5	3.75	asparagus	5	2.33	hyacinth	16	3.08
sassafras	2	3.00	avocado	16	2.71	cauliflower	27	1.96	yucca	1	2.88
aloes	1	2.92	pomegranate	8	2.63	broccoli	18	1.96	woodbine	4	2.87
yew	3	2.83	gooseberry	5	2.63	leek	3	1.96	anemone	8	2.54
acacia	4	2.75	mango	2	2.38	parsnip	8	1.92	cowslip	2	2.54

Notes. f = frequency and APR = average preference ratings. Higher numbers indicate greater likability. (From "Attitudinal Effects of Mere Exposure," by R. B. Zajonc, *Journal of Personality and Social Psychology Monograph Supplement*, 1968a, 9(2), 13. Copyright 1968 by the American Psychological Association. Reprinted by permission.)

it (Harrison, 1968; Saegert & Jellison, 1970). For example, we might turn from a favorite television program to watch the progress of a large, unidentified, and alarming insect marching across the ceiling. But our attentiveness to this worrisome creature would not signify that we liked it more than the television show.

Subsequent studies have suggested that this mere-exposure effect holds under a wide range of conditions (Harrison & Crandall, 1972; Zajonc, Swap, Harrison, & Roberts, 1971; Saegert, Swap, & Zajonc, 1973). However, other studies have found a curvilinear, inverted-*U* relationship such that stimuli of intermediate familiarity are rated most favorably (Berlyne, 1970; Harrison & Crandall, 1972; Stang, 1973b, 1974; Smith & Dorfman, 1975). Positing a curvilinear relationship between familiarity and liking is ever popular, for it provides a way of succinctly integrating all possible results. According to such theorizing, "mere-exposure" and "novelty" (liking for low-frequency stimuli) effects represent two myopic views of segments of the inverted-*U* curve (see Figure 3-2).

Berlyne (1970) has offered a two-factor theory to account for relationships of the type portrayed in Figure 3-2. He suggests that stimulus repetition has two effects. First, there is **positive habituation,** which refers to a reduction of uncertainty and conflict and hence to increased liking. The second factor, **tedium,** refers to a decrease in arousal with the result that the stimulus seems dull and boring. Over repeated exposures of the stimulus, both positive habituation and tedium increase. Early in the course of exposures, positive habituation is the strongest factor, with the apparent effect that familiarity leads to liking. Later in the course of exposures, the tedium factor gains in strength, and further exposure leads to decreased liking.

What establishes the inflection point in the inverted-*U* curve? That is, at what point does increasing familiarity start to generate disliking instead of liking? Thus far three factors have been identified. First, when stimuli are presented in repetitious, redundant sequences, the inflection point comes sooner than if during the sequence a number of different stimuli are interspersed (Berlyne, 1970; Harrison & Crandall, 1972; Stang, 1974). Thus a popular song heard 24 hours a day would be expected to become tedious and unpleasant after fewer repetitions than the same song played only a few times a day in a program containing many different songs. Second, the inflection point comes following fewer exposures if the stimuli are simple rather than complex (Saegert & Jellison, 1970; Smith & Dorfman, 1975). For example, a simple melody such as Ravel's *Bolero* or *Coming Through the Rye* would wear thin before a complex melody such as a Beethoven symphony. Third, the inflection point comes after fewer exposures when there is no delay between the last presentation of the stimulus and the rating of it than when these two events are separated

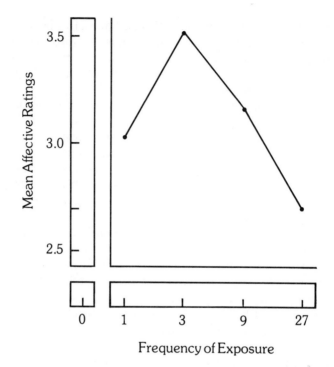

Figure 3-2. In this experiment, Chinese ideographs were shown 1, 3, 9, or 27 times in a row and were then rated in terms of the extent to which the subject thought they represented something good, favorable, or positive. As the figure shows, stimulus repetition led first to increased and then to decreased ratings of favorability. (From "Heterogeneity-Homogeneity of Exposure Sequence and the Attitudinal Effects of Exposure," by A. A. Harrison and R. Crandall, *Journal of Personality and Social Psychology,* 1972, *21,* 236. Copyright 1972 by the American Psychological Association. Reprinted by permission.)

in time (Stang, 1974). That is, having just heard a simple tune played endlessly, we might consider that tune less agreeable than if we were asked to evaluate it at some later time. In sum, although familiarity leads to liking, factors such as boredom may provide some limiting conditions.

MOTIVATION AND PERCEPTION

During the invasion of France in 1944, American paratroopers were provided with tin "crickets" for purposes of recognition. By clicking these crickets twice, they could identify themselves to other Americans moving around in the hedgerows. One legend has it that what one of these paratroopers heard as the reassuring sound of a tin cricket was in truth the bolt mechanism of an enemy rifle. This soldier's last error was an error in perceptual judgment. The unwanted sounds indicating the presence of an enemy were wishfully interpreted as the wanted sounds that heralded the presence of a friend.

Needs refer to biological or psychological deficits (such as a lack of food or sleep), and **motives** refer to preferences for broad classes of activities (for example, socializing or achieving). As implied in the paratrooper example, people sometimes select, emphasize, or even imagine stimuli that satisfy their needs and motives, while misperceiving, screening out, or ignoring stimuli that add to their frustrations and miseries. This behavior is called **selective perception.**

An illustration of the occasionally wishful nature of perception has been provided by Mann and Taylor (1969). They interviewed people waiting in line for football tickets, Batman *T* shirts, and chocolate bars. In each line there was a "critical point"—that is, people in line before this point would get what they were waiting for, but those in line after this point would not, for the supply would be exhausted before they could advance to the head of the line. Interviewees were simply asked to estimate the number of people in front of them. Although persons before the critical point tended to overestimate the number of people in front of them (attesting to the value of what they were waiting for), individuals standing in line after the critical point tended to *underestimate* the length of the queue, thus showing a cheerful optimism that the wait would not be in vain.

Values and Thresholds

The **Study of Values** (G. W. Allport, Vernon, & Lindzey, 1960) is a scale that measures people's underlying interests or values. This scale is based on the rationale that there are ideal types of people whom real people approximate to varying degrees. An **ideal type** is not an actual person; neither is it necessarily a good thing. It is an intellectual tool produced by abstracting and distilling the characteristics of people (or groups) and then forging these qualities into a unified coherent construct. The Study of Values assumes six such ideal types: (1) *theoretical man,* who is dominated by the discovery of truth; (2) *economic man,* who is "practical" and characteristically interested in what is useful; (3) *aesthetic man,* who, as a lover of form and harmony, judges all experiences from the standpoint of fitness, symmetry, and grace; (4) *social man,* who is dominated by a need for affection, respect, and love; (5) *political man,* who is interested in power; and (6) *religious man,* who is mystical and dominated by a need to understand and experience unity with the universe. Despite the titles, these ideal types are supposed to be applicable for women, too.

Scores on the Study of Values indicate the extent to which the respondent's values approximate the interests associated with each ideal type. After assessing subjects' values, Postman, Bruner, and McGinnies (1948) used a tachistoscope to present words that were related to each of the six value categories. The more important the value category was to the subject, the more easily seen the category-relevant words. F. H. Allport (1955) reports similar results in an unpublished study by Vanderplass and Blake, who spoke the value-related stimulus words at different levels of volume.

An important possible explanation for these findings is the operation of familiarity. The person who is interested in economics would probably read and discuss economic theory more than the person interested in practical things or in religion. This self-controlled exposure would make terms and ideas from economics familiar, with the usual effect of lowering the recognition threshold.

The Perceptual-Accentuation Hypothesis

According to the **perceptual-accentuation hypothesis,** the perceived dimensions or prominence of a stimulus is related to that stimulus' relevance to personal needs or motives. That is, whatever is important to you should loom bigger or brighter in your eyes.

Early tests of this hypothesis examined the perceived size of coins. Bruner and Goodman (1947) had children adjust the size of a circular spot of light until it appeared to be equivalent in size to coins of denominations running from a penny to a half-dollar. Control subjects matched the diameters of worthless cardboard disks the same size as the coins. Coin size was consistently overestimated, but cardboard-disk size was not. Even more intriguing was the finding that the greatest overestimation was made by children from financially poor families. Although several subsequent studies also found that valuable coins were seen as larger than valueless disks (F. H. Allport, 1955), other studies have not confirmed this finding. Experiments by Tajfel and Cawasjee (1959) and by Dorfman and Zajonc (1963) suggested that the actual size of the coin is important. In both experiments, subjects saw coins of large denomination and physical size[1] as larger than comparably sized valueless disks, but coins of small denomination and physical size as smaller than the valueless disks. Furthermore, perceptual-accentuation effects are contingent on sources of extraneous stimulation (such as background noise or room temperature), which have varied across different experiments, and on the type of back-

---

[1]Although in many cases the physical size of a coin is related to its value, exceptions do exist (such as nickel-dime differences).

ground against which the stimuli are presented (Dorfman & Zajonc, 1963; Zajonc & Dorfman, 1964). Support for the hypothesis that valuable coins loom bigger and brighter than valueless disks is thus highly uneven, and it is not presently possible to draw firm conclusions on the topic.

Other studies have investigated the perceptual accentuation of human targets. Kassarjian (1963) found that in the 1960 election Kennedy and Nixon supporters tended to overestimate the height of their preferred candidate. Dannenmaier and Thumin (1964) found that people judged high-status persons as taller than low-status persons, but P. R. Wilson (1968) has suggested that this study lacked adequate controls. Rump and Delin (1973) found that high status led not to an overestimation of height but to a more accurate estimation of height. They found that, although subjects were accurate when judging the height of short and tall high-status stimulus persons, they tended to overestimate the height of short high-status stimulus persons and underestimate the height of tall low-status stimulus persons. Rump and Delin suggest that our attention is drawn to a person who is of high status; our inattentiveness to low-status persons leads to many errors in judgment.

In one interesting, relatively recent study, needs were related to the perceptual accentuation of some interesting need-related qualities (Stephan, Berscheid, & Walster, 1971). In this experiment, sexual arousal was varied by having some men read a description of a sexy seduction scene and having others read a description of the sex life of herring gulls. Next (in what was ostensibly a different and unrelated experiment) the subjects were given a photo of a pretty blonde coed and a "background questionnaire" on which the coed had described herself in desirable terms. Half the men in each arousal condition were led to believe that the coed would be accessible because the experimenter had arranged a date, whereas the other half were led to believe that they would not get to meet her.

The sexually aroused men rated the coed as prettier and better looking than did the nonaroused men. Of the aroused men, those who thought the coed was accessible rated her as more sexually receptive than did those who did not expect to meet her. This finding suggests that objects must be relevant to the satisfaction of the need for certain kinds of distortions to occur. In terms of ratings of qualities that were unrelated to sexual needs (the woman's "personality" or "intelligence"), comparable perceptual distortions did not occur.

The perceptual-accentuation hypothesis certainly is interesting, and several studies have suggested that valued stimuli do seem big and bright in the observer's eyes. Yet the results of several of the studies just considered show that there are many qualifications and exceptions and that findings that seem to support the hypothesis may be explained by methodological artifacts instead. Furthermore, overestimation of valued stimuli may represent a number of different processes; simply labeling all of them "perceptual accentuation" may be a gross oversimplification. Thus, although the accentuation hypothesis organizes a number of findings, it is at best tentative and must be treated with caution.

The Perceptual-Defense Hypothesis

How would you react if you were reading a religious pamphlet that contained, in one sentence, an obscene adjective? According to the **perceptual-defense hypothesis,** you probably wouldn't even notice it. This hypothesis states that people have an inability to correctly perceive obnoxious, threatening, or psychologically painful stimuli.

Early support for this hypothesis came from McGinnies (1949), who tachistoscopically presented "dirty" words, such as *bitch, belly, penis,* and *whore,* and "neutral" words, such as *river, sleep, broom,* and *stove.* Thresholds were higher for the dirty words; that is, these words required more stimulation for the subject to report recognition. McGinnies also obtained a measure of emotionality through recording changes in electrical conductance of the skin brought about through palmar sweat. Subjects showed emotional reactions to dirty words under conditions of less stimulation than necessary for reporting recognition. This finding suggested that the process of defense was active.

An alternative explanation of McGinnies' results was offered by Howes and Solomon (1950, 1951), who said McGinnies was dealing with the effects of familiarity. They suggested that, since dirty words are less likely to appear in print, people have not had much practice reading them. Because of their infrequency, then, dirty words might be more difficult to recognize than neutral words. In support of this contention is the earlier-noted finding that *more frequent* words are easier to recognize (Howes & Solomon, 1951). However, word frequency and word favorability have been found to be positively correlated, so that less frequent words tend to be less pleasant (R. C. Johnson, Thompson, & Frincke, 1960; Zajonc, 1968a). Thus the difficulty in recognizing infrequent words could be that these words are unpleasant! Finally, it has been suggested that perceptual-defense results might reflect nothing more than a tendency to *report* neutral words. Perhaps subjects don't want to appear "dirty minded" to the experimenter, so they are reluctant to report the dirty words. Or perhaps people are likely to say those words that they use routinely in conversations (Broadbent, 1967). According to this last interpretation, perception would hardly enter into "perceptual defense" at all. What all this means is that, although dirty or unpleasant words are less likely to be reported, it is not at all clear what is involved. Once again we find that needs and motives may affect perception, but the findings are not entirely straightforward, and competing explanations abound.

ACCURACY IN PERCEIVING OTHERS

Given identical information about the target, are two people likely to be equally accurate in their judgments? Or are some people characteristically more perceptive than others? This issue has a long and troubled history. Highly informative, however, is a study by Cline and Richards (1960), whose procedures avoided many of the pitfalls of earlier research.

Cline and Richards filmed, in natural settings, interviews with a cross-section of adults from the Salt Lake City area. The ten interviewees, or targets, included a divorced waitress, a 22-year-old Chicano laborer, a 40-year-old married male occultist of Italian parentage, and even a geology major. The interviewers probed personal values, personality strengths and weaknesses, reactions to the interview, hobbies, activities, self-concept, and temper. Off camera, each target person completed a battery of nine personality tests. Both targets and five of each target's friends underwent close questioning. On the basis of all this information, the examiners constructed five judging instruments. These instruments were used by 50 judges for evaluating each target after viewing the films. The instruments included: (1) multiple-choice questions concerning the target's reactions to various situations, (2) scales measuring the extent to which various adjectives described the target, (3) a form on which the subject guessed the target's opinions, (4) a sentence-completion test on which the subject guessed how the target would finish incomplete sentences, and (5) an adjective checklist on which the subject indicated which member of a number of pairs of adjectives best described the target.

Results showed that, with any specific instrument, subjects who did well at rating the first five targets did well with the second five targets. The correlations expressing this accuracy across targets ranged from .67 to .79. Furthermore, subjects who tended to do well with one instrument tended to do well with other instruments. Although the correlations showing this generality across instruments were relatively low (.24 to .65), most were statistically significant. This study thus suggests that some people are characteristically more perceptive than others.

Judgmental Skills

Most likely, more than one type of skill is required for judging others accurately. Bronfenbrenner, Harding, and Gallwey (1958) have identified two such skills: *sensitivity to the generalized other* and *sensitivity to individual differences.*

Sensitivity to the generalized other refers to an awareness of the typical characteristics or responses of a large class or group of people of which the target is a member or representative. It is an ability to accurately recognize characteristics that a number of people (such as soldiers or Protestants or third-graders) have in common. For example, professors in some fields, such as social sciences and humanities, are very likely to be politically liberal, whereas professors in some other fields, such as agriculture and engineering, are very likely to be politically conservative (Lipset & Ladd, 1970). Awareness of these real differences can help us to make better-than-chance guesses about the political beliefs of professors whom we meet from various departments.

Sensitivity to individual differences refers to the ability to identify the ways in which individuals differ from one another and from the average member of their group. For example, before proclaiming that Professor X is a Republican because he teaches agricultural economics, it would be useful to seek cues indicating whether or not Professor X is an average or typical agricultural economist in this regard. Peak judgmental accuracy, of course, requires *both* sensitivity to the generalized other *and* sensitivity to individual differences. The skills are believed to be independent, in that a given person may possess neither, both, or one but not the other.

Correlates of Accuracy

The personal qualities correlated with accuracy in judging others have been summarized by G. W. Allport (1961). First, a good judge is *experienced:* he or she has been exposed to a wide variety of people in a wide variety of settings. Second, a judge who is *similar* to the target is more accurate than one who is dissimilar. Third, most studies have found a moderate relationship between *intelligence* and the ability to judge others; it is difficult to understand someone who is more subtle and complex than oneself. Fourth, at least some evidence suggests that, to the extent to which people have *self-understanding*, they will be understanding of others. Fifth, accurate judges are *well-adjusted;* they are "socially skillful" and "emotionally stable." Finally, although the good judge is successful in social relationships and reasonably warm and friendly, he or she is also somewhat *detached*.

The Curious Effect of Special Training

Conspicuously absent from Allport's list is the description of a good judge as one who is *trained in dealing with people*. Certainly one of the aims of training programs in clinical psychology, psychiatry, social work, and so on is to teach the trainee to correctly perceive others and to understand their problems. This training is expensive and time consuming. Is it worth it?

Seventy-two medical students made ratings of a patient after having been shown a physician-patient interview by Crow (1957). Next, half of the students underwent instruction in physician-patient relationships while the other half were given additional instruction in surgery or in internal medicine. All subjects were again given the judgmental task. Those who had undergone the special training in physician-patient relationships became *less accurate* than the controls who had not received special instruction.

Crow's experiment examined the effects of one relatively brief training course. What about an entire training program? J. H. Weiss (1963) gave three targets a number of tests and interviews. The interviews were prepared in the form of typescripts. Judges were 60 Ph.D.s in clinical psychology and 60 Ph.D.s from the physical sciences. The judges were given either the whole package of information about the targets or the test results without the typescripts, and their task was to give the same answers to multiple-choice questions as those given by the target. There were no overall differences between the trained clinicians and the untrained physical scientists. However, given partial information, the clinicians were superior; given full information, the physical scientists showed greater accuracy. Apparently the clinicians' accuracy decreased as a result of being given access to the idiosyncratic detail contained in the interviews.

Training programs have typically emphasized individual differences. They have taught practitioners to be very wary of basing judgments on a person's group membership. So much attention has been drawn to misconceptions about different groups that possible real differences are ignored. In the Weiss study, clinicians confronted with only the test results were forced to draw conclusions on the basis of their knowledge of groups of people with similar scores. Clinicians given access to the highly idiosyncratic interview material were trapped by a quagmire of detail into ignoring generalities. This does not mean that training programs cannot raise judgmental accuracy, but it does mean that some training programs might be revised to instill sensitivity to the generalized other as well as sensitivity to individual differences.

PART SUMMARY

Perception refers to the processes through which the individual receives, organizes, and interprets information from the environment. Social perception refers to these processes when other people are peripherally or directly involved. Perception of social and nonsocial targets is in many ways similar. However, unlike objects, people are sources of deliberate actions and are characterized by motives and intents. These qualities clearly enter into others' perceptions of them.

Perception involves the interaction of perceiver variables, situational variables, and target variables. Because perception always involves a combination of public and private determinants, it is unlikely that two people will ever perceive the same thing in exactly the same way.

People see what they expect to see. Expectancies may be established by immediately preceding experiences, by suggestion and other forms of social influence, and by fairly lengthy learning histories during which it is discovered that some stimuli have higher conditional probabilities than do others. Familiar stimuli are more easily detected or recognized than unfamiliar stimuli, quite possibly because they are more expected. Three additional effects of familiarity should be emphasized. First, to the extent to which the person is familiar with a class of stimuli, it is easy for him or her to make discriminations within that class. Second, unfamiliar stimuli attract attention. Third, a number of studies have suggested that, within fairly wide latitudes, familiarity with a stimulus leads to more favorable reactions to it.

Several lines of research suggest that people have a tendency to selectively perceive stimuli that are somehow related to their interests, motives, and needs. According to the perceptual-accentuation hypothesis, whatever is important to a person should loom bigger or brighter in his or her eyes. Although a number of studies on the perception of nonsocial and social targets seemingly support this hypothesis, it must be treated with caution. According to the perceptual-defense hypothesis, it is difficult to perceive threatening or humiliating conditions. People may be less likely to report seeing threatening stimuli, but it is not at all clear what is responsible for this effect. In many studies that purport to show an effect of needs and motives on perception, alternative explanations of results have not been successfully eliminated.

Results of a highly sophisticated study by Cline and Richards showed that people who are good judges of one quality or attribute tend to be good judges of other qualities or attributes; also, people who are accurate when judging one target tend to be accurate when judging other targets as well. Two of the skills that are required for accurate judgments are an ability to recognize the real differences that distinguish groups from one another and an ability to recognize differences among individuals from within the same group.

According to Allport, an accurate judge of others is characterized by experience, similarity to the target, intelligence, self-understanding, good adjustment, and an attitude of detachment. Some studies suggest that specialized training programs can lead to a reduction in accuracy of person perception when an extremely sharp focus on individual differences blurs differences due to membership in different classes or groups.

THE SITUATION

Take two identical cardboard disks of some shade of gray. Paste one disk against a sheet of black cardboard and the other against a sheet of white cardboard. Compared with the former disk, the latter will seem darker. The appearance of the identical disks varies as a function of the situation or context in which it is presented.

The situation or context is also a powerful determinant of how we see other people. Consider, for example, how you might judge two politicians after seeing their campaigns covered in the evening news. One politician is shown in a motorcade that is slowly making its way through a dense crowd of people. Next he is shown in a jam-packed auditorium. The other politician is shown in a motorcade passing occasional groups of cheering people. Next he is shown speaking in a sparsely filled stadium. The first politician would probably seem more popular than the second. Yet it could be that fewer people turned out to see the "popular" than the "unpopular" candidate. The impression of popularity may depend on the skill of their respective campaign managers. For example, one manager always plans motorcades for densely populated business districts at lunchtime (thus ensuring that there would automatically be some crowd) and limits the motorcades to a three- or four-block run (so that everyone who wants to see the candidate has to jam into a small area). Similarly, it is always arranged so that the halls and auditoriums in which the candidate speaks are just a little too small to hold the anticipated crowd. The important thing is not what impression the candidate makes on the live audience but how large the live audience appears in subsequent newsreels (Bruno & Greenfield, 1972).

There are three ways in which the situation or context in which we encounter other people affects our perception of them. First, the physical setting is likely to provide cues that can affect the perceiver's impression of the target. Second, a situation can involve two or more targets, each one of whom affects the perceiver's impression of the other. Third, the situation can affect perception by establishing a relationship between the perceiver and the target.

THE PHYSICAL SETTING AS A SOURCE OF CUES

As indicated in the discussion of the two politicians, the situation provides a source of information that can dramatically affect our impressions of others. For some other examples, think about how an impression of two people fighting would differ depending on whether this activity were occurring in a football game or in a restaurant, and how an impression of a tap dancer would vary depending on whether the dancing occurred on stage or on the hood of a car. In considering some of the ways in which physical settings can affect our judgments of emotions, we'll see that some settings are more informative than others.

The Setting and Judgments of Emotion

It is not necessary for us to know the context in which an emotion was photographed in order to make a reasonably accurate judgment of it (Chapter 8). However, it is clear that knowledge of the situation or context will affect the judgmental process (Frijda, 1969; Birdwhistell, 1970). For example, an elderly woman crying at a funeral might be judged as

sorrowful, but a woman crying at a wedding might be judged as overcome by joy.

An awareness of the situation or context, however, raises a certain danger: judgments may be made on the basis of how the perceiver *thinks* the target should react to the situation, and the target's facial expression and posture may not be given sufficient weight. For example, a woman crying at a wedding might be sad (because of the bride's choice of a husband), whereas a woman crying at a funeral might be happy (because of the prospect of a large inheritance). Snap judgments based on the context can thus be faulty or wrong.

Informative and Noninformative Settings

Settings vary in terms of the extent to which they are taken as revealing something about the target's character, ability, and motives. For example, one's impression of Parson Brown might be revised rapidly downward if he were seen riding in the limousine of a crime boss. On the other hand, this would not be the case if it were clear that he was a hostage held at gunpoint. Differences in the extent to which a situation allows us to infer motives or intents may account for seemingly conflicting findings on the role of "context" in the mere-exposure effect.

A vocal criticism of the mere-exposure studies described earlier is that the exposure manipulation takes place in a setting that is at worst emotionally neutral and probably "positively toned," since the psychology laboratory is associated with truth, science, knowledge, and all sorts of "good" things (Burgess & Sales, 1971). What if the stimulus were presented in an unpleasantly toned, *negative* context? If you were a convict, how would you feel about your cellmate after a decade or two of confinement? As a result of peeping out of your cell window and watching the hangman ply his trade, would the hangman "grow on you"?

Results of an experiment by Saegert, Swap, and Zajonc (1973) compelled the authors to conclude that liking results from exposure—even if the exposure takes place in a negative context. During the course of an experiment supposedly on taste perception, girls wandered from room to room where they encountered other women varying numbers of times. For some subjects this contact took place during the pleasant task of tasting soft drinks; for other subjects the contact took place in the context of sampling concoctions of citric acid, vinegar, and quinine. In both pleasant and unpleasant situations, increased exposure was associated with increased liking.

Perlman and Oskamp (1971), on the other hand, did not find increases in liking when targets were exposed in negative contexts. These researchers presented photographs of blacks and whites in varying frequencies. Photographs were posed with the model in negative contexts (for example, pushing a broom), neutral contexts (no props), or positive contexts (for example, standing behind a pulpit). The biggest increases in liking over exposures were found when the stimulus persons were presented in positive contexts. Some increases in liking occurred over exposure for stimulus persons presented in neutral contexts. Although stimulus persons presented in negative contexts were generally given the most unfavorable ratings, the neutral- and negative-context stimuli did not differ significantly in terms of shifts in liking over exposure.

How may we reconcile these apparently discrepant findings? Saegert and her associates defined "context" in such a way that their "negative context" cast no aspersions on the qualities of the target. The context was clearly separated from the personality, motives, and intentions of the person who was being rated. Perlman and Oskamp, on the other hand, defined "context" in such a way that the contexts might have revealed something about the targets' abilities and achievements. Their findings of increased liking over exposures when stimulus persons were presented in positive contexts, but no striking decrements over exposures when the stimuli were presented in negative contexts, are understandable if their positive context provided a firmer basis for inferring personal qualities than did their negative context. For example, a subject seeing the target as a highly trained professional may have concluded that this person had ability and motivation and subscribed to the cherished values of society.

A subject seeing the target pushing a broom may not have known whether to conclude that the target lacked competence and motivation or simply was the victim of a ruthless, and perhaps racist, world.

THE SITUATION AS EXPRESSING A RELATIONSHIP BETWEEN TWO OR MORE TARGETS

The situation can define or imply a relationship between two or more targets, thus affecting the perception of one, the other, or both. Consider, for example, a snapshot of a man and a woman standing before a preacher at an altar. Think about how your impression of this touching couple would change if the preacher were replaced with a judge and the church with a divorce court!

Expressions in Context

Cline (1956) prepared line drawings of faces in three-quarter view. There were no distinguishing features other than the profile, eye, eyebrow, and mouth. The faces' expressions, however, were quite different and were referred to as *Smiling, Glum,* and *Frowning.*

Each face was paired with each other face, and students rated different pairs on several scales. How each face was evaluated depended on the other face with which it was paired. When presented with *Smiling, Glum* was seen as an embarrassed or defeated person who was dismayed at having been bested by *Smiling.* Paired with *Frowning, Glum* became aloof, tough, and independent rather than put down. Paired with *Glum, Smiling* was seen as a gloating bully; yet, paired with *Frowning, Smiling* became a friendly peacemaker. With *Smiling, Frowning* was seen as passive and resentful, but, with *Glum, Frowning* was seen as actively domineering. According to Cline (1956, p. 157) "To see two people as mutually relevant causative agents in an action-reaction system is a basic and informative process in the perception of social events."

Contrast and Assimilation

One person can provide a standard for comparison that affects our judgment of a third person. In the earlier mentioned Rump and Delin (1973) experiment, in which subjects judged stimulus persons of various heights, the height of the experimenter was also varied. The taller the experimenter, the lower the estimated height of the stimulus person. An accentuation of the difference between two stimuli presented close together is called a **contrast effect.**

When two or more targets are seen as voluntarily associated (as in the case of friends or dating couples), they are likely to be seen as similar to each other. For example, although pairs of friends are known to be similar on a number of dimensions, Miller, Campbell, Twedt, and O'Connell (1966) found that people who knew both individuals tended to exaggerate the extent to which they had similar personalities. More recently, Sigall and Landy (1973) have shown experimentally that impressions of a person's desirability depend to some extent on the desirability of the company he or she keeps. A male target was presented as either the boyfriend of or unrelated to a female accomplice of the experimenter. In some cases the female accomplice was tastefully dressed and groomed; in other cases she was poorly dressed and wore an ugly wig instead of tasteful makeup. The most favorable overall evaluation of the target occurred when he was presented as the boyfriend of an attractive woman, and the least favorable evaluation occurred when he was presented as the boyfriend of an unattractive woman. Assuming or accentuating the similarity between two stimuli is called an **assimilation effect.**

THE SITUATION AS DEFINING THE RELATIONSHIP BETWEEN PERCEIVER AND TARGET

Finally, the situation can specify or define a relationship between the perceiver and the target and in this way affect perception. For example, in the context of a dating relationship a wild and uninhibited person might be perceived as highly desirable by the partner, but in the context of a marriage relationship the same wild and uninhibited person might be seen by the same partner as very undesirable. The same behaviors that are considered fun on a date may be considered irresponsible in a marriage. For another example, a perceiver who is a supervisor may favorably evaluate a supervisee as methodical, conscientious, and hard working. If, as a result of a dramatic promotion, the former supervisee becomes the perceiver's supervisor, this same target person may now be unfavorably rated as an obsessive-compulsive, tyrannical slave driver. Finally, consider how the comic overtones of the stereotyped country sheriff (as portrayed in Dodge commercials) would rapidly disappear if you, rather than someone else, were being questioned by the sheriff.

Anticipated Interaction Distance

A highly important situational variable is the actual or expected psychological distance that the situation imposes between the perceiver and the target. Mirels and Mills (1964) led college women to believe that they would be assigned a partner with whom they were to work at problem solving. The experimenters described the partner in highly unflattering terms. Yet, compared with ratings assigned to similarly described nonpartners, better ratings were accorded to the supposed future partners. In this case, subjects wishfully overevaluated a person whom they could not avoid.

More recently, judgments of a teacher's excellence and attractiveness have been related to the teacher's instructional style and to the expected degree of interaction with the teacher. To create impressions of formal and informal teachers, Firestone, Kaplan, and Moore (1974) taped experimental interviews presenting the teacher's views on student advising, grading, and philosophy of education. The formal teacher's comments indicated orderliness, carefulness, preparedness, intellectual precision, objectivity, and overall organization. The informal teacher's comments revealed friendliness, intellectual curiosity, looseness, personal concern for students, and an overall lack of organization.

Four sets of ratings of the two teachers were obtained. One measure did not involve specification of the teaching situation. The others involved rating the teachers in three different situations ordered according to psychological distance between the teacher and the students. Under close-interaction conditions, teachers were rated as instructors in an intimate, seven-person seminar. Under conditions of moderate distance, teachers were rated as instructors in a 30-person discussion section, in which some student-teacher interaction was likely. Under the distant-interaction conditions, teachers were rated as instructors in impersonal 250-person lectures.

As Figure 3-3 suggests, students were, on the whole, more favorably impressed with the informal teacher. However, although the informal teacher was given better ratings as a leader of a seminar than as a lecturer to a large group, the formal teacher was given better ratings as a lecturer to a large group than as a leader of a small seminar. The same hang-loose attitude that was relatively desirable in a small discussion section was relatively undesirable in a large lecture class. Similarly, the high degree of organization and rigidity that could prevent a free-ranging discussion in a small seminar was seen as useful in the large lecture setting.

Situation-Appropriate and Situation-Inappropriate Target Behavior

The situation defines the right and proper ways in which the target may act toward the perceiver. If a target behaves in ways that are "out of bounds," our evaluation of him or her is likely to be lowered. But what is improper in one situation is not necessarily improper in another. This

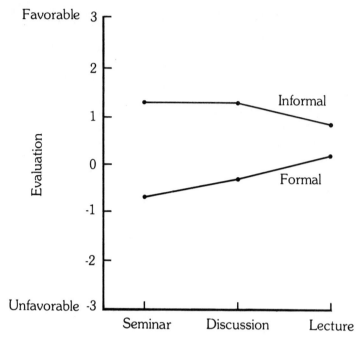

Figure 3-3. Attitudes toward teachers as a function of the teacher's formality and the anticipated interaction distance. (Adapted from "The Attitude-Gradient Model," by I. J. Firestone, K. J. Kaplan, and M. Moore. In A. A. Harrison (Ed.), *Explorations in Psychology.* Copyright © 1974 by Wadsworth Publishing Company, Inc. Used by permission of the publisher, Brooks/Cole Publishing Company, Monterey, California.)

was cleverly shown by Kaplan, Firestone, Moore, and Degnore (1971), who had students take part in an interview in which banal, impersonal questions were interspersed with probing, intimate questions. This interview was presented as a business interview, as a psychotherapeutic interview, or as a sex-inventory interview. Respondents were equipped with a device that allowed them to make continual ratings of the interviewer. In all settings, respondents evaluated the interviewer less favorably when intimate as compared with nonintimate questions were asked. However, the magnitude of this effect depended on the situation. The negative reaction to the interviewer when the intimate questions were posed was far more pronounced in the business-interview setting than in the psychotherapeutic or sex-inventory settings. Business interviews traditionally focus on bland material such as one's level of education, previous experience at a line of work, and so forth. In this setting a question about how often one masturbates is unexpected and shocking and generates very unfavorable impressions of the interviewer. In a psychotherapeutic or sex-inventory interview, however, such intimate questions are not quite so unexpected and shocking.

Situation, Task, and Cognitive Tuning

The situation may also impart to the subject a particular orientation toward the target that affects the organization of complex impressions. Zajonc (1960) told subjects that they would enter into deliberations concerning a hypothetical job applicant after reading a letter about him. Some subjects expected to transmit the information they read (transmitters), whereas others were led to believe that they would soon receive additional information (receivers). Both transmitters and receivers then arranged cards containing characteristics of the applicant into whatever groupings and subgroupings seemed natural to them. Transmitters described the applicant by more characteristics and arranged these characteristics into more categories than did receivers. Transmitters paid attention to specific details in the letter; in effect, they organized a fairly precise outline to help them during subsequent transmission. Receivers tended to use fewer but broader categories. Their lesser degree of organization made allowance for receiving new information that might not have been hinted at in the letter. **Cognitive tuning** refers to a mental set to receive and structure information in a way compatible with future task requirements.

Subsequent research has also shown that transmitters prefer information in nice, neat packages. A. R. Cohen (1961) found that transmitters accentuated the distinctive features of the target person and preferred not to receive conflicting information. Brock and Fromkin (1968) found that transmitters were better able to recall the polarized or distinctive features of the stimulus person. In this experiment, subjects spent more time listening to a tape presenting material supportive of earlier material than they spent listening to a tape presenting inconsistent or conflicting information. Using nonsocial stimuli, Mazis (1973) found that, compared with receivers and controls, transmitters preferred familiar, rather than novel, information. All these studies taken together support the idea that transmitters want nice, consistent impressions unmarred by the inconsistencies and conflicts that would make subsequent transmission difficult.

PART SUMMARY

Our perceptions of others are affected by the situations or contexts in which they are encountered. There are three general ways in which contexts influence social perception.

First, the physical setting may provide highly informative cues. In judging another's emotions, we are likely to be heavily swayed by the situation in which those emotions appear. This may or may not contribute to a high level of accuracy. In judging another's character or personality, we can consider the situation relevant to the extent to which the target's presence in that situation reveals his or her abilities, motives, or intents.

Second, the situation can express a relationship between two or more targets and thus affect our impressions of each. Facial expressions, for example, take on different meanings depending on the facial expressions of the other people present. One person can provide a standard for comparison that affects our judgments of another person. In cases in which two or more targets are seen as voluntarily associated, their similarities may be exaggerated.

Finally, the situation can alter perception of the target through defining the relationship between the perceiver and the target. Illustrative here are the findings that (1) people are sometimes rather wishful when they evaluate unpleasant people with whom they expect to interact; (2) warm but disorganized teachers are liked more when near than when distant, but formal and aloof teachers are liked more when distant than when near; (3) the same act on the part of a target may be interpreted differently depending on the psychological distance between the perceiver and the target; and (4) expected conditions can affect the way we organize an overall impression of another.

THE TARGET

Adolf Hitler had very bad breath (Mosely, 1971). As you probably know, observed or inferred personal qualities such as this are a major determinant of how we feel about others. Recent research on target variables has had two main thrusts. First, how are various items of information about a target integrated to form an overall impression of that target? This process is called **impression formation.** Second, how do a person's acts suggest something about his or her underlying qualities, motives, and intents? Making the leap "from acts to dispositions" is called **attribution.**

IMPRESSION FORMATION

Studies of impression formation are concerned with how various pieces of information about a person are selected, weighed, and combined to form an overall picture. Four important findings here are: (1) that negative information is given more weight than positive information; (2) that some perceived qualities contribute more to our overall impressions than do others; (3) that the perceiver may assume much after having seen little; and (4) that perceivers tend to average bits and pieces of evaluative information about the target when forming an overall impression of likability.

Positive and Negative Information

Mr. Gordon has a wife and two children. He has lived in a nicely maintained home in the same upper-middle-class neighborhood for years. A respected banker with a reputation as a "man with a heart," he has been praised repeatedly in the local newspaper for his demonstrations of civic pride and social responsibility. Then, one afternoon, he is arrested for making a pass at an undercover police officer in a local restaurant. When subsequent evaluations of Mr. Gordon are made, which do you think will be given more weight—ten years of responsible community leadership or one instance of "irresponsible" conduct?

Almost all evidence points to the conclusion that unfavorable, negatively toned information is considered more important than favorable or positively toned information. For one thing, the negative information is generally regarded as more *informative* than the positive information (Moore, 1974). For example, Leventhal and Singer (1964) described three target persons: one in favorable terms, one in neutral terms, and one in unfavorable terms. Subjects were then asked how satisfied they were with the presented information. The negatively toned information was considered the most adequate and informative and stimulated the least desire for more information. Lott, Lott, and Crow (1969) had subjects describe likable and unlikable targets. They found that it required more positive adjectives to describe the likable targets than it took negative adjectives to describe the unlikable targets—again suggesting that negative information is somehow more informative.

Moreover, a wide array of studies show that, when overall impressions are formed, negative information is given more weight than positive information. Summarizing studies of employment interviews, Mayfield (1964) concluded that interviewers would not necessarily hire people who divulged positive information, although they were fairly sure to reject people who divulged negative information. Unfortunately, this rule of thumb may not be so useful as it appears, for Mayfield also concluded that the same information that struck some interviewers as highly positive struck some other interviewers as highly negative. Since Mayfield's review, quite a number of studies have confirmed that people accentuate the negative. For example, S. Feldman (1966) examined the capacity of various adjectives to modify impressions. He found that negative adjectives lowered ratings more than positive adjectives raised them. In another study, subjects evaluated *pairs* of evil deeds, such as pocketing waitresses' tips and poisoning dogs. The fouler of the two deeds determined the overall ratings of the pair (Birnbaum, 1972).

Why is disproportionate weight given to negative information? Several possibilities have been discussed by Kanouse and Hanson (1972). One is that negative characteristics are more likely to negate or undo positive characteristics than positive characteristics are to negate or undo negative characteristics. For example, a person may have a reputation as an able and conscientious accountant. But would you hire this person to straighten out your firm's records if you suspected that the accountant had used his or her skills to embezzle funds from a previous employer? Most likely, the piece of negative information would undo the positive information, and the accountant would not be hired.

Other explanations focus on the sharp contrast provided by negative information. Reports about people are routinely favorable. There are at least two reasons for this. One is that our society is packed with rules, regulations, and socializing techniques to ensure that people will be "good" as opposed to "bad." The other reason is that there are strong biases toward reporting the desirable and the acceptable. Therefore, negative information contrasts with positive information as a foghorn contrasts with a string quartet. An implication of this line of reasoning is that, when *positive* information contrasts, it should gain in importance. Thus we might find ourselves very impressed when we discover that Frankenstein's monster raises flowers or that the Mummy is kind to children.

There may be some circumstances under which the addition of a tidbit of negative information raises overall impressions. First, inclusion of some negative material in a recommendation suggests that the person making the recommendation is candid and sincere and that the positive information is trustworthy. Second, just a touch of negative information can make a near-perfect person seem a bit more human and hence a bit more likable.

In a study by Aronson, Willerman, and Floyd (1966), male subjects listened to taped interviews of a person who was presented either as outstanding or as mediocre. In one condition the interview was routine, but in the other the interview ended with the interviewee clumsily spilling coffee all over himself. On the whole, the outstanding person received more favorable ratings than did the mediocre person, but the blunder had different effects on the ratings of the two targets. Although it led to less favorable ratings of the mediocre target, it led to more favorable ratings of the outstanding target. Spilling coffee made the mediocre person look like a clumsy oaf, but it gave the near-perfect person a welcome touch of humanity. Later research, however, showed that the blunder raised the likability of the near-perfect target only when the target was male and rated by other males. When the blunder was made by a near-perfect female, or if the perceivers were female, the blunder did not lead to raised evaluations (Deaux, 1972).

Central and Peripheral Traits

To study how we form overall impressions, Asch (1946) prepared two lists of personality-descriptive adjectives. One list read "intelligent, skillful, industrious, warm, determined, practical, and cautious." The second list was identical, except that the adjective *warm* was replaced with its opposite, *cold*. Each of these stimulus lists was read to a different group of subjects. Subjects were then given a list of different "response" adjectives and asked to check off those they felt described the target to whom the stimulus list applied. The subjects also wrote sketches describing their overall impressions of the targets.

Although the two stimulus lists differed by only one word, they created radically different impressions. Compared to the *cold* person, the *warm* person was described as more popular, wise, humorous, and imaginative. It was unlikely that *warm* simply led to improved ratings on all dimensions, because the *warm* person was not viewed more favorably in all respects. Further research showed that other substitutions (such as *blunt* for *polite*) did not cause major differences in the response adjectives chosen. Asch thus made a distinction between central and peripheral traits. **Central traits** are traits like warm and cold, which cause changes in the perception of other traits and hence contribute disproportionately to overall impressions. **Peripheral traits** are traits like blunt and polite, which do not precipitate changes in the impressions of other qualities. The discovery that traits vary in terms of centrality suggested to Asch that the impressions we form of others are not simply the sum of component parts but are, instead, dynamic wholes.

But are they really dynamic wholes? Wishner (1960) had a different view. In his (1960) study, 214 students rated introductory psychology teachers on the warm-cold dimension and most of the stimulus and response traits that had appeared on Asch's adjective checklist. Wishner found: (1) that there were low correlations between warm-cold and other stimulus traits (intelligent, skillful, and so on), which suggested that "warm" and "cold" provided new information rather than added to the strength of information already present; (2) that response checklist ratings correlated more highly with central-trait ratings than they did with peripheral-trait ratings; and (3) that the warm-cold ratings correlated most highly with those checklist items that showed the greatest shifts following the substitution of *warm* for *cold*. Wishner suggested that a trait should be considered central for traits that are correlated with it and peripheral for traits that are uncorrelated with it.

Wishner's study has been used both as a refutation of Asch and as a testimony to Asch's wisdom. On the one hand, by showing that it is possible to predict overall impressions from component traits, Wishner's investigation refutes the view that overall impressions of personality are different from the sum of their parts. On the other hand, the study supported the idea that some traits are more important than others in that changes in them trigger systematic variations in the perception of other traits. It added to Asch's view by providing a nonintuitive definition of central traits and by suggesting how to predict the effects of traits of different degrees of centrality.

Implicit Theories of Personality

A remarkable feature of impression formation is that, given minimal information, we tend to fill in gaps and develop rather complete pictures of the target. Bruner and Taguiri (1954) have suggested that we each develop our own informal, impressionistic theory of personality. These **implicit theories of personality** indicate to us what kinds of qualities or traits "go together" and hence result in our inferring or predicting some traits

or qualities after having seen what we take as evidence of other traits. Thus, on discovering that our new neighbor is a ballerina of international fame, we may leap to the conclusion that she probably wouldn't enjoy being a majorette for a drum and bugle corps or going on a date to the roller derby. Or, after discovering that a man has spent the family's welfare check on gambling rather than on milk and sneakers for his children, we may infer that he is given to strong drink, unfaithful to his wife, and most likely a thief.

Studies reviewed by Hastorf, Schneider, and Polefka (1970), Rosenberg and Sedlak (1972), and Schneider (1973) reveal the following about implicit theories of personality. First, these theories are developed at a very early age, although the theories held by children differ in many important ways from the theories held by adults. Second, people within a given culture seem to develop somewhat similar implicit theories of personality, but different theories will predominate in different cultures. Third, within any given culture, there are still considerable differences among the theories developed by different individuals. Fourth, these theories are to some extent valid, in the sense that the traits people see as going together actually are correlated. For example, in one study it was found that, when high school girls arranged items from a personality test into clusters of items that they thought went together, the clusters thus obtained agreed significantly with clusters obtained through the computer analysis of the personality-test responses of a large number of people (Stricker, Jacobs, & Kogan, 1974). Finally, implicit theories are also to some extent "ideal," in that the perceived correlation among the traits may exceed the actual correlation among the traits (Passini & Norman, 1966). Whatever their validity, implicit theories of personality at least give us the comforting illusion that other people are stable and predictable.

Summation and Averaging Models

Asked simply to state how much we like someone, we can usually answer with little hesitation. But such overall evaluations clearly depend on the favorability of the specific qualities and characteristics that we associate with that person. How do we combine these elements to form an overall impression? Two models have been advanced. One, the **summation model,** suggests that the values of the different pieces of information are simply added or summed. The other, or **averaging model,** suggests that the overall evaluation is the arithmetic mean or average of the components (Anderson, 1965, 1968a, 1971; Hodges, 1973).

Tests of the two models require some initial knowledge of the values of the components to be summed or averaged. This information has been thoughtfully provided by Anderson (1968b), who reduced G. W. Allport and Odbert's (1936) list of 18,000 personality traits to a more manageable 550. One hundred students rated the 550 words on seven-point scales. According to this list, the five nicest things you could call someone are sincere, honest, understanding, loyal, and truthful; the five nastiest things you could call someone are dishonest, mean, phony, cruel, and—the ultimate insult—a liar. The average scores ranged from 5.73 for sincere and honest to .26 for liar.

In many situations the two models would not offer different predictions. Whether averaged or summed, a person described as *sincere* (5.73) and *honest* (5.73) would be liked better than someone described as *phony* (.27) and a *liar* (.26). However, when we consider the combination of highly and moderately polarized information, different predictions are forthcoming.

Suppose we have two targets. Claude is described by two highly favorable adjectives, *sincere* (5.73) and *honest* (5.73). Maude is also described as *sincere* and *honest*, but to this description are added two moderately favorable adjectives: *persistent* (3.47) and *sophisticated* (3.72).

According to the summation model, our overall evaluation of Claude would be 5.73 + 5.73, or 11.46. Our evaluation of Maude would be 5.73 + 5.73 + 3.47 + 3.72, or 17.65. Thus we should like Maude better than Claude.

According to the averaging model, our overall evaluation of Claude would be (5.73 + 5.73)/2, or 5.73. Our evaluation of Maude would be (5.73 + 5.73 + 3.47 + 3.72)/4, or 4.65. Thus we should like Claude better than Maude.

Anderson (1965) conducted a study along these exact lines. The critical comparison was the relative evaluation of two highly positive traits as compared with two highly positive traits plus two moderately positive traits. Results contradicted the summation model and supported the averaging model. Addition of moderately polarized information lowered, rather than raised, evaluations. A number of subsequent studies by Anderson and his colleagues have continued to support the averaging model. In one recent test, it was found that the model could be used for interpreting how people combine impressions of individuals to derive an overall impression of a group (Anderson, Linder, & Lopes, 1973).

ATTRIBUTION THEORY

After irresponsibly leveling accusations at a prominent politician, a columnist prints a public retraction and apology. How would our impression of the journalist be affected by this seeming act of contrition?

To some extent, it would depend on the *perceived cause* of the apology. If the apology were voluntarily offered after the columnist discovered that his or her information was unreliable, we might conclude that the columnist was an honest and decent person who had owned up to an unfortunate mistake. If the retraction and apology were compelled by a stern court order, we might not be quite so lavish with our praise. In fact, if we agreed with the judge that the evidence of libel was overwhelming, we might consider the journalist to be either stupid or a cheap sensationalist.

As indicated earlier, "attribution" refers to the procedures by which the average individual infers the causes of behavior. Contemporary research on **attribution theory** deals with several broad issues. First, it seeks to determine the conditions under which people are likely to assign a cause to their own or to others' behavior. For example, if you were in a theater and saw a woman jump up and run toward the exit, would you wonder what prompted this action? Second, attribution theory deals with the conditions that lead to the inference of one cause of the behavior rather than another. For example, would you assign one cause to the woman's action if there were smoke in the theater and another cause if her exit were preceded by that of a small toddler? Third, attribution theory deals with the different consequences of assigning the behavior to one cause rather than to another. If you inferred that the woman was fleeing a holocaust, would you react differently than if you inferred that she was chasing an errant 3-year-old? The greatest proportion of empirical studies have addressed the second of these topics: how observers infer that someone's behavior is due to one cause rather than another.

Inferring Dispositions

Whenever we observe the actions or fate of other people, we have two basic options. We can explain their actions or fate as due to chance, luck, coercion, circumstances, or other factors that have little to do with the persons themselves. Or, we can find causes in the targets' abilities, motives, and personality characteristics. Let's use the term **dispositional inference** to refer to cases in which behavior or its consequences are attributed to some quality of the person. For example, if we infer that a student does badly on a test because he or she is stupid or poorly motivated, we would be making a dispositional inference. If we infer that a student does badly on a test because the test is unfair, we would not be making a dispositional inference.

For a person's behavior or life circumstances to seem revealing of some inner quality, they must not be easily explained as the result of capricious fate, environmental constraints, or situational circumstance. For example, suppose you are a waiter or waitress at a resort, and a customer fails to leave you a tip. Does this mean that he is stingy? Perhaps he was forgetful, or out of change. Perhaps your service was poor.

According to Jones and Davis (1965), we can make inferences about another's dispositions only if we see the person as having a number of options available and then making a *deliberate choice among them.* If the customer has no options, or if his behavior or circumstances are forced upon him by external factors, there is insufficient information to infer much about him. Of course, explanations alternative to the explanation that he is stingy might be eliminated one by one. If you had brought him change, the excuse that he was out of change would not hold. If he left a penny tip, then forgetfulness would not explain his lack of generosity. If you were certain that the service was flawless, then stinginess becomes an increasingly salient explanation of his failure to tip.

Kelley (1967) has listed four criteria that suggest to an individual observer that his or her impressions of someone (or something) are based on the inherent properties of the target (or entity) rather than on the observer's own characteristics or his or her own characteristics in combination with the target's characteristics. The criteria are *distinctiveness, consistency over time, consistency over modality,* and *consensus.* Comparing the evidence against these criteria would help you to decide whether the lack of a tip said something about the customer or something about you.

Distinctiveness refers to the extent to which the phenomenon is observed when the target is present but is not observed when it is absent. For example, if this man is the only customer who fails to leave a tip, this suggests something about him, rather than something about your service.

Consistency over time refers to the extent to which the phenomenon is observed each time the target or entity is present. For example, if he is served by you repeatedly and fails to leave a tip on each occasion, explanations of distraction or forgetfulness would seem to lose plausibility.

Consistency over modality refers to the extent to which the target is associated with similar phenomena under differing conditions. For example, if the customer refused to buy tickets to the Waiters' Ball or to donate a dime to the Orphans' Relief Fund, there would be further testimony to his inherent stinginess.

Consensus refers to the extent to which different observers report similar experiences of the phenomenon. Further evidence that he is stingy or cheap would be provided if other waiters and waitresses, bellpersons, and cab drivers all reported that he never tipped.

In short, you should feel that the customer's failure to tip reflected something about his underlying nature if he were the only customer not to tip, if he failed to tip on different occasions, and if he showed a lack of generosity when in other situations or when dealing with other people. If many customers failed to tip, if the customer in question sometimes left sizable tips, and if he showed generosity in other situations and when dealing with other people, a disposition to be stingy would not explain his behavior.

Several studies support Kelley's thesis that stronger dispositional inferences will be made when the evidence confronting the observer is consistent (Kepka & Brickman, 1971; McArthur, 1972; Karaz & Perlman, 1975). In one ingenious study, subjects were given information about racehorses' past performances, allowed to predict a winner, and then shown a videotape in which their horse won or lost (Karaz & Perlman, 1975). Consistency was varied by having the horse's performance in the videotaped race either the same as or different from its earlier performance. As expected, when the horse's performance in the videotaped race was consistent with its previous performance, people attributed its performance to qualities of the horse itself. When the horse's performance in the videotaped race was inconsistent with its previous record, subjects chalked its performance up to the circumstances of that particular race.

Dispositions fall into two categories: the target's *abilities* and the target's *intents*.

Attribution of Abilities

Observing that a person has repeated success at a task usually leads the observer to infer that the performer has task-relevant abilities (Weiner, Frieze, Kukla, Reed, Rest, & Rosenbaum, 1972). Observing repeated failure suggests that the person lacks such abilities. Once a low expectation is formed, a successful performance is likely to be attributed to chance. As Moore (1974) has noted, if a trained mathematician and a 4-year-old girl each give the correct answer to a tough math problem, in the former case the answer would be taken as testimony to the mathematician's brilliance, whereas in the latter case the answer would be dismissed as pure luck. A series of studies by Jones, Rock, Shaver, Goethals, and Ward (1968) suggests that the observed *pattern* of successes and failures is important in the attribution process.

In these studies, subjects observed live or filmed performers attempting to answer a series of difficult intelligence-test items. The performer answered half of the items correctly. In one condition, she began the series with mostly right answers but showed a performance decrement as the series progressed. In the other condition, she began with mostly wrong answers but improved over trials. Although in each case the performer got the same number right, subjects gave different ratings of the performers' abilities. The woman whose performance deteriorated was seen as having more ability than the woman whose performance improved—or than control performers who got the same number of right answers but in random order. Furthermore, the performer with the deteriorating performance was somehow remembered as having gotten more right answers. To reconcile high ability with poor performance on the last few trials, subjects suggested that the performer had lost interest in the task.

Expectations about performance may be built up in other ways, such as through a familiarity with how things tend to work in our culture. Some tasks, such as sewing or repairing carburetors, are sex linked in that women are trained for some and men are trained for others. Deaux and Emswiller (1974) suggest that, as a result, we expect women to excel at "feminine tasks" and men to excel at "masculine tasks." They hypothesized that, when a person performs well at a sex-appropriate task, the observer will feel that this good performance reflects aptitude and training; if a person performs well at a sex-inappropriate task, the observer will write the performance off as due to luck. To test this hypothesis, Deaux and Emswiller had subjects listen as male or female targets attempted to identify common objects that were camouflaged within a picture. In the feminine-task condition these objects consisted of such things as mops and double boilers, and in the masculine-task condition these objects consisted of such things as wrenches and tire irons. As the experimenter asked questions about what was in the picture, the target gave true or false answers. The target always answered 16 out of 25 correctly, a performance that subjects were led to believe was better than average.

Next, subjects rated the target's performance in terms of the extent to which they considered it due to ability or due to luck. As Figure 3–4 shows, identical performances at the masculine task were attributed to ability on the part of men but to luck on the part of women. The reverse did not hold true: women were not seen as more competent than men on the feminine task. Thus the hypothesis was only partially supported. These results most likely represent a repeatedly demonstrated tendency to devalue women's achievements in our culture (Chapter 4).

Many other factors will also influence attribution of ability. For example, Jellison, Riskind, and Broll (1972) found that, when people place reckless bets on their performance at a task requiring skill, they will be seen as more competent than cautious bettors. Cialdini, Braver, and Lewis (1974) found that, when we see one person yield to another person's arguments, we consider the former less intelligent than someone who does not yield. These latter investigators also found, however, that, when someone yields to one of our *own* arguments, we conclude that he or she must be very intelligent indeed!

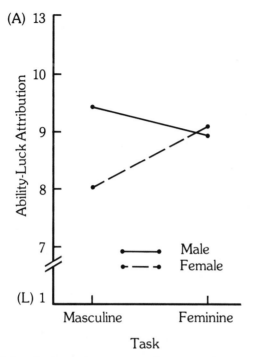

Figure 3-4. Ability-luck attributions as a function of sex of task and sex of performer. High numbers indicate attribution to ability and low numbers indicate attribution to luck. (From "Explanations of successful Performance on Sex-Linked Tasks: What Is Skill for the Male Is Luck for the Female," by K. Deaux and T. Emswiller, *Journal of Personality and Social Psychology,* 1974, 29(1), 82. Copyright 1974 by the American Psychological Association. Reprinted by permission.)

When we are in the course of observing others, an inference of ability may be one of the first inferences we make. Once sufficient information has been gained, attention is directed toward inferring other qualities. The reason why an attribution of ability comes first is that other attributions often hinge upon it. For example, we could not infer that Roger premeditatedly murdered Leroy unless we first inferred that Roger had the ability to control the circumstances leading to Leroy's demise. If the ability is lacking, the verdict is accidental death.

Attribution of Motives and Intents

Inferring intent is a complex process. It requires considering the options available to the person and then interpreting the chosen option in light of the rejected alternatives.

According to Jones and Davis (1965), **uncommon effects** serve as cues or tip-offs that reveal to the perceiver the target's intent. Generally, an action will have several effects, not just one. For example, an adolescent girl of vaguely Protestant background joins church U. Church U offers Sunday services, potluck dinners, and pastoral counseling and affords a sense of responsibility and a mantle of respectability. But what did the girl *intend* by joining this particular church? Why not church C, M, or P, which have very similar doctrines? Here, say Jones and Davis, we should compare the consequences of joining church U with the consequences of joining the other churches. Each church would have a number of features in common: Sunday services, religious music, and so forth. However, on close examination it turns out that all of the girl's friends belong to the church-U youth group and that only "unpopular" kids belong to the youth groups of alternative churches. Churches C, M, and P, on the other hand, expect daily prayers and unremitting attendance at solemn worship services. Here is an uncommon effect: church U promises more in the way of personal popularity and fun social events. There is now a basis for attribution. In the case of this teenager, sociability seems to have won out over religiosity.

The **assumed desirability of effects** also plays an important role in inferring intent. Many actions produce "mixed results"—some bad, some good. For example, giving up smoking is bad insofar as cigarettes have the contradictory but wonderful effects of being soothing pacifiers and providers of instant resolve, but giving up smoking is also good insofar as it decreases the likelihood of a lingering, hideous death. We assume that people are motivated by the favorable effects. That is, each time I give up smoking, I do so to preserve my health and extend my life, rather than to undergo a six-week case of the jitters.

Although the desirable effects may provide us with an instant "explanation" of another's actions, they do not tell us much about idiosyncratic, underlying qualities of a specific individual. According to Jones and Davis, compared with universally desired, universally sought consequences, *less universally sought effects* are more revealing. Thus we are more willing to draw a conclusion about someone who is willing to undergo discomfort or resist social pressure than about someone who is not. For example, the avoidance of punishment seems universally sought. According to folklore, George Washington risked punishment by admitting to his father that he had hacked at a cherry tree. Character won out over love of pleasure, and all good Americans have attributed his confession to the underlying disposition "honesty." On the other hand, if George had told his father that he not only was not responsible for the vandalized cherry tree but had no knowledge of its cover-up, people would be less willing to attribute him with honesty. He could be telling the truth in the latter case, but he could also be trying to get out of punishment. To the extent that there are a number of viable explanations of a given act, we tend to have less confidence in any one of them. This is known as the **discounting principle.** Several studies have suggested that, when people argue for something that is likely to elicit an adverse reaction from the audience (for example, arguing against unions to a Teamsters' local), they are likely to be seen as "truthful" even if they aren't particularly well liked (Jones & Davis, 1965).

Living up to role expectations prevents adverse reactions from people in interlocking roles. Disregarding one's role is likely to yield rejection from others. Since rejection is not often sought, it follows that when people behave in a way that is at variance with their roles, that behavior is seen as more informative about their true nature than is in-role behavior.

This effect has been shown by Jones, Davis, and Gergen (1961), who had subjects listen to recorded job interviews. The applicant was seeking to become either a submariner or an astronaut. Before the applicant gave his responses, the interviewer clearly defined the role of submariner or astronaut. Applicants then answered the questions in a manner consistent with or inconsistent with the role. Since, in accordance with the discounting principle, in-role answers could reflect either the applicant's true qualities or a response to the demands of the interview, subjects had little basis for inferring what this interviewee was "really like." However, there was only one possible explanation for the out-of-role behavior: an inner quality of the person. Subjects considered the out-of-role behavior to be more revealing and had more confidence in their judgments when rating the out-of-role than the in-role stimulus person.

More recent findings have also generally supported the discounting principle. Touhey (1972a) found that a perceiver was more likely to make dispositional inferences when role explanations were not available. Chaikin and Cooper (1973) found that out-of-role behavior increased the extremity of the evaluations made by the observers. The direction of the evaluations was determined by whether or not the out-of-role behavior resulted in favorable or unfavorable consequences for the observer. Thus it was difficult to "either respect or scorn" someone's actions if those actions were in role and hence revealed little about that person.

Biases, Errors, and Illusions

Many attribution processes could be impersonally accomplished by a computer. It is easy to imagine, for example, a computer deciding whether a certain level of performance suggests skill or chance. Yet, although in many ways attribution processes seem rational and sensible, there is also, as Deaux and Emswiller's results suggest, a bit of the subjective or human touch. Kelley (1967, 1972) has discussed some of the "errors, biases, and illusions" in attribution, and Jones and Davis (1965) have specified the ways in which the perceiver's relationship to the target influences attribution.

Kelley points to three biases in the attribution process. First, people tend to place insufficient emphasis on the situational causes of others' behavior and to liberally attribute these others with dispositions and traits. For example, after seeing a woman snap at her child, one is likely to conclude that she is "short tempered" and to dismiss the fact that the child had taunted her for three hours before she "blew her cool." Second, when the perceiver is interacting with the target, the perceiver is likely to see himself or herself as the cause of the target's behavior—provided that it reflects well on the self. Thus when a student improves, the teacher may see the improvement as a result of his or her own skill as a teacher; when a patient improves, a psychotherapist may attribute it to his or her clinical sensitivity and skill. On the other hand, if the student flunks out, "poor ability and low motivation" are blamed, and, if the patient attempts suicide, "pathology" is responsible. Third, if the target does something for gain, he or she is more likely to be seen as personally culpable than if the same thing is done to prevent loss or punishment. Perhaps in recognition of this, national leaders never order their troops into a neighboring country to take over the resources. Invasions are always proclaimed "self-defensive" by the invaders. In addition to these biases on the part of the observer, Kelley notes that attributions may be faulty because the situation is misleading. Consider the plight of a man who is spied by his girlfriend of long standing as he helps a female neighbor with her stuck zipper.

The perceiver's personal stake in the action is a focal point for Jones and Davis (1965). **Hedonic relevance** refers to the extent to which the target's acts further or hinder the perceiver's interests. We are more likely to explain an act or a circumstance as due to some quality of a person if it is hedonically relevant. For example, driving past a bus stopped by the side of the road, we might nonchalantly infer that there had been an equipment failure. On the other hand, if we were passengers on that bus, we might less nonchalantly make a number of unflattering inferences about the driver's ability and parentage. On a more upbeat note, if a bartender gives a beer "on the house" to someone else, we may see the act as reflecting a policy of management. If the bartender gives us the free drink (thus making the act hedonically relevant), we may see the act as reflecting friendliness and charity on the bartender's part.

Personalism refers to the extent to which the perceiver believes that an act was somehow caused or occasioned by his or her presence. Consider, for example, getting extremely poor service while trying to buy a ferry ticket across the river Styx. Perhaps everyone else there is also getting poor service (low personalism). Or perhaps only the hero of the story is getting poor service (high personalism). According to Jones and Davis, strong inferences are likely when a perceiver believes that the act was somehow related to his or her presence. In support of this, Potter (1973) has found that increasing personalism strengthens evaluative reactions to a target.

Attribution of One's Own Characteristics

E. M. Forster is credited with saying "How can I tell what I think until I see what I have to say?" (Kelley, 1967, p. 214). Although there are many roads to self-knowledge, a number of recent theorists have suggested that we do not always know why we do what we do when we do it, but instead we infer the causes of our thoughts, feelings, and actions *after* they have occurred (Schachter, 1964; D. J. Bem, 1967, 1972; Kelley, 1967; Nisbett & Valins, 1972). One line of research strongly suggests that, under certain conditions, people will infer their own emotions. In a recent study, Laird (1974) induced subjects to "smile" or "frown" without referring to happy or angry expressions. For example, while Laird was in the process of attaching electrodes to the subject's face, he would give instructions such as "Now I'd like you to contract these muscles" and "Pull your brows together," and in this fashion Laird induced a frown. Subjects reported feeling angry when frowning and happy when smiling. Furthermore, after subjects had been induced to smile, they found cartoons more humorous than after they had been induced to frown.

Very influential in a number of contexts is Schachter's two-factor theory of emotion (Schachter & Singer, 1962; Schachter, 1964). This theory suggests that a general state of excitement (physiological activation or arousal) combines with external cues to produce specific emotional states. This will occur, Schachter suggests, only if the person does not already have a convincing explanation of the bodily feelings associated with the heightened arousal.

Schachter and Singer (1962) induced arousal with an injection of epinephrine. Some injectees (informed subjects) were correctly told that this adrenalin-like substance would make them feel warm, flushed, and shaky and would increase their heartbeat rate. Others (uninformed subjects) were not given this information. The uninformed subjects, led to expect no effects, had to find external cues to explain their feelings to themselves. Schachter and Singer provided cues in abundance.

The Schachter-Singer project was fairly complex and involved a number of different conditions, but let's follow the fate of the epinephrine-injected subjects in the informed and uninformed conditions. After the shots, subjects in each of these conditions underwent either "eupho-ria" or "anger" treatments. Both treatments involved a secret confeder-ate, or "stooge," of the experimenter's.

In the euphoria condition, after the experimenter's departure the stooge engaged in a series of increasingly silly activities. Beginning with doodling and an improvised game of basketball (using crumpled scratch paper and a wastebasket), the stooge proceeded to zanier activities with paper airplanes and slingshots and, for a grand finale, twirled an impro-vised Hula-Hoop. In the anger condition, the subject and stooge were given a long and obnoxious questionnaire to complete. The first items seemed innocent enough, but questions became increasingly insulting, concluding with the item:

With how many men (other than your father) did your mother have extra-marital relationships?

4 and under: _____   5–9: _____   10 and over: _____

In this anger condition, the confederate grumbled and then became openly hostile and antagonistic toward the experimenter and question-naire.

Subjects' subsequent reports on their emotional states revealed that, once physiologically aroused, they found a label for their emotion by referring to the behavior of the stooge. This result occurred, however, only when the subject did not have a correct and adequate explanation that the trembling hands, warm and flushed feeling, and pounding heart were simply the results of the adrenalin-like substance. For all injected uninformed subjects, the biological states were the same, but whether these states were interpreted as euphoria or anger depended on the nature of external, social cues.

Other experiments have examined the hypothesis that people can infer their own likes and dislikes. Valins (1966) affixed fake electrodes to a group of male subjects. The electrodes were, in turn, connected to a device that purportedly amplified the subjects' heartbeats so that they were audible to the subjects. The heartbeats were actually fake, and their rate was controlled by the experimenter.

The men were then shown slides of nude females. When some slides were shown, the "heartbeat" rate remained fairly constant; when other slides were shown, there were audible changes of rate. Afterward subjects rated the various nudes and were allowed to keep photos of those whom they liked the best. Nudes that seemingly caused a change in heartbeat rate were evaluated more favorably, and pictures of these nudes were more likely to be chosen as prizes. In other words, having heard what they thought were changes in their heartbeats, subjects inferred that they must have been attracted to the associated women.

In two other ingenious studies using the heartbeat apparatus, people's feelings about snakes were altered (Valins & Ray, 1967). In the first study, subjects were unselected college students; in the second study, subjects were students who were particularly fearful of snakes. In each experiment, subjects were shown slides of snakes. Interspersed among the snake slides were slides of the word *shock*. Presentation of the *shock* slide was in fact followed by a mild shock. Heartbeat changes were associated with the *shock* slide but not with the pictures of the snakes. Then a test of snake avoidance was administered. For the unselected subjects this test consisted of six items, ranging from looking at a live boa to actually handling it. For snake phobics the test involved seeing how much social pressure was required to induce the phobic to touch the snake. In both experiments, snake avoidance was reduced for experimental subjects but not for control subjects, who believed the heartbeat-like noises were miscellaneous sounds unrelated to their physiological state.

How could this be? From noting a change in heartbeat on presentation of the *shock* slide, subjects inferred that they were afraid of the shock. From noting no change in heartbeat on presentation of the snake slides, they inferred that snakes did not elicit a comparable amount of fear. (One can only rejoice in the fact that the heartbeat machine did not break down, causing subjects to believe themselves dead.) In the beginning of the next chapter we will consider another social-psychological procedure through which fears of snakes may be reduced.

Let's conclude with a consideration of an interesting characteristic difference between the perceived cause of one's own behavior and the perceived cause of someone else's behavior. To some extent, people who believe that they are in charge of their own fate are likely to see other people as in charge of their own fate too (Sosis, 1974). However, Jones and Nisbett (1972) note that, although we tend to see other people's behavior as produced by some personal trait or inner quality, we tend to see our own behavior as caused by external, situational variables.

Why should it be that, if you see me drive my car into a ditch, you are likely to attribute my act to incompetency, drunkenness, or some other personal frailty, whereas I am likely to explain the same act as the result of external factors, such as an attempt to avoid running someone over or to evade a more serious accident? Jones and Nisbett suggest that both historical and attentional factors contribute. First, compared with the observer, the performer is more likely to be aware of the historical determinants that led up to the event. For example, as the driver I might be the only one who is aware that my brakes are spongy, my tires are bald, and a baby carriage is starting to roll down the street toward me. Second, the observer's attention is likely to be drawn to and focused on the performer, whereas the performer's attention is likely to be directed elsewhere. In other words, while you are staring at my out-of-control car and thinking "What an idiot!" I am staring at the baby carriage and thinking something else. In accordance with the attentional interpretation, Duval and Wicklund (1973) found that dispositional inferences are more likely when attention is drawn toward the target.

PART SUMMARY

Different pieces of information about a stimulus person, or target, are weighed and integrated to form an overall impression of the target. Negatively toned information is seen as more informative than positively toned information and is typically given more weight in overall evaluations. One explanation is that negative information is more likely to negate or undo positive information than positive information is to compensate for negative information. Other explanations are built on the presumption that negative information is relatively rare and, because of its novelty, attracts attention.

Asch has shown that certain substitutions (central traits) in a list of descriptive adjectives can cause changes in the meaning of other adjectives in the list, whereas other substitutions (peripheral traits) have few repercussions. Subsequent research suggests that a trait is best defined as central to the extent that it correlates with other traits and that, contrary to Asch's expectations, it is possible to predict overall impressions from component traits.

Given limited information about a person, a perceiver is likely to nonetheless develop a comprehensive, overall impression of him or her. This is a consequence of implicit personality theories, which suggest to the perceiver what kinds of traits intercorrelate. Implicit theories of personality are based in part on fact and in part on fiction. Although they may lack validity, they help us to see others as stable and predictable.

There are two models that describe how items of varying favorability are combined to form an overall evaluative impression. One model suggests that the values of each component item are summed; the other model suggests that the values are averaged. In the case of adding moderately polarized information to highly polarized information, the two models give different predictions. The preponderance of evidence supports the averaging model's prediction that the polarity of overall evaluations is reduced when moderately polarized information is combined with highly polarized information.

Attribution theory deals with the procedures people use to infer the cause of a person's behavior or circumstances. Dispositional inferences are likely when the criteria of distinctiveness, consistency over time, consistency over modality, and consensus are met. An attribution of ability is one of the first inferences made, since it is often a precondition for other attributions. Inferring motives, intents, personality, and attitudes is a complicated process that involves evaluating the target's actions in light of his or her unchosen alternatives. Choices that yield unpleasant consequences for the target and out-of-role behavior are seen as particularly informative.

The attribution process is subject to certain biases and distortions on the part of the perceiver. People tend to place insufficient emphasis on the situational causes of others' behavior. People also tend to see themselves as partially responsible when another person's actions or circumstances are favorable or socially desirable, but not at all responsible when the other's behavior or circumstances are undesirable. Perceivers are more likely to see the targets as personally responsible for their acts if these acts promote gains rather than prevent losses. Finally, perceivers are likely to see the targets' behavior as reflecting underlying personal qualities when the behavior is relevant to the perceiver.

People may infer their own attitudes and emotions. Also, historical and attentional factors may lead performers to see their own behavior or circumstances as situationally caused, whereas outside observers see the same behavior as the result of dispositional variables.

4
Social Learning

OBSERVATIONAL LEARNING

EARLY SOCIAL-LEARNING THEORY

Hullian Learning Theory
Same Behavior, Matched-Dependent Behavior,
*   and Copying*
Competence Hierarchies
Shaping

MODERN SOCIAL-LEARNING THEORY

THREE EFFECTS OF MODELS

Response-Facilitation Effects
Inhibition and Disinhibition Effects
Acquisition of New Responses

THE OBSERVATIONAL-LEARNING PROCESS

No-Trial Learning
Reinforcement as a Performance Variable
Guidance

A NOTE ON CLASSICAL CONDITIONING

Sources of Variability

PART SUMMARY

SOCIAL REINFORCEMENT

SOCIAL APPROVAL AND VERBAL OUTPUT

Social Reinforcement and Rate of Verbalization
Social Reinforcement and the Content of Verbalization
Awareness and Verbal Conditioning

SOCIAL REINFORCEMENT AND THE DEVELOPMENT
OF SELF-CONTROL

The Timing of Punishment and the
*   Development of Conscience*
Love-Oriented and Direct Punishment
Magnitude of Threat of Punishment

SOCIAL REINFORCEMENT AND SOCIAL INTERACTION

PART SUMMARY

OBSERVATIONAL LEARNING, SOCIAL REINFORCEMENT, AND SEX-ROLE BEHAVIOR

SEX ROLES IN NORTH AMERICA

SEX TYPING IN CHILDHOOD AND ADOLESCENCE

Models in the Home
Models in the Classroom
Sex Typing in Adolescence

MAINTAINING THE STATUS QUO:
REWARDS AND PUNISHMENTS IN ADULTHOOD

Women's Performance as "Inferior"
Employment Discrimination

A NOTE OF CAUTIOUS OPTIMISM

PART SUMMARY

A few years ago, some rather unusual advertisements were placed in community newspapers by Bandura, Blanchard, and Ritter (1969). These ads sought snake phobics—that is, people with strong, irrational fears of snakes—to take part in an experiment to eliminate their fear. A number of people responded, some of whom complained that their fear was so prominent that their activities were curtailed and their enjoyment of life consequently diminished. For example, they could not perform occupational duties in locales where there was a possibility that a snake might be encountered, and camping, hiking, hunting, and related activities were not viable recreation alternatives.

First the investigators measured the strength of the fear by means of a behavioral test of snake avoidance. This test involved several tasks requiring increasing intimacy with a large but harmless king snake. For example, an easy task for subjects was to approach the caged snake and look at it; a somewhat harder task was to touch the snake with a gloved hand; the hardest task for subjects was to allow the snake to crawl around in their lap while their hands were held still at their sides. Forty-eight people who failed this initial test were used in the experiment.

One group of experimental subjects watched a half-hour color film showing young children, teenagers, and adults having progressively more intimate contacts with snakes. The film began with individuals handling plastic snakes and ended with them caressing the large king snake, draping it around their necks, and letting it slither over their bodies.

A second group of experimental subjects watched through a window as an experimenter in an adjoining room played with a snake. Later each subject was invited to join the experimenter and snake. The experimenter, still playing with the snake, encouraged the subject to do the same. They began with relatively nonthreatening tasks, such as just touching the snake, and proceeded to more frightening activities.

Afterward subjects were again put through the earlier behavioral test. Subjects in the control group, who had not been exposed to fearless performers, scored as poorly as before. Subjects in the two experimental groups performed much more fearlessly and showed a substantial reduction of snake avoidance. They also showed an improved attitude toward reptiles in general.

Newly encountered or changing environmental conditions lead us to abandon old ways of behavior (for example, avoiding snakes) and to acquire new ones. **Learning** refers to a change or modification of behavior as a result of experience. **Social learning** refers to those cases in which the conditions surrounding the change include, in part, the actions, reactions, or fate of another person. In this chapter we will first consider how the *observed behavior* of one person affects learning on the part of another person. This is called **observational learning.** Then we'll consider how one person's actions and reactions can constitute *rewards and punishments,* which also modify people's behavior. This is called **social reinforcement.** After having thus gained some understanding of these basic processes, we will consider how they help explain the learning and performance of those behaviors considered appropriate for people of a given sex in our culture. Later discussions of aggression, altruism, conformity, and other topics will reveal that observational learning and social reinforcement are pervasive processes that affect many different behaviors in many different settings.

OBSERVATIONAL LEARNING

Aside from early speculation on the nature of "imitation," research and theorizing on the effects of observing the behavior of another person has had two phases. The first was spearheaded by N. Miller and Dollard (1941), who attempted to apply to human social learning principles that had been derived from studies of animals during the 1930s. The second phase was spearheaded by Albert Bandura (1962), who treated human social learning as a phenomenon in its own right, rather than as an extension of animal learning.

EARLY SOCIAL-LEARNING THEORY

There was tremendous optimism in the field of psychology in the 1930s and 1940s, when it was believed that general theories of behavior could be developed. Although primarily rooted in animal-learning studies, these theories were meant to be breathtaking in scope, systematically accounting for everything from conditioned reflexes in the dog to higher thought processes in people. One of the most prominent theories was developed by Clark Hull (1943). Developed over a span of 20 years, Hull's theory provided a launching pad for Miller and Dollard's (1941) empirical research in social learning.

Hullian Learning Theory

Hull suggested that learning requires four factors: drive, cue, response, and reinforcement. Response is nothing new to you, but the other concepts may need some explanation.

Drive is an inferred motivational state that links privations and deprivations to response strength. The presence of painful or unpleasant stimuli or the absence of comforts or necessities induces drive, which in turn energizes behavior. Thus a person exposed to the painful blare of a neighbor's stereo will respond more vigorously than a person who is left in silence, and a person who has gone for hours without drinking will drink more copiously than a person who has just downed two cans of Coke.

Cues are the distinctive stimuli that make a situation discriminable from other situations. Lights, bells, sirens, gongs, mothballs—any stimulus can serve as a cue.

Reinforcers are things or events that follow a response and, by reducing drive, result in a more favorable state of affairs for the learner and thus raise that response's probability. For example, being passed food after saying "please" would be satisfying to a hungry diner. This reward following the diner's simple courtesy should raise the odds that the diner will say "please" the next time he or she is hungry and wants some food passed. Over the years it has proved useful to make a distinction between a positive and a negative reinforcer. A **positive reinforcer** is one (such as food) whose *application* increases the likelihood of the response that it follows. A **negative reinforcer** is one (such as a cat-o'-nine tails) whose *withdrawal* increases the likelihood of the response that it follows. As Table 4-1 shows, both the application of a positive reinforcer and the withdrawal of a negative reinforcer are "reinforcing" in the Hullian sense that they result in a more favorable state of affairs for the learner and increase the likelihood of the response's performance. Unless otherwise specified, in the following discussion "reward" and "reinforcement" will refer to either one or both of these events.

Table 4-1. The effects of positive and negative reinforcers

	Positive Reinforcer	Negative Reinforcer
Application Following a Response	"Rewarding"—raises the probability of the response	"Punishing"—lowers the probability of the response
Withdrawal Following a Response	"Punishing"—lowers the probability of the response	"Rewarding"—raises the probability of the response

From *Explorations in Psychology,* by A. A. Harrison (Ed.). Copyright © 1974 by Wadsworth Publishing Company, Inc. Reprinted by permission of the publisher, Brooks/Cole Publishing Company, Monterey, California.

Learning involves a particular sequence of drive, cue, response, and reinforcement. The learner must (1) want something, (2) notice something, (3) do something, and (4) get something. Drive motivates behavior in the presence of the cue. The learner emits various responses until one is rewarded or reinforced. This reinforced response is strengthened and, over a series of such sequences, eventually learned. Later on, the motivated organism will make this learned response when the appropriate cues are present.

For example, suppose you have borrowed a friend's foreign car, and it is unlike other stick-shift cars that you have driven. You get it into first gear and move slowly into a blind intersection. You see that a cement mixer is about to enter the intersection at the same time. The fear of being killed produces instant drive. You decide to back up but are not familiar with the shift pattern; a quick scan of the car's interior reveals, to your horror, that the little plaque indicating the locations of the various gears has been ripped off. You jam the shift lever down and to the right, release the clutch, and nothing happens. Scratch response one; on to response two. You whip the lever down and to the left. When the clutch is released, the car begins to creep forward. You curse yourself for spending your last night on earth studying social psychology, but that doesn't get the car into reverse gear either. Your actions become more frantic as your drive is further increased by the rapidly diminishing distance between you and the cement mixer, which is now sounding its horn. Next response: shift up and to the right. This time the car jerks backward, out of harm's way.

The reward of having your skin saved (which you think of as relief and Hull thinks of as drive reduction) strengthens the up-and-to-the-right response when the appropriate cues are again present. Later, again faced with the problem of getting your car into reverse, you should not again have to try all the wrong possibilities. Learning has occurred. Fortunately for us, in most cases learning does not involve a very high level of drive such as that associated with a threat on our lives, and failure to learn is not a capital offense!

Operating within the framework of general behavior theories such as Hull's, psychologists have identified a number of principles that appear to affect the course of learning. Many of these principles involve the manipulation of reinforcement. For instance, once someone has learned a response to a given cue, he or she is likely to perform similar responses in the presence of similar, but not identical, cues. This is called **generalization.** An illustration might be a recruit in boot camp who frantically learns to salute everyone in uniform. However, if rewards follow the response in the presence of some cues but not in the presence of seemingly similar cues, the person is likely to learn to distinguish among them. This is called **discrimination learning.** For example, after receiving laughs and jeers for saluting other recruits, mail carriers, and police officers, a new recruit would soon learn to salute only in the presence of uniforms that signify superiors in the military ranking system.

Extinction refers to the weakening or dropping of unrewarded or punished responses (such as salutes to an equal). **Resistance to extinction** refers to the extent to which a response will be performed even though reinforcement no longer follows it. One of the most intriguing discoveries has been that responses that have been reinforced only a small percentage of the time will be more resistant to extinction than responses that have been reinforced a large percentage of the time. For example, Cowan and Walters (1963) rewarded children's aggressive acts with marbles. Later the children were given the opportunity to behave aggressively, but no more marbles were dispensed. They found that children who had been given marbles following each aggressive response were the first to give up responding aggressively, that children who had been rewarded for every third aggressive response less readily stopped responding aggressively, and that children who had been rewarded for every sixth aggressive response gave up their aggressive responses least readily of all. Reinforcement following some, but not all, performances of a response is called **intermittent reinforcement.** Why should intermittent reinforcement increase resistance to extinction? One possibility is that learning and extinction trials are more similar for the occasionally reinforced subjects. Whereas people who are reinforced after each performance notice quickly when reinforcement is withdrawn, people who have been reinforced only occasionally may not so readily detect the changed conditions.

Such principles, identified in the 1930s, 1940s, and 1950s, are very much with us today. However, the leading contemporary explanations of these principles are not necessarily in agreement with Hull's. For example, rewards and punishments do affect the likelihood of a response. However, whereas Hull believed that reinforcement was required for learning to occur, recent demonstrations (which we shall soon encounter) suggest that reinforcement has more of an effect on the performance of a response than on the learning of that response.

Same Behavior, Matched-Dependent Behavior, and Copying

Miller and Dollard (1941) discussed three cases in which one person appears to imitate the behavior of another. These instances are *same behavior, matched-dependent behavior,* and *copying.*

Same behavior refers to the situation in which two or more people are independently responding to similar or identical environmental conditions. Although they may be engaging in similar activities, in this case they are not actually attending to each other, and no imitation is involved. For example, two jungle explorers who are slapping themselves are probably not imitating each other but are responding independently to attacks by stinging gnats.

Matched-dependent behavior refers to the situation in which a leader emits cues that trigger an imitative response on the part of the observer or "follower." The observer's behavior is called matched-dependent behavior because the observer duplicates or *matches* the behavior of the leader, and the performance is *dependent* on cues provided by the leader. The leader is the more experienced person, who is able to correctly interpret the situation and make an appropriate response. The observer or "learner" is unable to understand the cues inherent in the situation but can easily understand the cues provided by the leader.

As an example of matched-dependent behavior, consider a new soldier's first day in battle. He is a replacement moving out on patrol with a battle-hardened sergeant. Artillery shells shriek overhead; all sound equally worrisome to the green recruit. At the sound of a certain shell, the veteran sergeant jumps into a ditch. The recruit, who is keeping a close eye on the sergeant, does the same. This action spares his life when a near-miss detonates.

As a beginner the new combatant is unable to distinguish among the various rushes, roars, and whines, although the battle-hardened sergeant can make these complex discriminations. The recruit can, however, easily understand the cues emitted by the sergeant when he jumps into a ditch. Over time, followers are likely to learn to interpret situations directly and to perform successfully in the absence of the leader. For example, toward

	The Old Sarge	The New Recruit
Drive:	Fear	Fear
Cue:	Sound of shell	Sight of Old Sarge jumping
Response:	Jumping into ditch	Jumping into ditch
Reinforcement:	Safety	Safety

Figure 4-1. The critical variables in matched-dependent behavior

the end of his combat tour, the former new recruit could be sent out on a solitary mission with at least some chance of survival. A specification of the critical variables in matched-dependent behavior is presented in Figure 4-1. The important difference between the model or "leader" and the learner is to be found in the nature of the cue. The sergeant responded directly to the sound of the artillery shell, whereas the recruit responded to the sergeant's jumping.

Copying is similar to matched-dependent behavior in that one person learns to mold his or her behavior after the behavior of another. The difference is that the copier also identifies and responds to cues of *sameness* and *difference* of results when comparing his or her behavior to that of the leader. For example, a first violinist of a great symphony orchestra and a student violinist might pull their bows across the strings in very similar ways, but, although the accomplished violinist's movements yield a melody, the student's seemingly identical movements yield horrendous screeches and squawks. For the student to learn through copying, it is necessary to respond to these differences in results and to modify his or her own bow-pulling procedures until the sounds produced are acceptably close to those produced by the maestro. Copying thus requires much more than just matching the behavior of the leader; it involves a careful assessment of results as well.

Miller and Dollard discuss a number of human and animal studies, most of which deal with matched-dependent behavior. In these experiments, leaders were first taught to make certain responses. Next, followers were rewarded with food (pellets for rats and candy for children) when they made the same response as the leader. In this way, rats learned to match the leader's choices in a *T* maze, and children learned to match a leader's choice of one of two locations in a room. In some experiments the importance of reinforcement was highlighted by rewarding the observer for responses that were *opposite* to those made by the leader. Under these conditions, mismatched responses were learned. Figure 4-2 shows the behavior of eight animals that were rewarded for choosing the direction opposite to that taken by the leader, as compared with the behavior of eight animals that were rewarded for going in the same direction as the leader.

Further studies reported in Miller and Dollard's book showed that, having learned to match the behavior of one leader, the learner would match the behavior of another; also, after learning to imitate at one task, there was a tendency to imitate at another. A learned **generalized tendency to imitate** such as this is necessary for explaining matched-dependent behavior under new or novel conditions.

Competence Hierarchies

Matched-dependent behavior is considered likely in a situation in which two people differ in competency. The reason why the less competent person will imitate the more competent person (rather than the other way around) is clear when we consider likely patterns of reinforcement. A competent person is, by definition, one who is good at securing rewards. A less competent person who matches his or her behavior is likely to secure similar rewards. Matching the behavior of someone less competent is likely to go unrewarded or even to be punished.

Four competence-ranking systems, or **competence hierarchies,** are discussed by Miller and Dollard. Knowledge of the two people's location within these systems allows educated guesses concerning who is likely to be the leader and who is likely to be the follower.

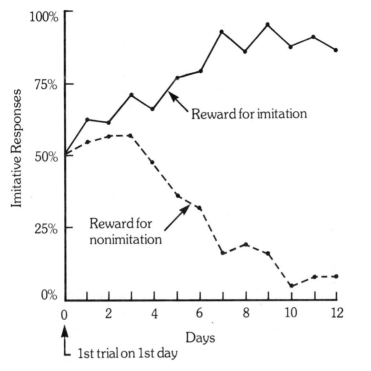

Figure 4-2. The learning of imitation and nonimitation by rats. (From *Social Learning and Imitation,* by N. E. Miller and J. Dollard. Copyright © 1941 by Yale University Press. Reprinted by permission.)

First, people are likely to imitate their *age-grade superiors.* Compared with the young child, the older child and adult have had more opportunity to master the environment; through matched-dependent behavior, the younger person can profit from this experience.

Second, people are likely to imitate their *superiors in the social-status hierarchy.* Members of higher social classes have better food, better homes, better medical care, and more security. Ignoring factors such as race (which may chain a person to low social class) or inherited wealth (which may endow comfort without responsibility), achievement of high social class may be a direct result of superior performance. Imitation of social-status superiors is reinforced when it gains for the person the better life associated with higher rank.

The third class of exemplary performers constitutes *superior technicians in any field.* Through careful choice of whom to imitate, it is often possible to gain good results at a task without any understanding of the underlying principles. For example, by matching a potter's motions, you might be able to produce a vase with an interesting glaze; by matching a mathematician's behavior step by step, you could conceivably coax the right answer from a slide rule.

Fourth, and finally, people are likely to match the behavior of their *superiors in the intelligence-ranking system.* The intelligence hierarchy cross-cuts all other hierarchies. **Intelligence** in this context refers to a very general ability to read environmental cues and to produce or improvise adaptive responses.

An interesting field study by Lefkowitz, Blake, and Mouton (1955) supports the idea that people are more likely to match the behavior of a high-status person than of a low-status person. The investigators studied pedestrians at an intersection where the flow of traffic was controlled by automatic lights. Under control conditions, 99% of the pedestrians waited for the *Walk* sign. Under a set of experimental conditions, in which a 31-year-old male who was made to appear of low status by being dressed in well-worn, scuffed shoes, soiled, patched trousers, and an unpressed blue denim shirt disobeyed the *Wait* sign, the percentage of pedestrians who obeyed the sign decreased to 96%. However, when this same dis-obedient male was made to appear of high status by being dressed in a freshly pressed suit, shined shoes, white shirt, tie, and hat, the percentage of pedestrians who obeyed the *Wait* sign dropped to 86%. Thus, seeing another person violate the *Wait* sign was a cue that elicited matched responses on the part of some observers. The degree of matched-dependent behavior was greater when the "leader" was of high rather than low status.

Shaping

Reinforcement theories such as Hull's suggest that, for learning to take place, the response must be emitted and then followed by reinforcement. In a rat's maze relatively few responses are available, other than turning left or turning right. Thus there is a reasonable probability that the rat will emit the "right" response so that the trainer can reinforce it. However, the requirement that a right response must be emitted can be a bit of a problem in most everyday situations in which the learner might make any of a number of responses. Might not a teacher or trainer have to wait forever for the right response to be emitted?

In this case, Skinner's method of successive approximations, or **shaping,** is of use. This process involves rewarding responses that come increasingly close to the desired response. During the early phases of learning, vague approximations of the response are rewarded. Later, more accurate performances are required. For example, in teaching a child to tie her shoes, a parent could first reward her for touching the shoes and then for slipping the shoes on her feet. Later the child would be rewarded only for attempts at tying some kind of knot. Finally, rewards would be withheld until the shoelaces were correctly tied.

In sum, Miller and Dollard attempted to account for human social learning with the same variables used to explain the maze learning of the rat. Following Hull, they suggested that learning requires a combination of drive, cue, response, and reinforcement. An organism, motivated by drive and in the presence of a cue, emits responses until one is followed by reinforcement. It is this reinforced response that is learned. Social learning differs from nonsocial learning in that the "cue" is provided by another person's behavior, rather than by an impersonal aspect of the environment. Matched-dependent behavior refers to activity that has been cued by similar activity on the part of another. Because of the likely pattern of rewards, we usually learn to match the behavior of people who are older, shrewder, or smarter than ourselves.

MODERN SOCIAL-LEARNING THEORY

Suppose you wanted to teach a child to tie her shoes. Would you wait until she tied them and then administer a reinforcement, or would you use the "expedient" of shaping, as discussed above? My hunch is that you would do neither. You would probably show her by putting on and tying your own shoes, all the while offering encouragement and providing a running verbal description of your activities. When we consider that much social learning involves demonstrations, instructions, and even physical assistance, the drive-cue-response-reinforcement theory advocated by Hull and his followers seems too narrow (Bandura, 1971b).

Contemporary social-learning theory as formulated by Albert Bandura and his associates differs from early social-learning theory in at least five highly significant ways (Bandura, 1962, 1965b, 1969, 1971a, 1971b, 1973). First, modern social-learning theory is cast in terms of modeling rather than in terms of matched-dependent behavior. **Modeling** occurs whenever an observer adopts the live, filmed, or verbally described behavior of another person, or "model." As we shall see, modeling effects are considerably more far-ranging than is matched-dependent behavior. Second, in contrast to early social-learning theory, modern social-learning theory suggests that it is not necessary for the observer to perform a response in order for it to be learned. Third, unlike Miller and Dollard, Bandura believes that reinforcement is not necessary for learning to occur. Fourth, unlike the earlier view, the contemporary view assigns importance to instructions, directions, and deliberate attempts to guide. Finally, Miller and Dollard's experimental demonstrations of matched-dependent behavior involved simple tasks and, with the exception of a few animal studies, generated little subsequent research; as we shall see, the present era in social learning has been marked by a wealth of diverse studies, often involving intricate and intriguing forms of social behavior.

Very important in Bandura's theorizing is the idea that people can fashion their behavior after that of nonpresent "filmed" and "symbolic" models as well as live models. A **filmed model** is one presented by means of a motion-picture or videotape recording. Many researchers prefer filmed to live models, because filming eliminates inadvertent variations in the model's behavior during different experimental sessions. We will pay particular attention to filmed models when we consider the effects of televised violence on aggression (Chapter 7).

Symbolic models are those whose behavior is portrayed through oral or written descriptions. Thus people may fashion their behavior after the *verbally described* behavior of Christian martyrs, of outlaws of the Old West, or of the heroes of Valley Forge. The effects of achievement imagery in fairy tales on later productivity (Chapter 2) may be a good example. In this case, models presented in fairy tales affected adult entrepreneurial activity.

THREE EFFECTS OF MODELS

Viewing a model's performance can have three effects on the observer. First, it can trigger or *facilitate* the performance of an already learned response that is similar to that performed by the model. Second, viewing a model's behavior can have *inhibiting* or *disinhibiting* effects—that is, lead the observer to suppress behavior that would otherwise be expressed or to express behavior that would otherwise be suppressed. Third, viewing a model's behavior can result in the learning or *acquisition* of the modeled response. Thus, observing a model can affect either the performance of already learned responses or the acquisition of new responses.

Response-Facilitation Effects

A model's response can serve as a stimulus that elicits an already learned response on the part of the observer. This is called **response facilitation.** One example would be when you look skyward after seeing someone else do so; another example would be when you join in with the familiar chant of the cheerleaders at a football game. Response-facilitation effects are distinguished from disinhibition effects (discussed below) in that the behavior in question is socially acceptable and hence unencumbered by restraints, and from acquisition effects in that no new responses are learned (Bandura, 1971b).

Inhibition and Disinhibition Effects

Observing a model's behavior can have inhibiting or disinhibiting effects. **Inhibition** refers to the suppression of a response that would otherwise be performed. For example, in a combat situation, soldiers can be very frightened, but they usually don't bolt toward the rear because of inhibition effects produced by a calm and courageous leader. **Disinhibition** refers to the performance of a response that would otherwise be suppressed. Examples of disinhibiting military models have been provided by Schultz (1972). In one incident, which occurred during World War I, members of an artillery battalion just behind a very active front line were trying to get some sleep. After receiving orders to report to regimental headquarters, the commander turned to his adjutant and said "Let's beat it," and the pair began running toward the rear. This behavior disinhibited the entire battalion, which ran rearward a full 6 miles.

Some of the most intriguing modeling research has dealt with inhibition and disinhibition effects. In some studies the model's behavior discourages the observer from expressing potentially harmful or dangerous impulses, and in other studies the model's behavior encourages the observer to engage in activities that are harmless but that the observer finds threatening. These particular studies involve learning as well as performance, since the observer's new self-control or freedom typically appears to be a permanent gain.

In one important line of research, observers are taught to inhibit their impulses for immediate pleasures and satisfactions. A strong link appears to exist between delinquent activity and an inability to inhibit impulses for immediate gratification. In one study, Mischel (1961) found that delinquent children preferred a small prize that they could have immediately to a more valuable prize that would be given to them in the future. This preference is called an **immediate orientation.** Nondelinquent children, in contrast, preferred the later, more valuable, prize to the immediate but smaller gain. This preference is called a **delay orientation.** A serious possibility is that, if delinquents could be taught a delay orientation, impulsive and delinquent activity might be reduced.

Several studies have related the observed behavior of others to the observer's delay-of-gratification orientation. Bandura and Mischel (1965) had children with either the immediate or delay orientation view a model who displayed the orientation that was opposite to their own. As expected, delay-orientation children began snapping up the smaller but immediate prizes, whereas immediate-orientation children began choosing the larger but future prize. In a more recent study, Stumphauzer (1972) extended these results to a sample of prison inmates. Young inmates who viewed an older prisoner waiting for rewards became more patient themselves, and this new self-control was retained when they were tested weeks after the modeling session.

In another series of studies, people who are fearful of performing certain harmless but threatening actions (for example, encountering a snake, approaching a puppy, or climbing a ladder) observe a model perform these responses without any adverse consequences. This observation usually helps the observers to overcome their inhibitions, with the result that they become capable of likewise fearless performances (Bandura, 1969, 1971a). The disinhibiting effect can be particularly pronounced when the observer sees that the model is initially frightened by the threatening circumstances but slowly overcomes his or her fears and begins coping with the threatening conditions over time (Meichenbaum, 1971). Procedures such as these are by no means limited to laboratory demonstrations; they are in routine use in psychotherapy.

Acquisition of New Responses

The third modeling effect is the transmission of new behavior. That is, observing a model's performance can lead to learning a new response. The responses thus learned may be lengthy and complex. One of the effects of the early modeling studies was to convince skeptics that social learning involved much more than merely learning to follow a leader to the left or to the right. In what might be regarded as a typical early modeling study (for example, Bandura & Huston, 1961; Bandura, Ross, & Ross, 1963a, 1963b), children would observe a model perform a variety of highly stylized responses, such as placing a colorful hat on her head at a rakish angle, marching in an exaggerated way to a pile of toys, and then playing with each one in unique and distinctive ways. Under many conditions, when the children were given the opportunity to perform in the same way, they reproduced strikingly large portions of these highly involved sequences. Let's now consider the conditions that Bandura believes make observational learning possible.

THE OBSERVATIONAL-LEARNING PROCESS

The research and theory of Bandura and his associates suggest that observational learning occurs in ways not quite identified by the early social-learning theorists. The contemporary theorists reject the drive-cue-response-reinforcement formulation of social learning and emphasize people's thought processes instead. As indicated earlier, the main features that distinguish Bandura from Miller and Dollard include Bandura's beliefs that (1) responses do not have to be emitted and reinforced in order to be learned, and (2) deliberate guidance has important social-learning effects.

No-Trial Learning

In accordance with Hull's principles, Miller and Dollard argued that a response had to be emitted in order to be learned. Yet, as Bandura points out, much behavior seems to be learned in the absence of overt performance. We all know of cases in which people perform reasonably well after simply observing someone else play a game, operate a tool or appliance, or work at a handicraft. For a response to be learned, it need not be performed; observation of the stimulus conditions on the one hand and the model's response on the other will often be sufficient.

Although learning does not require physical activity, it does require **cognitive,** or mental, activity. First the stimulus conditions and the model's responses must be attended to. Then these stimuli must subsequently be coded in the form of images and words and entered into memory. Later, under appropriate incentive conditions, they must be retrieved and translated into overt responses.

If observed behavior is translated into symbols and encoded into memory, activities that help this symbolic process should aid learning through observation, whereas activities that interfere with this process should impair learning. This result has been shown by Bandura, Grusec, and Menlove (1966). While watching a complex modeling sequence, some subjects verbally described the model's behavior (a procedure designed to facilitate the symbolization process), other subjects watched and were given no facilitating or inhibiting tasks, and still other subjects counted rapidly while watching the sequence (a procedure designed to impair the symbolization process). As expected, the first group of subjects showed the most learning and the third group showed the least.

In a later study, Gerst (1971) compared the effectiveness of different learning techniques. Subjects were shown intricate movements of the arms, hands, and fingers that had been drawn from the manual language of the deaf. They attempted to reproduce these intricate gestures, both right after seeing them and after 15 minutes of engaging in a distracting reading task. There were four conditions: Controls, who were asked to count backward while viewing the sequences (an activity that should interfere with encoding), achieved about 44% accuracy when they reproduced them. Verbal-description subjects, who gave matter-of-fact verbal descriptions of the sequences as they watched them, achieved about 51% accuracy. Imaginal-coding subjects, who closed their eyes right after viewing the sequence and vividly imagined it, achieved about 56% accuracy. The best reproductions (59% accuracy) came from the summary-labeling subjects, who were told to think of persons, animals, objects, or other familiar things that would remind them of the sequence. The summary-labeling group was clearly superior under conditions of delayed reproduction. Likening the modeled sequence to a familiar thing or event (no matter how idiosyncratic) thus proved to be an efficient way of organizing the novel sequence, entering it into memory, and later retrieving it.

A forceful illustration of the importance of symbolic coding has been provided by Bandura and Jeffery (1973). In this study, subjects viewed videotapes of various novel behavior sequences. Subjects in the coding conditions were then shown a distinctive letter or number at the time each sequence was shown, whereas controls were not given this memory aid. Next, some subjects were allowed to rehearse, either by actually performing the modeled responses (motor rehearsal) or by reviewing the distinctive letters or numbers that had been associated with each behavior sequence (symbolic rehearsal). The availability of symbols, coupled with the rehearsal of these symbols, was associated with a high level of performance, both during an immediate testing session and during a testing session one week after the sequences were shown. Contrary to what many early learning theorists would expect, motor rehearsal (practicing without the benefit of symbols) did *not* result in an improvement of performance. Taken together, the results of these studies suggest that observational learning depends very much on people's abilities to process information.

Reinforcement as a Performance Variable

As indicated earlier, contemporary social-learning theory departs from early social-learning theory by proposing that a response need not be reinforced in order to be learned. Rewards and punishments do play a role in contemporary theorizing—but as *performance,* rather than learning, variables. That is, although reinforcement may not affect the learning or acquisition of a response, it may very well affect the performance or emission of that response.

A study of children's moral judgments provides a clear illustration that reinforcement is not necessary for observational learning. In this study by Bandura and McDonald (1963), subjects were children who ranged in age from 5 to 11 and who had different orientations for evaluating right and wrong. There are two orientations, and each is believed to represent an interplay of maturational and experiential factors. In the course of the child's development, one orientation appears and then is superseded by the other (Piaget, 1948).

Children with the less mature **objective-responsibility orientation** assess the seriousness of an act in terms of the material damage done.

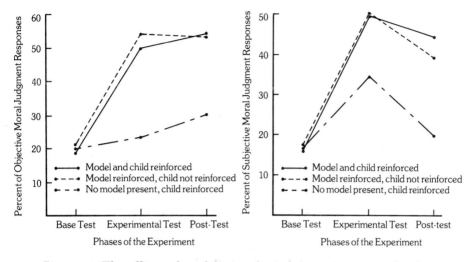

Figure 4-3. The effects of modeling and reinforcement on moral judgments. Left: Mean percentage of objective moral-judgment responses produced by subjective children on each of the three test periods for each of the three experimental conditions. Right: Mean percentage of subjective moral-judgment responses produced by objective children on each of the three test periods for each of three experimental conditions. (From "The Influence of Social Reinforcement and the Behavior of Models in Shaping Children's Moral Judgments," by A. Bandura and F. J. McDonald, *Journal of Abnormal and Social Psychology*, 1963, *67,* 278, 280. Copyright 1963 by the American Psychological Association. Reprinted by permission.)

Children with the more mature **subjective-responsibility orientation** assess the seriousness of an act in terms of the perpetrator's intent. Orientations are measured by presenting pairs of episodes and asking the child to tell which of the pair is naughtier. For example, the child might be asked "Who did the naughtier thing—Johnny, when he accidentally dropped and broke a whole tray of glasses while trying to help his mother, or Jimmy, who broke one glass while trying to steal cookies from the cupboard?" The objective-orientation child would assign greater blame to Johnny (because he did the most material damage), whereas the subjective-judgment child would assign more blame to Jimmy (because of the evil intent surrounding the mishap).

Subjects were assigned to one of three conditions. In the no-model-present, child-reinforced condition, there was no model but the child was reinforced for responses that were contrary to his or her orientation. In the model-reinforced, child-reinforced condition, both the model and the child were rewarded for judgments inconsistent with the child's orientation. In the model-reinforced, child-not-reinforced condition, only the model was rewarded. Afterward the child made moral judgments in the absence of the model.

Results (see Figure 4-3) clearly showed that both in the presence of the model and in subsequent isolation, children made judgments of a type contrary to their own orientation but of a type that the model had been rewarded for expressing. This occurred whether or not the child had been rewarded. Simply reinforcing the child for expressing judgments contrary to his or her own orientation had no effect. Children in this latter condition hardly ever made a response contrary to their own orientation and, as a consequence, gave the experimenters little or no occasion to administer the reinforcement.

A later study by Bandura (1965a) showed that, although reinforcement is not necessary for learning, it does affect performance. In this study, nursery-school children viewed a fake five-minute television program that showed an adult model aggressing against an inflated plastic "Bobo" doll. In this highly involved modeling sequence, Bobo was punched in the nose, pounded on the head with a hammer, kicked, and pelted with rubber balls. Each aggressive act was stylized and was accompanied by an appropriate verbalization, such as "Sockeroo, stay down!" or simply "Bang!"

There were three different endings to this film. In the model-rewarded condition, a second adult entered, proclaimed that the aggressive model was a "strong champion," and plied the model with candies and drinks. In the no-consequences condition, the model was neither rewarded nor punished. In the model-punished condition, the aggressive person was scolded, denounced, and spanked.

Next the subjects were taken to a room that contained a number of toys, including Bobo and all the paraphernalia used in the modeling sequence. The child was seemingly left alone to play with the toys but was in fact observed, so that the experimenter could record the extent to which the model's behavior was reproduced. Results at this point showed that, whereas the no-consequences and model-rewarded conditions did not significantly differ, subjects in these two conditions were more aggressive than were children in the model-punished condition.

If the experiment had concluded at this point, it would have seemed that the model-punished children had learned less. But next came an acquisition measure. The experimenter offered treats for each aggressive response that the child could perform. This situation erased all differences among the three groups. Model-punished subjects now performed as much of the aggressive sequence as did the other children. Thus, seeing the model punished did not result in failure to learn—only in a reluctance to perform the punished response. It would appear, then, that neither direct nor vicarious rewards (seeing the model reinforced, as in the Bandura and McDonald study) are necessary for learning but that, once a response has been learned, its *performance* depends on the promise of rewards.

What contemporary theorizing suggests, then, is that people are active interpreters of their environment rather than passive responders to changing environmental conditions. When their attention is directed toward a model, they can mentally connect the conditions confronting the model, the model's response, and the model's outcomes. They can form expectancies that, if they behave in a similar fashion under similar conditions, they will receive similar outcomes. Thus, seeing a model rewarded may instigate an imitative response because the observer expects the same goodies too (Lerner & Weiss, 1972). If the model is unrewarded or punished, the observer will not imitate the model, but this in no way shows that the model's response was unlearned. Numerous studies have confirmed Bandura's (1965a) finding that, when the appropriate incentive conditions are created, the responses of even a nonrewarded or punished model are likely to be imitated (Lerner & Weiss, 1972; Thelen, McGuire, Simmonds, & Akamatsu, 1974). Thus reinforcers might better be thought of as *incentives,* which draw forth or elicit various responses once they have been learned.

Guidance

If someone or something from another planet attempted to rear a human child using the procedures outlined in early textbooks on learning, this saucerian would no doubt be amazed by the disappointing results. The reason for this lack of success would be that (among other things), whereas directions, instructions, and other forms of guidance are in routine use throughout the world, they did not enter into the laboratory experiments on which early learning theory was based (Bandura, 1971b). In today's social-learning theory, however, directions, instructions, and guidance are accepted as important aids to the learning process. Directions and instructions provide, in effect, symbolic models that draw attention to the relevant behavior and perhaps instigate the first appropriate response. The effect of guidance was shown in an interesting experiment by G. M. White (1972).

In White's study, fourth- and fifth-graders played a bowling game and won small gift certificates. Present in the laboratory was a box marked "the Trenton Orphan's Fund." In addition to a no-model control condition, there were three modeling conditions. In the first, children watched an adult model donate some of the winnings to the orphan's fund. In the second condition, following the modeling sequence, children were given the opportunity to donate but no specific instructions to do so. In the third experimental condition, after viewing the generous model, children were given both the opportunity to make an offering and specific instructions to do so.

Next the children were left alone in the experimental room, won more gift certificates, and were again given the opportunity to make a donation. Control children were the stingiest, and children who had observed the model were somewhat less stingy. Children who had viewed the model and were given the opportunity to rehearse were somewhat generous, and children given specific guidance were the most generous of all. In other words, observation, practice, and guidance all encouraged charitable behavior, and the effects were cumulative.

A NOTE ON CLASSICAL CONDITIONING

Let's continue our discussion of observational learning with a brief consideration of how "Pavlovian," or classical, conditioning can occur through observation. In classical conditioning the pairing of an initially neutral stimulus with one that reliably elicits a response results in the initially neutral stimulus' eliciting an identical or similar response.

There are four components in this form of learning. The **unconditioned stimulus (UCS)** is a stimulus that, at the beginning of the learning sequence, reliably elicits a response, called the **unconditioned response (UCR).** The **conditioned stimulus (CS)** is one that, at the outset of the learning sequence, is neutral in the sense that it does not elicit a response comparable to the unconditioned response. The conditioning process involves presenting the conditioned stimulus just prior to the unconditioned stimulus. As a result of one or a number of pairings, the originally neutral conditioned stimulus will come to elicit a **conditioned response (CR),** which is, for all intents and purposes, similar to the unconditioned response. Figure 4-4 illustrates this process and shows how it may account for a child's cringing when a parent scowls. Responses that are learned in this way can be extinguished through repeated presentation of the conditioned stimulus alone.

Classical conditioning has been achieved using a wide variety of stimuli and subjects. It may account for many of our emotional reactions, both favorable and unfavorable. In the former case, a local and unknown politician may appear on stage just prior to a respected state or national leader, who brings the crowd roaring to its feet. Later the appearance of the local candidate alone may suffice to elicit tumultuous applause. Or, after several run-ins with the police, your heart might thump and "leap to your throat" when you discover that a police car with its red light and siren on has pulled up behind you.

According to Bandura (1969), a model's emotional response can serve as an unconditioned stimulus for an observer's unconditioned emotional response. Thus a child may feel and act disgusted after observing a parent act disgusted. A neutral stimulus that is present at the time the model's emotional response occurs can become a conditioned stimulus for the

Figure 4-4. Classical conditioning

observer's emotional response. A child may share a parent's disgust reaction to a Skid Row tenant and then, seeing another down-and-outer, feel disgust even though the face-making parent is not present.

In accordance with this finding, several studies have shown that viewing a person's emotional reactions elicits similar emotional reactions on the part of the viewer. For example, observers' emotional responses have been shown to fluctuate in correspondence with the emotions expressed by the hero in a film depicting "coming of age" ceremonies. When the hero was undergoing a hairdressing ritual, the observers' emotional responses were mild, but when the hero was having incisions made in his penis, observers' reactions perked up considerably (Lazarus, Speisman, Mordkoff, & Davison, 1962).

A number of early studies sought to determine if observing another person acquire a conditioned emotional response would result in the acquisition of that response by the observer. Commenting on such experiments, Berger (1962) noted that it was not always clear what triggered the observer's "conditioned response." Rather than responding to the supposedly conditioned stimulus (such as a buzzer), the observer could have been responding to the unconditioned stimulus (the performer's emotional response). However, Berger's own research and a recent study by Venn and Short (1973) provide support for the hypothesis that viewing another's emotional reaction to an otherwise neutral stimulus can result in that stimulus' eliciting a similar emotional reaction from the observer.

In Venn and Short's study, the conditioned stimuli were plastic figures of Mickey Mouse and Donald Duck. In one experiment nursery-school children watched a brief movie of a 5-year-old model who reacted neutrally when his mother attempted to give him one of the two toys but reacted with fear responses (such as screaming and withdrawing) when his mother attempted to give him the other toy. In another experiment the child model again acted neutrally when his mother attempted to give him the control toy, but in this case he reacted positively, with smiling and expressions of delight, when his mother gave him the experimental toy. Although the learning effects were not long lived, children showed more negative reactions to the stimulus that the model had been conditioned to fear and more positive reactions to the stimulus that the model had been conditioned to like than they did to the respective control toys.

Sources of Variability

Observational learning is a well-documented phenomenon. How, then, can we account for people's novel and innovative behavior? There are at least three reasons why our society is not one big chorus line.

First, our focus on observational learning should not obscure the importance of nonobservational or direct learning. Direct learning often results in the acquisition of novel responses. For example, if your car broke down in an isolated location, you might, through individual trial and error, discover a novel solution to your problem (such as replacing a lost cotter pin with a small piece of discarded baling wire). This original response would enter into your behavioral repertoire and help distinguish you from other people.

Second, each of us is continually exposed to a diversity of models who behave in different ways. Even when one model (such as a parent) predominates, competing models will have some impact. The end result is that an observer's behavior is likely to be a unique mosaic or blend, incorporating in a novel configuration elements of the behavior of several models. For example, a woman emerging from medical school has been exposed to live models in the form of her family doctor and her instructors in medical school. She has been exposed to filmed models, not only through instructional movies but also through doctor shows on television and theater screens. She has no doubt pored over many pages of material that verbally describes the appropriate behavior of physicians. The emerging picture is not the result of exposure to any one model but the result of exposure to a number of different models—live, filmed, and symbolic. And even if there had been only Marcia Welby, M.D., for a model, imperfect attentional and memory factors would have ensured that she would not have been a carbon copy of Marcia.

The third reason why we are not all alike is that, as Bandura notes, through modeling processes people can learn not only specific responses but also *styles* of responding. As a result, people exposed to creative, innovative, original models may themselves learn to be creative, innovative, and original. In other words, some novelty and originality may be the result of imitation!

PART SUMMARY

People learn through observing the behavior of others. Miller and Dollard attempted to account for human social learning in terms of the same principles used to explain the learning of the rat in the maze. Following Hull, they suggested that learning requires a combination of drive, cue, response, and reinforcement. The motivated organism responds in the presence of cues until one response is reinforced and learned. Social learning differs from nonsocial learning in that the "cue" is provided by another person's behavior, rather than by an impersonal aspect of the environment.

Although Miller and Dollard also discuss same behavior (which is not truly imitative behavior) and copying (which requires attention to sameness and difference of results), their analysis focuses on matched-dependent behavior. Matched-dependent behavior refers to activity that has been cued by a similar activity on the part of another. Consistent with Miller and Dollard's theorizing, it has been shown that both animals and humans can learn to match or mismatch a "leader's" responses. A consideration of likely patterns of rewards suggests that less competent individuals are likely to learn to match the behavior of more competent individuals.

Social-learning theory has made tremendous strides since Miller and Dollard's pioneering analysis of social-learning processes. The newer formulation by Bandura and his associates suggests that observing a live, filmed, or symbolic model's behavior can have three effects: (1) response facilitation, or the elicitation of an already learned response; (2) inhibition and disinhibition effects; and (3) the learning of simple or complex behavior sequences. According to contemporary theorizing, learning does not require response performance, since learning is a cognitive, or mental, activity. Reinforcement is not seen as necessary for learning but is treated, instead, as a performance variable. Contemporary social-learning theory also acknowledges various learning aids, such as guidance in the form of directions, instructions, and physical assists. An abundance of studies, including studies of classical conditioning, show that modeling effects are a widespread and varied phenomenon.

Given the pervasiveness of observational learning, we might expect people to be blurred carbon copies of one another. This is not the case, because novel behavior can result from nonsocial learning, exposure to a number of different models, and exposure to creative and innovative models.

SOCIAL REINFORCEMENT

According to Ripley's *Believe It or Not* (22nd series, 1974, p. 86), Charles Fane, British Envoy to Florence, Italy, was the most sensitive person in all history. He became desperately ill for six weeks because the British Foreign Secretary had omitted the word *very* in signing a letter "Your (very) humble servant."

Few of us are quite this sensitive to others' behavior toward us, but all of us can list actions with which others can make us feel comfortable or uncomfortable. By engaging in these actions at the appropriate times, people can reward us for behavior that they find acceptable and desirable and punish us for behavior that they find unacceptable and undesirable. Whether one adopts Miller and Dollard's view that reinforcement increases the strength of learning, or Bandura's view that reinforcers are not necessary for learning but provide incentives that motivate performance, there is simply no getting around the fact that, when responses are followed by rewards, they are likely to be repeated. When reinforcers are dispensed by other people, they are called **social reinforcers.**

Although any reinforcer can be considered "social" if it is administered by one person to another (Zajonc, 1966), some reinforcers, like love and approval, seem more social than others in that they can come only from other people. In the discussion that follows, we will emphasize the role of acceptance, approval, agreement, liking, and loving (as expressed through smiles, nods, Mm-Hmms, soulful glances, pats on the back, and squeezes on the knee) as **positive social reinforcers** and the role of rejection, disapproval, and disliking as **negative social reinforcers.**

SOCIAL APPROVAL AND VERBAL OUTPUT

The majority of studies on social reinforcement have examined the effects of approval and disapproval on subjects' verbalizations. In these studies, experimenters have attempted to manipulate the *rate* at which people speak and to affect the *content* of what they say. Studies that involve changing the rate or content of what people say through the manipulation of social approval are called **verbal-conditioning** studies.

Social Reinforcement and Rate of Verbalization

A compelling demonstration of the effects of social reinforcement on verbal output has been provided by Centers (1963). After appearing for an experiment, Centers' subjects found someone waiting who said:

> "Hi. I'm Johnny Martin and going to be in the experiment with you. You must have just missed Dr. Centers. I came early, and Centers told me the machine had broken down and that he had to go downstairs to get someone to fix it. He said he ought to be right back, but if he isn't, we're to wait for a full half-hour before we can leave. We'll get full credit for the experiment even if he doesn't come" [1963, p. 377].

Johnny Martin was actually the experimenter, and the study took place during a 30-minute wait in an anteroom. During the first ten minutes, the *operant level* was established. That is, the experimenter was unresponsive to the subject's comments, and the rate at which the subject verbalized without reinforcement was thus ascertained. During the second ten minutes, or *reinforcement phase,* the experimenter reinforced verbalizations by showing attention, agreement, sympathy, and understanding after each utterance. During the final ten minutes, or *extinction phase,* the experimenter either actively disagreed with each verbalization or reacted with icy silence.

As Figure 4-5 shows, the overall rate of verbalization, informative statements, and opinion statements increased during the reinforcement stage and decreased during the extinction phase. Only the rate at which subjects asked questions did not increase during the reinforcement phase. This exception can be understood when we consider that, as people become acquainted with each other, they typically turn from asking each other questions to volunteering information instead.

Although most verbal-conditioning studies involve one subject and one experimenter, verbal-conditioning effects have been obtained in group discussions in which the person who administers the reinforcement also contributes to the conversation. For example, Sarbin and Allen (1968) first identified students who spoke infrequently and students who spoke frequently in the course of a seminar session. They attempted to increase the rate of contribution of the infrequent participators by approving of everything they said, and to decrease the rate of participation of the frequent contributors by ignoring their offerings. Whereas the infrequent

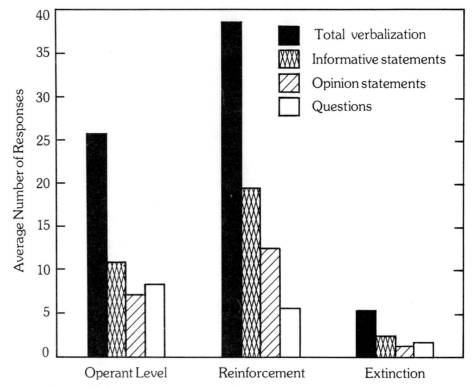

Figure 4-5. The reinforcement and extinction of verbal behavior. (From *Experimental Social Psychology,* by R. B. Zajonc. Copyright © 1966 by Wadsworth Publishing Company, Inc. Reprinted by permission of the publisher, Brooks/Cole Publishing Company, Monterey, California. Based on data from "A Laboratory Adaptation of the Controversial Procedures for the Conditioning of Verbal Operants," by R. A. Centers, *Journal of Abnormal and Social Psychology,* 1963, *67,* 334-339. Used by permission.)

participators were originally responsible for 5% of the contributions to the group discussion, at the end of the sessions they were responsible for 28% of the contributions. Frequent participators, who initially accounted for 29% of the contributions, were at the end responsible for only 19%.

Compared with the effects of approval, the effects of disapproval were relatively uneven and erratic. By way of explanation, Sarbin and Allen note that, although the experimenters did not agree with the frequent participators, other group members were not prevented from doing so. Another possibility is that, compared with the showing of approval, the withholding of approval was less consistently accomplished by the experimenters. Sarbin and Allen, noting that the withholding of approval conflicts with the customarily supportive role of an instructor, point out that they had trouble ignoring the contributions of the talkative students. Disagreeing and withholding approval are difficult tasks. Adams and Hoffman (1960) found that, when social approval is withdrawn, people may become upset, hostile, and angry. An experimenter is thus likely to be punished for withholding social approval!

Social Reinforcement and the Content of Verbalization

Studies of the effects of social approval and disapproval on what people say originated with Greenspoon (1955), who had subjects simply say out loud whatever words came to mind. Greenspoon increased the rate at which plural nouns were emitted by saying "Mm-Hmm" each time the subject said a plural noun. A number of related experiments followed Greenspoon's. For example, Quay (1959) was able to raise the rate at which people reported early-childhood experiences, and Adams and Hoffman (1960) manipulated the rate at which people made self-reference statements.

Several studies have suggested that social reinforcement affects verbal statements of opinion. In a telephone survey, Hildum and Brown (1956) were able to use approval to elicit statements for or against the "Harvard philosophy of education." Kranser, Knowles, and Ullman (1965) were able to influence attitudes toward doctors and medical science. Most importantly, Cialdini and Insko (1969) were able to influence stated opinions about psychologists. Other findings have been reviewed by Kanfer (1968) and by Marlatt (1972).

A major question is whether such manipulations have anything more than superficial and transient effects. Some evidence on this matter has been provided by Insko (1965). In his study he first contacted members of his University of Hawaii psychology class by telephone and asked if they agreed or disagreed with a series of statements concerning the creation of a special fun-filled week of festivities to be known as "Aloha Week." Half the subjects were reinforced with "Good" for expressing favorable views, and the other half were reinforced with "Good" for expressing unfavorable views. Consistent with earlier findings, there was an immediate effect such that subjects rewarded for "pro" responses were more likely to give additional "pro" responses on the phone than were subjects who had been rewarded for "con" responses. Later, subjects received a questionnaire containing items about a number of local issues, including

Aloha Week. Responses to this topic showed that earlier conditioned views had persevered over a week's time.

Awareness and Verbal Conditioning

Some theorists have agreed with Dollard and Miller's (1950) suggestion that verbal conditioning represents direct or automatic learning. According to this view, people responding to verbal-conditioning procedures are not necessarily aware that their response rates are changing or that the experimenter is approving of some responses while disapproving of others. Thus changes in response rates can occur at an unconscious level. Some other theorists have agreed with the alternative view—that people are active interpreters of their environment—and have suggested that verbal-conditioning effects require conscious and perhaps strenuous intellectual activity on the part of the learner (Spielberger, 1962; DeNike, 1964; Bandura, 1969; Page, 1969, 1972, 1974). According to this latter group of cognitive theorists, people form hypotheses during verbal-conditioning sessions. Social approval or disapproval tells them whether their hypotheses are correct or incorrect. Eventually, they successfully hypothesize what constitutes a "correct" response. Approval from the experimenter provides a source of motivation to perform this response.

Consider, for example, a study in which self-reference statements are reinforced. Discovering that, after he or she says "I feel a little warm in here," the experimenter smiles and nods, the subject may hypothesize that it was the allusion to the temperature that elicited the favorable reaction. To test this hypothesis, he or she grunts "Unseasonably warm," but this time the experimenter is unmoved, and the temperature hypothesis is rejected. Later, still floundering around, the subject might state "It seems to me that the hour should be up," and the experimenter agrees vigorously. After contemplating the similarities of the two winning sentences, the subject may uncover the pattern and discern that self-references including *me, myself,* and *I* bring forth the approval. To maintain the experimenter's stream of regard, the subject will work self-references into all of his or her sentences, and the experimenter will note with satisfaction that the subject has learned.

Thus, according to cognitive theories of verbal conditioning, learning requires conscious hypothesis testing and represents the discovery of a correct hypothesis. Awareness of the reinforcement contingencies (that is, what must be said in order to receive approval from the experimenter) is a *precondition* for learning, in that there will be no increase in the rate of "right" responses until the correct response has been discovered. In contrast, noncognitive theorists such as Dollard and Miller do not consider awareness to be a prerequisite for verbal conditioning. However, noncognitive theorists recognize that awareness may be a *correlate* of learning, since, after learning, a person may eventually recognize and be able to describe the reinforcement contingencies. The relative merits of cognitive and noncognitive explanations thus hinge on whether subjects are aware of the reinforcement contingencies at the time the conditioning effects first appear.

The awareness issue is a complex one, and the road to truth is fraught with methodological hazards. Since Greenspoon's day, experimenters have generally concluded experimental sessions by asking subjects to describe the reinforcement contingency. It would seem that in some cases experimenters were so vague in their questioning or so skirted the issue that many aware subjects went unidentified; in other cases the experimenters so bullied, badgered, and led their subjects that a false confession of awareness was obtained (Kanfer, 1968).

Despite many difficulties, the evidence seems to favor the cognitive interpretation (DeNike, 1964; Page, 1969, 1972, 1974; Hamilton, Thompson, & White, 1970; H. A. White & Schumsky, 1972). For example, DeNike (1964) rewarded college students for verbalizing human nouns. At several points subjects were told to jot down their thoughts about the experiment. About a third of the subjects were judged aware. Only these aware subjects showed learning; the unaware subjects did not differ from randomly rewarded controls. An impressive relationship was found between the dawning of awareness and conditioning. On the trials *before* the reinforcement contingency was identified, about 10% of the responses were human nouns, but, on trials *after* the reinforcement contingency was identified, about 30% of the responses were "correct."

Figure 4-6 shows the results of an experiment by Page (1972), who reinforced the pronoun *I*. At the end of Trial Block 5, all subjects were unaware. At the end of Trial Block 7, some subjects remained unaware but others had become aware. As Figure 4-6 shows, only the aware subjects learned. In another part of this experiment, Page instructed subjects either to "behave in such a way as to make me say Good" or to "behave in such a way as to avoid making me say Good." Under the former instructions, subjects increased their use of the pronoun *I*; under the latter instructions, 10 of the 12 subjects completely avoided the pronoun *I*, and received zero reinforcements. It is impossible to prove that verbal conditioning *never* occurs without awareness. However, these replicated findings (Page, 1974) that only aware subjects learn and that aware subjects can errorlessly reverse themselves when told to do so strongly support the cognitive position.

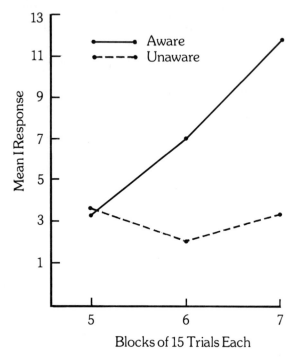

Figure 4-6. The role of awareness in verbal conditioning. This graph shows the mean selection of the pronoun *I* for subjects who were unaware of the reinforcement contingency at Block 5 but were separated into "aware" and "unaware" subjects at the end of Block 7. (From "Demand Characteristics and the Verbal Operant Conditioning Experiment," by M. M. Page, *Journal of Personality and Social Psychology,* 1972, *23*, 375. Copyright 1972 by the American Psychological Association. Reprinted by permission.)

SOCIAL REINFORCEMENT AND THE DEVELOPMENT OF SELF-CONTROL

Given the opportunity, the human infant will delightedly consume nutritionally unbalanced foods that promote tooth decay, will urinate or defecate on a shag rug, will play flamboyantly with his or her genitals, will peek when he or she shouldn't, and will behave in countless other uncontrolled, self-indulgent ways. A major task of society is to discourage such spontaneity when it is considered harmful to the performer or threatening to the social order. Two broad types of mechanisms, internal and external, have been devised to prevent the expression of some impulses and to limit the expression of others. Each type involves, in part, the regulation of behavior by means of socially administered rewards and punishments.

Behavior regulators that are *external* to the acting individual are based on the premise that, under conditions of surveillance, people will show exemplary behavior to avoid adverse reactions from others. Thus we have various "watchdog," or **social-control** agencies such as the police, the F.B.I., the Department of the Treasury, the Bureau of Consumer Affairs, school honor councils, and so forth. Mechanisms that are **internal** to the acting individual are described by such terms as *inhibitions, conscience,* and *superego.* **Internalization** refers to the individual's acquiring of society's prescriptions for behavior. We will use the term **conscience** to designate society's rules as embodied in the individual. Conscience is reflected in judgments of right and wrong, self-control, and feelings of unworthiness and guilt after self-control has failed.

Observational learning, of course, plays a major role in morality, since parents, teachers, and other adults model socially approved activities. We have already seen that children of parents who both preached and practiced altruistic behavior were more likely to be dedicated civil-rights workers than were children of parents who preached but did not practice charity (Rosenhan, 1970); moreover, the Bandura and McDonald (1963) study shows that, under some conditions, models can induce at least modest changes in the direction of more mature moral judgments. Highly relevant also are studies such as Stumphauzer's (1972), which show that models can help impart a delay-of-gratification orientation. Thus the present emphasis on rewards and punishments should not obscure the importance of observational learning.

The Timing of Punishment and the Development of Conscience

Punishment is a cheap and popular way of suppressing unwanted behavior and imposing society's standards. The extent to which punishment results in the internalization of society's standards would appear to depend on a number of factors, including the *timing* of the punishment. The effects of the timing of punishment on conscience development are clearly shown in a series of papers and studies by Aronfreed (1961, 1963, 1964, 1969; Aronfreed & Reber, 1965).

Aronfreed's basic experimental procedure is to confront a child with an array of toys and then tell the child that he or she may play with only some of the toys, since a certain one is being reserved for "older children." At that point the forbidden toy is not designated; the child finds out through being punished that the forbidden toy is the most attractive one present. After the child has chosen the forbidden toy, punishment is administered either as the child *initiates* the forbidden act (for example, picks up the toy), as the child *engages* in the forbidden act (holds or plays with the toy), or as the child *terminates* the forbidden act (puts down the toy). The test of internalization consists of leaving the child alone in the room with the toys. The toys have been gimmicked in such a way that it is possible to tell later if the child played with the forbidden toy during the experimenter's absence.

For the most part, the strongest internalization occurs when the punishment is associated with the *initiation* of the act. Aronfreed's explanation involves two sequential processes. First, through classical conditioning, the intent to commit the transgression becomes associated with anxiety (since the intent has been followed by punishment). Thus, preparing to perform a forbidden act makes one feel anxious. Second, people learn to reduce this conditioned anxiety by substituting for the transgression a harmless, nonforbidden act. In the experiment this would consist of playing with a nonforbidden toy, which is not anxiety provoking.

Punishment at the onset of an act leads to later nonperformance of the act.

Punishment at the termination of an act leads to feelings of guilt.

Punishment *following* the act produces an entirely different result. Under these conditions, intent does not become a conditioned stimulus that elicits anxiety, since the intent to transgress and the punishment are too removed in time. Instead, cues surrounding the termination of the act become associated with anxiety. Punishment following the act does not lead to response suppression but instead leads to feelings of guilt.

Language is accorded an important role in Aronfreed's internalization research. Language allows the child to anticipate the consequence of his or her actions. Language can also be used as a reward or punishment: considerable anxiety can be generated by phrases such as "You're gonna get it when your parents get home." In addition, language may help ward off feelings of anxiety and guilt. For example, children could learn to "confess" because they know that if they do so people will go easy on them.

One particularly interesting study (Aronfreed, 1964) shows how self-critical verbal behavior may serve to reduce anxiety. Children in this experiment played with a box that had four levers. Certain responses resulted in a buzzer sounding. Under experimental conditions the female experimenter would react with sharp disapproval to acts that triggered the buzzer, and she referred to the transgression as a "blue" act. Her characterization of the act as "blue" was made either at the onset or at the termination of punishment. Later the children were given the opportunity to criticize themselves by verbalizing "blue" after they had made the buzzer sound. Children whose acts were described as "blue" prior to the punishment did not resort to self-criticism, but children whose acts were described as "blue" following the punishment did engage in self-criticism. In the former case, "blue" was associated with an increase in anxiety (brought about by the anticipation of punishment), and the word "blue" was hence avoided. In the latter case, "blue" was associated with a decrease in anxiety (brought about by the termination of punishment), and hence referring to the act as "blue" restored a sense of comfort. Thus children may learn to criticize—but not inhibit—their own behavior.

Aronfreed's studies suggest that punishment at the initiation of an act leads to internalization, whereas punishment at the termination of an act leads to guilt. Verbal criticism by a parent at the onset of punishment is less likely to result in self-criticism on the part of the child than is verbal criticism that is associated with the termination of the punishment.

Love-Oriented and Direct Punishment

In addition to the timing of punishment, the type of punishment is also of importance. A distinction is often made between psychological or love-oriented punishment on the one hand and direct punishment on the other. **Love-oriented punishment** involves the withdrawal of affection, mild forms of disapproval coupled with explanations for the disapproval, gentle exhortations and admonitions, and enforced social isolation. **Direct punishment** consists of physical beatings and strong verbal assaults involving screams and imprecations. Love-oriented punishment seems to promote internalization, whereas direct punishment seems to produce rebellion (Aronfreed, 1969; McCandless, 1969).

There are several reasons for the superiority of love-oriented punishment. If Johnny clobbers his kid brother with the goldfish bowl and Mother withdraws her love, Johnny may regain her affection by behaving in more acceptable ways. On the other hand, if Mother clobbers Johnny in return, she can have three adverse effects. First, she would be an aggressive model. Second, she would increase Johnny's drive or arousal and through this motivational factor might strengthen Johnny's bad behavior and make peaceful activities difficult to learn. Third, Johnny could interpret her behavior as an attack, which is known to be an instigator of aggression (Chapter 7).

Magnitude of Threat of Punishment

Common sense might suggest that, the more severe a threatened punishment, the less likely a person should be to engage in the forbidden activity. However, some social psychologists have reasoned that a threat of mild punishment should lead to greater self-control than a threat of severe punishment. One aspect of dissonance theory (Chapter 5) is that we seek to justify our behavior in our own eyes. In the case of a severe threat, we can reason that we are not engaging in the activity because of the promised horrible consequences; no further justification is required. The activity itself remains attractive, and, when the threat of punishment is removed (as when the parent leaves the room or the teacher turns to the blackboard), its performance should remain likely. In the case of a mild threat, punishment alone may not quite rationalize exemplary behavior. To provide sufficient justification for not engaging in the forbidden activity, we may convince ourselves that the activity simply isn't that attractive. This devaluation would reduce our motivation to engage in the activity. When the threat of punishment is removed, the performance would still be unlikely.

The effects of varying the magnitude of threatened punishment on the evaluation of a forbidden activity have been explored by Aronson and Carlsmith (1963). After ranking toys in terms of attractiveness, a child was left alone with the toys and told not to play with the second most attractive one. In the mild-threat condition the experimenter told the child he would be annoyed if the child played with the toy; in the severe-threat condition he told that child that, if the toy was played with, he would become very angry and take away all the toys. After a ten-minute interval (during which no child played with the forbidden toy), the child's preferences were reassessed. In the mild-threat condition, in which there was only minimal justification for not playing with the toy, the evaluation of the forbidden toy was lowered. In the severe-threat condition, in which the avoidance of punishment was sufficient justification for not playing with the toy, the toy retained its initial attractiveness.

A more recent study by Lepper (1973) supports the general idea that mild threats lead to more self-control than severe threats. This experiment was similar to Aronson and Carlsmith's in that children were threatened to varying degrees for playing with a toy and in that the child's attitudes toward the toy were carefully assessed. As expected, except in certain subconditions (in which the experimenter had taken steps to stabilize the child's initial attitudes), the children given a mild threat devalued the toy more than the children given a severe threat or the nonthreatened controls. Furthermore, in this experiment the children given the mild threat were more resistant to temptation when taunted with the toy than were children in the other conditions. It was also found that the children given the mild threat were more likely to consider themselves honest than were the other children. Lepper argues for a self-attribution or self-perception (Chapters 3 and 5) interpretation of his results. Children who resist temptation under conditions of mild admonitions reason that they do so because they are "honest," and their self-inferred honesty will appear in other situations. Dissonance and attribution theories agree, however, that mild threats are more likely to yield greater resistance to temptation than are severe threats.

REINFORCEMENT AND SOCIAL INTERACTION

For purposes of analysis, we have been considering social reinforcement as a one-way process, with one person responding and the other applying or withholding reinforcers. In most natural settings we find that two or more people are, through various techniques, satisfying and disappointing each other. **Exchange theories,** as advanced by Homans (1961) and by Thibaut and Kelley (1959), suggest that the initiation, course, and termination of social interaction are governed by the obtained or expected pattern of rewards within the relationship.

The basic elements in Thibaut and Kelley's theory are response alternatives and outcomes. **Response alternatives** refer to the responses or courses of action available to each participant in the situation. **Outcomes** refer to the consequences or results of the interaction, as subjectively assessed by each of the participants. Outcomes in turn consist of two components: rewards and costs. **Rewards** are all the positive aspects of the outcome (achievement of a goal, entertainment, feelings of acceptance and self-esteem, and so forth), and **costs** are all the negative aspects of the outcome (effort expenditure, boredom, feelings of rejection and embarrassment, and so forth). Outcomes are expressed numerically. The numbers stand for the *subjective* values of the outcome, and, for convenience, they may be expressed as the algebraic sum of the rewards (+) and costs (−). For example, kissing a member of the opposite sex might have a reward value of +5; contracting the mumps, a cost value of −50. The outcome of kissing a person of the opposite sex who has the mumps can be expressed as −45.

Outcomes are truly interactive, in that they depend on the combination of response alternatives selected by each of the participants. For purposes of analysis, consider the simple case in which two bank customers discover that they are converging on the same teller's window. Each person's response alternatives would include (1) *proceeding*—that is, going ahead with the hope that the other person will defer—or (2) *diverting*—that is, choosing another, unoccupied teller at the other end of the bank. Table 4-2 depicts this situation and expresses hypothetical outcomes. A table that presents response alternatives and outcomes associated with each combination thereof is called a **matrix.**

Table 4-2. Response alternatives and outcomes: The bank-teller problem

		Customer II			
		Proceed		Divert	
		I	II	I	II
Customer I	Proceed	−1	−1	+1	−1
	Divert	−1	+1	−1	−1

As Table 4-2 shows, each customer (I or II) can rush ahead or defer to the other, and the outcomes experienced by each will depend on the combination of responses of the pair. The outcomes associated with each combination of responses are expressed as the intersection of the row and the column. If each person rushes ahead, the resulting clash might prove embarrassing and time consuming (as they dance around the teller's window) and hence lead to mildly negative outcomes for each. If one customer continues ahead and the other defers, the former gets quick service but the latter is delayed. Finally, if both change course, both are delayed

and experience negative outcomes. The outcomes in Table 4-2 are purely arbitrary and represent *my* rather mild feelings about such a situation. If the people or conditions change, so do the outcomes. For example, some people might find giving way to another person an unbearable humiliation, whereas others don't care. Or, if a taxi were waiting outside, a short delay could become costly.

In many cases such as this, the pattern of outcomes would be such that the issue of who proceeds and who diverts is no issue at all. For example, usually one customer would arrive ahead of the other, and this would alter outcomes. If the second customer did not defer, he or she would likely be considered rude and may feel guilty. This would make it too costly for the second customer to proceed, so he or she would make way for the first. Similarly, a customer with a mask and a gun might have no qualms about taking precedence over the other patrons, who would, in turn, have few misgivings about making way.

Anticipated and expected outcomes also govern the course of complex and extended interactions. On a first date, for example, the conversation is likely to flit around until the couple hits upon a topic of mutual interest—that is, one that provides each person with favorable outcomes in terms of interest and involvement. Similarly, the selection of activities can be understood in the same fashion. If each person likes classical music, then the concert is likely to win out over the football game. In a sustained relationship, conflicts of interest are inevitable. Patterns often develop whereby the people "trade off" so that each has his or her way about half the time. The general idea is that each person exchanges something for what is received in return, as in "You scratch my back and I'll scratch yours."

Outcomes also determine the initiation and termination of interaction. We may approach a stranger at a party and attempt to strike up a conversation because we have heard she is witty and amusing; by that, we mean that the rewards are expected to outweigh the costs. On the other hand, we may steer away from a prior acquaintance at the same party because we know he's a bore; by that, we mean that the trouble of talking to this person is not justified by the long, dry, dull monologue expected in return.

According to Thibaut and Kelley, the outcomes obtained in an ongoing interaction are continually being evaluated with respect to two standards. One, the **comparison level,** or **CL,** represents the level of outcomes that the person feels he or she has earned or otherwise "deserves." Outcomes falling above CL are considered satisfying, and those falling below CL are considered unsatisfying. For example, one person in a group of three roommates may cook substantial but bland meals when it is his or her turn and expect others to also cook mediocre meals when it is their turn. If one of the other roommates prepares fine French cuisine, the level of outcomes would be favorable, whereas if the other prepares nothing but franks and beans, dissatisfaction is likely to result. The **comparison level for alternatives,** or **CLalt,** is defined as the lowest level of outcome a person will accept and still hang in. A roommate given to serving nothing but bread and water or porridge would be inviting some reshuffling. If outcomes fall above CL, the person is happy with the relationship or the interaction. If outcomes fall between CL and CLalt, there are feelings of dissatisfaction. If outcomes fall below CLalt, the person will leave the relationship or terminate the interaction. CL and CLalt will depend very much on what the person is used to (or wants to be used to) and on the level of satisfaction expected in alternative relationships.

Thibaut and Kelley's formulation is especially suitable for dealing with influence and power. If person A can, by varying his or her behavior, make it desirable for person B to vary his or her behavior in a certain way, then A has **behavior control** over B, in that A can affect the likelihood of what B will do. For example, by being warm and affectionate when Bob suggests that they go out to dinner, and by being distant and aloof when Bob announces that he is going out drinking with the boys, Alice can raise the probability of a dinner date and lower the probability of a neglectful partner. The extent of Alice's behavior control over Bob depends on how much Bob has to gain by adjusting his behavior in the direction favored by Alice. If Bob doesn't care about Alice anymore, he may go out drinking with the boys no matter how cool Alice threatens to become.

Fate control refers to a situation in which one person can affect another's outcomes no matter what the other person does. Fate control is exemplified by medieval princes who, with a whimsical snap of the fingers, could award gold, land, and titles—or an extended session in the dungeon. Fate control can still be observed in the military, in the family, and in certain academic and employment settings.

The important thing about fate control is that it is readily converted to behavior control. For example, a boss controls the fate of individual employees, but the individual employee does not control the fate of the boss. The boss can motivate a high level of performance by offering good pay and can discourage poor performance by threatening dismissal. By keeping good employees and replacing bad employees, the boss can guarantee himself or herself an uninterrupted flow of good outcomes. The employees, on the other hand, can secure good outcomes only by adjusting their behavior to fit the requirements of the boss.

PART SUMMARY

One person's actions can serve as rewards and punishments that affect the likelihood of another person's behaviors. A large number of studies have examined the effects of social approval and disapproval on subjects' verbal behavior. Social reinforcement can affect both the *rate* at which people speak and the *content* of what they say. Approval and disapproval have been shown to affect expressed opinions, and a study by Insko suggests that changes induced by social reinforcement are neither superficial nor fleeting.

Early theorists saw the verbal-conditioning process as "unconscious and automatic." More recent, cognitive, theorists suggest that the verbal-conditioning process is dependent on active hypothesis testing on the part of the learner. These cognitive theorists suggest that an awareness of the reinforcement contingencies is a precondition for learning to occur. Although investigations of awareness are difficult to interpret, most recent studies suggest that an awareness of the reinforcement contingencies precedes the appearance of the verbal-conditioning effect. These studies show once again that people are active interpreters of their environment rather than passive responders to changing environmental conditions.

A major task confronting society is to teach the individual to inhibit the expression of some impulses and to limit the expression of others. Internalization refers to the learning of society's rules of conduct and the development of conscience. Highly important in the analysis of internalization are Aronfreed's studies of the effects of timing of punishment on the inhibition of responses. Aronfreed has found that internalization is greatest when punishment is administered at the initiation of the transgression. Aronfreed has also found that, when punishment follows the termination of the act, guilt is more likely than response inhibition; in addition, self-criticism is likely if a child's behavior is disparaged after the punishment has been terminated. Other studies suggest that psychological or love-oriented punishments encourage greater internalization than do direct punishments and that relatively mild and vague threats lead to greater resistance to temptation or response inhibition than do severe and specific threats.

Exchange theory suggests that the initiation, course, and termination of social interaction are governed by the obtained or expected pattern of rewards within the relationship. The basic concepts include response alternatives, or the courses of action available to the individual, and outcomes, or the values attached to various combinations of responses. Outcomes reflect a balance between what the person puts into the relationship, or costs, and what the person gets out of the relationship, or rewards. Outcomes are evaluated with respect to two standards: the CL, which represents the level of outcomes that the person feels were earned or somehow deserved, and the CLalt, which establishes the minimum acceptable outcomes for maintaining the relationship. When one person can affect another's outcomes, he or she can influence what that other person will do.

OBSERVATIONAL LEARNING, SOCIAL REINFORCEMENT, AND SEX-ROLE BEHAVIOR

Not too long ago I had lunch with a friend from the rhetoric department. Present at the table was a woman being considered for a position in that department. As an important university official walked by, my friend waved him over to the table and said "Bart, I'd like you to meet Dr. Ferne So and So, who is visiting us from Midwestern U." Bart glanced at me with a perplexed look (we had met briefly before), but it was soon replaced with a broad smile as he grabbed my hand, shook it, and warmly proclaimed "Glad to meet you, Vern."

Perhaps the reason for Bart's mistake was that in our society we still tend to think of professors as men. Some of our strongest expectations about a person are determined by that person's sex. As Bem and Bem (1970, 1973a) have noted, there are such strong assumptions concerning sex-appropriate behavior that it is difficult to even conceive of alternatives. Furthermore, society seems geared to ensure that people will behave in ways consistent with these assumptions.

To apply some of our knowledge of observational learning and social reinforcement, let's consider how social-learning processes help account for the process of **sex typing,** which refers to the acquisition of the emotional responses, personality, attitudes, and beliefs that are defined as appropriate for a given sex in a given culture (Mussen, 1969). The result of sex typing is an elimination of behavioral alternatives. Men do not really have the opportunity of staying home to cook and sew, and women do not get to go to the moon.

SEX ROLES IN NORTH AMERICA

Despite cross-cultural variation (Mead, 1935), there is impressive agreement within our own society concerning what constitutes masculine and feminine behavior (Broverman, Vogel, Broverman, Clarkson, & Rosenkrantz, 1972). We expect men to adopt the **instrumental role**—that is, to "get things done" and to take on tasks that are physically strenuous or dangerous. Men are taught to be autonomous, or independent, as well as dominating, aggressive, and emotionally inhibited, so that they can build bridges and transcontinental railroads, sail ships in heavy seas, climb mountains, and blow up enemy emplacements. We expect women to adopt **expressive** and **passive-dependent roles.** That is, they are taught to be warm and nurturant and to display their emotions (the expressive role), as well as to be meek, indecisive, submissive, and reliant on men (the passive-dependent role). Women's tasks (which are never done) center around ministering to others and handling routine chores such as cooking, cleaning, and rolling bandages.

Despite the Women's Liberation Movement, the Broverman et al. study found the traditional views of men as instrumental and women as expressive to be persistent and pervasive. There was consensus regardless of sex, marital status, or educational level. Furthermore, it was quite clear that the masculine characteristics were the more highly valued—except when masculine characteristics were assumed by women. In this case, masculine behavior was taken as symptomatic of poor mental health. Thus, although sex typing leads to a reduction in the number of alternatives open to each sex, the options open to women tend to be the less desirable alternatives.

SEX TYPING IN CHILDHOOD AND ADOLESCENCE

Differential treatment of boy infants and girl infants begins at birth. Although male infants initially receive more touching, rocking, holding, and other forms of direct physical contact, from 6 months or so on, female infants receive more physical contact (Lewis, 1972). There is thus a shift from proximal (close) to distal (distant) treatment for male infants and a shift from distal to proximal treatment for female infants. By age 2 or so, the physical contact accorded a child of either sex will decrease. However, Lewis suggests that this differential treatment shapes passive-dependent behavior on the part of girls but autonomous behavior on the part of boys. He also suggests that the physical contact mothers give their daughters in later infancy may explain why adult females are more likely to hug and kiss members of the same sex than are adult males.

Models in the Home

Identification refers to taking on the qualities or attributes of another person. This is a complex modeling process that, according to Mussen (1969), is based on an intricate developmental relationship, that occurs in the absence of training, and that involves fantasies of "being like" another person, as well as superficial resemblances in terms of behavior. Identification with a model of the same sex is seen as an important part of the sex-typing process. The widely accepted view is that boys identify with their fathers, whereas girls identify with their mothers. Lynn (1972) has challenged this simple notion, suggesting that the structure of the contemporary North American family makes this pattern of identification unlikely.

In most families the father is away from home during most of the daylight hours. It is the mother who tends and cares for infants of both sexes. Because the mother is an accessible model, Lynn suggests that both male and female infants will initially identify with her. Since this identification is appropriate for a daughter, it is allowed to continue. Since it is inappropriate for a son, it will be discouraged. The male is thus forced to find a more appropriate model. Because of the father's absence much of the time, the boy infant must piece together a masculine role model on the basis of observing not only his father but other male models, including neighbors, relatives, and TV heroes.

Lynn argues that these separate patterns of identification involve different types of learning activities. Identifying with the mother requires only passivity and docile acceptance. Identifying with a culturally defined role requires initiative and independence, an active exploration of different people and situations, and an abstraction of the characteristics that define the masculine role. As a result, the different styles of learning involved will carry over into later learning situations. Thus the typical female will surpass the typical male in passive tasks involving rote memory, verbal fluency, and language use, whereas the typical male will surpass the typical female in active tasks involving analytic ability and problem-solving skills (Lynn, 1972).

During the preschool years, provision of sex-appropriate toys, such as footballs and dolls, encourages the performance of sex-appropriate behavior. Reinforcement is also an element, as when a father beams proudly when his daughter plays with a doll but scowls when his son engages in the same activity. By the time children enter school, they have usually acquired quite a bit of knowledge about sex-appropriate behavior.

Models in the Classroom

Elementary-school teachers are often females who model and reward feminine virtues (McCandless, 1969). Indeed, Kagan (1964) found that, during the first and second grades, children are likely to view school as a feminine enterprise, although there is likely to be a shift in attitude when the child discovers that certain types of learning (such as math and science) are very useful for masculine occupations like engineering. A live, feminine model in the classroom will be partially offset by the symbolic masculine models that appear in textbooks.

In children's texts and storybooks, the heroes are typically men. Analyses of elementary-school readers (Child, Potter, & Levin, 1946; Fisher, 1970; Weitzman, Eiffler, Hokada, & Ross, 1972; Bem & Bem, 1973a) suggest that about 75% of the central characters are males. In their examination of prize-winning picture books, Weitzman et al. found that women were underrepresented in titles, central roles, and even illustrations. Where they did appear, they modeled traditional sex roles. Boys actively explored, offered information, provided solutions to problems, and led, but girls were timid, passive, and uncreative followers. Characterizations of adults were equally sex typed: although men engaged in a variety of occupations, women were presented as wives and mothers. Thus, even if a teacher is highly open minded, attempts to soft-pedal sex typing may be undermined by symbolic models in the textbooks.

At least two other factors also encourage the learning and performance of sex-appropriate behavior during the elementary-school years. First, off the school premises, many organizations, such as the Cub Scouts, Brownies, and Little League, are geared for providing males with masculine models and females with feminine models and for reinforcing sex-appropriate behavior. Second, sex typing is most likely facilitated in same-sex peer groups in which conformity pressures (Chapter 9) encourage sex-appropriate activities such as baseball and jacks.

Sex Typing in Adolescence

There would appear to be little or no let-up in sex typing during the years of junior and senior high school. Although children of the two sexes undergo a number of common educational experiences, girls are likely to be shunted into homemaking courses and away from manual-arts courses, whereas boys are given exactly the opposite treatment. Extracurricular activities remain divided along sex lines: athletics are prominent for boys, and social clubs are prominent for girls.

Abundant reading material aimed at this age group would seem to further reinforce sex typing. For the young adolescent female there are comic books and pulp novels dealing with romance, and for the later adolescent female there is *Seventeen*. For adolescent males, there are comics with two-fisted heroes and an abundance of magazines devoted to sports, outdoor activities, and mechanics. Coed magazines or comics such as *Archie* do not seem to seriously threaten traditional standards.

In sum, from earliest infancy through adolescence, children are exposed to persons who model sex-appropriate behavior. Children are likely to be rewarded for behaving in ways that are considered sex appropriate, and they are likely to be punished for behaving in ways that are considered more appropriate for members of the opposite sex.

MAINTAINING THE STATUS QUO: REWARDS AND PUNISHMENTS IN ADULTHOOD

It has been suggested that the sex-typing process diminishes the number of alternatives and options available to a person of a given sex. It has been further suggested that the alternatives that are made inaccessible to (or at least difficult for) women tend to be the more desirable alternatives. In adulthood, women continue to be confronted with conditions that encourage them to engage in the less desirable activities usually reserved for their sex, rather than in the more desirable activities usually reserved for the opposite sex. That is, an adult woman is likely to go unrewarded or even be punished for attempting to step out of her place.

Women's Performance as "Inferior"

An artistic or creative accomplishment by a woman is less likely to be rewarded with praise than is an identical accomplishment by a man. This fact remains true even when women do the evaluating (Goldberg, 1968). A limitation to this generalization was found by Pheterson, Kiesler, and Goldberg (1971), who had women evaluate works of art that were presented as either male created or female created and as either contest entries or contest winners. If the artwork was still in competition (that is, if the judges had not yet rendered a decision), then the work was rated more favorably when attributed to a man than to a woman. However, if the artwork had already been judged and had been awarded a prize, then

the work was likely to be evaluated as equally good whether it had been attributed to a man or to a woman. The authors suggest that, if the outcome of an evaluation is in doubt (as when a contest is still in progress), people simply expect the man to do better, and such expectations can contribute to his becoming the winner. In other words, man's ability and effort are rewarded, whereas equal ability and effort on the part of the woman remain unreinforced.

A recent study within the framework of attribution theory (Chapter 3) shows that, when a woman does succeed, she is likely to be seen as very highly motivated. This result has been offered by Feldman-Summers and Kiesler (1974), who had subjects view identical performances of men and women. In the first study, subjects were given sheets of problems that supposedly had been worked on by either a man or a woman. In some cases the stimulus person had answered 90% of the problems correctly, and in other cases only 20% of the problems were answered correctly. In the second study, subjects evaluated successful and unsuccessful male and female physicians. In some cases the physicians were described as having made it on their own and in other cases as possibly having received some help from a father who was also a physician. In both experiments, subjects indicated the extent to which they thought the various performances were due to ability, motivation, task difficulty, and luck.

Women were seen as more highly motivated than men in both experiments; that is, subjects of both sexes believed that the women were forced to *try* harder. In the second experiment it was also found that, whereas men explained the successful male's performance in terms of ability, they explained the successful female's performance in some other way, such as in terms of her being helped out by her father. Perhaps in response to Women's Lib, females felt that the male had an easier task, since he did not have to overcome sex barriers to become a doctor. Taken together, the results show that successful women are seen as having to be especially motivated, to overcome a lack of ability, and to succeed despite the handicap of being a woman in our society. Feldman-Summers and Kiesler suggest that, in a situation in which ability is more important than motivation, attributional processes might result in a man's being selected over a woman, even if the two candidates have identical records. This prediction would seem to be borne out in studies of employment discrimination.

Employment Discrimination

Nowhere is differential reinforcement as clear as in the employment setting. In academia, for example, women tend to be underemployed. Compared with men, women tend to get jobs at less prestigious universities and, within a university, to hold lower-level jobs (Rossi, 1970; Cates, 1973). The possibility that the women are actually less qualified would not seem to explain the results of an experiment by Fidell (1970). She prepared two resumés of academic training and qualifications that were identical in every respect, except that in one case the person described was a man and in the other case, a woman. These resumés were sent to prospective employers. Although the two candidates had identical qualifications, the male candidate was evaluated more positively—and seen as more suitable for a high-level appointment. Once again, a given level of accomplishment was more likely to be rewarded when it was attributed to a man. And once a woman is in a job, there are many barriers to promotion (O'Leary, 1974).

Legislation makes overt discrimination illegal, but it is difficult to identify subtle forms of discrimination and then formulate and enforce laws against them. An example of a very subtle form of discrimination is the segregation of job advertisements in newspapers. In Pittsburgh the National Organization for Women (NOW) filed a complaint against the *Pittsburgh Press* for separating jobs into columns headed "Jobs—Male Interests" and "Jobs—Female Interests." Although a disclaimer was included stating that this procedure was for the "convenience of readers," there was a strong suspicion that this policy tended to discourage female applicants, since reading between the lines might suggest "Women need not apply."

To test this hypothesis, Bem and Bem (1973b) presented want ads, either sex segregated (and with the same disclaimer as in the *Pittsburgh Press*) or alphabetically listed without headings, to a group of subjects. Under segregation conditions only 46% of the women questioned were as willing to apply for male-interest jobs as for female-interest jobs, even though the male-interest jobs were preferable in terms of salary, fringe benefits, and opportunity for advancement. However, when the ads were presented alphabetically and without headings, 81% of the women were as interested in applying for the jobs originally classified as male-interest as for the jobs initially classified as female-interest.

A NOTE OF CAUTIOUS OPTIMISM

Observation of models and social reinforcement encourage the learning and performance of sex-appropriate behavior. However, there are some signs that conditions may be changing in the direction of greater flexibility and more behavioral options for both men and women. Three of the major encouraging factors are: (1) technological change, (2) changing patterns of identification, and (3) changing patterns of social reinforcement.

First, it has long been noted that there are biological bases for the two sex roles. Lynn (1972) suggests that the biological basis for the expressive or passive-dependent role includes women's smaller size, lesser muscle mass, lower energy, and less restless activity. These differences would appear to be biologically based, because they appear before birth and can be altered through hormone injections. However, technological developments in the last 50 years or so seem to have rendered such biological differences inconsequential. Just as 100 years ago the Colt revolver "equalized" the weak and the strong, electric motors, hydraulic mechanisms, and the family station wagon have equalized men and women today.

Second, we can probably expect new patterns of identification within the family. Lynn, you will recall, suggested that, although a little girl identifies with her mother and in the process learns to be passive-dependent and expressive, a little boy identifies with an abstract role model and in the process learns to be independent and instrumental. However, this process assumes a traditional family in which the woman stays home and the man goes to work. As more and more women gain employment, daughters as well as sons may be forced to identify with abstract role models.

Finally, patterns of reinforcement may be changing in such a way as to allow more options for each sex. This trend is most clearly shown in the opening up of new employment opportunities for women. Women are still discriminated against and underemployed. However, an analysis of census data and opinion polls has led Wattenberg (1974) to conclude that conditions for women have improved dramatically since 1940 and that a goodly amount of this improvement took place in the last decade. In 1940, for example, only 27% of women aged 35 to 44 worked, but, by 1970, 50% of the women in this age bracket were in the labor force. Among older women (45–64) the figure rose from 20% to 48% in the same 30-year period. Wattenberg argues that women did not simply trade one distasteful job (doing dishes at home) for another (doing dishes in someone else's home): the percentage of women employed in menial jobs (domestic service) halved between 1960 and 1970, and the increase in the labor force stems from women's moving into increasingly higher-status positions. Wattenberg does not claim that there is equality; he carefully notes that women are underrepresented in many occupational categories, including "chairman of the board." What Wattenberg does suggest is that, if we look at trends over the last 30 years, we find that today's women have more options available, and there is no reason to expect a discontinuation of this trend in the future.

Recently Sandra Bem (1972, 1974, 1975) has been studying individual differences in people's abilities to adopt either the instrumental or the expressive role. She has used the term **androgynous** to refer to individuals who are able to behave either instrumentally or expressively, depending on inclination and situation, and she has developed a scale for measuring this psychological quality (S. Bem, 1974). Students of both sexes who scored as androgynous were, for example, able to show "masculine" independence when pressured to conform and "feminine" playfulness when given the opportunity to interact with a kitten. The androgynous individual may someday come to define a new and more human standard of psychological health (S. Bem, 1975).

PART SUMMARY

Modeling and social reinforcement encourage the learning and performance of sex-appropriate behavior. In our society, women are expected to be expressive and passive-dependent, and men are expected to be independent and instrumental. Feminine roles are generally considered to be less desirable than masculine roles.

Sex typing, or the learning of sex-appropriate behavior, begins during the early months as a mother decreases the amount of physical contact accorded a son but increases the amount accorded a daughter. Very important during the preschool years is the complex modeling effect called identification. According to Lynn, girls identify with the mother, but boys identify with a culturally defined masculine role model. These separate patterns of identification require passive-dependent behavior on the part of girls and active exploration and mastery on the part of boys.

Elementary-school teachers are usually feminine models. Symbolic masculine models are likely to dominate reading materials. During the school years, organizations such as the Boy Scouts and Girl Scouts provide sex-appropriate models and reward sex-appropriate behavior, and sex typing is further encouraged by conformity pressures exerted by same-sex peers. Sex typing continues through adolescence.

In adulthood, women are likely to go unrewarded for trying to engage in certain culturally desirable activities traditionally reserved for men. First, a high level of performance on the part of a woman is less likely to be favorably evaluated than is an identical level of performance on the part of a man. Second, women are less likely to be rewarded with prestigious and high-paying jobs than are men with similar credentials.

Changing conditions may result in a greater number of options remaining open for members of both sexes. First, technological advancements are rendering inconsequential certain biological differences between the sexes. Second, female infants as well as male infants may now be encouraged to identify with abstract role models rather than with specific individuals. Finally, patterns of reinforcement seem to be changing, as shown by the opening up of occupational opportunities for women. As a result of the interplay of such factors, both men and women may gain the freedom to choose either the instrumental or the expressive role, depending on inclination or situation. This freedom may lead to new, high levels of psychological well-being.

5

Attitude Formation
and Change

COGNITIVE-CONSISTENCY THEORIES

DISSONANCE THEORY

Dissonance in Free-Choice Situations
Dissonance in Forced-Compliance Situations
Self-Perception Theory as an Alternative
   to Dissonance Theory

CONGRUITY THEORY

BALANCE THEORY

The ABX System
Experimental Tests of Balance and ABX

STRENGTHS AND LIMITATIONS

PART SUMMARY

FUNCTIONAL THEORIES

KATZ' FOUR FUNCTIONS

Adjustive Attitudes
Ego-Defensive Attitudes
Value-Expressive Attitudes
"Knowledge" Attitudes

KELMAN'S PROCESSES OF ATTITUDE CHANGE

Compliance
Identification
Internalization
An Experimental Investigation

STRENGTHS AND LIMITATIONS

PART SUMMARY

190

PERSUASIVE COMMUNICATIONS

SOURCE CHARACTERISTICS

Credibility
Likability

PRESENTATION CHARACTERISTICS

Media
Order of Presentation
Forewarning Effects
Distraction and Persuasion

CONTENT CHARACTERISTICS

One- and Two-Sided Presentations
Fear

PART SUMMARY

One day each June, as the temperature soars toward 100°, I don cap and gown and march with others through the dust to the football field, where our college commencement ceremonies are held. Included in the festivities are two speeches. One is made by a distinguished guest and the other by a graduating senior. Although there is admittedly some variability in these speeches over the years, usually one speech reflects pride in national accomplishments and optimism about the future, whereas the other reflects anger about national shortcomings and pessimism about the future.[1] The essentials of each speech can be summarized as follows:

> "This, the best-educated class of all time, is about to march proudly forth from this citadel of wisdom into the greatest society the world has ever known. As Americans, the graduates will enjoy an unparalleled standard of living. They will eat quantities of fine food, live in luxurious homes, drive sleek and powerful cars, and engage in leisure activities that are the envy of people the world over. They will work shorter hours and make more money doing more meaningful work than workers in any other land. I know that this wonderful class will contribute to the insightful and energetic leadership that in the last decade has raised our national educational level, cut

---

[1]For elaboration of these themes, see Wattenberg (1974).

our incidence of poverty in half, raised individual purchasing power, and made tremendous inroads into eliminating the universal plagues of hatred, oppression, and unequal opportunity."

"The poor jokers who have played the Establishment's game and struggled through this apathetic diploma factory are about to enter one large insane asylum. As Americans, they will live out their years eating artificial foods, breathing poisonous air, dwelling in cardboard and plastic homes, risking their lives in overpowered, unsafe automobiles, and futilely seeking relief at the crowded beaches and parks that provide occasional islands in the sea of junkyards that indelibly stains the surface of this dying planet. As Americans, those who find jobs will work at dull, meaningless tasks for paper money, which will be traded for shoddy goods and incompetent services. Hopefully, those few seniors who are neither junkies nor tools of the Fascist Establishment will try to create a new civilization free of slums, poverty, hatred, and oppression."

Listeners from another planet may wonder if the two speakers are referring to the same educational institution, society, and leadership practices. Listeners in the audience, however, show no confusion. We learn early in life that, with few (if any) exceptions, any discriminable person, thing, event, or set of conditions is likely to be judged more favorably by some people than by others. Learned emotional, intellectual, and behavioral responses to persons, things, and events are called **attitudes.** In our discussion **attitude holder** will be used to refer to the person who maintains an attitude, and **attitude object** will refer to the person, thing, or event about which the attitude is held.

The concept of attitudes has long been considered one of the most distinctive and indispensable in social psychology (G. W. Allport, 1954a; McGuire, 1969). Its special status stems from its ability to appeal in one way or another to social psychologists with many different orientations. Attitudes are both a part of the person and an expression of the person's culture. Attitudes can be viewed as the result of individual psychological processes and of social-influence processes. In turn, attitudes have implications for both the adjustment of the individual and the operation of the society.

Since Plato's time many writers have found it convenient to view attitudes as consisting of three interrelated components: the *affective*, the *cognitive*, and the *behavioral* (Hovland & Rosenberg, 1960). The **affective component** is the emotional component. It consists of the feelings of pleasure, displeasure, or ambivalence that the attitude object elicits. For example, one Presidential candidate may elicit a strong positive emotional reaction from you, such as admiration and pleasure, whereas the alternative elicits a strong negative emotional response, such as revulsion and hostility. The **cognitive component** is the intellectual component of an attitude. Also called the "belief" component, it consists of what the attitude holder sees, thinks, knows, or reasons about the attitude object. For example, you may "know" that, if elected or appointed, one Presidential candidate will lead the country to peace and prosperity, whereas the other will take the country down the trail to disaster. The action or **behavioral component** of an attitude refers to the attitude holder's predisposition to respond. Someone who has a favorable attitude intends to promote the interests and welfare of the attitude object, whereas someone with an unfavorable attitude intends to somehow work against it. For example, during an election year you will be "all set" to vote for one candidate rather than for the other.

Attitudes, then, are often treated as packages that combine feelings, thoughts, and actions. Usually the three components tie together (Fishbein & Ajzen, 1974). That is, liking something, believing it useful, and promoting its interests would seem to go together, as would disliking something, believing it harmful, and working against it. Nonetheless, many times when we compare people's feelings, beliefs, and stated intentions on the one hand with what they actually do on the other, we find startling inconsistencies. In other words, attitudes and actions sometimes conflict.

The first study to suggest an inconsistency between attitudes and actions was conducted by LaPiere (1934). He found that hotels and restaurants that indicated on a mailed questionnaire that they did not serve Orientals would nonetheless provide accommodations to Orientals who showed up in person. More recently, Campbell (1969) reported that, although the church shapes strong beliefs about right and wrong, these beliefs seem to have little effect on churchgoers' actual moral behavior. In another study, Kothandapani (1971) found that people's feelings and beliefs regarding birth control did not provide very good predictors of actual use of contraceptives. Reviews by McGuire (1969) and Wicker (1969) also reveal inconsistencies between what people say and what people do.

Several factors would seem to complicate the relationship between attitudes and behavior (Fishbein, 1967; Ajzen & Fishbein, 1973; Fishbein & Ajzen, 1974; Kelman, 1974). Three of the factors are (1) the lack of specificity of most attitudinal measures, (2) the influence of unmeasured attitudes on behavior, and (3) the pattern of rewards and punishments in the situation in which the attitude holder acts. For purposes of illustration, suppose we ask Mr. and Mrs. Bigott what they think about having an Oriental move in next door. The Bigotts reply that they don't like

Orientals, know that they are up to no good, and would be violently opposed. Yet, when an Oriental couple moves in, the Bigotts act friendly toward them and even invite them over for dinner. Why?

The first possibility is that our attitude measurement may be faulty and not capture the situation as it actually unfolds. In the abstract form in which the questions are worded, the Bigotts may think of a retired coolie who is both an opium fiend and a Communist agitator. They may fantasize the deterioration of the house next door, strange vegetable material growing all over the neighborhood, the stench of mysterious food, and a herd of Chows and Pekingese digging up their rose garden. In fact, the new neighbors may be upper-middle-class people who work hard, carefully maintain their home, and quote the Bible rather than Chairman Mao. Because attitude measures are usually nonspecific and abstract, there is considerable room for misinterpretation of the question.

A second explanation for the Bigotts' behavior is that other, unassessed attitudes might have affected their reactions toward their new neighbors. The Bigotts may not like Orientals, but they do like well-to-do Republican bankers who share their interest in roses. If the newcomers fall into enough of these liked categories, the Bigotts may feel that, on the whole, the Orientals add to the quality of the neighborhood.

Finally, the pattern of rewards and punishments in the specific situation may prevent the Bigotts from acting on their prejudices. For example, they may refrain from sharing their distaste for Orientals because standards of fairness and equality are prevalent in their All-American neighborhood, and departure from these standards would elicit a stern reaction from the other neighbors. Another possibility is that the new arrivals appear to be tough customers (holding black belts in karate), and, to avoid possible injury, the Bigotts go out of their way to be friendly to the new neighbors.

Thus inspecific measures, unassessed attitudes, situational constraints, and other factors can all contribute to a discrepancy between what people say and what people do. Yet, when these factors are carefully taken into account, we can do an improved job of predicting from attitudes to behavior. For example, by increasing the specificity of measures, Wicker and Pomazal (1971) were able to reduce the slack between attitudes toward psychological research and actual participation in such research. Although the relationship between attitudes and actions can become very complicated, as Kelman (1974) has put it, attitudes are nevertheless "alive and well" in the sphere of action.

There are two basic thrusts in the field of attitude research. One deals with attitudes as they are found. It involves estimating the proportion of people within a group, community, or society who have particular attitudes, such as for or against a person or product. The second thrust—on which this chapter is based—emphasizes the experimental investigation of the conditions that cause people to form or change their attitudes. In this case, emphasis is on the dynamic relationship between cause and effect. Our discussion will be organized around three approaches to attitude formation and change: the cognitive-consistency approach, the functional approach, and the persuasive-communications approach.

COGNITIVE-CONSISTENCY THEORIES

An entire family of attitude theories is based on the idea that people strive to see the world as orderly and consistent. Each of these theories begins by specifying its basic parts or elements. As we shall soon see, these elements may be the affective, cognitive, and behavioral components of a single attitude; a number of different, interrelated attitudes; or even the attitude holder's friends and enemies and their attitudes. Each theory goes on to specify the possible relationships among its elements. Some of these relationships are hypothesized to be psychologically consistent, stable, and unlikely to change, whereas other relationships are hypothesized to be inconsistent, unstable, and likely to change. Each consistency theory also provides formulas or rules for defining consistent and inconsistent states.

A person who is experiencing inconsistency is expected to juggle elements or redefine the relationships among them in such a way as to achieve consistency. In the process of preventing or eliminating inconsistency, the person forms and changes attitudes. Thus, consistency theories suggest that attitude formation and change reflect motivation to impose order on the world about us. As we shall see, impressions of order may sometimes require a distortion of perceptions or a misjudgment of evidence. The consistency theories that we will consider are *dissonance theory, congruity theory,* and *balance theory.*

DISSONANCE THEORY

Dissonance theory, initially formulated by Leon Festinger (1957), is without question the most prominent member of the cognitive-consistency family. This theory examines the relationship between two or more **cognitions,** or "items of information," which Festinger (1957, p. 3) has defined as "any knowledge, opinion, or belief about the environment, oneself, or one's own behavior." Two types of relationships are possible: consonant and dissonant.

Consonance exists when one of the cognitions *follows from* or *is implied by* the other. Formally stated, given two cognitions, *A* and *B*, if *A* implies B (or if B follows from A), they stand in consonant relationship. Less formally, whenever expectations are confirmed, we have consonance (Aronson, 1968). Consonance is likely in four kinds of situations: (1) when two cognitions are logically consistent; (2) when thoughts, feelings, and actions are congruent with **mores**—that is, social customs of ethical or moral significance; (3) whenever a specific instance is consistent with more encompassing rules or principles; and (4) when a cognition is consistent with past experience.

Dissonance, on the other hand, exists if one of the cognitions follows from or is implied by the *opposite* of the other. Formally stated, A and B are dissonant if A implies *not* B or if B follows from *not* A. Less formally, whenever expectations are disconfirmed, dissonance is aroused. Thus dissonance is likely: (1) when the two cognitions are logically inconsistent, (2) when attitudes or actions violate social mores, (3) when a specific instance conflicts with more encompassing rules, and (4) when an event conflicts with past experience. Examples of consonant and dissonant relationships are presented in Table 5-1.

Both consonant and dissonant relationships can involve more than two cognitions. In some cases people are confronted with a large number of interrelated cognitions, some of which are consonant and some of which are dissonant. The overall degree of dissonance varies as a function of the number and importance of the dissonant cognitions in proportion to the number and importance of consonant cognitions (Sherwood, Baron, & Fitch, 1969). Thus:

$$\text{Dissonance} = \frac{\text{Importance and number of dissonant cognitions}}{\text{Importance and number of consonant cognitions}}.$$

Dissonance is an aversive state that the person tries to avoid or reduce. This may involve changing one cognition, changing the other, or adding new cognitions to achieve a favorable balance.

Consider the case of a student who believes that all Samaritans are selfish but then finds himself aided by a Samaritan delegation to an international student conference. One technique he might use to reduce his dissonance would be to abandon the prejudice that all Samaritans are selfish. A second technique would be to reinterpret the helpful act so that it supported the prejudice. He could decide, for example, that the Samaritans were only trying to give a good impression so they would get preferential treatment at the conference. The third possibility would be to add new cognitions that supported one of the two dissonant cognitions. For example, the student could seek out so many testimonials about the rude and inconsiderate behavior of Samaritans that the one helpful act recedes into total insignificance.

Table 5–1. Possible consonant and dissonant relationships

Case	Cognition A	Consonant Cognition B	Dissonant Cognition B'
1. Consistent or inconsistent with principles of logic	If one pencil costs 5¢, a dozen pencils will cost 60¢.	The college bookstore wants 60¢ for a dozen nickel pencils.	The college bookstore wants 98¢ for a dozen nickel pencils.
2. Consistent or inconsistent with social mores	According to the campus honor code, thou shalt tell the truth, the whole truth, and nothing but the truth.	I told the instructor frankly that I didn't take her exam because I wasn't prepared for it.	I told the instructor that I didn't take her exam because my grandmother died—but I didn't mention that it happened on October 3, 1951.
3. Consistent or inconsistent with encompassing rules or principles	The less you eat, the more you lose.	I cut out bread, beer, potatoes, pie, and butter and lost 20 pounds.	I cut out bread, beer, potatoes, pie, and butter and still gained weight.
4. Consistent or inconsistent with past experiences	I've found exchange students from Samaria to be selfish and inconsiderate.	At the conference some Samaritan students parked their car in such a way that I couldn't get mine out of the lot.	At the conference some Samaritan students gave my car a push after the battery went dead.

Dissonance theory has generated more research than any other social-psychological theory. In fact, we have already encountered some of this research. In Chapter 2, for example, we saw that people may lower their opinion of good-quality merchandise when it is sold at a bargain-basement price. The cognitions "This aluminum foil is inexpensive" and "This aluminum foil is of good quality" are dissonant, and, to avoid or reduce this dissonance, shoppers apparently developed the attitude that the foil was not of good quality. In the discussion to follow, we will consider two major research themes: (1) dissonance reduction and attitude change in free-choice situations and (2) dissonance reduction and attitude change in forced-compliance situations. Many additional examples of dissonance research will be encountered in the remaining chapters of this book.

Dissonance in Free-Choice Situations

In a **free-choice situation,** a person is confronted with two or more alternatives and must choose one. Each alternative may be generally pleasant (as when you get to choose your own graduation gift) or generally unpleasant (as when you have to choose one of two obnoxious courses to fulfill an annoying university requirement), but each alternative is also likely to have both some advantages and some disadvantages. Once a choice has been made, the perceived undesirable qualities of the chosen alternative and the perceived desirable qualities of the rejected alternative will become dissonant with the knowledge of the choice. **Postdecisional dissonance** refers to dissonance following a choice. In the process of reducing this dissonance, the person develops a *more favorable* attitude toward the *chosen* alternative and a *less favorable* attitude toward the *rejected* alternative. Variations in attitudes toward the alternatives are not a cause of the choice; they are a result of the choice.

To illustrate, let's consider a coed who is confronted with the choice of living in the college dorm or renting a private apartment off campus. Table 5-2 lists some of the advantages and disadvantages our hypothetical student associates with each alternative.

Let's suppose that she chooses the off-campus apartment. In this event, the cognitions in columns *A* and *D* are consonant in that they support her choice. The cognitions in columns *B* and *C* (which imply that she should have made the opposite choice) are dissonant. Dissonance reduction could take the form of (1) reassessing the importance of the various cognitions, (2) somehow redefining the cognitions so that they become consonant with the choice, or (3) adding new cognitions to categories *A* and *D*. Thus she could (1) decide that the cognitions listed in

Table 5-2. Possible consonant and dissonant elements following the choice of college and off-campus housing

Off-Campus Apartment	
A. *Advantages*	B. *Disadvantages*
1. No regimentation; minimum house rules	1. High cost
2. More spacious quarters	2. Distance from campus
3. Complete freedom to choose roommates	3. Necessity of cooking
4. Flexible menu and eating schedule	4. Full year's lease

College Dormitory	
C. *Advantages*	D. *Disadvantages*
1. Low cost	1. Oppressive regimentation; many house rules
2. Proximity to classes	2. Cramped quarters
3. Cooking not a necessity	3. No roommate selection
4. Nine-month lease	4. No menu selection

A and *D* are the only ones that matter; (2) redefine the chosen alternative's liabilities as assets, such as by deciding that the apartment's distance from campus is advantageous because it encourages an invigorating and healthy daily walk; (3) redefine the rejected alternative's assets as liabilities, such as by finding fault with the dormitory food; (4) find new benefits of apartment living, such as the freedom to keep pets; and (5) find new disadvantages of dormitory living, such as a dehumanizing lack of privacy.

The basic dissonance-theory prediction is thus that, following a choice, the chosen alternative will gain in relative attractiveness. In an early study, Brehm and Cohen (1959) found that children who made a choice of toys raised their evaluation of the chosen toys and lowered their evaluation of the rejected toys. An entirely different approach was taken in a field study by Knox and Inkster (1968), who had bettors at a racetrack estimate the chances that their preferred horse would win. Subjects evaluated the horse either just before or just after they had made their decision firm by placing their bets. Increased attractiveness of the chosen alternative was shown by a greater conviction that the bet-upon horse would win.

Postdecisional dissonance and attitude change are not an inevitable consequence of a choice. The likelihood and magnitude of postdecisional dissonance depend on two factors. The first factor is the *relative attractiveness* of the various alternatives. When the alternatives are of highly unequal value, little or no dissonance will follow from choosing the better of the pair. For example, the choice of thick eyeglasses over blindness would produce little dissonance. Each alternative is unattractive, but blindness is so much more unattractive an alternative that the choice of wearing eyeglasses follows. However, as the alternatives become *equal* in value, the likelihood and magnitude of dissonance following a choice will increase. For example, choosing to invest a given amount of money in one stock rather than in another should arouse considerable dissonance and noticeable attitude change.

In an early study by Brehm (1956), women first rated a number of small appliances, such as a radio, a desk lamp, and a coffee maker. They were then told that they would get to keep one of these appliances as a gift. Most women were also told that, since there weren't enough of each appliance to go around, they would have the choice of one of a pair of items that the experimenter would select. In one experimental condition, designed to generate high dissonance, women chose between a pair of items that they had rated as approximately equal in attractiveness. In another experimental condition, designed to generate low dissonance, women were given two alternatives of unequal desirability. In a control condition, women were not given a choice but were assigned an item by the experimenter. Next, some women were allowed to read "manufacturers' fact sheets," which aided in the discovery of new consonant elements. The most striking result was that women in the high-dissonance condition, who had been given the opportunity to find consonant elements, showed the greatest tendency to raise their evaluation of the chosen alternative relative to their evaluation of the rejected alternative.

The second factor that affects the likelihood and magnitude of postdecisional dissonance is the *similarity of the consequences* of the different choices. If the alternatives yield *similar* consequences, choosing one does not mean giving up all the satisfactions to be derived from the other, and very little dissonance should result. For example, if the choice were between two washing machines, the choice of one does not mean giving up the advantages to be derived from the other. Each washer does the same basic job, each costs about the same amount, each comes with similar standard features, and each looks the same at 15 paces. If the alternatives yield *dissimilar* consequences, choosing one means giving up the satisfactions associated with the other, and dissonance should result. For example, a laundry washer and a dish washer each have definite advantages and disadvantages, and choosing to enjoy the advantages of one is choosing to sacrifice the advantages of the other. This kind of choice should result in considerable attitude change.

The importance of dissimilarity of consequences has been shown by Brock (1963), who had children indicate liking for three toys and for three crackers. They were then given a choice between two similiar items (for example, two items of food, such as a graham cracker and a cheese cracker) or between two dissimilar items (for example, an item of food and a toy, such as a yo-yo). Again decisions were followed by attitude change, and in this experiment the changes were most pronounced when the choice was made between two dissimilar items as compared to two similar items.

In sum, dissonance theory suggests that, following a decision, there will be a spreading apart of alternatives such that more favorable attitudes develop toward the chosen alternative and less favorable attitudes develop toward the rejected alternative. This effect will be pronounced to the extent that the alternatives are of equivalent value and to the extent that the consequences of the alternatives are dissimilar rather than similar. However, we should note that attitude change of this type is itself likely to induce dissonance, since the attitude holder's new attitudes will be inconsistent with his or her old ones. Thus we have the paradox that the act of reducing dissonance generates new dissonance! But it seems that dissonance induced by a discrepancy between initial and present attitudes is likely to be reduced through a distortion of memory. It has been found that, when subjects whose attitudes have recently changed are asked to recall their earlier views, they tend to remember them as consistent with their newly formed attitudes (Goethals & Beckman, 1973).

Dissonance in Forced-Compliance Situations

Forced compliance exists when a person is induced to openly say or do something that conflicts with a private conviction or belief. Since the public statement or action cannot be retracted, dissonance reduction is likely to take the form of a change in the private belief. However, this change will occur *only* if the person is made to feel responsible for the decision to engage in the attitude-discrepant act. If **external justifications** are available—that is, rationalizations or excuses that allow the attitude holder to believe that he or she had "no choice" but to engage in the act— dissonance reduction through attitude change is unlikely.

We have already encountered an example of this situation in our discussion of the relationship between severity of threat and attitudes toward a forbidden act (Chapter 4). Children threatened with severe punishment did not change their attitudes toward a forbidden toy, but children threatened with mild punishment decided that the forbidden toy was not so enticing as they had originally thought. Thus dissonance between the cognitions "This is a nice toy" and "I am not playing with this nice toy" was reduced by developing less favorable attitudes toward the toy. Although threat provided the external justification for an attitude-behavior discrepancy in this particular study, in most studies monetary rewards serve this purpose. The basic prediction is that, the larger the reward for the attitude-discrepant act, the greater the external justification and the less likely that there will be attitude change in the act's direction. The trick in getting this prediction to work is to pressure or coax "high-dissonance" subjects *just enough*—so that they engage in the attitude-discrepant act but do not end up feeling they had "no choice" but to go ahead and do it.

One of the most well-known dissonance studies was a forced-compliance experiment by Festinger and Carlsmith (1959). After participating in the dull and uninteresting task of slowly rotating a seemingly endless series of pegs, subjects were falsely told that the study dealt with the effects of expectancies on performance. They were then asked to tell a person who was misrepresented as the next subject that the experiment was interesting and fun. Some subjects were coaxed into doing so for a paltry $1, whereas others were offered $20. After the subjects had told these lies about the experiment, their private reactions were assessed. Subjects paid $1 reported that the experiment was more enjoyable than did subjects paid $20. The $1 subjects had insufficient external justification for the lie, and dissonance reduction occurred through developing favorable attitudes toward the dull and uninteresting task. The $20 subjects experienced little or no dissonance and showed little or no attitude change because they could rationalize "I only said it for the money."

By far, most forced-compliance studies involve **counterattitudinal role playing.** As in the Festinger and Carlsmith study, the subject is asked to openly advocate a point of view that is inconsistent with what he or she really believes. The subject does not simply state the discrepant position; usually, he or she is asked to try to adopt the other side's point of view and to come up with arguments to support the other side.

Other theories share with dissonance theory the prediction that counterattitudinal role playing results in attitude change in the direction of the public statements. **Incentive theory,** for example, suggests that a number of rewards are associated with counterattitudinal role playing (Elms, 1969, 1972). The role player may derive satisfaction both from the discovery that he or she has the intellectual flexibility to adopt novel views and from the approving nods of the experimenter. According to incentive theory, these rewards account for the counterattitudinal role player's attitude change. Furthermore, incentive theory predicts that, the larger the incentives or rewards, the greater the attitude change. This prediction stands in sharp contrast to dissonance theory's prediction that, when incentives for engaging in an attitude-discrepant act are varied, small incentives should result in greater dissonance and attitude change than should large incentives.

Several studies confirm the dissonance prediction. In 1959, city police intervened during a student disruption at Yale University. Most students felt that the intervention was unwarranted, and charges of police brutality followed. Shortly thereafter, Cohen offered varying amounts of money for writing essays that praised the police and their activities (reported in Brehm & Cohen, 1962). Subjects paid 50¢ showed the most favorable attitudes toward the police action, subjects paid $1 showed the next most favorable attitudes, and subjects paid $5 or $10 showed the least favorable attitudes. The difference between the 50¢ and $1 subjects in this experiment is of particular interest, since each amount of money is believable. A criticism of studies that offer larger amounts of money, such as $20, is that subjects may not believe that they will really receive this amount (they usually don't receive it).

Dissonance theory also suggests that increasing the negative consequences associated with an attitude-discrepant act should have effects similar to those resulting from decreasing the positive consequences or external justifications associated with the act. Thus the theory leads to the prediction that, the more effort expended in counterattitudinal role playing, the greater the dissonance and the greater the attitude change. To test this hypothesis, Zimbardo (1965) had role players speak into a microphone and hear their own words come back at them. In the low-effort conditions, they heard their own words as spoken; in the high-effort conditions, the words were heard .25 second after they were spoken. Delayed auditory feedback, as in the high-effort condition, makes it difficult to read aloud even simple passages. As expected, subjects in the high-effort conditions showed the greatest attitude change following counterattitudinal role playing.

Unfortunately for the simplicity of the story, not all studies have confirmed the dissonance hypothesis of a negative relationship between incentive magnitude and attitude change. A whole string of experiments have produced results in line with the incentive-theory prediction of a positive relationship between incentive magnitude and attitude change following a counterattitudinal role-playing session (W. A. Scott, 1959; Elms & Janis, 1965; Janis & Gilmore, 1965; Rosenberg, 1965).

In one relatively recent series of six experiments, results included one statistically significant confirmation of the dissonance prediction, one statistically significant confirmation of the incentive prediction, and four sets of results that didn't show much of anything at all (Collins, Ashmore, Hornbeck, & Whitney, 1970)! Clearly, the question thus becomes one of identifying the conditions under which the dissonance-theory prediction prevails. It would appear that this is likely to happen (1) when the role player feels that he or she has freely chosen to play the counterattitudinal role and (2) when the decision to play the role has some undeniable consequences. Otherwise, the incentive-theory prediction is likely to prevail.

First, for counterattitudinal role playing to produce dissonance effects, people must feel that there was a real degree of choice about engaging in the attitude-discrepant act (Linder, Cooper, & Jones, 1967; Holmes & Strickland, 1970; Sherman, 1970; Collins & Hoyt, 1972). The bribe or coercion that reduces freedom of choice provides external justification for the attitude-discrepant act, and there is thus no need for dissonance reduction. Instead, people will respond to bribes and threats in the manner in which incentive theory predicts. In support of this finding, Holmes and Strickland (1970) had subjects write counterattitudinal essays concerning student involvement in academic and administrative decision making within their university. Low-incentive subjects were given no credit for doing so, normal-incentive subjects were given one hour of credit toward their course requirement, and high-incentive subjects were told that they would earn two hours of class credit. Under no-choice conditions the experimenter took it for granted that the subjects would write the counterattitudinal essay, whereas under free-choice conditions the experimenter stressed that the decision to write the essay was entirely up to the subjects. As Figure 5-1 shows, when the subjects felt that they had voluntarily made the decision to write the essay, dissonance predictions were confirmed; when they were not given complete freedom of choice, high incentives led to greater attitude change.

Second, the dissonance prediction will hold only if the decision to engage in the attitude-discrepant act has meaningful consequences (Collins & Hoyt, 1972). Role playing under conditions of anonymity may be a case in which small incentives would generate little dissonance and yield little attitude change (Carlsmith, Collins, & Helmreich, 1966). Under conditions of anonymity the subject's attitude-discrepant act is known only to the experimenter, and the experimenter knows that the subject is faking. Counterattitudinal role playing is thus of little consequence. On the other hand, if subjects role-play before someone who does not know that a lie is in progress, the counterattitudinal role playing has the serious implication that the role player is coming across as someone or something that he or she is not. Under conditions of deliberate misrepresentation, counterattitudinal role playing is not so easily dismissed as a lark. To examine this hypothesis, Carlsmith and his associates offered incentives of 50¢, $1.50, or $5.00. Some subjects expressed the counteropinion in private essays and others in public confrontations. As expected, under conditions of anonymity, larger incentives are associated with

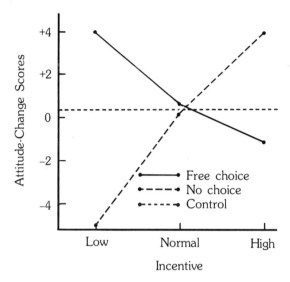

Figure 5-1. Attitude change following counterattitudinal role playing under conditions of varied incentives and freedom of choice. (From "Choice Freedom and Confirmation of Incentive Expectancy as Determinants of Attitude Change," by J. G. Holmes and L. H. Strickland, *Journal of Personality and Social Psychology,* 1970, *14,* 43. Copyright 1970 by the American Psychological Association. Reprinted by permission.)

greater attitude change, but, under conditions of public presentation, larger incentives are associated with less attitude change. In sum, only when a person feels that he or she has had some choice and is hence *personally responsible* for some *real consequences* should there be an inverse relationship between incentive magnitude and attitude change as a result of counterattitudinal role playing.

At least two other explanations have been offered to account for the fact that some studies have found a positive relationship between incentive magnitude and attitude change whereas other studies have found a negative relationship between these two variables. Conolley (1970) and Wilhelmy and Duncan (1974) found a U-shaped relationship between incentive magnitude and attitude change. That is, as incentive magnitude was increased from a small to a moderate amount, attitude change decreased, but, as magnitude was raised from a moderate to a large amount, attitude change increased. The first or downward portion of the curve was consistent with dissonance theory, and it might be taken as reflecting increasing external justification, lessening dissonance, and hence less attitude change. The second or upward portion of the curve is consistent with incentive theory, and it might be taken as reflecting increasing satisfaction and hence increasing attitude change. These researchers suggest that, as the magnitude of the incentive approaches "sufficiency," there is less and less dissonance to be reduced and hence less attitude change, but, as the point of sufficient justification is reached (moderate-sized rewards in these experiments), further increases in incentive magnitude start acting as bribes. Whether dissonance or incentive effects are found would depend on whether the experimenter is manipulating incentives within the zone of "insufficient justification" (low to moderate rewards) or within the zone of "oversufficient justification" (moderate to high rewards).

A second explanation, favored by the incentive theorists, is that for the most part incentive results are found; the occasional dissonance results are caused by negative emotions generated by the large monetary rewards used in some dissonance studies. According to Elms (1972), when people consider various alternatives, they are likely to "scan" the positive and negative features of each one. A counterattitudinal role player is encouraged to look only at the positive features associated with the counterattitudinal position; this behavior is called **biased scanning.** Large, unexpected monetary rewards offered for very little in return might generate emotions such as embarrassment, suspiciousness, and guilt, which impair the scanning process. According to this line of reasoning, if large incentives did not generate these disruptive, negative emotions, then dissonance predictions would not be supported. In studies by Janis and Gilmore (1965) and Elms and Janis (1965), subjects engaged in counterattitudinal role playing for large and small incentives. To generate negative emotions that would inhibit biased scanning, the experimenters told some subjects that the experiment was sponsored by a rather questionable group such as the Russian Embassy; other subjects were assured that the experiment was sponsored by a respectable, trustworthy source such as the U.S. Department of State. As expected, when the sponsor was trustworthy (thus calming negative feelings), greater incentives yielded more attitude change. Thus one possibility is that small incentives sometimes yield greater attitude change than large incentives because large incentives generate negative emotions.

What, then, are we left with? First of all, there is absolutely no question that counterattitudinal role playing is a potent attitude-change technique. Under some conditions the noncommonsensical dissonance-theory prediction of an inverse relationship between incentive magnitude and attitude change prevails. But under many other conditions, larger incentives for the discrepant act lead to greater attitude change in the direction of the counterattitude—exactly as incentive theory predicts. It is possible that dissonance is aroused and reduced by means of attitude change only under special circumstances, such as when the person feels that he or she chose to engage in the attitude-discrepant act and when there are undeniable consequences of such a choice. Another possibility is that, if rewards are manipulated in the low-to-moderate zone, dissonance effects are likely, but, if rewards are manipulated in the moderate-to-high zone, incentive effects are likely. Finally, there is the possibility that dissonance findings have nothing to do with dissonance but represent something else, such as negative emotions that interfere with the biased-scanning process. One thing does seem certain: there will not be a speedy resolution of this lively controversy.

Self-Perception Theory as an Alternative to Dissonance Theory

Daryl Bem (1967, 1972) has offered an alternative explanation of free-choice and forced-compliance results. According to his **self-perception theory,** people infer their own attitudes from a knowledge of their behavior and the conditions surrounding it. In the case of attitude change in a free-choice situation, the choice provides some *behavioral evidence* on which to base differential ratings of chosen and rejected alternatives. Thus the coed who was moving into an off-campus apartment would have new evidence (her behavior) that would allow her to conclude that the apartment was better than the dorm. The process is similar in the case of attitude change in the forced-compliance situation. After advocating a position at variance with their own initial position, the role players are confronted with new hard evidence (the attitude-discrepant behavior) suggesting that their true attitudes are not what they thought they were prior to the role-playing session. In effect, the role player would reason "This is what I said—this is what I must believe."

Furthermore, the smaller the incentive, the stronger the basis the role player has for concluding that the counterattitudinal position is the true position. As we saw in Chapter 3, if no gains or small gains follow behavior (in this case, the attitude-discrepant act), then that behavior is taken as reflecting the person's underlying attitudes and dispositions. Thus, if a person engages in an attitude-discrepant act for a small incentive, he or she would reason "I couldn't be saying this for the money. It must be what I really believe." On the other hand, when large gains follow behavior, then that behavior may reflect either the person's real attitudes or an attempt to secure the gains. Thus, if a person engages in an attitude-discrepant act for a large incentive, he or she might reason "I'm saying this for the money. It isn't what I really believe." Role playing for small incentives would thus provide a firmer basis for inferring one's own attitudes than would role playing for large incentives.

On the basis of observing your own behavior, then, you would make a judgment concerning your own attitudes in the same way that you would make a judgment about another person's attitudes on the basis of observing his or her behavior. According to self-perception theory, attitude change in free-choice and forced-compliance situations represents an "interpersonal judgment in which the observer and the observed happen to be the same individual" (Bem, 1967, p. 183).

To test self-perception theory, Bem has observers infer the attitudes of people who are engaging in counterattitudinal role playing or participating in other types of "dissonance" studies. If the observers correctly infer the participants' attitudes on the basis of observing the participants' behavior, then it is plausible that the participants might be using similar reasoning processes about themselves. Bem suggests that, if observers cannot correctly infer the participants' attitudes on the basis of observing the participants' behavior, then the participants must be responding to something private, such as cognitive dissonance. Thus Bem notes that, if "interpersonal simulations" of dissonance experiments produce findings that parallel dissonance results, doubt would be cast on the validity of dissonance theory.

To show that interpersonal simulations would produce dissonance results, Bem had subjects read partial descriptions of the Festinger and Carlsmith (1959) study in which subjects were paid different amounts for claiming that the experiment they had participated in was fun and exciting. He also gave them details of the Cohen (reported in Brehm & Cohen, 1962) experiment in which varying amounts were offered for writing in support of unwarranted police actions. Observers were then asked to indicate how they thought these original subjects really felt. As observers, they presumably did not experience dissonance. Yet they answered that the original subjects receiving small amounts of money for the attitude-discrepant act must have really felt that way, whereas the original subjects who received large amounts of money probably did not.

Quite a few interpersonal simulations have confirmed these findings, but there have also been studies that have failed to support the self-perception hypothesis (Bem, 1972). According to critics of self-perception theory (Mills, 1967; Jones, Linder, Kiesler, Zanna, & Brehm, 1968), one of the problems in such studies is that the observer is not aware that the act he or she is observing is discrepant with the original participant's initial position. Proponents of dissonance theory argue that, if the original participant's initial position were made clear to the observer, then the observer might not be so hasty to infer this person's attitudes on the basis of observing an attitude-discrepant act. In response, Bem and McConnell (1970) argue that participants in forced-compliance situations aren't able to remember their premanipulation attitudes after they have engaged in the attitude-discrepant act. Thus, although outside observers may not be aware of the cognitive inconsistency that, according to dissonance theory, plagues the counterattitudinal role player, the actual role players may not be aware of this inconsistency either!

At present, the battle between dissonance and self-perception theories centers around the effects of varying the salience of the subjects' initial attitudes—that is, their attitudes before they engage in the role playing. An attitude is made salient to the extent that a person is forced to clearly state it and to reflect upon it. According to self-perception theory, increasing the salience or extremity of the pre-role-playing attitude should weaken or eliminate attitude change following the role playing, because it would make the self-perception process difficult. For example, being sensitized to the fact that a few minutes earlier one stoutly maintained a viewpoint different from the one just recently expressed should make it difficult to infer that one "really believes" in the more recent position. (Recall from Chapter 3 that inconsistency makes dispositional inferences difficult.) According to dissonance theory, increasing the salience of the initial attitude should strengthen attitude change, because the more prominent the initial position, the more dissonant the role-played position. At least two recent studies have supported dissonance theory's prediction of a positive relationship between the salience of initial attitudes and attitude change in forced-compliance situations (Ross & Shulman, 1973; Green, 1974).

CONGRUITY THEORY

In our second consistency theory, **congruity theory,** there are three elements: P, S, and O. The first element, P, is the perceiving person or attitude holder who is trying to see the world as orderly and consistent. The other two elements, S and O, are both attitude objects. S is the source. The source is a person (such as the President), a group (such as the justices of the Supreme Court), or a thing (such as a newspaper) that will at some point express or imply a relationship to the third element, O. This third element may be a person, or it may be an impersonal entity such as a product or a law.

Congruity theory attempts to relate P's liking for both S and O, on the one hand, to the expressed or inferred relationship between S and O, on the other (Osgood & Tannenbaum, 1955). For example, if you (as P) like the *New York Times (S)* but are against a law legalizing marijuana *(O),* congruity theory would attempt to predict how you might reassess your attitudes toward both the *Times* and the law if the *Times* came out in favor of the law. The relationship between S and O is called a **bond** and may be a positive or **associative bond** (goes with, likes, favors, endorses, and so forth), as in the foregoing example. Alternately the bond between S and O may be a negative or **dissociative bond** (dislikes, leaves, blames, and so forth), which would be the case if the *Times* came out against, rather than for, the law legalizing marijuana. Consistency and stability in this theory are called **congruity;** instability and conditions for change are called **incongruity.**

The operation of congruity theory is best described in three steps and by presenting P's attitudes toward S and O as points on seven-point scales running from +3 (like very much) to −3 (dislike very much). At Step 1, S and O are unrelated and are independently evaluated by P. At Step 2, an associative or dissociative bond relates S and O in P's mind. At Step 3, P shows new attitudes toward both S and O. P's new attitudes toward both S and O are no longer independent; that is, P's attitude toward each is partly determined by his or her attitude toward the other. In the case of an associative bond, this drama unfolds in Figure 5–2.

We begin with S and O at different points on the scale. When an associative bond or relationship is formed between S and O, incongruity exists if they lie at *different* points on the scale. In the case of an associative bond, incongruity is reduced by reassessing S and O so that they end up at the same point on the scale.

Suppose it is a Presidential election year. Senator Phoghourne, whom P likes very much, has just received his party's nomination. Senator

Figure 5–2. An example of congruity theory. According to congruity theory, if P likes Senator Phoghourne (black man in white suit) but does not like Governor Twaddlebottom (white man in black suit), Phoghourne's choice of Twaddlebottom as a running mate will cause P to re-evaluate both Phoghourne and Twaddlebottom.

Phoghourne has not yet given any indication of his choice for a Vice-Presidential running mate. One possibility (unknown to *P*) is Governor Twaddlebottom, whom *P* does not particularly like. At this point Senator Phoghourne and Governor Twaddlebottom are unrelated in *P*'s mind (Step 1, Figure 5–2).

However, much to *P*'s disappointment, Senator Phoghourne selects Governor Twaddlebottom as his running mate (Step 2, Figure 5–2). According to the rule stated above, incongruity results. In this particular example, the incongruity is reduced by lowering the evaluation of Phoghourne and raising the evaluation of Twaddlebottom an equal amount (Step 3, Figure 5–2).

Although a downward re-evaluation of the more favored element and an upward re-evaluation of the less favored element are to be expected when an associative bond is formed, these variations do not always involve an equal amount of change in attitude toward each of the two elements. In the resolution of incongruity, the more polarized, or extreme, attitude does not change as much as the less polarized attitude. Thus, if Phoghourne were initially $+2$ and Twaddlebottom were more highly polarized at -3, an associative bond would result in more of a downward re-evaluation of *S* than an upward re-evaluation of *O*. Formulas for computing the meeting point may be found in Zajonc (1968b) and in Kiesler, Collins, and Miller (1969).

The effects of the formation of a dissociative bond are a bit more complex. A dissociative bond creates incongruity and forces for change when *S* and *O* are *not* equidistant in opposite directions from zero at the time the bond is formed. If, for example, Senator Phoghourne pointedly rejected Governor Twaddlebottom as a running mate, there would be no change given initial ratings of $+2$ and -2 (which are equidistant from zero). However, if ratings were $+3$ and -2, or if they were $+2$ and -1, $+1$ and -2, or -1 and $+3$, there would be incongruity, and its resolution would involve re-evaluating *S* and *O* so that they were equidistant in different directions from zero. Formulas for these computations also can be found in the above-cited sources.

Studies of incongruity theory have involved varying the initial position of *S* and *O* and the nature of the bond and then seeing if attitude change follows the prescribed formulas. In the course of this research, Osgood and Tannenbaum (1955) found a need for two correction factors for predicting attitude change. First, there is the **assertion constant.** Attitudes toward the source of the assertion, *S,* are expected to change less than the attitudes toward the object of the assertion, *O.* So, in the example above, the attitude toward Phoghourne should change slightly less (about .17 point, in case you like to know such details) than the attitude toward Twaddlebottom. Second, there is a **correction for incredulity.**

This factor deals with the problem that people do not necessarily believe the communication that associates S and O. The greater the incredulity, the less believable the assertion becomes, and incredulity tends to moderate the amount of attitude change.

BALANCE THEORY

The third and final member of the cognitive-consistency family that we will consider is **balance theory.** Originally formulated by Heider (1946, 1958), balance theory assumes a normal state and a tendency for conditions to return to this normal state after they have departed from it. The principle that conditions will return to a normal state is called **homeostasis.** The set of relationships that fulfill the conditions of a normal state are referred to as **balanced relationships,** whereas inconsistent relationships that depart from the normal state are referred to as **imbalanced relationships.** Balance theory suggests that the tendency to seek or create order among elements represents an ability that is provided as a gift of the organism's nervous system. The approach is highly phenomenological; that is, it deals with relationships as experienced by the attitude holder. Achieving balance, like reducing dissonance, may require a distortion of perceptions or a misjudgment of evidence.

The basic elements are people (P, O, Q) and objects or impersonal entities (X, Y, and Z). As in the case of congruity theory, relationships among elements are referred to as bonds, which may be either positive or negative. In balance theory a **positive bond** ($+$) refers to a state of association or connectedness (such as "Dasher is a member of Santa's reindeer team" or "The Seven Dwarfs kept Snow White") or to a state of liking ("Cinderella loves the good life"). A **negative bond** ($-$) refers to a state of dissociation or disavowal ("Rudolph was excluded from the reindeer team") or to a state of disliking ("Cinderella hates household drudgery").

In the case of two-element or **dyadic relationships,** balance exists if the bonds connecting the two are all positive or all negative. For example, the belief "Nelson and Jerry like each other" would be balanced, but the belief "Nelson has unrequited friendship for Jerry" would not be balanced, because in this second instance there is one positive and one negative bond. To resolve this imbalance and achieve consistency, the attitude holder can alter his or her perception of one of the bonds. Thus, consistency could be achieved by believing that Jerry secretly returns Nelson's affection (two positive bonds) or that Nelson actually hates Jerry (two negative bonds).

In the case of three-element or **triadic relationships,** a state of balance exists when all three of the bonds are positive or when two of the

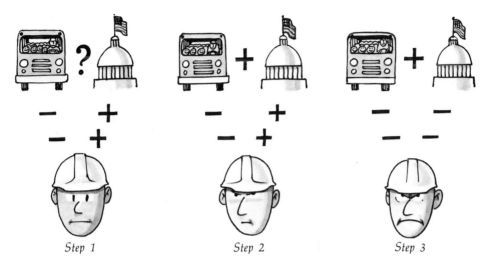

Figure 5-3. Balance theory. According to balance theory, if Bozo dislikes busing and likes the Supreme Court (Step 1), but the Supreme Court comes out in favor of busing, imbalance occurs (Step 2). To achieve balance, people might perceive Bozo as disliking the Supreme Court (Step 3). Other ways of achieving balance would be to see Bozo as favoring busing or to misperceive the Supreme Court's decision as actually being against busing.

bonds are negative and one is positive. If two of the bonds are positive and one is negative, or if all the bonds are negative, imbalance exists. An easy way to remember this is to algebraically multiply the signs of the three bonds. If they come out negative, as when $(-)(-)(-) = (-)$, then they are imbalanced. As with two elements, when there is imbalance, one of the bonds is likely to be misperceived in such a way as to restore a balanced state of affairs. As in the case of congruity theory, the operation of balance can be illustrated as a three-step process (Figure 5–3). Our elements are Bozo, busing, and the Supreme Court.

As perceivers, we know that Bozo likes $(+)$ the Supreme Court but is not very happy about $(-)$ busing (Step 1). When the Supreme Court renders a decision in favor of $(+)$ busing, we have imbalance (Step 2). To reduce this imbalance, we might perceive Bozo as disliking the Supreme Court (Step 3). As perceivers, then, we might replace the imbalanced, two-pluses-and-one-minus state of affairs with the balanced, one-plus-and-two-minuses state of affairs. However, there are two other ways in which we might achieve balance. One of these other possibilities for Step 3 would be to perceive Bozo as favoring busing, and the other possibility would be to misperceive the wordy Supreme Court ruling as actually being against busing. Thus, to achieve consistency in our perception of the Bozo/busing/Supreme Court triad, we may misperceive one of the bonds.

Thus far we have been adopting the perspective of someone outside the triad. However, the bonds in this example would also be important for Bozo, who can at once be a perceiver and an element in the triad. That is, Bozo should respond to the Supreme Court's decision by developing less favorable attitudes toward the Court, by developing more favorable attitudes toward busing, or by misperceiving the Supreme Court's decision. Thus Figure 5-3 could represent attitude change on Bozo's part, as well as an outsider's perception of the situation. Before reviewing the evidence supporting Heiderian balance theory, it would be useful to consider a closely related formulation.

The ABX System

An important version of balance theory that closely follows the version just described is the **ABX system** of Newcomb (1961, 1967), which also deals with triadic relationships. This theory differs from Heider's, however, in that at least two of the elements (A and B) must be people, whereas the third element, X, can be a person or an impersonal object. The relationship between A and B is one of attraction ($+$) or disliking ($-$). The bonds between each person and X are referred to as orientations, which are very similar to the ($+$) and ($-$) bonds discussed above.

The conditions for consistency (which Newcomb describes as *symmetry*) are exactly the same as the principles for balance discussed earlier. That is, if all bonds are positive, or if two bonds are negative, conditions are stable. What this means is that, if two people like each other, they will have similar attitudes toward X; if they dislike each other, they will have dissimilar attitudes toward X. Either attraction or attitudinal similarity can serve as the independent variable in this "social" version of balance theory.

There is, however, an important difference between Heider's and Newcomb's theorizing. Both a situation in which A and B liked each other but had different attitudes toward X and a situation in which A and B disliked each other but had similar attitudes toward X would be equally inconsistent. Yet, whereas Heider did not distinguish between these two cases, Newcomb (1967) suggests that the former situation is preferable to the latter. A negative feeling between the person doing the rating and the other person in the relationship is more aversive than imbalance. As we shall see, people may be willing to put up with a little inconsistency if it helps maintain cordial relations with someone else.

Experimental Tests of Balance and ABX

Balance theory and *ABX* have given rise to three general hypotheses. First, when people are given imbalanced or **unbalanced relationships** (relationships that are incomplete in that one of the bonds is not specified), they should "see" or "complete" the relationship in ways that produce the all-positive or two-negative-and-one-positive state of affairs. Second, if balanced relationships are more natural and harmonious than unbalanced relationships, they should be easier to memorize or learn. Third, for the most part, people should like or prefer balanced or symmetrical relationships to unbalanced or asymmetrical relationships.

The first and most direct hypothesis is that people will fill in missing bonds or misperceive existing bonds to achieve the all-positive or two-negative-and-one-positive state of affairs. Morissette (1958), in a test of a formalized version of balance theory offered by Cartwright and Harary (1956), presented subjects with some of the bonds in triadic relationships and had them "predict" the remainder of the bonds. They found that the relationships were completed in accordance with balance theory. Burdick and Burnes (1958) assessed a subject's liking for B and varied B's relationship to X. On the basis of knowing these two bonds, they were able to use balance principles to predict A's liking for X.

In accordance with the *ABX* system, Newcomb (1961) found that, after a group of strangers moved into a large house, those who had similar attitudes tended to develop liking for one another, whereas those who had dissimilar attitudes tended to dislike one another. Furthermore, the people who liked one another tended to develop similar attitudes, whereas the people who disliked one another tended to develop dissimilar attitudes. In the next chapter we will see that telling two people that they have similar attitudes leads to their liking each other.

In a study engagingly titled "My Enemy's Enemy Is My Friend," Aronson and Cope (1968) induced some subjects to like the experimenter by having the experimenter flatter them. Other subjects were induced to dislike the experimenter by having the experimenter treat them in a very insulting manner. Next the subjects overheard the experimenter's supervisor either praise or berate the experimenter. Subjects were then asked by another party to do the favor of making phone calls for the supervisor. Liking for the supervisor was inferred from the number of phone calls the subject was willing to make. As we would expect, when the subject liked the experimenter, he or she liked the supervisor best when the supervisor appeared to also like the experimenter. When the subject disliked the experimenter, he or she liked the supervisor best when the supervisor also disliked the experimenter.

The second major hypothesis derived from balance theory is that balanced or symmetrical relationships are easier to learn than their inconsistent counterparts. Support for this hypothesis has come from Zajonc and Burnstein (1965a, 1965b), who had subjects memorize all the bonds in triadic relationships and who kept track of the number of errors made before all bonds were learned. The relationships involved two hypothetical men, and the remaining elements were integration, birth control, and *Newsweek*. For the most part, balanced relationships were learned with fewer errors.

Yang and Yang (1973) hypothesized and confirmed that people who were already anxious would have a particularly difficult time learning nonbalanced relationships. Although a small degree of anxiety is beneficial for learning, a high degree of anxiety is detrimental. Yang and Yang's results suggest that the person's pre-existing or dispositional anxiety and the additional anxiety or discomfort generated by nonbalanced relationships can combine to have an adverse effect on learning. More recently, Cottrell (1975) found that people who used balance rules to memorize triads did better than did rote-memorizing controls, and Picek, Sherman, and Shiffrin (1975) found that, compared with nonbalanced relationships, balanced relationships were better recalled.

The third major hypothesis generated by balance theory is that people will prefer or like balanced relationships more than they like imbalanced or unbalanced states. In an early test of this hypothesis, Jordan (1953) presented subjects with hypothetical situations involving two people and an impersonal entity. Half of these situations were balanced, and the other half were not. On the whole, balanced relationships were rated more favorably. Physiological reactions to balanced and imbalanced relationships, measured by Burdick and Burnes (1958), reflected more favorable emotional responses to the balanced triads. "Preference" studies down through the years have been generally supportive of balance predictions, although effects have sometimes been minimal and may be outweighed by a host of other variables (Brickman & Horn, 1973; Crockett, 1974; Gutman, Knox, & Storm, 1974).

However, some of these "preference" studies have found support for Newcomb's hypothesis that balanced states will not necessarily be liked more than imbalanced states if balance depends on a negative bond between the perceiver and the other person. Representative is a study by Price, Harburg, and Newcomb (1966), who had each subject think of himself or herself as *P* in a triadic relationship with another person, *O*, and an impersonal entity. Balanced states were not more pleasant than imbalanced states when balance involved a negative bond between *P* and *O*. That is, subjects found that they preferred the state of two positives and one negative to ill will between themselves and the other person. Although this preference for imbalance has been found repeatedly when the subject is instructed to take the viewpoint of *P*, it has not often been found when the subject responds as an outside observer of hypothetical situations (Aderman, 1969).

STRENGTHS AND LIMITATIONS

Each consistency theory has unique strengths and weaknesses. Dissonance theory has generated many times the number of studies generated by all other consistency theories combined. Yet this same degree of interest has also aroused an abundance of criticisms (Aronson, 1968; Kiesler, Collins, & Miller, 1969; D. J. Bem, 1970, 1972; Elms, 1972). A major strength of Osgood and Tannenbaum's congruity theory is that it has the mathematical precision that balance theory sorely lacks, although, compared with balance theory, congruity theory applies only to a limited range of situations. But rather than make endless comparisons among individual consistency theories, let's consider three major criticisms that have been aimed at the whole cognitive-consistency family.

First, it has been suggested that most people most of the time remain unflinching in the face of dissonance/incongruity/imbalance (D. J. Bem, 1970). For example, Wrightsman (1969) found that people who took a strong law-and-order position were *less* likely than others to obey a law requiring them to purchase and display a vehicle-registration sticker, even though the cognitions "I am for law and order" and "I am breaking the law" are dissonant. One possible explanation is that people don't experience inconsistency all that often, because elements that seem related to an outside observer are kept isolated in "logic-tight" mental compartments. A judge, say, may never relate the belief that he or she is not prejudiced with a decision just rendered that further disadvantages already disadvantaged minorities. Another possibility is that attitude holders are aware of these inconsistencies but are not motivated to do anything about them. Indeed, some theorists have suggested that people find pleasurable a moderate amount of incongruity, disconfirmation of expectations, and other conditions that violate consistency principles (Berlyne, 1960, 1972).

The second major criticism is that consistency theories do not take individual differences into account. For example, although results of a study by I. Silverman (1971) generally supported consistency theory, about 20% of a group of people who were supporters of Senator Edward Kennedy did not respond to the "Chappaquiddick incident" (in which a female companion of the Senator's was drowned) either by lowering their opinion of the Senator or by trying to absolve him from all blame in the affair. Functional theories, which we will discuss next, have been more accommodating of individual differences.

Third, with the exception of congruity theory, consistency theories do not adequately specify what form inconsistency reduction will take. For example, consider again the case of Bozo, the Supreme Court, and busing. Following the Supreme Court's decision, Bozo could eliminate inconsistency by raising his opinion of busing, by lowering his opinion of the Supreme Court, or by misinterpreting the evidence. Furthermore, people may find ingenious ways of eliminating inconsistency that are not specified by the theories themselves (Brown, 1965). In laboratory experiments it is possible to take steps to close off various avenues of inconsistency reduction. In natural settings, however, there are likely to be several possibilities for inconsistency reduction and no good way of predicting which one will be chosen. Despite such difficulties, consistency theories have clearly been a dominant influence in social psychologists' attempts to understand attitude formation and change.

PART SUMMARY

The most popular topic in social psychology is the study of attitudes, which are learned emotional and intellectual responses to persons, things, and events. Many writers have suggested that there are three components to attitudes: an affective or emotional component, an intellectual or belief component, and an action or behavioral component. Although these three components often mesh to form a coherent package, there is sometimes a low correspondence between what people feel, believe, and intend to do and what they in fact end up doing. The correspondence between assessed attitudes and behavior is likely to be low because of the lack of specificity of the attitude measures, because of a moderating effect of unassessed attitudes, and because of the pattern of rewards and punishments in the situation.

Cognitive-consistency theories are the most conspicuous theories of attitude formation and change. After defining basic parts or elements, consistency theories specify both the relationships among the elements that are psychologically consistent and unlikely to change and the alternative relationships that are psychologically unstable, inconsistent, and likely to change. Change involves a redefining of elements or a juggling of relationships to impose consistency.

Dissonance theory is the most prominent member of the cognitive-consistency family. Dissonance theory begins with two or more cognitions, or items of information. Dissonance exists when one of the cognitions follows from or is implied by the opposite of the other. Dissonance is an aversive state that the individual tries to reduce by changing one cognition or by adding new consonant elements. Two central research themes have been dissonance reduction and attitude change in free-choice and in forced-compliance situations.

In a free-choice situation, the person chooses one of two or more alternatives. Following this choice, the perceived undesirable qualities of the chosen alternative and the perceived desirable qualities of the rejected alternative are dissonant. To reduce this dissonance, the person finds ways to increase the attractiveness of the chosen alternative and to decrease the attractiveness of the rejected alternative. This spreading apart of alternatives following a choice will be great to the extent that the alternatives are of equal value and that the alternatives have dissimilar rather than similar consequences.

In a forced-compliance situation, a person is coaxed into saying or doing something that conflicts with his or her private beliefs. To the extent that there are few or no external justifications for this attitude-discrepant act, there will be attitude change in the direction of the act. In support of this hypothesis, dissonance theorists cite experiments showing a negative relationship between the magnitude of the incentive for the attitude-discrepant act and subsequent attitude change. However, many other experiments have supported incentive theory's prediction of a positive relationship between incentive magnitude and attitude change. Dissonance theorists suggest that dissonance effects in forced-compliance situations require that the person feel that he or she chose to engage in the attitude-discrepant act and that this choice led to some significant consequences. Incentive theorists counter that dissonance effects result when large incentives interfere in the biased-scanning process. Still another possibility has been suggested by Bem, who argues that both free-choice and forced-compliance results can be understood as a self-perception or self-attribution process.

A second major consistency theory is congruity theory. The elements in this theory are a perceiver, P, a source, S, and a third entity, O. According to congruity theory, P's attitude toward S and O will depend on S and O's relationship to each other. If S and O are elevated differently, an association between S and O will cause a lowered evaluation of the initially more favored member of the pair and a higher evaluation of the initially less favored member of the pair. If, on the other hand, S disavows or rejects O, there will be, under some conditions, a higher evaluation of the initially more favored element and a lowered evaluation of the initially less favored element. Precise formulas allow one to predict the meeting point in the former case and the resultant degree of discrepancy in the latter case.

The third major consistency theory is balance theory, which assumes a normal state and a tendency for conditions to return to this normal state if they depart from it. The focus is usually on three-element, or triadic, relationships. The elements are connected by positive or negative bonds. Balance exists when all bonds are positive or when one bond is positive and two bonds are negative. Balance studies suggest: (1) that, when people are presented with imbalanced or unbalanced relationships, they tend to "see" them or complete them in a balanced fashion; (2) that balanced relationships are easier to learn and memorize than imbalanced relationships; and (3) that in most cases people prefer or like balanced relationships more than they like imbalanced or unbalanced relationships. An exception to this last generalization is that a person may not prefer balance when it depends on an unfriendly relationship between himself or herself and someone else.

Consistency theories are among the most influential theories in social psychology. Although one can make many critical comparisons among the different theories, three important criticisms are applicable to the class. First, people seem able to withstand considerable amounts of dissonance/incongruity/imbalance. Second, consistency theories seem to do a poor job of taking individual differences into account. Third, consistency theories do not always specify what form inconsistency reduction will take. Despite these difficulties, however, consistency theories have been very popular in the field of social psychology.

FUNCTIONAL THEORIES

Functional theories of attitudes suggest that people form and maintain attitudes that satisfy their ulterior needs and motives. A simple but intuitively compelling example of such an attitude is provided by the resident of Death Row who vociferously maintains that the death penalty should remain abolished. Although, as Kiesler, Collins, and Miller (1969) note, this approach to attitudes invites an unending list of needs or motives, functional theories attempt to explain a diversity of attitudes by referring to a highly limited number of motives or goals.

Three functional theories have been advanced. The two theories developed by Katz (1960) and by Smith, Bruner, and White (1956) are quite similar, so our discussion here will follow the more developed theory of Katz. Then we will turn to a somewhat different functional theory proposed by Kelman (1958, 1961).

KATZ' FOUR FUNCTIONS

Katz (1960) posits four uses or functions of attitudes: the *adjustive function*, the *ego-defensive function*, the *value-expressive function*, and the *knowl-*

edge function. Each of a person's attitudes can serve one or more of these functions.

Adjustive Attitudes

An attitude serving the **adjustive function** helps to maximize rewards and minimize punishments. Thus we have favorable attitudes toward attitude objects associated with direct rewards and satisfactions and unfavorable attitudes toward attitude objects that are associated with frustrations and punishments. Adjustive attitudes may represent emotional associations that were classically conditioned during past experience with the object, or they may represent perceived means for obtaining desired ends. A favorable attitude toward beverages that were earlier associated with comfort and well-being and an unfavorable evaluation of beverages that produced nausea and vomiting would reflect the classical-conditioning process. Hostility toward legislation that would place restrictions on one's business (for example, strict price controls) and strong enthusiasm for legislation that would prevent or lift such restrictions would reflect the instrumental or utilitarian basis for adjustive attitudes.

Changes in adjustive attitudes are based on varying patterns of rewards and punishments. For example, when down and out, a person may clamor for larger welfare checks (for the satisfaction of more to eat); after having struck it rich, the same person may argue that welfare rolls and payments should be heavily pared (for the satisfaction of lower taxes). Studies showing changes in expressed attitudes as a function of social approval thus yield results consistent with the idea of adjustive attitudes (Chapters 4 and 9).

Ego-Defensive Attitudes

Ego defenses are unconscious processes that serve to protect the person from unwanted perceptions or impulses by blocking them from awareness or by distorting them so that they take a less threatening or offensive form. Attitudes serving the **ego-defensive function** thus protect people from unpleasant truths about themselves or about the harsh realities of the real world. Thus a person may form an attitude because it helps to explain away personal inadequacies ("I lost, but it's a stupid game!"), to impart a sense of security ("It's just a lot of talk—the Commies have no real military capacity!"), or to substitute pleasant conditions for unpleasant conditions ("Heck, we'll whip those North Vietnamese in two weeks flat!").

The ego-defensive function would seem to provide a basis for many prejudicial attitudes. A person may gain a sense of superiority by finding fault with members of other groups. Since such attitudes are based more on the psychological functioning of the attitude holder than on the characteristics of the attitude object, efforts on the latter's part to change the former's attitudes should have little or no impact. Thus, to counter Glenda's allegation that Jews would rather run bars and nightclubs than go into respectable businesses, Golda might go into banking. Glenda's response might be that Jews think of nothing but money and are always trying to buy their way into Christian society.

Changing ego-defensive attitudes would seem to require techniques that give people insight into their own psychodynamics. After ascertaining his subjects' level of defensiveness, McClintock (1958) examined the effects of different appeals on prejudice. The informational appeal attempted to reduce prejudice by stating some facts. The interpretational appeal involved presentation of a case study, complete with an analysis emphasizing the sinister unconscious processes that lead to prejudice. Although the effectiveness of the informational appeal was not affected by the person's level of defensiveness, the interpretational appeal produced more attitude change in subjects of moderate defensiveness than in subjects of low or high defensiveness. Subjects low in defensiveness did not base their prejudices on ego defenses, so the interpretational approach was not tailored to their motives. The finding that people high in defensiveness were not affected by the interpretational approach seems inconsistent with functional theory, but perhaps they were so defensive that they simply could not be reached on the basis of McClintock's procedures.

Value-Expressive Attitudes

Whereas attitudes serving the ego-defensive function may conceal the person's true nature, attitudes serving the **value-expressive function** serve to reveal one's deepest values and to proclaim to the world what kind of person one considers oneself to be. Thus, value-expressive attitudes offer two kinds of satisfactions. First, there are satisfactions in revealing **values,** which are defined as judgments of attractiveness, desirability, and worth that are based on abstract concepts (beauty) and broad classifications (Communists). Second, there are satisfactions in "proclaiming to the world" one's true nature. Such proclamations have the positive feature of leading to a sharper self-concept and a stronger sense of identity.

Value-expressive attitudes can be changed by convincing people that their present attitudes somehow fail to reflect their underlying values or are somehow inconsistent with their self-concepts. Thus, some advertising campaigns have urged 50-year-old men to display their hidden identities as hairy-chested devils by giving up their stodgy family sedans for cramped cocktail lounges on wheels that are misrepresented as rugged sportscars. Other campaigns have encouraged women to express both their femininity and their liberated status by smoking special skinny cigarettes. After all, paying more money for less tobacco would not seem to serve the adjustive function.

"Knowledge" Attitudes

People seek to make sense out of their world, and attitudes serving the **knowledge function** assist with this effort. This does not necessarily mean that people are avid knowledge seekers in the same sense as a philosopher or a social psychologist, or that they are always careful about what source of knowledge they choose. But they do want to understand the events that impinge on their lives, so they may explain various social woes by forming the attitude that the Communists (Fascists, Jews, Catholics, hippies, vegetarians, Episcopalians) are taking over the country. Changing knowledge-based attitudes would require re-education and strong informational appeals.

KELMAN'S PROCESSES OF ATTITUDE CHANGE

A second functional theory has been offered by Kelman (1958, 1961). This approach is classified as functional because, for the most part, it also points to extrinsic satisfactions as determinants of attitude formation and change. Furthermore, as in the case of the preceding theory, this theory suggests that a given attitude can be acquired in different ways and that knowledge of why an attitude is held is useful for understanding the conditions under which that attitude is likely to change. According to Kelman, attitudes may be based on *compliance, identification,* or *internalization.* Each type of attitude is formed in a different way and is likely to be altered by different types of influence. Kelman's approach focuses on the various types of influence attempts or processes that induce attitude change.

Compliance

A **compliance-based attitude** is one that has been adopted in order to secure favorable reactions from other people. Thus an employee may curry favor by voicing views remarkably similar to those of the boss when the boss is present, and the adolescent may favor the clothing styles and mannerisms of other adolescents to gain acceptance from his or her peers. Such attitudes will change immediately if the person moves to a new situation with a new set of demands; although they are publicly expressed, compliance-based attitudes are not privately accepted. The process for changing this type of attitude is to change the **social effect** of the attitude—that is, the pattern of rewards and punishments. For example, an adolescent who professes to like blue jeans and sweatshirts may suddenly come to prefer old clothes from the funky '50s if other adolescents begin to show scorn for blue jeans and sweatshirts but admiration and praise for pleated trousers, skinny-collared dress shirts, bow ties, and green sweaters with white reindeer designs. Studies showing the effects of approval and disapproval on expressed opinions (Chapters 4 and 9) are consistent with the concept of compliance-based attitudes.

Identification

Identification-based attitudes are adopted to establish or maintain an intrinsically satisfying relationship with another person or group. This satisfying relationship may be based on identification (as discussed in Chapter 4), or it may be based on reciprocal roles (that is, two interlocking roles), with the attitude holder in one of the two intermeshing positions. As an example of the former, a little girl may adopt her mother's political views because she wants to be "like" Mother. In the latter case, a little boy may adopt his father's positive attitude toward athletics because it can lead to a more satisfying father-son relationship (attending games together, having mutual interests for discussion, and so forth).

Identification-based attitudes are both publicly expressed and privately maintained. However, such attitudes are not intrinsically satisfying; they are based on conscious or unconscious hopes of establishing and maintaining a satisfying interpersonal relationship. The process of changing this kind of attitude requires changing the **social anchorage** of the attitude—that is, inducing the other person to change his or her attitudes with the expectation that the attitude holder will follow suit.

Internalization

An **internalization-based attitude** is motivated by a feeling of satisfaction stemming from ideas and acts that are compatible or congruent with one's underlying value system. According to Kelman, an attitude that is congruent with an underlying set of values produces *intrinsic* satisfactions. Attitudes at the internalization level are reflected in both public expression and private acceptance. Change would require manipulating value congruence—that is, convincing people that their attitudes are incongruent with their underlying values. Internalization-based attitudes are considered the most difficult to change.

At this point we might pause to compare Katz' four functions with Kelman's three bases. There are some similarities, and there are also some differences. First, there is a similarity between adjustive attitudes and compliance-based attitudes, in that each type can be changed by altering the pattern of rewards and punishments. However, whereas Katz takes a broad view of what constitutes rewards and punishments (including conditioned feelings of satisfaction and dissatisfaction), Kelman emphasizes rewards and punishments in the form of social approval and disapproval. Katz' ego-defensive attitudes and knowledge attitudes do not have parallels in Kelman's theory, and Kelman's ideas about identification are not paralleled in Katz' theory. Both value-expressive and internalization-based attitudes provide intrinsic satisfaction for the attitude holder. For the most part, however, Katz and Kelman agree that attitudes are often maintained not because they are intrinsically satisfying but because they satisfy certain ulterior motives.

An Experimental Investigation

As indicated earlier, Kelman suggests that any attitude could rest on any of the three bases, and the process of attitude change will be different with each base. To change an attitude based on compliance, the influence attempt would have to involve changing the social effect of the attitude; to change an attitude based on identification, the influence attempt would have to involve changing the social anchorage of the attitude; and to change an internalization-based attitude, the influence attempt would have to alter value congruence. An experimental test of all the facets of this theory would be very difficult, but one has been undertaken by Kelman (1958).

The experiment took place prior to the 1954 Supreme Court decision on desegregation. Subjects were black college students attending black colleges. Before the experiment, these subjects expressed the opinion that all colleges, white and black, should be desegregated. Kelman presented these subjects with appeals arguing the alternative view that, if the Supreme Court decision was for desegregation, a number of private colleges should remain all-black to perpetuate black culture and tradition.

There were three different tape-recorded appeals—each geared for different types of attitudes. To affect compliance-based attitudes, the communicator was presented as the president of an independent foundation who would not hesitate to withdraw funds from the subjects' college if they happened to disagree with him. Subjects who maintained favorable attitudes toward desegregation because such attitudes were associated with rewards would be expected to change their views when it was made clear that their prodesegregation stance could result in the loss of financial support. To affect identification-based attitudes, the communicator was presented as the kind of person the students would want to be like: a highly attractive black student spokesman. In the third appeal, aimed at internalization-based attitudes, the communicator's arguments for segregation were supposedly based on the embodiment of Afro-American values as derived from careful research and "the evidence of history."

Afterward, questionnaires were administered in such a way that they would tap the effects of the different appeals on compliance-, identification-, and internalization-based attitudes. Although a bit uneven, results tended to support the general hypothesis that each appeal would affect attitudes at the associated level but not at other levels. For example, some subjects were told that their questionnaires were to be shown to the communicator. The compliance-oriented appeal affected responses under these conditions, whereas the other appeals did not. Moreover, if the communicator, when shown the questionnaire, could not identify the subjects and hence could not punish them by withdrawing funds from their school, then the compliance-oriented appeal had no effect. Similarly, the identification-based appeal had its most pronounced effects on attitudes under conditions designed to maximize the subjects' identification with the attractive student spokesman. Thus the results suggest that there may be different motivational bases for attitudes, each one of which requires different procedures for inducing attitude change.

STRENGTHS AND LIMITATIONS

Functional theories offer a number of attractions. First, they address a long-suspected relationship among attitudes, personality, and motives. Individual differences are therefore accorded importance, rather than neglected. Second, by highlighting that the same attitude may result from different underlying motives, these theories avoid oversimplification. Third, they offer some clear statements concerning the conditions under which attitudes will change. Finally, they are consistent with studies of social reinforcement and attitude change.

Functional theories would appear to have one outstanding weakness: they have generated very little new research and thus have received very little in the way of direct confirmation. (You may have noticed that, although the discussion of consistency theories was crammed with studies and results, the discussion of functional theories was an almost uninterrupted narrative.) Why should this be? One possible explanation is that no one likes the ideas. This reason seems unlikely, since for the past 15 years these ideas have been given generous space in discussions of attitudes. If the ideas had been rejected, functional theories would have receded into history a decade ago.

A more likely possibility (brought to my attention during an informal conversation with a functional theorist) is that, although social psychologists like the functional theorists' ideas, they have been too timid to rise to the extraordinary challenge of testing them experimentally. Compared with testing consistency theories, testing functional theories is a very difficult task. For example, a dissonance study can be made very complicated, but the backbone usually remains one of a small number of well-proven manipulations—such as having the subjects engage in counterattitudinal role playing. Functional theories do not have the very practical advantage of being accompanied by a set of well-known, basic experimental procedures. At present there are no pat techniques for determining the functions an attitude serves, and there are no pat procedures for inducing attitude change once these functions have been discovered. The lack of research is certainly a liability. But perhaps functional theories retain a role of importance in discussions of attitudes because it is hoped that someone will accept the challenge and that this liability will eventually be overcome.

PART SUMMARY

Functional approaches suggest that people form and maintain attitudes because they satisfy extrinsic motives. Katz has identified four such functions. First, attitudes serving the adjustive function serve to maximize satisfactions and minimize dissatisfactions. Changing these attitudes requires varying the associated pattern of rewards and punishments. Second, attitudes serving the ego-defensive function protect the person from unpleasant truths and harsh realities. Changing these attitudes requires giving the person insight into his or her own personality. Third, attitudes serving the value-expressive function serve to proclaim central values or to express one's identity. Change in this case requires convincing people that their present attitudes are inconsistent with their values or with their real, inner self. Finally, attitudes serving the knowledge function help the person make sense out of the world. Changing this type of attitude would require an informational appeal.

Kelman's functional approach focuses on the conditions under which one person will accept influence from another. Compliance-based attitudes are based on favorable reactions from another person; changing them requires changing their social effects. Identification-based attitudes are based on establishing or maintaining intrinsically satisfying relations with another person; changing these attitudes requires varying social anchorage. Internalization-based attitudes are intrinsically satisfying because they are compatible with underlying values. Change in this case requires the manipulation of value congruence.

On the positive side, functional theories accommodate personality variables, help us avoid oversimplification by pointing out that the same attitude may have different bases or underlying motives, clearly specify the conditions for attitude change, and are consistent with what we have already learned about social approval and verbal conditioning. On the minus side of the ledger, they have generated very little research, possibly because experimental tests of functional theories are difficult to perform.

PERSUASIVE COMMUNICATIONS

Would you react differently to a *New York Times* editorial than to a *Daily Worker* or *National Lampoon* editorial? How would an advertisement for a new toothpaste have to be worded to get you to buy? Would your reaction to an appeal to donate funds differ if the appeal came through a personal phone call rather than through a mass mailing? Let's now broaden our perspective and consider attitude change as a possible result of one person's making an appeal to another to change his or her views. In addressing the highly practical issue of how one person gets another to change his or her attitude, we go beyond the attitude holder to consider characteristics of the person who is making the appeal, the content of the appeal, and the way the appeal is made.

The material in this section is not organized within specific theoretical frameworks, as in the preceding sections of the chapter. Instead, it is organized around empirical research—an approach to attitudes urged and built upon by Carl Hovland and his associates at Yale University (Kiesler, Collins, & Miller, 1969). Rather than designating a kind of theory, the **communications approach** thus designates research based on the theme question "Who says what to whom, how, and with what effect?"

The discussion to follow centers around three independent variables: (1) the characteristics of the **source,** or person who makes the appeal; (2) the characteristics of the presentation, or method of the appeal; and (3) the characteristics of the content, or material contained in the appeal. But we will not lose sight of the characteristics of the attitude holder, who might now be better thought of as an audience for the attitude-change appeal.

SOURCE CHARACTERISTICS

Studies of source characteristics examine the effects of the qualities or attributes of the person making the appeal on the audience's attitude change following the appeal. Two important variables of the source are credibility and attractiveness.

Credibility

Credibility refers to the "believability" of the source. This variable in turn rests on two other factors: (1) the *perceived expertise* of the source, or the extent to which the source is seen as bright and knowledgeable, and (2) the *perceived trustworthiness* of the source, or the extent to which the source is seen as making a fair and unbiased presentation. Of course, the hypothesis has been that more credible sources are more persuasive, and for the most part this simple, straightforward hypothesis has been substantiated. We will consider expertise and trustworthiness individually.

Studies that have varied expertise have repeatedly found that persuasivness increases with the perceived competence and knowledge of the source. For example, Crisci and Kassinove (1973) have found that, following a recommendation to buy a book, mothers were more likely to comply if the communicator was presented as "Doctor" rather than as "Mister." The simple explanation for this kind of finding is that, as rational information processers in search of truth, we try to match experts' opinions (which tend to be reasoned and based on fact) while mismatching the opinions of the village idiot. However, an alternative analysis has been offered by Jellison (1974), who has shown that, when a source is presented as competent and knowledgeable, people lose confidence in their own abilities. He suggests that this loss of confidence in the presence of an expert makes the person vulnerable to the expert's arguments. Consistent with this interpretation is the finding that, up to a point, increasing the expressed self-confidence of the source increases the persuasiveness of the appeal. Presumably, a high degree of self-confidence on the part of the source leads to self-doubt on the part of the audience. However, a very high degree of self-confidence and the appearance of being "cocky" may anger or alienate the audience and make it resistant to change (London, McSeveney, & Tropper, 1971).

At least two conditions limit the effects of variations in the source's expertise. First, if the audience considers itself familiar with the issue and views itself as expert, the competence of the source becomes inconsequential (Insko & Schopler, 1972). Second, no matter how "expert" the source, a patently ridiculous assertion is likely to be rejected out of hand. This result has been shown in a study by Bochner and Insko (1966). In this experiment, "Sir John Eccles, a Nobel-Prize-winning physiologist" or "Mr. Harry J. Olson, director of the Fort Worth Y.M.C.A." argued in favor of reduced sleep each night. The amount of sleep advocated varied from eight hours down to no hours. As the amount of sleep advocated declined from eight hours to four hours, the appeals of both sources were about equally effective. When only three or two hours of sleep were advocated, subjects were more influenced by Sir John than by Harry. However, when *no* sleep was advocated, subjects were relatively uninfluenced by either source. Thus, to the extent that the source undermines its credibility by virtue of its appeal, variations in expertise will not yield variations in persuasiveness.

Studies that have varied the perceived trustworthiness or "objectivity" of the source have also been guided by an intuitively compelling hypothesis—specifically, that a source who seems to be speaking frankly and without ulterior motives should be more persuasive than a source who stands to profit through a biased, manipulative presentation. Tests of this hypothesis have involved raising or lowering the audience's suspicions.

As we saw in our discussion of attribution theory (Chapter 4), if a speaker makes a statement that is self-damaging, it is likely to be interpreted as truthful and sincere. Thus a fairly reliable procedure for reducing the audience's suspicions is to have the source take a stand that seems harmful to his or her self-interests. In one study an imprisoned criminal was found to be more persuasive when he argued that the courts should have more power rather than less, but a prosecutor was more persuasive when he argued that the courts should have less power rather than more (Walster, Aronson, & Abrahams, 1966). In another study it was found that an antiwar statement had more impact when it was attributed to a U.S. Army general than when it was presented without an author; moreover, when the antiwar statement was attributed to the general, it had more impact than a prowar statement attributed to the same source (Koeske & Crano, 1968).

Other techniques for altering the audience's suspicions have not met with as much success. To lower subjects' suspicions and encourage attitude change, Walster and Festinger (1962) had subjects "eavesdrop," or overhear the source make the appeal. The hypothesis was that, if the audience believed that the source was unaware of its presence, the audience would also believe that the source was being honest and candid, since there would be no reason for the source to lie. According to this hypothesis, you should, for example, be more likely to believe the President if you overheard him talking to his wife in the White House pantry than if you heard him addressing you and other fellow Americans on national TV. Although some support was gained for this "eavesdropping hypothesis," not all subsequent studies have yielded confirming results (McGuire, 1969).

Commonly noted in discussions of credibility is the sleeper effect, first noted by Hovland, Lumsdaine, and Sheffield (1949). The **sleeper effect** is a delayed rather than immediate attitude change following a persuasive communication. That is, if the audience's attitudes are assessed shortly after hearing an appeal from a low-credibility source, the appeal will seem to have had little effect. If the attitudes are measured days or weeks later, attitude change will supposedly appear. One explanation of the "sleeper effect" is that, after some time has passed, the attitude holder remembers hearing the arguments in favor of the new position but does not remember that they came from a low-credibility source. However, Gillig and Greenwald (1974) were unable to obtain a reliable sleeper effect in seven separate studies involving more than 600 subjects. Noting inadequacies in earlier data that were presented as supporting the concept, they suggest that the sleeper effect be "laid to rest."

Likability

On the basis of commercials, we would never infer that crime bosses prefer luxury car X, alcoholics prefer wine Y, or morticians wear only creep-proof underwear Z. The basis for a source's attractiveness varies somewhat—good appearance, professional status, popularity as an athlete or entertainer—but, to my knowledge, no sponsor has ever deliberately had people with *dislikable* qualities sing their product's praises.

In general, the more attractive the source, the more persuasive the appeal (Keasey & Keasey, 1971; Darley & Cooper, 1972). Attitude theories very nicely accommodate this commonsense finding. Balance theories suggest that, given a liked source, balance requires sharing the same attitudes as the source; given a disliked source, attitudes should be dissimilar to those of the source. Although most advertisers seem to follow the procedure of having a liked source embrace their product, a few have had a disliked source criticize or disavow the product. For example, burglars might complain that an alarm device makes their job difficult, or bugs and germs may shriek against various sprays and cleansers. Functional theories also offer an easy accounting of this principle. For example, forming and maintaining an attitude at the identification level would depend on the valence or attractiveness of the person with whom the attitude holder is identifying.

However, under certain limited conditions an unattractive source may be more persuasive than an attractive source. According to dissonance theory, if a person voluntarily chooses to listen to a source arguing a position with which the person disagrees, an attractive source would provide external justification for listening, and no attitude change would result. If, on the other hand, the person chooses to listen to an unattractive source, there will be no external justification for listening. To reduce the resulting dissonance in the latter case, the person must decide that the message itself is worthwhile, and there would thus be attitude change in the direction advocated by the source. Recent experimental support for this hypothesis has come from Cooper, Darley, and Henderson (1974), who found that deviant-appearing sources induced more attitude change in listeners than did more liked, conventional-appearing sources.

From this general line of theorizing it also follows that, if you "sample" a product you are sure you won't like, there should result greater liking for the product if you were coaxed into the act by someone who is unattractive rather than by someone who is attractive. Sources of varying degrees of attractiveness urged Army reservists to eat fried Japanese grasshoppers in an experiment by Smith (1961). In one condition, the source acted in a "friendly, warm, permissive manner," smiled considerably, told the reservists to take it easy and enjoy themselves, and so forth. In another condition, the source acted in a "formal, cool, official manner," did not smile, told the reservists they could not smoke, and gave sharp answers to questions.

The friendly source was far more effective at inducing subjects to eat the grasshoppers. But, once the act was performed, reservists coaxed by the friendly source showed little improvement of attitudes toward the delicacy when compared with subjects who had eaten the grasshoppers for the unfriendly source. The latter reservists could not justify eating the grasshoppers by saying "I did it for him; he's a nice guy." They had to reduce their dissonance by saying "Grasshoppers? Mm-mmm, good!" However, it should be emphasized that unattractive sources get better results than attractive sources *only* in the special case in which dissonance is aroused. For example, we would not expect an unattractive person to be more persuasive if people left the room as soon as he or she began to speak, or if he or she failed to get people to try a "free sample" of the disliked product.

PRESENTATION CHARACTERISTICS

Presentation characteristics refer to the method of making an appeal and the conditions under which the appeal is made. **Presentation variables** include (1) media, (2) order of presentation of the arguments, (3) forewarning—that is, whether or not the audience is warned that the source will attempt to change its attitudes, and (4) the presence of distractions at the time the appeal is made.

Media

Media refers to the agencies or means of presentation. In general, it would appear that in-person, face-to-face appeals are more persuasive than filmed, televised, or recorded appeals and that written appeals are often just so much wasted paper (McGuire, 1969). For example, Lamm (1967) had subjects in one room participate in an attitude-change discussion while subjects in other rooms either observed and listened or simply listened. Discussants showed the most shift from their original position, observers showed the second most attitudinal shift, and listeners showed the least attitude change.

There are many reasons for the superiority of in-person appeals, particularly those made on a person-to-person basis. The audience is more likely to pay attention to the local canvasser at the door than to the televised national politician and more likely to be concerned about the expectations and reactions of the in-person source. The in-person source, in turn, can better gear the appeal to the audience (changing the line of argument if he or she notes boredom or other adverse reactions) and has a better chance of manipulating approval and disapproval. Finally, an in-person source has all channels of communication open. In addition to communicating through the meaning captured by the actual words, he or she can communicate through postures, gestures, and tenor of voice. The availability of these nonverbal channels can immensely facilitate the communication process (Chapter 8).

Order of Presentation

After ascertaining initial attitudes, Lund (1925) had students read written communications arguing one side of an issue; he then measured the resulting attitude change. The students were then given communications arguing the other side of the issue, and their attitudes were again assessed. The first communication produced more attitude change. A **primacy effect** refers to the finding that information presented early in a sequence has more impact than information presented late in the sequence.

Subsequent research has been about equally likely to find a **recency effect**—that is, that the information presented late in the sequence has more persuasive impact than the information presented early. Commenting on the discrepancy between Lund's findings and contradictory findings by Hovland and Mandell (1957), Elms (1972) suggests that in this particular instance, by issuing conflicting counterarguments, Lund produced a drop in his own credibility. Because of differences in procedure, Hovland and Mandell were less likely to be perceived by the audience as up to some form of trick.

Other resolutions of the inconsistency between primacy and recency findings have pointed to attentional and learning factors. Jones and Goethals (1972) suggest that, as a result of diminishing attention, information presented first will have an advantage. If special steps are taken to ensure undiminished attention on the audience's part, then the most recently presented material will have the advantage.

N. Miller and Campbell (1959) have offered an alternative explanation based on well-documented learning phenomena. According to their analysis, the first side of an argument is learned better and interferes with the learning of the second side. This interference is called **proactive inhibition.** If proactive inhibition is overcome and the second side is learned, that side tends to be remembered better than the first side. Again drawing on findings from the area of verbal learning, it follows that, when the second side comes immediately after the first, proactive inhibition is great and a primacy effect will predominate. When a reasonable time interval separates the two presentations, proactive inhibition is minimal and a recency effect will prevail. Thus, if you find yourself going second in a debate, remember that you are going to have to work a little harder to maintain the audience's attention; also, if possible, give the audience a break or intermission before you begin.

Forewarning Effects

Forewarning means telling the audience that an attempt will be made to induce it to change its attitudes. There are at least two reasons why we might expect forewarning to make an audience resistant to a persuasive appeal. First, forewarning may raise the audience's suspicions, with the result that the audience dismisses the source's arguments ("He's only saying that to get me to go along with him"). Second, as we shall see in Chapter 8, people don't like to be manipulated, and being warned that the source is intending to manipulate them may produce a reverse or "boomerang" effect. However, there are also reasons why we might expect forewarning to increase the audience's receptivity to a persuasive appeal. For example, forewarning might make it clear what the source has in mind, and, to receive approval from the communicator, the audience may decide to "go along" with the source. Or perhaps if people feel that they voluntarily chose to listen to the source, consonance would require that their attitudes change in the direction advocated by the source. In accordance with all these conflicting ideas, experimental studies have found that forewarning sometimes stiffens the audience's resistance and sometimes leads to greater attitude change in the direction advocated by the source (Cooper & Jones, 1970; Dean, Austin, & Watts, 1971; Heller, Pallak, & Picek, 1973; S. W. Hollander, 1974).

A promising reconciliation of these findings can be found in the self-esteem theory developed by Cooper and Jones (1970) and by S. W. Hollander (1974). According to this resolution, if people expect to receive a persuasive communication, they can avoid the possibility of looking gullible to others if they change their attitudes in the direction of the appeal *before* the appeal is made. To preserve self-esteem in this way, the audience must have information concerning the speaker's topic and the direction of the speaker's arguments. Studies that have made topic and direction clear have generally found that forewarning enhances attitude change (S. W. Hollander, 1974). An audience that is merely told that an attempt will be made to induce attitude change does not have sufficient information to protect its self-esteem through precommunication attitude change. When forewarnings are not explicit in terms of topic and direction, they will encourage a stiffening of the audience's resistance or even a "boomerang" effect.

Distraction and Persuasion

According to the **distraction hypothesis,** an audience that is distracted at the time the attitude-change appeal is made will show more attitude change than will an undistracted audience. In a recent review of tests of this hypothesis, R. S. Baron, Baron, and Miller (1973) cited 19 confirmations and 7 disconfirmations of this effect.

Several interpretations have been offered to account for the finding that distraction increases persuasion. Dabbs and Janis' (1965) "affect" explanation suggests that a pleasant activity (such as drinking Pepsi and eating peanuts) puts the person into a good mood, with the result that he or she is agreeable and easily persuaded. However, this affect interpretation would not seem to account for all the findings, since it has also been found that neutral or unpleasant distractions can also facilitate attitude change.

The effects of neutral and negative distractions might be understood in terms of the "counterargument-disruption" hypothesis and the "effort" hypothesis. The counterargument-disruption hypothesis (Festinger & Maccoby, 1964) suggests that, when people listen to a speaker, they are likely to think of counterarguments, and distraction serves to disrupt this process. According to the effort hypothesis (Zimbardo, 1965), distraction makes it effortful to attend to the communication. The increased effort imposed by a distraction creates dissonance, which is reduced by attitude change in the direction of the source's position. Like the "affect" hypothesis, these two concepts seem to have some merit, but neither can account for all the results (R. S. Baron et al., 1973). For example, dissonance theory does not easily account for "affect" results. Furthermore, there remain lurking in the background a few findings that show a negative relationship between distraction and persuasion.

A promising resolution to this controversy suggests that distraction affects two variables: *receiving* the message and *yielding to* the message (Regan & Cheng, 1973). If the message is difficult to understand but persuasive when understood, distraction makes it difficult to follow the line of arguments, with the result that much of the message's impact is lost. If, however, the message is easy to understand but not particularly convincing when understood, then distraction affects yielding, with the result that persuasive impact is increased. In other words, distraction will hinder reception but facilitate yielding. Thus, when the message is simple, distraction assists attitude change; when the message is complex, distraction impairs attitude change.

CONTENT CHARACTERISTICS

Content variables are perhaps the most obvious ones. Yet they are the most difficult to discuss, not only because there are so many of them but also because they are so closely tied in with characteristics of the audience that, for the most part, no simple rule of thumb can be offered. There is more than a little truth to the old adage "Know thy audience." Here we will consider two content variables: (1) the effects of ignoring as compared with acknowledging opposing points of view and (2) the effects of basing an appeal on fear.

One- and Two-Sided Presentations

In a **one-sided presentation,** the source does not acknowledge or discuss opposition views and arguments. In a **two-sided presentation,** the source acknowledges and discusses opposing views, although not necessarily in a fair and impartial manner. Ignoring the opposition's point of view seems to increase persuasive impact when the audience is already in agreement or when the audience is not particularly bright. Discussing both sides of the issue or refuting the opposition's arguments increases impact if the audience is initially opposed to the source's position or is intelligent. As Elms (1972) notes, audiences in disagreement have most likely already heard the opposing arguments, and smart audiences are likely to think them up themselves. In both cases, some discussion of the opposition's viewpoint would seem to be required. Furthermore, a two-sided presentation may prevent the audience from going along with the opposition when it is exposed to the opposition's arguments in the future.

According to **inoculation theory** (McGuire, 1969), acknowledging counterarguments will stiffen the audience's resistance to those counterarguments if they are encountered in the future. Inoculation theory draws a parallel between resistance to disease and resistance to persuasion. When a person is inoculated against a disease, the injected serum gives him or her the disease in a very weak form. The body then manufactures counteracting antibodies that provide a later defense against the illness in strong form. According to McGuire, when one is making an appeal, some mild arguments against one's own position will cause the listeners to generate what might be thought of as "cognitive antibodies." These antibodies make the person resistant to subsequent strong arguments from people favoring the opposing points of view. In general, the experimental evidence has shown that people's attitudes are less likely to cave in in the face of strong counterarguments if they have earlier been exposed to mild versions of these same counterarguments (McGuire, 1969).

Fear

Attitude-change campaigns are often aimed at getting people to give up an activity that they find pleasurable (smoking, drinking, drug use, promiscuity) or to engage in an activity that they find bothersome or down-right unpleasant (use seatbelts, see a physician, remove oily rags from the basement). The most obvious arguments in such cases center around the negative consequences of failure to comply. However, attempting to ram home the fear of cancer (or alcoholism, or venereal disease, or impalement on a steering column) is tricky business, since fear can impair as well as facilitate the attitude-change process.

Although fear can motivate attitude change, there are at least three ways in which fear can diminish the impact of a persuasive communication (Janis, 1967, 1971; Elms, 1972). First, whereas a slight amount of anxiety facilitates learning, massive amounts of anxiety impair learning. High-fear appeals may be so generally upsetting that it becomes difficult to learn the recommended preventive measures. Second, the extreme unpleasantness of frightening material may undermine persuasiveness by making the source seem unattractive. Third, according to the **defensive-avoidance hypothesis,** extremely threatening material may cause the audience to avoid or reject the message because it is too painful to con-template (Janis & Terwilliger, 1962; Janis, 1967, 1971).

A large number of studies have attempted to relate fear and attitude change, and there have been many seemingly conflicting findings (Higbee, 1969). However, some order can be imposed on this chaos if we consider that different amounts of fear may have very different effects (Janis, 1967,

1971; Elms, 1972). Under conditions of *very low fear*, people may remain indifferent and inattentive to the message; thus there would be no motivation for attitude change. Under conditions of *moderate fear*, people may be motivated to attend to the message and to follow precautionary recommendations, such as brushing their teeth more regularly or using seatbelts. Under conditions of *very high fear*, people may begin to defensively avoid the attitude-change communication. Thus it is widely accepted that we can make sense out of fear and attitude-change results if we posit a curvilinear, inverted-*U* relationship between fear and attitude change, with maximum attitude change being likely under conditions of intermediate fear.

In one study (Krisher, Darley, & Darley, 1973) three different degrees of fear were aroused. Subjects were adults who were susceptible to mumps. In one condition, mumps were described to subjects in a matter-of-fact way. Although possible complications involving the brain and the testes were mentioned, the message focused on the fact that contracting the mumps would result in a loss of valuable time. In this condition only a low level of fear was aroused. In a second condition the message emphasized the dangerous and painful aspects of contracting mumps in adulthood, and subjects were shown slides depicting gory operations. In this condition a moderate amount of fear was aroused. In the third condition, which aroused the highest degree of fear, subjects were given the same message as in the second condition; however, their fear was intensified by a machine that supposedly showed that their heart was pounding furiously as they listened to the message. (In Chapter 3 we saw that people may infer that they are afraid by listening to changes in what they believe to be their heartbeat rate.) Next, subjects were told that they could get a vaccination against the mumps and were asked if they intended to do so. Subjects in all conditions indicated an intent to be vaccinated. Yet only 20% of the low-fear subjects and 30% of the high-fear subjects reported for the inoculation, whereas 70% of the intermediate-fear subjects followed through with this precaution.

The optimal amount of fear to build into a message—that is, the amount that produces the strongest motivation without triggering defensive reactions—is very difficult to pinpoint. It depends partly on the audience's anxiety level before the message is presented. For example, Niles (1964) found that, whereas subjects who were initially high in anxiety were more influenced by a relatively low-fear appeal, subjects initially low in anxiety were more influenced by a relatively high-fear appeal. In effect, as the amount of fear in the message is increased, already anxious subjects may begin to defensively avoid the message sooner than will nonanxious subjects. Furthermore, to the extent that a person is already aware of some of the arguments, he or she is likely to have adapted to some of their frightening qualities and can therefore take stronger fear appeals before beginning to defensively avoid the meaning of the message. Thus the "optimal" amount of fear should be greater for people who are already somewhat familiar with the issues.

It would also appear that amount of fear interacts with the specific recommendations in the appeal to determine whether the recommendation will be accepted. Generally, if the recommendation is for some sort of long-term behavior change, such as giving up smoking or using seatbelts, moderate fear provides better results than high fear or low fear. However, if the recommendation is for an immediate action, such as signing a pledge or getting an X ray or inoculation on the spot, high fear may be more effective than low fear or moderate fear (Leventhal & Niles, 1964; Leventhal, Singer, & Jones, 1965). Perhaps specific instructions about what to do here and now allow one to cope realistically with the situation and preclude the operation of ego defenses that provide as "protection" only a wishful distortion of reality.

PART SUMMARY

The communications approach to attitude formation and change addresses the question "Who says what to whom, how, and with what effect?" Three important factors are characteristics of the source, or the person who makes the appeal, characteristics of the manner in which the appeal is made, and characteristics of the content of the appeal.

Important source characteristics include credibility and likability. Credibility, or believability, refers to expertise and trustworthiness. In general, expert sources are more persuasive than inexpert sources, but this effect will be limited by the expertise of the audience and by the plausibility of the arguments. Trustworthy sources are more persuasive than nontrustworthy sources. Liked sources usually induce more attitude change than disliked sources. However, if choosing to listen to an attitude-discrepant message induces dissonance, a disliked communicator can induce more attitude change than a liked communicator.

Presentation characteristics refer to the method of making an appeal and the conditions under which the appeal is made. Studies of presentation variables reveal four major findings. First, face-to-face appeals have more impact than recorded or written appeals. Second, studies of the order of presentation of opposing sides show that, if the audience's attention can be maintained, or if the two presentations are separated in time, the second side will have greater impact; otherwise the first side will have greater impact. Third, forewarning an audience that an attempt will be made to change its attitudes is likely to increase attitude change if the speaker's topic and position are made clear. If, however, forewarning is not so explicit, it may make the audience resistant to the appeal. Finally, distracting the audience adversely affects the reception of a message, but encourages yielding. As a result, distraction is likely to add to the persuasive impact of a simple but faulty message and to detract from the persuasive impact of a complex message.

Two important content characteristics of persuasive communications are one- and two-sided presentations and fear. Acknowledging and discussing opposing points of view would appear to be a good strategy if the audience is intelligent or has already heard the opposition's arguments. According to inoculation theory, a two-sided argument may also provide a useful form of insurance if the audience is likely to hear opposing arguments in the future. Moderate fear generally results in greater attitude change than does low or high fear. The optimal amount of fear to build into a message depends on the audience's pre-existing anxiety level and on the audience's familiarity with the issue.

6
Attraction
to Others

AFFILIATION

MOTIVES FOR AFFILIATION

Others as a Source of Assistance
Others as a Source of Stimulation
Others as a Source of Information
Others as a Yardstick for Self-Evaluation

FEAR AND AFFILIATION

The Reduction of Individual Risk
The Reduction of Fear
Social Comparison and the Reduction of Uncertainty
Affiliation, Fear, and Anxiety

AFFILIATION AND FREEDOM FROM INNER RESTRAINTS

Anonymity and Deindividuation
Diffusion of Responsibility and Deindividuation
Modeling and Deindividuation

PART SUMMARY

LIKING

PROPINQUITY AND LIKING

RECIPROCITY OF LIKING

SIMILARITY AS A BASIS FOR LIKING

Perceived Similarity as a Cause of Liking
Belief Incongruence: Dissimilarity and Disliking
Interpretations of the Similarity-Liking Relationship
Similarity and Liking: Some Limiting Conditions

DIFFERENCES AS A BASIS FOR ATTRACTION

The Completion Principle
The Complementarity Hypothesis
The Duplication Theorem

PART SUMMARY

LOVE

THE LOVE SCALE

A THEORY OF PASSIONATE LOVE

THE CHOICE OF A ROMANTIC PARTNER
Physical Attractiveness
Playing Hard to Get
Dating and Mating as a Marketplace Phenomenon

SOCIAL INFLUENCE AND LOVE
Parental Influence
Peer-Group Influences
The Influence of Formally Organized Groups
Endogamy and Exogamy

PART SUMMARY

In the late 1880s, General Georges Boulanger was one of the most respected and admired persons in all of France. Furthermore, he had high aspirations: to revise the French constitution and to take over as dictator. After his party scored a major but not decisive victory in the elections of 1889, crowds surged into the streets of Paris and demanded that their hero march to the presidential palace and take over the reins of government. As it so happened, he was dining near the palace. His lieutenants urged him to lose no time, for his hour had struck. However, General Boulanger wanted to go elsewhere—home to the arms of his lover, Madame de Bonnemains. When he returned to his headquarters some hours later, his disheartened aides informed him that the crowds had gone home and that it was too late. At the most crucial moment of his life, General Boulanger chose being with his lover over staging a coup d'etat. He never got another chance to become dictator. General Boulanger and Madame de Bonnemains were forced to flee to Belgium, where she soon died of tuberculosis. Two months after that, he committed suicide on her grave (Shirer, 1971).

In this chapter we will consider the conditions that make one person a compelling source of attraction for another. Research and theory in this area of interpersonal attraction have addressed three general problems, which we'll touch upon in turn. First, we will consider affiliation, the most general process of seeking out and associating with others. Second, we will consider liking and will attempt to understand why some people are more attractive than others. Finally, we will consider romantic love, which has emerged only recently as a topic for scientific inquiry.

AFFILIATION

Affiliation refers to associating with others independent of such considerations as special liking or loving for them. Among the reasons why people affiliate are: to satisfy situationally induced needs, to cope with stressful circumstances, and, in some cases, to gain freedom from inner restraints and engage in impulsive, antisocial activities.

MOTIVES FOR AFFILIATION

Certain kinds of situations give rise to personal needs that in turn motivate affiliative behavior. When there are certain kinds of work to be done, when people are understimulated, and when people feel that they have important gaps in their knowledge or feel uncertain about themselves, they are likely to seek out others. Thus, needs for *assistance, stimulation, information,* and *self-appraisal* may propel us into association with one another.

Others as a Source of Assistance

Within many species, organisms can achieve in concert what they cannot accomplish alone. For example, the salp—which looks much like a 60-foot-long parachute floating in the ocean—is actually a gigantic colony of millions of sea squirts arranged radially around a long central cavity. Their mouths are on the outside and their discharge ports on the inside; gulping and squirting water, the whole colony moves through the water by jet propulsion. Hingston (1932) has provided a graphic description of how groups of ants attack an insect many times their size and simply stretch its limbs until it expires. He also reports seeing ants link together to form a living bridge over which other ants may travel. Concerted activities within monkey bands, baboon troops, and other primate groupings have been noted repeatedly (Scott, 1969; Elms, 1972).

The available evidence suggests that "people" discovered very early in the course of evolution that some tasks that were impossible for the individual could often be accomplished through coordinated efforts (Howell, 1965). *Paranthropus* males (1,750,000 B.C.) divided the work on a hunt and banded together to do battle with their brighter relative *Australo-*

pithecus. A major element of sociological theorizing is that societies are based on the **division of labor**—that is, the assignment of different tasks to different people. One way or another, the butcher and the baker must get together in order to make a sandwich. By creating conditions of mutual dependency, the division of labor imparts a feeling of solidarity and belonging (Durkheim, 1902).

Thus, much affiliative behavior can be traced to the simple discovery that other people are useful or necessary for getting something done. As we shall see in Chapter 10, "assistance from others" is not always beneficial, and sometimes people can accomplish more or perform better when working by themselves. However, for the most part, the fact that there is a mastodon to barbecue, a crop to harvest, or a piano to move provides ample justification for getting together.

Others as a Source of Stimulation

In contrast to traditional discussions of motivation, which stress quiescence or freedom from tension as a sought-after end state, contemporary discussions point out that organisms are often motivated to seek increased levels of stimulation (Berlyne, 1960, 1966, 1971; Sales, 1971; Sales, Guydosh, & Iacono, 1974). Animals will depress bars, open latches, and engage in problem solving to view complex and unusual stimuli. Humans often show preferences for spelunking, mountain climbing, parachuting, competitive sports, and other activities that require strenuous effort and involve some risk of personal injury. The stimulation involved would appear to be intrinsically satisfying.

Prolonged periods of low levels of stimulation have been shown to be aversive and to have debilitating effects (Heron, 1957). In **sensory-deprivation** experiments, stimulation is reduced by having subjects wear heavy gloves and slippers, ear plugs, and translucent goggles that admit only diffuse, unpatterned light. Under such conditions subjects show irritability, confusion, and a decline in test performance (Zubek, 1969). In the absence of external stimulation the mind may turn inward, sometimes with terrifying results. Sensory deprivation can result in bizarre visual hallucinations (Heron, Doan, & Scott, 1956), and, although a month or so in "the hole" may not produce any devastating effects, continuing solitary confinement can lead to psychotic breakdowns (Martin, 1954).

Other people provide rich and varied stimulation. Thus, when a person feels understimulated, he or she may seek out others for company. Because of sheer boredom, we may go out on dates with people we don't really like, attend social festivities that we have ridiculed in advance, or join a club whose interests we do not really share. The same general principle may hold for nonhumans.

People differ in their needs for stimulation, and Sales (1971) has related such individual differences to extent of involvement in social activity. In one of Sales' studies, subjects were assembled into groups and asked to discuss what would happen if everyone were born with an extra thumb on each hand. Compared with men with a low need for stimulation, men with a high need showed greater involvement in the discussion. For females, this correlation was not significant—most likely because of norms prescribing that women play a passive role in this kind of social situation.

In another study, Sales found that subjects of both sexes who had a high need for stimulation attended more closely to a complex dialog. Additional research revealed that, compared with subjects with a low need for stimulation, subjects with a high need for stimulation showed a greater preference for complex as compared with simple tartans and were more likely to try to find stimulating things to do (poking through the contents of purses and pockets, pacing around, and so forth) when instructed to wait in a room alone. These last findings are important because they suggest that the greater attention to social stimuli on the part of the high-need subjects reflects a general need for stimulation rather than a specific need for social stimulation. In line with other theorizing suggesting that there is an optimal level of arousal (Berlyne, 1960, 1966, 1971), Sales goes on to propose that, although underaroused people will seek stimulating social activities, people who are already excited may prefer normally boring conditions.

Others as a Source of Information

Cognitive clarity refers to an understanding of what has happened and what is likely to occur next (Schachter, 1959). People feel uncomfortable when there are gaps in their knowledge, and gossip, rumor, and a comparison of notes and impressions provide a way to gain relevant information when the situation is unclear. Thus the search for cognitive clarity may motivate people to affiliate with others. In a simple experimental demonstration of this principle, Schachter and Burdick (1955) had the principal of a girls' school enter a classroom, point to a girl who was an accomplice, and say without explanation "Miss K., get your hat, coat, and books, and come with me. You will be gone for the rest of the day." The observers spent the remainder of the day discussing the situation in an attempt to make some sense of it.

Others as a Yardstick for Self-Evaluation

According to Festinger's (1954) **social-comparison theory,** people have a need to evaluate their opinions and abilities. Often evaluation is accomplished through reference to the physical world. For example, the opinion that the flavor of watermelon is enhanced by salt can be tested by salting and tasting a watermelon. However, in many cases a physical referent such as a salted watermelon is not available. When there are no such nonsocial means of evaluation, people will evaluate their opinions and abilities by comparing them with those of others.

In choosing someone as a standard for self-evaluation, the person is likely to seek out someone who is similar to him- or herself, since an individual whose abilities or opinions are very divergent from one's own would not allow an accurate comparison. For example, a college sophomore who is trying to evaluate his or her own intelligence is unlikely to learn much from a comparison with inmates of an institution for the mentally retarded or with this year's Nobel Prize Winners. We tend to employ social comparison when we are *uncertain* about ourselves.

Social-comparison theory has been extended by Schachter to encompass emotions. According to him:

> In a novel, emotion producing situation, unless the situation is completely clear cut, the feelings one experiences or "should" experience may require some degree of social interaction and comparison to appropriately label and identify a feeling. We are suggesting, of course, that the emotions are highly susceptible to social influence and that, as has been suggested for opinions, a need for social evaluation of the emotions may be active [1959, p. 26].

Thus, people who are in a state of arousal and have no ready explanation for that arousal will compare themselves with others in an attempt to define their feelings or emotions. Also following Festinger, Schachter suggests that people will seek for comparison purposes people whom they perceive as experiencing a similar state. Schacter hypothesized and found that people affiliate under conditions of emotional uncertainty and that they generally choose to affiliate with people who are in a similar emotional state (Schachter, 1959, 1964).

Recent experimental support for Schachter's hypothesis has been provided by Mills and Mintz (1972). In their experiment, subjects were given caffeine. Some of the subjects were correctly informed that they had been given the stimulant, whereas others were falsely told that they had been given an analgesic (pain killer) that would not have an arousing effect. Subjects who had been given the caffeine but could not explain the resulting arousal (since they thought they had taken the analgesic) were more likely to choose to affiliate with other participants in the experiment than were either caffeine subjects or control subjects who had been given a nonarousing placebo. As we shall see, further support for the hypothesis that emotional uncertainty prompts affiliation has been obtained in a number of other experiments.

FEAR AND AFFILIATION

Have you ever read a really *good* ghost story about a group of people who remain together for a night in a haunted house? Although a few such stories exist, a far more common theme is the victimization of isolated individuals, such as the city slicker whose car breaks down in the country during a thunderstorm or the too-inquisitive stranger who can't resist forcing his way into a long-deserted chamber. Writers seem to sense that terror multiplies when the person confronted with frightening circumstances is all alone.

It has repeatedly been found that the presence of companions reduces both the magnitude and the frequency of reactions to aversive or stressful conditions (Epley, 1974). There are at least three general reasons why people under stress might seek to be with others. First, being with others can *reduce the actual danger* inherent in the situation. Second, being with others may result in a *direct reduction of fear*. Third, threatening or frightening circumstances may generate *emotional uncertainty*, which in turn prompts affiliative behavior.

The Reduction of Individual Risk

To some extent there is truth in the old adage "There's safety in numbers." For one thing, people who band together can eliminate or reduce objective hazards by establishing an active defense. Thus early Westerners gathered at a fort or some central location when an attack was imminent, police officers patrol "hot" areas in pairs, and we are encouraged not to swim alone in troubled waters. Furthermore, if the source of concern has only a limited capacity or desire to inflict harm or injury, affiliation can be helpful to the individual in that it lowers the likelihood that any one person will be victimized. The more speeders who simultaneously rush by a lone patrol car, the less likely any individual speeder is to get a ticket. In this connection it might be noted that mountain lions, sharks, and other predators often victimize the weakest member of the flock, school, gaggle, or herd. Elimination of the stragglers can sometimes increase the survival chances of the group. That is, the weak and deformed are eliminated from the gene pool, and they no longer compete for scarce resources, such as food in winter (Lorenz, 1966).

Like most old adages, "safety in numbers" also has some important limitations. First, the "predator" may be able to handle two or more potential victims as a group but not be able to handle each of them as individuals. Thus two pranksters caught red-handed are wise to run in opposite directions. Second, although banding together may increase defensive capacity, it can also increase attractiveness as a target. In military operations, individual stragglers may be ignored in favor of massed targets and pockets of resistance.

The Reduction of Fear

Results of studies of animals and humans alike suggest that, under threatening conditions, affiliation can lead to a reduction of fear, although it is not clear that simple companionship is sufficient to account for this reduction (Epley, 1974). On the basis of learning theory, we would expect a learned association between the presence of others and a feeling of well-being. After all, other people comfort us when we are children and are experiencing distress.

To begin with the animal studies, an early experiment by Rasmussen (1939) found that thirsty rats anticipating shock at a fountain would keep drinking longer when in the presence of another rat than when in isolation. This result suggests less fearfulness in the group situation. Davitz and Mason (1955) reported that rats were less likely to be immobilized by fear if a companion was present, and Morrison and Hill (1967) found that a companion had a calming effect on a rat even if the rat had been raised in isolation. In an experiment by Latané and Glass (1968), rats confronted with threatening circumstances were less likely to freeze or defecate (both symptoms of fear) when in the presence of another active rat than when in the presence of a semisocial stimulus (an anesthetized rat) or a nonsocial stimulus (a toy car). Although the anesthetized rat had some calming effect, the greater calming effect of the unanesthetized rat suggested to the researchers that interaction and mutual responsiveness are necessary for maximal fear reduction to occur. Thus it would appear that, with reasonable reliability, the presence of a companion can have a calming effect on a rat under stress.

Evidence suggesting that members of the same species, or **conspecifics,** have a fear-reducing effect for humans comes from two types of studies. In the first type, subjects are threatened and placed with others, and then measures of fear are obtained. In the second type, subjects are threatened and then given the option of waiting alone or waiting with others for the threatened events to transpire. The former type of study can provide direct evidence that affiliation lessens fear; the latter or "preference" type of study, however, can provide at best indirect or circumstantial evidence. Because it cannot be assumed that a preference for being with others indicates that actually being with others reduces fear, preference studies are open to alternative interpretations in terms of social-comparison theory. For this reason the preference studies will be set temporarily aside pending a reconsideration of social-comparison theory in the next section.

One of the first studies to investigate whether affiliation leads to a reduction in reported fear was conducted by Wrightsman (1960). Subjects were shown a tray of syringes, needles, cotton swabs, and so forth and were told that they would be given painful shots that would have a number of noxious side effects. After reporting their level of fear, they either remained alone, were told to wait in the presence of three other people with whom they were not allowed to talk, or were told to wait in the presence of three other people with whom they could talk. Fear was then reassessed.

In analyzing his results, Wrightsman separated subjects into two groups: firstborns and later-borns. Earlier findings (Schachter, 1959) had suggested that firstborn children might be more comforted by the presence of others than would second- and later-borns. The explanation advanced for these findings was that firstborns are likely to receive more attention from their parents than are later-borns, with the result that they would form a stronger conditioned association between the presence of others and the alleviation of unpleasant circumstances. Results showed that affiliation led to a reduction of reported fear, whether or not talking was permitted. However, this effect occurred only in the case of firstborns.

Although MacDonald (1970) did not find that affiliation reduces fear, at least two studies have generally supported the idea that a companion can comfort a human who is fearful. First, in a study that involved *only* firstborns, Amoroso and Walters (1969) found that subjects who were allowed to affiliate after being threatened with shocks reported less fear and showed fewer physiological indicators of fear than did controls. Second, Buck and Parke (1972) threatened both firstborns and later-borns with shocks and found that both groups were calmed by the presence of a companion. However, there was some evidence in Buck and Parke's data that the firstborns were more comforted than the later-borns. On the whole, then, it would seem that a threatened person who is in the presence of others shows less fear than a person who is in isolation, and at least some evidence suggests that this comforting effect is greatest for firstborn people.

How can we account for the findings that conspecifics can have calming effects for both animals and humans under stress? There are at least three nonexclusive possible explanations: (1) companions can *interfere with the performance of the fear response;* (2) companions can be *fearless models* that encourage courageous performances; (3) through the process of classical conditioning, companions may *elicit conditioned responses of contentment and well-being.*

First, conspecifics can serve as a source of distraction, which interferes with the performance of the fear response. Through a process of elimination, Morrison and Hill (1967) concluded that the calming effect companions had on rats that had been raised in isolation probably stemmed from the companion's distracting properties, since "learned reassurance" of one form or another would not seem to explain this particular result. In his recent review of the literature, Epley (1974) also highlighted the possibility that the companion may have an interfering effect. Epley notes, for example, that calming effects are most likely when the subject and the companion are allowed unrestricted interaction. Inconsistent with the "distraction" or "interference" interpretation are other findings showing that nontalking companions (whom we would expect to be less distracting than talking companions) can be as comforting as companions who are allowed to talk (Schachter, 1959; Wrightsman, 1960).

Second, there may be modeling effects, with the result that the timid take heart from the bold. Some of the Morrison and Hill (1967) results support this interpretation, as do the earlier findings of Davitz and Mason (1955), who reported that rats taught to fear a flickering light were more calmed by fearless than by fearful companions. In the Buck and Parke study, it was found that people who were affiliated with a calm and sympathetic companion reported less fear than did people who were affiliated with a less calm model. Several other studies involving humans also suggest a positive relationship between the companion's courage and fear reduction (Epley, 1974).

The third possibility is that conspecifics are reassuring because they have been associated with rewards and gratifications in the past. One is, after all, at some point fed and cared for by conspecifics (for example, one's parents), and many of the early rewards and gratifications are experienced in the presence of a family or other group of conspecifics. As a result of classical conditioning, conspecifics should elicit feelings of contentment and well-being, particularly in the case of firstborns. According to this interpretation, if the presence of a conspecific has been associated with pain or with unhappy circumstances, there will be no calming effect. For example, we would not expect a child to be comforted by the presence of a wicked step-parent who is given to beating the child mercilessly.

Thus there is reasonable evidence that the presence of a companion reduces fear. Affiliation under stress might therefore be motivated by an attempt to reduce fear. However, still another explanation of affiliation under unpleasant conditions exists. Many of the "preference" studies, which give threatened subjects the choice of waiting alone or waiting in the presence of others, support a social-comparison interpretation of affiliation under stress.

Social Comparison and the Reduction of Uncertainty

In one experiment, Schachter (1959) assigned women to one of two conditions, which we shall here designate as low fear or high fear. The procedures used for varying fear were comparable to those used by Darley (1966) in the fear and conformity study discussed in Chapter 2. Women in both conditions were told that they would receive electric shocks. Women in the low-fear condition were told that the experiment would be enjoyable and that the shocks would resemble a "tickle" or "tingle." Women in the high-fear condition were told that the shocks would be intense and very painful, although there would be no "permanent damage." Each woman was then told that there would be a short delay before "Dr. Zilstein" arrived and the experiment could begin. She was then offered the choice of remaining by herself or waiting with "some of the other girls here." In the low-fear condition, only 33% of the subjects chose to wait with others, but in the high-fear condition, 63% chose to affiliate. In the latter condition the correlation between reported fear and desire to affiliate was .88.

Schachter favored a social-comparison interpretation of the findings. He suggested that the threat manipulation generated emotional uncertainty, which each subject sought to reduce by comparing herself with other women. Affiliation under stress, then, may reflect an attempt to identify and evaluate one's feelings. Consistent with this interpretation are the results of other experiments reported in Schachter's monograph. In one experiment all subjects were threatened with strong shocks. Next, some subjects were offered the choice of waiting alone or waiting with another, similarly threatened, subject. Other subjects had to choose between waiting alone or waiting with someone who had not been threatened with intense shocks. Results indicated that "misery loves company— but only miserable company." Whereas 60% of the subjects grabbed the opportunity to wait with other fearful subjects, none of the subjects given the opportunity to wait with nonfearful subjects chose to affiliate. This result is consistent with social-comparison theory's hypothesis that people are motivated to compare themselves with similar others, since this choice allows the most accurate self-appraisal. In another study, Schachter found that, when subjects threatened with strong shocks were told that they could wait with another person but could not talk about the experiment with him or her, they still chose to affiliate. This finding suggests that affiliation was not prompted by a desire to start a conversation for purposes of distraction or by an attempt to achieve cognitive clarity. Enforced silence did not preclude the social-comparison process, because we need not talk to compare our emotions to the emotions of others.

The relationship among fear, emotional uncertainty, and affiliation has also been examined by Rabbie (1963), who told a group of four subjects either that everyone present would receive a strong shock or that only one of the four would receive a strong shock (the unlucky designate was not specified). Fear was at least as great in the four-in-four as in the one-in-four condition, but greater affiliation was found in the uncertain, one-in-four condition. Gerard and Rabbie (1961) found that, when subjects were given information about others' reactions to the threatening circumstances (that is, provided with a basis for comparison that did not require affiliation), affiliation was reduced. In a similar vein, Teichman (1973) has argued that a clear and structured threat situation that generates little uncertainty is less likely to result in affiliation than is a less-structured, vague, and ambiguous situation.

Affiliation, Fear, and Anxiety

Under some kinds of stressful conditions, people prefer isolation over affiliation. To explain this effect, it is necesssary to make a distinction between fear-arousing circumstances and anxiety-arousing circumstances. **Fear,** say Sarnoff and Zimbardo (1961, p. 357), "is aroused whenever persons are confronted by an external object or event that is inherently dangerous and likely to produce pain. . . ." **Anxiety,** on the other hand, is a feeling of vague apprehension and dread that is aroused by certain objectively innocuous conditions. These particular conditions have discomforting properties because they trigger unconscious, childhood-based fears, insecurities, and needs. Because people know that their unsettled reactions to seemingly harmless conditions are inappropriate, they are "loath to communicate their anxieties to others" and hence prefer to endure them alone.

Sarnoff and Zimbardo (1961) created fear in one group of subjects by using the now-familiar shock manipulation; they created anxiety in another group by leading the subjects to anticipate engaging in infantile oral activities while the experimenters ostensibly measured physiological reactions to oral stimulation. In the low-anxiety condition, subjects were told that they would play for a brief time with whistles, kazoos, and a pipe and would blow up a balloon. In the high-anxiety condition, subjects were told that they would spend a great deal of time sucking on baby bottles, oversized rubber nipples, pacifiers, and lollipops. Both fearful and anxious subjects were then given the choice of waiting alone or waiting with another person. As expected, fear and affiliation were positively related, but anxiety and affiliation were negatively related. These findings have been confirmed by Buck and Parke (1972) and by Firestone, Kaplan, and Russell (1973), who also found that anxious subjects who did choose to affiliate preferred to do so with nonanxious, dissimilar others. Anxiety results would thus seem to be a "mirror image" of fear results.

Taken together, the fear and anxiety studies suggest that a person facing stressful circumstances may be caught between conflicting motives. On the one hand, there may be a desire to affiliate to reduce emotional uncertainty. On the other hand, there may be a desire to avoid others to protect oneself against a loss of esteem from them. The risk of embarrassment would thus appear to limit the drive for social comparison.

In sum, it is well documented that under conditions of stress people are motivated to affiliate with others. Affiliation under stress promotes an active defense and minimizes individual risk. It can also bring about a direct reduction of fear as a result of response interference, modeling, or classical conditioning. Affiliation under stress may also result in the reduction of uncertainty through the social-comparison process. However, certain factors such as the risk of embarrassment can limit the stress-affiliation relationship.

AFFILIATION AND FREEDOM FROM INNER RESTRAINTS

Being with others usually seems to have a restraining effect on what we do. In public we often feel that we must be on our "best behavior," censoring our speech and hiding strong emotions. Yet it would appear that, under certain conditions, affiliation with others can reduce inner restraints, facilitate the expression of intense emotions, and prompt anti-social activities. Some affiliative behavior, then, may be motivated by a desire for freedom from inner restraints.

Affiliation with others will be disinhibiting under conditions of **deindividuation,** which is defined as a "state of affairs within a group such that the individual member is not seen or paid attention to as an individual" (Festinger, Pepitone, & Newcomb, 1952). In a deindividuated group, members are "submerged," losing their personal identity. Thus submerged, they feel a loss of concern about adverse reactions from others and a weakening of inner controls based on fear, guilt, shame, and commitment.

As early as 1896 the French sociologist LeBon suggested that, cloaked in the anonymity of a crowd, people lose some of their personal responsibility. To examine this phenomenon in the laboratory, Festinger and his associates defined deindividuation in terms of an inability on the part of the members of the group to remember "who said what" during a group discussion. They found in a study of small groups of men a correlation of .57 between an inability to remember who said what and the number of derogatory statements made about parents, such as "No matter how much I try to think that my folks are good to me, the fact remains that they've done me wrong." A high level of anxiety makes learning and recall difficult, and some investigators suspect that in all-female or mixed-sex groups there is such a high level of anxiety prior to the discussion that there will be a general inability to recall who said what, regardless of the direction that the discussion session takes (Cannavale, Scarr, & Pepitone, 1970).

At least ten factors have been hypothesized as reducing individual inhibitions within a group (Zimbardo, 1970). Perhaps the three most carefully documented causes of lowered restraints are *anonymity, diffusion of responsibility,* and *the presence of uninhibited models.*

Anonymity and Deindividuation

Several studies have examined the effects of anonymity on rowdyish behavior (Singer, Brush, & Lublin, 1965; Zimbardo, 1970; Diener, Westford, Dineen, & Fraser, 1973). Under control conditions, designed to heighten a sense of individual identity, subjects are likely to be given name tags, greeted and addressed as distinct individuals, and made to spend some time getting to know one another as distinct personalities. Under experimental or "deindividuation" conditions, subjects' names are not used, and they are likely to be dressed in uniforms that minimize their individual identity. For example, subjects may wear lab frocks, slouch hats that partially cover their faces, or even gowns and hoods reminiscent of those worn by members of the Ku Klux Klan. Using such procedures, Singer et al. found that deindividuated subjects were more likely to use obscenity in speech, and Zimbardo found that deindividuated subjects were more likely to inflict pain and punishment on an innocent victim.

In the Zimbardo experiment, subjects were induced to administer shocks to a female victim who was in actuality an accomplice of the experimenter's. The duration of each shock was controlled by the subject. The victim receiving the shocks was either good natured and altruistic or obnoxious and self-centered. Each victim groaned in misery as the subjects delivered the shocks. Both victims received rougher treatment at the hands of the deindividuation subjects. Control subjects responded to the wails of the nice woman by decreasing the amount of shock they administered and to the wails of the insufferable wretch by increasing the amount of shock delivered. Deindividuated subjects, on the other hand, indiscriminately shocked both victims.

A confirmation of the findings of greater hostile activity in deindividuated groups comes from Diener et al. (1973). Both anonymous and identifiable subjects were told that they were to help train a person who was trying to remain a pacifist in the face of harassment. As they "trained" the pacifist by bombarding him with wads of newspaper, rubber bands, sponge-rubber bricks, and plastic pellets shot from a toy pistol, hidden observers rated the level of aggressiveness. Both male groups and female groups were more aggressive when the members were anonymous than when they were identifiable. However, when individuals rather than groups "trained" the pacifist, anonymity did not affect aggressiveness.

Other studies have related anonymity to pilfering and stealing. Fraser, Kelem, Diener, and Beaman (1975) found that anonymous trick-or-treaters who were in groups were more likely to steal extra candy and money in the absence of perceived adult surveillance than were children who were identifiable or not members of a group. Zimbardo (1970) found support for the hypothesis that deindividuated behavior is more likely in urban areas than in settings less characterized by anonymity. In this study, identical cars were abandoned, hoods open, one in metropolitan New York and the other in suburban Palo Alto, California. The New

York car was stripped in 26 hours. The Palo Alto car was untouched for a week—except by a passerby who considerately closed the hood when it began to rain.

Diffusion of Responsibility and Deindividuation

Diffusion of responsibility refers to a decrease in feelings of personal responsibility for a decision or act as a result of an increase in the number of people making the decision or engaging in the act. That is, the more people involved in a decision or act, the less personally responsible each individual will feel. When responsibility is spread around like this rather than placed squarely on the shoulders of the individual, undesirable behavior becomes more likely (Mathes & Kahn, 1975).

In Mathes and Kahn's very elaborate experiment, subjects participated alone, in groups in which they could not communicate with the other members, or in groups in which they could communicate with the other members. The experiment was presented to the subjects as two different experiments that followed each other. For the "first experiment," subjects wrote creative essays that were read by a secret accomplice of the experimenter's. This confederate ostensibly judged the merits of the essay and then fined the writer accordingly. To create a strong desire for revenge, this judge heavily criticized the essay and levied a large fine. To create a very weak desire or no desire for revenge, the judge complimented the essay and levied only a nominal fine.

In what was presented as the "second experiment," the subject adopted the role of a judge and levied fines against the former tormentor, who was now doing a poor job of trying to memorize nonsense words. "Revenge" was measured by the size of the fines levied against the former judge. As expected, subjects in all conditions who had been motivated to seek revenge in the first part of the experiment fined the former judge more heavily than did subjects who had earlier been treated leniently. Revenge-motivated subjects who were in a group of similarly motivated individuals reported feeling less responsible for seeking revenge and engaged in greater retaliatory behavior than did revenge-motivated subjects who were alone. There was no significant difference between the revenge-motivated subjects from groups in which communication was allowed and the revenge-motivated subjects from groups in which communication was not allowed. This latter finding suggests that an explanation of greater revenge taking in groups does not need to draw on the concept of social interaction. Thus, diffusion of responsibility alone seems adequate to account for the results.

Modeling and Deindividuation

When a group has one or more disinhibited members, modeling effects will encourage impulsive and antisocial behavior. As we shall see in the next chapter, aggressive models have a powerful aggression-eliciting effect. Most studies on this topic have examined the effects of a model on the antisocial behavior of an individual observer. However, a study of the effects of an aggressive model on an interacting *group* of observers has recently been published by Diener, Dineen, Endresen, Beaman, and Fraser (1975).

In this study, groups of eight subjects were to be sent into a room that contained wads of newspaper, styrofoam bats, rubber bands, and a pacifist-in-training who was awaiting molestation. Before being allowed to attack the pacifist, subjects were shown a movie that was supposedly intended to give them some idea of what the room looked like but that in fact presented a modeling sequence. In a nonaggressive film a person was shown pacing around the room and talking to the pacifist, whereas in an aggressive film a person was shown hitting and clubbing the pacifist, dragging him around the room, and so on. Two other variables were manipulated. First, the experimenters attempted to vary the subjects' feelings of personal responsibility. Some subjects were reminded that, even though they were taking part in a scientific study, they were free individuals who were responsible for their own actions at all times. Others were told that the experimenter assumed full responsibility for anything that happened in the experiment. Second, the experimenters manipulated expectations, or "set." Some subjects were told that the experiment was all a game, whereas others were told that it was a study of aggression. The aggressive modeling sequence, the disavowal of responsibility, and the game set all led to greater aggression toward the pacifist. The strongest single effect was due to modeling: subjects who had viewed the aggressive sequence were *four times* as aggressive as subjects who had viewed the nonaggressive sequence. Furthermore, subjects who had seen the aggressive model, who were made to feel unresponsible for their behavior, and who were led to view the whole thing as a game were *38* times as aggressive as subjects who had viewed the nonaggressive model, who felt responsible for their actions, and who had been told that the experiment involved aggression.

Some affiliative behavior, then, may be motivated by a desire for freedom from inhibiting inner restraints. This type of potentially dangerous freedom is likely in groups in which members are anonymous and feel little personal responsibility and in which uninhibited models are present. Deindividuated behavior is not always violent and destructive, and, according to Zimbardo (1970), people are likely to derive pleasure from becoming reindividuated following an episode of running amok.

PART SUMMARY

Affiliation refers to the most general process of seeking out others. There are four situationally induced needs that prompt affiliative behavior. First, in some situations people seek out others for the simple reason that they need help in accomplishing a task. Second, under boring or underarousing conditions, people may seek out others to fulfill a need for stimulation. Third, people feel uncomfortable when there are gaps in their knowledge, and they may seek out others to fill in these gaps and thus achieve cognitive clarity. Fourth, according to social-comparison theory, when physical referents are absent, people may seek out others to evaluate their abilities, opinions, and emotions.

The relationship between threatening circumstances on the one hand and affiliative behavior and fear reduction on the other is very complex. There are at least three reasons why a person confronted with threatening circumstances might be motivated to seek out others. First, affiliation can reduce the actual danger inherent in the situation, either by promoting an active defense or by minimizing individual risk. Second, affiliation may result in a direct reduction of fear. A companion can reduce fear by offering distraction that interferes with the fear response, by providing a courageous model, or by merely being a conditioned stimulus that is associated with contentment and well-being. Third, according to social-comparison theory, threatening circumstances can generate emotional uncertainty, which in turn motivates affiliative behavior. In some cases, threatening circumstances give rise to feelings of anxiety rather than fear. When this occurs, there would appear to be a negative relationship between stress and affiliative behavior.

Finally, affiliation can provide freedom from inner restraints and prompt impulsive or antisocial behavior. This effect occurs in deindividuated groups. Deindividuated behavior is likely when the members of the group are anonymous, when there are feelings of shared rather than individual responsibility, and when the group contains uninhibited models.

LIKING

Congenial cowboy Will Rogers was famous for saying that he had never met a person he didn't like. A careful reading of his sweeping endorsement of personkind, however, reveals the possibility that he still found some people more likable than others. Whatever the words we choose, attraction is selective. Considering any pair of my acquaintances at a given point in time, I usually find one member of the pair more attractive than the other.

Liking and friendship have been of major interest to social psychologists. In this section we can focus on only a few of the major contributants to liking. First, we will consider the fact that people who are put into contact with each other usually end up liking each other. Second, we will consider the reasons why liking is often mutual and reciprocal. Third, we will consider the ways in which two people's similarities and differences provide a basis for friendship. It should be noted, however, that material presented in other parts of this book also deals with the determinants of liking. For example, studies of impression formation (Chapter 3) and of attitudes (Chapter 5) certainly help shed light on the reasons why one person likes another.

PROPINQUITY AND LIKING

Propinquity refers simply to nearness in space. With amazing regularity, it has been found that people thrown into contact with one another are likely to become friends. Festinger, Schachter, and Back (1950) report that the more likely residents were to encounter each other as they walked through the grounds of a housing complex, the more likely they were to become friends. Students who sit near each other in class are likely to form friendships, and this process can be disrupted by assigning the students new seats in the course of the term (Byrne, 1961). More than one study that compared the addresses of people who obtain marriage licenses found some support for the old notion that people end up marrying "the boy or girl next door" (Berscheid & Walster, 1969). We cannot dismiss all these findings by saying that friendship caused the people to locate near each other, for in many cases the pairs of friends were initially strangers who had been thrown together by circumstance.

Very convincing evidence of the effects of propinquity on friendship comes from Priest and Sawyer's (1967) study of the development of friendships in "Pierce Tower," a newly opened residence hall for 320 University of Chicago males. The tower consisted of four two-story "houses" stacked on top of one another. Each 80-man house was given a separate identity, with its own lounge, housefather, government, and planned activities. Within each story, rooms were arranged on a rectangular perimeter outside a core containing service facilities.

Each autumn and spring for the first four years of the residence hall's existence, the men were given questionnaires to fill out. All the dorm's residents were listed, and each man indicated whom he recognized, whom he talked to, and whom he liked. On the basis of these responses, all possible pairings of men within the hall could be assigned to one of six friendship categories, which, in ascending order of friendship, were *nonrecognition, recognition, talk, like, friend,* and *best friend.* These categories were then related to four degrees of proximity, which, in ascending order, were *towermates, housemates, floormates,* and *roommates.*

Substantial relationships between propinquity and attraction were found. For example, considering the "like" relationship, 93% of the roommate pairs liked each other, 48% of the floormate pairs liked each other, and 39% of the housemate pairs liked each other—but only 20% of the towermate pairs liked each other. Moreover, on any given floor, as the distance between two people's rooms decreased, the likelihood of a close relationship increased. Whereas 93% of the roommates liked each other, 57% of the people in adjacent rooms liked each other, 50% of the people 2 to 7 rooms apart liked each other, and 44% of the people 8 to 13 rooms apart had reciprocal liking.

More recently, Segal (1974) mailed state police trainees a questionnaire that asked respondents to indicate, among other things, who their best friends were at the academy. Trainees at this academy were assigned to dormitory rooms and to seats in classes on the basis of the alphabetical order of their last name. Thus, men whose names were close together in the alphabet were physically close in the academy. She found correlations in excess of .90 between trainees' proximity in the alphabetical roster and the likelihood that they would be friends! This finding should remind us, incidentally, of the difficulty with accepting correlational evidence as proof of a causal relationship. Although men whose names were close together in the alphabet were likely to become friends, the first letter of the last name was certainly not the cause of this friendship. Instead, a third factor (such as Cadet Acock and Cadet Adair's being assigned to the same room) was responsible.

Certainly under normal conditions some sort of contact is a precondition for liking to occur. But why does propinquity typically lead to liking? Shouldn't it be just as likely that contact would lead to disliking? There are at least three explanations for why close contact is likely to lead to friendship.

First, sheer familiarity may be a factor. Since we have already reviewed evidence that repeated contact with another person may lead to more favorable feelings about him or her (Chapter 3), we need not dwell again on this point.

Second, exchange theory offers some suggestions. When two people are forced to interact (as when they are dumped into the same room by a capricious housing authority), their options are to coordinate activities and live together in friendship or to ignore and frustrate each other and endure in misery. The rewards of friendship and the punishments from conflict and rivalry should certainly promote a cordial relationship.

Third, a dissonance-reduction explanation is also possible. Being in regular contact with another person and disliking that other person are dissonant. Whereas we can't always reduce this dissonance by leaving the situation (as in the case of cellmates), we can reduce it by deciding that the other person is likable. In Chapter 3 we saw that the anticipation of future interaction leads to favorable evaluations even of obnoxious people (Mirels & Mills, 1964).

RECIPROCITY OF LIKING

Although imbalances can and certainly do occur, feelings of liking are usually mutual and reciprocal. Backman and Secord (1959) told subjects that certain other people in a group would be likely to find them attractive. The subjects tended to choose these designated "likers" when instructed to form a team. In their study of naturally formed friendships within Pierce Tower, Priest and Sawyer (1967) found that each man tended to like each other man to the extent that he was liked in return.

A straightforward demonstration of the "rule of reciprocity" comes from an experiment by Sigall and Aronson (1969), who told male subjects that they were to receive an evaluation of the strengths and weaknesses in their personalities by a woman who was a first-year student in clinical psychology. Half the men received a favorable evaluation and the other half an unfavorable evaluation. To simultaneously investigate the effects of physical attractiveness on liking, the experimenters had half the men rated by a woman who was tastefully made up, whereas the remainder were rated by the same person who appeared without makeup and wearing a frizzy, off-color wig that was "so unflattering as to border on the grotesque." Women raters who had given favorable ratings to the subjects were more favorably rated by the subjects than were woman raters who had given unfavorable ratings. Thus an important variable in interpersonal attraction is the extent to which the attractor finds the attracted attractive! In addition, results showed that the woman was rated more favorably when she was made to appear physically attractive.

Certainly the "rule of reciprocity" is not inviolable. When another's liking for us is accompanied by childish or excessive demands, or when it seems attributable to some sort of ulterior motive, we are likely to be put off. However, for the most part we tend to like people who like us. Both exchange theory and balance theory offer some explanation for this finding.

An exchange-theory explanation of the rule of reciprocity comes from considering likely patterns of rewards. Most of us want to be liked, and, when other people like us, we find it rewarding and satisfying. Reciprocity of liking can be thought of as a barter or trade: you be my friend, and I'll be yours. On the other hand, unrequited friendship is frustrating and punishing. It involves investment of the self with no dividends in return. In the case of unrequited friendship, outcomes fall below an acceptable level, and the person is likely to shop around for a better deal.

An alternative explanation comes from balance theory, which predicts that we will be attracted to people who have the same feelings about us that we have about ourselves. Quite reasonably, this means that, if we *like* ourselves, we should be attracted to people who also like us. Similarly, if we *dislike* ourselves, then we should be attracted to people who dislike us.

Although some studies have found that subjects with negative self-evaluations like negative evaluators better than positive evaluators (Dutton & Arrowood, 1971), other studies have found the completely contradictory result that subjects with negative self-evaluations prefer positive evaluators to negative evaluators (Skolnick, 1971). An interesting resolution comes from Dutton (1972), whose results suggest that, if the subject's self-evaluation is tentative and unstable, a negative evaluation from someone else serves as an unhappy confirmation of a suspected truth; as a result, the negative evaluator will be disliked. If, on the other hand, the subject is reasonably certain about his or her undesirable qualities, then the balance-theory predictions are confirmed.

SIMILARITY AS A BASIS FOR LIKING

A common approach to the study of friendships involves studying the ways in which the characteristics of two people combine to determine the degree of mutual attraction. Overwhelming evidence shows that people are likely to choose as friends those who somehow resemble themselves. To convey the generality of the similarity-liking relationship, Table 6-1 lists some of the dimensions on which friends have been shown to be more similar than nonfriends. The studies summarized in the table use many different methods, and some of the correlational studies may show that people who are friends become similar over time. In fact, Newcomb (1961) has offered clear evidence that this can happen. However, as we shall soon see, there is also ample evidence that similarity *causes* liking.

It is useful to make a distinction between actual and perceived similarity. For example, several studies have suggested that friends are

Table 6.1. A partial roster of the dimensions on which friends have been found to be similar*

Age	Height	Personality
Attitudes	Income	Physical appearance
Class standing	Intelligence	Politics
Deafness	Interests	Race
Deviance	Mental health	Religion
Educational level	Military rank	Smoking behavior
Eye color	Occupation	Social status

*Drawn from reviews by Berscheid and Walster (1969), Lindzey and Byrne (1968), Insko and Schopler (1972), and Rubin (1973).

similar in personality (Lindzey & Byrne, 1968). However, outside observers may see or perceive friends as having more similar personalities than they in fact have (Miller, Campbell, Twedt, & O'Connell, 1966). Furthermore, when a relationship is going well, friends or spouses may tend to exaggerate their similarities, but, in times when satisfaction with the relationship is low, they may tend to underemphasize their similarities and stress their differences (Byrne & Blaylock, 1963; Levinger & Breedlove, 1966). Finally, even though similarity is a potent basis for attraction, two people will not be drawn to each other if their resemblances go undiscovered. For example, if, on encountering a person of another race, we automatically assume that he or she shares none of our interests and beliefs, we may avoid striking up a conversation. However, if the conversation had been held, a number of mutual interests might have emerged.

Perceived Similarity as a Cause of Liking

Perhaps the best evidence that similarity *causes* liking comes from applying the **phantom-other procedures** developed by Byrne and his associates (Byrne & McGraw, 1964; Byrne & Nelson, 1965). After subjects express their attitudes, they are presented with a questionnaire that purportedly shows the attitudes of another person. In actuality, there is no other person, and the questionnaire has been carefully prepared by the experimenter in such a way that the views expressed coincide to some degree with the subjects' views. The extent to which agreement on a specific issue will contribute to interpersonal attraction will depend somewhat on the nature of the people involved and the importance they attach to the issue (Clore & Baldridge, 1968; Touhey, 1972a). However, for the most part the *proportion* of the phantom other's attitudes that are similar to the subject's attitudes determines the extent to which the subject finds the "other person" attractive (Byrne & Nelson, 1965; Byrne, Gouaux, Griffitt, Lamberth, Murakawa, Prasad, Prasad, & Ramirez, 1971; Insko & Wetzel, 1974). The linear relationship between attitudinal similarity and attraction is not culture bound, since it has been found in Mexico, Japan, India, and even Texas (Byrne, Gouaux, et al., 1971). Although there have been some disconfirmations (Wright & Crawford, 1971), perceived attitudinal similarity is such a dependable contributant to liking that "phantom-other" procedures are a popular method for manipulating interpersonal attraction for experimental purposes.

One interesting line of research suggests that a person who starts out taking positions that are different from the subject's but ends up agreeing with the subject will be liked better than a person who is equally agreeable throughout. Byrne, Lamberth, Palmer, and London (1969) had subjects listen to a tape recording of another student expressing 24 attitudes. The proportion of attitudes that were similar to the listener's was in all cases .50, but the experimenter varied the sequence in which the similar attitudes were expressed. Although there was a sharp decrease in liking for the phantom who started out showing similarity to the listener but then began expressing dissimilar attitudes, there was an increase in liking for the phantom who "yielded" by starting out in disagreement but ending up in agreement. When there was neither an increase nor a decrease in the proportion of similar attitudes expressed over trials, there were no changes in the subject's liking for the target.

Yielding to another person's point of view appears to reinforce that person's responses. Lombardo, Weiss, and Buchanan (1972) conducted an experiment that paralleled some of the verbal-conditioning studies that were reported in Chapter 4. These studies, you will recall, showed, among other things, that social approval increases the rate at which people verbalize opinions. Consistent with this result, Lombardo and his associates found that subjects voiced their attitudes more rapidly in a condition in which they were followed by a confederate who expressed similar attitudes than in a condition in which similar views were not expressed. However, they also found that a confederate who at first disagreed but later yielded to the subjects' point of view had more of an effect on the rate at which the subject responded than did a confederate who agreed with the subject throughout. Subsequent withdrawal of agreement led to extinction (in this case a decrease in the speed with which the subject voiced additional attitudes).

These and other findings suggest a "recency effect" in interpersonal attraction. That is, we seem to be particularly attracted to someone who has only recently begun agreeing with us or giving us favorable evaluations (Aronson & Linder, 1965). A highly plausible interpretation of this recency effect is that former disagreement provides a dark background against which the new stream of agreement flows in sharp contrast (Mascaro & Graves, 1973).

Belief Incongruence: Dissimilarity and Disliking

A highly influential theory of prejudice is based on perceived dissimilarity. According to Rokeach's theory of **belief congruence,** people do not reject other people simply because they belong to a different racial group; rather, they reject them because they believe that people of other races must have attitudes, values, and beliefs that are different from their own. Thus it is the perception of attitudinal dissimilarity, or "belief incongruence," that causes prejudicial attitudes (Rokeach, Smith, & Evans, 1960).

In an early test of this theory, Stein, Hardyk, and Smith (1965) followed phantom-other procedures and had adolescents rate teenaged stimulus persons who were either similar or dissimilar to the raters. In some cases the questionnaire indicated that the stimulus teenager was of the same race as the rater, and in other cases it indicated that the stimulus teenager was of a different race.

Subsequent ratings revealed that subjects responded primarily in terms of beliefs and only secondarily in terms of race. The race effect tended to be one of preferring not to have intimate contacts with a person of another race in front of a third party (such as a parent) who might not understand. Stein et al. also argue that, when there is little evidence available about a person of a different race, then people may automatically assume a lack of belief congruence. Whether attitudinal similarity will be more important than racial dissimilarity will thus depend on whether the similarities are revealed before the parties jump to the conclusion that their beliefs are dissimilar.

The use of phantom-other procedures in comparisons of belief congruence and race has been criticized on the basis that the race manipulation is rarely forceful. That is, although the beliefs are usually spelled out in detail, race is usually presented as background information like "age" or "year in school." However, Hendrick, Bixenstine, and Hawkins (1971) found that, when race was made salient by using videotaped stimulus persons, there was again a strong effect of belief congruence but only a weak or negligible effect of race.

Unfortunately, this evidence does not mean that we can eradicate prejudice through an advertising campaign intended to convince blacks and whites that they have similar attitudes. Some people will always respond to others simply on the basis of race, especially in the context of an intimate relationship (Goldstein & Davis, 1972). Also, social pressure can encourage prejudice and discrimination even on the part of people who would otherwise live up to standards of fair play and equality (Silverman, 1974).

Interpretations of the Similarity-Liking Relationship

Insko and Schopler (1972) have reviewed four interpretations of the similarity-liking relationship. First is the *balance-theory* interpretation, which is, of course, specifically geared for dealing with this relationship. Balance or symmetry requires that people who share orientations or attitudes like each other, whereas people with dissimilar attitudes must dislike each other.

A second explanation involves *anticipated rewards.* When people have similar views, arguments and disputes should be minimal and mutually satisfying activities easy to find. For example, if you and your roommate both like situation comedies, then you can enjoy them together on TV. However, if you prefer situation comedies and he or she prefers athletic events, at least one of you will have to be disappointed.

Third is a *social-comparison* evaluation. As we saw in our discussion of Festinger's social-comparison theory and Schachter's research on affiliation under stress, people who are similar to oneself provide the best sounding boards for evaluating abilities, opinions, and feelings. For example, if you are the curator of a museum of natural history, only another, like-minded curator can help you evaluate and come to grips with your tender thoughts about your gammaracanthukatylodermogammarus. In this case, reduction of uncertainty provides the reward for hobnobbing with like-minded people.

Finally, there is the *implied-favorable-evaluation* interpretation, which suggests that, when people discover that they have attitudes in common with someone else, they anticipate that this other person will like them. In order to be liked, they seek out such persons.

These explanations, Insko and Schopler note, are by no means mutually exclusive. In a sense, they can all be boiled down to the idea that people who are similar to us offer rewarding associations because they help us achieve balance, because they are easier to get along with, because they provide a better yardstick for self-understanding, and because they like us in return. Each of these factors can contribute to the similarity-liking relationship.

Similarity and Liking:
Some Limiting Conditions

We do not, of course, expect similarity to lead to liking under all conditions. Someone highly similar to you could prove to be dull and unexciting (what could you possibly have to discuss with someone who is completely like minded?), or excessive similarity could rob you of valued feelings of individuality. Furthermore, if someone has a major shortcoming, you may like this person better if he or she is dissimilar rather than similar to you.

Novak and Lerner (1968) presented subjects with "partners" who were either similar or dissimilar. Half of the time the partner was presented as normal and the other half as mentally unstable. The "normal" partner was liked better when similar, but the "abnormal" partner was liked better when dissimilar. The idea that someone with an emotional problem is in many ways similar is threatening, for there is the clear implication that a breakdown could happen to you yourself. It is less discomforting to be with a disturbed person who is different in many respects, since it is implied that you will be spared the affliction. In a similar experiment, Taylor and Mettee (1971) confronted different subjects with partners representing all combinations of similar/dissimilar and pleasant/obnoxious. Not too surprisingly, the most liked partner was the similar-pleasant one, but once again it was found that the psychologically blemished person was easier to tolerate if he or she was dissimilar rather than similar to the perceiver.

DIFFERENCES AS A BASIS FOR ATTRACTION

Some theorists believe that two people can be different in such a way that their differences provide a basis for mutual attraction. The *completion principle* and the *complementarity hypothesis* each suggest that two people can be drawn together because one offers something that the other lacks. For example, a strong but stupid armed robber and a puny but clever pickpocket might get together because they feel that, as a team, they can get rich and enhance their reputations.

The completion principle and the complementarity hypothesis do not necessarily deny the importance of similarity as a basis for attraction. As Murstein (1972) notes, similarities may limit the field of choice. However, once the field has been limited, the choice may be made on the basis of unfulfilled needs. For instance, the strong but stupid armed robber might be drawn to many criminals on the basis of similarity of interests, but he might be particularly attracted to the weak but clever thief who can provide the brainpower for some really big-time jobs.

The Completion Principle

The **completion principle,** formulated by Cattell (1934), suggests that one individual may be drawn to another because of:

> a desire to possess characteristics . . . which are felt by the individual to be necessary to his self-concept or to his or her general social life. . . . For example, a socially awkward person might especially value a partner who is socially adroit and poised. Moreover, a person who is not managing his affairs too intelligently would obviously experience gains from a wiser partner. It is not part of the principle that this must occur consciously [Cattell & Nesselroade, 1967, p. 351].

Support for this principle was found in a comparison of stable and unstable marriages (Cattell & Nesselroade, 1967). In the more successful marriages, wives provided an emotional expressiveness, a cautiousness in the face of risks, and a relaxed manner that the husbands lacked. The husbands, on the other hand, provided tough mindedness, an adventurous spirit, and get-up-and-go.

The Complementarity Hypothesis

According to the **complementarity hypothesis** (Winch, 1958), two people are drawn together because they have needs that mesh together in such a way that the satisfaction of one person's needs involves the satisfaction of the other person's needs. For example, the "good woman" and the "bad man" may fall in love because each can satisfy important needs of the other. At the risk of oversimplification, the good woman may find the bad man attractive because he appeals to her hidden sexual longings or because she finds the possibility of reforming him an irresistible temptation. The bad man may find the good woman attractive because she promises to interject stability into his life. As another example, a person who needs to be dominant may be drawn to a person who needs to be submissive. As the former gets his kicks from kicking, the latter gets his kicks from being kicked. The complementarity hypothesis differs from the completion principle primarily in that it requires the meshing and interlocking of specific satisfactions.

The history of the complementarity hypothesis has been rather stormy. Original support for the hypothesis came from a study of 25 married couples by Winch, Ktsanes, and Ktsanes (1955), who assessed the

strength of 15 different needs in each spouse. Their finding that people with needs to be submissive or receptive tended to have spouses with needs to be dominant or assertive was interpreted as supporting the complementarity hypothesis. However, this particular study has been sharply criticized (Tharp, 1963), and reviews of the literature have shown that a large number of studies have yielded results that are not complementary to the complementarity hypothesis (Lindzey & Byrne, 1968; Berschied & Walster, 1969).

Yet it may still be that complementarity is an important basis for attraction under certain limited conditions. Kerckhoff and Davis (1962) studied dating couples moving toward marriage. In the first stage of a dating relationship, similarity in social class was important; as the relationship developed, similarity in underlying values and interests gained in importance. Further progress toward marriage depended on the extent to which the two people fulfilled complementary needs. This study suggests that different factors are important at different points in a relationship. Supportive of this view are Bermann and Miller's (1967) findings that, with roommates, need complementarity played an important role in stable relationships (that is, relationships that were important to the women and that the women wanted to maintain) but did not play much of a role in unstable relationships.

Whether or not complementarity will provide a basis for attraction will also depend on the specific needs involved. For example, people who like each other may have similar needs for achievement but dissimilar needs for dominance (Bermann & Miller, 1967). Thus, when the intensity of a relationship and the nature of the specific needs are taken into account, need complementarity may help to predict interpersonal attraction.

Paralleling the hypothesis of need complementarity are hypotheses suggesting that people are drawn together on the basis of role complementarity (Murstein, 1971; Seyfried & Hendrick, 1973; Wagner, 1975). According to these hypotheses, two people's liking for each other will depend in part on how well each fulfills the role he or she is expected to play in the relationship and on how well the two roles intermesh and provide a "fit." For example, Seyfried and Hendrick (1973) found that females were more attracted to masculine men than to feminine men (although males were less motivated by role complementarity). In a study of camp counselors, Wagner (1975) found that attraction is dependent on both compatibility of people's needs and the extent to which their behavior fulfills each other's role expectations. Of course, role complementarity does not invariably lead to liking; an executioner and a condemned criminal occupy interlocking roles, but I would not expect these two people to be fond of each other.

To conclude, we might note that the complementarity hypothesis is very difficult to test. Usually an investigator will examine the complementarities between two people, which makes the number of possible complementarities studied very limited. People have a number of relationships with a number of different people, and they have a wide array of needs. A person's needs may indeed mesh with those of his or her friends. However, the specific needs examined in the study may mesh with the needs of a friend other than the one whom the researcher is studying. We cannot expect complementarities for every specific need in every specific relationship.

The Duplication Theorem

An interesting form of role-compatibility theorizing has been offered by Toman (1971), whose **duplication theorem** suggests that the child's position within the family will determine the course of his or her adult relations with peers outside the family. The child's age and sex create a role preference that may or may not mesh with the role preference of another person.

For example, within the family the older brother (of a sister) is used to a position of seniority and leadership with regard to the opposite sex, whereas the younger sister (of a brother) is used to leadership and protection from a person of the opposite sex. Similarly, the older sister (of a brother) is used to a position of seniority and leadership with regard to the opposite sex, whereas the younger brother (of a sister) is used to being led and protected by a female. In adulthood, a marriage between an older brother (of a sister) and a younger sister (of a brother) might be expected to work, and so should a marriage between an older sister (of a brother) and a younger brother (of a sister). However, marriage between an older brother and an older sister shouldn't work (since each is used to being boss), and neither should marriage between a younger brother and a younger sister (since each is used to being bossed). Thus, according to Toman, when adults choose as a friend or mate someone who allows them to duplicate the roles they learned in childhood, the relationship should be stable and enduring; when they choose a friend or mate who is used to a role that conflicts with their own, the relationship is likely to flounder. In support of this theory, Toman presents a number of divorce statistics showing a high divorce rate among partners who fail to duplicate earlier role relationships.

In sum, despite some early problems with Winch's theory of complementary needs, there is growing evidence that the way in which two people's characteristics mesh will affect the way they feel about each other. Complementarity between certain kinds of needs provides a basis for attraction in some situations. Complementarity in terms of role expectations is also an important determinant of interpersonal attraction.

PART SUMMARY

Attraction is selective, in that there are some people whom we like, some whom we dislike, and some who leave us indifferent. Propinquity refers to nearness in physical space. Although it seems equally plausible that being thrown into contact with another person will provide a basis for either liking or disliking, the typical finding is that propinquity leads to friendship. This can be understood as a mere-exposure effect, as an exchange phenomenon, or as a result of dissonance reduction.

In general, people like those people who like them in return. This rule of reciprocity can be understood in terms of exchange theory or in terms of balance theory. An interesting derivation of balance theory suggests that people who *dislike* aspects of themselves will like people who also dislike these same aspects. This prediction is supported only when the person is reasonably certain about his or her own lack of worth.

A common approach to the study of attraction involves comparing the interrelationship of two persons' psychological qualities. Compared with nonfriends, friends have been found to be similar on a number of dimensions. Some of the best demonstrations that perceived similarity causes liking come from experiments in which the subject rates a "phantom other," who is made to appear similar or dissimilar to the subject. In general, attraction increases with the proportion of attitudes the two people discover they have in common. One theory of prejudice suggests that people dislike those of different races because of perceived dissimilarity. The linkage between similarity and liking can be interpreted in terms of balance, rewards and costs, social comparison, or expected evaluations from others. The similarity-linking relationship can be reversed when the other person has a major flaw or shortcoming.

Certain kinds of differences can also contribute to interpersonal attraction. The completion principle suggests that people seek out others who possess qualities that they themselves lack. The complementarity hypothesis suggests that, when two people have needs that fit together in such a way that the satisfaction of one person's needs will result in the satisfaction of the other's, they will be drawn together. The extent to which complementarity affects attraction depends on the intensity of the relationship and the specific needs assessed. Closely related are findings that compatibility of role expectations is also an important determinant of the satisfactions to be derived from a relationship.

LOVE

People have long been fascinated with predicting and controlling the course of romantic love. Early New Englanders, for example, developed a rich folklore dealing with courtship, love, and marriage (Emrich, 1970). The woman who wanted to predict love was told such things as "If a skunk comes by, it is the sign of a new courtship." If she wanted to take a more active role, she was told "If you can walk around the block with your mouth full of water, you may be married next year." Men, on the other hand, were assured "You can secure a girl's love by pulling a hair from her head." Today these quaint procedures can still gain your true love's attention—provided, of course, that he or she is an anthropologist or a psychiatrist!

Despite centuries of interest, it has only been in the last ten years or so that social psychologists have devoted serious efforts to dealing scientifically with love. Our discussion of love is organized around four topics. First, we will consider the development of an objective test to measure love. Second, we will discuss a theory of passionate love. Third, we will look at some factors that affect the choice of a romantic partner. Finally, we will consider the ways in which people outside the devoted duo (parents, friends, and so forth) can affect the course of a romantic relationship.

THE LOVE SCALE

Zick Rubin (1970, 1973) reasoned that romantic love—like intelligence, vocational interests, and mental disorders—could be measured by means of a pencil-and-paper test. He proceeded on the assumption that love is a *multifaceted attitude* that can be measured by responses to a standardized set of questions. Because his project was innovative, potential items for his love scale had to be based on speculation. To help validate the love scale (in a way that will be spelled out shortly), Rubin concurrently developed a liking scale. Questions for the liking scale were drawn from earlier research on liking.

Rubin started out with a very large number of questions. After they had been submitted to groups of judges, who suggested some changes, 70 items were presented to about 200 students. Each of the students answered the items with reference to a girlfriend or boyfriend and with reference to a "platonic friend" of the opposite sex. By intercorrelating responses to all items, Rubin was able to identify those items that clustered together and seemed to measure loving and liking and to eliminate those items that did not cluster together. The result was two 13-item scales (Rubin, 1970). The items on the love scale represent three components of romantic love: (1) **affiliative and dependent need,** or the person's desire to be with and dependent upon the partner, (2) **predisposition to help,** or the person's interest in showing kindness and consideration toward the partner, and (3) **exclusiveness and absorption,** or the extent to which the person emphasizes the relationship at hand at the expense of other relationships.

Although the study that will now be reported involves these 13-item scales of loving and liking, subsequent refinement has resulted in two nine-item scales (Rubin, 1973). The improved, nine-item scales, which Rubin is presently using in his research, are presented in Table 6-2.

After the items had been selected, a large number of dating (but not engaged) couples completed each scale with reference to their dating partner and with reference to a same-sexed friend. Analysis of their responses focused first on establishing the scales' reliability and validity. Reliability was shown by the high internal consistency of each scale; that is, responses to items within each scale were positively correlated. This finding suggested that the scale measured one attribute in a systematic way rather than two or more attributes in a haphazard way (Chapter 2). Validity was shown in two ways. First, differences in scores were pretty

Table 6–2. Nine-item versions of the love scale and liking scale

Love Scale

1. I feel that I can confide in _____ about virtually everything.
2. I would do almost anything for _____.
3. If I could never be with _____, I would feel miserable.
4. If I were lonely, my first thought would be to seek _____ out.
5. One of my primary concerns is _____'s welfare.
6. I would forgive _____ for practically anything.
7. I feel responsible for _____'s well-being.
8. I would greatly enjoy being confided in by _____.
9. It would be hard for me to get along without _____.

Liking Scale

1. I think that _____ is unusually well adjusted.
2. I would highly recommend _____ for a responsible job.
3. In my opinion, _____ is an exceptionally mature person.
4. I have great confidence in _____'s good judgment.
5. Most people would react favorably to _____ after a brief acquaintance.
6. I think that _____ is one of those people who quickly wins respect.
7. _____ is one of the most likable people I know.
8. _____ is the sort of person I myself would like to be.
9. It seems to me that it is very easy for _____ to gain admiration.

Note: Respondents mentally fill in the name of the other person in the blanks. They respond to each question on a scale ranging from "Not at all true; disagree completely" to "Definitely true; agree completely." Responses to each item are then scored from 1 to 9, with 9 indicating the greatest loving or liking. (Adapted from "Measurement of Romantic Love," by Z. Rubin, *Journal of Personality and Social Psychology*, 1970, *16*, 265–273. Copyright 1970 by the American Psychological Association. Reprinted by permission.)

much as one would hope. For example, people tended to score higher on love for their dating partner than on love for their friend. Second, the scales were validated by showing that, although there were high intrascale or within-scale correlations, there was only a relatively low correlation between the scores obtained on the two different scales. This evidence, which shows that the scales measure two different types of relationships, shows **discriminant validity.**

Men and women responded to the scales in somewhat different ways. It appeared that the women tended to discriminate more carefully between loving and liking. They also tended to like their boyfriends more than they were liked in return; the boyfriends were more likely to reciprocate love than liking. Moreover, in accordance with cultural norms that allow women's relationships to be more intimate, intense, and emotional than men's relationships, women expressed more love for the same-sexed friend than did men.

Rubin's next step was to try to predict behavior on the basis of love scores. In this part of the study, half the subjects were dating couples who scored high on the love scale and the other half were couples who scored low on the love scale. These strong-love and weak-love couples showed up for the experiment either with their own partner or with somebody else's partner. As they waited in a room, unseen observers carefully recorded the amount of time they spent looking into each other's eyes. As expected, strong-love couples who were together spent more time gazing into each other's eyes than did weak-love couples who were together. And, since strong-love subjects did not spend a comparable amount of time looking into the eyes of somebody else's partner, Rubin concluded that there was honoring of the musical pledge "I only have eyes for you."

Rubin is actively continuing his study of love. He has, as noted above, been refining his scales and his conception of love. He has also been following the course of relationships over time. Among his findings have been that, the longer a relationship endures, the less changeable it becomes and that romantic partners who score high on either the love scale *or* the liking scale develop a stronger relationship over time (Rubin, 1973). We will soon consider additional evidence suggesting that, for a relationship to endure, it is helpful to like, as well as love, one's partner.

A THEORY OF PASSIONATE LOVE

Theories that seem more than adequate when applied to other phenomena in some ways fall flat when applied to passionate love (Walster, 1971). Consider, for example, the fate of "social-reinforcement" notions. If a person becomes nasty and abusive with a friend, no one is surprised when the punished "friend" terminates the relationship and seeks companionship elsewhere. If a person becomes nasty and abusive with a lover, no one is surprised if the lover's feelings of passion are intensified. Furthermore, on the basis of what we know about the effects of withdrawal of reinforcement, we might infer that the best way for a person to disengage from a romantic relationship would be to flatly refuse to see the erstwhile lover. Yet we all know that this procedure can have some very sticky consequences. To avoid a "blowup," it is safer to follow a slow program of gradual disinvolvement: the number of evenings the pair gets together starts to slowly taper off, and the person initiating the breakup shows decreasing amounts of enthusiasm while cautiously revealing that alternative relationships are gaining in attractiveness (Goffman, 1952).

Walster (1971) has suggested that Schachter's two-component theory of emotion may serve to explain passionate love. (As you will recall from Chapter 3, this theory suggests that a general state of physiological activation or arousal combines with external cues to produce a specific emotional state.) The necessary arousal may be brought about through any stimuli that "usually produce sexual arousal, gratitude, anxiety, guilt, loneliness, hatred, jealousy, or confusion." The cues can take many forms: a well-turned ankle, bulging biceps, mood music, leather boots, or whatever. Thus, exciting circumstances such as a public execution or a bullfight can fan the fires of passionate love—provided that present in the situation are cues to help the person define the emotional state as passion. When the cues in the situation change so that the person attributes the arousal to something else, passion should die.

A main advantage of this theory is that it explains why punishing or upsetting circumstances can intensify feelings of passion. Sexual frustration—being told "no"—could *increase* feelings of love by raising the rejected one's level of arousal. Sexual gratification, on the other hand, could *reduce* passion by weakening the "arousal" component of love.

To test the hypothesis that seemingly irrelevant arousing circumstances fan the fires of passion if appropriate cues are present, Dutton and Aron (1974) studied men who were approaching one of two foot bridges. The first bridge, expected to generate a high amount of arousal, was a 5-foot-wide, 450-foot-long suspension bridge constructed of wooden boards attached to wire cables. The bridge had very low handrails of wire cable and a pronounced tendency to tilt, sway, and wobble, thus sensitizing users to the rocks and rapids 230 feet below. The second bridge, which was expected to generate little or no arousal, was made of heavy cedar planks and ran a mere 10 feet above a small rivulet.

As each man crossed the bridge, he was approached by either a male or a female interviewer. After requesting cooperation on a psychology project, the interviewer asked the subject to make up a story about a picture and then gave the subject a piece of paper indicating where he or she could be found to discuss the experiment.

In the case of the male interviewer, there was very little sexual imagery in the projective-test stories, and virtually no subjects called "to discuss the experiment." In the case of the female interviewer, people made

up sexier stories, particularly in the vicinity of the high-arousal bridge. Furthermore, whereas only 12% of the low-arousal subjects called the female experimenter for "debriefing," 50% of the high-arousal subjects contacted her after the experiment. To eliminate the possibility that hairy-chested devils frequent hairy-chested bridges and only sexless twerps frequent secure bridges, Dutton and Aron conducted an additional study in the lab, where subjects could be randomly assigned to arousal conditions. This study, too, showed that arousal coupled with the presence of a pretty experimenter combined to spur men's sexual interest.

THE CHOICE OF A ROMANTIC PARTNER

Although liking and loving may be distinct states, to some extent they are caused by the same variables. Similarity and proximity, for example, contribute to romantic involvements as well as to friendships (Barry, 1970), and much of the research on the completion and complementarity hypotheses has involved loving—or at least married—couples (Kerckhoff & Davis, 1962; Cattell & Nesselroade, 1967; Toman, 1971). However, when we turn from the choice of a friend to the choice of a romantic partner, other variables, such as physical appearance and "hard-to-get" behavior, start to enter in.

Physical Attractiveness

In an attempt to understand what leads to a continuing dating relationship, Walster, Aronson, Abrams, and Rottman (1966) arranged dates for a large number of college freshmen. In return, these freshmen completed a number of personality tests and were rated by a panel of interviewers. After the ball was over, the investigators compared the couples who wished to continue dating with the couples who did not. None of the personality measures explained the difference. Wanting to continue to date the partner, asking for a date, and accepting a date depended only on the partner's physical attractiveness. At least three reasons have been advanced to explain why good looks are an asset in a romantic relationship.

First, as Dion, Berscheid, and Walster (1972) note, physical appearance is immediately recognizable, whereas other assets—such as consideration, warmth, or sense of humor—take time to be revealed. Thus, good looks may be particularly likely to have a strong initial impact. Over time, however, it may develop that the muscle man or beach bunny is socially inept and a terrible bore, with the result that the relationship is discontinued. Consistent with the idea that good looks may become less important as a relationship deepens is Stroebe, Insko, Thompson, and Layton's (1971) finding that, although people showed more interest in dating good-looking as compared with not-so-good-looking people, physical appearance did not have much of an influence on "considering the person for marriage."

Second, there is considerable agreement in our culture about what constitutes good looks. Having a good-looking partner in a romantic relationship has the special advantage that it confers prestige. We are no doubt conditioned early in life to be "turned on" by certain characteristics of the opposite sex, and "good looks" is certainly one of these characteristics.

A third reason why attractiveness is important is that, on the basis of our implicit theories of personality (Chapter 3), we may *automatically assume* that a person who is physically attractive possesses a number of other desirable attributes as well. To test this hypothesis, Dion, Berscheid, and Walster (1972) had subjects rate unattractive, average, and attractive stimulus persons. The more attractive stimulus persons were rated as having more socially desirable personality traits and were, moreover, expected to lead happier, better lives. The generality of this "what is beautiful is good" effect was demonstrated in another study by Dion (1972), who found that a transgression committed by an attractive child was evaluated as less serious and less likely to reflect an enduring tendency toward antisocial behavior than was an identical transgression committed by an unattractive child. However, the extent to which this phenomenon holds depends on what qualities are rated, since good-looking people are also assumed to be vain, egotistical, snobbish, and likely to have an extramarital affair (Dermer & Thiel, 1975).

Although on the basis of computer-dating studies one might expect to find only stunning couples, glancing into parked cars at a drive-in movie would reveal that quite a few average-looking people find dates. This fact might seem to conflict with the Walster et al. findings, but it is important to note that, in such computer-dating studies, experimenters arrange the dates and thereby break the ice. Once a person is thus assured of a date with an attractive partner, he or she can go ahead and enjoy. However, having to hustle your own date is a zebra of a different stripe. In this case people generally choose as a partner someone who is about as good looking as they themselves (Walster, Aronson, Abrams, & Rottman, 1966; Murstein, 1972; Huston, 1973).

We may be motivated to date the best-looking person in the world, but we also want to be spared the pain and embarrassment of rejection. As a result, we usually attempt to estimate the likelihood of rejection before making a bid. This requires contemplating our own attractiveness in relation to the attractiveness of the other person. If we decide that the other person is so much better looking than us that rejection is highly probable, we are likely to have a dampening of interest. If we decide that the other person is beneath our league, there is again a dampening effect. The likelihood of dating should be greatest when the partner is of equal attractiveness to the self: both persons can feel happy that they are doing the best they can do.

Although some early studies failed to support the matching hypothesis, there have since been some encouraging results (encouraging at least for those of us with mediocre-to-poor looks). Murstein (1972), for example, has found that dating couples were less discrepant in terms of attractiveness than were randomly matched pairs. Huston's (1973) research has provided the following findings: (1) men believed that rejection by an attractive woman was more likely than rejection by an unattractive woman; (2) to the extent that the men saw themselves as attractive, they felt that an attractive woman would be likely to accept their offer of a date; (3) when acceptance was guaranteed, men selected a more attractive woman to date than when acceptance was not assured.

Playing Hard to Get

Folklore down through the ages suggests that the woman who is "hard to get" is the most attractive catch. There are at least three theoretical reasons why this belief should be true (Walster, Walster, & Berscheid, 1971). First, dissonance theory suggests that the trouble and effort involved in winning a hard-to-get woman may generate dissonance, which will be reduced by overrating the woman. Second, men may learn or infer that a woman who is hard to get (because she is so much in demand) offers more attractions than a woman who does not generate competition. Third, a woman who is hard to get will be frustrating. Frustration raises arousal, and, as we know from the theory of passionate love, raised arousal may intensify romantic yearnings.

To test the hypothesis that a hard-to-get woman is an attractive woman, Walster and her associates conducted a number of studies. In one study they predicted that, the more romantic interest a stimulus person expressed in a subject, the less that stimulus person would be liked, because she would be "too easy to get." Results, however, showed a positive relationship between romantic interest and the ratings of the stimulus person (Walster, Walster, & Berscheid, 1971). In another experiment some women were instructed to play hard to get, whereas others were instructed to eagerly accept offers to a dance. Elusiveness had no impact on attractiveness (Lyons, Walster, & Walster, 1973). In still another study a bona fide prostitute played hard to get by telling certain "Johns" that she was choosy about her clientele and might not agree to see them again, whereas other "Johns" were not led to anticipate difficulty arranging meetings in the future. The hard-to-get treatment neither fanned the fires of passion during the initial encounter nor affected the number of times the "Johns" attempted to arrange additional visits (Walster, Walster, & Lambert, 1973). All told, five experiments *disconfirmed* the hypothesis that the hard-to-get woman is the more desirable woman.

However, before discounting the hard-to-get variable as irrelevant, it is necessary to consider the recent arguments of Walster, Walster, Piliavin, and Schmidt (1973). Careful interviews of male students revealed a number of advantages *and* disadvantages of hard-to-get and easy-to-get women. A hard-to-get woman offers prestige, but she may stand a man up or humiliate him in front of his friends. An easy-to-get woman would not be difficult to date, but she might be hard to discourage if the man lost interest or might embarrass the man in front of his friends by being overly affectionate. Thus comparisons of the two types of women might have yielded discouraging results because the pros and cons of one kind of female had to be weighed against the pros and cons of the other.

Walster and her associates suggest that there are two components of "playing hard to get." First, there is the component of how hard or easy the woman is for an *individual man or subject* to get. Second, there is the component of how hard or easy the woman is *for other men* to get. The woman who is selectively hard to get (specifically, easy for the subject to get but hard for all other men) should offer maximum appeal. If she is easy for the subject to get, then the subject is assured of a prestigious date; if she is hard for "other men" to get, then the potential trauma of losing her to another man is avoided. Support for this hypothesis was found in an experiment in which men rated uniformly hard-to-get, uniformly easy-to-get, and selectively hard-to-get women. The woman who was easy for the subject to get but hard for other men to get was rated as the most attractive on virtually all rated dimensions (Walster, Walster, Piliavin, & Schmidt, 1973).

Dating and Mating as a Marketplace Phenomenon

In applying exchange theory to the subject of dating and mating, Rubin (1973) has argued that the choice of a partner represents a trade-off in which both persons get the best they can with what they have to offer. Occupational status, education, intelligence, wealth, good humor, reputation, character, and prospects are, like good looks, social assets that can be bartered in the process of seeking a date or mate. The trade-off may involve similar assets (as in the case of two people of equivalent attractiveness), or it may involve entirely different assets. In the latter case the most obvious example is a trade of sexual prowess and good looks for money and prestige, as when a handsome but penniless young man is drawn to a rich but elderly dowager. I agree with Rubin (1973, p. 82) when he argues that "although we may prefer to believe otherwise, we must face up to the fact that our attitudes toward other people are determined to a large extent by our assessments of the rewards that they hold for us." The argument loses some of its harsher tone when we consider that the "commodities" traded may include such delightful assets as a sharp mind, a good sense of humor, and a keen esthetic appreciation.

SOCIAL INFLUENCE AND LOVE

A common theme in love stories is interference or meddling on the part of outsiders. As the loving pair whimpers "Why don't other people leave us alone?" parents question the partner's background, friends try to push the couple together or pry them apart, and self-styled counselors of all descriptions bombard the couple with a steady stream of unsolicited advice. The simple fact is that no dating couple is an island, alone and by itself. Parents, peers, and even society at large promote some romantic relationships and discourage others.

Parental Influence

Parents have a vested interest in their offspring's selection of a mate. From their point of view, choice of the "wrong person" can result in a loss of social status or in the abandonment or dilution of cherished family

values. On the other hand, selection of the "right person" can perpetuate all that is good in the family and, in some cases, raise the family's fortunes. We are all familiar with cases in which people have been at least temporarily disinherited, disowned, or otherwise disavowed because they became involved with someone who was not gainfully employed, who had an inadequate education, or who belonged to the "wrong" religious denomination.

Although, when we think of parental meddling, we are likely to think of a blowup prompted by sudden recognition that the family name is about to be sullied, parental influence is pervasive, long term, and often subtle. Beginning in infancy, the child is exposed to the "right" kind of values, with the hope that he or she will be drawn to what the parents consider the "right" kind of people later on. The child's social activities may be structured so that he or she is likely to come into contact only with *acceptable* other children (such as through enforced attendance at dance lessons, debutante balls, church youth groups, and private schools). Furthermore, some father-son and mother-daughter talks represent direct attempts at swaying the child. Such parental influence is not always shunned. Parents are usually perceived (correctly or incorrectly) as a source of guidance and wisdom and as having their offspring's best interests at heart. Adolescents report real concern about their parents' reactions and typically hope their attitudes and activities will be approved of (Douvan & Adelson, 1966).

Actively meddling parents, however, run the risk of intensifying romantic feelings. To study this **Romeo and Juliet effect,** Driscoll, Davis, and Lipetz (1972) asked seriously committed dating couples and marriage partners to complete two scales dealing with love and parental interference. The love-scale items were in many respects similar to those used by Rubin, although they were developed independently. The **Parental Interference Scale** asked the extent to which parents tried to meddle, had a bad influence on the relationship, took advantage of or rejected the partner, and criticized the partner. Couples completed the questionnaires twice, approximately six to ten months apart.

Responses to the scales showed a positive, significant correlation between parental interference and feelings of love. But did the interference *cause* intensification of love? Driscoll et al. note—and then discard—several alternative explanations. First, maybe parental opposition becomes great only if the couple seems seriously involved. Intensification of love could then cause an increase in interference. This alternative, the researchers suggest, seems unlikely, because a comparison of responses to the first and second administrations of the questionnaires shows that parental interference occurs first. A second possibility is that parental interference could successfully break up couples with low levels of love, leaving only couples with a high level of love intact. If this "selective-attrition" explanation were true, however, one would expect parental interference to break up relationships between the first and second administrations of the scales. Since this did not happen, this alternative can also be discarded. A third possibility—that background characteristics resulted in both parental interference and intense love—was not revealed by the available measures. What we are left with, then, is the explanation that active parental interference raises love to new heights.

The Romeo and Juliet effect is quite understandable in terms of several theories. First, active interference may make the relationship harder to maintain, and dissonance theory suggests that expending trouble and effort to maintain a relationship would make that relationship attractive. Second, according to a theory that will be presented in Chapter 8, when one person tries to impair the freedom of another (such as by trying to stop a son or daughter from dating someone from the "wrong side of the tracks"), the second person will find the discouraged act attractive and be motivated to perform it. Finally, interference is frustrating. In accordance with the theory of passionate love, frustration could intensify passion by increasing the arousal component of this emotion.

Two other findings of the Driscoll et al. study are of interest. First, although parental interference had an influence on both married and unmarried couples, it affected the unmarried couples more than the married ones. Second, among married couples, variables other than parental interference bore a very close relationship to love intensity. For example, feelings of love were highly correlated with trust in the partner, a lack of criticism from the partner, and an absence of hurtful and obnoxious be- haviors on the part of the partner. (These correlations were present but were much smaller in the case of the unmarried couples.) Premarital love is associated with romance and passion, which are more likely to be af- fected by parental interference. Marital love is associated with friendship and companionship, which are less affected by parental influence.

Peer-Group Influences

In social psychology, a **peer group** is a group of individuals of sim- ilar ages and interests and with similar rights and obligations. Peer groups exert pressure on individual members to conform, and such pressures may be particularly intense during adolescence (Chapter 9). A person's peer group is thus likely to affect when dating begins and who is dated. Peers offer the adolescent approval for choosing some kinds of partners but not for choosing others.

Within an adolescent group there is often consensus concerning the desirable qualities of a date. The specific characteristics endorsed change from group to group and over time. In the 1950s the ideal man might have been the football hero, whereas in the 1970s he may be the one most heavily into popular music or psychedelic drugs. In the 1950s, premium might have been placed on background and manners, and in the 1970s it might be placed on openness and honesty. Whatever the group standards, dating the "right" kind of person signifies success and is rewarded with prestige and approval. Dating the "wrong" kind of per- son leads to ridicule and rejection. In some settings a "dating and rating" game develops, with the winner being the person who gets the most dates with the most popular people.

Peer groups also dictate the right and proper procedures for dating. For example, several years ago a relationship might have begun with a Coke date, then proceeded to movie dates, and only later advanced to expressions of affection. In the 1970s the idea of going on a Coke date and parking in lovers' lane seems to be rather quaint. Yet it would still appear true that there are group standards indicating appropriate levels of involvement at different points in a relationship. Nowadays, physical contact may precede the sharing of ideas, hopes, and aspirations.

The Influence of Formally Organized Groups

Formally organized groups also encourage some kinds of romantic relationships and discourage others. One function of church groups is to help people meet and date people with similar backgrounds. Miss Morgenstern will never become Mrs. Morgan if she is never allowed out of the synagogue. Other groups may be blind (or partially blind) to religious background but encourage associations among people of equivalent social status. In a provocative paper, sociologist John Scott (1965) has argued that the traditional fraternity and sorority system was important in this regard.

According to Scott, in the early years of this century the American middle class began to send its daughters to state colleges so that they would be easily accessible to middle-class boys. The problem was that state colleges did not carefully discriminate among students on the basis of race, creed, color, or national origin. As a result, although Daughter was likely to meet someone of reasonable intellectual competence and with bright "prospects" for the future (since he would be armed with a college diploma), the boy might nevertheless lack what prejudiced parents would politely call a "suitable background."

As an antidote to this problem, the traditional sorority system gathered girls of similar ethnicity, religion, background, and social status into one residence unit. There they were occupied with various group activities (planning teas, building papier-mâché floats, and so forth) that minimized contact with people from other races or religions and from poor families. Dating was encouraged, but only with members of fraternities that were "matched rather nicely on the basis of ethnicity or class." There were planned picnics, parties, and dinners, and concerted efforts were made to arrange dates for difficult cases. The sorority also served as a school of upper-class behavior where girls learned how to "dress with expensive restraint . . . make appropriate conversation, and drink like a lady." Rejection of one's bid to join a sorority was a cause of distress, not only because it implied that one was substandard but also because it severely lessened one's chances for a "good" marriage. Once a coed was in a sorority, proposals were not likely to be forthcoming from men of higher-status fraternities and were not likely to be accepted from members of lower-status fraternities. The quality of one's spouse thus rested on the quality of one's sorority. According to Scott, the system worked, in that sorority girls got engaged faster than nonsorority girls, and they got what were considered to be the better "catches."

Scott's observations are now well over ten years old. Since they were written, the Women's Liberation movement has reduced the premium placed on getting married. Policies and laws now prohibit discrimination on the basis of race, creed, color, or national origin (although people may still understand when they are not really wanted). Fraternities and sororities are on the decline in many locations, and those that thrive seem to have been reorganized along new lines. Yet Scott's basic hypothesis—that certain groups have the function of promoting "suitable marriages"—remains reasonable. It still appears that people are encouraged to marry people with similar backgrounds.

Endogamy and Exogamy

An **endogamous choice** refers to selecting someone of one's own group, class, or kind for purposes of dating and mating, whereas an **exogamous choice** refers to choosing someone who is not a member of one's own group, class, or kind. As we have seen, within broad limits, social pressures foster endogamy.

Encouraging people to date and mate with those who are from the same "group" (loosely defined) has at least three beneficial consequences (DeLamater, 1974). First, there is a perpetuation of the status quo. Group values and traditions can thus be preserved down through the generations. Second, to the extent that common interests, values, and needs contribute to marital success, the pathway to marriage should be smoothed and the marriages themselves given a basis for stability. Third, such in-group choices may strengthen the group by providing new emotional bonds that help cement the members together. Of course, there are also some limits to pressures for endogamy. The ultimate expression of endogamy would be the choice of a romantic partner from one's own immediate family. Although this has been known to happen for purposes of preserving power or wealth (the crowned heads of Europe at one time consisted of an intricate network of siblings, cousins, aunts, and uncles), marrying someone who is a first cousin or closer is generally discouraged in Western society.

DeLamater (1974) has also listed four reasons why exogamy might be preferable to endogamy. First, pressures toward endogamy narrow the range of options. Diversity is limited, and the opportunity for fulfilling unique needs is reduced accordingly. Second, within many small groups, unregulated endogamous choices can lead to disruptive competitions and rivalries, which impair the group's normal functioning. One can well imagine the fate of an expedition in which male and female scientists spend more time fighting for each other's favors than tending their instruments. Third, endogamous choices reduce the number of linkages between the group and the larger society. Exogamous choices, on the other hand, can provide the social glue that binds the smaller social unit (such as the folks of Warren, Rhode Island) to the larger collectivity (the people of the U. S. A.). Finally, when it comes to romance, a person from one's own group may simply seem less exciting. Lambert, Rothschild, Altland, and Green (1972, p. 86) note:

> A . . . new living pattern has been created in coeducational dorms on several college campuses throughout the country (*Life*, November 20, 1970). At first glance, it appears that such living arrangements tend to deemphasize sex and place it in a more practical perspective. When a boy sees a girl every day, she becomes more of a friend and less of a sex object. Apparently, the familiarity of daily living breeds a nonromantic heterosexual relationship.

In an exploratory study of the social factors that regulate intimate relationships within college residence units, DeLamater (1974) surveyed students within a small residential college (fewer than 400 students) that was part of a larger university community (more than 30,000 students). Students were asked if they were having an "intimate physical relationship" and, if so, whether their partner was also a member of the college. Students who were not actively involved were asked whether they would prefer to date a college member.

Results revealed an interesting sex difference. In terms of involvement in actual relationships and preferences for future relationships, women showed a desire for men *outside* the immediate community. Men were more likely to be involved with (or to want to be involved with) someone from *inside* the residential college. Many reasons were cited for the choices. However, the issue of accessibility was a recurrent theme. Men evaluated "access" favorably; they were attracted to women within the college because these women were handy and convenient. Women evaluated access negatively; their preference for an exogamous choice often reflected a desire to inhibit gossip. Thus men were motivated to make endogamous choices for reasons of convenience and women to make exogamous choices for reasons of privacy.

PART SUMMARY

In the last decade or so, experimentally oriented social psychologists have begun to seriously study romantic love. In a pioneering attempt, Rubin developed a scale to measure romantic love. Comparing responses to this scale with responses to a scale of liking provides some evidence of reliability and validity and shows that liking and loving are conceptually distinct. The love scale has been used to predict the amount of time people spend gazing into each other's eyes.

Passionate love does not seem easily explained in terms of rewards and punishments, since frustration and misery sometimes fan the fires of passion. Walster suggests that this phenomenon can be understood in terms of Schachter's two-component theory of emotion. Passionate love would thus involve a general state of activation or arousal and the presence of cues that cause the person to think "This must be love."

A number of factors affect choice of a romantic partner. As in liking relationships, similarity, propinquity, and interlocking needs are of consequence. Physical appearance is also important. On the one hand, people are interested in as good-looking a partner as possible, but, on the other, they are afraid that someone who is better looking than they will reject them. The consequence is that a person may prefer to date someone who is of equal attractiveness. A woman is likely to be highly valued by a given man if she plays "easy to get" for that man but "hard to get" for other men. Rubin suggests that good looks, brains, money, and other social assets are used in trade-offs in dating and mating. Each of us does the best we can with what we've got.

Romantic involvements are very much affected by outside social influences. Through the instilling of values, the control of their children's social environment, and direct guidance and counseling, parents try to ensure that their child will become involved with someone they consider to be the "right kind of person," and their influence is often accepted. However, parental meddling can also intensify a love relationship. Peer groups offer guidance about whom, how, and when to date. Within groups of adolescent peers, there is likely to be consensus concerning what constitutes an acceptable date. Dating this kind of person earns social approval. Formally organized groups, such as prep schools, church groups, and traditional sororities and fraternities, encourage people of similar backgrounds, values, and class standing to become interested in one another.

An endogamous choice is the selection of a partner from one's own group; an exogamous choice is the selection of a person from a different group. Each kind of choice has important personal and social consequences. In a preliminary study of these choices, DeLamater found that women had a preference for intimate relationships with men who were not part of the same living unit, whereas men preferred involvement with women who were part of the same living unit. The women showed a concern for privacy, but the men were more concerned with convenience.

7

Harmful and Helpful Behavior

AGGRESSION

BIOLOGICAL BASES FOR AGGRESSION

People's Fighting Instincts
The Bad-Blood Hypothesis

FRUSTRATION AND AGGRESSION

Instigation
Inhibitions
Displacement and Catharsis
Frustration as One Source of Arousal

SOCIAL LEARNING AND AGGRESSION

Aggression as a Socially Learned Response
Facilitation and Disinhibition Effects
Reinforcement and Aggression
Implications for Reducing Violence in Society

PART SUMMARY

HELPING BEHAVIOR

THE HELPER

Personality Variables
Feelings of Competence
Mood

THE VICTIM

Character
Dependency
Reciprocity

THE SITUATION

Severity of the Situation
Modeling Effects

The Bystander Effect
The Urban Setting

PART SUMMARY

By his own admission, convicted killer Carl Panzram bent his whole mind to figuring out different ways to injure and punish his enemies, and he considered everyone to be his enemy (Gaddis & Long, 1970). One of his plans was to place a large contact bomb in the middle of a railroad tunnel so that, when the engine of a passenger train struck it, it would explode and wreck the train. Then he would pump poison gas fumes into the tunnel, don a gas mask, enter the tunnel, and rob the bodies. In the late 1920s, when this plan was devised, many more people traveled by train than is the case now. Panzram estimated that he could gather $50,000 to $100,000 from about 300 or 400 dead passengers.

But this was only the beginning of his plan. The money obtained from the great train robbery was to be invested in war industry; then, to ensure big dividends, a war was to be touched off between England and the United States. Panzram expected to accomplish this latter feat either by sinking a British battleship in New York harbor (and making it look as if the U. S. navy had done it) or by blowing up an American ship in the middle of the Panama Canal (and making it look as if *England's* navy had done it).

Fortunately, this man's fantasies ran well ahead of his performance capabilities, although he did manage to kill 25 people before he got his opportunity to spit at the hangman on the way down. Carl Panzram, suggested noted psychiatrist Karl Menninger, was the "logical product" of the harsh prison system of the times (Gaddis & Long, 1970).

In this chapter we will consider some of the causes of our most ignoble and noble behaviors. In the first half of the chapter we will consider the conditions under which one person is likely to inflict pain and injury on another. In the second half of the chapter we will consider the conditions under which one person is likely to act unselfishly in another person's behalf.

AGGRESSION

Definitions of aggression must take into account both behavior and intent. A strictly behavioral definition might define aggression as behavior that results in personal injury or in the destruction of property. However, according to this definition, a doctor who administers an injection or a flustered hostess who drops a trayload of filled coffee cups on the new white shag rug would have to be defined as aggressive. To accommodate both behavior and intent, let's define as **aggression** any activity, either physical or verbal, that has as a goal the infliction of harm or damage on someone or something (Berkowitz, 1969a). Intent may be stated, or it may be inferred by the observer (Bandura, 1973). Because people engaging in aggressive activity may attempt to disguise their motives, and because the processes we use to infer people's intents involve a strong element of the subjective (Chapter 3), there is always a chance that a person's behavior will be mislabeled. For example, a spiteful murder may be dismissed as an accidental shooting, or an accidental shooting might be adjudged to be a spiteful murder.

Aggressive activity always has been, is, and may remain a major part of human life. Some of the earliest records of people describe military activity, and today we are constantly bombarded with factual and fictional accounts of aggression and violence. Why do people make one another suffer so? Although there are many answers to this question, three views of aggression dominate the behavioral and social sciences today. The first is that aggression is biologically determined by an inbred, aggressive drive. The second theory is that aggression results from frustration, or the blocking of goal-directed activity. A third view is that observational learning and social reinforcement explain much human aggressive activity. Let's consider each of these explanations in turn.

BIOLOGICAL BASES FOR AGGRESSION

Today more than three million species of animals stalk the face of the earth and swim its seas and oceans. Although the popular view of the jungle as a "war of all against all" is essentially incorrect, because not every species fights with every other species, one does find creatures of many sizes and shapes destroying conspecifics or other animal life. Barnacles of the species *Balanus balanoides* eliminate barnacles of the species *Chthamalus stellatus* by brute force: the latter are simply undercut and lifted off, or perhaps squashed. Ants are ferocious fighters; their clashes leave the battleground littered with severed abdomens, legs, and antennae (Hingston, 1932). Certain species of dragonflies use their wings to beat others out of the air (Wilson, 1969).

There would appear to be almost constant warfare between large, neighboring families of rats. The female rat is likely to be the murder specialist. After she slinks up to a victim that is innocently munching away at its feeding place, a sudden pounce and a quick nip through the carotid artery keep the struggle brief (Lorenz, 1966).

Quite a few writers have catapulted to fame with amusing stories about skull-bashing baboons and other primates that tear one another limb from limb. Ardrey (1961) has described the meeting of two groups of howler monkeys:

> When the two groups sight each other, each on the fringe of its territory, all break into a total rage. Males, females, juveniles and infants become ants on a hot plate, leaping through the branches, scudding through the tree-tops, screeching, barking, chattering in frenzy. The forest cathedral becomes a green asylum for its insane inhabitants, and the howls of apparent melancholia become the shrieks of the totally demented.*

The naturalists who have observed such phenomena have not felt that modeling and reinforcement provide compelling explanations of aggressive behavior; rather, they find it tempting to look to biology for an answer. Thus a number of theorists have suggested that aggression is instinctive, or somehow bred into the organism in the course of evolution. Two barnacles fight over the best spot on a rotting ship's hulk and two rats attack each other because the immediate environment is not sufficient to sustain life in both of them. The aggressive survive, and over generations the pacifists are forcibly eliminated from the gene pool.

People, like barnacles, are the product of evolution. Thus it is also tempting to describe human aggression as instinctive. Ardrey (1961, 1966), for example, suggests that humans have a natural instinct to kill and that war is a hand-me-down from the days when there were conflicts over crops of bananas. Theories suggesting that much of our behavior is instinctive and the product of evolution are called **ethological theories** of behavior (Lockard, 1971; Nelson, 1974).

People's Fighting Instincts

The most influential ethological theory of aggression is that formulated by Konrad Lorenz (1966). According to him, humans have a fighting instinct that they share with members of other species. Aggressive behavior has two components: an "internal" component and an "external" component. The internal component is aggressive energy or **aggressive drive;** this self-generating, spontaneous energy builds up over time without

*From *African Genesis*, by R. Ardrey. Copyright © 1961 by Literate S. A. Reprinted by permission of Atheneum Publishers, Inc.

outside provocation. The external component of aggression is an aspect of the environment called a releaser. In ethological theory, a **releaser** is a stimulus that elicits a biologically preprogrammed behavior or series of behaviors. When sufficient aggressive energy has been built up within the nervous system, the presentation of a releaser will trigger an aggressive outburst. This drains off the aggressive energy, and presentation of another releaser will not again trigger an outburst until the organism has had a chance to replenish the energy supply.

Intraspecies aggression can serve the useful functions of weeding out the lame and infirm and of spreading out populations geographically, thus ensuring that the number of organisms in an area does not exhaust the food supply. However, there is an important evolutionary difference in intraspecies aggression between nonhumans and humans. As nonhumans developed the instinct of aggression, they also developed inhibitions against aggression. Thus aggression is often "ritualized" among nonhumans. With much puffery, two beasts may snort, paw, growl, snap, and so forth, but neither gets hurt because the more faint-hearted of the pair submits. For example, one wolf may throw itself down and bare its throat—a gesture of submission or appeasement that causes the other to cease the attack before bloodshed occurs. But in the case of humans the instinct to aggress (and the capability for engineering machines of destruction) has evolved far more rapidly than the aggression-inhibiting mechanisms. People who attempt to submit or show appeasement by falling on their knees and begging for mercy are still liable to have their heads blown off.

According to Lorenz, because it is biologically generated, aggressive energy is a fact of life. However, although it cannot be eliminated, it can be rechanneled along relatively harmless lines. For example, rather than having it out with switchblades, two people might fight each other with pillows or styrofoam bats; rather than hassling over national boundaries, rivalrous nations might engage in vigorous sports contests. Lorenz also encourages people to laugh and make friends—although, according to the theory, nothing can prevent the buildup and discharge of aggressive drive (Bandura, 1973).

Explaining aggression as instinctive or innate has a certain appeal. For one thing, it is incontestable that people have both the physical and the mental capacity to aggress. Moreover, this kind of explanation suggests a certain satisfying continuity within the species. Another reason for the attractiveness of ethological explanations is that they are both general (in that they apply to a wide array of organisms) and parsimonious (in that few concepts are needed). And, as Wilson (1969) points out, we can derive a certain feeling of comfort from viewing our sins as only animal sins with their origin in the dim evolutionary past.

On the other hand, the validity of ethological theories of human aggression is at best suspect. Lorenz, Ardrey, and similar theorists have been challenged on almost every point except literary style (Berkowitz, 1969b; Montagu, 1968; Elms, 1972; Bandura, 1973; Nelson, 1974).

The first major point of criticism involves the fact that evidence of instinctive regulators of aggressiveness, even among nonhumans, has been shown to be highly equivocal. For example, Elms (1972), a social psychologist, roamed a forest in pursuit of howler monkeys and found them to be relatively mild mannered in their dealings with one another; according to Bandura (1973), animals do not possess innate signals for stopping each other's attacks. Nelson (1974) notes that, although reviewers from outside the field of ethology have been willing to assume the validity of Lorenz' animal evidence (but feel that his findings do not apply to humans), reviewers who share Lorenz' interests in animals feel that his conclusions are fundamentally wrong. There is considerable agreement that Lorenz and Ardrey have ignored controlled observation in favor of more easily gained evidence.

Although there are doubts about the impact of instincts, there are no doubts about the impact of learning and other environmental factors on animal aggression. Among numerous studies cited by Bandura (1973) is one by Kuo (1930), who raised kittens under three conditions: with rat-killing mothers, by themselves, or with rats as companions. Whereas 85% of the kittens raised with rat-killing mothers became rat killers, 45% of the isolates and only 17% of the kittens raised with rat companions became rat killers. When non-rat-killing kittens that had been reared in isolation were exposed to a rat-killing model, 82% became rat killers. Only 7% of the non-rat-killing kittens that had been raised with rat companions killed rats even following exposure to a rat-killing model.

A second criticism of ethological theories is that, even if instincts were adequate to account for aggression among barnacles, dragonflies, and ants, it would not necessarily follow that the same explanation would apply to humans. Pointing out that two European armies fighting over the Ukraine are in some ways analogous to two groups of ants fighting over a sugar cube does not lead to the conclusion that the underlying principles are the same. There are tremendous differences among species (compare yourself to a praying mantis), and animals cannot be construed as simple versions of humans (Lockard, 1971).

Perhaps the major objection to instinct interpretations of aggression is that they cannot account for the variability in human aggressive activity (Berkowitz, 1969a, 1969b; Bandura, 1973). People will sometimes fight even though they are well fed and their homes are secure, and people will sometimes not fight even though they are hungry and crowded. When people do fight, they fight not only with fang and claw but also with pen, grenade, gas, rocket, flamethrower, fire hose, and mace—none of which is successfully used by relying on biologically preprogrammed behavior sequences. Human fighting often involves highly organized armies that have only the most rudimentary counterparts among other species. To staff these armies, appeals to people's aggressive instincts usually have to be supplemented with some form of draft or conscription. At best, instincts can account for only a limited amount of human aggressive activity.

The Bad-Blood Hypothesis

If, as is well known, animals can be bred to be violent, could violent, aggressive behavior also run in human families? Such "bad-blood" interpretations of violent people have been around for more than a century. In the 1870s a man by the name of Dugdale traced the history of seven generations of a large New York family. Their high rate of participation in criminal and antisocial acts suggested to Dugdale some sort of hereditary taint. "This illustrious family tree," notes McNeil (1966), "contained so many varieties of personal and social ugliness that it cost the state of New York approximately $1,300,000 during only 73 years of its existence." It wasn't until years later that this and other "bad-seed" studies were recognized as preposterous. Members of these families share not only similar genes but also similar environments.

In the 1960s, however, new evidence was found suggesting a genetic basis for individual differences in aggression. A certain chromosomal aberration that can occur only in men—known as the **XYY genotype**—was found to be present in the genetic composition of a number of men incarcerated in a hospital for the criminally insane.

The incidence of the XYY pattern is rare, but a recent review suggests that there is a definite association between the XYY genotype and institutionalization for antisocial behavior (Hook, 1973). For example, in one study there were no XYYs in 2040 "normal adult males," but, in a maximum-security hospital, 7 out of 197 tested, or 3.6%, were XYY. Summarizing a large number of studies, Hook suggests that the maximum rate of occurrence of the XYY genotype in the population at large is 0.4%, but among male inmates of "penal-mental" institutions it is about 2%, or five times the maximum base rate. There are some problems here, because the XYY chromosome is associated with certain physical traits that may themselves be related to aggression, and the "statistics" might have been collected in such a way as to exaggerate the degree of association between XYY and violence (Owen, 1972; Bandura, 1973; Hook, 1973). However, even if the XYY pattern invariably leads to aggression, 98 out of 100 locked-up brutes do not show the XYY anomaly. Thus this explanation, even if "real," is of little practical significance. Once again a purely biological argument is insufficient to explain human variability.

As Wrong (1963, p. 78) has noted, *"In the beginning, there is the body."* Humans are biological organisms, which makes some behavior impossible, some behavior possible, and some behavior probable. People are blessed or cursed with the capacity to aggress. To understand when, where, and how they use this capacity, we must turn to a consideration of environmental factors.

FRUSTRATION AND AGGRESSION

People hope and aspire, but, unlike in B movies, their dreams do not always come true. The pathway to happiness is fraught with hazards and obstacles. The instructor announces a test next Monday, and a planned weekend trip has to be postponed. A sought-after job opens up, but it is given to somebody else. You come to the end of a mystery novel and discover that the last three pages have been torn out.

Frustration refers to the smashing of hopes, the thwarting of desires, and the appearance of obstacles that keep people from reaching their goals. According to the **frustration-aggression hypothesis,** the natural consequence of frustration is aggression (Dollard, Doob, Miller, Mowrer, & Sears, 1939). Although people may seem to greet frustrations with acceptance and aplomb, close examination should reveal that the aggressive response is not destroyed but merely "delayed, disguised, or otherwise deflected from the immediate goal." According to frustration-aggression theorizing, the strength, direction, and form of aggression are determined by two factors: *instigation* and *inhibition.*

Instigation

The strength of the instigation, or motivation to aggress following frustration, is said to be affected by three variables: (1) the strength of the blocked behavior, (2) the extent of the frustration, and (3) the total number of frustrated responses.

First, the more highly motivated the frustrated behavior, the greater the instigation to aggress. Being stopped by a police officer while driving to the travel agent's to pick up your tickets to Europe should be less of an instigator than being stopped while rushing to the airport to catch your plane. In addition, the frustration-aggression theorists note that, since the motivation to achieve a goal increases as that goal becomes nearer, the timing of frustration is important. Thus, if you were forced to cancel your trip to Europe a few weeks in advance, there would be less instigation to aggress than if your plans had been upset only a few days before your departure.

Second, the greater the extent of the frustration (that is, the more effectively it blocks the response), the greater the instigation to aggress. For example, you may not be ready to leave on your trip to Europe until you have located your dark glasses, camera, and airplane tickets. Although an inability to locate any of these items would be upsetting, an inability to find the airplane tickets would be particularly frustrating. Dollard et al. present numerous crime statistics purporting to show that greater magnitudes of frustration are associated with greater incidences of antisocial acts involving property damage and violence.

Third, the number of responses frustrated will also determine instigation to aggress. Minor frustrations may add up and result in an outburst far out of proportion to the most recent frustration. For example, you might not have "blown up" at the inept baggage handler if earlier that day you hadn't gotten a ticket while driving to the travel agent's and been seriously delayed by an inability to find your sunglasses, camera, and plane tickets.

Inhibitions

Learned inhibitions determine the form and direction of aggression following instigation to aggress. Usually, the strongest tendency is to aggress against the frustrating agent, which makes some sense if it removes the obstacle (as when a strikebreaker, or "scab," shoves through a picket line). However, direct aggression is often punished (as many crippled scabs have found out). As a result, people learn to control their reactions to frustrations. The infant has to wait for food, the child is frustrated by the teacher's demands, and the adolescent is frustrated by a rejecting date. Socialization involves learning the inhibition of aggression toward parents, teachers, and peers.

In an ingenious field study, Doob and Gross (1968) examined the hypothesis that frustrated people will be less likely to respond aggressively if the frustrator is of relatively high social status. One of the experimenters drove up to a traffic light and stopped just as it turned red. The unwitting subject was the person in the car stopped immediately behind him. When the light turned green, the experimenter kept his vehicle stationary. The question was how long the subject would wait before angrily beeping the horn.

In the high-status condition the experimenter was neatly attired in a sports jacket and white sport shirt. He drove a nearly new luxury car that had been carefully washed and polished for the occasion. In the low-

status condition the experimenter was not neatly attired and drove an old, beat-up, and initially inexpensive auto.

When the high-status frustrator blocked the intersection, only 50% of the subjects honked, but, when the low-status driver did so, 84% of the drivers honked. Considering only honkers, there was a longer wait before honking at the high-status driver. Finally, there was the statistically insignificant observation that, although no subjects attempted to bump into the high-status car with their own vehicle, two subjects rammed the low-status car from behind.

Displacement and Catharsis

The tension generated by frustration will not erupt into aggression if the frustrated person can find a goal that is a satisfactory substitute for the blocked goal. A substitute goal will reduce the instigation to aggress to the extent that the original need is satisfied. For example, the person who seeks great wealth as a Shakespearean actor may be mollified if he or she acquires a large sum for acting in a television situation comedy. However, satisfactory substitute activities are not always available, and, when frustration cannot be undone, the aggressive drive will not simply evaporate. It must somehow be discharged.

If learned inhibitions or other factors prevent aggressive behavior toward the frustrator, aggression is likely to be directed toward a target that is as similar as possible to the frustrator but that does not have the power to retaliate. Aggression directed toward such a substitute animate target (as when a man takes it out on his children after having been denied a raise) or toward an inanimate target (as when a 98-pound weakling kicks a chair after a 200-pound bully walks off with his girl) is called **displaced aggression.**

The *perceived intent* of a frustrator would appear to affect displacement of aggression. An **arbitrary frustration** is one that is seen as willfully imposed, as when your roommate deliberately, and with malice aforethought, sets a torch to your term-paper notes. A **nonarbitrary frustration** is one seen as unintended, as when your roommate accidentally incinerates your notes in the course of housecleaning. Typically, less aggression is directed toward the frustrator when the frustration is seen as accidental or nonarbitrary.

In an ingenious study of displacement, Burnstein and Worchel (1962) had groups of subjects try to pool information to reach a decision. Within each group was a secret accomplice of the experimenter's who frustrated the group by interrupting the discussion, thereby preventing the group from making the decision. In the arbitrary-frustration condition, the interruptions were made attributable to the willful operation of an obstreperous and obnoxious personality. In the nonarbitrary-frustration condition, the confederate entered wearing a hearing aid, which ostensibly broke down just before the discussion—a sad accident that forced him to keep asking for clarification.

Aggression was measured by means of votes to oust the confederate from the group and by means of questionnaires designed to tap potentially hostile attitudes. In some conditions, subjects raised their hands as the experimenter polled them individually; in other conditions, subjects cast secret ballots. Public- and private-rejection conditions were included to see if the possibility of adverse reactions from others inhibited the expression of aggression.

Compared to subjects in the nonarbitrary-frustration condition, subjects in the arbitrary-frustration condition were far more likely to vote against the stooge. Thus frustration led to more direct aggression when the frustrator was seen as acting willfully and deliberately. However, responses to the questionnaires revealed that the nonarbitrary-frustration subjects felt just as aggressive as the arbitrary-frustration subjects, but they displaced their aggression onto other targets, such as the experimenter. Finally, subjects were more likely to be rejecting when they cast secret ballots than when they voted openly, which suggests that social norms inhibit aggression toward accidental frustrators such as the physically handicapped. Nonarbitrary frustration, then, would appear to lead not to less aggression but to a redirection or displacement of the aggression.

Catharsis refers to the release of pent-up emotions. In the context of the frustration-aggression hypothesis, catharsis refers to the venting or drawing off of aggression. Formally stated, the occurrence of any act of direct or displaced aggression is assumed to reduce the instigation to aggress. For example, after frustrating each other in a number of different ways, a verbal "blowup" between spouses should release the pent-up frustrations and thereby "clear the air" so that the process can start all over again.

An implication of the catharsis principle is that aggression might be controlled or reduced by providing people with some sort of safe outlet for expressing their aggressive impulses. (A close analogy would be drawing off steam from a boiler so it does not explode.) They could smash up a junk car, shoot up beer bottles, rip up newspapers, or beat up a Bobo doll. Another implication of the catharsis principle is that people can vent their aggression vicariously—that is, through watching others aggress.

The catharsis principle is a bit tricky to assess because it is, in fact, several different principles (Doob, 1970; Konečni & Doob, 1972; Doob & Wood, 1972). A distinction must first be made between catharsis through engaging in aggressive activity and catharsis through watching someone else engage in aggressive activity. A distinction must also be made between catharsis through the infliction of pain or injury on one's tormentor and catharsis through the infliction of pain or injury on someone or something other than the tormentor. When these distinctions are drawn, we discover that the principle bandied about as "the catharsis principle" is thus an amalgam of at least four principles, involving all combinations of whether or not the annoyed individual engages in the aggressive activity and whether or not the victim of the aggression is the person responsible for the annoyance. It is not too surprising, therefore, that studies bearing on the catharsis principle yield conflicting results.

Let's consider findings bearing on three versions of the catharsis principle right now but wait a bit before considering findings relevant to the fourth version. First, it appears that, when an individual is allowed to hurt a former tormentor, the likelihood of subsequent aggression against the tormentor is decreased (Konečni & Doob, 1972; Doob & Wood, 1972). This finding is consistent with the already noted version of the catharsis principle suggesting that a heated exchange between a husband and wife may clear the air so that tensions can again start building up. Second, under some conditions at least, harming someone other than one's tormentor can reduce subsequent aggression toward that tormentor. In one study it was found that, compared with annoyed subjects who had no chance to aggress, annoyed subjects who had the chance to injure a third, neutral party were less aggressive when later given an opportunity to harm the tormentor (Konečni & Doob, 1972). Thus there is also some support for the version of the catharsis principle suggesting that "kicking the cat" might keep a person from foolishly aggressing against a nasty boss. Third, seeing someone else harm one's tormentor can reduce one's subsequent aggression toward that tormentor (Doob, 1970; Doob & Wood, 1972). Thus there is also at least some support for the version of the catharsis principle suggesting that an annoyed employee who sees his or her irritating supervisor being annoyed by the supervisor's supervisor may subsequently feel less aggressive toward the immediate supervisor. In sum, there is evidence to support three of the four versions of the catharsis principle.

However, before we fully accept the catharsis principle, four points must be emphasized. First, note that, in each case of reduction of aggression through catharsis, the person was described as somehow annoyed or tormented. In the absence of insult or injury, harming another or seeing another harmed could be expected to *increase* subsequent aggression. As we shall soon see, such an increase could occur as a result of modeling effects. Second, as Doob and his associates have noted, it is not a foregone conclusion that in the three situations just discussed a "draining off of aggressive tensions" was responsible for the reduced aggression. Something else, such as a feeling that the tormentor had gotten "paid off" or gotten what he or she "deserved," could have been responsible. Third, note that cathartic activity would not seem to be a helpful way to reduce violence in our society, for it depends on aggressive activity! Finally, we must reserve our evaluation of the catharsis principle until we have considered the fourth (and perhaps most common) version, which suggests that the likelihood of aggression is reduced when a person sees someone else inflict injury on someone or something that has not been a personal annoyance. We'll discuss research relevant to this aspect of the catharsis principle later in this chapter, after considering a social-learning analysis of aggression.

Frustration as One Source of Arousal

In the 35 years or so since the appearance of the frustration-aggression hypothesis, numerous studies have yielded results generally consistent with it (Sears, Hovland, & Miller, 1940; Miller & Bugelski, 1948; Burnstein & Worchel, 1962; Azrin, Hutchinson, & Hake, 1966; Doob & Gross, 1968). However, it has become clear over the years that the connection between the two variables is actually quite loose (Bandura &

Walters, 1963; Berkowitz, 1969a; Bandura, 1973). For one thing, aggression is only one response to frustration. Instead of leading to aggression, frustration could lead to **stereotyped responding** (senseless repetition of an act, such as running one's fingers through one's hair or tapping a pencil on the table) or to **regression** (a reverting to childish, infantile modes of behavior). Or, as Berkowitz (1969a) notes, frustration may not lead to much of anything if the person doesn't really expect to reach the goal anyway; in this case, rather than "pumping up" aggressive tendencies, repeated frustrations may lead to apathy and withdrawal. Furthermore, aggression often appears in the absence of frustrating circumstances, as when shoving, jostling, smashing bottles, and ripping up the bleachers follow a team *victory* rather than a frustrating defeat. Because of all this variability, the original frustration-aggression hypothesis is not adequate to account for people's aggressive activity.

Berkowitz (1969a) has proposed a modification of the theory, stating that the effect of frustration is to produce a generalized drive or arousal. Whether or not aggression ensues depends on the presence of aggression-related cues in the situation. These cues may be internal (such as thoughts) or external (such as a waving fist). In a sense, aggression is "pulled out" by appropriate cues rather than "pushed out" by strong emotionality—although, when emotionality is very high, very little "pulling out" may be required. Thus, whereas Miller and Dollard dwelt on cues as *inhibitors,* the contemporary view is to consider cues as triggers or *elicitors* (Berkowitz, 1969a, 1974; Bandura, 1973).

The general procedure for testing the arousal-cue formulation has been to create conditions of high and low arousal by means of frustration or other manipulations while at the same time varying the accessibility of cues thought to elicit aggression. The greatest aggression is predicted under conditions in which arousal is high and the aggressive cues are present. Typically, aggression is measured in terms of the amount of shock the subject tries to administer to a confederate. The confederate either is cast in the role of being punished for making mistakes while trying to learn or is cast in a position in which he or she is being "signaled" by means of electric shock.

An interesting example of such research comes from Berkowitz and LePage (1967), who induced a high or low level of arousal and then gave subjects the opportunity to administer shocks to a confederate. Present in the laboratory were either two badminton rackets or a shotgun and a revolver. Under low-arousal conditions, the subjects administered little shock to the confederate, and the presence of the weapons had no effect. Under high-arousal conditions, subjects delivered significantly more shocks in the presence of the weapons than in the presence of the badminton rackets, which suggests that the weapons were aggression-eliciting stimuli. Although a few later studies did not find weapons to be aggression-eliciting stimuli (Buss, Booker, & Buss, 1972), some of the failures to confirm the finding might have resulted from the use of sophisticated or experiment-wise subjects who were concerned about how the experimenter would evaluate them if they aggressed against one another (Turner & Simons, 1974).

It is quite possible that everyday frustrating situations also contain aggression-related cues. Although it may appear in these situations that "frustration" leads to aggression, the aggressive act could also be contingent on specific cues. Again consider the case of being stopped and ticketed by a police officer while rushing to the airport to catch a plane. Afterward you may yell at your spouse or companion, and maybe even run over a stray animal or two. In addition to blocking "goal-directed behavior," being ticketed would also expose you to a number of aggression-related cues. Police officers are usually decked out with mace, clubs, handcuffs, and, no doubt, an imposing revolver. If the "frustrating" officer were wearing a green blazer and carrying a badminton racket, aggressive reactions on your part should be much less likely.

The arousal-cue line of reasoning has three important implications. First, nonfrustrating conditions that raise arousal should also lead to aggression if the appropriate cues are present. As one example, pain can be quite arousing. Whereas losing a finger to a power saw will not necessarily lead to aggression (since aggressive cues are not likely to be present), losing the same finger on the battlefield (where aggressive cues are abundant) may very well lead to aggressive behavior. More than one medal winner has earned his laurels wiping out an enemy emplacement after having a pinky or part of an ear shot off. As another example, being attacked can be quite arousing. A person who is shoved, jostled, or otherwise abused is likely to experience a pounding heart, flushed cheeks, and sweating palms—all of which are indicators of arousal. The common observation that being insulted or attacked elicits aggression is not at all surprising when we consider that associated with an attack will be an abundance of aggressive cues provided by the attacker.

A clear demonstration of how nonfrustrating arousal can affect aggression has been provided by Geen and O'Neal (1969). To manipulate aggressive cues, the experimenters showed some subjects a film clip of an aggressive boxing sequence and showed other subjects a nonaggressive film. Next, subjects were given the opportunity to deliver shocks to a confederate. During this part of the experiment, arousal was manipulated by presenting or withholding white noise, which is known to have arousing properties. (White noise contains all the sounds of the spectrum; you can hear it by listening to the sea or, if you live in Iowa, by cupping a beer mug to your ear.) The most shocks were delivered by subjects who had seen the aggressive film and who had been aroused by the white noise.

The second implication of arousal-cue research is that, if there are no aggression-eliciting cues present in the situation (or if the person has been taught to respond to these cues in a nonaggressive way), frustration should facilitate nonaggressive responding. After observing ten groups of children in a free-play situation, Davitz (1952) trained five groups in aggressive play and the other five groups in nonaggressive, or constructive, play. Aggressive training consisted of teaching four competitive games. For example, in "Scalp," a piece of cloth was tied around the arm of each child. The object was to tear the scalps from others while protecting one's own. In "Break the Ball," each child was provided with a Ping-Pong ball and instructed to break other people's balls while protecting his or her own. Constructive training consisted of teaching children to work cooperatively on murals and jigsaw puzzles.

The experimenter then passed out candy bars to all the children and began showing a movie. Frustration was induced by stopping the projector as the climax of the movie approached and by snatching back the candy bars before they could be eaten. The children were immediately placed again in a free-play situation, and their behavior was filmed. These films were later coded for aggressive activity by two independent judges.

In the aggressive-training group, 70% of the subjects showed increased aggression following frustration. In the constructive-training group, 55% of the subjects showed increased *cooperative* activity. As a result of learning, constructive, not destructive, activity was energized by frustration.

The third implication of arousal-cue theory is that, in the absence of arousing circumstances, aggression-related cues should be unlikely to elicit aggression. That is, any aggressive tendencies elicited by cues alone will idle in "low gear" and not erupt into overt action when the motivational or "drive" component is absent. After showing some children an aggressive film, Hanratty, O'Neal, and Sulzer (1972) frustrated some of them by withholding attractive toys. Later, nonfrustrated children did not aggress, even if they had seen the aggressive movie. Frustrated children did aggress, but only if they had seen the aggressive film.

An interesting series of experiments by Berkowitz and his associates has identified the kinds of cues that are likely to elicit aggression. Berkowitz and Geen (1966) found that observed violence is particularly likely to elicit aggression if the cues present in the observed violent situation are also present in the situation in which the viewer has the opportunity to aggress. In this study, subjects were given the opportunity to administer shocks to a stooge who was introduced either as *Bob* Anderson or as *Kirk*

Anderson. Subjects were shown a film clip, either of an exciting but non-violent race or of a brutal fight scene in which one of the combatants was named *Kirk*. Arousal was also manipulated. Of the aroused subjects shown the aggressive film, more shocks were delivered to a confederate named *Kirk* than to a confederate named *Bob*. The idea, then, is that, if the potential victim or target of aggression is somehow associated with the observed violence, aggression is more likely.

More recently, Berkowitz and Alioto (1973) found that the viewer's interpretation of observed violence is also important. Subjects were shown a film clip either of a prize fight or of a rough football game. Some subjects were told that the film portrayed professional athletes doing their job, whereas other subjects were told that they were watching grudge matches in which the victors had intended to soundly beat and even hurt the losers. Aroused subjects who had been led to interpret the film as aggressive shocked an earlier tormentor more vigorously than did subjects who thought they had viewed professional athletics. In another experiment, subjects were shown a war film that was presented either as fact or as fiction. Subjects who were led to believe that the events portrayed were real were more aggressive than were subjects who thought they were watching fiction. Thus subjects may discount aggressive cues present in an aggressive behavior sequence if the action is presented as nonaggressive or as fictional. Other studies of aggressive cues have been discussed by Berkowitz (1974).

Taken together, the experiments reviewed in this section suggest that some of the limitations of the frustration-aggression hypothesis can be overcome if we interpret frustration as a source of arousal that, like other sources of arousal, is likely to result in aggression when the aggression-related cues are present. This reformulation takes us a long way toward understanding why frustrated people sometimes fail to aggress and why nonfrustrated people sometimes inflict injury and damage.

SOCIAL LEARNING AND AGGRESSION

One of the most influential analyses of human aggressive behavior has come from the modern social-learning theorists, who argue that most, if not all, human aggression is explainable in terms of observational learning and social reinforcement (Bandura & Walters, 1963; Baron & Liebert, 1971; Bandura, 1973). According to this analysis, (1) aggressive responses are socially learned; (2) observing an aggressive model is likely to prompt aggressive activity on the part of the viewer; and (3) patterns of rewards and punishments affect the likelihood that an aggressive response will be performed. After discussing each of these points in turn, we will consider some of the implications for reducing violence in society.

Aggression as a Socially Learned Response

People do not instinctively know how to activate grenades, spray one another with poison gas, or deliver a deft karate chop to the neck. These and other aggressive responses are learned from watching others. At least three types of evidence suggest that social learning has a potent effect on human aggressive activity.

First, carefully controlled laboratory studies show that children learn complex and involved aggressive responses as a result of watching these responses being performed by models. For example, Bandura, Ross, and Ross (1963a) found that children performed a number of novel aggressive responses after observing these responses on the part of a live human, a filmed human, or a cartoon character. Not only did the models transmit novel aggressive responses, but they also reduced the child's inhibitions against performing earlier-learned or improvised aggressive responses.

Second, case histories and field studies of aggressive and nonaggressive people suggest that aggressive models were highly influential in aggressive people's lives. For example, in a comparison of aggressive and nonaggressive children from intact, middle-class homes, Bandura and Walters (1959) found that aggressive boys' parents repeatedly modeled and reinforced combative attitudes and behavior. Highly informative about the effects of filmed models are Eron, Huesmann, Lefkowitz, and Walder's (1972) findings that the extent to which 8-year-old boys viewed violence was positively correlated with their level of interpersonal aggressiveness ten years later. Results of several studies show that the most plausible interpretation of this kind of relationship is that the viewing of violence was the cause and aggressiveness was the effect (Bandura, 1973).

Third, studies of aggressive groups, such as delinquent gangs, the military, and certain warlike societies, usually reveal strong aggressive models and a pattern of reinforcements conducive to aggressive behavior. Comparable nonaggressive groups lack these models and reinforcements (Bandura, 1973). The person born into a slum neighborhood, for example, is likely to be brought up surrounded by angry, aggressive people and is likely to gain approval and status for acting tough and defiant. In the military, potential combatants undergo months of training in fighting. One aim of the training is to help recruits overcome their fear of lethal weapons, and the other aim is to show them how to use these weapons to terrorize others. Good learners are rewarded with promotions and medals. Finally, in societies characterized by a high degree of aggressiveness, children may be trained from birth to engage in combat. For example, Bandura notes that, among the highly warlike Dani of New Guinea, male children are exposed to increasingly warlike situations and encouraged to learn increasingly useful warlike skills. The developing male child first plays a game called "spear the seed," then advances to practice using real spears on inanimate objects, and then begins to use harmless spears on real human opponents. As an adolescent the Dani male is taken to the battlefield to watch actual combat from a distance. All this training prepares the Dani warrior to enter into the daily battles that characterize the tribe's relationship with its neighbors. The Dani fight not to obtain food or territory but to appease the spirits of previously slain warriors. Since new warriors are always slain in the process of atonement, the war is never ending.

Facilitation and Disinhibition Effects

Social-learning theory suggests that viewing an aggressive model should have response-facilitation and response-disinhibition effects (Chapter 4). Thus, seeing someone else aggress should raise the likelihood of an aggressive response on the part of an observer, even when new learning is not involved. This prediction is diametrically opposed to a prediction forthcoming from the catharsis principle.

Earlier we saw that "the catharsis principle" is perhaps best regarded as having four different versions and that there has been at least some support for three of these versions. Specifically, some evidence suggests that, if an annoyed person is allowed to act aggressively toward a tormentor, to act aggressively toward a nontormentor, or to view a third person tormenting the tormentor, the amount of subsequent aggression that the annoyed person will direct toward the tormentor is likely to be reduced. But the catharsis principle also suggests that aggression will be reduced if a person views *someone else* aggressing against someone or something that has *not* been a source of personal annoyance. Thus a person should feel less aggressive after watching a bloody massacre in a movie, even though the people slain had never been a source of personal annoyance. However, the idea that a cathartic effect results from watching someone else aggressing against a third party who has not harmed the viewer is unsupported by most of the research data. Although one study suggests that this effect occurs (Feshbach & Singer, 1971), this experiment has been severely criticized (Ball-Rokeach, 1971; Bandura, 1973). If this particular version of the catharsis principle works, it would appear to do so under a very limited range of conditions and on a (for now) nonpredictable basis. Viewing violence on television or in the movies raises, rather than lowers, the observer's level of aggressive activity.

Social-learning theory's prediction that the observation of violence begets more violence has been repeatedly confirmed. Hanratty, Liebert, Morris, and Fernandez (1969) found, using direct and unequivocal measures of aggression, that children who watched an aggressive film of a clown being attacked were more likely to aggress than were controls. Baron and Kepner (1970) reported that subjects who viewed an aggressive model were more aggressive than control subjects and that controls, in turn, were more aggressive than subjects exposed to a nonaggressive model. Berkowitz (1970a) found that women who had recently heard Don Rickles' hostile humor rated a victim in such a way as to lower the likelihood that she would get a job. Liebert and Baron (1972) noted that children who had viewed a segment from the violent crime program *The Untouchables* were more likely to hurt another child than were children who had viewed a nonviolent racing sequence. Furthermore, you have probably noted that, in many of the studies by Berkowitz and his colleagues, the aggression-related cues were embedded in film clips of people fighting. The roster of studies could be lengthened, but the research just cited would seem to lay bare the facts. When social-learning principles are pitted against predictions based on one major version of the catharsis principle, social-learning theory will win almost every time (Baron & Liebert, 1971; Bandura, 1973).

Reinforcement and Aggression

According to Bandura's social-learning analysis, the likelihood of an aggressive act will depend in part on the patterns of rewards and punishments that the potential aggressor associates with the situation. Reinforcers may be external to the aggressor (a captured city, cheers from a gathered throng) or internal to the aggressor (feelings of pride or guilt).

In quite a few cases, very tangible external rewards may prompt aggressive behavior, as when a big child bullies a small child and is rewarded by gaining possession of a prized toy. Indeed, in many cases aggressive activities seem to be oriented toward achieving external tangible goals, such as a toy, a sack of gold, or a piece of land; the infliction of pain and injury is only an incidental factor (Bandura, 1973; Berkowitz, 1974; Tedeschi et al. , 1974). Thus a mob that overthrows a tyrant may be more interested in obtaining food than in beating the tyrant into a bloody pulp, and an armed robber may be more interested in getting some money to enjoy the good life than in slitting the victim's throat. Tyrants who relinquish power gracefully and robbery victims who pay up often spare themselves considerable pain and discomfort. External rewards follow successful acts of aggression so often that some writers have suggested that psychologists would do better to talk in terms of the "exercise of coercive power" than in terms of aggression (Tedeschi et al. , 1974).

Social reinforcement is a second external regulator of aggressive activity. As indicated earlier, groups such as delinquent gangs, which are characterized by a high degree of aggressive activity, usually reward members' violent attitudes and actions with approval and with promotions within the status-ranking hierarchy. Unambiguous evidence of the effects of social reinforcement on aggression comes from Geen and Stonner (1971), who had subjects punish a "learner's" errors. Under experimental conditions the experimenter responded to the subject's administration of shock to a victim with verbal approval in the form of "That's good!" or "You're doing fine!" As Figure 7-1 shows, only the socially reinforced subjects delivered increasingly greater shocks to the inept learner.

Finally, there are internal regulators in the form of pride or guilt. Inflicting pain on another person may initially be rewarding because it exacts compliance from the victim, but, as a result of the classical-conditioning process, another person's suffering may become rewarding in its

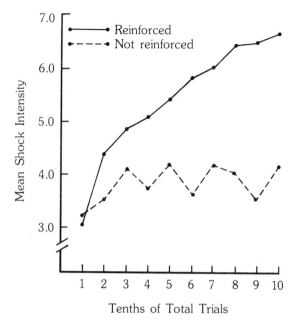

Figure 7-1. The effects of reinforcement on administering shock to a victim. (From "Effects of Aggressiveness Habit Strength on Behavior in the Presence of Aggression-Related Stimuli," by R. G. Geen and D. Stonner, *Journal of Personality and Social Psychology*, 1971, *17*, 151. Copyright 1971 by the American Psychological Association. Reprinted by permission.)

own right. On the other hand, inflicting harm on another person may make us feel anxious and guilty. Relevant here is Aronfreed's research (Chapter 4) implying that firm but reasoned punishment at the beginning of a child's agressive act is likely to lead to strong internal controls against aggression. Aggression is not uniformly self-rewarded or self-punished without regard to the victim or to the circumstances. For example, ordinarily humane people may commit atrocities in time of war, and heartless brutes may feel guilty for swearing in front of their parents.

Implications for Reducing Violence in Society

Instinct theories offer little in the way of workable plans for reducing and controlling the level of aggression within society. The catharsis principle offers the disheartening suggestion that aggression is needed to reduce aggression. Social-learning theory, on the other hand, offers a number of remedies, many of which have withstood testing both in the lab and in the field. Bandura (1973) concludes his book on aggression by tracing some of the practical implications of social-learning theory for reducing and controlling aggression. In this section we will consider: (1) what might be done to modify the behavior of aggressive individuals; (2) how the prevalence of aggressive models on television might be reduced; (3) what might be done to make police and prisons more effective protectors of the peace; and (4) why society must attempt to eliminate the frustrations it imposes on the disadvantaged segments of the population.

First, social-learning theory has a number of implications for helping violent individuals control their aggressive behavior and seek nonaggressive solutions to their problems. According to Bandura, highly aggressive people often resort to violence because they do not have the skills for getting what they want through peaceful means. For example, nonviolent people may have the verbal skills necessary to talk their way out of a tough situation, but violent persons can get out only by using their fists. As another example, a well-educated, middle-class person can achieve the good life through holding a well-paying, middle-class job, but the lower-class person may believe that he or she can achieve the good life only by resorting to armed robbery.

Bandura suggests that violent people be offered the chance to socially learn nonaggressive ways of coping with problems and of achieving their various goals, and he proposes four steps for doing so: (1) nonaggressive modes of behavior should be modeled; (2) learners should be given guidance and the opportunity to practice their new modes of response; (3) it should be arranged that the learner's nonaggressive responses be successful—that is, followed by reinforcement; (4) if possible, action should be taken to ensure that aggressive solutions to problems go unrewarded.

Second, although Bandura does not advocate censorship of the media, he does point out that the amount of televised aggression and violence is high. He also points out that all the available evidence suggests that reducing the amount of televised violence would reduce viewers' subsequent aggressive behaviors. Bandura proposes that tallies be kept of the number and intensity of violent acts on different shows and that these figures be publicized, à la *Consumer Reports.* Sponsors can decide whether they want their names associated with high-violence shows. In other words, if it will later be made explicit that "the preceding brutalizations have been brought to you by Belva's Bagel Bakery," Belva might think twice before sponsoring a brutal show.

Third, although giving credit where credit is due, Bandura notes that police, jailors, and other peace officers may sometimes provoke or encourage violent outbursts. This is particularly likely when the officer behaves more harshly than the suspect feels is warranted considering the severity of the suspected offense (Toch, 1969). Bandura suggests that keepers of the peace be given more training in nonbelligerent treatment of suspects and convicts, and that a pattern of rewards be established that favors non-violent processing of clients. Furthermore, he proposes that the rewards accorded to prison guards (or correctional officers, as they are euphemistically called in California) be made contingent on their success at rehabilitation. For example, salaries at correctional facilities might be negatively correlated with the number of offenses committed by persons recently released from the institutions.

Finally, in light of Merton's (1957a, 1957b) theorizing, it should be added that society must continually appraise itself. If certain features of society systematically block off socially approved ways or channels to privileges or goals, the people denied those advantages are likely to resort to individual force and collective riots. Giving everyone a fair chance at the good life is not merely an ideal; it is a practical way of minimizing criminal activity and civil disobedience.

In sum, the social-learning principles discussed in Chapter 4 are fully applicable for understanding aggression. Although it is a disappointment to biologists who like to think in terms of quivering neurons and to psychoanalysts who like to think in terms of seething psychic cesspools, human aggressive activity is largely understandable in terms of observational learning and social reinforcement. The social-learning analysis strikes some people as "evangelical" and has been criticized for obscuring the search for nonlearning contributors to aggression (Berkowitz, 1974; Pepitone, 1974). However, in my personal estimation, the application of modern social-learning theory represents a great leap forward in the study of aggression.

PART SUMMARY

Aggression refers to behavior that is intended to inflict injury on someone or something. As a major aspect of human life, aggression has long commanded the interest of psychologists. The three major approaches to understanding aggression are the biological approach, the frustration-aggression approach, and the social-learning approach.

Behavior that we interpret as aggressive is found in many species. Culture and learning do not seem to explain why one insect fights with another, so Lorenz and others have looked to evolution for an explanation. Rougher, tougher species should have a better chance of obtaining scarce resources and surviving. The victors that stalk the earth today have a self-generating aggressive drive that erupts into behavior when the appropriate releasing stimulus is present. Furthermore, individual differences within a species may be related to genetic variables, such as the XYY chromosome. Certainly our biological structures must provide us with the capacity to aggress. Explaining aggression in terms of evolution and heredity provides a general and parsimonious explanation, and the idea that our sins have their origin in the dim evolutionary past is to some people comforting. However, evidence for innate aggressiveness, even among nonhumans, is equivocal. If it were conclusively shown that nonhumans possessed an aggressive instinct, it would not automatically follow that humans were propelled by analogous forces. The overriding difficulty of instinct interpretations of human aggressiveness is that they cannot account for the variability in human aggression.

According to the frustration-aggression hypothesis, frustration, or the blocking of goal-directed activity, motivates aggression. The strength of the motivation or instigation to aggress depends on the strength of the blocked response, the extent of the blocking, and the number of responses blocked. The form and direction of aggression following frustration depend on learned inhibitions. When learned inhibitions prevent the expression of aggression toward the frustrator, the aggression will be displaced onto other targets. Although there is a linkage between frustration and aggression, frustration can lead to many responses other than aggression, and aggression often appears in the absence of frustration.

Associated with frustration-aggression theorizing is the catharsis principle. This principle suggests that, if a person engages in aggressive activity or observes someone else engaging in aggressive activity, that person's subsequent aggressiveness will be reduced. On close inspection the "catharsis principle" would appear to be four different principles. First, aggressing against a tormentor will reduce one's subsequent aggression toward that tormentor. Second, aggressing against a nontormentor will reduce one's subsequent aggression toward a tormentor. Third, viewing someone else aggressing against one's tormentor will reduce one's subsequent aggression toward that tormentor. Fourth, observing someone aggressing against a nontormentor will reduce the viewer's subsequent level of aggression. Although there is some evidence in support of the first three versions of the catharsis principle, the fourth version is unsupported by the research data. Observing someone else aggressing against a nontormentor is likely to raise, rather than lower, the viewer's subsequent aggression.

Recent researchers have advanced an arousal-cue formulation suggesting that frustration often does lead to aggression but, for this to happen, aggression-related cues must be present in the situation. Frustration is cast as a source of drive or arousal. Considerable evidence suggests that, in the absence of the appropriate cues, frustration and other arousing circumstances will not lead to aggression. Furthermore, aggression-related cues will have little or no effect if the organism is not motivated to perform. The observed violence of others is a major source of aggression-related cues.

Observational learning and social reinforcement account for much aggressive behavior. Through observational learning, we learn how to aggress. This result has been shown in laboratory demonstrations, case histories of aggressive and nonaggressive people, and comparisons of aggressive and nonaggressive groups. Viewing an aggressive model has response-facilitation and response-disinhibition effects. Thus, aggressive modeling raises the likelihood that the viewer will engage in similar aggressive behavior. This result is clearly shown in studies that have related filmed and televised aggression to viewers' performance of aggressive responses. Patterns of reward and punishment also affect the likelihood that an aggressive response will be performed. Rewards for aggression include material gain, social approval, and feelings of satisfaction or pride.

The social-learning analysis offers a number of remedies for our violence-riddled society. First, modeling and social reinforcement might be applied to help violent individuals learn to solve problems and achieve goals through nonviolent modes of responding. Second, the incredible level of violence that characterizes television fare might somehow be reduced. Third, police officers, jailors, and other people who deal with aggressive persons might be better trained in nonbelligerent ways of handling suspects or inmates. Finally, violence would likely be reduced if all segments of the population were given equal access to the "good life," so that no one would feel compelled to resort to aggressive activity to attain this goal.

HELPING BEHAVIOR

An urgent message reached Sacramento County Deputy Sheriff and criminology student Robert Ruh as he sat taking an anthropology final. Two youths, discouraged over unemployment, disaffected with the Establishment, and having little else to do, had held up a sporting-goods store and obtained a plentiful supply of firearms and ammunition. They then proceeded to a bank, where they took 25 hostages and then issued a demand for one million dollars and a getaway car. By this time the bank was surrounded by police bristling with guns. The youthful desperados demanded to negotiate with Deputy Ruh, because he had gained their confidence during an earlier investigation.

Corporal Ruh, despite his wife's protestations, stripped to the waist, clasped his hands behind his head, and entered the bank to negotiate the release of the hostages. One of the desperados "went a little crazy" when the million dollars arrived. However, after 4 hours and 44 minutes of begging, cajoling, and alternating threats and promises, the youths released the hostages and surrendered. The corporal's risk of his own life was repaid with the lives of 25 hostages and of the two gunmen themselves (S. Ross & Kupferberg, 1974).

We'll turn now to a consideration of the conditions that lead to the performance of unselfish acts. We can define **helping behavior** as voluntary acts that benefit other people. This kind of behavior is widespread within our society. Almost any newspaper contains stories of people who risk life and limb to help others. Moreover, Americans donate millions of dollars to charity each year. In terms of less dramatic assists, Darley and Latané (1970) found that 85% of Manhattan passersby were willing to offer minor assistance in the form of giving the time or directions. They also found that 72% of the passersby who were told "My wallet was stolen" were willing to give the experimenter a dime; 65% were willing to give a dime even if no reference had been made to a stolen wallet.

On the other hand, seeming indifference to another's plight is also widespread within our society. Pleas for funds often fall on deaf ears, and bystanders have ignored accidents, injuries, and requests for assistance. Perhaps you have already heard about Catherine Genovese. Returning to her New York City home late one night in 1964, she was attacked by an assailant who stabbed her to death, slowly and brutally, over a half-hour period. At least 38 people heard her screams; none went to her aid personally or even called the police.

Since this particular incident, social psychologists have shown a keen interest in establishing the conditions under which one person will help another. Also known as **altruistic** or **prosocial behavior,** helping behavior has been related to three factors: (1) the qualities of the potential benefactor or *helper*, (2) the qualities of the potential beneficiary or *victim*, and (3) the qualities of the *situation.*

THE HELPER

A number of "helper" characteristics have been identified as correlates of altruism. These characteristics include personality variables, feelings of competence, and mood.

Personality Variables

Armed with batteries of tests, social psychologists have sallied forth to identify the personality correlates of helping behavior. Schwartz (1968), for example, has developed a 24-item Ascription of Responsibility or **AR Scale.** High scorers are aware that their actions have consequences for others ("Being very upset or preoccupied does not keep a person from doing anything considerate he ordinarily would"), whereas low scorers tend to shift responsibility for the fate of others away from the self ("You can't blame basically good people who are forced by their environment to be inconsiderate of others"). Schwartz and Clausen (1970) found that, compared with subjects who scored low on the AR measure, high scorers were quick to offer help to someone who was faking a seizure; 65% of the high scorers took direct actions, whereas only 47% of the low scorers so acted. Furthermore, high scorers were less likely than low scorers to be inhibited from helping by the presence of other bystanders (the inhibiting effect of bystanders will be discussed shortly.)

Reviews of personality studies by Krebs (1970) and by Gergen, Gergen, and Meter (1972) suggest that helping behavior is modestly but positively correlated with strength of social and religious values, conscience development, and "general friendliness." However, correlations between personality measures and altruism have often been very low, possibly because as we saw in Chapter 1, many studies do not adequately take situational factors into account. Personality measures are correlated with helping behavior, but the measure that predicts helping behavior in one situation will not necesssarily predict helping behavior in another situation (Gergen et al., 1972).

Feelings of Competence

Whether a person is likely to offer help depends on the extent to which he or she feels competent. This means, quite reasonably, that a person who has never changed a flat tire might not stop to help a stranded motorist, and that a person who has not been trained in mouth-to-mouth resuscitation might not attempt to offer first aid. When a person feels competent, he or she is likely to offer assistance because the costs of helping (in terms of effort, risk, and danger) will tend to be low (Harris & Huang, 1973). However, it has also been shown that the specific area of competence need not be relevant to the emergency at hand for it to affect helping bahavior.

Before asking them to donate blood, Kazdin and Bryan (1971) had their subjects take part in one of two tasks. One was a physical exam (the outcome of which would reveal whether the person was in good physical condition to give blood), and the other was a test of creative ability (the outcome of which would reveal nothing about the person's condition for giving blood). Within each group, half the subjects were made to feel highly competent by being told that they were in the pink of condition or that they were highly creative; the other half were informed that they were of average health or ability. Whereas 26 of the 48 competent-feeling subjects volunteered to give blood, only 10 of the 48 average-feeling subjects volunteered to do so. The area of competence did not make a difference. Thus, even though it was irrelevant to their ability to give blood, subjects made to feel competent by being called "creative" were likely to help out.

Two possible explanations for their findings are suggested by the authors. First, risk taking might have been increased by the high-competence manipulation. That is, the "competent" subject who was rewarded for taking a chance with the test might have been willing to take another chance by volunteering to give blood. Second, discovering that we are of superior status may enhance our sensitivity to the less fortunate people in this world. A third possibility is also mentioned but is dismissed: that success generated a good mood, which increased affection for other people. Although Kazdin and Bryan do not feel that their results were compatible with this alternative, other studies, cited in the next section, are quite compatible with it (Isen, 1970; Isen & Levin, 1972).

In passing, we might note that, under certain limited conditions, displays of failure or *incompetence* may raise the likelihood of altruistic behavior. This is likely to happen when failure has harmed the person's image, and helping another individual offers the opportunity to repair the damage. Results of a study by Isen, Horn, and Rosenhan (1973) suggest that Good Samaritans of this kind are trying to repair their image not in their own eyes but in the eyes of other people.

Mood

Situationally induced moods also affect helping behavior. One such mood is guilt, and another is the recently alluded-to "glow of good will" that accompanies satiety, good fortune, and other happy circumstances.

If you are made to feel responsible for harming another, you may try to expiate your guilt by helping that person. For example, a number of pedestrians in Toronto were confronted with the sight of a man dropping computer cards onto a wet sidewalk (Konečni, 1972). In a control condition the experimenter dropped the cards about 12 feet away from the unwitting subject. In a restitution condition the experimenter brushed against the subject and made it appear that the subject had knocked the cards out of the experimenter's hands. Whereas 16% of the control subjects helped, 39% of the presumably guilty-feeling restitution subjects helped. Moreover, for every card that was picked up by a control subject, three or four cards were picked up by a restitution subject. Konečni also found that, when an observer saw one confederate knock the cards out of another confederate's hand, people would sympathetically help out, although, if the confederate dropped them himself, such aid was not likely to be forthcoming. A number of other studies of guilt—and some problems with the generalization that guilt leads to helping behavior—will be discussed in the next chapter when we consider the ways in which one person may attempt to induce guilt in another person in order to manipulate this second person's behavior.

The **warm-glow hypothesis** suggests that, if success, good fortune, or delicious food puts the person in a good mood, that person is primed to offer help to others. To test this hypothesis, Isen and Levin (1972) induced good moods either by distributing cookies to library users or by having users of public telephones find "lost" change when entering the booth to make a call. In the library study, cookie-fed subjects were more likely than controls to agree to take part in a psychology experiment; in the telephone study, people who had been delighted by finding a dime were more likely than controls to help a nearby victim pick up a number of papers that had dropped out of a manila folder.

THE VICTIM

Following a major accident that results in more casualties than their emergency room can handle, some hospitals leave the old or derelict untreated in order to attend to the young and well-to-do (Glaser & Strauss, 1968). In many less critical situations also, the characteristics of the person in need will affect the likelihood that help will be given. Recognizing this fact, pairs of hitchhikers may choose to have the female stand by the side of the road and wag her thumb while the male, luggage, and assorted pets hide out of view. Three important qualities of the potential beneficiary of a helpful act are character, dependency, and the extent to which the victim has helped the benefactor in the past.

Character

To whom would you be more likely to give "change for a phone call"—a neatly dressed businessperson carrying a briefcase or a shabbily dressed hobo from Skid Row? Certainly the similarity of the needy to ourselves is an important factor in our decision of whether or not to help. For example, Emswiller, Deaux, and Willits (1971) had "hippie" and "straight" experimenters request a dime from "hippie" or "straight" passersby. They found that subjects were more likely to give money to similar than to dissimilar people. Similarity may also account for why people in different cultures seem more likely to help out compatriots than foreigners (Feldman, 1968).

The actual or attributed character of the person in distress is also a powerful determinant of our willingness to offer help. In a field study by Piliavin, Rodin, and Piliavin (1969), casually dressed male experimenters staggered and then collapsed on the floor of a New York City subway

train. In one condition the victim carried a cane; in the other he smelled of liquor and carried a bottle tightly wrapped in a brown paper bag. The victim who appeared to be ill received spontaneous help on well over 90% of the trials, but the victim who appeared to be drunk was spontaneously aided on only about 50% of the trials. Why should people be more willing to help a person who appears ill than a person who appears drunk?

One possible explanation is that the cost of helping a drunk is greater. Firsthand experience or complex attribution processes, coupled with implicit personality theories, could lead people to believe that the drunk might be belligerent and, in his alcoholic haze, might injure or embarrass them.

Intimidation and threat certainly can inhibit the offer of aid. Allen (1972) had a confederate enter a subway heading *uptown*. Within earshot of the subjects, this person asked a second confederate (the misinformant) if the train was going *downtown*, to which the misinformant replied "yes." Thus bystanders were given the opportunity to help the first confederate by correcting the misinformation supplied by the second.

Four threat conditions were established by some play-acting just prior to this incident. In one condition the misinformant had been leafing through a muscle magazine. A third confederate tripped over his outstretched legs, whereupon the misinformant sprang to his feet, balled his hand into a fist, and hollered "Watch out, buddy! You want to get hurt?"

In this condition, in which there was a high risk of physical threat, subjects were least likely to correct the misinformant. In a second condition the misinformant responded to the tripping with a snappy "What's the matter, baldy, can't you see without your toupee?" A risk of embarrassment was almost as effective as a risk of violence in deterring assistance from the witnesses. In the third condition the misinformant did not respond to the tripping incident. In the fourth condition the misinformant not only did not respond to the incident but also was self-effacingly unsure when giving the wrong directions to the victim. Whereas less than 40% of the threatened subjects corrected the misinformant, about 80% of the witnesses in these last two conditions attempted to help out.

A second reason why people are reluctant to help a drunk is that they may feel he has brought his plight upon himself and that his fate is only a just reward for his evil ways. According to Lerner's (1970) **just-world hypothesis,** people like to believe that they live in a fair and equitable world in which they get what they deserve. Moreover, they will act in such a way as to perpetuate this belief. A person who is perceived as guilty, villainous, or somehow unworthy may go unaided, because help for this person would be more than he or she deserved. A person perceived as innocent may not only be rescued but be given special compensation to balance out the discomfort and distress he or she has experienced.

An interesting aspect of the just-world hypothesis is that, if a person is not in a position to rescue or compensate an innocent victim, he or she may reassess the victim's culpability. If an honest, hard-working businessperson suffers irreparable financial loss, for example, we may decide either that the world is cruel and unfair or that the person is actually dishonest and lazy. Since we are motivated to maintain a belief in a just world, our dissonance is, in this case, reduced by devaluing or derogating the victim. Although some results suggest that subjects will derogate or devalue an innocent victim (Lerner & Simmons, 1966), these experiments might have been conducted in such a way that, in the course of the manipulations, the character of the "innocent" victim was impugned (Godfrey & Lowe, 1975). Thus something other than a need to believe in a just world could have accounted for the results. If it is abundantly clear to the observer that the victim has only the best of motives, derogation is unlikely (Godfrey & Lowe, 1975).

Finally, there is a possible evolutionary explanation for ignoring the ignoble. Altruistic behavior can have survival value for the group. The shot-up soldier who is rescued and patched up may go out and fight another day. However, helping those who drain the group's resources or who work against its interests leads to a decrease of the group's strength, and a society of lazy parasites could result. Thus survival chances may be best if we are quick to aid contributing members but slow to aid the nonproductive or destructive among us. As in the case of other attempts to account for complex human behavior in terms of evolutionary factors, this explanation of altruism has met with a chilly reception (Campbell, 1972).

Dependency

People are more likely to come to the aid of a victim who is specifically dependent upon them than they are to rescue a victim who can secure aid from other sources. For example, if you were the only rescuer present in the waters, you might take greater risks to save survivors of a capsized boat than you would if a Coast Guard cutter were drawing near. The importance of dependency has been shown both in the laboratory (Berkowitz & Daniels, 1963, 1964; Thalhofer, 1971) and in the field (Schaps, 1972; Pomazal & Clore, 1973).

In one study, Berkowitz and Daniels (1964) hypothesized that people would be more willing to help someone who was in a position of high dependency and that they would be particularly sensitive to the dependent person's plight if they had recently received help themselves. First, some subjects were aided by a confederate as they undertook an experimental task, whereas other subjects did not get this assistance. Next, all subjects reported for what was presented as an entirely different experiment. They were told that they were to do work for a "supervisor" who was, in fact, a second confederate (not the one who had helped them earlier). To create conditions under which the supervisor was in a position of high dependency, the experimenters told some subjects that the supervisor could get a high rating and a chance at a monetary prize only if they, the subjects, performed well under the supervisor's direction. To create conditions under which the supervisor was in a position of low dependency, the experimenters led other subjects to believe that their output was not intimately linked to the supervisor's ratings and chances. Helping was measured by how hard the subject worked to produce for the supervisor.

Subjects whose supervisors were highly dependent outperformed subjects whose supervisors were not so dependent, and the best performance came from subjects in the high-dependency condition who had themselves been given help. Thus dependency led to helping, and being helped earlier sensitized the helper to the supervisor's plight. Since the help the subjects had received had been from someone other than the supervisor, the greater helpfulness of these subjects could not be explained as an attempt to pay back a favor. Subsequent research suggests that people will help a dependent person even when the person being helped will gain a prize that will not be shared with the helper and even when he or she will remain unaware of the helper's assistance and hence be unable to reward the Good Samaritan with gratitude (Berkowitz, 1968). Berkowitz suggests that there is a **norm of social responsibility**—that is, an unwritten societal rule stating that we must help other people even if we gain in return nothing more than a feeling of satisfaction for being a good human being.

If the costs of helping are sufficiently high, increased dependency may not lead to more helping. In an ingenious field study, Schaps (1972) examined the coeffects of dependency and cost on altruistic behavior. Subjects were shoe salesmen who were confronted by a female customer who demanded to see pair after pair of shoes. Under conditions of high dependency the woman limped into the store with a broken heel, and under conditions of low dependency she entered with the shoes she was wearing in serviceable condition. In the high-cost conditions the store was relatively crowded with customers, and in the low-cost conditions the clerks were less busy. (Since shoe salesmen work on a commission basis, they could lose a great deal of money by sticking with one customer when the store is busy.) Helpfulness was measured by the number of pairs of shoes shown, the time spent with the customer, and the number of trips back to the stock room for more shoes. Results indicated less helping under high-cost than under low-cost conditions. The bogus customer was likely to get more help when she was highly dependent, but only if the store wasn't busy at the time. Thus feelings of satisfaction for being a good neighbor may sometimes be outweighed by more tangible rewards, such as commissions.

Reciprocity

When the lion was dependent on Daniel, Daniel was good enough to pull a painful thorn from its paw. Later, when Daniel was dependent on the lion, the lion went without dinner, much to Daniel's benefit. More modern reports also suggest that the likelihood of a dependent person's receiving aid depends on the extent to which he or she has been helpful in the past (Goranson & Berkowitz, 1966; Greenberg & Frisch, 1972; A. Kahn & Tice, 1973). These findings are consistent with the **norm of reciprocity,** which suggests that we pay back kindness with kindness and cruelty with cruelty.

After having some subjects receive help and other subjects be denied help, Goranson and Berkowitz (1966) gave all subjects the opportunity to help a supervisor. In some cases the supervisor was the woman who had given or denied help, and in other cases the supervisor was a second confederate. The initial aid was sometimes made to appear voluntary and sometimes not.

There were three major findings, each of which suggests that receiving a favor from another person produces an indebtedness that the recipient is motivated to repay. First, subjects were less likely to help the supervisor if she had earlier refused to help the subject than if she had been helpful. Second, more aid was given to the supervisor when she, rather than the second confederate, had earlier aided the subject. Finally, subjects were more likely to reciprocate if the supervisor's earlier aid had been voluntary rather than compulsory.

This third finding suggests that we are more likely to return a favor that reflects good intentions than a favor brought on by coercion or accident. On the other hand, we may not be likely to help out another person simply because he or she stated an intention to help us at an earlier point in time. When people claim good intentions, their sweet-sounding words may in fact reflect good intentions, or they may represent an attempt to "butter us up" to get something in return. Because such stated intentions may raise suspicions like this, we often tend to feel that their actions speak louder than their words. A. Kahn and Tice (1973) had a confederate either state an intention to help or not help the subject or state no intention at all. The confederate then actually helped a lot or a little. Later reciprocation by the subject depended not on what the confederate said, but on what he or she did. On the other hand, in a second study, in which the subjects "accidentally" overheard the confederate stating good intentions, the subjects had no reason to doubt the confederate's sincerity. In this case, good intentions on the confederate's part were sufficient to lead to good deeds on the subject's part.

THE SITUATION

Characteristics of the situation will also affect whether or not a person will grant a request or intervene in an emergency. Compare, for example, how you might respond to a voice from behind asking "Got the time?" when in a dark alley at 2:00 A.M. with how you might respond to the same request when on campus at 2:00 P.M. Our discussion of helping behavior concludes with a consideration of four important situational variables: (1) the severity of the situation, (2) modeling effects, (3) the number of bystanders present, and (4) the setting of the emergency.

Severity of the Situation

One analysis of the conditions under which a bystander will intervene in an emergency situation suggests that the likelihood of assistance depends in part on the degree of arousal of the bystander (Piliavin, Rodin, & Piliavin, 1969; Piliavin & Piliavin, 1972). According to this analysis, observing an emergency is physiologically arousing, which affects the likelihood that the observer will take some action. Thus we might expect an observer to be less motivated to do something under conditions of a mild or relatively nonarousing emergency (the overturning of a tricycle) than under conditions of a severe or relatively arousing emergency (the overturning of a school bus).

However, there is not necessarily a one-to-one correspondence between the severity of the emergency and the likelihood of direct aid, since the cost of helping may also increase as an emergency becomes severe. Although there may be little effort or risk involved in helping a slightly bruised child out of a puddle, applying tourniquets and trying to move children with unknown injuries from a smoldering overturned school bus involve effort, risk of personal injury, risk of being sued, and the likely ruination of a set of clothes. Thus the person who is a witness to a stressful, gory accident is highly motivated to do something, but this motivation, rather than being expressed through direct intervention, may appear as indirect intervention (informing the police) or as flight from the scene. Consistent with this line of argument, Piliavin and Piliavin found that a nonbloodied victim (low cost of helping) was more likely to receive direct aid than was a bloodied victim (high cost of helping) but that the bloodied victim was more likely to receive indirect help. Also consistent are Staub and Baer's (1974) findings that the likelihood of intervention is increased when escape from the situation is made more difficult; when escape is difficult, the costs of *not* helping are increased.

Modeling Effects

The observed helpfulness of others is certainly a major contributor to altruistic behavior. In one demonstration of this modeling effect, Bryan and Test (1967) had a woman stand by the side of a busy street. Next to her was a car with a flat tire. The car's trunk was wide open, and a fully inflated tire was in view. Under modeling conditions, motorists approaching the woman first passed another woman stranded by the side of the road. At this site the woman was being helped by a man who was changing the tire. Excluding drivers who stopped to try to pick the woman up, 58 motorists halted under modeling conditions, whereas only 35 halted under no-model control conditions.

The same investigators also had a woman dressed in a Salvation Army uniform stand by a kettle, ringing a bell. Under modeling conditions a male walked up to the kettle and made a small donation. In line with expectations, although there were 84 donors under these conditions, there were only 56 donors under control conditions. Later, Wagner and Wheeler (1969) had sailors overhear a model's response to a request for funds to help bring the family of a dying sailor to his bedside. Compared with subjects who overheard a control model saying he'd "think it over," those overhearing a model who generously donated $20 gave more money. Overhearing a third, selfish model who refused to give anything resulted in the least generosity. In a somewhat similar experiment by Macauley (1970), a subject actually put her wallet away after hearing a model refuse to make a donation!

Macauley suggests that models can also have "boomerang effects." Seeing a generous person, we may feel so bad about our inability to be equally generous that we make no donation at all. After seeing a tightwad refuse to contribute, we may proudly donate to gain a sense of superiority. However, the most recent experimental evidence suggests that, even though people may react to a selfish, exploiting model with moral indignation and disdain, they will still follow the model's behavioral example (Mason, Hornstein, & Tobin, 1973).

One of the Bryan and Test findings was that white shoppers were less likely to drop money into the kettle after having been exposed to a black model than after having been exposed to a white model. Whether or not the female solicitor was white made no difference. This result suggests that the similarity between the model and the potential helper as well as victim may be important. In a different test of this hypothesis, Hornstein, Fisch, and Holmes (1968) carefully prepared wallets containing money, fictitious papers, and an identification card. The wallets protruded from envelopes, which also included a cover letter from a previous finder (the symbolic model) who had later lost the whole package. In a condition intended to highlight the similarities of the model and the helper, the cover letter was apparently written by a fellow American; in a condition intended to highlight dissimilarity, the letter was written in halting English by a foreign visitor to our shores. The letters additionally expressed positive or negative feelings about returning the wallet. Whereas about half the subjects exposed to the American symbolic model returned the wallet, only about one-third of the subjects exposed to the foreign symbolic model did so. Furthermore, whereas subjects exposed to the American model were less likely to return the wallet if the original finder had expressed negative feelings about being helpful, subjects exposed to the foreign model were unaffected by the model's feelings. Hornstein et al. conclude that, when a person who is similar (and hence a useful comparison point) feels bad about an act, the observer is deterred from such activity.

The Bystander Effect

One of the shocking aspects of the Genovese murder described earlier was the large number of people who could have come to her assistance. We now have evidence suggesting that the likelihood of a given observer's offering aid might have been higher if that observer had thought that he or she was the only one to hear the pleas. This hypothesis is suggested by a series of studies reported by Latané and Darley (1969). The approach taken by these researchers and their associates represents a highly preferred research strategy: they conducted a series of interrelated experiments and obtained convergent results.

Subjects in one of these experiments (Darley & Latané, 1968) entered individual cubicles to take part in a group discussion via intercom. The size of the group was varied, and the experimenter pointed out that he would not be listening to the ongoing discussion but would be stationed nearby.

Each person in the group made some preliminary remarks over the intercom. The first person to respond was a male confederate who indicated a susceptibility to seizures. The second time the confederate talked, he began stuttering. Monopolizing the intercom, he gasped and eventually lost all coherence. The experimenters measured how far this fake seizure had to progress under various conditions before the subject would leave his or her cubicle and seek assistance. The more people there were who could offer help, the less likely it was that a given individual would do so. For example, 85% of the solitary observers promptly reported the incident, but only 31% of those who thought other bystanders were present did so. Increasing inactivity as a function of the number of other people present is called a **bystander effect.** It can occur in nonemergency as well as in emergency situations (Levy, Lundgren, Ansel, Fell, Fink, & McGrath, 1972).

Several other studies have replicated and extended these results. In one experiment, mentioned at the beginning of Chapter 1, smoke billowed into a room containing an isolated subject, a subject with two confederates, or three subjects. Although isolated subjects promptly reported the emergency, this response was inhibited in the two group conditions. Thus bystanders may even inhibit people from acts that can preserve their *own* skins! In another experiment, as subjects waited alone, with a friend, or with a stranger, they heard a female in the next room trip, fall, and injure herself (Latané & Rodin, 1969). Aid was less likely when there were two individuals present, but pairs of friends were more likely to offer assistance than were pairs of strangers. In a third experiment the investigators moved into the field and had two confederates walk out of a liquor store with a case of beer while the manager busied himself in a back room. Once again, solitary witnesses were more likely to report the theft than were individuals in groups. The presence of models and other variables will certainly contribute to whether or not a bystander effect is obtained. However, taken together, these results strongly suggest that the likelihood of any given individual's intervening in an emergency is decreased if he or she knows that other bystanders are present.

The explanation of the bystander effect offered by Latané and Darley involves tracing out a series of four decisions a person must make before intervening and considering the ways in which other bystanders may influence each of these decisions. These four decisions are described as follows: (1) the witness must decide whether or not he or she is watching an emergency; (2) the witness must decide whether or not he or she has any responsibility for doing something about the emergency; (3) the witness must decide that there is a course of action available; (4) the witness must decide whether or not to implement that course of action.

First, the witness must interpret the event as an emergency. Is a man lying in a doorway in a diabetic coma, or is he only drunk, happily sleeping it off? To interpret the situation, people in groups of bystanders may look to one another for guidance—and interpret one another's seemingly nonchalant reactions as indicating that an emergency is not in progress. As we would predict from social-comparison theory, people are particularly unresponsive if the unmoved fellow bystanders are similar rather than dissimilar to themselves (Smith, Smythe, & Lien, 1972). Solitary observers do not have social cues to tip the scales against defining the situation as an emergency.

If other bystanders' reactions reveal concern, intervention is unlikely to be inhibited at this decision point (Bickman, 1972; Clark & Word, 1972). The importance of the clarity of the situation has been underscored by Clark and Word, who found that all of the groups exposed to a nonambiguous emergency contained at least one helper, whereas only 30% of the groups exposed to an ambiguous emergency contained at least one helper. They note that the bystander effect may be less pronounced in groups of friends because friends find it easier to detect concern in one another's facial reactions.

Second, the witness must feel some personal responsibility. Such feelings of responsibility may be less pronounced if other bystanders are present. According to this diffusion-of-responsibility explanation of the bystander effect, as the number of bystanders is increased, each one feels less responsibility individually (Latané & Darley, 1968). The attitude develops that "someone else" ought to do something about the situation. This feeling may be particularly likely if other bystanders are seen as more competent than oneself. For example, Schwartz and Clausen (1970) found that subjects in group conditions were less likely to intervene in a medical emergency when they were led to believe that one of the other people present was medically trained.

Conversely, responsibility is less likely to diffuse if a bystander believes that he or she is the person best able to do something about the situation. Ross (1971) found less of a bystander effect when children rather than other adults were bystanders, and Ross and Braband (1973) found that subjects paired with a blind person responded as frequently and as rapidly to an emergency as did subjects who were alone. Clear evidence of the effects of inhibiting the diffusion process comes from Bickman (1971), who had individuals or pairs of people overhear an accident. There were two group conditions. In one condition both the first and the second bystanders were close enough to help the person in distress, but in the other condition the second bystander was located a quarter of a mile away and heard the accident over an intercom. As expected, the second bystander's presence did not inhibit the first's helping behavior when the second bystander was unable to help, but it did inhibit the first's helping behavior when either bystander was equally able to intervene.

The third step in the intervention process is to decide what kinds of measures may be taken, and the fourth step is to implement these measures. At these points, people are likely to be concerned about how other bystanders will react to their reactions. Will they look incompetent or foolish? Will people laugh at them for getting excited? Thus, anticipated adverse reactions on the part of other bystanders can tip the scales against intervention.

All told, it would seem that, when a person is confronted with an emergency, the rewards are biased in favor of inaction, and the bias is particularly pronounced if other bystanders are present.

The Urban Setting

Some people from small towns have the uneasy feeling that, whereas in their home town people would spring to their aid in an emergency, in a city like New York, Chicago, or Los Angeles they could be murdered in front of a thousand pairs of eyes and nobody would pay any attention. Is there any rational basis for such an attitude? The city certainly offers joys in terms of diversity and stimulation, and I would never claim that the people of upstate New York are necessarily bigger hearted than the people of Manhattan. Yet there are certain facets of urban living discussed by Milgram (1970) that could discourage Good Samaritanism in large cities.

Because people in cities are jammed together physically, they may

compensate by maintaining psychological distance. An unwritten law of city life is "Mind your own business," and there are other rules aimed at keeping large numbers of people with very different backgrounds from clashing. Then, too, cities provide points of concentration for burglars, drug peddlers, cutthroats, and criminals of all description. Since urban life is often perceived as more dangerous than rural life, it is also less likely to promote a sense of mutual trust. In one unpublished study it was found that, although 75% of all city subjects responded to a stranger by shouting through the closed door, in a small town about 75% of the subjects opened the door to talk to the stranger (Altman, Levine, Nadien, & Villena, 1969). Indifference to others may be encouraged by competition over scarce resources such as subway seats. Furthermore, deindividuating conditions associated with urban life may lead to a loss of the inner controls that encourage adherence to the norm of social responsibility.

A very important factor that Milgram discusses is **information overload,** which refers to the fact that city dwellers are bombarded by more stimulation than they can adequately code or process. An emergency situation simply may not stand out from the incredible hubbub of city life. Problems that do register may not be acted upon because there are so many of them ("If you helped all the unfortunates on the way to school, you'd never get there") or because there are other, "more pressing" demands.

A major characteristic of urban life is living by the clock. Time pressures and helping behavior have been related in an interesting study by

Darley and Batson (1973). Theology students reporting for the experiment were told that they were to go to another location and deliver a talk. Half of them were told to hurry because time was short, but the remainder were not rushed. Within each of these conditions, half the subjects were told that the talk would be on the parable of the Good Samaritan, whereas the other half were led to anticipate talking on nonhelping topics. As expected, time-pressured subjects were less likely to stop and offer help to a shabbily dressed man slumped, coughing and groaning, in a doorway. Furthermore, help was not more likely to be forthcoming from the subjects rushing to talk on Good Samaritanism. Thus the time pressures of city life may be expected to discourage helping behavior.

PART SUMMARY

Helping behavior refers to voluntary acts that benefit others and are not easily explained in terms of selfish motives. Such behavior is widespread in our society, but also widespread is a seeming indifference to the plight of others. In recent years social psychologists have devoted considerable energy toward identifying the conditions under which one person will help another rather than stand idly by. Altruism has been related to characteristics of the helper, of the victim, and of the situation.

Helper variables include personality, feelings of competence, and mood. Although studies of personality correlates have had some success, the results have been mixed. A major shortcoming of some of these studies has been an attempt to predict helping across situations. As noted in an earlier chapter, more promising procedures may be those in which the specific helping situation is also taken into account. Transient states have also been related to helping behavior. Feelings of competence induced by immediately preceding success, as well as a good mood induced by immediately preceding satisfactions, raise the likelihood of helping behavior.

Victim variables include real or perceived character, dependency, and the extent to which the victim has earned favors from the helper. First, people seem less willing to help unsavory characters than people of relative social worth. This attitude can reflect fearfulness, a belief that the victim brought the plight upon himself or herself and therefore deserves to suffer, or even an evolutionary phenomenon. Second, one person is more likely to help another if that other is particularly dependent upon him or her. Third, in accordance with the norm of reciprocity, people are most likely to offer aid to those who have helped them in the past.

Situational variables include the severity of the emergency, the presence and actions of models, the number of bystanders present, and (in a somewhat different sense) the hustle and bustle of the city. First, severe emergencies will elicit a high degree of arousal in the observer, but whether or not this arousal motivates direct intervention will depend on other factors, such as the costs involved in helping. Second, the observed selfish or unselfish behavior of others affects altruism. Third, as the number of witnesses to an emergency increases, the likelihood of any individual's intervening will decrease. One prominent explanation of this bystander effect is that intervention requires a series of steps, each one of which may be affected by the presence of other people. When other witnesses are present, the individual may be less likely to define the situation as an emergency, may feel less responsible personally, and may fear ridicule for taking inappropriate action. Finally, factors associated with urban life (such as a lack of trust, input overload, and time pressures) may foster nonintervention in emergency situations.

8

Interaction in the Dyad

COMMUNICATION

SETTING THE STAGE: ENVIRONMENT AND INTERACTION

Sociofugal Environments
Sociopetal Environments
Planning Environments

NONVERBAL COMMUNICATION

Proxemic Communication
Kinesic Communication
Paralinguistic Communication
The Uses of Nonverbal Messages

SOCIAL PENETRATION: THE DEVELOPMENT OF AN INTERPERSONAL RELATIONSHIP

The Depth and Breadth of a Relationship
Rewards, Costs, and Penetration
Self-Disclosure as Social Penetration

PART SUMMARY

COOPERATION IN THE DYAD

EXPERIMENTAL GAMES

SOCIAL STRATEGIES AND SOCIAL MOTIVES

PERSONALITY AND COOPERATION

THE "OTHER PERSON" AND COOPERATION

Friends and Strangers
Strategy of the Other Person

THE SITUATION AND COOPERATION

Outcome Values
Communication Opportunities
Group Atmosphere

THE EXTERNAL VALIDITY OF PDG RESEARCH

PART SUMMARY

INFLUENCE IN THE DYAD

TACTICS OF INFLUENCE

Ingratiation
Pacing of Demands
Guilt Manipulation

THE MANIPULATIVE PERSONALITY

INFLUENCE ATTEMPTS AND BOOMERANG EFFECTS

PART SUMMARY

I think I had the same feeling about John Kennedy that I'd had about Proxmire the first time I'd met him: a sense of disbelief that this wealthy, glamorous man who was thinking about running for President actually gave a damn about what I thought of anything, much less Presidential politics. I know I was flattered, and I suppose that was part of what made me as excited as I was the next morning—so excited, in fact, that I got there a half hour before our breakfast meeting and sat in my car until 9 A.M.*

As we shall soon see, flattery may get you somewhere, even if you are neither glamorous nor of high rank. In this chapter we turn to a consideration of how two people influence and respond to each other as they interact in the dyad, or two-person group. First we will discuss where and how two people are likely to trade information with each other and how the type of information traded changes as their relationship progresses. Second, we will consider some of the conditions that make it likely that two people will abandon selfish interests and coordinate their activities for mutual gain. Finally, we will discuss flattery and other tactics that two interacting people use to gain favors and compliance from each other. This chapter thus provides a shift of emphasis toward social interaction— that is, the mutual and reciprocal processes that go on within and between groups.

*From *The Advance Man,* by J. Bruno and J. Greenfield. Copyright © 1971 by Jerry Bruno and Jeff Greenfield. Reprinted by permission.

COMMUNICATION

Communication refers to the transmission of information and affect (feelings) from one person to another. Less formally, communication in the dyad is an information-trading process through which two people get to know each other's feelings, beliefs, and intentions and develop some sort of a relationship with each other. An essential component of interaction, communication is the basic social process upon which all other interpersonal processes depend.

In our discussion of interaction we will consider three issues: (1) the influence of the immediate setting on the likelihood that two people will learn about each other and develop a relationship; (2) nonverbal communication, such as through facial expressions, gestures, and tenor of voice; and (3) the process of information trading as a determinant of the course of a relationship. These factors, as we shall see, are highly inter-related.

SETTING THE STAGE: ENVIRONMENT AND INTERACTION

To some extent, whether or not people will interact and develop a relationship is determined in advance by the immediate environment. Certain locations are conducive to social interaction, whereas other locations discourage or prohibit it (Sommer, 1969; Mehrabian, 1971). **Sociofugal environments** are those that seem to drive or keep people apart, and **sociopetal environments** are those that draw people together and encourage intimacy. An example of a sociofugal environment would be a row of solitary-confinement cells; an example of a sociopetal environment would be the communal baths at the Esalen Institute, a West Coast encounter-group (Chapter 10) center.

Sociofugal Environments

In sociofugal environments, communication and intimacy are discouraged by physical barriers or by rules against interaction that are accepted and enforced by area occupants (Sommer, 1967). People may either simply pass through sociofugal areas enroute to sociopetal ones, or they may deliberately choose a sociofugal area for purposes of isolation. In the former case, two strangers boarding an elevator are likely to station themselves in opposite corners in the rear of the elevator, face away from each other, and spend the brief time consumed by the ride examining either their shoes or the elevator's ceiling—even though each is on his or her way to a party and is looking forward to an evening of intense interaction. In the latter case, people may seek out a library because it provides some isolation from other people and may assume that others have chosen it for the same reason (Sommer, 1967).

Robert Sommer studied users of a large reading room in a university library. The room contained 18 large rectangular tables, each accommodating 12 people, 6 on each side. The investigator arrived at the library when it opened and simply recorded the order in which users arrived and their choice of seats. Until the time when no unoccupied tables were left, about 80% of the entrants chose an unoccupied table. When no "new" tables were left, the most favored seats were those that were distant from the already occupied seats. For example, a chair four seats removed from an occupied position was about 25 times as likely to be selected as was a chair adjacent to an occupied position. Forced to choose between two equidistant locations, people preferred the one in which eye contact with others was minimized. Eye contact, which is considered an indication of intimacy (Argyle & Dean, 1965), is to be avoided with strangers in public places.

Not only do library users *abide* by social standards against interaction, but they also help to enforce them. **Territorial defense** refers to the techniques used to keep others away. One type of technique, referred to as an **agonistic display,** involves looking as tough, menacing, or obnoxious as possible, with the hope that the potential intruder will be scared away. Dogs, for example, ward off trespassers by crouching, perking up their ears, curling back their upper lip, and snarling. Library users may ward off potential tablemates by staring, glaring, leering, and sneering. However, such displays may seldom be required; since people feel uncomfortable and defensive when they realize that they are about to intrude on others (Efran & Cheyn, 1974), their anxieties may prevent them from intruding in the first place.

A second technique is to use **markers** to bound or stake out areas that are to remain private (Sommer & Becker, 1969; Becker, 1973; Fisher & Byrne, 1975). Markers are, in effect, "keep out" signs. In the animal kingdom, markers may be auditory (a snake's rattle), olfactory (dog manure by the fire hydrant), or visual (bear-claw marks on a tree). Humans spread out books and papers on top of library tables, and they use jackets, briefcases, and other large objects (such as feet) to protect adjacent or opposite chairs.

Markers also serve to "reserve" a space when the user is temporarily absent, although nothing reserves a space so well as a live person (Becker, 1973). Sommer and Becker (1969) marked library places with either (1) two notebooks and a textbook, (2) a stack of four library journals, (3) four scattered library journals, (4) a sports jacket draped over the back of a chair, or (5) notebooks and a sports jacket. Whereas all unmarked control chairs were occupied within about 20 minutes, only 32% of the reserved chairs were occupied within two hours. The personal markers, such as the sports jacket and the notebooks, were able to entirely ward off intruders. Impersonal markers, such as the library journals, only delayed occupancy.

An alternative to defense ("fight") is withdrawal ("flight"). Flight often involves subtle attempts to increase psychological distance by shrinking back. Confronted by a too-intimate stranger, we can draw our legs back under the chair, shift away from the intruder, pull in our arms close to our body, and studiously avoid eye contact. However, if the intruder seriously violates sociofugal taboos and is oblivious to agonistic displays and markers, we might resort to flight.

Outright flight was elicited in the library by Felipe-Russo and Sommer (1966). In *Condition I* the female experimenter, sitting down next to a female victim and seeming completely oblivious to her presence, unobtrusively slid her chair sideways toward the victim and attempted to maintain a distance of about 12 inches between her shoulders and the victim's. If the victim attempted to slide her chair away, the experimenter would take up the slack. In *Conditions II–V* the experimenter sat somewhere near the subject but did not crowd her. For example, in *Condition II* she kept her chair about 2 feet away and in *Condition V* about 5 feet away. In the *Control* condition the experimenter did not sit at the same table as the subject. As Figure 8-1 shows, at the end of a half-hour "crowding" session, 90% of the controls remained at their place, but only 30% of the most highly crowded subjects had not left.

Sociopetal Environments

Sociopetal environments encourage social interaction. Living rooms, lobbies, lounges in residence halls, group-therapy rooms, certain restaurants, and nightclubs are a few of the areas intended to support communication and the development of interpersonal intimacy. Yet the intended use and actual use of a space are sometimes discrepant. We all know of beautiful living rooms where conversations falter. Given that interaction is considered socially appropriate in such settings, the extent to which interaction occurs depends largely on furniture arrangement. This is because furniture establishes the *distance* between the potential conversants and also their physical *orientations* vis-à-vis each other.

As any ham radio operator or patron of the long-distance telephone can tell you, proximity is not a prerequisite for interaction. However,

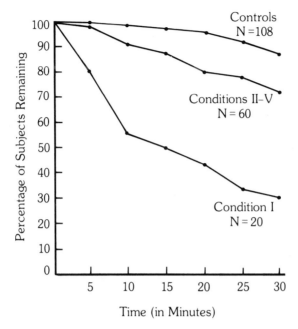

Figure 8-1. Percentage of victims remaining at each five-minute interval after invasion. Conditions *II–V* did not differ and hence were lumped together for purposes of the final analysis. (From "Invasions of Personal Space," by N. J. Felipe-Russo and R. Sommer, *Social Problems,* 1966, *14*(2), 213. Copyright © 1966 by the Society for the Study of Social Problems. Reprinted by permission.)

whether or not a conversation will develop is clearly affected by the sheer distance between the two potential conversants. Sommer (1965) placed two couches face to face in a room through which a large number of people passed during a hospital "open house." The distance between the two couches was varied systematically. People sitting on the two couches conversed freely when the spread was about 5½ feet, but conversations were dramatically curtailed when the distance was increased. Living rooms in which the furniture is arranged along the walls may also discourage conversations.

Although no relationships will profit if the two people are forced to scream at each other from across the room, it is unlikely that there is one "optimal" distance for interaction. For example, interactions with your date might be discouraged if he or she were 18 feet away, but interaction with the President of the United States might be discouraged if he were 18 inches away. One can be "too close for comfort," as well as "too far away."

Furniture arrangements also establish physical orientations. Consider, for example, a 5-foot-square table with two chairs at each side. All seats at that table are within conversation distance of every other seat. But two people placed in seats that are side by side, catercorner, or directly across from each other would have different orientations.

Mehrabian and Diamond (1971) assigned pairs of subjects face-to-face, catercorner, or parallel seats that represented, respectively, 0°, 90°, or 180° orientations (these figures representing the sum of the angles that both subjects would have to turn for face-to-face contact). The subjects' conversations were recorded, their behavior was coded by hidden observers, and, afterward, they completed questionnaires. The 180° seating arrangements, which had people facing in the same direction (as when seated on a sofa), curtailed communication relative to the two conditions in which the people could see each other. However, this result did not hold for *all* types of communication: "negative" messages, involving criticism and complaint, were easier to deliver in the parallel "sofa" arrangement. One possible reason why the side-by-side arrangement is *less* conducive to intimacy is that it seriously impairs communication through gestures and facial expressions. The impact of this kind of communication will be discussed shortly.

We should note, however, that, just as there is no one best "distance," there is no one seating arrangement that is "best" for all purposes. Sommer (1965) showed students diagrams of rectangular tables with one chair at the head, one at the foot, and two chairs along each side. They were asked to indicate preferred seating arrangements under four conditions: (1) conversation, which involved chatting before class; (2) cooperation, which involved studying together for an exam; (3) coaction, which involved studying for different exams; and (4) competition, which involved seeing who could complete a series of puzzles first. Conversing subjects preferred the corner-to-corner or directly opposite seating relationships. Side-by-side seating was preferred by subjects who imagined studying together, perhaps because this arrangement would make it easier to look at each other's notes, books, and so forth. Competing tasks called for maximizing the distance between the two interacting people.

Planning Environments

Research of the type reported by Sommer (1969, 1974) and Mehrabian (1971) makes it possible for architects, designers, and interior decorators to plan environments that better fit the needs of their human users. For example, a formal living room with the major pieces of furniture all lined up along each wall, as in the palaces of Edinburgh, Potsdam, or St. Petersburg, is fine—but only if you are king, kaiser, or czar. If you are not royalty and do not want to remain imperially distant from your guests, you may want to place your major pieces of furniture fewer than 6 feet apart and aligned along the 0° or 90° orientation. Since not all arrangements are best for all people and all purposes, easily movable furniture (such as inflatable chairs and huge bean bags) is convenient because it can be rearranged to fit the mood of the occasion.

Incorporating flexibility and variety would seem particularly important in public places that accommodate individuals and groups with varying needs for intimacy. In airport waiting rooms, for example, one finds both lone individuals and small, interacting groups. Seats arranged row upon row in the nonintimate 180° orientation would best accommodate voluntary isolates, and clusters of chairs arranged in the 0° and 90° patterns would best accommodate interacting groups. Movable furniture could solve the problem, but apparently planners fear that movable furniture would be moved right out of the public places. For the most part, furniture in public places is bolted to the floor or cemented to the ground. It thus can severely frustrate individual users and provoke vandalism (Sommer, 1974).

As an example of how social psychology can contribute to architecture and design, consider Mehrabian's (1971) proposal that restaurants be fitted with zig-zag-shaped tables. Tables such as those shown in Figure 8-2 would require about 20% less space per person than would square tables. There should be little apprehensiveness about joining a stranger at such a table, since it would not be necessary to face someone directly across. Notice that person *D* can take a seat very close to *C* but, by directly facing the counter, avoid eye contact with *C*. However, for *C* and *D* to converse, only a slight amount of reorientation would be necessary. Through additional swiveling, *D* could converse with *A*, *C*, *F*, or *E*. Although it is unlikely, it would also be possible for *B* and *D* to converse. In the future we can expect an increasing amount of interplay of the ideas of social psychologists, architects, and designers.

NONVERBAL COMMUNICATION

A principal character in the film *2001: A Space Odyssey* is a computer called HAL. In addition to handling such routine computer tasks as monitoring all systems and plotting courses and speeds, HAL experiences emotions and *interacts* with the astronauts. In a sense, it is possible today to interact with computers such as by playing chess or tic-tac-toe. Interaction with HAL, however, did not require pushing buttons, reading printouts, or monitoring flashing lights. HAL conversed in idiomatic English.

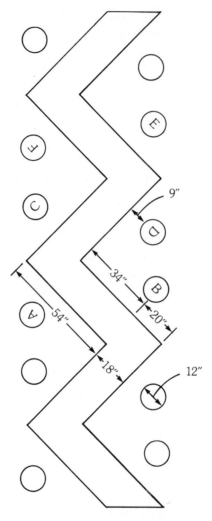

Figure 8-2. A basic module for zig-zag furniture arrangements in public eating, drinking, and entertainment spots. (From *Silent Messages,* by A. Mehrabian. © 1971 by Wadsworth Publishing Company, Inc., Belmont, California. Reprinted by permission of the publisher.)

Alphonse Chapanis (1971) points out that we are far short of building a conversational computer like HAL, for many reasons. Not only must HAL understand the dictionary definitions of spoken words, but it must understand shades of meaning imparted by pauses, inflections, emphases,

rate of delivery, and tone of voice. Visual stimuli such as postures, gestures, and facial expressions add new complexity.

The importance of such factors is illustrated in some of Chapanis' (1973) own work. Two-person groups were assigned problems that required discussion for solution. These discussions took place through (1) written notes, (2) teletyped communications, (3) telephone communications, or (4) face-to-face interaction. A comparison of written communications with typescripts of oral communications revealed a striking difference. Compared with the written communications, the typescripts were almost indecipherable. Yet, as one would expect, solution time was shorter under the telephone and face-to-face conditions than under the two written-communications conditions. Since the written communications involved more foresight, planning, organization, and care, the advantage of oral communication lay elsewhere—in the manner of speaking. Chapanis concludes that, until we can formally specify the gradations in meaning conveyed by manner of speaking, a conversational computer like HAL will not be possible.

Nonverbal communication (or "covert" communication) refers to the transmission of information and affect that are not put into words. Because of our intellectual preoccupation with words, we are likely to be somewhat neglectful of the role of communication through postures, gestures, and tenor of voice. The three major forms of nonverbal communication are *proxemic, kinesic,* and *paralinguistic.*

Proxemic Communication

Proxemic communication refers to the transmission of information and affect through spatial arrangement. We have already seen that distance and orientation can promote interaction, but now let's consider the ways in which these factors can serve to express a relationship as well. The next time you're waiting in line in a theater, try to observe dating couples. Some will be standing a couple of feet apart; some, inches apart. They also will show varying degrees of body contact. There is considerable agreement among observers that people who are voluntarily located close to each other have a closer or more intimate relationship than do people separated by some distance (Altman & Taylor, 1973; Mehrabian, 1971; Allgeier & Byrne, 1973).

Anthropologist Edward Hall (1959) has described four "zones" that reflect how people are feeling about each other at the time the zone is in use. **Intimate distance** extends from skin contact to about 18 inches. This is the zone for the most intimate relationships. It is the "distance of mattresses and wrestling mats." In this zone there is maximal opportunity for communication. Each person dominates the other's visual field, there is a close-up view of the other person's facial expression, touching is often involved, and each person can sense the other's body warmth and odors. **Personal distance** ranges from 1½ to 4 feet. It is the appropriate distance for close interaction. **Social distance** extends from about 4 to 12 feet. It signifies a less casual, more formal relationship. **Public distance** extends from about 12 feet onward. It is used for formal interactions, such as those between minister and congregation or politician and followers. Thirty feet, notes Hall, is the distance usually set around important public figures. He noted, for example, that during the 1960 Presidential campaign an invisible barrier kept friends this distance from John F. Kennedy until the nominee invited them, one by one, to step across.

Hall points out that these zones are arbitrary and culturally conditioned. What constitutes "social distance" in one culture constitutes "personal distance" in another. Representatives of the two cultures may thus have difficulty in discovering an acceptable distance for a conversation. For example, one of my students described inadvertently stepping backward into a basket of fresh fruit while bargaining in a Mideastern marketplace. The Mideasterner kept moving closer to attain the "appropriate" distance for bargaining, while the American kept moving farther away with the same goal in mind.

Orientation, like distance, can also serve an expressive function. Sommer (1965, p. 343) notes a certain metaphorical quality to some of the earlier-described relationships between tasks and seating arrangements. People competing sit "across from each other," people cooperating sit "on the same side," people conversing sit "in a corner," and people co-acting choose a "distant relationship." In a later study, Lott and Sommer (1967) found that seating preferences can also reflect social status. Upper-class college students choosing seats at a table preferred the cozy 90° orientation when sitting with an equal-status person (such as a classmate) but preferred being separated by the full width of the table when positioning themselves vis-à-vis superiors (the dean of their college) or inferiors (flunking freshmen).

Kinesic Communication

Kinesic communication is the transmission of information through facial expressions and gestures. Kinesics is perhaps the most heavily researched area of nonverbal communication. Let's consider, in turn, communication through facial expressions and communication through gestures.

Facial expressions are highly informative about the nature of an emotion. Several observers witnessing a person's facial reactions often agree on the emotion he or she is experiencing, and, it would seem, they are more likely to be right than wrong. In one early study, Ekman (1964) took pictures of people during two phases of an interview. During the stress phase the interviewer deliberately disagreed with and criticized the interviewee (thus presumably upsetting the interviewee), and during the catharsis phase the interviewer revealed that the criticism was faked (thus presumably relieving the interviewee). Subjects were highly successful at identifying the phase in which each photograph was taken. In a number of later experiments, "senders," or stimulus persons, have looked at emotionally loaded slides (sexy nudes, grisly burn victims, and so forth) while observers who cannot see the slides judge the sender's emotions. For the most part, these studies reveal that facial expression is a good transmitter of feelings (Buck, Savin, Miller, & Caul, 1972; Buck, Miller, & Caul, 1974). Many other studies confirm that people's nonverbal responses change as a function of the stimuli they are encountering and that these nonverbal responses serve a communicative function (Duncan, 1969; Wiener, Devoe, Rubinow, & Geller, 1972; Ekman, Friesen, & Ellsworth, 1972; Ekman, 1973; Rosenthal, Archer, DiMatteo, Koivumaki, & Rogers, 1974).

At least six categories of emotions (and certain "blends" of two or more emotions) appear to be reliably communicated through facial expression. These categories are *happiness, sadness, anger, fear, surprise,* and *disgust.* Ekman, Friesen, and Tomkins (1971) attempted to relate these emotions to activity in three facial areas. Their procedures were complex, but, basically, they had judges classify emotions by referring to: (1) the brow and the forehead, (2) the eyes, and (3) the area below the eyes, especially the mouth and the jaw. Over six emotion categories, 49% of the judgments based on the brow and forehead were correct, 67% of the judgments based on the lower face were correct, and 73% of the judgments based on the eyes were correct. Although these overall figures suggest that each of the three facial regions reveals something about emotions, it should be noted that, for specific emotions, certain facial areas were more revealing than others. For example, eyes did not seem to reveal "disgust" or the lower face "sadness," despite all our preconceptions about "downturned mouths." On the other hand, happiness, anger, and disgust were most clearly registered on the lower face, and sadness and fear most clearly registered in the area of the eyes.

Are facial displays of emotion culturally learned? Or is a given emotion expressed the same way in every culture? Ekman and his colleagues suggest that happiness, sadness, and the other emotions are expressed identically in such different cultures as Borneo, Brazil, Japan, New Guinea, and the United States (Ekman, 1970, 1972; Ekman & Friesen, 1969, 1971; Ekman, Friesen, & Ellsworth, 1972). This does *not* mean, however, that people from each culture will have identical facial reactions when confronted with a specific stimulus, because *evoking stimuli* and *rules of emotional display* will vary from land to land.

Evoking stimuli trigger an emotional reaction. Any given reaction (such as disgust) may be aroused by different stimuli in different cultures. In the United States, for example, a shrunken head may give rise to feelings of disgust and a chiliburger with ketchup may give rise to feelings of delight. In Borneo the head may give rise to delight and the crimson chiliburger to feelings of disgust. Once disgust or delight has been evoked, the natural facial expression of the members of the two cultures should be quite similar. That is, the American's expression in response to the chiliburger should be the same as the Borneon's to the head, and the Borneon should respond to the chiliburger as the American responds to the head.

Display rules are socially learned strategies for managing and controlling facial reactions. There are four such strategies. **Deintensification** refers to an attempt to "tone down" a reaction. Thus a combat leader who is frightened out of his wits may attempt to look only mildly apprehensive. **Intensification** refers to an attempt to exaggerate an emotion. For example, mildly appreciative of a gift necktie, a person may attempt to convey unbounded joy. **Neutralization** refers to an attempt to look neutral (as in a game of poker), and **masking** refers to an attempt to replace one expression with another (as when a guest feigns delight on hearing that the hostess is going to serve liver and spinach casserole).

Display rules vary from culture to culture and may hide cross-cultural similarities in facial reactions. For example, Orientals are supposed to mask negative feelings with polite smiles. Ekman (1970) showed 25 Japanese subjects a film that varied in content, from neutral scenes to a depiction of a hideous body mutilation. When a compatriot was present, the stoicism of the Orient prevailed. But when the subject thought he was alone (and display rules were rendered inoperative), he showed the same fear, anger, and disgust reactions that were typical of the American viewers.

Whereas facial expressions reveal the *type* of emotion experienced, for the most part the body and limbs reveal the *intensity* of the emotion— through shivering, fidgeting, shaking, quivering, tensing up, and so forth. An important exception is the hands, which reveal more than emotional intensity (Ekman & Friesen, 1972; A. A. Cohen & R. Harrison, 1973).

We all know, for example, that an open hand waggled sideways suggests one thing, whereas an up-and-down motion of a hand balled into a fist suggests something else. Ekman and Friesen (1972) have identified three different communicative functions of the hands. First, hands can be used to produce **emblems,** which substitute for a verbal communication. A beckoning motion toward a waiter in a crowded restaurant would be an example. Second, hand movements can serve as **illustrators,** complementing and supplementing verbal communications. For example, hand motions may be used to emphasize something, to point to an object or place, or to convey the rhythm or pacing of an event. Finally, there are **adaptors,** which are activities that help one to deal with a situation. For example, a highly nervous person may fidget with his or her keys to draw off tension. Adaptors are not necessarily meant to communicate, as are emblems and illustrators, but they can be informative because they reveal stress or anxiety.

Paralinguistic Communication

Paralinguistic communication refers to the transmission of information and affect through one's manner of speaking. It is communication through sighs, pauses, tenor of voice, rate of delivery, and so forth. For example, if a husband's voice trembles and soars and his speech is punctuated with lengthy pauses and "uhs" as he describes a harmless evening with the boys, he may convey an impression of untruthfulness. The communicative value of paralinguistic communication is illustrated in the Chapanis studies cited earlier. Although subjects in the two oral-communication conditions solved the problems faster than did subjects in the two written conditions, subjects interacting face to face did not do significantly better than subjects conversing on the telephone. Thus, with the two tasks involved, improved performance was attributable to the availability of paralinguistic, rather than proxemic or kinesic, cues.

Some social psychologists are keenly interested in the judgments people make on the basis of other individuals' tone of voice. This is a challenging research problem, for it involves separating what is said from how it is said. For example, if someone chirps in a bright and bouncy tone of voice "I feel wonderful today," it would seem that a rating of this person as "happy" would reflect both content and presentation.

In one study, Davitz and Davitz (1959) asked subjects to express different feelings such as anger, fear, and pride. However, speakers were instructed to use letters of the alphabet instead of words. Other subjects, serving as judges, listened to tape recordings of these sessions and attempted to identify the faked emotions. They did far better than could be expected by chance alone. Anger, nervousness, and sadness were the most accurately conveyed emotions, and pride, jealousy, love, and fear were the least accurately conveyed.

When people are expressing emotions they really feel (rather than faking such emotions on the directions of the experimenter), the elimination of "content" becomes a bit more troublesome. It might be possible to eliminate this factor, however, by comparing judgments of recordings and judgments of written transcripts of the recordings. The difference would be due to paralinguistic cues. An expensive technique for eliminating content is to use filters that allow intonations to be heard but make the words unrecognizable. An inexpensive technique (for the poor but patient researcher) is to cut the recording tape into segments, slice these into subsegments, randomize the subsegments, and then glue them back together for playing.

Using filters, Milmoe, Rosenthal, Blane, Chafetz, and Wolf (1967) found that the feelings reflected in a physician's speech affected his or her degree of success at getting alcholics to seek treatment. For example, doctors who used an angry tone of voice were not very effective, no matter how sweet their words. It has also been found that the tone of a mother's voice correlates with her child's behavior (Milmoe, Novey, Kagan, & Rosenthal, 1968). Compared with little girls whose mothers' voices did not betray anxiety, those whose mothers had "anxious" tones of voice tended to be more cautious.

People take turns speaking in conversations, and paralinguistic cues are important for the turn-taking process. When we are about to relinquish the floor, our voice may trail off, but, if we intend to continue, we may respond to an attempted interruption by speaking louder. The greater the difference in amplitude between the person who is trying to butt in and the person who is trying to keep speaking, the more likely it is that the interruption attempt will succeed (Meltzer, Morris, & Hayes, 1971).

When one person is trying to cut in on the other, a certain amount of "retaliation" is likely. In response to an interruption, the "defender" is likely to invigorate his or her own speech (Morris, 1971). In addition, we might note that paralinguistic cues can reveal the extent to which the conversants have gotten to know each other. As their dyadic interaction progresses, each person speaks less hesitatingly, and the number of filled pauses (pauses filled with "ers" and "ahs") diminishes (Lalljee & Cook, 1973).

According to Mehrabian (1971), certain seemingly minor changes in phrasing can make major differences in meaning. For example, in response to "How do you like the fried chicken I fixed?" you could reply "I like your fried chicken" or "I really like fried chicken." Both are positive expressions, but the latter response leaves the quality of the chicken in question ambiguous and gives an impression of less liking. Or, although "Why not get together sometime?" and "Let's get together sometime" both superficially indicate an interest in reuniting, the "Why not?" form, suggests Mehrabian, reflects indecision and doubt. Psychological studies of syntax would seem to be a promising area for future research.

The Uses of Nonverbal Messages

Nonverbal communication becomes fascinating when nonverbal messages are the only form of communication or when the nonverbal and verbal communications conflict. Nonverbal messages can take the place of, modify, or contradict verbal messages.

First, gestures and expressions often substitute for the spoken word, as when a man puts his fingers to his lips to silence chattering children. More interesting are those cases in which we feel a person *unwillingly* reveals something about himself or herself. For example, if a professor offering academic advice to a student sucks in her stomach, adjusts her blouse, and pats her hair into place, we might infer that she has something other than the midterm exam on her mind. In this regard it is far easier to censor our choice of words than to carefully control our facial expressions, postures, and gestures. For example, Ekman and Friesen (1969) have shown that attempts to maintain a poker face may come to naught because a smile or frown briefly and uncontrollably flashes across the face. Although these slips may last but a fraction of a second, some observers are very good at detecting them.

Second, nonverbal cues can "modify" verbal messages. For example, a politician may issue a written statement proclaiming the utmost dedication to racial equality. Yet the verbal presentation of that statement could convey a lack of conviction or enthusiasm.

Finally, nonverbal cues may directly contradict the spoken word. Consider again the earlier example of an errant husband protesting his innocence in an uneven, falsetto voice while tugging on his collar with one hand and rubbing his sweaty brow with the other.

When people receive seemingly contradictory messages, which do they believe? Perhaps we are aware of the comparative ease with which verbal statements can be suppressed or changed around. After comparing responses to pictures, typewritten messages, filtered recordings, and so forth, Mehrabian (1971) concluded that communicated feeling rests 55% on facial expression, 38% on voice, and only 7% on what is said.

We might note in conclusion that some people do a better job than others of understanding nonverbal messages. This finding has been revealed through widespread administration of the **PONS,** or Profile on Nonverbal Sensitivity (Rosenthal et al., 1974). The PONS is a 45-minute film containing two-second excerpts of episodes in which an actress enacts various behaviors, such as discussing her divorce, talking to a child, or ordering food in a restaurant. Viewers make multiple-choice judgments of the episodes on the basis of the excerpts. Each excerpt provides the viewer with one of 11 combinations of proxemic, kinesic, and paralinguistic cues. For example, in one excerpt the voice may be filtered and the face hidden, although postures and arm movements are visible. In general, adults do better than children and women do better than men at judging the messages in the excerpts. Some people remain accurate judges even when the excerpts are reduced to a fraction of a second. However, it is worth noting that, when the excerpts are extended from two seconds to five seconds, people do so well that the PONS fails to discriminate among them.

SOCIAL PENETRATION: THE DEVELOPMENT OF AN INTERPERSONAL RELATIONSHIP

Social penetration is a term coined by Altman and Taylor (1973) to refer to the processes through which two people progress from strangers to casual acquaintances to close friends and beyond. Social penetration may never begin (as when two strangers pass in the night), may advance to a given level and then stop (as when a dating couple decide that they will be "just friends"), or may progress to a deep and meaningful level but then be thrown into reverse (as in the case of a divorce). The social-penetration process is thus a sounding-out process through which people get to know about and become increasingly involved with each other. **Social depenetration** refers to a deintensification or termination of a relationship.

The Depth and Breadth of a Relationship

Altman and Taylor (1973) have made an interesting distinction between the depth and the breadth of a social relationship. Given any area or part of our lives, some of our attitudes and experiences are shallow, in that we are willing to share them with almost anyone; others are deep, in that they are highly personal and, because of fear of ridicule or rejection, we are willing to share them only with a trusted few. The extent to which people in a group are willing to express such potentially explosive material would define the **depth dimension** of the relationships within the group. For example, in the area of sex, a relationship within which people discussed the secondary sex characteristics of mammals would be considered shallow, whereas a relationship within which people discussed their personal sex hang-ups in detail would be considered deep.

The **breadth dimension** is defined in terms of the number of the participants' needs and interests or "parts of their lives" that enter into the relationship. For example, a marriage relationship (in which people live together, enjoy sex together, share similar outside interests and experiences, and frequently discuss many different topics and issues) would be characterized as broad, whereas a relationship that touches on only one or two aspects of each participant's life (such as an interest in stamp collecting or in furthering a political cause) would be narrow. As the process of penetration continues, people trade increasingly intimate information touching on increasingly larger numbers of aspects of their lives. Stability in a relationship would seem to require that penetration along the depth and breadth dimensions proceed hand in hand. Thus it is hypothesized that a relationship that is intimate only in terms of one aspect of the participants' lives (for example, sex) is likely to fail.

Rewards, Costs, and Penetration

According to Altman and Taylor, three factors hasten or restrain the growth of an interpersonal relationship. First, there are the *personal characteristics* of the participants, which include such variables as similarity, need complementarity, and other determinants of attraction that were discussed in Chapter 6. Thus, for example, people with similar interests and values are likely to make initial contact with each other; development of their relationship may depend on such variables as complementarity and completion. Second, there are the *situational contexts*, or interaction settings, which were discussed earlier in this chapter. For example, less penetration is likely in a library than in a cocktail lounge. Third, there are the *outcomes of the exchange* in terms of rewards and costs. Thus, whether

you will want to increase or decrease the breadth and depth of a relationship with another will depend on what you feel you are getting out of the
relationship, what you feel you deserve in the relationship, and what you
feel you could get out of other relationships (Chapter 4).

Altman and Taylor emphasize that *past* outcomes and *anticipated
future* outcomes, as well as *present* outcomes, enter into the decision to increase or decrease the level of involvement of a relationship. For example,
a woman might go out on a date with a man who is grumpy and no fun
at all. If this low outcome represented her only experience with the man,
the likelihood of a continuing relationship would be low. However, if
they had dated for several months prior to this particular evening (and
she had secured good outcomes on these dates) or if she believed that he
had just had a bad day (and hence expected better outcomes in the future), one negative experience might have little overall impact on the
course of the relationship. As another example, after accumulating a large
pool of generally favorable outcomes over a period of ten years of marriage, one partner would probably not run right out and have an affair
the moment the spouse becomes ill, even though from the immediate
perspective having such a fling might be more attractive than nursing the
spouse back to health.

Self-Disclosure as Social Penetration

The actual, ongoing process of developing a relationship is perhaps
best illustrated in the self-disclosure research touched on in Chapter 1.
In this kind of research, two subjects or a subject and an experimenter
discuss topics that can be analyzed in terms of the breadth and depth
dimensions. As we noted in Chapter 1, there is a strong reciprocity effect;
that is, when one party in a relationship is willing to reveal his or her
inner self, the other party is likely to respond in kind (Savicki, 1972;
Derlega, Harris, & Chaikin, 1973). Two people must work together to
deepen and broaden their relationship, and, if their self-disclosures lose
synchronization, their attraction to each other may diminish (Jones &
Gordon, 1972).

There are two explanations for reciprocity of self-disclosure. The
one we encountered in Chapter 1—the reinforcement or exchange interpretation—suggests that each person is motivated to self-disclose in order
to induce the other person to self-disclose in return. According to an alternative, modeling interpretation, one person's self-disclosure may have
response-facilitation or -disinhibition effects that prompt similar disclosures on the part of the other person (Marlatt, 1970).

Exchange and modeling interpretations offer different predictions
concerning the effects of self-disclosure by someone who is *outside* the

relationship. According to the exchange interpretation, self-disclosure should beget self-disclosure only within the interacting dyad, where intimacy can be repaid with intimacy. According to the modeling interpretation, self-disclosure on the part of a noninteracting outsider should also beget self-disclosure, since all that is required is a model to prod things along. In support of the exchange interpretation, Davis and Skinner (1974) found that listening to disclosures on the part of a tape-recorded model did not elicit as much self-disclosure from subjects as did listening to the same disclosures on the part of an interviewer with whom the subjects were interacting. Since the interviewer "went first," subjects were apparently paying the interviewer back for the information they had just received.

In addition to the other person's disclosures, personality and situational factors will affect a person's self-disclosures. Some people are simply more willing to self-disclose than others, and in our society, which ridicules men who express tender feelings or weep, it may be particularly difficult for men to self-disclose (Jourard, 1971). We might also note in passing that some situations may give rise to instant but short-lived intimacy. Two strangers on an airplane may discuss their financial woes and sex hang-ups and may gaily parade the skeletons from their respective family closets, secure in the knowledge that, since they will never see each other again, the potentially damaging material will never be used against them.

PART SUMMARY

Some locations or environments are conducive to interaction whereas others are not. Sociofugal environments discourage interaction by means of physical barriers or by means of rules curtailing interaction. For example, in a library, users tend to stay away from others and to engage in tactics to keep others away. Sociopetal environments encourage communication and intimacy. Given that interaction is acceptable, the extent to which it will occur depends largely on furniture arrangement. Although there is no one "best" distance, conversations tend to trail off if participants are much more than about 5 feet apart. Interaction is encouraged by face-to-face seating and discouraged by side-by-side seating. Research on the impact of environments on interaction has a number of implications for planning areas to better fit the needs of their human users.

Communication refers to the transmission of information verbally or silently. Because of our preoccupation with words, it is easy for us to neglect the important role of nonverbal communication. Major forms of nonverbal communication are proxemic, kinesic, and paralinguistic.

Proxemic communication is the transmission of information and affect through spatial location. Considerable theorizing and evidence suggest that the physical closeness of two or more people reveals the extent to which they like each other. Certain seating arrangements may reflect the task at hand and the relative status of the people in the group.

Kinesic communication is communication through expressions and gestures. Facial expressions reliably express happiness, sadness, anger, fear, surprise, and disgust. Different emotions may be most clearly etched on different parts of the face. Emotions are expressed in the same way in all cultures, although evoking stimuli and norms regulating the expression of emotions may vary from land to land. Postures and gestures are more communicative of the intensity of an emotion than of its type. However, hand movements can serve a number of communicative functions.

Paralinguistic communication refers to the transmission of information through one's manner of speaking. Studies of paralinguistic communication suggest that people can, with some accuracy, judge others' personality or moods by listening to their tone of voice. Paralinguistic cues are important for turn-taking in conversations.

Nonverbal messages can replace, alter, or contradict the spoken word. Mehrabian has concluded that conveyed emotion depends mostly on facial expression, next on the tone of voice, and only minimally on the words selected.

Social penetration refers to the processes through which two people come to know each other and develop a relationship. Relationships have both depth and breadth dimensions. Each dimension is reflected in the kinds of information the two people share with each other. Depth refers to whether the information is personal or intimate, and breadth refers to whether the shared information touches on many different aspects of the two persons' lives.

At least three types of variables affect the social-penetration process: the personal characteristics of the participants, the contexts or interaction settings, and the outcomes. Altman and Taylor's analysis breaks down outcomes into past outcomes, present outcomes, and anticipated future outcomes. Even if immediate outcomes are low, the person may not leave the relationship because of pleasant memories or because of the promise of better times in the future.

The actual penetration process is clearly illustrated in self-disclosure research. To the extent that one person in a relationship is willing to reveal his or her inner self, the other person is likely to respond in kind. Such reciprocation would appear to represent an exchange, rather than a modeling, phenomenon. Personality and situational factors also affect the self-disclosure process.

COOPERATION IN THE DYAD

Cooperation refers to the coordination of efforts for mutual rewards. The defining characteristic of cooperation is that the rewards following the effort are distributed between the two or more participants. Students studying together for better grades, passengers helping to push a car out of a snowbank, a person exchanging a check for an interest in a business, and world leaders attempting to replace the nuclear arms race with less dangerous activities all illustrate human cooperative activity.

EXPERIMENTAL GAMES

Without question, the laboratory study of cooperation in the dyad was one of the most prolific research areas of the 1960s. In these studies, experimenters used specially contrived tasks that are easily described in the language of Thibaut and Kelley (1959), which was discussed in Chapter 4. Each member of the dyad is provided with a limited number of carefully defined response alternatives (usually two), and each person's outcomes are contingent on both his or her own and the other person's responses. To translate response alternatives and outcomes into experimental procedures, the experimenters seat each subject before a control panel outfitted with one red and one blue button and a number of lights to inform him or her of the combinations of choices. It is explained that, on signal, each will make a choice in ignorance of the other's choice and that, when both have responded, a light will illuminate on the control panel indicating the combination of the responses. They are given payoff matrices that describe the possible combinations of responses and outcomes (which may be symbolic or monetary). Typically, there are a number of "iterations," or trials. These tasks are referred to as **experimental games**—"experimental" for transparent reasons and "games" because the participants can win or lose money or points in varying amounts.

By far the most popular experimental game is the **Prisoner's Dilemma Game,** or **PDG.** The PDG received its strange name from a problem hypothetically confronted by two armed-robbery suspects who were apprehended by the police and put into separate cells (Luce & Raiffa, 1957). Although certain that the pair was responsible for the robbery, the district attorney had too little evidence to convict them on anything more than a minor, trumped-up charge that carried a very light sentence. To obtain a conviction on the more serious count, the D.A. asked each prisoner individually to turn state's evidence. If the prisoner did so, said the D.A., he would be let off free, although his partner would be convicted. If both confessed, the deal would be off, but the D.A. would urge some leniency in sentencing. Thus, if both criminals remained silent, each would get off easy. However, by remaining silent, each criminal would run the risk that he would end up with the maximum sentence by virtue of the other person's confessing. If both confessed, even though the judge might show some leniency, they would be worse off than if they had remained silent. In this case, refusing to confess is cooperative, in that it promotes light sentences for both parties; confessing is competitive, in that it promotes personal gain at the expense of the other person.

In the laboratory, cooperative and competitive responses take the form of a depressed blue or red button, and the "payoffs" are poker chips or small monetary prizes rather than years of freedom. The specific outcomes associated with any combination of responses can vary within considerable latitudes and still constitute a PDG (Gallo & McClintock, 1965), but Table 8-1 shows a typical PDG payoff table, or matrix. Al-

Table 8-1. A Prisoner's Dilemma Game (PDG) matrix

| | | Player II's Response | |
		Blue	Red
Player I's Response	Blue	Player I +5¢ Player II +5¢	Player I −4¢ Player II +6¢
	Red	Player I +6¢ Player II −4¢	Player I −3¢ Player II −3¢

though initially it might appear that selection of the competitive red choice would maximize personal gains, long-term considerations demand that the other person's needs be taken into account and that the cooperative blue choice predominate. Otherwise, the two players will repeatedly end up in the red/red cell, where they both lose.

SOCIAL STRATEGIES AND SOCIAL MOTIVES

Early research focused almost exclusively on the PDG. This game has proven particularly useful for the analysis of **social strategies**—that is, overt responses of cooperation and competition. Social strategies, however, must be distinguished from **social motives,** which refer to the personal needs satisfied by a social strategy. Presumably, a strategy is employed because it "does something" for its chooser. Yet a given strategy might satisfy any of a number of different motives. Three such motives identified by McClintock (1972) are *own gain, joint gain,* and *relative gain.*

Own gain refers to motivation to do as well as one can. It is a "nonsocial" motive, in that the other person's gains and losses are irrelevant. For example, an own-gain male would choose a response that nets him 10¢ and someone else 20¢ over a response that nets 5¢ for each. Before we conclude that this person is altruistic, we might note that he would also choose a response that nets him a 10¢ gain and the other person a 20¢ loss over a response that nets 5¢ for each. Under conditions of own-gain motivation, the only issue of consequence is what one can do for oneself. Own-gain motivation is shown when a player is unresponsive to variations in the outcomes experienced by others.

The person motivated by **joint gain** seeks outcomes that include rewards for others, as well as for himself or herself. This is a highly social motive. Sensitive to and motivated by others' needs, the joint-gain person cooperates and typically prefers the blue response in the PDG.

Relative gain is also a social motive. However, rather than seeking rewards *for* others, the person seeks rewards *relative to* others. For example, motivated by relative gain, you might prefer a response that gains you nothing but leads the other person to lose 5¢ to a response that gains each of you 5¢. Although winning no money, you would be glad to be "a nickel up" on somebody else. The relative-gain motive is most clearly assessed by the red alternative to the **Maximizing Difference Game,** or **MDG** (Table 8-2).

Many different factors have been related to cooperation in experimental games, and there have been several extensive reviews of the research (Gallo & McClintock, 1965; Vinacke, 1969; Wrightsman, O'Connor, & Baker, 1972). We'll consider in turn how characteristics of the individual participant, characteristics of the partner, and characteristics of

Table 8-2. A Maximizing Difference Game (MDG)

		Player II's Response	
		Blue	*Red*
Player I's Response	*Blue*	Player I +6¢ Player II +6¢	Player I 0¢ Player II +5¢
	Red	Player I +5¢ Player II 0¢	Player I 0¢ Player II 0¢

the situation affect levels of cooperation. It is important to remember that, for the most part, the PDG and MDG have been used to assess social strategies rather than social motives. This is because the "cooperative" and "competitive" responses could represent more than one motive (Table 8-3).

Table 8-3. Social strategies and social motives

Response Choice	*Strategy*	*Possible Motives*
PDG		
Blue	Cooperation	1. Joint Gain
Red	Competition	1. Own Gain
		2. Relative Gain
MDG		
Blue	Cooperation	1. Joint Gain
		2. Own Gain
Red	Competition	1. Relative Gain

PERSONALITY AND COOPERATION

It appears that some people have a more cooperative orientation than others and that this orientation will show up in a number of ways, including the way they play experimental games. For example, although not all results are in complete accord, at least three studies have found that people who favor friendly international endeavors, the easy flow of communication among nations, and friendly negotiated solutions to international disputes are more cooperative or more responsive to their partners than are people who tend to distrust other nationalities, favor restricting the flow of international commerce, and advocate military solutions to disputes (Lutzker, 1960; McClintock, Harrison, Strand, &

Gallo, 1963; McClintock, Gallo, & Harrison, 1965). Thus, cooperative attitudes in the sphere of international relations bear some relationship to cooperative behavior in the dyad.

According to Kelley and Stahelski (1970), "cooperators" and "competitors" have different views of the world, especially concerning the cooperativeness of other people. Competitors tend to see all other people as very much like themselves, whereas cooperators recognize variations in human nature and see some people as more cooperative than others. The competitor, who thinks everyone else is competitive, is blind to the other person's cooperative overtures. The cooperator, sensitive to individual differences, will respond to others on a tit-for-tat basis. Paired with another cooperative person, the cooperator will cooperate at a very high level. Paired with a competitive person, the cooperator will compete in an attempt to induce the partner to cooperate. As a result, the pairing of a cooperator and a competitor results not in the inflexible competitor's becoming cooperative, but in the flexible cooperator's becoming competitive! The cooperator's competitiveness reinforces the competitor's belief that "It's a cutthroat world." When it comes to a mixed-motive situation in which people can choose to cooperate or to pursue selfish ends, one bad apple spoils the two-apple barrel.

In one recent study that did not use experimental games, D. W. Johnson (1975) first assessed children's predisposition to cooperate on three different tasks. A composite score on these tasks was then related to the children's ability to take the perspective of other people. Johnson reasoned that the ability to take the perspective of another—that is, to put oneself in the place of another and understand how the other person sees and feels about conditions—is an important component of the cooperative orientation. One measure of perspective taking assessed the children's cognitive ability to understand how other people *perceived* conditions, and the other measure assessed the children's affective or emotional ability to understand how other people *felt* about conditions. Whereas the cognitive ability to view conditions the way others did was unrelated to the children's orientations, the affective ability to understand how other people felt about conditions was clearly related to cooperativeness. In other words, a person with a cooperative orientation may be distinguished from a person with a competitive orientation partly on the basis of the former's ability to appreciate how another person will feel when an action is taken that will yield that other person satisfactions rather than disappointments.

Although it makes some sense to think of people as varying in the extent to which they adopt a cooperative orientation toward interpersonal relations, the search for personality correlates of people's orientations has not met with much success. In a recent review of the many studies that have attempted to relate personality-test scores and cooperative game-playing strategies, Baxter (1972) noted that scores on 17 different personality measures were unrelated to cooperative game-playing behavior. Scores on 11 measures were unreliably related to cooperation; that is, some investigators found significant relationships but others did not. Five personality measures have been successfully related to cooperation, but in the case of four of these measures there had not been any attempts to replicate the findings. One personality measure does seem to yield scores related to cooperative game-playing behavior. At least three studies have found that a person's need for achievement (Chapter 2) is correlated with cooperativeness. People who are concerned with standards of excellence and who prefer to engage in success-related activities tend to be more cooperative than people who score low on measures of need for achievement.

Several reasons have been advanced for the failure to identify personality correlates of game-playing strategies. One such explanation is that experimental games provide such limited and formal conditions that individual differences based on personality have little chance for expression (Vinacke, 1969). A second possibility is that investigators have not yet identified the personality variables that would correlate with cooperation or competition (Baxter, 1972). A third explanation is that personality measures can predict game strategy, but only if they are used in combination. That is, if attempts are made to consider combinations of personality variables, a correlation between personality measures and cooperation may emerge. A fourth, and very likely, possibility is that personality variables may typically be outweighed by situational factors. Whereas personality factors may influence strategies early in an experimental game, they lose importance as the game progresses and the subjects get caught up in it (Wrightsman, 1966; Terhune, 1970; Wrightsman et al., 1972). Thus personality-based cooperative or competitive propensities seem to be outweighed by such factors as whether one is confronted with a friendly or a cutthroat "partner."

THE "OTHER PERSON" AND COOPERATION

A number of studies have attempted to relate game-playing strategies to various characteristics of the "other person" or partner. Partner variables include who the partner is and what strategies he or she adopts when playing the game.

Friends and Strangers

We would certainly expect people to be more cooperative when dealing with friends than with strangers or enemies, and studies using the PDG and MDG have generally found this to be the case (Oskamp & Perlman, 1966; McClintock, 1972). In one study, players given prior information that led them to perceive their partners as friendly were more cooperative than were players who were given no prior information; moreover, the no-prior-information subjects were more cooperative than subjects who had been led to believe that their partner was unfriendly and hostile (McClintock & McNeel, 1967). A later study, which used naturally formed pairs of friends, confirmed this finding (McClintock, Nuttin, & McNeel, 1970).

Friendship, however, is not invariably a basis for *unconditional* cooperation. Children who liked each other, disliked each other, or had no specified relationship played a PDG-type game for Swingle and Gillis (1968). Initially, children paired with friends were the most cooperative. However, it was arranged that, halfway through the experiment, the partner became either *more* or *less* cooperative than he or she had been in the first half of the game. Subjects whose friends switched in the direction of cooperation became more cooperative, but subjects whose friends switched in the direction of competition became more competitive. Strategy shifts on the part of nonfriends did not elicit reciprocity of comparable magnitude. One explanation for this change in strategy with friends but not with nonfriends is that, when dealing with strangers, we prefer to adopt a rather neutral, middle-of-the-road posture. Or perhaps, although we are particularly eager to cooperate with friends when they show a willingness to do so too, we may also feel particularly hurt and vengeful when they let us down.

Strategy of the Other Person

The norm of reciprocity (Chapter 6) clearly suggests that one person should be cooperative to the extent that the other is cooperative. To test this straightforward hypothesis, several investigators have "rigged" their experiments so that the two players interact with a simulated partner rather than with a real one. Each subject believes that he or she is interacting with the other person present, but in fact the outcomes represent a combination of his or her responses and a response secretly made by the experimenter. Thus the experimenter can control for each person what the "other player" seems to do.

In one study a comparison of subjects whose simulated partners cooperated on 83% of the trials with subjects whose simulated partners cooperated on only 17% of the trials revealed no differences in the overall levels of cooperation (Bixenstine, Potash, & Wilson, 1963). In another study, which compared the level of cooperation elicited by simulated others who adopted 85%, 50%, or 15% cooperative strategies, there were again no differences in cooperation (McClintock et al., 1963). In fact, there seem to be many failures to support the hypothesis that cooperation from one person leads to cooperation from another.

However, as Zajonc (1966) has noted, these findings may be easily understood when we consider the likely patterns of reinforcement in these studies. The "responses" of the simulated partner did not depend in any way on the real player's choice. They were programmed in advance by the experimenters and were *unconditional*, in that nothing the subject did could change them.

When the "partner" is preprogrammed, the competitive choice offers the best rewards. If the simulated partner is unconditionally cooperative, the subject can take advantage of the partner without risking retaliation. The subject soon discovers that, whatever he or she does, the partner will be cooperative and let the subject win, and the winnings are the greatest when the subject chooses the noncooperative alternative. If, on the other hand, the simulated partner is competitive, the real player discovers that it is not possible to induce the partner to cooperate, since again the preprogrammed partner is uninfluenced by his or her actions. Here, too, the noncooperative choice leads to the best outcomes, because it minimizes the losses that will be incurred.

However, *conditional* cooperation on one person's part may elicit cooperation from the other. A large number of experiments have arranged that, if a subject makes a competitive choice, the simulated other will retaliate in kind, but, if the subject makes a cooperative choice, the simulated other will also cooperate. As careful reinspection of Table 8-1 should reveal, under these conditions cooperation is rewarded and competition is punished. The most common finding has been that under these conditions subjects quickly learn to cooperate; in other words, reinforcement does reign supreme (Vinacke, 1969; Oskamp, 1972; Wrightsman et al., 1972). What these studies seem to suggest is that cooperation may be brought about by a series of steps during which the person indicates an increasing willingness to repay cooperation in kind. By his or her series of responses, each person slowly influences and adapts to the other, with the result that they begin to coordinate efforts for mutual rewards (Vinacke, 1969).

The process of developing cooperation can be particularly difficult if the two players have the potential to threaten each other. Using the **Trucking Game,** Deutsch and Krauss (1960, 1962) asked each of two female subjects to take the role of an operator of a small, independent trucking firm, either Acme or Bolt. Each woman's task was to move her truck from a starting point to a destination. The starting points and the destinations were shown on a map (see Figure 8-3), and the two trucks' progress was recorded by a counter. Subjects were told that they would

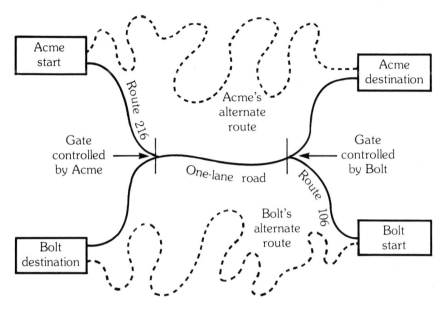

Figure 8-3. Road map for the Trucking Game. (From "The Effect of Threat on Interpersonal Bargaining," by M. Deutsch and R. M. Krauss, *Journal of Personality and Social Psychology,* 1960, *61,* 183. Copyright 1960 by the American Psychological Association. Reprinted by permission.)

receive an imaginary payoff of 60¢ "minus expenses" for each trip completed. Expenses were incurred at the rate of 1¢ per second for delivery.

As Figure 8–3 shows, there were two routes available to each trucker. One was a private road that was roundabout and hence expensive to use. The other, public, road was short and direct. The complication, however, was that a one-lane stretch on the public road could be used by only one truck at a time. If both trucks rushed onto this stretch, there would be an impasse and an expensive waste of time. The way to win the most money at the Trucking Game is to take turns using the one-way public road.

Subjects in some conditions were provided with a gate that they could use to block off the one-way stretch to the other person. In the no-threat condition, neither woman had a gate; in the unilateral-threat condition, one woman had a gate; in the bilateral-threat condition, both women had a gate. The index of cooperation was the total amount of time elapsed for both players to reach their destinations.

Results showed that joint gains were made in the no-threat condition. Losses were incurred in the two threat conditions, and these losses were twice as great under conditions of bilateral as under conditions of unilateral threat. Unilateral-threat subjects with a gate did do better than their powerless partners. However, it was also found that, when facing a partner with a gate, a subject did better if she did *not* have a gate with which to retaliate. The greatest losses were incurred when each woman had the capacity to escalate the conflict. When people have the means to coerce each other, they are tempted to use these means to win, and friendly negotiation becomes unlikely.

THE SITUATION AND COOPERATION

A seemingly endless list of situational variables has been explored by experimental-games researchers. Three of the more intriguing types of situational variables are *outcome values, communication opportunities,* and *group atmosphere.*

Outcome Values

Although in most experiments cooperation yields the best long-term gains, the initial level of cooperation typically is low and is likely to decrease over trials. One explanation of subjects' self-defeating behavior is that the payoffs are so low that they have no real value for the subjects (Gallo & McClintock, 1965). Thirty trials of unrelenting cooperation will rarely yield each person a dollar.

However, attempts to increase cooperation by raising the payoffs have yielded conflicting results. McClintock and McNeel (1966) found that an increase in incentives led to greater cooperation in an MDG, and, by using real rather than token payoffs, Gallo (1966) was able to increase cooperation on a version of the Trucking Game. Yet Gumpert, Deutsch, and Epstein (1969) found that increasing the payoffs on a PDG lessened cooperation. In their study, subjects were more cooperative when playing for token rewards ("imaginary dollars") than when playing for real cash. In other experiments a comparison of various incentive conditions showed no significant differences in average level of cooperation (Gumpert et al., 1969; Knox & Douglas, 1971).

These inconsistencies probably reflect several different factors. First, subjects may not believe it when the experimenter tells them that they have the opportunity to walk away with a lot of money (even in those rare cases when the experimenter is telling the truth). As a result, the believable small incentives may have more motivational value than the unbelievable large incentives. Second, within the range of believable payoffs, monetary values may appear insignificant in contrast to other intangible satisfactions, such as delight at being "one up" on one's opponent during an MDG (Gallo, 1968). A third factor is suggested by Knox and

Douglas' (1971) study in which subjects played the PDG for either pennies or dollars. Although the two conditions did not result in a difference in average number of cooperative responses, there was greater variability in the high-payoff conditions. This finding suggests the possibility that, when stakes are high, people become excited or aroused and that this increased arousal magnifies their pre-existing response tendencies. If this hunch is true, we would expect that, under high-incentive (arousal) conditions, pairs of cooperators would become more cooperative and pairs of competitors would become more competitive.

Communication Opportunities

Communication is highly important for working out differences and for pursuing a mutually advantageous course. For example, the breaking off of diplomatic relations, and hence communication, between countries often signals a war. At exactly that time when representatives of each nation should be discussing constructive alternatives, they are moving toward conditions for which only military solutions remain possible. The results of several studies suggest that both nonverbal communication (in which people see each other and communicate through postures, gestures, and facial expressions) and verbal communication (in which people can discuss their differences) can facilitate cooperation. Working outside the laboratory, Dorris (1972) found that an unconditional cooperator could, by appealing to moral standards, elicit reciprocal cooperation, even though his or her unconditional cooperation could have been seriously exploited. Working within the experimental-game paradigm, Voissem and Sistrunk (1971) found that cooperation increased over trials when subjects were given the opportunity to pass written messages stating what they intended to do and what they expected their partner to do. Greater cooperation was found when subjects could communicate after every trial than when they could communicate only after every tenth trial.

The importance of proxemic and kinesic communication has been shown by Wichman (1970) and by Gardin, Kaplan, Firestone, and Cowan (1973). Wichman reported that subjects who were isolated from each other were the least cooperative, those who could see or hear each other were somewhat cooperative, and those who could both see and hear each other were the most cooperative of all. In the Gardin et al. study a number of variables were manipulated, including proximity, orientation, and eye contact. Figure 8-4 shows that, with people in the 0° or face-to-face orientation, there was greater cooperation when there was no barrier to eye contact. In the case of side-by-side seating (in which subjects would in any case have difficulty studying each other's faces), the difference between the barrier and no-barrier conditions did not attain significance.

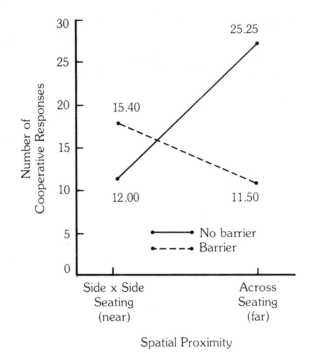

Figure 8-4. Cooperation as a function of spatial proximity and the availability of eye contact. (From "Proxemic Effects on Cooperation, Attitude, and Approach-Avoidance in a Prisoner's Dilemma Game," by H. Gardin, K. J. Kaplan, I. J. Firestone, and G. A. Cowan, *Journal of Personality and Social Psychology*, 1973, *27*, 16. Copyright 1973 by the American Psychological Association. Reprinted by permission.)

It would seem that it is easier to hurt or take advantage of an anonymous nonentity than someone who is looking you in the eye.

Group Atmosphere

Some studies suggest that the group's mood or atmosphere affects cooperative activity. Oskamp and Perlman (1965) raised or lowered cooperation by having subjects first participate in a rigged discussion during which the other group members advocated cooperation (or competition) through such statements as: "I think people in general are too competitive. I think we'd be better off if we cooperated a little more. I'm going to push the left button."

In another study the same investigators compared subjects from two different colleges (Oskamp & Perlman, 1966). One was a small liberal-arts school that appealed to students interested in becoming artists or scholars or in entering service-oriented fields such as social work. The other college appealed to students interested in business, law, and other competitive careers. Again, group standards fostering cooperation were associated with more cooperative responses on the PDG. Other studies, discussed by McClintock (1972), show cross-cultural differences that are presumably interpretable in terms of national standards of cooperation and competition. A comparison of second-, fourth-, and sixth-grade children from Japan, the United States, Greece, and Belgium showed that at all age levels the children from Japan—the country showing the highest degree of economic competitiveness (as reflected in tremendous leaps in manufacturing and the export of goods)—were the most competitive. Thus the extent to which groups encourage and approve cooperative activities and cooperative solutions to problems will affect the extent to which group members choose cooperative or competitive strategies. One explanation for these findings is that modeling and social approval affect cooperative human activity.

THE EXTERNAL VALIDITY OF PDG RESEARCH

Without question, the PDG and its many variants have dominated social-psychological studies of cooperation. Experimental games may provide the ultimate in control. Usually the two or more players cannot see each other and are forbidden to converse. "Interaction" involves pushing a button without knowing what button one's partner has pushed. The advantage of such minimal social contact is that, because the situation is stripped of most of its usual superfluities, it is possible to manipulate one or a small number of independent variables while holding others constant. Recording and analyzing interaction are easy when the number of response alternatives is only two. Precisely because experimental-games research takes place under such highly artificial and contrived conditions, these researchers are usually among the first to be singled out when criticisms of the laboratory method begin flying. The thrust of this criticism is that experimental-games research has low external validity —that is, tells us little or nothing about cooperation in the "real world."

Critics have pointed to the differences between the laboratory and the natural setting and have argued that these differences make generalization from one to the other impossible. Perhaps representative of the criticisms are those made by Pruitt (1967) and by Gergen (1969). Pruitt notes, for example, that: (1) although in experimental-games studies people are usually not allowed to communicate, in real life they almost always have this opportunity; (2) although in the laboratory people do not have the opportunity to tentatively try out their decisions and then reverse them if the results are unfavorable, in real life this opportunity is usually present; (3) although in the laboratory payoffs are in the form of pennies, tokens, or imaginary money, in real life the payoffs are often large and meaningful; (4) the pattern of outcomes available in experimental games is not often paralleled by the pattern of outcomes available in real life; and (5) although social rules and customs concerning the appropriateness of cooperation are not present in the lab, they are present in real-life situations. To Pruitt's list we might add two additional criticisms from Gergen. They are that: (6) the assumption that pushing the blue switch is a cooperative response is too simplistic, and (7) in most cases people are not limited to one or two response alternatives but have many different options.

At present we *cannot* freely generalize from cooperation in dyads playing experimental games to cooperation in dyads behaving in naturalistic settings. However, two points bear emphasis. First, many social psychologists (myself included) are firmly convinced that experimental games provide useful analogies or prototypes for studying cooperation and competition in social interaction. Lave (1965) argues that the Prisoner's Dilemma Game does capture the choices of cooperating and competing as they are routinely encountered in the marketplace and on Capitol Hill, and Deutsch (1969, p. 1091) has described himself as "brash enough to claim that the games people play as subjects in laboratory experiments may have some relevance for war and peace." Second, in a step-by-step fashion, researchers have been increasing the degree of correspondence between cooperation in experimental games and cooperation in naturalistic settings. For example, as we have already seen, investigators have attempted to make payoffs more meaningful, have allowed opportunities for communication, and have introduced social standards relevant to cooperation into the lab. Cooperation, like most social processes, is very complex. I agree with experimental-games researchers who suggest that starting with the simplest possible situation (such as an experimental game) and then increasing its complexity by adding one variable at a time may ultimately prove to be the best way to capture and understand cooperation in "real-life" settings.

PART SUMMARY

Cooperation refers to the coordination of efforts for mutually beneficial results. The use of experimental games has been popular for studying cooperation under carefully controlled conditions. Each subject is given a limited number of carefully defined response alternatives, and gains and losses are based on the combination of the subjects' choices. By far the most popular such game is the Prisoner's Dilemma Game, or PDG. One response is defined as cooperative, since it leads to gains for the other person as well as for the self. The second response is defined as competitive, in that it promotes personal gains at the expense of the other person.

Overt responses in experimental games are referred to as social strategies, whereas the needs satisfied by these responses are referred to as social motives. The three social motives discussed by McClintock are own gain, joint gain, and relative gain.

Social strategies have been related to personality variables, the nature and behavior of the other player, and situational variables. Several studies suggest that some people have a more cooperative orientation than others and that it shows up in a number of ways, including game-playing behavior. Compared with cooperators, people with competitive orientations tend to see other people as competitive and have difficulty adopting other people's emotional perspectives. For the most part, attempts to correlate personality measures and game-playing strategies have led to disappointing results.

The "other person" is important both for who he or she is and for what he or she does. Friends tend to be more cooperative than strangers, as well as more responsive to shifts in each other's strategies. As an analysis of the patterns of rewards suggests, unconditionally cooperative behavior does not necessarily elicit cooperation from the partner. Cooperation in the dyad develops through a slow process whereby each person gradually influences and adapts to the other. This process is likely to be impaired if the people can threaten each other.

Three important situational variables contribute to cooperative behavior. First, in the experimental situation, variations in monetary payoffs do not necessarily have easily predictable effects on cooperation and competition. Second, an increase in opportunities for communication can facilitate cooperation. Third, a cooperative atmosphere within a group can encourage cooperative behavior on the part of group members. Although it is not possible at present to easily generalize from cooperation in the laboratory to cooperation in the field, experimental-games research may ultimately lead to an understanding of cooperation in real-life settings.

INFLUENCE IN THE DYAD

Intentionally and unintentionally, people act in ways that cause others to respond in a satisfying, rewarding manner. Through begging, cajoling, needling, wheedling, flattering, demanding, harping on insecurities, and appealing to strengths, they induce each other to meet their stated or implicit demands. In a sense, almost every social-psychological process can be viewed as an instance of interpersonal influence. Here, however, we will reserve the term **interpersonal influence** to refer to the means through which one person induces another to comply with an overt or unspoken request.

To some extent, very simple reinforcement principles account for much of the interpersonal-influence process. The person who controls the resources can call the shots. In some cases the school principal can raise the salary of an exemplary teacher and lower the salary of a teacher who seems too unconventional. The police officer is backed up not only by the authority of the legal system but also by clubs, guns, chemical sprays, and all the other "musts" for maintaining control. The parent, spouse, and lover may be "minded" because they have the power to dispense or withhold love, affection, and allowances. The doctor's orders to give up smoking or the lawyer's frank advice to settle out of court may be accepted because their opinion offers the lure of a longer or better life.

TACTICS OF INFLUENCE

Although it seems to offer a satisfyingly simple way of handling interpersonal relations, open use of promises and threats is often impossible or ill advised. In about half of all cases, the distribution of power (in terms of who controls the rewards and the punishments) is not convenient for the party who wishes to do the influencing. Also, when one person openly attempts to manipulate another, the other may become resentful and uncooperative. Perhaps to compensate for possible unfavorable distributions of power and for a general lack of enthusiasm for being bossed around, people often use "low-pressure" influence tactics to exact compliance or gain favors from each other. Three "soft-sell" tactics are: (1) *ingratiation*, (2) *the pacing of demands*, and (3) *guilt manipulation*.

Ingratiation

When one person is dependent on another (as when an employee with no other job possibilities needs a raise, or when a prisoner needs a favor from a guard), the imbalance of power can be reduced through tactics of ingratiation (Jones, 1964). **Ingratiation** refers to any activities aimed at putting oneself in the good graces of another. These activities include agreeing with the other, cheerfully doing favors, complying with requests, and, according to Schneider and Eustis (1972), matching the other person's level of self-disclosure. To maintain the pleasant stream of agreement, flattery, and favors, the advantaged member of the pair will grant the ingratiator concessions and favors. In a small-group setting in which a leader or supervisor has the power to dispense rewards to a number of subordinates, friendly and compliant subordinates are particularly likely to get good results if the group contains some hostile, noncompliant subordinates as well (Kipnis & Vanderveer, 1971).

Ingratiation under conditions in which people are made dependent on each other has been discussed by Jones, Gergen, and Jones (1963), who formed pairs of one Navy R.O.T.C. freshman and one Navy R.O.T.C. upperclassman. Each member of a pair was seated in a separate cubicle. The subjects were told that they would be given the opportunity to share their attitudes with each other. In one condition, designed to highlight the subjects' dependency on each other, they were told that the aim of the exercise was to find compatible commander-subordinate pairs and that it was important to receive favorable evaluations from the partner. In another condition, subjects were simply told to express themselves accurately. It had been arranged that, before expressing his own opinion, each member of the pair would see a very unpopular, contrived opinion that was misrepresented as coming from the partner. Subjects in the experimental or high-dependency condition agreed more with the partner's unpopular opinion than did subjects in the low-dependency, control condition. Presumably the freshmen were attempting to curry favor with their superiors, and the upperclassmen were trying to elicit good will from the freshmen to prove their skill as "leaders." Furthermore, the relatively powerless, dependent freshmen claimed more agreement than did the relatively powerful upperclassmen.

Successful ingratiation requires a certain amount of tact and diplomacy. If the ingratiator's ulterior motives show through the façade of friendliness, the target of the influence attempt is likely to feel "used" and thus react adversely. Jones reports an unpublished study of Dickoff (1961), who told female interviewees that they were being evaluated by a hidden observer. In one condition, subjects were told that this observer would ask for a favor after the interview; in another condition the possibility of being asked a favor was not raised. Within each condition, one-third of the subjects were given very favorable ratings by the observer, one-third neutral ratings, and the remaining third unfavorable ratings. The subjects then evaluated the observer.

As we would by now expect, there was clear reciprocity: subjects' ratings of the observer were about as favorable as the observer's ratings of the subjects. However, the observer who might have ulterior motives was rated less favorably than her pure-of-heart counterpart, and this difference was most pronounced when the subject had herself been given a very favorable rating.

A certain amount of suspiciousness may exist when there is an unequal distribution of power. In a recent study by Kleinke, Staneski, and Weaver (1972), it was found that, when a job applicant flattered the interviewer by repeatedly using the interviewer's name, the applicant was perceived as an insincere phony who was attempting to curry a favor. However, in a situation in which something like a job was not in the balance, a person who used another's name received very favorable ratings.

To conclude our discussion of ingratiation, it is useful to consider Berscheid and Walster's comment on the use of flattery and compliments. According to these authors, a compliment is a "gift horse whose mouth is usually examined quite carefully" (1969, p. 62). A patently false compliment is likely to be rejected because it suggests ulterior motives. A patently true compliment will fail to make a good impression, because the recipient has simply heard it too often before to pay attention to it anymore. Berscheid and Walster suggest that compliments are most likely to be accepted when the recipient is *uncertain* about the extent to which he or she possesses the extolled virtue.

Pacing of Demands

A belief of door-to-door salespeople seems to be that, if a person can be induced to comply with a small request, he or she will later be more likely to accept a larger demand. Peddlers of encyclopedias, for example, may request a few minutes of your time to "ask you some questions"; only much later does the $500 contract appear.

To examine this **foot-in-the-door-hypothesis**—that a large request is more likely to be accepted if it has been preceded by a small request—Freedman and Fraser (1966) contacted housewives by telephone and asked them to answer a series of harmless questions about household products. Three days later the women were recontacted and confronted with the large request of allowing a team of five or six men to inventory the household products stashed in all the rooms, closets, and cupboards. Other women were approached only with this larger request. Whereas 52.8% of the two-contact subjects complied with the larger request, only 22.2% of the one-contact subjects were agreeable. Although in this study the women did not actually have to go through with the larger favor, a more recent study found that women who had been asked to wear a pin to publicize an anticancer drive were more likely to actually donate money to the drive than were one-contact controls (Pliner, Hart, Kohl, & Saari, 1974).

A second study by Freedman et al. sought to discover if the small request had to be similar to the large request for the foot-in-the-door effect to occur. There were four first requests, representing all combinations of two issues (safe driving and the prevention of forest fires) and two types of tasks (posting a small sign in the window and signing a petition). The large request, which came two weeks later, was to allow the posting of a huge "Drive Carefully" sign on the front lawn.

Whereas only about 17% of the one-contact controls agreed to the large request, 76% of the same-issue, same-task subjects complied. However, subjects in the other two-contact groups were also more agreeable than the one-contact controls. Thus compliance with a small request did not have to involve the same issues and tasks that the large requests involved. The authors suggest that compliance with the first request altered the women's self-perception. From observing their own behavior, they decide that they are the "kind of persons" who do this sort of thing. The Pliner et al. findings are also consistent with the self-perception interpretation.

More recently, Cialdini and his associates have found that preceding a modest request with an outrageously large request that the person is sure to refuse raises the likelihood that the modest request will be acted upon favorably (Cialdini, Vincent, Lewis, Catalan, Wheeler, & Darby,

1975). In one experiment some subjects were asked to commit themselves to two years of weekly volunteer work (all subjects refused). Subjects in a one-request control group were spared the large demand. Then all subjects were asked to grant the smaller request of agreeing to do two hours of volunteer work on one Saturday afternoon. Experimental subjects who had been confronted with the large request were more likely to grant the smaller request than were controls. Contrast would be one possible explanation; that is, perhaps the small request seems smaller if one has been exposed to the large request than if the large request has not been presented. However, contrast was eliminated as a causal factor because other subjects who were asked to choose to grant either the small or the large request (and hence were able to contrast them) were not more likely to volunteer than were the one-request controls.

The results of this experiment and two others reported by Cialdini et al. are interpreted in terms of the norm of reciprocity. The authors suggest that, when the person making the large request shifts to a smaller request, he or she is, in effect, making a concession by going a little bit easier on the subject. The subject reciprocates this concession by meeting the modest demand. Thus the requester who shifts from an outrageous to a reasonable demand indicates a willingness to meet the subject halfway, and, by granting the small request, the subject responds in kind. In the control conditions the requester makes no concessions, so the subject does not feel indebted.

Guilt Manipulation

Have you ever seen a movie plot like this? Person A (perhaps Joan Crawford) is responsible for a horrible accident in which person B (perhaps Bette Davis) is crippled for life. Joan then devotes the rest of her life to catering to Bette's every whim. Of course, toward the end of the movie it usually develops that Bette wasn't really crippled—or that she had regained all her powers some years back. Faking allowed her to retain control over Joan. This theme is based on the idea that, if a person is made to feel responsible for harming someone else, guilt alleviation may take the form of volunteering to help this person or complying with his or her requests.

High school students awaiting an experiment by Freedman, Wallington, and Bless (1967) were confronted by a confederate who claimed to have just taken part in the experiment. In the experimental or guilt condition the confederate described in great detail the "Remote Associates Test" used in the experiment; in the control condition this test was not mentioned. When the subjects entered the laboratory, the experimenter made a statement about how important it was for them never to have heard of the Remote Associates Test. Either because they were well paid or because they did not want to disappoint the experimenter, both experimental and control subjects denied any knowledge of the test. Later the lying, and presumably guilty, subjects were more likely than the controls to do the favor of taking part in an additional experiment.

The finding that people who feel they have done some harm will offer to grant a favor or comply with a request has been confirmed in the field. As noted in Chapter 7, Konečni (1972) found that subjects who felt responsible for causing an experimenter to drop a number of cards were more likely than controls to help the experimenter retrieve the cards. In another study, by Regan, Williams, and Sparling (1972), it was found that, when guilty people cannot make amends to their victim, they may find someone else to help. In this investigation a male experimenter asked women in a shopping center to take his picture. When they tried to do so, the camera malfunctioned. Under control conditions, subjects were made to feel that the malfunctioning was not their fault, whereas under guilt-arousing conditions the experimenter implied that the subject had broken the camera. Next, subjects had the opportunity to help a different experimenter who was carrying a broken grocery bag. Whereas 55% of the experimental subjects helped the second experimenter, only 15% of the control subjects tried to be of assistance.

Before you try to play "victim," however, you had better consider four other lines of evidence. First, Freedman et al. (1967) also induced guilt by having subjects upset a pile of index cards carefully arranged on a table. (This feat was accomplished by secretly pulling the legs out from under the table as the subject tried to squeeze by.) Half the subjects were then given the opportunity to do a favor for the owner of the cards, and the other half were given an opportunity to do a favor for someone else, who had not been wronged. Again the guilty parties were more likely to grant the favor than were the innocent controls, but only if the person whom they could help was not the same person they had harmed. The authors suggest that, on the one hand, a guilty person wants to make amends, but, on the other hand, he or she wants to avoid contact with the victim. A subsequent experiment by the same researchers supported this interpretation. When guilty subjects could help an injured party without actually coming into contact with him or her, they were quite likely to do so.

A second limitation to the guilt-helpfulness phenomenon is suggested by the just-world hypothesis (Chapter 7). Rather than attempt to expiate our guilt by helping the victim in one way or another, we may justify or rationalize the transgression by convincing ourselves that the victim got exactly what he or she deserved (Lerner & Simmons, 1966; Lerner & Matthews, 1967). Other ways of evading rather than atoning for guilt through helping others include convincing ourselves that the transgression did not really do the victim that much harm (Noel, 1973) or engaging in self-punitive behavior (Wallington, 1973).

Third, Cialdini, Darby, and Vincent (1973) found that, if something positive happens to the transgressor between the time he or she begins to feel guilty and the time he or she gets the opportunity to help, the motivation for helping the victim may be removed. According to their **negative-state relief hypothesis,** charitable behavior that follows harm-doing represents an attempt to reduce the unpleasant feelings that come about after committing a transgression or even after seeing a transgression committed. If something other than charity or compliance restores a sense of well-being, helpful activity will not occur. Thus, in the case of a guilt-induced business transaction, the brandy, champagne, and fine cigars might best remain hidden until after the final papers have been signed.

Finally, it would appear that the victim who overplays or underplays the magnitude of his or her grievance is likely to get nothing. Discussing the results of research in which the magnitude of the harm and the magnitude of compensatory acts were covaried, Berscheid and Walster note:

> . . . a compensatory act is most likely to be performed if it will replace an eye for an eye. Acts which will replace a glass eye for an eye or three eyes for one eye should have lower performance probabilities. The finding that "victims" get exactly what they deserve—no more, no less—has the interesting implication that if the victim magnifies the extent of his suffering to such an extent that the harmdoer has no hope of making full restitution, the harmdoer is likely to make no restitution at all [1967, p. 346].

THE MANIPULATIVE PERSONALITY

Are some people more manipulative than others? Christie and Geis (1970a), among others, have developed and refined scales that predict **Machiavellianism,** or the use of deceit, cunning, and opportunism in interpersonal relations. These **Mach scales** (which come in several versions) are named after the 16th-century Italian Niccolo Machiavelli, whose name is synonymous with exploitation. Scale items, which include "I think most people would lie to get ahead" and "I do not blame a person for taking advantage of someone who lays himself open for it," are based on Machiavelli's writings. The rationale underlying these scales is that a person who thinks like Machiavelli is likely to act like Machiavelli. Typically, studies compare people who score toward the two extremes of the scale (that is, "high Machs" and "low Machs").

From the studies presented by Christie and Geis (1970a) emerges an interesting profile of the high Mach. This person's chief distinguishing characteristic is a tendency to show little emotional involvement with others. Other people are viewed as things to be manipulated, not as objects of fondness. Whereas low Machs show empathy and a concern for others, high Machs tend to adopt a "cognitive orientation"—that is, they deal with others on an intellectual basis.

The high Mach is also an influencer, not an influencee. This fact is best shown in various attitude-change studies. Face-to-face discussion and counterattitudinal role playing are more likely to produce attitude change in low Machs than in high Machs (Geis, Krupat, & Berger, 1965; Rim, 1966; Harris, 1966). In informal groups, high Machs are most likely to take over leadership, to channel the group's discussion and activities, and to dictate the course of events.

Finally, high Machs are theorized to have a lack of concern about conventional morality, with its hampering prescriptions ("Do unto others as you would have them do unto you") and proscriptions ("Do not covet thy neighbor's stereo system"). In general, comparisons have *not* revealed differential lying and cheating, usually because they have involved temptations to which even low Machs will succumb. However, there is some evidence that high Machs either experience less shame or guilt than low Machs or can hide it better. This has been shown by Exline, Thibaut, Hickey, and Gumpert (1970), who had confederates try to induce high and low Machs to cheat on a test. Later the subjects were openly implicated by a stooge. One measure of ability to hide guilt was the time the subject spent "looking the experimenter in the eye" (which, according to earlier research, gives an impression of honesty). Low Machs discreetly averted their gaze, but high-Mach culprits unflinchingly maintained eye contact. Furthermore, as the confrontation continued, eye contact from low Machs decreased, whereas eye contact from high Machs increased. There was also an (insignificant) tendency on the part of high Machs to be less likely to "crack" and confess their guilt.

A central issue, of course, is whether high Machs are better manipulators and get what they want more often than low Machs. Geis (1970) devised a special three-person dice game faintly reminiscent of Parcheesi. Successful performance required making and breaking coalitions, usurping positions of power, and inducing others to make moves favorable to oneself. As a group, high Machs were more successful than middle or low Machs. Another game (Christie & Geis, 1970b) involved splitting $10 between any two of three players. Somehow, high Machs tended to end up in the winning duo.

Braginsky (1970) offered high- and low-Mach children 5¢ for each quinine-flavored cracker they could talk a middle-Mach child into eating. High Machs were more successful than low Machs, but different strategies were used by boys and girls. In the act of exacting compliance, little-boy

Machs were more likely to falsify the facts, whereas little-girl Machs were more likely to omit crucial parts of the truth.

Singer (1964) conducted a study to investigate whether high-Mach students manipulate their teachers into assigning them high grades. With ability held constant, there was a significant positive correlation between men's Mach scores and their academic grade-point average. For women, something else was a better predictor of grades. Singer found that for "noticeable" women (that is, women who sat in the front of the classroom, saw the instructor after class, and visited the instructor frequently during office hours) there was a correlation between physical attractiveness and grades.

Although high Machs are often presumed to be evil and sinister, Christie and Geis note that they have many desirable qualities. In many respects they tend to be well adjusted, they maintain a firm grip on reality, and they have a knack for getting things done. They are not vicious or vindictive but are often friendly, affable, and outgoing. Some of the nicest people I know are high Machs. Christie and Geis (1968) report that, as a group, social psychologists have scored higher on the Mach scale than any other segment of the population tested.

Let's note in conclusion that Machiavellianism is a matter of degree. The extent to which most of us use cunning and guile no doubt varies from situation to situation. Most people are neither invariably manipulators nor invariably defenseless "soft touches."

INFLUENCE ATTEMPTS AND BOOMERANG EFFECTS

Suppose you wanted to visit one of our national parks this summer but had not yet decided on which one. Imagine how you would react if you received in the mail a bus ticket stamped "Not Valid for Yosemite National Park" and a letter reading:

Dear _____ :

We are pleased to send you this complimentary bus ticket. You may use this ticket to go anywhere in the United States, Canada, or Mexico, with the exception of Yosemite National Park. It is indeed our pleasure to make you this gift, but again let us stress that under no circumstances may you go to Yosemite National Park.

Sincerely,
The Authorities

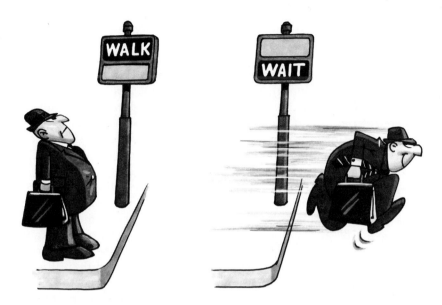

A specific prediction of how most people would react comes from Brehm's (1966) theory of **reactance.** Brehm says that we each have a set of **free behaviors**—that is, responses that we feel we can choose to perform. For example, right now your free behaviors might include studying other material, writing letters, chatting with your friends, getting something to eat or drink, going for a walk, taking in a movie, or embarking by bus for Yosemite (if you had sufficient money). Reactance results when a free behavior is eliminated or is threatened with elimination, such as when a person is told that he or she cannot engage in an activity or when someone tries to pressure the person into an alternative activity. The predicted result is that the threatened or eliminated alternative gains in importance and desirability, and thus the person is motivated to exercise or restore his or her freedom of choice by engaging in the forbidden act. Therefore, according to reactance theory, the letter and bus ticket should have the effect of raising the attractiveness of a trip to Yosemite and perhaps prompting an immediate departure by car, bicycle, or Pogo stick.

Tests of reactance have involved posing a threat to a response alternative and then assessing the changes in that response alternative's attractiveness and probability of performance. For example, Worchel and Arnold (1973) have found that threatening to censor a communication increased people's desire to hear the communication and caused the potential listeners to change their attitudes toward the position to be advocated in the communication. Mazis (1975) found that women who had been deprived through legislation of phosphate-based detergents rated these detergents more highly than did women who were allowed to use these environmental pollutants. The amount of reactance and "boomer-ang" seems to depend on: (1) the magnitude of the threat or the likeli-hood that it will be carried out (Regan & Brehm, 1972); (2) the importance of the free behaviors that are threatened (Brehm & Cole, 1966); and (3) the number of free behaviors threatened (Sensenig & Brehm, 1968).

Using both verbal and monetary threats, Regan and Brehm (1972) endangered supermarket shoppers' freedom to choose to buy or to refuse a king-sized loaf of sandwich bread. All subjects were handed cards. To vary verbal threats, the experimenters gave subjects in the low-threat-to-freedom condition cards asking them to "please try" the bread; sub-jects in the high-threat condition were given cards telling them that they *would* buy the bread. To vary threat monetarily, the experimenters gave subjects in the low-threat condition a card containing money to cover the cost of the bread; subjects in the high-threat condition were given a card containing both the cost of the bread and a small bribe. Female shop-pers were more likely to buy the bread if politely asked than if strongly urged and when given the exact compensation than when given the extra bribe. Male shoppers, on the other hand, were unaffected by the threat manipulation; they were as likely to buy the bread when strongly urged as when politely asked and when given the extra bribe as when given exact compensation. The authors suggested that, whereas women are knowledgeable and discriminating supermarket shoppers who jealously guard their prerogatives, less knowledgeable and nondiscriminating men do not consider supermarket choices to be free behaviors, and for this reason they did not show reactance. Another possible explanation for the results is that the male subjects were so engrossed in their carefully prepared lists that they didn't take the time to read what was printed on the card!

Another study suggests that being forced to choose an alternative that is already preferred may prompt a person to change his or her mind. For example, after wishing all day for a pot-roast dinner, coming home and being told that you *have* to eat pot roast could elicit grunts and curses. In this study, Sensenig and Brehm (1968) first assessed attitudes on a num-ber of different issues. Then subjects were told that they would write short essays on five of the issues covered on the questionnaire. Unthreat-ened subjects were asked which side of the issue they wanted to support, but threatened subjects were told which side of the issue to support. Of the latter, some subjects were told which side to support only on the first issue (low threat), whereas others were told which side to support on all five issues (high threat). In fact, all subjects ended up writing from the point of view that they had initially favored. Attitudes were then reas-sessed.

Threatened subjects, who were told to adopt positions that they already held, tended to shift away from these initial positions. Furthermore, this shift was most pronounced under high-threat conditions, which suggests that anticipation of threats to freedom in the future leads to greater exercise of freedom in the present. A recent, somewhat similar, experiment has revealed that observing a threat posed to the freedom of another person can arouse reactance and attitude change in an observer (Andreoli, Worchel, & Folger, 1974).

PART SUMMARY

Although simple reinforcement principles seem to account for a large proportion of interpersonal-influence effects, the open use of bribes and threats may be impossible or ill advised, either because the distribution of power may not favor the person who is making the interpersonal-influence attempt or because openly manipulative behaviors can have a backlash or boomerang effect. As a result of such considerations, people often resort to subtle or low-pressure influence attempts.

Three tactics of influence are ingratiation, the pacing of demands, and guilt manipulation. Ingratiation refers to a range of tactics aimed at putting oneself in another's good graces. To maintain the stream of praise and complicity, the high-status or advantaged person in the relationship may grant concessions and favors to the low-status or disadvantaged person. Concessions and favors become less likely when the high-status person believes that the ingratiating behaviors are insincere and based on ulterior motives. Regarding the pacing of demands, a large request that has been preceded by a small request is more likely to be granted than is the large request presented by itself. Also, a small request that has been preceded by a large request is more likely to be granted than is a small request that has been presented by itself. Research on guilt manipulation shows that, if a person can be made to feel that he or she has harmed someone, that person may offer to do favors for the victim in order to expiate the guilt and restore a feeling of well-being. The guilt-compliance relationship is subject to several limitations.

Research by Christie, Geis, and others shows that people vary in the extent to which they use guile and deceit in dealing with others. To assess these individual differences, these researchers developed Mach scales, based on the writings of Machiavelli. People who scored high on these scales tend to be intellectual rather than emotional in their dealings with others and tend to influence others more than they are influenced in return. Several studies have shown that high Machs are more likely to get their way than are low or middle Machs. However, Machiavellianism is a matter of degree, and manipulative behaviors may often be situation-specific.

According to the theory of reactance, when freedom of choice or behavior is imperiled, people will take action to maintain or restore their freedom. Several studies have shown that forbidden fruits are the sweetest and that people are motivated to engage in forbidden activities.

9
Interaction
in Small Groups

COMMUNICATION AND INFLUENCE WITHIN THE SMALL GROUP

SOCIAL DIFFERENTIATION AND LEADERSHIP

Participation as a Cause of Leadership Status
Task and Socioemotional Leadership

COMMUNICATION FLOW

Spatial Factors
Status Factors

PART SUMMARY

CONFORMITY

THE ESTABLISHMENT OF GROUP NORMS

Norms in Society
Reference-Group Phenomena

CONFORMITY AND THE DISTORTION OF JUDGMENTS

Antecedents of Conformity

ACTION CONFORMITY: THE BEHAVIORAL STUDIES OF OBEDIENCE

Antecedents of Obedience
Evolution, Autonomy, and the Agentic State

NONCONFORMITY

Anticonformity and Independence
Minority Influence

PART SUMMARY

ENCOUNTER GROUPS

ORIGINS OF THE ENCOUNTER-GROUP MOVEMENT

The Depersonalization of Social Relations
The Rise of Humanistic Psychology

THE CULTURE OF THE ENCOUNTER GROUP

Encounter-Group Norms
The Encounter-Group Leader

SOME EFFECTS OF PARTICIPATION

Potential Risks
Potential Benefits

PART SUMMARY

From the perspective of an extraterrestrial being circling the earth in a satellite, there would appear to be an infinite number of ways in which ships could cross the Atlantic. Yet, despite this seeming freedom, observation over time would reveal that for the most part transatlantic shipping follows a very few prescribed routes. The observer might infer that some points on the ocean are more important than others (for example, what we know as New York and Liverpool). Closer examination would reveal that these more prominent points have certain social resources (a large population and abundant industry) and certain physical resources (sheltered harbors) that distinguish them from other coastal points.

From the perspective of an observer of a small group, there are many ways in which communications could pass across a table. Yet, again despite a seeming lack of constraints, observation over time would reveal that for the most part communications tend to follow a few prescribed channels. This observer might infer that some of the people are more important than others. Closer study would reveal that these more prominent people have certain social resources (such as popularity and an ability to get things done) and certain physical or "geographical" resources (for example, a seat at the head of the table) that distinguish them from others in the same group.

In this and the following chapter we'll adjust our sights to focus beyond the dyad onto small groups containing more than two people. A small group, you will recall, is defined as one in which each member has the opportunity for face-to-face interaction with each and every other member. In this chapter we'll consider (1) the flow of communication and influence within the small group, (2) conformity, and (3) encounter groups, which may serve as vehicles for the development of self-understanding and of social skills. In the following chapter our discussion of group dynamics will continue with a consideration of performance and problem solving in small groups.

COMMUNICATION AND INFLUENCE WITHIN THE SMALL GROUP

Placed together in a group, people will act in ways that make them distinguishable from one another. For example, some persons will participate more than others and will exert more influence on the group as a whole. The process through which interacting individuals distinguish themselves is called **social differentiation.** The exercise of influence to coordinate the activities of group members in pursuit of a common goal is called **leadership.** The processes of social differentiation and leadership have been carefully observed by Bales and his associates (Bales, 1950a, 1950b, 1953, 1956, 1958, 1970; Bales & Slater, 1955; Slater, 1955; Burke, 1972).

SOCIAL DIFFERENTIATION AND LEADERSHIP

To study social differentiation and leadership, Bales and his associates have used a coding system (Chapter 2) called **Interaction Process Analysis,** or **IPA.** This system provides a method for quantifying and analyzing the natural flow of communication within a small group. The crux of the system is that each act of behavior can be classified into one of a limited number of categories.

A group of four or five people is assembled in a room equipped with a one-way mirror. (Observers in an adjoining room can see the group but cannot be seen in return.) The observers record the person who is acting, the person to whom the act is addressed, and the nature of the act. Each act can be classified into one of 12 categories. Bales reports that a skilled observer can reliably record 20 acts a minute.

The 12 categories used in Interaction Process Analysis are presented in Figure 9-1. It is important to note that these categories are the original ones used over a time span of about two decades. Relatively recently, Bales has made some changes in his coding system. The modified system is very close to the original system, but, if you are thinking of working with IPA, you should certainly acquaint yourself with the newer version (Bales, 1970). The earlier system is presented here because it is the one that has been used in the research we will discuss.

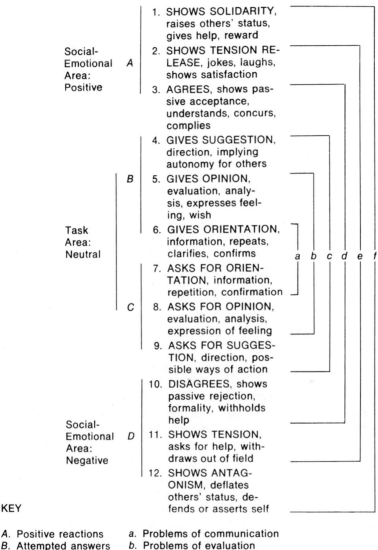

Social-
Emotional   *A*
Area:
Positive

1. SHOWS SOLIDARITY, raises others' status, gives help, reward
2. SHOWS TENSION RE-LEASE, jokes, laughs, shows satisfaction
3. AGREES, shows passive acceptance, understands, concurs, complies

B

4. GIVES SUGGESTION, direction, implying autonomy for others
5. GIVES OPINION, evaluation, analysis, expresses feeling, wish

Task
Area:
Neutral

6. GIVES ORIENTATION, information, repeats, clarifies, confirms
7. ASKS FOR ORIEN-TATION, information, repetition, confirmation

C

8. ASKS FOR OPINION, evaluation, analysis, expression of feeling
9. ASKS FOR SUGGES-TION, direction, possible ways of action

10. DISAGREES, shows passive rejection, formality, withholds help

Social-
Emotional   *D*
Area:
Negative

11. SHOWS TENSION, asks for help, withdraws out of field
12. SHOWS ANTAG-ONISM, deflates others' status, defends or asserts self

a b c d e f

KEY

A. Positive reactions
B. Attempted answers
C. Questions
D. Negative reactions

a. Problems of communication
b. Problems of evaluation
c. Problems of control
d. Problems of decision
e. Problems of tension reduction
f. Problems of reintegration

Figure 9-1. Coding categories used in Bales' Interaction Process Analysis. (From *Interaction Process Analysis,* by R. F. Bales. Copyright 1950 by Robert F. Bales. Reprinted by permission.)

As Figure 9-1 indicates, the categories themselves may be grouped. The letters *a* through *f* represent different sequential problems that face any forming group. Problems of *communication* involve deciding what the situation is like. Problems of *evaluation* refer to forming attitudes toward the situation. Problems of *control* and *decision* involve attempting to do something about the situation. Problems of *tension reduction* and *reintegration* have to do with establishing and maintaining effective human relations within the group. The most important distinction is a broad one: that between socioemotional (social-emotional) and task categories. **Socioemotional acts** are positive and negative emotional responses toward others in the group (Categories 1–3 and 10–12). **Task acts** are emotionally neutral behaviors that are relevant for completing the job or task confronting the group (Categories 4–9).

Social differentiation has been shown by Bales and Slater (1955; Slater, 1955) who applied IPA to 20 groups of three to six people. These all-male groups met on four occasions and each time were instructed to discuss administrative problems and to offer recommendations. The ongoing interaction was recorded, and after each session subjects ranked all the members of the group (including themselves) in terms of (1) who provided the best ideas, (2) who offered the most guidance, and (3) who seemed best at leadership. They also indicated how much they liked the other members of the group.

The analysis showed that some people participated more heavily in the discussion than others. Furthermore, the amount of inequality was greatest in the six-person groups. Whatever the size of the group (within the limits studied), the highest participator was responsible for about 42% of the output. As the size of the group was raised from three to six members, the communications of the lesser participators decreased to compensate for increases in the high participator's output. There was also social differentiation in terms of the kinds of contributions different people made. Whereas some people's contributions tended to fall into the task categories, others' contributions tended to fall into the socioemotional categories. Additional evidence of social differentiation came from the questionnaire data, which revealed that the person who was ranked the highest on one dimension (for example, best ideas) was rarely ranked highest in another category (for example, best liked).

An additional finding was that group members became more differentiated from one another over successive meetings of the group. For example, at the end of the first meeting the same person was ranked tops in terms of both offering ideas and being liked in 57% of the cases, but at the end of the fourth session this was true in only 8% of the cases. During the first session, the men who initiated the most acts were described as offering the best ideas and the most helpful guidance. At the end of the fourth session, they were openly and consistently rated as "leaders." Recently it has been shown that outside observers' rankings of group members on the different dimensions correspond closely to the rankings made by members within the group (Stang, 1973a; Stein, Geis, & Damarin, 1973).

Participation as a Cause of Leadership Status

It has repeatedly been found that there is a close correspondence between rate of participation and leadership status within the small group. For example, in addition to the studies just cited, we might note an interesting investigation by Strodtbeck (1951), who related talking time of spouses to "decisions won" in 34 marriages. In 14 of the 19 couples in which the husband won, he was the most talkative; in 10 of the 15 couples in which the wife won, she was the most talkative. However, we might ask whether leadership status is caused by a high rate of participation or whether it is simply a symptom of a "commanding personality."

Strong experimental evidence supporting the hypothesis that a high rate of participation causes group members to rate people as leaders has come from Bavelas, Hastorf, Gross, and Kite (1965), who assigned discussion problems to four-person groups. In front of each person were green and red signal lights that could not be seen by the other members. Subjects were told that, if they made a valuable contribution to the discussion, their green light would illuminate, but, if they detracted from the discussion, their red light would come on.

During the first part of the experiment the discussion proceeded naturally, and high and low participators were identified. During the second phase a low participator was given the rewarding green light for talking, whereas high participators were given the punishing red light for talking. The low participators' rate of contribution increased and remained at a high level during a third phase. Through this procedure the leadership ratings of the original low participators were raised. If the other participants know that the low participator's behavior has changed because of conniving on the part of the experimenter, increased participation will be unrelated to leadership ratings (Hastorf, Kite, Gross, & Wolfe, 1965). However the Bavelas et al. experiment clearly shows that a high rate of participation is a cause, not just a correlate, of leadership status.

Task and Socioemotional Leadership

An extremely important finding of Bales and his associates was that the person who scored highest in terms of ideas and guidance and was eventually recognized as "the leader" was *not* necessarily the most liked. In his efforts to get things done, this person tended to be aggressive, to frequently disagree with people, and, occasionally, to show open antagonism. By monopolizing the floor, he frustrated other potential contributors. The term **task leader** has been used to refer to this member—the one who provides the best ideas and the most guidance and who contributes the most toward achieving the objective at hand.

There are three ways in which a group can manage the tensions induced by the task leader. Two of these techniques would prevent the group from ever attaining its goal. First, group members could scapegoat by picking a low-status member and venting their frustrations upon that person. However, this tactic would drive members out of the group one by one, and the group would disintegrate before reaching its objectives. Second, the group could attempt to overthrow the task leader. Unfortunately, he or she would soon be replaced by another, and the group would be in constant revolution. The third and most workable solution appears to be for some other member of the group to smooth over ruffled feathers and keep everybody calm. By engaging in socioemotional activities, this person helps the group release tension and maintain good morale. This person is called the **socioemotional leader** and is the best-liked member of the group.

In an attempt to refine the distinction between task and socioemotional leaders, Burke (1968) obtained a number of measures and intercorrelated them. He found that task leaders: (1) provide "fuel" for discussion and introduce many ideas and opinions; (2) stand out as "leaders" in the discussion; (3) supply the "best" ideas; (4) offer guidance and keep the discussion moving; (5) make the most influence attempts; (6) have the most success at molding the group's opinions; and (7) provide the most clarification of points in the discussion. Socioemotional leaders, on the other hand: (1) are the best liked; (2) do the most to keep relationships cordial and friendly; and (3) make more tactful comments to soothe hurt feelings. It would thus appear that, in small, informal groups, there are two leadership roles ("getting things done" and "keeping things calm") that will be filled by different people. The two leaders, it develops, work hand in hand. For example, they interact more with each other and agree more with each other than with other members of the group.

It must be emphasized that this differentiation between task and socioemotional leadership roles is expected only in a small, informal group. In such groups the high participator *takes* a role of power and influence. This action generates the antagonism that in turn encourages the emergence of a socioemotional leader. Burke (1972) reports that, if the high participator does not unilaterally assume leadership but is instead elected or appointed by a higher authority, heavy-handed purposive activity is less likely to raise the ire of group members, and the need for complementary leaders is lessened. Thus, when a leader's task activity is seen as "legitimate," or is considered right and proper by the group members, one leader may be sufficient. (Leadership in industrial work groups, the military, and other settings in which task activity is considered "legitimate" is discussed in Chapter 11). In addition, the extent to which "getting things done" and "keeping things calm" will conflict depends on the nature of the group and of the task. For example, in a group whose goal is to have a good time, there may be little conflict. On the other hand, in a group whose task is to choose which members to pitch out of a lifeboat so the others can survive, doing the job and soothing ruffled feelings are likely to conflict.

COMMUNICATION FLOW

As indicated earlier, communication in the small group does not proceed in a haphazard fashion but instead flows along established channels. Two important factors that affect the flow of communication within the small group are spatial factors and social status.

Spatial Factors

Our discussion of the effects of the immediate environment on interaction (Chapter 8) has implications for understanding how the setting may affect the rate and flow of communication within the small group. For example, if two people are seated more than 6 feet or so apart, sheer distance should tend to discourage communication. Here we'll consider what happens when a small group sits around a table with each person within easy earshot of everyone else.

The person's location at a table is tied in with his or her characteristic rate of participation (Hare & Bales, 1963). Whoever sits at a **high-talking seat** sends more than the average number of messages, and whoever sits at a **low-talking seat** issues fewer than the average number of messages. At a rectangular table the head chair is a high-talking seat, even when it is not reserved for a formally organized leader. The second most frequent contributor is likely to be the person at the foot of the table (that is, the end away from the door to the room). People who sit at the corners of a rectangular table contribute the least to the discussion. Communications are most likely to be directed toward someone directly across the table (the 0° orientation) and least likely to be directed toward someone sitting adjacent and parallel (the 180° orientation).

To some extent these findings can be understood by measuring distances from chair to chair, computing angles, and so forth. But there is a complicating factor. People with dominant personalities—who might be expected to participate heavily in the discussion on the basis of personality factors alone—initially choose high-talking seats, whereas less dominant people are more likely to defer and take low-talking positions (Hare & Bales, 1963).

A partially occupied circular table may approximate other geometrical configurations that contain high- and low-talking seats. At a fully occupied circular table, it is difficult to identify high- and low-talking seats, but it is possible to make educated guesses concerning the *sequence* in which people will speak. Steinzor (1950) found that a speaker is most likely to be followed by the person sitting directly across. People have more of a stimulus impact on a person directly across than on a person located at an angle. Group members sitting next to each other are relatively cut off from nonverbal cues (Steinzor, 1950).

Status Factors

People's prestige or status within the group is highly related to communication flow. Usually we are most comfortable conversing with people of equivalent social status (Riley, Cohn, Toby, & Riley, 1954; Hurwitz, Zander, & Hymovitch, 1960). For example, at "mixers" where freshmen (low-status people) and faculty (high-status people) are supposed to get to know each other, strong efforts may be required to keep people within each echelon from interacting only with one another.

There are several reasons why people might feel most comfortable talking to their social equals. First, equal status may be associated with similar interests. Incoming students have their orientation experiences to discuss and may see the college as a bureaucratic adversary; the faculty may prefer to philosophize about administrative issues and campus policies and may see the university as more of an old friend. Second, when a low-status person chooses to interact with a person of equivalent status, he or she is less likely to be ignored, rebuffed, or rejected than when attempting to interact with a high-status person. Although at a mixer it is unlikely that a freshman would be flatly ignored by a faculty member, faint enthusiasm can be almost as stinging! Third, interacting with people of equal status may help the high-status individuals to maintain their exalted positions. Secrecy can contribute to an air of superiority that would vanish if a stupid or foolish remark slipped out. A faculty member, for example, might be reluctant to reveal to a student how little he or she knows about the workings of the college. To help maintain status distinctions by discouraging communication, groups may establish special segregated facilities (faculty or officers' clubs, doctors' lounges, vice-presidents' dining rooms, and places designated "Authorized Personnel Only") and employ highly technical jargon (which allows professionals to talk to one another without low-status eavesdroppers' being able to understand). Finally, we might note that a uniform, stethoscope in the pocket, expensive set of clothes, and other such items may create a status boundary that keeps low-status people away. Knowles (1973) found that subjects were less likely to walk through an interacting group of people partially blocking a hallway when these people were older and nicely dressed than when they were younger and casually dressed.

Messages that cross status boundaries are usually directed upward. Hurwitz, Zander, and Hymovitch (1960) staged a conference for approximately 24 low-status and 24 high-status mental-health professionals. The lows directed more communications toward the highs than the highs did toward the lows. Riley et al. (1954) noted an upward flow of communication during their field study of adolescent girls, and Kelley (1951) and Cohen (1958), among others, have found upward flows of messages in experimentally created hierarchies. There are at least four possible explanations of this finding, and all of them are based on the assumption that low-status people are unhappy with their miserable position in the group.

First, in the Hurwitz et al. study, low-status mental-health professionals wishfully overestimated the extent to which they were liked by the high-status professionals. The authors suggest that this overestimation represents a certain defensiveness on the part of the low-status person. Uneasy about the imbalance of power, the low-status person may direct communications upward in order to ingratiate.

A second possibility is that, by interacting with higher-status people, the low-status person raises his or her own status in the eyes of an observer. This explanation can be understood in terms of congruity theory (Chapter 5). Initially the high-status person is at the positive end and the low-status person at the negative end of the -3 to $+3$ favorability scale. If an associative bond is formed (as when the two converse), they will be drawn together on the favorability scale. The low-status person should become more liked and the high-status person less liked. Assuming that the low-status person makes an ingratiating overture that is difficult to reject, he or she has something to gain and the high-status person has something to lose.

A third possibility, offered by Kelley (1951), suggests that low-status people fantasize about occupying high-status positions. According to this interpretation, hobnobbing with the elite is an imagined substitute for actual status.

The fourth possibility is that upward communications are aimed at objective improvement of one's position in the group. If this is true, then informing people that they have reached a point on the status pyramid beyond which they may not advance should terminate the upward flow. In an experiment by Cohen (1958), some subjects were told that they could not advance in status and other subjects were told that further advances were possible. Compared with subjects chained to their positions, subjects who could advance spent a relatively greater amount of time talking with superiors than with equals, issued longer statements to superiors, wasted less time chatting about task-irrelevant topics, and were less critical of their superiors. A chance for advancement thus increased both the upward flow of communications and the number of ingratiating behaviors.

PART SUMMARY

Placed together in a group, people engage in behaviors that distinguish them from one another. This process of social differentiation has been examined using Interaction Process Analysis, a scheme for classifying social behaviors into 12 categories. Application of this technique to small groups reveals inequality of participation in group discussions. In the course of interaction, two group leaders emerge—a task leader whose contributions are directed toward getting things done and a socioemotional leader whose contributions are directed toward maintaining cordial relations within the group. This sharp differentiation of leadership roles is less likely in more structured groups in which task-directed activity is considered legitimate.

The communication flow in small groups follows established channels. People in some seats at a table characteristically participate more than people in other seats. Although this pattern may reflect "geographical" advantages, other possibilities cannot be ruled out. Social status is another important determinant of communication flow. Communication flows most easily among equal-status people. When status boundaries are broken, communications tend to flow upward, perhaps to enhance the prestige of the lower-status person.

CONFORMITY

Pioneering social psychologist F. H. Allport (1924) conducted a series of experiments that compared the behavior of people in isolation with the behavior of people in groups. One task was judging odors, which ranged from vile to fragrant. When a comparison was made between the ratings of people who were alone and the ratings of people who were together, the latter were less extreme; that is, the unpleasant odors were rated as less unpleasant and the pleasant odors as less pleasant in the "together" condition than in the "alone" condition. This effect occurred even though in the group setting subjects had not been allowed to talk to one another. Did the presence of others in close quarters impair or confuse the subjects' sense of smell? Virtually identical results were obtained when the entire experiment was repeated using judgments of weights. According to Allport, his subjects felt that they were more likely to be "at odds" with others if they went too far than if they didn't go far enough. As a more recent study of attitudes suggests, professing moderation on an issue is likely to protect one from criticism and ridicule (Cialdini, Levy, Herman, & Evenbeck, 1973).

Allport's finding of moderation in groups is an example of **conformity,** which we can define as group-induced uniformities in individual group members' thoughts, feelings, and actions. Research in this area has had three major thrusts. The first began with Sherif's (1936) examination of the formation of group standards, the second with Asch's (1952) examination of the effects of group membership on the distortion of perceptual judgments, and the third with Milgram's (1963) research on obedience.

Two types of social influence, *informational* and *normative,* contribute to observed conformity (Deutsch & Gerard, 1955). Each type is

geared to a social need or "dependence" on the part of the individual (Jones & Gerard, 1967).

Information dependence refers to the person's dependence on others for understanding or interpreting environmental conditions. For example, in a group faced with a difficult investment problem, the person unskilled in the vagaries of the stock market would be more information dependent than would a licensed stockbroker. He or she should thus be likely to rely on the investment recommendations of the others in the group. **Informational social influence** refers to pressures to accept information that the group provides as evidence of reality. Thus, from following the drift of the group discussion, the beginning investor may decide that petroleum investments have a better future than aerospace investments.

Effect dependence refers to the person's dependence on others for good outcomes or rewards, such as care, protection, acceptance, love, and social approval. For example, a geologist stationed at an isolated base in Antarctica would be more effect dependent on his or her small group of coworkers than would a geologist stationed at U. C. L. A., because the latter would have other sources of socially-administered rewards and gratifications available. **Normative social influence** refers to pressures to live up to expectations in order to secure socially administered rewards and to avoid socially administered punishments.

Information and effect dependence may or may not coincide. Children are highly dependent on others both for understanding the world and for securing good outcomes. Among adults, one could accept the esoteric arguments of an impersonal television panel that human life existed on Mars a million years ago (high information dependence but low effect dependence), or one could fake agreement with prejudicial remarks solely to secure favorable reactions from others (low information dependence and high effect dependence). The distinction between informational and normative social influence is very useful for understanding the conditions under which conformity becomes likely.

THE ESTABLISHMENT OF GROUP NORMS

Muzafer Sherif (1936) was struck by the observation that human activities are *socially regulated*. Discussing how people satisfy their needs, for example, he noted:

> When we observe people in the search for food, shelter, or mates, we conclude that these activities run in certain prescribed channels. People do eat, mate, and enjoy the security of shelter; but how and under what circumstances they will eat, mate, and enjoy shelter are, to a great extent, regulated by customs, traditions, laws, and social standards. This is true for every individual, living in every society we know, primitive or highly developed [1936, p. 1].

The basic regulating mechanisms are called **social norms.** These are socially devised standards that provide a framework for interpretation and evaluation. Norms define degrees of acceptability and unacceptability. Failure to abide by norms is an offense punishable by ridicule, rejection, and feelings of failure or guilt.

Sherif's basic hypotheses about group norms can be summarized quite succinctly. First, interacting people will develop group norms that affect their judgments and behavior. For example, a group of amateur golfers may agree that a score in the high 80s constitutes a good game and is a cause for celebration. Second, different groups can be expected to develop different norms. For example, although a golf score in the high 80s may be very acceptable within a group of amateurs, it might be very unacceptable within a group of professionals. Third, norms that are originally external to the individual later become internalized. For example, an amateur golfer who is practicing alone might feel very satisfied with a score of 88 and immediately retire to the golf-course bar. A professional who got the same score under the same conditions might become upset and vow not to leave the course until a better performance is achieved.

To test these three hypotheses, Sherif had subjects sit in a darkened room and view a pinpoint of light that was about 20 feet away. Under such conditions a pinpoint of light will appear to move, and this apparent motion is called the **autokinetic effect.** Each time the light was illuminated, subjects were asked to state how far it moved. Some subjects did so first alone and then in groups of two or three. Other subjects did so first in groups and then alone.

In support of the hypothesis that interacting groups will develop norms, Sherif found that, whereas the individual judgments prior to group participation showed great variability, there was relatively little variability among judgments within each group. In support of the hypothesis that different groups develop different norms, he found that, although judgments within groups tended to converge around a common point, these points of convergence varied from group to group. Finally, in support of the hypothesis that group norms established at one point in time affect solitary judgments at a subsequent point in time, he found that, when group judgments preceded individual judgments, the individual judgments tended to fall into the range established by the group.

Within his laboratory Sherif created a **microculture**—a simplified, miniature society that enables us to study social processes under controlled conditions. Another helpful feature of the microculture is that, whereas social change proceeds at its own pace in the larger "real-world" society, or **macroculture,** social change in the microculture can be sped up, thus making it possible for the experimenter to observe what happens to norms over several generations (Jacobs & Campbell, 1961; MacNeil, 1965; Weick & Gilfillan, 1971). In such studies the investigators create norms and then remove people from the group, one by one, replacing them with new members. There may be several complete turnovers of membership (generations) before the norms lose force. Another instance of the persistence of norms over generations is to be seen in the long-term survival of standards within certain organizations. For example, the U. S. Navy has a gradual turnover leading to a complete change of membership every 30 years or so. Nonetheless, many of the values and standards of 150 or 200 years ago remain in force today.

Some norms are more likely to persist over generations than others. In studies by Jacobs and Campbell (1961) and MacNeil (1965), norms that were originally unrealistic, silly, grotesque, or arbitrarily imposed decayed more rapidly over generations than did realistic norms based on an honest group consensus. Weick and Gilfillan (1971) qualify this finding by showing that the decay of highly arbitrarily imposed norms occurs only when there is a better alternative available. They had subjects perform tasks following norms that prescribed either an easy way to go about the task or a difficult way to go about the task. Whereas the easy strategy was perpetuated indefinitely, the difficult strategy decayed over generations. But when it is not easy to find a better way of proceeding, even highly arbitrary norms will persist over generations.

Perhaps "long-standing traditions" and "proud heritages" have their appeal because we recognize that scrutiny over generations has not revealed enough flaws and inadequacies to lead to their abandonment. Newer standards and values may or may not be good enough to pass the test of time. Long-established business firms often try to capitalize on their lengthy histories. Thus we may see large bronze plaques near the front doors proudly proclaiming "Since 1775." Newer firms may get some mileage out of plaques inscribed "Since 1975"—if it is obvious the plaque has been constructed to last a thousand years.

Norms in Society

Adherence to norms seems to be a universal phenomenon. Travel magazines report the quaint customs, traditions, and ways of doing things that are accepted within various cultures. In the articles we are reminded that in one society feminine beauty involves long, droopy breasts and carefully distended lips; in the advertising section we are reminded that in another society feminine beauty involves artificially lifted breasts and carefully painted lips. Newspapers report polls informing us that people from the same segment of society (broadly defined in terms of such criteria as ethnic background, geographical location, age, economic situation, and so forth) tend to have similar attitudes. The behavior of some business people in slavishly adhering to custom and tradition could leave us with the impression that, to advance beyond a certain rung on the organizational ladder, it is necessary to drive a Buick and send one's children to private school. Common experience suggests that, although clothing styles, hairstyles, and gadgets such as Hula-Hoops and smiley buttons are hard to anticipate, when they appear they are adopted almost simultaneously by large portions of the population.

Perhaps we are so sensitized to the possibility of conformity that we too hastily find examples. Conformity is a social process, and behavioral uniformities must somehow be related to the group. Four motorists busy changing tires by the side of the road are behaving similarly. However, we would be reluctant to call this activity conformity; they are simply engaging in *same behavior*—that is, responding independently to mishaps that have befallen each of their vehicles. My hunch is that much independent action, which has involved little or no social influence, has been erroneously identified as "conformity."

In a field setting, where we must deal with conditions as they are found, how can we tell if uniformities in behavior represent conformity? For example, would conformity be demonstrated if an overwhelming percentage of California's grape pickers voted Democratic? Three criteria—although by no means foolproof—are useful for helping us to distinguish between same behavior and conformity. First, in addition to similarities within groups, are there differences between groups? Such differences would provide circumstantial evidence that the similarities within groups are somehow caused by the group. Second, does the person who acts in a seemingly conforming manner when in the group setting behave differently when alone? Although group norms also regulate the behavior of isolated individuals, a shift such as this must be taken as evidence of conformity. Finally, is there behavior change as the person moves from one group with one set of norms to another group with another set of norms? Such changes suggest responsiveness to the social-influence process. Studies by Newcomb (1943, 1963) and by Lieberman (1956) provide good evidence of conformity.

During the 1930s the political norms at Bennington College were more liberal than those at most other colleges of the day. Newcomb (1943) assessed the political attitudes of Bennington freshmen, sophomores, juniors, and seniors. Presumably each successive group had greater exposure to the liberal college norms. He found more uniformly liberal attitudes among the upperclasswomen. Furthermore, he made these assessments for four consecutive years. As students progressed from freshman to senior status, they became increasingly liberal. The comparison of different groups and the demonstration of increased conformity as a function of time in group make this study particularly interesting. In a follow-up investigation, Newcomb (1963) discovered that the women had maintained their new liberal orientation over the years. For example, 51% of these women favored Kennedy in the 1960 election, although given their educational level, places of residence, and income, one would have expected only 25% to have favored Kennedy over Nixon. Why didn't these women revert to their former ways after leaving college? Newcomb found that they tended to marry liberal men and to choose liberal friends. Thus the norms of their later groups were compatible with the Bennington norms.

Adherence to group norms has also been shown by Lieberman (1956), who found attitude change as workers move from group to group. Factory workers promoted to the rank of foreman became more pro-management and less pro-union, but, when a business recession forced them back into the production line, they readopted their earlier views. Election to union stewardship, on the other hand, resulted in more pro-union and fewer promanagement attitudes. After their elective term expired, these workers, too, tended to revert to their earlier attitudes.

Reference-Group Phenomena

A **reference group** is any group that provides standards by which we can evaluate ourselves and adjust our behavior accordingly. Newcomb (1953) has made a distinction between positive and negative reference groups. **Positive reference groups** provide standards that we endorse, and **negative reference groups** provide standards that we disavow or oppose.

A very important aspect of a reference group is that it need not be present in order to exert an influence on individual behavior. People sometimes adopt the standards of groups that are distant in space (Chinese revolutionaries) or in time (the 12 Apostles) or that never existed, except as symbolic models (the gods of Mount Olympus). As Table 9-1 shows, reference groups and membership groups (that is, the groups to which the person actually belongs) may or may not coincide.

Table 9-1. Examples of overlapping and nonoverlapping reference and membership groups

| | | *Membership Group* | |
		U. S. Army	*Enemy Army*
Reference Group	*U. S. Army*	Douglas MacArthur	(Classified)
	Enemy Army	Benedict Arnold	Tojo

The co-effects of membership groups and reference groups have been shown in a now-classic field study conducted by Siegel and Siegel (1957). First they learned that college women who lived in high-status but low-comfort "row houses" (so called because they were located on what used to be "sorority row") were more authoritarian than women who lived in dorms. They also found that freshmen who *wanted* to live in these row houses were more authoritarian than those who wanted to remain in the dorms. (The common assumption is that, if a person wants to belong to a group, that group constitutes a reference group for that person.)

About a year later, as the result of a housing lottery and of some reassessment on the part of some of the subjects, the women who had earlier aspired to live in row houses could be divided into three groups. First, there were those who wanted to belong to the row houses and were accepted into the row houses. These women had authoritarian reference and membership groups. Second, there were those who still aspired to row-house membership but had not yet been accepted. These women had authoritarian reference and nonauthoritarian membership groups. Finally, there were those women who no longer wanted to belong to the row houses and who had not gained entry. These women had nonauthoritarian reference and membership groups.

Because all the women were members of a liberal academic community, subjects in all groups showed a *drop* in authoritarianism over the duration of the study. However, the drop was *smallest* for those with authoritarian reference and membership groups, *intermediate* for those with authoritarian reference groups and nonauthoritarian membership groups, and *largest* for those with nonauthoritarian reference and membership groups. These findings from the field thus imply that a group will exert the most influence on the individual when it serves as both a reference and a membership group and the least influence when it is neither a reference nor a membership group.

Miller (1963) has suggested that each person has as many reference groups as there are parts to his or her personality. Sometimes the standards maintained by a person's different reference groups will conflict. For example, our reactions on passing an X-rated movie house would depend on whether we were referring to the standards of our Saturday night drinking group or our Sunday morning church choir. However, conflict is usually averted because the standards of different reference groups are salient in different situations. Reactions on driving by an X-rated movie theater should be determined by the cues present in the situation—that is, whether a beer keg or our recently cleaned choir robe is in the back seat of the car.

An interesting line of research shows that, if one person disparages or criticizes another's reference group, the second person may defend the group by trying to disprove the charge. This result has been found by Buss and Portnoy (1967), who studied people's willingness to withstand pain after the experimenters disparaged reference groups of different degrees of importance and praised rivalrous groups.

Before beginning the actual experiment, Buss and Portnoy ascertained their subjects' strength of identification with eight different reference groups. From these eight they selected three of different degrees of importance. The most important was nationality (American), the second most important was gender, and the least important was college. They also selected associated **comparison groups**—that is, groups believed to be rivalrous with the reference groups. For each reference group except gender, there were two comparison groups: a strong-comparison group (a group with which the reference group was highly rivalrous) and a weak-comparison group (a group with which the reference group was not particularly rivalrous). For example, for the most important reference group, the strong-comparison group was Russians and the weak-comparison group was Canadians.

In the actual experiment, Buss and Portnoy measured how much electric shock each subject could tolerate, with the excuse that they were conducting a study of the reactions of people in general. They increased the voltage of current applied to the subject's finger until he or she demanded that the procedure be discontinued. Next, one of the experimenters initiated a conversation with the subject. This conversation was very general and casual, except that under experimental conditions it included an invidious comparison between one of the reference groups and an associated strong or weak comparison group. For example, in the high-importance/strong-comparison condition, the experimenter remarked that Americans couldn't take punishment as well as the Russians. Then the experimenter again measured pain tolerance. As hypothesized, it was found that, the more important the reference group, the greater the increase in shock tolerance. Furthermore, this increase was greater when the experimenter had mentioned a strong-comparison group than when a weak-comparison group was mentioned.

CONFORMITY AND THE DISTORTION OF JUDGMENTS

In one of the most widely publicized studies in social psychology, Asch (1952, 1956) had subjects participate in groups that were trying to match the lengths of different lines. The experimenter showed a standard line and a set of comparison lines, and each person in turn indicated which of the comparison lines was the same length as the standard. Unknown to the subject (who was the last person allowed to respond), every other member of the eight-person group was a carefully coached accomplice of the experimenter's.

From the subject's point of view, the first two trials went smoothly, and the third trial promised to be another simple one, since the task was remarkably easy. However, on this third trial, the first person to respond called out a wrong answer, and so did the second and the third. Each successive member of the group of confederates, or **false majority,** agreed on a wrong answer on this and on other critical trials.

According to Asch, subjects looked perplexed and bewildered; some became fidgety and others highly subdued. Despite such signs of tension, in about two-thirds of the cases they nonetheless made independent judgments that repudiated the answers of the false majority. In the remaining third of the cases, however, subjects yielded and made errors that conformed with the estimates of the false majority. Stated another way, control subjects who made private written estimates erred on about 7% of the trials, but experimental subjects erred on about 33% of the trials. Asch's startling finding was thus that one-third of the subjects yielded to the pressure of the group.

Do yielders merely report agreement with the group, or do they actually see things in the way prescribed by the group? At least one experiment suggests that a false majority can actually induce perceptual distortion. In this study, Flament (1958) more or less duplicated Asch's procedures. However, in addition to having subjects announce their answers publicly, he had them manually adjust a bar until it matched the length of the standard. The others in the group could not see how the subject adjusted the bar and hence could not criticize the subject's response. The judgments of the false majority affected the private matching responses as well as the public verbal responses, leading Tajfel (1969) to conclude that social influence can induce changes in what people perceive as well as in what they say they perceive. Nevertheless, as we shall see, in many other studies it has been found that group pressures and standards affect public responses (that is, what people say) more than they affect perceptions or privately maintained beliefs.

How do you think you might react if you were a subject in Asch's experiment? Given that two-thirds of his subjects did not yield to the false majority, the odds are with you if you stoutly insist that you would have retained your independence. However, we might note in passing an interesting attribution study by Wolosin, Sherman, and Mynatt (1972), who found that, although people had a tendency to see others as "sheep" who would go along with the false majority, they tended to consider themselves highly resistant to the majority's influence. If people were in fact as independent as they claim to be, Asch's results would not have been possible.

Antecedents of Conformity

Asch's technique has provided the basis for a host of studies aimed at uncovering the antecedents of conformity. Three classes of variables have been explored: properties of the individual, properties of the task, and properties of the group. Most of these studies, however, have followed Crutchfield's (1955) and Tuddenham's (1959) lead in mechanizing experimental procedures so that a large number of subjects can participate in the experiment simultaneously and so that a cumbersome group of confederates is not needed. In these studies, five or so naïve subjects separated from one another by partitions are seated before panels festooned with an imposing array of lights and switches. The experimenter explains that the task is to respond to multiple-choice questions by throwing the switch corresponding to the best answer; each person's response will appear on everybody's control panels. Each person is led to believe that he or she will be the last to respond. By furiously flipping switches in a back room, the experimenter creates the impression of a false majority.

Properties of the Individual. Given identical tasks and conditions, some people conform when others do not. Major sources of individual differences in conformity include (1) competence, (2) personality, and (3) history within the group.

First, people who are relatively incompetent or unskilled are more likely to conform than people who are relatively competent or skilled. Generally, younger children are believed to be less skilled than older children or adults, and Tuddenham (1959) found that children tend to be more conforming than adults. More recently, in a study of first-, fourth-, seventh-, and tenth-graders from Oconomowoc, Wisconsin, it was discovered by Allen and Newtson (1972) that conformity on stated opinions, visual judgments, and reward preferences decreased over age. In a study of adults, Crutchfield (1955) found that conformity correlated $-.63$ with ratings of "intellectual competence" and $-.51$ with scores on the Concept Mastery Test, an advanced measure of intellect. In other studies, experimenters have increased subjects' resistance to pressures to conform by leading them to believe that they were competent relative to the other members of the group (Ettinger, Marino, Endler, Geller, & Natziuk, 1971). The extent to which the person thinks he or she is competent may be more important than actual competence (Stang, 1972). The inverse relationship between perceived relative competence and conformity is fairly easily understood in terms of informational social influence. A person who lacks the relevant skills and abilities to cope with a problem is information dependent and must accept others' solutions as correct. The young, less intelligent, and less skilled are hence likely to be highly susceptible to informational social influence.

Second, a number of personality variables have been associated with conformity, although once again the relationship between personality and social behavior is rather modest, since situational factors are not usually entered into the equation (Hollander & Willis, 1967). In an early study by Crutchfield (1955), 50 men underwent exhaustive psychological testing, which included an Asch-type situation. Conformity correlated $-.33$ with a measure of "ego strength" and from $-.30$ to $-.41$ with various scales from Gough's California Psychological Inventory. Conformity also correlated with authoritarianism, as assessed both by a paper-and-pencil test and by behavioral measures. (The relationship between authoritarianism and conformity has been verified by Malof and Lott, 1962, and by Steiner and Johnson, 1963.) A more recently examined correlate of conformity is the extent to which the person has high **self-esteem**— that is, feels powerful, significant, and worthwhile (Constanzo, 1970; Stang, 1972). Genuine self-esteem—as compared with a nervous display of bravado—is, of course, negatively correlated with conformity. Because people with low self-esteem are likely to be unsure of themselves and sensitive to rejection by others, we would expect them to be susceptible to both informational and normative social influence.

Third, the person's prior experiences in the group are important. Endler (1965, 1966) has demonstrated reinforcement effects; in his experiments, social approval for agreeing with the false majority predictably increased conformity, whereas reinforcement for increased defiance led to nonconformity. Perhaps the person's reinforcement history affects his or her feelings of competence or self-esteem.

Hollander (1958, 1960, 1964) has offered the interesting hypothesis that a record of exemplary behavior within the group may be rewarded with increased latitude for occasional outbursts of nonconformity. Thus, we might expect nonconformity now and then from people who have built up good will within the group.

Idiosyncrasy credits is the term coined to designate the accumulation of favorable impressions within the group. These credits may be earned in a number of ways, the two most salient being (1) by repeatedly demonstrating competence and (2) by living up to the expectations of the group. In turn, idiosyncrasy credits may be exchanged for freedom from criticism or rejection following nonconforming, individualistic acts. Once spent, these credits must be replenished to purchase additional freedom. For example, a radical pronouncement on the part of a monk who has for years been the model of the monastery would likely be met with more tolerance from his conservative peers than would the same statement made by a monk with a history of running roughshod over church tradition. However, repeated infractions of the norms without replenishing good will would eventually result in idiosyncrasy-credit bankruptcy (the monk would, in other words, exhaust his bishop's patience). The analogy between money and idiosyncrasy credits leads to many interesting hypotheses. For example, a new member of a group, who has not had time to build up a balance of idiosyncrasy credits, should be accorded less freedom for nonconformity than a senior member of the group who has had ample opportunity to establish good will. In a sense, senior members of a group have "paid their dues" and are rewarded with increased freedom from censure.

Properties of the Task.   A number of task variables have been related to conformity. These include (1) task difficulty, (2) task content, and (3) the extent to which each individual's response is made known to the other members of the group.

First, there is task difficulty. It is not clear that difficulty is strictly a property of the task, since a task can be defined as difficult only relative to the skills and abilities of the individual performer. Nevertheless, as we might expect, experimenters who have increased the difficulty or ambiguity of the task have generally found increased conformity. Asch (1952) discovered that conformity in the line-judgment task could be increased by reducing the difference between the standard and the comparison line chosen by the false majority. Kelley and Lamb (1957) found that, although pleasantness ratings of relatively nondescript substances could be influenced by a false majority, judgments of undeniably bitter substances could not thus be swayed. Deutsch and Gerard (1955) reported that conformity was increased when the task was made difficult by forcing subjects to rely on memory instead of on visible stimuli.

Increased ambiguity or complexity increases information dependence. When the task is difficult, the person is forced to turn to others for answers. As Hollander and Willis (1967) note, under such conditions conformity influences are particularly likely to be accepted if the others in the group are presented as credible, prestigious, and competent.

Second, there is the content of the judgment task. For example, we would expect less conformity in a line-judgment task on which judgments may be based in part on physical reality than in an autokinetic task on which there are no physical referents for determining the one right answer. No doubt the content of the judgment task affects conformity in countless ways. Of particular interest is whether the issue at hand stresses male-related or female-related activities.

Sistrunk and McDavid (1971) obtained a pool of 100 statements about a variety of "everyday opinions and matters of fact." On the basis of judges' ratings, it was possible to select "masculine items," which were of greater interest, relevance, and familiarity to men than to women; "neutral items," which were of equal interest to men and to women; and "feminine items," which were loaded more toward women's interests than toward men's interests. Items were prepared in a booklet entitled "Inventory of General Information."

After each item in the book was a figure supposedly representing the majority response of 200 college students to that item. On critical trials the majority response ran counter to the factually correct judgment or (in the case of opinion items) was randomly determined.

With only slight modifications, the "Inventory" was given to four different samples of subjects. Results showed that men were more likely to yield in the direction of the false norms when confronted with a neutral or feminine item than when confronted with a masculine item. Women, on the other hand, were more likely to yield when responding to a masculine item.

Different interests are associated with males and females. Through the sex-typing process, we gain expertise in the areas of interest to our own sex but remain relatively unskilled in the areas of interest to the opposite sex. The result is that we are typically less susceptible to informational social influence when confronted with an item loaded toward our own sex than when confronted with an item loaded toward the opposite sex.

This study has a very important implication. As Sistrunk and McDavid note, some earlier studies found that women tended to be more conforming than men. The usual interpretation was couched in terms of sex-role prescriptions: women are taught to be passive and conforming. An alternative explanation is that the experimental tasks (typically selected by male experimenters) have been masculine oriented. If the items in these earlier studies had dealt with such things as the number of eggs in an Angel food cake, we might long ago have drawn the conclusion that men are the more conforming of the two sexes.

A third task variable is whether or not the individual's response will be made known to the other members of the group. According to Thibaut and Kelley's (1959) analysis, three steps are required for enforcing group norms. First, the norms are stated. Second, the group members are kept under surveillance. Third, the members who abide by the norms receive social approval, whereas those who ignore the norms receive social disapproval. If the group member's response is made privately (for example, in a voting booth), then the second and third steps for norm enforcement are irrelevant. Since there would be less risk of censure or rejection for failure to conform, we would expect less conformity under conditions of private or anonymous responding. In accordance with this line of reasoning, several investigators have found greater conformity when the person's response is made known to the group than when the person's response is made known only to the experimenter. In an early study using the line-judgment task, Deutsch and Gerard (1955) found that subjects who performed under the usual face-to-face conditions conformed more than did subjects hidden from each other by partitions. More recently it has been found that subjects who thought their responses could be heard by others in the group responded to jokes with about as much laughter as did the other group members (Nosanchuk & Lightstone, 1974). Also, people contacted by a committee that urged them to get out and vote were more likely to do so if they thought the committee would search records to find out who voted than if they thought their failure to vote would go undetected (Gross, Schmidt, Keating, & Saks, 1974).

A discrepancy between public and private responding would seem likely when the person is effect dependent and his or her senses or motives prescribe one course of action while the group's norms prescribe another. That is, when there is little doubt about the objective facts or about what one wants, normative social influence may lead to public conformity but not to private acceptance. Public conformity with private independence represents a handy way of dealing with normative influence without completely forsaking personal convictions or interests.

On the other hand, a discrepancy between public and private responding would appear unlikely when the person is information dependent and needs to refer to group standards to understand some aspect of reality. Informational social influence is thus likely to guide the course of private interpretations as well as the course of public pronouncements. Consistent with this line of reasoning is Hood and Sherif's (1962) finding that in the autokinetic situation, in which an independent answer is difficult to derive, conformity is likely even when responses remain private. Subjects in this experiment "overheard" others making autokinetic judgments. Some overheard judgments that ranged from 1 to 5 inches, and others overheard judgments that ranged from 6 to 10 inches. Later solitary judgments tended to fall within the overheard range. Thus, when the facts are ambiguous or the person does not really know what he or she wants, informational social influence is likely to lead to both public conformity and private acceptance.

Properties of the Group.   Properties of the group provide a third set of variables that affect individual conformity. Here we will consider the size and the unanimity of the majority. Another important variable, cohesiveness, will be discussed separately in Chapter 10.

Despite what one might expect, there is no straightforward relationship between the size of the majority and individual conformity. As part of his original series of experiments, Asch varied the number of stooges from none to 16. Control subjects averaged .08 errors or "yields" on the critical trials. Subjects with one stooge averaged .33 errors or yields, subjects with two stooges 1.53 errors, and subjects with three stooges 4.00 errors. Contrary to common sense, increasing the size of the false majority to 8 or 16 did not further increase conformity. Although some subsequent investigators have obtained similar leveling effects, others have not. Gerard, Wilhelmy, and Conolley (1968) found increases in conformity when they compared groups of two, three, four, five, six, seven, and eight.

Gerard and his associates have attempted to specify the conditions under which increasing the size of the false majority beyond three or four leads to greater conformity. Although their results were not conclusive, their hypothesis is of sufficient interest to warrant further consideration. They suggest that only the first few answers will carry any weight if later responses are perceived as dependent on the first group members' answers. People who give dependent answers are, in effect, "sheep" whose opinion means nothing. However, if each person is seen as giving an answer that is independent of the others', each answer should help budge the subject in the direction of greater conformity.

Unanimity of the majority is required for inducing maximum conformity on the part of the individual—at least in an Asch-type situation in which the other group members are trying to get the individual to abandon the evidence confronting his or her senses. In one variation of his experiment, Asch (1956) arranged for the subject to have a partner who was a stooge and who agreed with him on all trials. In another variation the subject had a partner who deserted him halfway through the experiment. In a third variation the subject had a partner who joined him halfway through. Any rift in the majority had a clear liberating effect on the naïve subject. When a partner was present, conformity decreased.

Faced by a false majority, we may accept support from people whom we'd normally reject under other conditions. Malof and Lott (1962) had white subjects scoring high or low on a measure of prejudice receive support from white or black partners. As expected, low-prejudice subjects accepted support from both types of partners. Contrary to expectations, prejudiced subjects also accepted a significant amount of support from blacks.

As Asch noted, the presence of a partner has two effects. First, it breaks the unanimity of the majority. Second, it provides the subject with social support. Two studies suggest that both of these factors can reduce conformity.

First, Allen and Levine (1969) presented subjects with a number of opinion, judgment, and information items. In one condition there was the usual false majority. In another condition there was a partner. In a third condition there was an "extreme dissenter" who made a judgment even more incorrect than that made by the false majority. Conformity was diminished by the presence of the "extreme dissenter," who did not corroborate or support the subject's judgment but did break the unanimity of the group.

Second, Gerard and Greenbaum (1962) have found evidence for the mechanism of social support. In their experiment the partner chimed in *after* the subject. Results clearly indicated that the Johnny-come-lately partner had the effect of bolstering the subject's confidence in his or her own judgments. Furthermore, the later the partner spoke up, the greater the boost in the subject's self-confidence. Thus, both the breaking of unanimity and social support contribute to the defiance of a false majority.

In sum, a number of variables affect the likelihood that an individual will conform. In general, people who are younger, less competent, and low in self-esteem will conform more than people who are older, more competent, and high in self-esteem. Conformity becomes more likely when the task is made difficult and when it is geared toward people whose interests differ from the subject's. Finally, although there is no clear relationship between the size of the majority and conformity, there is a very clear relationship between the unanimity of the majority and conformity. The presence of a partner can liberate the person from the influence of the false majority.

ACTION CONFORMITY: THE BEHAVIORAL STUDIES OF OBEDIENCE

The Sherif and Asch procedures utilized judgmental tasks. In the last ten years or so, a series of spectacular and controversial experiments has carried the study of conformity beyond the realm of what people think and say and into the realm of what they do (Milgram, 1963, 1974). Asch and Sherif dealt with **signal conformity,** in which the group's judgments are taken as cues that elicit similar judgments on the part of the individual member. Milgram and his associates have dealt with **action conformity,** in which the group's prescriptions are translated into overt action. For example, agreeing with other tenth-grade girls that worn-out blue jeans are more attractive than Bonwit Teller's, Peck and Peck's, or J. C. Penney's finest would be an example of signal conformity. Wearing the worn-out jeans to a dance while expensive clothes remain hidden in the closet would be an example of action conformity.

In action-conformity studies, an individual experimenter or group of confederates explicitly demands that the subject inflict pain and injury on a victim. Compliance with explicit demands is called **obedience.** Although such behavior is sometimes valued (for example, when motorists avoid accidents by obeying traffic police), journalists, novelists, and social reformers have tended to focus on the undesirable consequences of obedience. George Orwell, in his frightening novel *1984,* describes in sickening detail a society in which people slavishly obey an evil government. Monstrous atrocities during World War II and, more recently, at My Lai during the Vietnam War have been attributed to obedience.

Obedience to superiors on the part of members of military and paramilitary organizations and obedience to stern parents on the part of children confronted with plates of unpalatable vegetables are typically expected. Obedience to total strangers on the part of an average American citizen is not so typically expected. At least, that was the case until Milgram's (1963) initial obedience study was conducted.

In this classic experiment, 40 men, ranging in age from 20 to 50 and representing many walks of life, were recruited through a newspaper ad that offered $4.50 for participating in a "memory" experiment. Arriving at the Yale psychology laboratory, each subject was introduced to a 47-year-old, mild-mannered confederate who was misrepresented as another participant in the experiment. The experimenter explained to the pair that he was interested in the effects of punishment on learning. The stooge, he explained, would be a "learner" who would memorize responses to different words, whereas the real participant would be a "teacher" who would administer punishing shocks each time the learner made a mistake.

The confederate, or victim, was strapped into a chair, and electrodes were fastened to his wrist. The real subject was seated in an adjoining room before an impressive "shock generator," which consisted of a panel with 30 lever switches arranged horizontally and ordered in terms of shock intensity from 15 to 450 volts. Groups of switches were labeled with descriptions ranging from "Slight Shock" through "Danger: Extreme Shock" and "XXX."

During the learning sequence, the victim proved singularly inept. After each mistake or failure to respond, the experimenter ordered the subject to administer an increased dosage of shock. If the subject balked, the order would be repeated, accompanied by such prods as "The experiment requires that you continue" and "You have no other choice; you *must* go on."

Milgram's subjects were neither apathetic nor sadistic. Control subjects, left to their own choices, selected shocks almost entirely from the lower ranges of the board. When told to increase the shock, many experimental subjects showed signs of extreme tension: they sweated, stuttered, trembled, groaned, bit their lips, and nervously fumbled with cigarettes. In one case an "initially poised" businessman was reduced to a "twitching, stuttering wreck" (p. 377), and in another case a man suffered a seizure "so convulsive that it was necessary to call a halt to the experiment" (p. 375). Whereas the most cynical estimate Milgram obtained prior to the experiment was that about 3% of the subjects would obey throughout, he found that all subjects obeyed up to 300 volts and 26 out of 40 (that is, 65%) delivered the maximum shock.

Antecedents of Obedience

Subsequent research has dealt with four variables hypothesized to affect obedience (Milgram, 1965a, 1965b, 1974). These include (1) the sponsoring institution, (2) the immediacy of the victim, (3) the immediacy of the experimenter, and (4) group pressure.

First, one possible explanation for the high level of obedience in the initial study is the prestige of the setting. The authoritative experimenter represented an "institution of unimpeachable reputation" and was probably seen as knowledgeable and trustworthy. To examine the possibility that the prestige of the university was responsible for obedience, Milgram duplicated his basic procedures in a mildly dilapidated commercial building in a neighboring industrial town (Milgram, 1965a). Changing the alleged sponsor of the project from Yale University to "Bridgeport Research Associates" did not appreciably reduce obedience. Almost half the subjects administered the full range of shocks.

A second variable hypothesized to affect obedience is the immediacy of the victim—that is, whether the victim is near and whether the suffering can be heard and seen (Milgram, 1965b). In warfare, for example, it might seem easier to kill invisible, impersonal enemies than identifiable individuals who are staring us in the eye. One American submarine commander noted that, for the most part, the enemy did not represent a pair of staring eyes (Grider & Sims, 1973). Because of this impersonality, he felt that sinking ships and sending unknown numbers of unseen people to watery graves were not in the least disconcerting. On the other hand, he responded with dismay on an occasion when his men took shots at a fully visible enemy hopping around on a skiff.

Like this submarine commander, subjects in the early obedience studies did not seem to enjoy viewing their victim. To examine the hypothesis that obedience would decrease with nearness to the victim, Milgram (1965a) established four experimental conditions. In the "remote-feedback" condition, the victim was in another room and his sufferings could not be seen or heard by the subject. In this condition, 65% of the men administered maximum shocks. In the "voice-feedback" condition, in which the victim's vocal reactions could be clearly heard, 62.5% of the subjects went all the way. In the "proximity" condition, in which the

victim was only 18 inches from the subject, 40% of the subjects showed maximum obedience. In the "touch-proximity" condition, in which the subject was required to forcibly hold the victim's hand on the shock plate, "only" about one-third of the subjects administered the maximum shock. In this experiment, then, the closer the victim, the more likely the subject was to defy orders.

A third important variable is the extent to which the person is under surveillance by the authority who is making the demands. In a further study the distance between the subject and the experimenter was varied. In one condition the experimenter was in the same room as the subject; in another condition, orders were delivered by telephone; in the most distant condition, orders came through a tape recorder. Obedience decreased with surveillance: compared with the most closely monitored subjects, only about a third as many subjects given taped orders administered the maximum shock. Furthermore, when the experimenter was absent from the room, subjects would sometimes pretend to obey but in actuality administer only a very weak shock. Such "cheating" provides an easy way of reconciling orders and conscience.

A fourth important variable is group pressure. To examine this variable, Milgram contrived groups varying in composition (1965b, 1974). For the most part, results paralleled those found in studies of signal conformity. In one variation, in which the others in the group democratically decided to keep upping the shocks, subjects to some extent went along, even though the experimenter was absent and even though it was possible for the subject to ensure that only a minimal level of shock was actually delivered. Other groups were created that were nonobedient. One of the two confederates in the group had been instructed to disobey the experimenter at the 150-volt level and the other at 210 volts (Milgram, 1965b). As our discussion of the disinhibiting effects of models and of the effects of a rift in the group would lead us to predict, obedience was reduced. Under these conditions only 10% of the subjects went all the way.

An interesting finding of the group studies was that obedience depended in part on the subject's role within the group (Milgram, 1974). In one variation the subject, instead of having to throw the switches, was given the subsidiary but essential task of reading off the words the victim was to learn. This time a full 37 out of 40 subjects obeyed throughout, which suggests that, when a group is faced with a sorry task, a subsidiary role may be easier to fulfill than a central role. Consistent with this line of thought are Kilham and Mann's (1974) recent findings that a person who gives orders to another to administer the shock and is hence one step removed from the act is more obedient than the person who throws the switches. Presumably, compared with a person in a central role, a person in a peripheral role feels less responsible for the group's actions.

Without question, Milgram's obedience research is considered among the most important in social psychology. It demonstrated that the run-of-the-mill middle-class American man would follow orders to hurt another person. No longer is it possible to look at Nazi Germany or Stalinist Russia and smugly state "It can't happen here." It also identified some of the conditions under which obedience becomes less likely. Finally, the stressful techniques employed by Milgram sharpened psychologists' interest in the ethical issues associated with research (Chapter 2). Now let's consider how Milgram (1974) has recently explained his findings.

Evolution, Autonomy, and the Agentic State

Drawing heavily on evolutionary concepts, Milgram (1974) has recently provided a rather speculative explanation of obedience. Organized social life, he notes, provides survival benefits for both the individual and the group, and creatures that can organize socially have better chances of survival. Social organization takes the form of hierarchical structures, in which each person accepts as a leader the person above. Smooth operation of the structure requires unity of purpose and action, which necessitates the individual's accepting control from others. Independent action and self-regulation also have a certain survival value. For example, were it not for conscience, the violent death rate might soar to such an extent that the group would be threatened with extinction.

People, Milgram suggests, are thus able to operate in two states: the agentic state and the autonomous state. In the **agentic state** the person is controlled by the social hierarchy and sees himself or herself as an "agent" of another person or of the organization. In the **autonomous state** the person is controlled by internal regulators, such as the conscience. In certain situations—such as on the battlefield or in the laboratory—there is an **agentic shift:** self-functioning and personal responsibility are replaced by functioning within the hierarchical system and compliance with the will of the group. To explain this shift, Milgram points to both developmental and situational factors.

The child's first learning experiences, Milgram notes, are in the family, where there are rules and regulations in abundance and where a strong respect for authority is instilled. At the age of 6 or so, the child is sent to school, which is in itself a system of authority. Whether or not one later enters an authoritarian occupation, the first 20 years are spent functioning as a subordinate in a system in which compliance is rewarded and defiance is punished. This situation, coupled with other routine events (for example, being exhorted by ministers and having run-ins with the police), usually results in a personal acceptance of the social order or hierarchy.

The immediate, situational factor that is responsible for the agentic shift is the "perception of a relevant authority." For example, subjects in Milgram's research entered into the experimental situation with the expectation that "someone will be in charge" and that they were to "do as they were told." All the experimenter had to do was identify himself. In other situations in which people expect someone to be "in charge," badges, uniforms, and gold braid may serve to identify the relevant authority.

Although there is consensus that the obedience research is among the most important in social psychology, this attempt to explain obedience in terms of inbred characteristics has met with a cool reception (Wrightsman, 1974). Milgram's theory would not seem likely to generate new, testable hypotheses, and it does not do an adequate job of explaining individual differences in obedience. As we saw in our discussion of Lorenz' theory of aggression, explanations of human social behavior that are based on evolution and inbred characteristics are not popular among social psychologists, because they do not sufficiently account for the variability in human social behavior. As presently formulated, Milgram's explanation of his important findings does not promise to be an exception to this rule.

NONCONFORMITY

Often people do not bend to the will of the group. We all know of renegades who order American food at Chinese restaurants (thus forcing the rest of us at the table to settle for the modest Nanking Dinner for Three instead of the more scrumptious Imperial Dinner for Four). More seriously, not long ago at the campus where I teach, the colonel in charge of the Army R.O.T.C. relaxed standards concerning the appropriate length for cadets' hair. Photographs of cadets with shoulder-length hair made the national news, and a number of irate veterans and retired officers protested to the colonel's superiors. Yet the colonel did not reverse his decision. In some cases a refusal to conform may have altered the course of history. For example, in 1868 an attempt was made to impeach President Andrew Johnson. The Republicans behind this move needed 36 votes in the Senate to ensure impeachment, but they were sure of only 35 votes. As Jahoda (1959) notes, although every conceivable pressure was brought to bear on the one hold-out Republican, this Senator remained firm, and the motion to impeach President Johnson was not carried.

A conformist behaves in accordance with the perceived norms of a group. How should we best describe the behavior that violates such norms? Is it adequate simply to view conformity and nonconformity as opposite ends of a continuum? Willis and others have suggested that a distinction must be made between two kinds of nonconformity (Willis, 1963, 1965; Stricker, Messick, & Jackson, 1970).

Anticonformity and Independence

The two types of nonconformity are anticonformity and independence. Only one of these two kinds of nonconformity represents freedom from social influence. **Anticonformity** (also known as counterconformity and negativism) involves behaving in ways that are contrary to those prescribed by the group. Thus, if everyone in the group is clean shaven and wears a coat and tie, the anticonformist will grow a beard and wear grubby clothes. If everyone in the group is bewhiskered and wears grubby clothes, the anticonformist will be clean shaven and wear a coat and tie. The anticonformist does the *opposite* of what the group expects, quite possibly to maintain a false sense of personal freedom (*false* because, like the conformist's behavior, the anticonformist's behavior is dependent on that of other people).

In the other type of nonconformity—**independence**—the nonconformist is aware of the group norms but assigns them relatively little weight when reaching a decision. He or she may accept the group's ways that seem reasonable and appropriate and reject the group's ways that seem unreasonable and inappropriate. For example, if members of his group are generally bewhiskered and bedraggled, the independent may be clean shaven (because it is more comfortable) but still renounce wearing a coat and tie (again because of comfort considerations). The independent is capable of evaluating and, when necessary, *resisting* social norms. True independence is considered difficult to achieve. Most of us seem to be quite variable, conforming in some situations but not in others.

Minority Influence

Certainly the bulk of research in the area of conformity has examined the conditions under which an individual is likely to conform and the processes through which his or her conformity is brought about. However, several investigators have examined the conditions under which the group will abandon its majority position and adopt the viewpoint advocated by the minority (Moscovici, Lage, & Naffrechoux, 1969; Nemeth & Wachtler, 1973; Moscovici & Nemeth, 1974).

In Asch's research, unanimity was essential for inducing conformity. When this *inter*individual consistency represented by the majority is translated into *intra*individual consistency represented by an adamant and unchanging individual, the minority may be able to sway the majority. That is, the minority may be able to bring the majority around to its point of view if it steadfastly maintains its minority position over a number of occasions or trials. This point was illustrated in a study by Moscovici et al. (1969), who showed blue colors to groups of six people. Within this group of six were two confederates who stoutly maintained that the color was actually green. Although under control conditions subjects mistook blue for green on the average of 1 out of 400 trials, under experimental conditions subjects mislabeled the hue as green on about 8½% of the trials. Thus a *consistent* minority with a clear position in which it obviously believes may be able to budge the majority opinion a small amount.

In the Moscovici et al. study, the minority was a group of two. Thus there was still some interindividual consistency, although it was a far cry from that shown by a unanimous majority of six or eight people in the Asch studies. However, to eliminate the possibility that some of the Moscovici et al. results might have required two agreeing dissenters, Nemeth and Wachtler (1973) examined the effect of an individual deviate on the majority opinion. In this experiment, subjects were shown art works that were labeled "Italian" or "German." Under control conditions, subjects showed a consistent preference for the "Italian" masterpieces. Under experimental conditions, subjects indicated preferences in the presence of a confederate who consistently chose one type of art. In one experimental condition the confederate invariably chose the relatively unpopular "German" masterpiece, whereas in the other experimental condition the confederate was unrelenting in his preference for the popular "Italian" selection. As expected, the repetitious choice of the unpopular "German" art resulted in experimental subjects' showing more of a preference for it than did controls. However, it was also found that subjects in the second experimental condition, in which the confederate invariably chose the relatively popular "Italian" works, also showed a greater preference for the relatively unpopular "German" art. This latter finding—that someone who adopted an extreme majority position could budge people in the direction of the minority point of view—was unexpected. Perhaps one explanation is that this effect is a reactance phenomenon (Chapter 8). The authors propose that, when a person advocates a minority position, he or she is showing courage and is introducing new elements that cause the majority to consider the positive features of the minority's choice. However, when someone overendorses the majority position, this person's rigidity raises questions of prejudice and fairness. Although further research is clearly needed, the Nemeth and Wachtler study suggests that either consistently advocating the minority position or overadvocating the majority position can induce change away from the point of view held by the majority.

PART SUMMARY

Conformity refers to group-induced uniformities in social behavior. Two types of social influence contribute to conformity. Informational social influence refers to accepting information from others as evidence of reality. Normative social influence refers to abiding by group standards in order to secure approval and to avoid disapproval and rejection.

A major feature of human life is that activities are socially regulated. Norms are socially devised standards that provide a framework for interpretation and evaluation. By comparing autokinetic judgments made by individuals who were alone with judgments made by individuals who were in groups, Sherif showed that interacting people will develop group norms, that different groups will develop different norms, and that norms developed in the group setting will later regulate "alone" behavior.

In the natural setting, same behavior may be misperceived as conformity. Conformity is a social process; thus uniformities in behavior must somehow be related to the group. Field studies of conformity become compelling when they show that, in addition to within-group similarities, there are between-group differences, that there are differences between public actions and private thoughts, and that a change in group membership is followed by a change in the individual's attitudes or behavior.

It is not necessary for a person to belong to a group in order to be influenced by its standards. Positive reference groups are those whose standards the individual accepts, and negative reference groups are those whose standards the individual rejects. Reference groups, like membership groups, affect individual behavior. When a person's reference group is criticized or disparaged, the person may try to disprove the criticism.

A historic event in social psychology was Asch's finding that, on about one-third of the critical trials, subjects abandoned the evidence confronting their senses and agreed with the incorrect but unanimous judgment of a group. On the heels of this discovery has come a host of experiments aimed at understanding the antecedents or causes of conformity. This search has involved properties of the individual, properties of the task, and properties of the group.

Properties of the individual that are related to conformity include competence, personality, and history within the group. First, the younger and less skilled are more conforming than the older and more skilled.

Second, although measures of authoritarianism and self-esteem, as well as a few other personality measures, correlate with conformity, attempts to predict conformity on the basis of personality measures have been somewhat disappointing, since situational factors usually are not adequately taken into account. Third, reinforcement and other "historical" factors affect conformity. It would seem that a record of adherence to group norms may raise the group's tolerance for an outburst of nonconforming activity.

There are three principal task variables. First, studies of task difficulty suggest that, when the task is made difficult or ambiguous, conformity will increase. Second, if the judgment task is biased toward the interests of one gender, members of that sex are less likely to conform to the false majority than are members of the opposite sex. Third, whether judgments are made publicly or privately will help to determine conformity. Normative social influence is more likely to have an impact on public statements than on private beliefs, whereas informational social influences may affect both of these dependent variables equally.

Two important group properties are size and unanimity of the majority. Some studies have found that increasing the size of the false majority beyond four or so reliably increases conformity, whereas other experimenters have failed to find this result. One interesting hypothesis worthy of further examination is that for such increases to affect conformity, each stooge's judgment must be perceived as independent. It has been found that any rift in the unanimity of the majority is likely to encourage defiance of the false majority.

Obedience refers to compliance with the explicit demands of other people. Milgram found that adult Americans from different walks of life continued to obey an experimenter's orders to inflict painful shocks on a "victim," even though they showed strong feelings of stress and guilt when doing so. Subsequent studies have examined variables suspected of affecting levels of obedience. When the suffering victim was brought closer to the subject, when the experimenter's surveillance was reduced, and when the subject was placed into a defiant group, obedience was decreased.

A recent and rather speculative theory suggests that obedience has its roots partially in evolution and partially in learning and situational factors. Survival chances are best for organisms that can function either autonomously or as members of an organized hierarchy. Humans can function either way. Because of developmental and situational factors, the perception of a relevant authority triggers a shift from the autonomous state (in which we perceive our behavior as self-controlled) to the agentic state (in which we perceive our behavior as under the control of another person). Like other attempts to account for complex and variable human social behavior in terms of evolution and instincts, this theory has met with a cool reception.

Willis and others have offered an important distinction between anticonformity (which involves doing the opposite of what the group prescribes) and independence (which involves assigning group norms relatively little weight). A person who holds a minority position may sway the majority in his or her direction by consistently advocating this position. A person who overespouses the majority position may also budge the majority in the minority's direction.

ENCOUNTER GROUPS

After dinner the ten strangers gathered in a comfortable room. They knew they were all there to learn about themselves and the ways they relate to others. The fate of the group was in the hands of the members. The permissiveness of the situation and the promise of new experiences generated anticipation and excitement on the one hand but anxiety and fear on the other.

At first the conversation was mere chitchat: impersonal and abstract. As boredom threatened, the talk became more specific, concrete, and personal. A woman revealed that behind her unusually pretty face hid frustration and despair. A friendless man tentatively reached out and was embraced by the group. A particularly responsive chord was struck in a woman who felt she had been in a meaningless marriage for 25 years. A young black woman felt able, for the first time, to be a person first and a "Negro" second. Feelings of affection, kinship, sorrow, and anger rippled through the group. After a weekend the members separated, determined to reach out to others and to more fully experience life.

This particular group, described by Solomon (1971), is only one of thousands or tens of thousands that have been formed across the land in the past decade or two. The genus or class is known as the **laboratory-training group,** or **t-group** (Egan, 1970, 1971). The purposes of such groups include: (1) increasing self-awareness, (2) increasing sensitivity to others, (3) increasing sensitivity to small-group processes, (4) improving skills at diagnosing problems in human relations, and (5) improving leadership skills on both task and socioemotional dimensions (Campbell & Dunnette, 1968). Here we'll follow Egan (1970, 1971) and emphasize those groups in which personal and interpersonal issues are the primary focus. In these **encounter groups,** other goals, such as learning about group dynamics and organizational behavior, are not necessarily eliminated but are made secondary to the goal of dealing with "personal and interpersonal deficiencies and potentialities" (Egan, 1970, p. 10).

Encounter groups are much easier to experience than to describe. The task of description is made difficult by (1) the dozen or so major varieties of such groups, (2) the differences in methods and procedures within each variety, and (3) the variability resulting from the unique inputs of the different people who make up individual encounter groups. There is, however, considerable agreement concerning members' *expectations* for such groups. People feel they will profit personally and interpersonally from their participation. For example, in a sample of 1133 participants, Bebout and Gordon (1972) found that at least 75% expected to (1) increase their capacity for deeper relationships, (2) discover how they were seen by others, (3) freely express emotions, (4) gain sensitivity to others, (5) share experiences, (6) find joy and self-fulfillment, (7) change their ways of getting along with people, (8) meet new people and make friends, (9) learn to help others, and (10) discover their inner selves. A tall order indeed!

ORIGINS OF THE ENCOUNTER-GROUP MOVEMENT

For thousands of years people have survived without encounter groups. Why should such groups appear at this point in history? Are they simply a fad, or are they a serious response to a sequence of major events? My guess is the latter. Contributing to the rise of encounter groups are (1) the depersonalization of social relations and (2) the rise of humanistic psychology.

The Depersonalization of Social Relations

The quality of people's relationships with one another appears to be on the decline. Compared with a century ago, people are transient, and hence their relationships are likely to be transient (Toffler, 1970). The increased mobility provided by the automobile and the airplane, the rise of superbusinesses that shunt employees all over the globe, the desire to move to a fancier neighborhood as finances permit—these and many other factors seem to have created a nation of wanderers, in which people don't really have much of a chance to get to know one another on an intimate basis. Moreover, the rise of the "bedroom community" means that we work with some people, live with others, and often spend our spare time with still others. With most acquaintances we share only a very few parts of our lives. This compartmentalization has produced what Toffler (1970) has described (with a certain sexist bias) as a "modular man," who interacts with a large *number* of people—but only in very limited ways with any given person. Even the family is on the decline.

Within a given home we find fewer people representing fewer generations, and, judging by divorce rates, even these small constricted families
have a short life expectancy.

The population explosion and the rise of the supercities may also be
contributing to the depersonalization of social relationships. As we noted
in Chapter 7, the city fosters strong norms of uninvolvement. Although
surrounded by millions of other people, individuals may feel isolated, indifferent, and powerless. Because of rapid technological change, increased
mobility, and the rise of impersonal metropolises, then, superficial, narrow social relationships may be replacing broad, deep relationships. As a
result, the experience of living may be becoming less rewarding. The interest in encounter groups may be traced, in part, to these conditions
(Altman & Taylor, 1973).

The Rise of Humanistic Psychology

The second major factor contributing to the encounter-group movement is the rise of humanistic psychology. Until perhaps the 1950s, psychology had devised only two models of people. One, the **behavioristic
model,** suggested that people could best be regarded as collections of
learned habits. The second, or **psychoanalytic model,** suggested that people are buffeted about by unconscious fears and hidden forces.

Now a third, **humanistic model** has been proposed that is dramatically different. People are viewed neither as mere responders to reinforcers nor as psychic cesspools, but as conscious, free, whole beings who set
goals and then actively strive to attain them. A major component of humanistic theorizing is that people have immense unutilized potential that
they seek to develop. Utilization of human potential—or **personal growth**
—cannot be strictly defined but includes (1) developing faith and trust in
other people and in the world, (2) developing the capacity to communicate, (3) developing self-determination and responsibility for oneself,
and (4) developing a sense of interdependence with others without surrendering personal freedom (Gibb, 1972). This kind of learning can take
place in many ways, but findings from classical group dynamics, group
psychotherapy, and organizational psychology suggest that small groups
can provide a particularly useful vehicle.

THE CULTURE OF THE ENCOUNTER GROUP

The encounter group provides a cultural island unencumbered by
many of the restrictions of society. A membership of 12 people or so
ensures that the group is small enough so that each person can engage in

intense interaction but not so small that this intensity becomes burdensome. Usually the group meets for a two- or three-hour session each week over a period of several weeks, although this schedule may be compressed into an intensive week, a weekend, or even a single night.

Encounter-Group Norms

Certain norms or ground rules govern the interaction. These rules may be very informal, or they may be explicitly stated in advance. No one set of ground rules applies to all groups (for example, in some groups physical violence is tolerated, but in others it is not), but quite common are *emphasis on the here-and-now, norms of self-disclosure, a climate of support, and feedback and confrontation.*

First, the *here-and-now* is emphasized over the "there-and-then." Ruminating about the past is considered unlikely to lead anywhere. Yesterday's errors are errors only because they make us unhappy today; talking about the past usually places intellect over emotion (a no-no); and, worst of all, such discussion is usually totally irrelevant to relationships within the group. Participants are thus encouraged to forget the past and deal with their present feelings about others in the group. To maximize involvement, group leaders also encourage them to be specific and concrete and to speak to particular individuals rather than make vague allusions to the group as a whole (Egan, 1970).

Second, there are *strong norms for self-disclosure.* A major cultural ban is therefore held in abeyance: members are urged not to conceal their thoughts and feelings but to drop the facades they use to get along in many daily social situations and to freely and candidly express themselves. According to Egan (1970), concealment of the inner self may be a major source of anxiety. For example, a person may hide a shortcoming or failure from others and then worry about adverse reactions if the word somehow gets out. A common result of revealing personal shortcomings in the encounter groups is that the person discovers that other people are more accepting than was anticipated. Yet norms of openness and honesty are not meant to encourage people to take things out on the group or to be emotional exhibitionists.

A third important ground rule is for a *climate of support,* which facilitates self-disclosure, the expression of emotion, and attempts to relate to others. There are three phases of support: antecedent, concurrent, and consequent. The antecedent phase involves *encouraging* the person to make the revelation or express the emotion. The concurrent phase requires *listening* when he or she engages in self-expression. That is, members must avoid preoccupation with other external events and avoid reveling in their own fantasies or concentrating on their own relationship to the person. The consequent phase involves *accepting*. Here a distinction must be made between **acceptance** (which refers to an unconditional regard for the person as a worthwhile human being) and **approval** (which refers to a positive reaction to or endorsement of a specific act). For example, if one person displays a romantic interest in another, the second should not feign reciprocity but also should not try to deprive the first person of his or her status as a valued member of the group by means of ridicule or belittlement. An encounter group, then, is a permissive group in which experimentation is encouraged.

Fourth, most encounter groups require *feedback and confrontation*. Feedback involves responding to another person's statements or activities in a way that enables the other person to know that he or she has triggered a reaction and to understand exactly what that reaction is. Confrontation is a special kind of feedback whereby one person points out to another some sort of discrepancy or inconsistency in his or her statements or behavior. For example, Jane may point out to Jennifer that, although Jennifer is professing great liking for Jonathan, she is all the while vigorously shaking her head "no," thereby implying that she feels otherwise.

Feedback and confrontation can easily degenerate into two people's venting hostility on each other. Responsible confrontation requires involvement and concern. Egan (1970) suggests that the rules for responsible confrontation should include (1) considering possible harmful effects of the confrontation; (2) making the strength of the confrontation proportional to the needs, sensitivities, and capabilities of the confrontees; and (3) trying to separate feelings, hypotheses, and facts during the confrontation.

The Encounter-Group Leader

In many encounter groups a leader evolves from within the ranks, and a whole class of *t*-groups is described as "leaderless." There has been a pronounced tendency to avoid the term *leader* and to substitute less authoritarian-sounding terms such as *trainer, resource person,* or *facilitator*. Whatever one's choice of terms, there is usually some particular person in the group who is handsomely paid to keep an eye on things.

Lieberman, Yalom, and Miles (1973) have identified four functions that are served by encounter-group leaders. First, they stimulate the group members to self-disclose, confront one another, express their emotions, contribute to the discussion, and so forth. Second, leaders express care and concern for the group and its members. Third, they provide intellectual input by explaining, clarifying, and interpreting occurrences within the group. Fourth, leaders serve an executive function by setting ground rules and limits, handling scheduling and timing problems, and so forth.

In an analysis of 15 leaders with different backgrounds and orientations, Lieberman et al. identified seven factors or types of leadership activity that helped the leader to fulfill the four functions just noted. These seven factors are *intrusive modeling, cognitizing, command stimulation, managing or limit setting, attention focusing, mirroring,* and *affective support.*

Intrusive modeling refers to eliciting responses from group members by direct demands and exhortations and by serving as a model group member. This factor involves confronting and challenging group members, drawing attention to oneself, expressing one's own feelings, and being a pacesetter for self-disclosure.

Cognitizing refers to teaching or instructional behaviors. This factor would include providing concepts for understanding oneself and the group; explaining, clarifying, and interpreting; and providing some sort of intellectual framework for personal and social change.

Command stimulation involves attempts to get responses through invitations, questions, and suggestions. This factor differs from intrusive modeling in that the leader displays emotional neutrality and does not personally model the desired reactions.

Managing or limit setting refers to establishing ground rules, helping the group to set goals, conducting exercises, starting and stopping sessions, and other "housekeeping" behaviors. Actions included in this category are stopping confrontations before they get out of hand and intervening when the group is beset by problems that block personal and interpersonal growth. Such problems would include cynicism, prolonged periods of silence, horseplay, intellectual discussions, and the avoidance of emotion by speaking in generalities and by pursuing purely intellectual insights.

Attention focusing refers to behaviors that direct attention toward specific people or issues within the group. This factor involves calling on specific people to contribute to the session, highlighting similarities and differences among group members, and pointing out the subtle relationships that members have with one another, inside or outside the group.

Mirroring refers to reflecting occurrences within the group. This function includes summarizing past events, rephrasing members' statements and expressions, and reminding the group of its decisions and goals. Although most encounter-group leadership behaviors are directed toward reaching future goals, mirroring is "reactive" in that it is a response to pre-existing conditions.

Affective support is the seventh and final factor. It involves providing approval, praise, and encouragement; protecting members who are under attack; and offering friendship, love, and affection to the group. Thus the final function of encounter-group leaders is to be warm and supportive in their own relations with others.

SOME EFFECTS OF PARTICIPATION

The encounter-group movement has generated heated debate. The people I know who conduct such groups have certainly found more to praise than to berate. My informal discussions with many satisfied participants suggest that the encounter-group experience can be entertaining and exciting and can provide a stimulus that leads to a new personal awareness, a new sensitivity to others, and a new meaning to life.

On the other hand, encounter groups have most certainly had some rather vocal critics. Certain group procedures (particularly self-disclosure and confrontation) bear an uncanny resemblance to the tactics used in brainwashing (Schein, 1958), and this similarity does not set well with those who think encounter groups may be aimed at undermining democratic principles (Skousen, 1967). Sigmund Koch (1974) suggests that terms such as *openness, honesty,* and *personal growth* have been bandied about so freely that they have become empty and meaningless. With sexist overtones, he notes that *t*-groups:

> . . . provide, in effect, a convenient psychic whorehouse for the purchase of well-advertised existential "goodies": authenticity, freedom, wholeness, flexibility, community, love, joy. One enters for such liberating consummation but inevitably settles for a psychic striptease" [1972, p. 34].

Encounter groups range from dull conferences, through groups with norms and leaders as just described, to totally uninhibited affairs that, to the outsider, represent little more than wild abandon and chaos. Depending on what type of group one is referring to, virtually any attitude can be justified. We will focus on the question of what is likely to happen as a result of participating in groups that are neither inane conferences nor showcases for emotional exhibitionism. We'll consider the potential risks and the potential benefits of encounter groups such as those run by many college counseling centers. In assessing risks and benefits, we need not rely only on personal testimonials and speculative arguments, since research results are now pouring in (Gibb, 1970, 1971; Bebout & Gordon, 1972; Lieberman et al., 1973).

Potential Risks

In encounter groups, emotions run high (an encounter group can be likened to a charm school thrown into reverse gear). Caught up in a wave of emotionality and relentlessly confronted by others, wouldn't a person —particularly a shy and sensitive person—be likely to "crack up"? Stories circulate about wrecked marriages, psychotic behavior, unemployment, and other hideous aftereffects of encounter-group participation.

As Lieberman et al. note, it is very easy to underestimate or overestimate the percentage of encounter-group members who become encounter-group casualties. Typically, group leaders have close contact with members for the duration of the sessions and then never see them again. Any casualties that occur after the group is terminated are thus likely to go undetected. On the other hand, each time someone "freaks out" in the middle of a session, word of the incident is likely to spread quickly. As the story is told and retold, it may enter into the folklore as five or six separate cases, thus enhancing the impression of danger in encounter-group participation.

Another problem is that, when psychological misfortune befalls an encounter-group member, it is not clear whether participation in the group was the responsible factor. People who are having difficulty in understanding themselves or others may be particularly motivated to seek out and join encounter groups. Personal or social maladjustment could be a cause rather than an effect of encounter-group participation. Even when researchers use control groups and objective measures, results can be difficult to assess. For example, Lieberman et al. found that, whereas only 2 control subjects (4%) entered psychotherapy within nine months after the study commenced, 18 encounter-group participants (13%) entered therapy during the same period of time. However, less than half of the encounter-group members who sought psychotherapy could be considered group casualties. In some cases the group membership was a constructive experience that led participants to realize that they needed psychotherapy; in some other cases the group members found participation so enjoyable that they wanted to continue to seek self-understanding through therapy.

Lieberman et al. also used self-report and other measures to detect casualties among their 150 or so encounter-group participants. They found that about *10%* of their experimental subjects underwent a destructive experience of one degree or another in the course of participation. Although several causes were identified, in most cases the harmful experience could be traced to an aggressive, highly obtrusive, and nonsupportive leader. Most other studies suggest that severe casualties are few (Reddy, 1972). Rogers (1970), for example, reported that, of 600 participants, only 2 (0.3%) had nervous breakdowns; in another study of 14,200 participants, only 33 (or 0.2%) had to quit their group for this reason (National Training Laboratories, 1969). However, it should be noted that a nervous breakdown is a rather extreme criterion for declaring a casualty and that in most cases optimistic figures do not take into account breakdowns that occur after the group is over.

Thus there is a risk of undergoing a destructive experience in the course of encounter-group participation. The odds of such a harmful occurrence may be low, and the extent of the damage may not be great. However, the possibility that one might become a casualty should certainly be taken into account. It should also be cautioned that all the figures cited here apply only to groups sponsored by reputable, competent organizations that are willing to be objectively assessed. What happens in freelance groups run by minimally trained or untrained leaders is anybody's guess.

How can people who are interested in joining an encounter group minimize their individual risk? Shostrom (1969) has offered what I consider to be some very sensible pointers for the encounter-group aspirant. First, people should think seriously about joining, not do so on impulse. Second, people should consider the size of the group. In a group of fewer than 6 people the situation may get too intense, and in a group of 20 or so there is unlikely to be much individual feedback. Third, except in special cases, people are usually better off in a group of strangers than in a group of friends. Fourth, people should be leery of groups that have a behavioral ax to grind—for example, a group whose members feel that everyone should be anti-intellectual or pro-Eastern religions. (An exception to this rule would be when you happen to share this preference.) Fifth, people should learn something about the background and qualifications of the leader. Shostrom admonishes aspirants never to participate in a group whose leader lacks formal connections with a professional organization one can check with. He urges people to ignore newspaper ads for groups, since professional ethics prevent trained professionals from advertising in this way.

We need to be concerned about who runs our encounter groups, because in some cases they are run not by competent professionals but by quacks or by people whose only qualifications are intense interest coupled with participation in one or two groups themselves. In my opinion, groups led by people with missing or vague credentials should not routinely be given the benefit of the doubt. Legally, anyone can run an encounter group. If people do so to satisfy a personal need to be a source of goodness or wisdom, if they confuse self-disclosure with exhibitionism, if they confuse encouraging people with forcing them into doing things they really don't want to, and if they cannot tell the difference between responsible confrontation and senseless attack, then the stage is set for encounter-group casualties.

Potential Benefits

Having considered the risk factor, let's now consider possible positive effects of encounter-group membership. Reviewing the outcomes of groups intended to enhance managerial skills, Campbell and Dunnette (1968) concluded that the effects were generally in line with the objective of increasing perceptiveness and sensitivity to interpersonal relations; furthermore, many of the beneficial effects were apparent "back home" in the work setting. A review by Gibb (1971) of more than 200 studies is also encouraging. According to Gibb, the most common finding is that social perceptiveness increases as a result of participation. People are also likely to end up feeling better about themselves, and there is likely to be less of a discrepancy between what people feel they are and what they'd like to be. Gibb cautions, however, that many groups are too brief in duration to produce optimal and long-lasting effects.

A very ambitious study of several hundred group participants has been reported by Bebout and Gordon (1972). Their project involved four administrations of a battery of tests: before participation, during participation, immediately after participation, and three to six months after participation. Variables included self-concept, self-esteem, self-actualization, alienation, interpersonal values, relations with friends, and perception of change. Outcomes depended to some extent on the nature of the group, and none of the groups seemed to have much impact on productivity or problems at school or at work. However, the evidence suggested that participation led to an increase in self-esteem, self-actualizing tendencies, and sensitivity to others, as well as to a reduction in feelings of loneliness.

Perhaps the study most likely to satisfy even the most hard-nosed experimentalist is the one by Lieberman et al. (1973). Subjects were randomly assigned to one of 17 different encounter groups or 2 control conditions. A battery of tests and questionnaires was administered, extensive interviews were conducted, and the researchers kept in touch with subjects for several months after the last group session had been held. In addition, sessions were tape recorded and carefully analyzed by outside observers.

Given the tremendous variability in the orientations of the leaders, group norms, and group composition, it is not too suprising that different people experienced different outcomes. On the whole, participation seemed to have a modestly beneficial impact on the participants. About 60% of those who did not drop out felt they had benefited (a figure that would be rather disappointing to the leaders, who had estimated benefits for 90% of the participants). Both experimentals and controls were seen as improved by their friends. Relative to subjects in the control group, subjects who had participated in an encounter group reported themselves to have become more change oriented and more growth oriented and to have achieved greater congruity between their "real" self (what they thought they were) and their "ideal" self (what they thought they would like to be). On a number of measures, change was apparent immediately after the sessions concluded but did not endure for very long afterward. An across-the-board comparison of experimental and control subjects suggests that the benefits of participation were modest.

Studies such as Lieberman et al.'s and Bebout and Gordon's allow for a rather precise analysis. When we include such variables as leader characteristics, group norms, and participant characteristics, it becomes possible to estimate with some certainty whether encounter-group participation will be a constructive or a destructive experience. For example, in Lieberman et al.'s study, leaders who showed a great deal of caring for the group and who took time to explain, interpret, and clarify group processes usually produced beneficial effects. Leaders who were excessively reliant on intrusive modeling and who failed to intercede when the interaction began to get destructive generally had detrimental effects. Laissez-faire or impersonal leaders did not have much effect at all. Group norms and expectations were also important. To some extent the best outcomes were experienced by groups in which many norms had developed and in which the members (rather than the leaders) were responsible for the

development of the norms. Those groups in which members were coerced into activities that they preferred not to engage in were likely to yield casualties. Characteristics of the participants were also important, but no one pattern of characteristics was evidenced by those individuals who profited most from encounter-group participation.

Should you try an encounter group? It's entirely up to you. In making your decision, however, you may want to take into account some of the potential risks and potential benefits outlined in this section.

PART SUMMARY

The various forms of laboratory-training or *t*-groups are intended to increase self-awareness, sensitivity to others, leadership skills, and an understanding of small-group problems and processes. The encounter group focuses directly on personal and interpersonal issues. Contributing to the emergence of encounter groups have been the depersonalization of social relations and the rise of humanistic psychology.

Encounter groups are places for experimentation and are unencumbered by many of the restrictions of society. Norms support emphasis on the here-and-now, self-disclosure, supportiveness, and feedback and confrontation. Most groups contain a special member who is charged with stimulating group members, expressing care and concern, interpreting occurrences within the group, and serving in an executive capacity. Several different types of behavior are shown as leaders fulfill these functions.

The encounter-group movement has been lavished with praise and heaped with scorn. Evaluative research suggests that there are some risks associated with encounter-group participation. Many studies have been conducted, and the balance of the evidence suggests that reputable groups usually do little harm and sometimes do some good. Predicting the outcome of encounter-group participation requires that characteristics of the leader, the group, and the participants be taken into account.

10
Performance in Small Groups

INDIVIDUAL VERSUS GROUP

SOCIAL FACILITATION

Coaction and Audience Effects
The Drive-Habit Interpretation
Mere Presence versus Evaluation Apprehension

WHEN ARE TWO HEADS BETTER THAN ONE?

The Quality of Individual Contributions
Rules for Combining Individual Contributions
Type of Task and Group Performance

DECISIONS INVOLVING RISK

Extremity Shifts
Familiarization Theory
Value Theories
Diffusion-of-Responsibility Theory
Information-Exchange Theory

PART SUMMARY

GROUP PROPERTIES AND GROUP PERFORMANCE

COMMUNICATIONS NETS

Centrality and Performance
Centrality and Satisfaction

CONFORMITY AND GROUP PERFORMANCE

Conformity and Productivity
Conformity and Problem Solving

COHESIVENESS AND PERFORMANCE

Antecedents of Cohesiveness
Cohesiveness, Conformity, and Productivity
Cohesiveness and Problem Solving:
  The Groupthink Phenomenon

PART SUMMARY

They were not only inseparable as brothers, but their very minds seemed to complement each other. They would bat a problem back and forth for hours, until almost invariably a solution appeared—the joint product of two brains working in perfect harmony [Lord, 1969, p. 85].

As this description of Wilbur and Orville Wright suggests, the pooling of individual skills and abilities sometimes leads to brilliant ideas and dazzling performances. Although there is considerable evidence supporting the claim that "Two heads are better than one," there is also some evidence supporting the conflicting claim that "Too many cooks spoil the broth." One of the goals of this chapter is to specify the conditions under which each of these claims applies. We will consider the ways in which participation in a group affects individual performance, problem solving, and decision making. We will also discuss various group properties and the ways in which they affect the group's level of performance.

INDIVIDUAL VERSUS GROUP

There are two general procedures for comparing individual performances with performances in groups. **Social-facilitation** research (so called because many early results suggested that the presence of others had a beneficial effect on performance) focuses on the individual and compares the performance of an isolated individual with that of an individual in a group. The second type of research focuses on the collectivity, or the group. It examines what happens when there is a pooling of individual abilities, efforts, and performances resulting in some sort of group product or score. Although there are several ways of conducting such research, a common technique is to compare the collective performance of a number of noninteracting individuals with the combined performance of the same number of interacting individuals. Conventionally, the collection of noninteracting individuals is called a **nominal group,** which means, literally, a "group in name only." (Although this definition conflicts somewhat with the definitions of groups discussed in Chapter 1, we will follow this convention.) A common finding is that the sum or average of individual performances in a nominal group is not the same as the pooled or combined performances of interacting people in a "real" group. After considering the relatively simple case of social facilitation, we will discuss what happens when there is a combination of individual efforts, judgments, and decisions in a group.

SOCIAL FACILITATION

In the 1890s a bicycle craze swept the nation (Throm, 1952). During that era it was discovered that cyclists who were racing against one another rode much faster than cyclists who raced alone against the clock (Cottrell, 1972). To test the hypothesis that competition has a beneficial effect on performance, Triplett (1897) moved into the laboratory and had children wind line around a reel, either alone or in the presence of two other children engaged in the same task. Even though in both conditions the children were urged to "go as rapidly as possible to make a record," children working in isolation did not perform so well as children in groups.

Coaction and Audience Effects

Coaction refers to two or more members of the same species engaging in identical tasks in the presence of each other. As Zajonc (1965) and Cottrell (1972) have noted, Triplett's finding that coaction has a beneficial effect on performance has been repeatedly confirmed. Allport (1924) had subjects perform a number of different tasks, either in separate rooms or around a table. Subjects under coaction conditions more speedily crossed out vowels on a printed page, completed more multiplications, thought of more associations to words, and reported more dramatic effects from an illusion. Chen (1937) observed 36 ants excavating nests. He observed them working alone, in groups of two, in groups of three, and then again working alone. Under coaction conditions the speed with which excavation began increased by a factor of six, and the amount of earth excavated increased by a factor of three.

Why do coactors perform more energetically than isolated individuals? One possible explanation is "competition." Improved performance might stem from rivalry, or a desire to do better than the others. Yet this explanation seems inadequate because it does not seem to apply to Chen's ants.

Another possible explanation is modeling (Chapter 4). The performance of each person (or insect) might have a disinhibiting effect or a response-facilitation effect, which improves the performance of each other person (or insect). Indeed, other findings from Chen revealed that an ant would perform more energetically when paired with an industrious than with a lazy partner. Yet the presence of others often improves performance even when the others present are not performing. **Audience studies** involve comparisons of solitary performances with performances in the presence of passive spectators.

A classic example of an audience study is provided by Travis (1925), who examined underclass students' performance at a pursuit rotor. This device closely resembles a phonograph turntable. Near the rim of the revolving disk is a spot or "target" about the size of a dime. The task is to hold a pointer on the target while the disk revolves. Performance is measured in terms of the amount of time the pointer remains on target. Except at very low speeds, this is a challenging task.

Travis' subjects practiced by themselves for several sessions. The initially rapid rate of improvement tapered off, and, after two consecutive sessions of no further improvement, the pursuit rotor was considered to have been mastered. Then came a session during which each subject performed before four to eight upperclass students. A comparison of the 10 *best* alone trials with *all* 10 audience trials revealed that 18 of the 22 subjects did better in front of an audience.

Over the succeeding 50 years, many other studies yielded results suggesting that coactors or spectators energize performance (Zajonc, 1965; Cottrell, 1972). In one recent study, Chapman (1973) had children listen to amusing material either alone, in the presence of spectators who could not hear the stimulus material, or in the presence of a coactor who was allowed to share the mirth and merriment. Results revealed both social-facilitation and modeling effects. Isolated children laughed less than children who were in the presence of an audience, and these latter children did not laugh so much as children in the coaction condition, in which modeling effects could occur.

Although some of the beneficial effects of coactors may be attributed to social learning, modeling effects cannot explain the beneficial influence of passive spectators on performance. Yet before we conclude that co-action and audience effects are always beneficial, let's note that all the studies just described measured *performances of simple or well-learned responses.* When we consider the effects of coactors or spectators on the *learning of new responses,* there emerges a strikingly different pattern of results.

One person who obtained such different results was Pessin (1933), who had subjects memorize lists of nonsense words. Each subject learned one list alone and one list in the presence of a spectator. Under alone conditions, subjects required an average of 9.85 trials to memorize all the words; under audience conditions, they required 11.27 trials. Thus Pessin's subjects did *worse* in the presence of others. Using animal subjects, Gates and Allee (1933) found a detrimental effect of coaction on learning. These experimenters trained cockroaches to run an E-shaped maze to avoid an aversive bright light. Isolates reached the security of a dark bottle about twice as fast as did coactors. During the early learning trials, for example, isolates ran the maze in an average of about 5 minutes, whereas pairs required about 12 minutes and groups of three about 18 minutes. More recently, Higgs and Joseph (1971) found that subjects presenting a partially learned Indian folktale made more mistakes in front of a large than in front of a small audience, which suggests that, the more people present, the likelier it is that the learner will make errors. Confirmation that coactors and spectators have detrimental effects when people are trying to learn has been provided by Martens (1969) and Martens and Landers (1972).

Zajonc (1965) was the first person to make sense out of seemingly conflicting coaction and audience findings by pointing out that, *although the presence of others facilitates the performance of well-learned responses, it impairs the acquisition of new responses.* And, indeed, studies following Zajonc' interpretation have for the most part supported this contention (Martens, 1969; Zajonc, Heingartner, & Herman, 1969; Hunt & Hillery, 1973). For example, Martens (1969) had subjects learn a difficult hand-eye coordination task that involved hitting a moving target. Attaining proficiency took longer and involved more errors when the subject was learning in the presence of an audience. On the other hand, after the task had been mastered, spectators had a beneficial effect on performance.

The Drive-Habit Interpretation

To explain the seemingly conflicting effects of the presence of others on learning and on performance, Zajonc (1965) turned to drive-habit theory (Hull, 1943). This theory suggests that the strength and direction of behavior are based on two factors. One is drive, which, you will recall, is a broad motivational state that underlies variations in the organism's level of activity (Chapter 4). Drive determines the strength of a response. The second factor is habit, which is a learned stimulus-response connection that determines the direction or nature of the response. Drive serves to energize a habit, with the result that the strength of the drive will determine the forcefulness of the performance of the associated response.

Zajonc suggests that the presence of a conspecific strengthens drive; as a result, responses will be performed more forcefully. The response that will be energized is the dominant response, which is, by definition, the response most likely to occur in the situation. If the task is simple or well learned, the dominant response is usually the correct response. In this case the presence of others would strengthen the "right" response, with beneficial effects. Alternatively, if the task is not well learned, the presence of others would strengthen incorrect responses, with an apparent detrimental effect. Thus the presence of others *facilitates the emission of*

the dominant response, and whether or not this facilitation will yield a beneficial effect depends on which response is dominant. Accordingly, Hunt
and Hillery (1973) found that, on a simple maze in which dominant responses were likely to be correct, coacting subjects made fewer errors
than did subjects performing in isolation. On a complex maze, in which
dominant responses were likely to be wrong, isolates made fewer mistakes than coactors (see Figure 10–1).

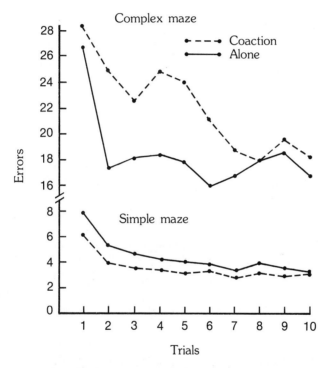

Figure 10-1. The effects of coaction and task difficulty on performance at a maze. (From "Social Facilitation in a Coaction Setting:
An Examination of the Effects of Learning over Trials," by P. J.
Hunt and J. M. Hillery, *Journal of Experimental Social Psychology,*
1973, *9,* 566. Copyright 1973 by Academic Press, Inc. Reprinted
by permission.)

In one direct test of the hypothesis that the presence of others facilitates the emission of a dominant response, Zajonc and Sales (1966) taught
people a number of different responses that varied in strength. They did
so by showing the subjects different made-up or nonsense words differ-

ent numbers of times. Prior research had shown that the most frequently presented word would be the dominant response.

Each subject saw and pronounced different words 1, 2, 4, 8, or 16 times. Next the words were flashed on a screen so quickly that it was difficult or impossible to recognize them. On special **pseudorecognition trials,** there was just a flash of lights, and no word was presented. However, subjects were required to tell the experimenter the "word" they thought had been presented. When such guesses were made by isolated individuals, guesses included a greater variety of words, representing subordinate as well as dominant responses. When such guesses were made before a spectator, they were more likely to be the words shown most frequently in the first part of the experiment. The results thus confirmed the hypothesis that the presence of an audience facilitates the emission of a dominant response.

Mere Presence versus Evaluation Apprehension

Although Zajonc' application of drive-habit theory to "social-facilitation" findings does a nice job of resolving some seeming inconsistencies, there remains a controversy concerning the *source* of increased drive in the presence of others. Zajonc' **mere-presence** interpretation suggests that the perception that there is another, similar organism present is sufficient to increase drive. Cottrell and his associates have disputed this interpretation, proposing instead that the drive increment results from the subject's recognition that other people will be evaluating his or her performance (Cottrell, Wack, Sekerak, & Rittle, 1968; Cottrell, 1972). This is the **evaluation-apprehension** interpretation of social-facilitation effects.

To compare the adequacy of these different explanations, Cottrell et al. (1968) established dominant responses following procedures similar to Zajonc and Sales'. However, in addition to control or "alone" conditions, recognition trials were conducted under two experimental conditions, "mere presence" and "audience." In the mere-presence condition, two other people were in the laboratory. Supposedly awaiting a perception experiment, they were accommodating their eyes by wearing blindfolds. In the audience condition, the two confederates posing as early arrivals for the perception experiment did not wear blindfolds. Audience confederates sought and were given permission to watch the subject perform while waiting for their own experiment. Results showed that the alone and mere-presence subjects did not differ on the pseudorecognition trials, whereas the audience subjects were more likely to guess the more familiar words. Thus, when the possibility of evaluation was eliminated by having the spectators don blindfolds, strengthening of the dominant response did not occur.

Completely different procedures were used by Henchy and Glass (1968) to vary the ability of the audience to evaluate the subjects. In one condition the two spectators were presented as "experts in perception and learning" who would be observing the subject's performance very closely. In another condition the audience was presented as students who were interested in watching the experiment. In a third condition no spectator was present, but subjects were led to believe that their behavior was being filmed for subsequent analysis by an expert. Finally, there was the usual "alone" control condition. Results showed greater facilitation of the dominant response under the two conditions in which subjects were sensitized to being evaluated by experts than under the conditions in which they were being evaluated by nonexperts or performed alone. Particularly intriguing are the results from the "filming" condition: when no audience was present—but subjects were led to expect subsequent evaluation by an expert—strengthening of the dominant response did occur. Several subsequent studies, which have also varied the extent to which the subject perceives that he or she is undergoing evaluation, would seem to support Cottrell's evaluation-apprehension interpretation (Martens & Landers, 1972; Gore & Taylor, 1973; Sasfy & Okun, 1974).

Although it is clear from these studies that evaluation apprehension raises arousal, it is not so clear that these results *exclude* mere presence as a source of arousal. For example, in the Henchy and Glass experiment there were weak social-facilitation effects in the condition in which the spectator was not supposed to be in a position to evaluate the subject. Furthermore, "mere-presence" would seem more plausible than evaluation apprehension as an explanation of the results of animal studies. Using cockroaches, Zajonc, Heingartner, and Herman (1969) found that the presence of spectator roaches impaired maze learning but facilitated performance once the maze had been mastered. Although we cannot be sure that these creatures were unconcerned about being judged by their peers, evaluation apprehension does seem rather unlikely.

Thus we have the possibility that *both* mere presence and evaluation apprehension increase drive. The mere presence of others may energize responses, and sensitizing people to the possibility of evaluation may raise their drive to a higher level yet. Indeed, Cohen and Davis (1973) have found that the performances of "mere-presence" subjects fell between the performances of "control" and "evaluation-apprehension" subjects. Whatever the subtleties of this particular issue, it is clear that the presence of coactors or spectators who have full use of their faculties improves performance and impairs learning.

Social-facilitation research shows that group membership can have a beneficial or a detrimental effect on individual performance at an individual task. We turn now to a consideration of group performances, which involve a pooling of individual abilities and efforts.

WHEN ARE TWO HEADS BETTER THAN ONE?

Reeves (1970, p. 334) has noted that the "multiple escalation of our potential through groups is the foundation of American industrial greatness." In a sense, this assertion is impossible to contest. As Reeves has noted, certain achievements are not possible for the individual; the Grand Coulee Dam, for example, remained only a dream until six major contracting companies pooled all their resources. Certain other achievements, however, are possible for either the individual or the group. In these cases it is useful to know whether groups are superior to individuals ("Two heads are better than one") or whether individuals are superior to groups ("Too many cooks spoil the broth").

Judging by the number of committees, task forces, work groups, and so forth that one encounters in society, there seems to be a basic faith that the group is superior to the individual. Indeed, there are many potential advantages to working in groups. First, there can be a pooling of skills and resources. If the task involves manual effort, there are more arms and legs, and, if it involves problem solving, there are more heads, each one of which may contain at least a few good ideas. Second, in a group there can be a division of labor such that each person works on only one small part of the overall project, with the result that the task is completed faster. Third, within the group, people can stimulate one another and coax forth new ideas. Fourth, because they are sensitized to others' reactions, people in groups may stop and think before they act and hence be less likely to carry through with foolish ideas. Fifth, groups may provide motivational advantages. Members can offer one another support and encouragement, which can supply an extra incentive for good individual performance.

On the other hand, there are certain difficulties that typically arise when we try to work together in groups. First, the members of the group have to be organized: rules for concerted action must be formulated and enforced; each person must understand the task and be willing to do his or her part; plans must be made to divide the work up in an effective and equitable way; conflicts of interest must be resolved and uncooperative people brought into line. Second, certain problems require new or unusual solutions. Within a group, established patterns of communication, social norms, and conformity pressures may keep new or unusual solutions from being uncovered. Thus, for example, although a group may have the potential to generate a large number of ideas, fear of negative evaluations by other group members can limit the variety of the ideas offered. Third, group membership can have an adverse effect on motivation. The increase in drive brought about by the presence of others will be a disservice if the task is novel or poorly learned. Finally, whereas people in isolation may stick to the task, people in groups may spend a considerable amount of time chatting or "clowning around."

Because of such factors, the question "Which is superior—the individual or the group?" does not have a single answer. Whether an individual or a group has a performance advantage depends on such things as the quality of the contributions or inputs of the individual members, the way the members' contributions are pooled or combined to produce a group product, and the nature of the task or problem confronting the group.

The Quality of Individual Contributions

In a judgmental task, the quality or accuracy of individual judgments will affect whether or not "two heads are better than one." For a long time it was thought that a judgment made by an individual would be inferior to a group judgment derived by averaging the contributions of a number of individuals. Knight (1921) was one of the first people to state this hypothesis. In her study, students estimated room temperature. Individual judgments ranged from 60° to 80°, and any individual judgment was likely to be quite a bit off from the actual temperature. However, the estimate derived from averaging a group of individual judgments was 72.4°, only .4° off from the true temperature. Shortly thereafter, Gordon (1924) had college students rank weights. (These weights differed so slightly in some cases that people could not easily rank them from lightest to heaviest.) She then correlated their individual rankings with the true or actual rank order. The average correlation between an individual's estimate of the order and the true order was .41. She also obtained group rankings (by averaging the individual rankings of a number of people) and correlated these group rankings with the true order. When group rankings were based on the judgments of 5 individuals, the correlation between estimated order and true order was .68. When group judgments were based on the contributions of 10 and 20 people, the correlation was still higher, and when group judgments were based on the contributions of 50 people, the correlation rose to a staggering .94. Subsequent studies involving judgments of personality traits, the numerosity of buckshot, and the number of beans in a bottle all suggested that group judgments were superior to individual judgments and that, the larger the number of people contributing to a group judgment, the greater the superiority of the group (Lorge, Fox, Davitz, & Brenner, 1958).

This finding reflects a statistical inevitability (Zajonc, 1962, 1966). Any individual judgment will contain a certain amount of error. A fundamental assumption of statistics is that errors are random and cancel one another out. All that is accomplished by combining individual judgments into a "group score" is a reduction in error through increasing the chances that different people's small mistakes will cancel one another out. The judgments need not come from different individuals for this effect to occur. Stroop (1932) showed that averaging 50 judgments by one individual led to an increase in accuracy fully comparable to that obtained by combining 50 different individuals' single judgments into a group score.

Another statistical inevitability (Zajonc, 1962, 1966) is that a pooling of individual judgments will increase accuracy only if the majority of individuals making judgments have a fair chance of being correct (as was the case in the studies just cited). However, if the majority of the individuals are fundamentally wrong, combining individual judgments should compound the errors and lead to a *decrease* in accuracy under "group" conditions. A study by Klugman (1945) lends some support to this idea. During World War II, Allied strategy was to seek victory in the European theater and only then devote full resources to victory in the Pacific. The war in Europe thus progressed much faster than the war in the

Pacific, where events did not suggest a forseeable end. In 1944 Klugman had soldiers predict the dates of the two armistices. In the case of the treaty with Germany, where the "handwriting was on the wall," the pooled judgments were superior to the individual judgments. In the case of the armistice with Japan, this superiority on the part of pooled judgments was not maintained.

Thus, knowing the quality of individual judgments is important if we want to predict the effects of combining them to reach a group verdict. If, in a group, each person's contribution is given equal weight and is not influenced by the contributions of the other group members, group judgments should be better than individual judgments if the individual judgments are better than could be expected by chance alone. If individual judgments are worse than would be predicted by chance, then individual judgments will be better than group judgments. In other words, competent and astute individuals should profit by combining their judgments; incompetent individuals might do better by leaving one another alone.

Of course, this discussion of the effects of pooling individual contributions is a simplification, because the assumptions that individual judgments will be given equal weight and that each individual judgment will not be influenced by the other judgments are not always met. For example, people will have differential influence in a discussion (Chapter 9), so we might expect some people's contributions to be given more weight than other people's. If the leader is so designated because of his or her expertise and is very influential in the discussion, then even in a group in which the average member is incompetent there may be some gains for the members by staying in the group. If, on the other hand, the most influential person in the group is incompetent, astute members might be wise to drop out. As this discussion suggests, the *way* in which individual contributions are pooled also has an effect on the quality of a group decision.

Rules for Combining Individual Contributions

Let's suppose that three school systems are attempting to hire new teachers. In one system a decision is made individually, by the principal. In a second system a decision is based on the majority vote of two out of three people—for example, principal, superintendent, and president of the PTA. In a third school system there are again three decision makers, but the decision is based on unanimity. In this last case, each decision maker has the power to veto—that is, can overrule any applicant he or she does not like.

Let's further suppose that, on the average, one out of five candidates will prove acceptable to any given interviewer. Application of simple formulas for estimating probabilities suggests the following: In the first system, about five candidates would have to be interviewed before an acceptable teacher was found. In the second system, about eight applicants would have to be interviewed before any two interviewers reached agreement. In the third system, about 125 candidates would most likely be required. Thus, if speed is one criterion, the individual decision maker would seem most efficient. Under conditions of unanimity rule (as in the third system), the larger the number of decision makers, the harder it should be to reach agreement.

Because unanimity is so hard to achieve, there is a strong temptation to believe that it must be right. For example, a single interviewer could base a choice of a teacher on his or her own idiosyncratic likes and dislikes (for example, ignoring a teacher's ability to work with children and choosing one who could work well with the PTA), which could spell disaster in the classroom. Although unanimity rule might seem to solve this problem, in fact it would not. Under conditions of unanimity rule, a wrong-thinking decision maker could veto the objectively best alternative because it does not meet his or her idiosyncratic needs.

Smoke and Zajonc (1962) have derived formulas for predicting the likelihood that group decisions will be correct given the rule the group uses for reaching a decision and the probability that any given member is correct. Figure 10–2 shows $h(p)$, the probability that the group response will be correct given p, the probability that any individual is correct. These particular computations are based on a group of five persons. As you can see, simple majority (three out of five) is the most likely to be correct, and an individual's decision can be better than a unanimous decision. Smoke and Zajonc also show that, the larger the group, the greater the advantage of a simple majority over unanimity rule. For all these formulas to work, however, we must once again assume that, on the whole, the people with the best ideas are neither more nor less influential than the less clever members of the group.

Type of Task and Group Performance

A third important determinant of group performance is the nature of the task. In a penetrating analysis of group problem solving, Kelley and Thibaut (1969) have identified some conditions under which the performance of the group will be *worse* than the performance of the best-performing member, about *equal* to the performance of the best-performing member, and *better* than the performance of the best-performing member.

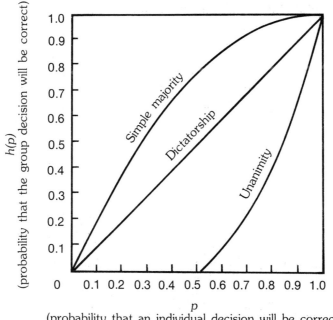

Figure 10-2. Probability that a group decision will be correct given the rule used for deriving a decision and the likelihood that an individual decision will be correct. (Adapted from "On the Reliability of Group Judgments and Decisions," by W. H. Smoke and R. B. Zajonc. In J. Criswell, H. Solomon, & P. Suppes (Eds.), *Mathematical Methods in Small Group Processes.* Copyright 1962 by Stanford University Press. Used by permission.)

Group performance is typically *worse* than the performance of the best-performing member when the problem can be approached from many different angles. In this case it is difficult for the people in the group to reach agreement concerning the best way to proceed. Ideas offered by different members tend to disrupt people's chain of thought, and each person confuses the others. Thus, with very complicated problems that do not have one right solution, the group tends to handicap the most proficient individual members.

Group performance is about *equal* to that of the best-performing member when the group is tackling an **insight problem.** Solutions to such problems involve few steps and, once found by one person, can immediately be recognized as correct by other persons. For example, in the "coat-rack" problem, subjects are given two long thin planks and a clamp and are told to construct a coat rack. The solution requires

viewing the clamp as a hook, and using it to brace the two planks between the ceiling and the floor. Once such a solution is found, it suddenly
seems obvious to all, and there is an "Aha" experience.

Let's consider what might happen in noninteracting nominal groups
and in real groups grappling with this problem. We can suppose that each
person will eventually derive the solution alone, but it will take each one
a different amount of time. The fastest person figures it out in 20 minutes,
the second fastest in 50 minutes, the third fastest in 70 minutes, and the
slowest person in 100 minutes. Individual or "nominal-group" performance can be expressed in terms of the average amount of time taken to
derive the solution, which in this case would be $(20 + 50 + 70 + 100)/4$,
or 60 minutes. But in the real or interacting group, the answer provided
by the fastest thinker would immediately be accepted by each of the
others. All would, in effect, have the solution in the same amount of time
as the fastest, which in this example is 20 minutes. Since only one person
can be the most proficient in the group, all other members profit when
the group's performance is raised to be in line with this person's. The
average savings in thinking time per person is 40 minutes, and the slowest
member of the group has saved 80 minutes.

Group performance is *better* than that of the most proficient member
if no one has the complete solution but each person has something to
contribute toward it. For example, Faust (1959) had subjects solve series
of anagrams, or words in which the letters have been scrambled. After
solving one anagram—and only then—the group could proceed to the next.
Usually one person was able to solve the first anagram but not the second,
whereas someone else could solve the second but not the first. Members
of the group thus pooled their abilities and insights. Again, this superiority of groups would seem to occur when the tasks or problems can be
broken down into a number of smaller subtasks or segments and when
the various members of the group have complementary skills.

DECISIONS INVOLVING RISK

Should an adventurer remain in the court of Spain or set forth on
a dangerous voyage to discover a new path to the Orient? Should an
appliance manufacturer stick with a stodgy line that has been enjoying
moderate sales for years or switch to some radical new designs? Should a
governor retain state office or resign in the hope of attaining the Presidency? Many such decisions are based in part on an element of chance.
Risk refers to the probability of attaining a prize or reward (or avoiding
a punishment or penalty) under anticipated conditions. As the probability
of a favorable outcome decreases, a decision is said to become "risky."

A major interest in social psychology in the last decade or so has been the risk taking of individuals as compared with the risk taking of groups.

To compare individual and group risk taking, many investigators have followed the procedures of Stoner (1961), who confronted subjects with hypothetical situations and asked them to make recommendations. These **choice dilemmas** require choosing between a more certain but less attractive alternative and a less certain but more attractive alternative. "Risk" in this case is defined in terms of how big a chance the respondent urges *another* person to take. One such dilemma, for example, deals with whether a person should elect to live out his or her days as an invalid or undergo an operation that might prove fatal. The respondent is provided with a number of probabilities or odds that the operation will be a success (9 in 10, 7 in 10, 5 in 10, 3 in 10, and 1 in 10) and is told to indicate the *lowest* probability of success he or she would find acceptable for recommending that the operation be performed.

Other dilemmas are concerned with whether a person should invest money in low-yield, "blue chip" securities or in more risky securities that offer rapid growth potential; whether a football player should choose a play that is certain to produce a tie score or a more difficult play that could lead to either a victory or a defeat; and whether a physicist should work on a long-term, significant, but very difficult problem or on an easier but less important problem. All told, there are 12 choice dilemmas on the **Choice-Dilemma Questionnaire (CDQ).** In each case, respondents indicate the *minimum* acceptable odds for recommending the gamble. Choosing the gamble on the basis of low odds of success (such as 1 in 10) is considered risky, and choosing the gamble only if the odds are high (such as 7 in 10) is considered conservative.

Extremity Shifts

Stoner's subjects were graduate students in industrial management. First they made individual decisions concerning dispositions of the various dilemmas. Experimental subjects were then formed into groups of six and were instructed to discuss the problems and to reach a unanimous recommendation. Control subjects restudied the problems and rated them alone a second time. Finally, subjects in both conditions again made private ratings. From what we know about conformity, we might expect a convergence of judgments toward a position of moderation; that is, risky people should become less risky and conservative people less conservative. However, Stoner found that group decisions were *more* risky than individual decisions and that this new riskiness was to some extent maintained in the individual decisions that followed group participation. The unexpected move toward greater risk was termed the **risky shift.** As Cartwright (1971) notes, a new level of riskiness following group discussion shows only a shift toward risk; it does not mean that an individual will be more conservative than a group when each is confronted with a risk-taking problem for the first time.

These findings triggered an avalanche of studies, about 80% of which used the CDQ (Cartwright, 1971). A fair number of these investigations, using both the CDQ and other measures of risk taking, have found evidence suggesting a group-induced shift toward risk (Cartwright, 1971; Clark, 1971; Pruitt, 1971; Clark & Willems, 1972). For example, Wallach, Kogan, and Bem (1962) gave the CDQ to more than 200 undergraduates and found risky shifts in 14 out of 14 groups of males and in 12 out of 14 groups of females. In another series of studies, this same trio sought a risky shift under conditions in which the risk-taking problems were not hypothetical and the outcomes of the subjects' decisions had some personal consequences (Wallach, Kogan, & Bem, 1964). In one of these studies, subjects selected questions to answer from old College Board exams. Perceived riskiness was varied by telling subjects that between 10% and 90% of the people attempting to answer a given question had failed. Cash prizes were offered for correct answers, and larger prizes were associated with the more difficult questions (that is, the questions that had most frequently been missed). There were several conditions, and, for the most part, risky shifts predominated. In another study by the same authors, an elaborate procedure was used to emphasize the negative consequences of failure. Subjects were told that, while taking part in a simple task, they would be subjected to various kinds of stimuli that could produce very unpleasant side effects, such as headache, nausea, dizziness, and stomach cramps. If they were incapacitated and could not complete the task, they would not get paid. They had to choose between a condition in which both the likelihood of the side effects and the amount of pay were low and a condition in which both of these factors were high. In most cases there was again a shift toward greater risk taking in the discussion-group situation.

However, there is also a large body of studies that have not supported the risky-shift finding. Lonergan and McClintock (1961), for instance, found no differences between individual and group bets on a modified wheel of fortune. More problematic yet are the findings of shifts in the conservative direction. Several investigators were able to rewrite the choice dilemmas in such a way that group decisions favored the less risky alternatives (Pruitt, 1971). In an experiment by Zajonc, Wolosin, Wolosin, and Sherman (1968), subjects bet which of two lights would come on. One option gave subjects a .6 chance of winning 4¢, and the other gave them a .4 chance of winning 6¢. Each choice was equally rational, because in the long run one could expect to win an average of 2.4¢ per trial. Half the subjects placed 160 bets alone and then 160 bets in groups, whereas the other half of the subjects bet first in groups and then as individuals. There was a shift toward greater conservatism in the groups. In a later study by some of the same authors, additional evidence of a conservative shift was obtained (Zajonc, Wolosin, & Wolosin, 1972).

These findings do not eliminate the possibility that interacting in groups can increase risk taking, but they do mean that the well-publicized risky-shift phenomenon has considerably less generality than was once thought. It is dependent on the subjects selected, the procedures used, and the specific tasks involved. Furthermore, the finding of shifts in a conservative direction suggests that the "risky shift" may be a part of the larger and more general phenomenon of **extremity shifts** (Cartwright, 1971; Insko & Schopler, 1972). To understand group-induced shifts in risk taking, then, we need a theory that explains greater polarization of decisions under group conditions, and it is better to think in terms of extremity shifts than in terms of "risky shift" alone. Unfortunately, as Cartwright (1971) notes, many of the early explanations focused on shifts toward the risky end of the continuum and are ill equipped to accommodate conservative shifts.

Because the risky shift did not fit in with pre-existing theories, the early risky-shift findings generated a host of interpretations, many of which did not withstand even cursory examination. Following Clark

(1971) and Pruitt (1971), we can classify the hardier theories as *familiarization theory, value theories, diffusion-of-responsibility theory,* and *information-exchange theory.*

Familiarization Theory

As shown in Chapter 3, novel stimuli often elicit feelings of discomfort, but these apprehensions are likely to disappear as the stimuli become familiar. Bateson (1966) has suggested that, since the problems presented in choice dilemmas are novel and unusual, people approach them with anxiety. Discussing these problems in the group setting results in their becoming familiar, and, with apprehensions lessened, it becomes easier to take a chance. According to this line of reasoning, anything that leads to increased familiarity with the choice dilemmas should result in a risky shift. In support of this theory, Bateson (1966) and Flanders and Thistlethwaite (1967) have shown that, when isolated subjects thoroughly acquainted themselves with the choice dilemmas, there was a shift comparable in magnitude to that produced by the group discussion. However, at least half a dozen studies have not supported the familiarization hypothesis (Pruitt, 1971), and the theory does not seem to easily account for conservative shifts.

Value Theories

A family of explanations of extremity shifts revolves around the premium our culture places on dash and derring-do. The best known is Brown's (1965) hypothesis that risky alternatives are often socially desirable alternatives. People may regard their relatively conservative "alone" decision as risky. Then, placed in the group, they discover that they are cowards compared with the riskier members. Following this social comparison, they shift in the direction of greater risk in order to prove their mettle. Under conditions in which conservative courses of action are culturally valued, social comparison should lead to a conservative shift.

A second interpretation based on interpersonal comparisons and social values is that, during isolated judgments, people favor an extreme alternative but assume that others would be more moderate in their choices. To live up to the assumed group norms, they choose a moderate alternative. However, in the group they discover that other members also seem to be leaning toward the risky (or conservative) extreme. This discovery has a disinhibiting effect that frees them to make an extreme judgment too (Levinger & Schneider, 1969; Pruitt, 1971).

Because there are several versions, theories involving values are perhaps the most difficult to assess. However, a recent study by Baron, Roper, and Baron (1974) reveals a difficulty in relying on a simple value interpretation of extremity shifts. These investigators hypothesized that, if value theory is correct, group discussion should lead to a shift in the direction of the socially desirable extreme even when risk taking is not involved. In our society, generosity and charity are considered more desirable than stinginess and selfishness. In a comparison of individual and group decisions concerning personal pledges to the Iowa Bengali Relief Fund, Baron et al. found group decisions to be less generous than individual decisions (see Figure 10-3). Since stinginess is regarded as undesirable, this "stingy shift" conflicts with the obvious value-theory prediction. As the authors note, another value might have been operating

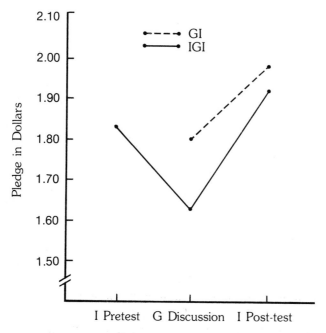

Figure 10-3. The stingy shift. The graph shows mean personal donations in the individual and group conditions. In the GI condition, subjects made decisions first in groups and then as individuals. In the IGI condition, subjects first made individual decisions, then group decisions, and then individual decisions again. (From "Group Discussion and the Stingy Shift," by R. S. Baron, G. Roper, and P. H. Baron, *Journal of Personality and Social Psychology*, 1974, *30*, 542. Copyright 1974 by the American Psychological Association. Reprinted by permission.)

in this experiment. Specifically, we also value not coercing others, and, as subjects sat around trying to decide how much money to pledge, this value might have outweighed the value usually placed on generosity. Nonetheless, the stingy-shift phenomenon is damaging to value theory because it shows that we cannot always predict an extremity shift on the basis of one relevant value. Other factors must be entered into the equation.

Diffusion-of-Responsibility Theory

According to the diffusion-of-responsibility interpretation, there is a fixed amount of responsibility for any given decision or action. As noted in earlier contexts, this responsibility may weigh entirely on one individual's shoulders or may be distributed among a number of people in a group. In the course of a group discussion, emotional bonds are formed that make diffusion likely. The result is that each member feels less personally responsible and hence less culpable if an undesirable event comes to pass. Freed of responsibility, the individual is more willing to take a chance in a group situation.

Certain findings are consistent with this interpretation of extremity shifts. For example, although Wallach, Kogan, and Bem (1964) found for the most part that groups induced shifts in the direction of choosing difficult or risky questions to answer, there was an interesting exception. When one member of the group was assigned complete responsibility for answering the question for the whole group, and was aware that the whole group's fortune hinged on his or her performance, that individual tended to become conservative. However, some other findings conflict with diffusion-of-responsibility notions. Baron, Roper, and Baron (1974) noted that, if their stingy shift were caused by diffusion of responsibility, one would expect both initially generous and initially stingy subjects to become less charitable in the group situation. Instead they found that only the initially generous subjects became stingy in the group setting. They interpret this result as showing that generous subjects were reluctant to try to embarrass or otherwise force the tightwads into contributing more money. On the whole, the batting average of the diffusion-of-responsibility theory seems to have been pretty good. However, this interpretation also seems a bit too limited to account for all extremity-shift phenomena.

Information-Exchange Theory

Information-exchange approaches suggest that new information is brought out in the course of the group discussion that may cause people to reassess their initial position. The importance of information flow was shown by Lamm (1967), who limited the number of channels for communication and found that under conditions of decreased communication there was decreased shift. That is, Lamm found the greatest shifts when subjects participated in face-to-face discussions, lesser shifts when subjects watched and listened through a one-way screen, and the smallest shifts when subjects merely listened to the discussion.

According to Vinokur (1971a, 1971b), persuasive arguments are brought out in the course of group discussions. These arguments cause the members to reassess the alternatives and change their decisions. Each alternative has some arguments in its favor. When the isolated individual chooses an alternative, selection is on the basis of the arguments that he or she has been able to uncover. Vinokur suggests that, when people are placed into interacting groups, the arguments others have found will also be uncovered. If the majority of arguments favor riskier alternatives, then there will be a risky shift; if the preponderance of arguments favor conservative alternatives, there will be a conservative shift. A shift will be unlikely if it is very easy for the average person to uncover the arguments (there will be few new arguments left to be brought out in the group) or if it is very hard for the average person to uncover them (if no one in the group is able to discover them, then they cannot be introduced).

A large number of recent results are consistent with the idea that people are rational beings who consider the arguments, assess the probabilities and values of various outcomes, and then render rational decisions. In one study, members of the group argued either for the position they had initially chosen or for a different position. Only when these people had argued their true position, and hence were able to use their best arguments, did extremity shifts occur (Burnstein & Vinokur, 1973). This result suggests that the uncovering of new and persuasive arguments is an important prerequisite of extremity shifts. In another study, Burnstein, Vinokur, and Trope (1973) varied both social comparison and the number of persuasive arguments. According to value theory, social comparison should affect extremity shifts because it allows people to discover that they are too moderate by other people's standards, but the number of persuasive arguments should not make much difference. According to information-exchange theory, the number of persuasive arguments should affect extremity shifts, but social-comparison processes should not make much difference. It was found in this study that, whereas a discrepancy between one's own position and another's position (social comparison) was not related to extremity shifts, the number of persuasive arguments was clearly and predictably related to such shifts.

Information-exchange theory has the advantage that it can account for risky shifts, conservative shifts, and no shifts. "Familiarization" results can be understood if we recognize that, in the process of familiarization, a subject is likely to uncover new arguments. Certain "value" results are also interpretable within the information-exchange framework. Although it has been noted that extreme risk takers are admired, Burnstein, Vinokur, and Pichevin (1974) found that the cause of this admiration was not that these people adhered to a social ideal but that observers believed that someone willing to take an extreme position must have some very good reasons for his or her choice. Thus the information-exchange interpretation of group-induced extremity shifts is very promising.

Perhaps few tasks are as difficult as assessing the complex jumble of studies which constitute extremity-shift research. Some investigators have found one kind of shift, some investigators have found another kind of shift, and some investigators have found no shifts at all. Each interpretation of extremity shifts has had some confirming and some disconfirming experiments, and on occasion the same experiments have been cited by one author as supporting one particular theory and by another author as refuting the exact same theory. (My own feeling is that at present information-exchange theory seems to be doing better than the others.) At this point only two conclusions are inescapable. First, well-publicized findings that groups can be "riskier" than individuals hold true only under a limited range of conditions; under alternative conditions, individuals can be "riskier" than groups. Second, any satisfactory explanation of extremity shifts must do an equally good job of explaining risky and conservative shifts.

PART SUMMARY

Social-facilitation research examines changes in individual performance under coaction and audience conditions. A wide range of coaction and audience studies suggests that the presence of others improves performance but impairs learning. Zajonc' mere-presence interpretation suggests that the presence of others raises drive, which in turn energizes the dominant response. If the dominant response is "right," there is a beneficial effect on behavior, but, if it is "wrong," there is a detrimental effect on behavior. The evaluation-apprehension hypothesis suggests that the source of drive is the performer's perception that he or she is to be evaluated by others. Although it has been shown that raising the likelihood and closeness of evaluation has response-strengthening effects, "mere presence" is not necessarily excluded as a source of drive.

Many studies have examined what happens when individual performances are combined to yield some form of group performance source. In some cases, groups are absolutely necessary for accomplishing the task at hand. In other cases the task can be tackled either by individuals or by groups. Although there is a widespread belief in the superiority of group endeavor, the relative superiority of groups depends on the abilities of the group members, the procedures used in deriving a group product, and the nature of the task.

Early studies showed that individual judgments were inferior to judgments representing the average of the judgments of group members. Pooling judgments by a number of individuals (or pooling a number of judgments by one individual) may have the effect of reducing error variance. If each member of the group has a good chance of being right, pooled judgments will be superior to individual judgments, but, if each member of the group has a good chance of being wrong, the pooling of judgments will only exaggerate the errors.

Procedures for combining individual judgments into a group judgment are also important determinants of the quality of group performance. Group decisions, particularly if they require unanimity, take a long time to reach. Assuming that each person makes an independent judgment and that each individual's judgment is given equal weight, a decision is most likely to be right if it is reached by a simple majority and least likely to be right if it is reached by unanimity.

The nature of the task can also affect the performance of individuals and groups. When the task is complex and requires consistency of approach, group performance is worse than that of the best-performing member. If the solution requires few steps and, once discovered, is easily understandable by all, group performance is about equal to that of the best-performing member. If no one person has the solution but each person can contribute to it, group performance is typically better than that of the best-performing member.

Stoner compared risk taking by isolated individuals with later risk taking by individuals in interacting groups. His finding of a shift toward greater risk taking in the group setting has been replicated by some later researchers but not by others. Although shifts are common, they may occur in the conservative as well as in the risky direction. Theoretical explanations must cover both kinds of extremity shifts. Familiarization explanations suggest that group discussion leads to a lessening of anxiety associated with risks. Value theories suggest that risk taking is a cultural norm that becomes salient in the group setting. Diffusion-of-responsibility theory suggests that people in groups are less likely to feel guilty if something goes wrong. Finally, information-exchange theory, which has the capacity to integrate many findings, suggests that whether or not a risky or conservative shift occurs depends on the number and nature of the arguments advanced. Because of the number of findings in this controversial area, many of these theories are difficult to assess. What does seem clear is that extremity shifts are common and that any adequate theory must take both kinds of polarizations into account.

GROUP PROPERTIES AND GROUP PERFORMANCE

The British Secret Service was in the business of turning out agents and operatives (spies and saboteurs) for duty behind enemy lines in World War II. To ferret out the most promising candidates, all nominees underwent extremely rigorous testing. Since many assignments required teamwork, some of this testing took place in groups. The groupstacle (group obstacle) course, described by Morgan (1957), required that a team of six men carry a 10-foot log over a 400-yard course. It was necessary to work the log over a 10-foot-high wall, under a heavy tarpaulin stretched out on the ground, over a 20-foot-high tree branch, and across a deep, muddy stream. The course record was 4 minutes 16 seconds. In highly efficient teams there was enthusiasm, good humor, loyalty, and friendship. Other, less coordinated teams could not finish within the allotted 45 minutes. In these teams there was hostility, distrust, and dissension.

As Morgan's report suggests, some groups perform at a better level than other groups. A major research interest in the area of problem solving and productivity is identification of the factors accounting for the different performances of different groups. Among the group properties or variables studied are (1) lines of communication within the group, (2) conformity, and (3) cohesiveness, or group spirit and morale. Another important factor related to group performance—leadership—is discussed separately in the next chapter.

COMMUNICATIONS NETS

Communication patterns within groups have dramatic effects on the efficiency with which the groups accomplish different tasks and also on the level of satisfaction expressed by group members. To study this variable, experimenters construct communications networks or **nets,** which require that communications flow along artificially imposed channels. Typically, subjects are seated around a table and separated by partitions, informed of the restrictions, and given a task to complete. Examples of some five-person nets—the wheel, the Y, the chain, the circle, and the comcon—are presented in Figure 10-4. Lines designate the approved channels, and circles represent the five members of the group. In the **wheel,** for example, all communications must pass through the person in the middle, whereas in the **circle** each person may communicate only with the person on his or her immediate left and right. **Comcon** is an abbreviation for "completely connected": each member of a comcon net

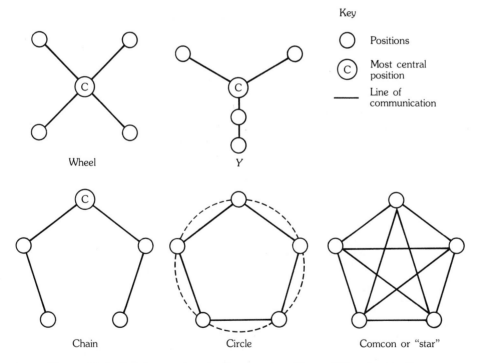

Figure 10-4. Some communications nets. (From "Communications Networks," by M. E. Shaw. In L. Berkowitz (Ed.), *Advances in Experimental Social Psychology,* Vol. 1, p. 113. Copyright 1964 by Academic Press, Inc. Reprinted by permission.)

has a direct channel to every other person, and communication can flow without restriction.

At least 20 nets have been examined experimentally (Shaw, 1964; Collins & Raven, 1969). The organizing concepts are distance and centrality. **Distance** is measured by the number of people a message must pass through to get from one person to another by the shortest route. **Centrality** refers to the location of a position with respect to all other positions. A position is said to be central within a network to the extent that a large number of messages must pass through it. In the wheel, for example, position C is central in that the person in that position serves as a sort of switchboard operator or clearinghouse for messages between all the other participants. At the other extreme are the circle and the comcon, in which no position is more central than any other. In the circle everyone can communicate with the person on his or her left or right, and with the remaining two people through only one intermediary.

Centrality and Performance

In one early study, Leavitt (1951) compared the circle, chain, Y, and wheel. Each of the five persons in the nets was given a card showing five (out of a possible six) symbols. Only one of the five symbols appeared on everyone's card, and the task was to discover this common symbol by passing messages along the authorized channels. In terms of the number of messages required for solution and the number of errors made, performance was better in the more centralized wheel and Y than in the less centralized chain and circle.

Using math problems, Shaw (1954) obtained completely different results. Subjects in the decentralized circle found the solutions faster and corrected their mistakes more promptly than did subjects in the centralized wheel. The key here seems to be the difficulty of the task involved (Shaw, 1964; Harshberger, 1971). Centralized nets are more efficient when the task is simple and the person in the central position merely collects and distributes messages. Less centralized nets are more efficient when the task is complex and requires a voluminous flow of messages. Under these latter conditions, the person in the central position may have trouble maintaining the necessary pace. Shaw's (1964) comparison of subsequent studies using simple tasks (identification of colors or symbols) with those using complex tasks (math, word-arrangement, sentence-construction, or discussion problems) confirms this hypothesis. Shaw has also noted that, since the tasks facing real-life discussion groups are likely to be complex, the general rule of thumb is that decentralized nets will be the most efficient.

Centrality and Satisfaction

Although Leavitt's subjects performed better in the more centralized networks, they preferred the less centralized nets. Virtually all subsequent investigations have also found this result (Shaw, 1964; Collins & Raven, 1969). Greater satisfaction within the decentralized nets stems from the greater freedom that the average member has to function in the group.

Disliking of centralized nets is not so commonly reported by the people assigned central positions within them. Because these people are critical for getting the job done, they enjoy positions of power and influence. Indeed, as we might expect from our discussion of communication and leadership in the last chapter, people placed in these high-participation positions are likely to be rated as "leaders" after the sessions are over. Cohen, Bennis, and Wolkon (1962) had the same subjects participate in both wheels and circles. During the shift from one net to another, some subjects were promoted from a position of less-than-equality (peripheral position in the wheel) to a position of equality (position in the circle) or to a position of greater-than-equality (hub of the wheel). Other subjects were demoted. Although demotions generally resulted in a lowering of satisfaction and promotions in a raising of satisfaction, a demotion from greater-than-equality to equality lowered satisfaction less than a promotion from less-than-equality to equality raised satisfaction.

On the whole, the results of these and other studies challenge an early assumption that the imposition of a rigid organization on a group is invariably beneficial. A high degree of organization can lead to increased efficiency when the task is simple. However, such structuralization can lead to decreased efficiency when the task is complex. Furthermore, for the most part a high degree of organization is a source of dissatisfaction for the average member of the group.

CONFORMITY AND GROUP PERFORMANCE

Group norms coordinate the activities of the group's members, and it seems reasonable to expect that conforming to group norms should yield dividends in terms of level of performance. Indeed, in some cases the level of efficiency and productivity of a group of nonconformists falls below that of a group in which each person conscientiously abides by group standards. However, the relationship between conformity and group performance is not a simple one. Whether conformity raises or lowers group performance depends on the specific norms of the group. Moreover, pressures to conform may limit the expression of novel and unusual solutions to the problems confronting the group.

Conformity and Productivity

If group norms favor productivity, then conformity will be associated with a high level of group performance. If, on the other hand, group norms favor shirking work and socializing or place a minimal emphasis on performance, then increased conformity will be associated with a decrease in group performance (Roethlisberger & Dickson, 1939; Homans, 1950; Schachter, Ellertson, McBride, & Gregory, 1951; Berkowitz, 1954).

Norms of low productivity sometimes develop in the industrial work setting. Although the overall goal of the organization is to produce as much as possible, norms within the work group may place a ceiling on members' performance. The fear is likely to develop that outstanding performance today could lead to higher minimal standards tomorrow. That is, workers are afraid that, if the boss discovers that they can perform a little better than he or she thought, this high level of performance may be expected to become routine. To prevent this from happening, production may be slowed down or hidden and not reported until some later time.

Conformity and Problem Solving

Some problems call for novel solutions. However, conformity to established ways of doing things may inhibit the flow of creative solutions. Because group members are fearful of ridicule or rejection for departing from established ways, they may not voice unorthodox ideas.

Brainstorming represents an attempt to deal with the inhibiting effects of group membership (Osborn, 1957). The procedure is to create an informal atmosphere that encourages complete freedom of expression. Participants are sternly admonished to withhold criticism until all ideas have been presented, and they are encouraged to elaborate on one another's ideas, no matter how ridiculous they initially sound. Later the alternatives are evaluated and their practicality assessed. An interacting group is considered important, because members can stimulate one another to new heights of creativity. Advocates of this procedure suggest that people can think up more and better ideas in a brainstorming group than they can think up in isolation or in a group that is not following brainstorming instructions.

Unfortunately, the results are not quite so simple as brainstorming buffs might have us believe. The brainstorming package involves two variables that have to be separated. One variable is the use of instructions to express oneself freely, elaborate on all ideas, and withhold censure and criticism. Such instructions can be given to individuals as well as to groups. The second variable is the type of group the individual is working in—that is, whether it is interacting or nominal. When subjects who are given brainstorming instructions are compared with controls who are not, the typical finding has been that more and better ideas are produced following brainstorming instructions (Shaw, 1971). However, when brainstorming instructions are given to all subjects, and then a comparison is made of nominal-group and real-group performances, it does not seem that people in interacting groups spur one another on to new levels of ingenuity.

In accordance with this last point are the findings of Taylor, Berry, and Block (1958), who compared the number and quality of solutions to problems given by a real group, consisting of four people who interacted and brainstormed, with those given by a nominal group, consisting of four isolated individuals whose solutions were pooled for purposes of analysis. Problems included listing the practical advantages or disadvantages that would be encountered if we each had three thumbs, exploring the difficulties that would arise if people averaged 6'8" tall and weighed twice as much as they actually do now, and devising ways for our educational system to handle a 50% rise in the number of students. Nominal groups devised more solutions to these problems, and the quality of their solutions was adjudged higher. In a different study, which involved research scientists and advertising personnel as subjects, Dunnette, Campbell, and Jaastad (1963) also found that nominal groups operating under brainstorming instructions did better than interacting groups operating under brainstorming instructions. Once again it would seem that a real-group setting can have an inhibiting influence that stifles creativity. The results of these studies do not suggest that one person working alone necessarily did a better job than four persons working together. What they do suggest is that, with the types of creative problems involved and the types of instructions given, four individuals working alone performed better than four individuals working in a group.

More recent research suggests that the extent to which the constraining effects of group membership impair problem solving depends on the phase of the problem-solving process. Vroom, Grant, and Cotton (1969) gave real and nominal groups "real-life" administrative problems to solve. The problem solving was separated into two phases: in the generation phase, alternatives were introduced; in the evaluation phase, the alternatives were appraised. Nominal and real groups were compared in each of these phases. The most striking finding was that the real groups came up with fewer and lower-quality solutions than did the nominal groups; moreover, the real groups required about eight times as much time for solution as the nominal groups. However, a finer breakdown traces this difference mostly to the generation phase. There was some evidence that interaction during the evaluation phase led to better assessments of the various alternatives.

In sum, in accordance with brainstorming principles, there may be a beneficial effect when people are told not to censor their ideas. However, there may be more liberation in isolation than in the interacting group, since it is difficult to defer our judgments of others' ideas and to expect that others will withhold their criticisms of our ideas in return. Recent findings suggest that a combinatorial approach, involving individual, followed by group, sessions, may be best. In this way, ideas that come out more freely in the individual setting can be more carefully assessed in the group setting.

COHESIVENESS AND PERFORMANCE

Perhaps some of you *Late Show* addicts have shared with me the following thrilling experience. A steaming jungle appears on the screen, with a road in the foreground. Very softly, just audible amid the gibbering monkeys and shrieking parrots, can be heard the approaching tramp of marching feet. The footsteps gain in audibility, and then, around a corner in the road, the men suddenly appear. Dressed in tatters, and suffering from vitamin deficiencies, anemia, and bunions, they nonetheless march in perfect cadence to the snappy, whistled strains of *The Colonel Bogey March*. These bedraggled troops, led by Alec Guinness, are somehow superior to the better-fed, better-dressed enemy guards hovering on the fringes. At least, this is how I remember a scene from *The Bridge on the River Kwai*.

Some groups have a certain sparkle, verve, and sense of purpose, whereas others are lackluster and apathetic. This camaraderie has long been noticed by militarists, who have imbued it with magical powers. Early in World War I, for example, it was supposed to compensate for German machine-gun bullets, and late in World War II for overwhelming Allied superiority. Today we speak of "cohesiveness" and recognize that it is an important variable in many groups—civilian as well as military.

As noted in Chapter 2, cohesiveness refers to the extent to which members are interested and involved in the group. Lott and Lott (1965) have suggested that cohesiveness may be regarded as the degree of unification within the group. Unification implies a shared frame of reference and common motives. Measures of cohesiveness usually involve an assessment of whether or not the members find the group attractive (Cartwright, 1968). Attitudinally, cohesiveness would be revealed by the extent to which the group members like one another or the group as a whole.

Behaviorally, cohesiveness would be revealed by approach behavior directed toward the group. For example, prompt and regular appearances for group activities would imply high cohesiveness, whereas tardiness, absenteeism, membership turnover, and quick exits after meetings would indicate low cohesiveness.

Cohesiveness is important as both an independent and a dependent variable. Since cohesiveness is considered a desirable end state, we will investigate some of its antecedents. Because cohesiveness has some implications for productivity and problem solving, we will also consider some of its consequences.

Antecedents of Cohesiveness

For the most part, the antecedents of cohesiveness have been sought in terms of the rewards and satisfactions provided by group membership (Cartwright, 1968). In Thibaut and Kelley's (1959) terms, the extent to which outcomes within the group are more favorable than outcomes obtainable elsewhere determines the group's cohesiveness. There are three principal ways in which groups can provide favorable outcomes: (1) by offering important socioemotional rewards, (2) by sponsoring activities that the members find intrinsically satisfying, and (3) by enabling the members to attain goals they could not achieve as individuals.

First, a friendly, supportive group is likely to be cohesive because it satisfies the members' social and emotional needs. This kind of satisfaction is particularly common in singles clubs and other groups established for the unlucky in love; in associations of the blind, hard of hearing, or otherwise physically handicapped; and in organizations of ex-convicts, ex-mental patients, and other people who may have special difficulties in satisfying their social needs. Lewin, Lippitt, and White (1939) found that groups with democratic and permissive atmospheres were more cohesive than autocratic groups in which orders came down from the top, and Likert (1961) reported that work groups led by considerate and understanding leaders were more cohesive than groups led by inconsiderate leaders. More recently, in a study of Alaskan bush camps, Traylor (1973) found a negative correlation between the number of rough-and-tumble jokes that made fools of group members and an attitudinal measure of cohesiveness.

Second, a group is likely to be cohesive if it engages in activities that the members find intrinsically satisfying. Hobby clubs are a good example. Collectors get together to compare notes and acquisitions, to trade, and to regale one another with catastrophic stories such as the one about the $200 postage stamp that was inadvertently slapped onto a postcard and mailed.

Third, a group is likely to be cohesive if it allows the members to achieve goals that they could not achieve as individuals. Reaching a goal is particularly likely to increase cohesiveness when a high degree of cooperation among group members is required. One interesting study shows that intragroup cooperation coupled with intergroup competition may be particularly satisfying. Myers (1962) put 30 three-man R. O. T. C. rifle teams into competitive leagues in which they tried to outshoot one another and another 30 teams into noncompetitive leagues in which they shot against impersonal standards. Over time the competitive teams became more cohesive than the noncompetitive teams. This effect occurred whether or not the competitive team scored well, which suggests that working together for a common end was sufficient to produce rewards and satisfactions. Of the competing teams, those that were the most successful in the competition were the most cohesive. (Intragroup cooperation coupled with intergroup competition will be considered again in Chapter 12.)

Although most investigators have pointed to rewards and satisfactions as determinants of cohesiveness, some theorists have suggested that frustration and disappointment can bring about cohesiveness. According to dissonance theory (Chapter 5), under certain conditions, high costs, rather than high rewards, may make a group attractive to its members. Aronson and Mills (1959) reasoned that dissonance would arise if people underwent trouble or expense to join a group that turned out to be dull and listless. They further hypothesized that, to reduce this dissonance, the members would raise their evaluations of the group.

To test this hypothesis, the researchers asked a group of women to take part in a group discussion of sex. In a no-initiation control condition, subjects entered the discussion immediately, whereas subjects in two other conditions were told that it was first necessary to take an "embarrassment" test to qualify for participation. In the mild-initiation condition this test consisted of reading aloud nonobscene sex-related words; in the severe-initiation condition it consisted of reading aloud obscenities and sexually explicit prose. The discussion, which took place over an intercom, was rigged to be dry, dull, and poorly conducted. Next the experimenters measured the attractiveness of the group by having the subjects rate the group and the discussion on a number of evaluative scales. In accordance with dissonance-theory predictions, subjects in the severe-initiation condition found the group more attractive than did subjects in the other two conditions. Apparently, then, the harsh initiation gave rise to dissonance, which was reduced by overevaluating the group.

A criticism leveled at this study is that the results are open to a number of alternative, nondissonance interpretations (Gerard & Mathewson, 1966; Elms, 1972). Most of these alternatives hinge on the experiment's sexy nature. For example, one possible explanation for the findings is that, in the severe-initiation condition, women were so excited or aroused by the initiation that even a dull discussion sounded good. Another possibility is that the women in this condition were relieved to discover that the discussion wasn't as dirty as the initiation implied. A third interpretation is that the women who underwent the severe initiation were so happy to pass the test that they gave the group a favorable rating. A fourth explanation is that these women were given reason to expect that later sessions might perk up (obviously, the severe initiation had little relationship to that day's discussion).

At least some of these alternatives were eliminated in an experiment by Gerard and Mathewson (1966), in which women were given electric shocks. Some women, the "initiates," were told that the shock was part of an initiation procedure designed to see if potential group members could remain objective in the face of discomfort, whereas other women, the "noninitiates," were told that the shock was unrelated to their eventual participation in the group discussion. Within each condition, half the women received mild shocks and the other half received severe shocks. Half of the initiates in each of the two shock conditions were told that they had passed the screening test, whereas the other half were told that they had failed. Then, all subjects listened to a tape of a "previous discussion" by the group they were expecting to join. This recording contained a boring conversation on cheating in college. Subjects then rated the group and the discussion.

Consistent with the suffering-leads-to-cohesiveness hypothesis, it was found that, of the initiates, those who received the severe shocks liked the group more than did those who received the mild shocks. This result supports the Aronson and Mills findings. However, in the case of the noninitiates, greater shock was associated with decreased liking for the group. This finding would seem to eliminate arousal interpretations of severity-of-initiation results. It was also found that the women who were told that they had passed the initiation did not like the group more than the women who had been told that they had failed. This finding would seem to eliminate the possibility that severe-initiation women liked the group better simply because they were more relieved at having passed the test. By replicating Aronson and Mills' findings using very different procedures and by systematically eliminating a number of alternative explanations of severity-of-initiation results, Gerard and Mathewson provided further confirmation for the hypothesis that, under certain conditions, costs, rather than rewards, are associated with attraction to a group. Remember, however, that, for dissonance reduction to raise cohesiveness, a "price of admission" must be associated with membership, and joining must to some extent be voluntary. In the absence of either or both of these conditions, we would expect dull and uninteresting groups to be less cohesive than stimulating and exciting groups.

To conclude our discussion of the antecedents of cohesiveness, we should note that some studies have measured cohesiveness in terms of the feelings of attraction between each possible pair of people in the group. In effect, cohesiveness is some sort of aggregate friendship score. It is not too surprising that by this procedure the same factors that lead to interpersonal attraction lead to cohesiveness. Thus propinquity, similarity, need complementarity, and other "liking" variables discussed in Chapter 6 have been associated with group cohesiveness (Lott & Lott, 1965).

Cohesiveness, Conformity, and Productivity

Cohesiveness, conformity, and productivity are closely interrelated. Cohesiveness increases conformity. Increased conformity, as we already know, can lead to either better or worse performance, depending on the nature of the group's norms. First let's consider some studies that have related cohesiveness to conformity, and then we'll look at some studies that have related cohesiveness to productivity.

In a now-classic study, Festinger, Schachter, and Back (1950) studied uniformities of opinion in two student housing developments. One development consisted of apartments in barracks-like structures, and the other was made up of U-shaped clusters of cottages. Apartment entrances were arranged so that residents rarely encountered one another as they moved around the area. Because of this lack of contact, the apartment dwellers were not really involved with one another, and they constituted, at best, a low-cohesive group. Among the apartment dwellers there was little uniformity of opinion. The cottage entrances, on the other hand, were arranged in such a way that residents frequently encountered one another. The cottage dwellers were interested in and involved with one another, and in these high-cohesive groups there was considerable uniformity of opinion. Apparently contact led to cohesiveness, which in turn led to conformity.

It would appear that cohesive groups are characterized by a high degree of communication and interaction, which are in turn responsible for a high degree of conformity. Back (1951) compared interaction in low-cohesive and high-cohesive dyads. High cohesiveness was induced by telling the two people that they'd like each other, by stressing the importance of group goals, or by inducing the members to believe that the dyad was prestigious. Members of the pair were then instructed to combine efforts and produce a story about some pictures. Communication within the dyad was carefully recorded. More influence attempts were made and accepted in the high-cohesive than in the low-cohesive dyads. Furthermore, in the high-cohesive dyads influence attempts were rather evenly distributed, whereas in the low-cohesive dyads one person attempted to dominate the other. In a later study, Lott and Lott (1961) gave 15 groups of students from ongoing organizations topics to discuss. An index of group cohesiveness was obtained from a questionnaire, and scores were correlated with communication levels (a tally of the frequency of communications) and conformity (defined in terms of uniformity of opinions). Cohesiveness correlated .43 with communication and .54 with conformity, showing a close interrelationship among these variables.

Group members will direct communications toward nonconformists or "deviants" in an attempt to swing them back into line; if this attempt fails, the deviants will be rejected by the group. This tendency to reject nonconformists is particularly pronounced in highly cohesive groups (Schachter, 1951; Janis, 1971, 1974). Treatment of deviants was studied experimentally by Schachter (1951), who planted confederates within ongoing discussion groups. One confederate, "the mode," was instructed to agree with the consensus of the naïve majority. A second confederate, "the slider," was instructed to initially disagree with the group's consensus but to later adopt the majority view. The third confederate, or "pure deviant," adamantly maintained a position that conflicted with the viewpoint of the group. High cohesiveness was established in some groups by having the members engage in an activity that they found fun and exciting, and low cohesiveness was established in other groups by having members engage in a noninteresting discussion task. In addition, Schachter arranged that the issue on which the pure deviant noncon-formed was either of high relevance or of low relevance with respect to the group's avowed interests. He reasoned that, because relevant issues are more important to the group than irrelevant issues, reactions to the nonconformist would be more intense under high-relevance conditions.

Later, subjects were instructed to nominate group members for various committee assignments and to privately indicate whom they would like to see ejected from the group. Results indicated that: (1) within each group the deviant was more likely to be rejected than was the mode or the slider; (2) greater rejection occurred in the high-cohesive groups, as indicated by the exclusion measure; and (3) greater rejection occurred in the high-relevance group, as indicated by the committee-nomination measure.

Since cohesive groups are happy groups and have an overall sense of purpose, one might expect them to also be highly productive. And, indeed, summarized in Lott and Lott's (1965) review is a host of studies suggesting that this is the case. In various experiments, high-cohesive groups have completed more puzzles, done more arithmetic problems, produced stories of higher quality, done better carpentry, and proven to be more combat ready than low-cohesive groups. However, the greater sensitivity to group norms in the more cohesive groups obscures any clear relationship between cohesiveness and high performance. For example, Seashore (1954) studied the relationship between cohesiveness and pro-ductivity in almost 300 industrial work groups. Although there was little correlation between these two variables, workers in the highly cohesive groups consistently produced at about the same level, whereas workers in less cohesive groups showed greater variability in performance. In other words, in the more cohesive groups there was greater adherence to the group's norms of productivity, whatever those norms might be.

Two early experimental studies show that cohesiveness can either raise or lower productivity, depending on whether group members urge one another to reach new, high levels of performance or, alternatively, to hold back on their production. Schachter, Ellertson, McBride, and Gregory (1951) brought together groups of young women and assigned them the task of constructing cardboard checkerboards. Cohesiveness was varied by telling some women that the other members of their group were particularly likable and by telling other subjects that there was no particular reason why they should find the other persons in the work group attractive. During the work session, notes were passed to the women urging either a work speedup or a work slowdown. Results showed a greater receptivity on the part of the high-cohesive groups—but only in the case of the message to slow down. Why did the speedup communication fail to have the anticipated effect? Subjects in Schachter et al.'s high-cohesive groups may have been unable to increase their production because they were already working at maximum speed. In a study by Berkowitz (1954), three-man teams making ashtrays on an assembly-line basis received notes, allegedly from other workers, that contained messages such as "Let's try to set a record" or "We don't have to wear ourselves out making these ashtrays." Not only were the high-cohesive groups more responsive to the speedup communications, but their improved performance was maintained during a later phase when no communications were passed.

Cohesiveness and Problem Solving: The Groupthink Phenomenon

After studying accounts of how U. S. Presidents and their small circles of select advisers have made group decisions, Janis (1971, 1974) hypothesized that "the more amiability and esprit de corps" in a group of decision makers, the less likely it will be that decisions will reflect independent, critical thought. Janis coined the term **groupthink** to refer to the mode of thinking and problem solving in which loyalty to the group and the seeking of agreement replace innovation and objective evaluations. Among the results of groupthink were the decision to escalate the Vietnam War during Lyndon Johnson's administration, the Cuban "Bay of Pigs" invasion plans of John Kennedy's administration, and the decision that led to the conflict between U. S. and Red Chinese troops in Korea.

Janis noted striking parallels between these high-level policy-making groups and groups of sophomores participating in laboratory studies of conformity. In both cases, sessions were marked by a type of conformity in which consensus was more important than the evidence, and reactions to deviants were stern. Not all cohesive groups will suffer from groupthink. A serious deterioration of critical thinking in cohesive groups is most likely when the group is confronted with a crisis that it cannot or will not discuss outside the small circle.

Among the many symptoms of groupthink are: (1) a shared illusion of invulnerability, which generates false optimism and lack of caution; (2) direct pressures on deviants; (3) a fear of disapproval, which keeps new alternatives from emerging, even though each person may secretly be nursing the same idea; (4) an illusion of unanimity such that, when someone representing the majority view speaks, his or her pronouncement is seen as accepted by everyone else in the group; (5) a failure to explore the moral or ethical consequences of group decisions, stemming largely from a fervent belief that the group is morally right; (6) the emergence of "mind guards," who protect the leader from criticism; and (7) group efforts to rationalize or deny all ill omens. Two other symptoms are likely if the group is dealing with some sort of rivals or "opposition." First, there will be a shared and mistaken belief that the leaders of the opposition are evil and stupid. Second, there will be an air of detachment that helps minimize the emotionally stressful aspects of the decision. For example, alternatives may be stated in terms of megatons and body counts, which say nothing about human suffering.

When such symptoms are present, problem solving is likely to be poor. Only one or two alternatives will be considered, and the nonobvious risks and drawbacks associated with the preferred alternative probably will not be discovered. Once an alternative has been rejected, it is unlikely to be reconsidered for hidden advantages. Facts and figures may be interpreted in wishful ways. Moreover, the group is likely to be so sure of the success of its strategy that it fails to establish contingency plans to deal with unforeseen circumstances.

Several safeguards will minimize the deterioration of critical thought. Some involve seeking information and evaluations from people who are not spellbound by the group's magic. For example, each member of the group could discuss deliberations with outsiders, or a few nonmembers might be brought in to attend the group's meetings. In addition, a problem could be assigned to more than one group for the purpose of uncovering new alternatives and arguments. Other safeguards involve changing the procedures for the meetings. Roles might be redefined so that group members become critical evaluators rather than agreeable yes people, one person could be appointed devil's advocate, and part of the session might be spent trying to view things from the opposition's perspective. Finally, after a tentative decision has been reached, there should be a "second-chance" meeting for voicing last-minute doubts and reconsidering all the deliberations. Although most of these safeguards require lifting the mantle of secrecy and all may mar the amiability or cohesiveness of the group, the benefits in terms of quality of decisions should be more than compensatory.

PART SUMMARY

Group productivity and problem solving are affected by a number of group variables, including lines of communication within the group, conformity, and cohesiveness. Communication channels influence the efficiency with which the group solves problems and the members' satisfactions with the group. Centralized communications networks are more efficient for dealing with simple problems, and decentralized networks are more efficient for dealing with complex problems. For the most part, the average group member expresses greater satisfaction with the decentralized networks.

Conformity is associated with good performance when the group norms favor a high level of productivity. When norms favor goldbricking, featherbedding, or putting a ceiling on performance, conformity will lead to a low level of productivity. Conformity can also inhibit the expression of novel or unorthodox solutions to problems, with the result that many good ideas go unvoiced. Brainstorming is a set of procedures designed to eliminate this inhibiting effect of group membership. Although brainstorming instructions can lead to more and better ideas, comparisons of nominal and real groups cast doubt on the overall value of brainstorming. Certain recent results suggest that people should think up ideas in isolation but then evaluate them in an interacting group.

Cohesiveness refers to the degree of unification of the members of a group. It is usually assessed in terms of the extent to which the group's members find one another or the group attractive. Most explanations of cohesiveness point to the satisfactions provided by the group. Groups may be attractive because they satisfy the members' needs for supportive social relationships or because they sponsor activities that the members find intrinsically satisfying or that enable them to attain otherwise inaccessible goals. If a person voluntarily undergoes a severe initiation to gain membership in a worthless group, dissonance reduction may lead to cohesiveness by raising the initiate's evaluation of the group.

Variations in cohesiveness, in turn, affect conformity and productivity. Cohesiveness, influence attempts, and the rejection of deviants are all positively intercorrelated. Studies relating cohesiveness and productivity suggest that cohesiveness leads to adherence to the group's norms of productivity. Since norms may encourage or discourage productivity, cohesiveness does not guarantee a high level of output. In some groups, cohesiveness may lead to a deterioration of problem solving. Attempts to achieve agreement replace critical thought. This phenomenon of "groupthink" may be prevented by bringing people with fresh perspectives into the group or by changing group norms and procedures.

11

Behavior
in Organizations

THREE PERSPECTIVES ON ORGANIZATIONS

THE "RATIONAL" PERSPECTIVE

Scientific Management
Bureaucracy

THE HUMAN-RELATIONS PERSPECTIVE

THE OPEN-SYSTEMS PERSPECTIVE

Specialized Subsystems
Systems Development

PART SUMMARY

MOTIVATION, SATISFACTION, AND PERFORMANCE IN ORGANIZATIONS

EXTRINSIC REWARDS, SATISFACTION, AND PRODUCTIVITY

Individual Rewards
Group Rewards

INTRINSIC REWARDS, SATISFACTION, AND PRODUCTIVITY

Theory X and Theory Y
Hygienic Factors and Motivators
Sources of Intrinsic Satisfaction
Humanizing the Job

COMPARISON, SATISFACTION, AND PERFORMANCE

Discrepancy Theory
Equity Theory

PART SUMMARY

LEADERSHIP IN THE ORGANIZATIONAL SETTING

LEVELS OF LEADERSHIP

DIMENSIONS OF LEADERSHIP BEHAVIOR

Closeness of Supervision, Satisfaction, and Performance
Consideration as a Determinant of Satisfaction and Performance
The Contingency Model

PARTICIPATIVE DECISION MAKING

PART SUMMARY

ORGANIZATIONAL ADAPTATION AND CHANGE

INTERNAL CONFLICT

ENVIRONMENTAL CHALLENGE AND ORGANIZATIONAL RESPONSE

Coping with Input Overload
Systems Research

INDUCING ORGANIZATIONAL CHANGE

Models of Organizational Change

THE CHALLENGE OF THE FUTURE

PART SUMMARY

In Columbus, Ohio, an 11-year-old girl had to stay home from school for four days. She had defied a regulation against eating on the school bus and had been banned for consuming one gumdrop. In London a man hurled a chair through the window of a citizenship and immigration office, stating that it was the only way to draw attention to his case. In Deep River, Ontario, a government official mailed some forms to Ottawa. They were returned by the designated recipient with a letter explaining that they had to be resent by registered mail—"to insure delivery." Then there was Michael Patrick O'Brien, who remained on a ferry boat between Hong Kong and Portuguese Macao for nearly a year because he had lost his passport and officials at each end were unwilling to grant him a new one.

These and other incidents reported by Mooney (1963) are merely extreme versions of the frustrations each of us has experienced filling out forms, trying to converse with a computer, or wearing out shoe leather while attempting to correct a simple "administrative error." As our pleas fall on deaf ears and our tempers wear thin, we are likely to think of the rules of the "bureaucracy" as deliberately and fiendishly intended to be as illogical, irrational, and impractical as possible. Yet such frustrations are unintended consequences of rules and procedures that were intended to be logical, efficient, and fair.

Larger than small groups but smaller than societies, organizations are much easier to point to (the University of Minnesota, the Franciscan Monks, New Jersey Bell) than to define. One of the more satisfactory definitions has been offered by Cyert and McCrimmon (1968, p. 568), who state: "An **organization** is a system having a complex hierarchical structure that operates within an amorphous environment with which it interacts." Let's go over each part of this definition in turn.

By referring to organizations as **systems,** Cyert and McCrimmon point out that organizations have a number of interdependent and functioning parts (participants, work groups, departments, divisions, and so forth). An organization is thus a dynamic, not a static, entity. **Structure** refers to channels of communication, lines of power and influence, role prescriptions, and all other factors that reduce the number of behavioral options available to the organizations's members and pattern or standardize interaction within any group. The **hierarchical structure** refers to the unequal distribution of power among the organization's members. To some extent, organizations can be viewed as held together by a chain of command, and an analysis of an organization would involve following the flow of influence from the president at the top of the pyramid to the errand runner at the bottom. Referring to this hierarchical structure as "complex" acknowledges (1) that in many cases there is no one single pyramid that adequately describes the overall distribution of decision-making responsibility and influence and (2) that some managerial practices tend to blur, rather than emphasize, lines of authority. Finally, the statement that an organization interacts with its environment serves to remind us that organizations do not exist in a social vacuum.

Cyert and McCrimmon's approach to organizations involves consideration of (1) participants, (2) goals, (3) roles, and (4) environment. First, organizations contain many people. Even though over a period of years there may be a complete turnover of membership, at any point in time there is a collection of people. If they are to remain in the organization and contribute to it, their personal needs and motives must be satisfied.

Second, organizations have goals. Later we will consider organizations as representing the merging of individual interests to solve common problems or to reach mutual goals. However, we have to be wary here of oversimplification, for within an organization different people may pursue different goals. For example, within many universities it is possible to find some professors dedicated to achieving excellence in teaching and others dedicated to advancing the frontiers of knowledge. Since research takes time away from teaching, and vice versa, these goals may conflict.

Third, organizations prescribe various roles. These roles define the behavior that is deemed necessary for the attainment of organizational goals. The functions of these roles are as follows: (1) because within the organization different members must perform different functions, roles define the areas of specialization; (2) roles coordinate the activities of different people (for example, at a brewery the bottles have to be filled at one station before the caps can be put on at the next); (3) as we saw in our discussion of secondary relationships, roles make it easy to substitute one person for another, thus alleviating problems of absenteeism and turnover; (4) by defining who is to accept orders from whom, roles help maintain order. Thus organizational roles ensure predictability of behavior and reliability of performance. Cyert and McCrimmon point out that in addition to the "preprogrammed" component of roles, which ensures this predictability and reliability, there is also a "discretionary" component, which allows some flexibility for the individual organizational member. This discretionary aspect helps the individual find satisfaction within the organizational setting.

Finally, the surrounding environment of any organization must be taken into account. Any organization is intimately interrelated with other organizations and with society at large. An appliance firm, for example, takes workers, minerals, energy, and other natural resources from the environment and sends finished appliances (via department stores) back into the environment. Any given manufacturer will be influenced by its competitors' actions, by related industries (steel, petrochemicals), by legislation (safety laws, for example), by trade unions, and by an endless list of other factors. Full recognition of this intimate relationship between an organization and its environment has only recently gained prominence in organizational theory and research.

Our discussion of organizations is divided into four parts. First, we will consider three major perspectives on organizations. Second, we will discuss the kinds of satisfactions that draw people to organizations and ensure good performance. Third, we will focus on leadership and decision making in the organizational setting, with special reference to "democratic" decision-making practices. Finally, we will consider a few of the ways in which organizations adapt to changing environmental conditions, as well as the kinds of changes in organizational practices that would seem to be required for organizations to meet the challenge of the future.

THREE PERSPECTIVES ON ORGANIZATIONS

An analysis of contemporary organizational theory and research would most likely reveal three major influences. Although these three influences are in some ways supplementary, each reflects a different perspective on an organization and its members. First, there is the *rational perspective*, which views organizations as analogous to machines. Second, there is the *human-relations perspective*, which stresses the socioemotional needs of individual participants and the dynamics of the work group. Third, there is the *open-systems perspective*, which attempts to describe the intricate complexity of organizations. This third, most recent, perspective has had a revolutionary impact on the field of organizational psychology.

THE "RATIONAL" PERSPECTIVE

One early approach was to view an organization as analogous to a machine, with the organization's human members representing cogs and wheels within it. These human cogs and wheels were taken as "givens," rather than as sources of variability. The approach was called "rational" not because it was the most logically derived or factually correct, but because it characterized the organization's members as objective, impartial, and fully responsive to impersonal rules. Decision makers, for example, were conceived of as aware of all the different alternatives and their likely consequences and were seen as able to unfailingly choose the "best" alternative in an impartial and unfeeling manner. Human needs and motives were thus either ignored or treated in very simplistic fashion. Two analyses that emphasize the rationality of organizational members are the "scientific management" and "bureaucracy" approaches.

Scientific Management

Taylor's (1911) school of **scientific management** dates from the beginning of the 20th century. Taylor hoped to "systematize" the performance of organizational members in the interest of efficiency—that is, his intention was to "stop the loafing" (Tannenbaum, 1966). Scientific management involved three components (March & Simon, 1958).

First, each worker was to be instructed in the *one best way* of performing a highly specialized job. This one best way was determined by time and motion analyses. Armed with a stopwatch, the analyst would time different procedures and select the most efficient one. In general, the principles of motion economy fell into three categories, related to (1) the use of the human body, (2) the arrangement of the work place, and (3) the design of tools and equipment. For example, smooth, continuous motions of the hands were deemed preferable to zigzag motions; there was to be a fixed location for all tools and materials; and levers, switches, handwheels, and so forth were to be positioned so that operation of them did not require a change of posture or body position.

Second, a *strict hierarchical organization* was imposed. The supervisor would establish the conditions surrounding the job and would tell the worker exactly what to do and when to do it. Discipline was harsh and rules rigidly enforced.

Third, to motivate good performance, very substantial *financial incentives* were offered. For example, the worker of that era who was making $1 a day might be offered $1.50 or more for absolute compliance with the new procedures.

To some extent, scientific management worked. About a 61% increase in pay led to as much as a 362% increase in output (Tannenbaum, 1966). Time and motion analyses and the engineering of tools and equipment for efficient use are very much with us today (Chapanis, 1965). However, scientific management had some very serious shortcomings. First, as we shall soon see, it ignored the subtleties of human motivation. Second, it did not take into consideration informal work-group norms that sometimes fostered low productivity. Third, it overlooked the relationship of different parts of the organization to one another and to the larger environment. For example, in one steel plant, increased efficiency led to the layoff of 75% of the employees. Company-owned housing went unrented, and the company-owned store went bankrupt (Tannenbaum, 1966). Thus, although Taylor's system produced immediate changes on the production line, it did not provide compensatory readjustments elsewhere.

Bureaucracy

Bureaucracy refers to a form of organization in which rationality and impersonality are developed to the highest degree. An impersonally applied system of rules ensures reliability and conformity. From the descriptions offered by Merton (1952, 1957a), Weber (1952), Katz and Kahn (1966), and others, the following picture emerges. (This picture, of course, represents an ideal type, which actual bureaucracies would approximate to varying degrees.)

Bureaucracies are aimed at reducing the variability in human behavior by devising and applying rules. Procedures are carefully specified, and penalties are attached to failures to conform. There is a well-defined hierarchical structure. All authority originates at the top but may be delegated downward in the chain of command. There is a clear-cut division of labor, and the official relationships among members are formal and impersonal. Each "department" has its own functions and does not meddle in the business of other departments. Bureaucracies tend to be secretive, in that their techniques and procedures are not usually publicly discussed. For the most part workers are reasonably well educated; they are drawn to bureaucracies for security rather than for spectacular advancement.

Bureaucratic organization does ensure predictability of behavior. However, it also has certain unintended and undesirable consequences. Since the bureaucrat is worried about adhering strictly to the rules and justifying all actions in the eyes of superiors, absurd as well as sensible regulations are sometimes enforced. Impersonal rules cannot cover all situations. Thus, as illustrated in the episodes that introduced this chapter, the idiosyncratic needs of individuals are seldom taken into account. The preoccupation with rules and regulations means that bureaucracies are often insensitive to changing environmental conditions. Traditional rather than innovative, they may not rise to meet the challenge of changing times. As a result, the bureaucracy is poorly integrated into the larger environment. As we shall see at the end of this chapter, this form of social organization may have outlived its usefulness.

THE HUMAN-RELATIONS PERSPECTIVE

In contrast to the rational perspective, the human-relations approach emphasizes the psychological needs of the organization's members and closely attends to processes within small, informal work groups. The subtlety of human motivation in the work setting first became apparent during studies conducted between 1927 and 1932 at Western Electric's Hawthorne plant in Chicago (Roethlisberger & Dickson, 1939; Homans, 1950).

In one study the researchers were trying to determine the effects on productivity of varying illumination. The mystifying finding was that, whether illumination was increased or decreased, there was a spurt in productivity. It turned out that the workers were responding to the "interest" shown in them by the experimenters. This phenomenon has become known as the **Hawthorne effect.** Contrary to popular myth, sheer attention cannot be pinpointed as the sole responsible factor. To establish rapport with the workers, the researchers attempted to maintain a friendly atmosphere, and they gave the workers considerable autonomy.

A second important finding of the Hawthorne studies was that groups of men who wired electrical panels developed informal norms that affected their productivity. Although these norms dictated that it was wrong to be a "chiseler" and fail to produce, they also set an upper limit on performance. As indicated in the last chapter, such ceilings may be imposed because the workers fear that a high level of performance will cause the boss to set higher minimal standards for productivity. This study illustrates the importance of small-group dynamics within the larger organization.

These findings, coupled with concurring evidence from the labs of group dynamicists, added the human touch to organizational theory. As a result, 30 or so years of effort have been addressed to such questions as "What kinds of procedures lead to both personal satisfaction and a high level of performance?" and "How may small-group norms contribute to, rather than distract from, the attainment of organizational goals?" Some partial answers to such questions will be presented later.

The human-relations approach added important new dimensions to our understanding of organizations, but it has two major limitations. First, it places little emphasis on relations among groups within the organization. Second, like the rational approach, it is inattentive to the organization's interaction with the larger environment.

THE OPEN-SYSTEMS PERSPECTIVE

The third major perspective on organizations, **open-systems theory,** began in the late 1950s as an attempt to integrate all the behavioral and social sciences, from cellular biology to sociology (Miller, 1955). It is intended to apply to cells, organs, and individuals right through to groups, organizations, and societies. In recent years the theory has been applied primarily to the study of groups and organizations (Katz & Kahn, 1966; Buckley, 1967; Aldrich, 1971).

According to open-systems theory, there are certain principles that hold true for individuals, small groups, organizations, societies, and organizations of societies—each one of which is a **system.** Every system processes materials or information, much as a computer processes information. That is, something is fed in at one end, something happens to it inside, and a finished, or at least partially processed, product is discharged from the other end. For example, at an automobile-manufacturing concern, metal, glass, and plastics are brought in; after these materials are sent down the assembly line, a finished automobile emerges. As another example, at your college naïve high school graduates are sent down an assembly line of sorts (beginning, perhaps, with remedial English and ending up with a senior seminar on Chaucer) and are transformed into sophisticated college graduates.

Figure 11–1 shows this general process in diagrammatic form and helps to acquaint us with some of the relevant terminology. **Inputs** refer to the information, energy, or materials that enter the system from the environment. Inputs pass through **boundaries,** which separate the system from the larger environment. These boundaries may be very visible, as in the case of a brick wall, a guardhouse, or a barbed-wire fence, or invisible, as in the case of admissions tests and other barriers that exclude people on the basis of ability or other such factors. However, they are invariably permeable enough to allow inputs to enter the system. **Throughput** refers to the information or material as it is being processed (for example, an automobile moving down an assembly line or a student working his or her way from English 1 to English 2). By reacting to the **output,** the environment provides **feedback**—that is, information that the organization can use for future guidance. For example, if two new automobiles are simultaneously introduced by the same firm, and the public reacts favorably to

Figure 11-1. Basic concepts of open-systems theory. According to this theory, business firms and other organizations are analogous to computers. Raw materials or inputs enter the system through its boundaries. This material is processed (throughput) and then discharged into the environment (output). The environment's reactions to the finished product (feedback) allow the organization to modify its practices for greater success.

one but not to the other, production of the popular one will be increased and production of the unpopular one will be discontinued.

Two features of open-systems theory should be immediately emphasized. First, by describing a system as open, full acknowledgement is given to the importance of the surrounding environment. Second, since open-systems theory can be applied to groups of all sizes, large, complex organizations and societies can be described as consisting of a number of different subsystems. For example, the Army has four combat arms (artillery, armor, infantry, and air defense), four combat support arms (corps of engineers, signal corps, military intelligence, and military police), and a number of noncombat support arms (quartermaster corps, medical services, and so forth). Each of these arms, like the Army itself, can be viewed as a system. Further breakdowns are also possible. For example, the first battalion of the second brigade of the third division may be treated as a system. Whether we are dealing with a system, a subsystem, or a supersystem depends on one's point of reference. As an analytical tool, open-systems theory has all the adaptability of a zoom lens.

Specialized Subsystems

Katz and Kahn (1966) suggest that, within large and complex organizations, different subsystems often serve specialized functions. Most organizations have five main subsystems. The **production system** deals with the central productive processes—that is, turning out the automobiles, friars, or advertising slogans. **Maintenance systems** offer the rewards that bring people into the organization, ensure reliable performance, and handle problems of absenteeism and turnover. **Boundary systems** separate the organization from other organizations and from the environment. **Adaptive systems** are concerned with research and development. They analyze feedback of varying types, ranging from hard facts concerning yesterday's sales to anticipated trends for tomorrow. Finally, the **managerial system** cuts across all other systems and provides synchronization.

Society can also be viewed as a system, and, if we adjust our zoom lens once again, we find that there are five different types of organizations serving specialized functions for society, just like the five different subsystems within organizations. First, there are **production organizations,** which create wealth, manufacture goods, and provide services such as dry cleaning and television repair. This class would include General Motors, MGM, and Kentucky Fried Chicken. Second, **maintenance organizations** socialize people for their roles in society. Examples are the school, the church, and various rehabilitational facilities. Third, there are **boundary organizations,** which would include customs and immigration services and, quite likely, prisons, jails, and other detention facilities such as mental hospitals. Fourth, **adaptive organizations** are those that create knowledge and plan for the future, such as research firms, many universities, and some government commissions. Finally, there are **managerial organizations** or political organizations, which coordinate and control people and resources. Examples would be governmental organizations such as a city council, a state legislature, or the U. S. Senate.

Systems Development

According to the analysis of Katz and Kahn, organizational development follows a more or less set three-step order. First comes a crude production system. Second, developing almost side by side are the managerial and maintenance systems. The third stage involves the development of "supportive structures"—the boundary and adaptive systems.

The first step in the development of an organization is cooperation in pursuit of common goals. Cooperation involves forming a simple production system. For example, a number of members of a small community might get together and form a volunteer fire department. Through this cooperation they can afford one another a level of protection that would not be provided by unorganized individuals.

The second step is the development of managerial and maintenance systems. These systems develop hand in hand to solve the ultimate problem of organizing: somehow reconciling the needs of the organization and the needs of the individual members. The managerial system handles the needs of the organization; the maintenance system attends to the needs of the individual. In the case of a volunteer fire department, for example, the different members will have different needs and hopes that may interfere with the mission (as when a firefighter prefers sleeping in to snuffing out a blaze). As a result, rules are formulated and enforced. The managerial system enforces these rules and, in the process, frustrates personal needs. To compensate, the maintenance system is established to provide rewards for membership and faithful performance. The volunteers thus might select a "chief" to enforce the rules and also hold beer busts and other fun activities to attract and hold members. Over time we might expect the managerial system to grow to encompass a board of commissioners, a chief, assistant chiefs, captains, lieutenants, and so forth and the maintenance system to include a payroll division, a personnel department, and so forth.

The third step entails the development of supportive structures at the boundaries of the system. As the fire department grows from a small group of volunteers to a large metropolitan force, it must have a steady stream of materials, personnel, and funds. A large fire department can be expected to have a purchasing department for procuring equipment ranging from hooks and ladders to toilet paper, a recruiting squad for bringing in new personnel, and, quite possibly, public-relations experts, lawyers, and lobbyists.

Once begun, systems growth tends to follow the **maximization principle.** That is, the system (and each subsystem within it) strives to become larger and more powerful and to gain control of as many resources as possible. There are several reasons for this snowballing effect. Competitive pressures encourage expansion since, if a competitor's growth is not matched, one's own organization may be muscled out of business. Thus each of two fire stations may vie for resources so as not to be rendered unnecessary by the other. Moreover, temporary pressures may force an increase in the size of a subsystem. Once acquired, people are difficult to eliminate from the payroll. Expansion in one subsystem induces strains in other subsystems that may be alleviated only by similar expansion. For example, after hiring additional firefighters to protect a new housing development, it may be necessary to hire new personnel clerks. In this way organizations become bigger and more complex.

Open-systems theory thus provides a common denominator for comparing organizations that are, on the surface, tremendously different. Full acknowledgement is given to the complexity of organizational phenomena and to the interplay between the organization and the environment. In the last decade this approach has revolutionized thinking about organizations.

PART SUMMARY

Organizations are social systems that have complex hierarchical structures and that interact with the larger environment. The components of an organization include participants, goals, roles, and environment. Three major perspectives on organizations are the rational perspective, the human-relations perspective, and the open-systems perspective.

From the rational perspective, organizations are analogous to machines and organizational members serve as unemotional cogs and wheels within the machine. One rational model, the scientific-management model, suggests that maximum worker efficiency can be produced by combining time and motion analyses, strict hierarchical control, and substantial monetary incentives. Another rational model, the bureaucratic model, suggests that organizations should be based on a system of rules. Scientific management can increase productivity, and bureaucracies do encourage reliability of behavior. However, neither model fully acknowledges the complexity of human motivation, the importance of the small work group, or the interplay between organization and environment.

The human-relations perspective focuses on the needs of individual organizational members and on informal dynamics within small work groups. This approach grew out of the findings that good performance can be motivated by social rewards as well as by money and that informal norms may develop in a work group that interfere with the attainment of organizational goals. Although the human-relations approach has made an indelible mark on comtemporary organizational psychology, it does not adequately take into account intergroup relations or organization-environment interaction.

Open-systems theory suggests that certain principles hold for all systems, ranging from individual organisms to small groups to societies. Social systems process material or information just as a computer does. The major concepts are inputs, throughput, output, feedback, and boundaries. Since the concepts, terms, and principles can be applied to groups of many different sizes, large and complex systems can be viewed as consisting of a number of subsystems. Within large organizations, subsystems have five specialized functions: production, maintenance, boundary, adaptive, and managerial.

Fully developed organizations undergo three stages of development. First, coordination of efforts in the pursuit of common goals leads to a production system. Second, managerial and maintenance systems evolve to articulate individual needs and organizational goals. The third stage is the development of systems that coordinate the organization with the larger environment. Once formed, systems tend to become larger and more complex. The relatively recent open-systems approach is highly influential in contemporary organizational psychology.

MOTIVATION, SATISFACTION, AND PERFORMANCE IN ORGANIZATIONS

Because all organizations are run by human effort, no organization can afford to neglect the problem of human motivation. Discussions of individual motivation and behavior in organizations are usually geared in one of two directions (Vroom, 1969): either toward understanding the *personal satisfactions* gained by the organization's members or toward understanding the *level of productivity* achieved by the organization's members. The reason for this split is that the conditions that make for happy workers do not necessarily raise productivity in such easily understandable terms as number of units of output per hour. A positive relationship between satisfaction and performance is likely when (1) the performance in question represents a valued skill, (2) the individual has internalized a well-defined set of job values, and (3) high levels of interaction in the work setting result in the individual's speedily receiving favorable evaluations when the job is well done (Likert, 1961; Nathanson & Becker, 1973). When the work does not draw heavily on the worker's abilities, when the person holds the job because of necessity rather than because of desire, and when there is little or no immediate positive feedback, then satisfaction and productivity are at best only loosely related. For example, in a review of 20 studies, Vroom (1964) found correlations between satisfaction and productivity ranging from −.31 to +.86, with a median correlation of only +.14.

However, before the boss decides to cancel the coffee break and rip out the Muzak, he or she should be aware that member satisfaction contributes to good outcomes for an organization because it leads to a low level of voluntary absenteeism and turnover (Ross & Zander, 1957; Vroom, 1964, 1969; Lawler, 1973). Absenteeism interrupts scheduling and creates a need for overstaffing, and, when people quit, costs of recruitment and training are boosted. According to Lawler (1973), finding and training someone for a low-level job often costs about $2000, and finding and training someone for a managerial job often runs five to ten times that person's monthly salary.

For an organization to function properly, three kinds of behavior are required. First, people must join and remain in the organization. Second, people must engage in dependable role performance. Third, people must display spontaneous and innovative behavior in response to unanticipated organizational problems. These three types of behavior are not necessarily motivated by the same forces. Katz (1964) and Katz and Kahn (1966) have identified four **motivational patterns,** which, taken collectively, ensure all these behaviors. These patterns are: (1) legal compliance, (2) the seeking of external rewards, (3) the exercise of self-determination and self-expression, and (4) the internalization of organizational values.

Legal compliance refers to the acceptance of organizational role prescriptions because they stem from a higher power or authority. Such prescriptions can be backed up by external force (such as a dock in pay, a dismissal from the job, or a sentence of 30 days in the brig). Such force is rarely necessary, however, since people usually accept the organization's duly formulated rules and regulations as legitimate and binding. According to Katz and Kahn, legal compliance can reduce absenteeism and ensure that work performance falls at or above the minimally accept-able level. However, an atmosphere of coercion may encourage high turn-over. Organization members will not be motivated to perform beyond the call of duty, and there will be little innovative behavior.

External rewards include monetary compensation, promotions, and fringe benefits. These rewards are "instrumental" in that they have value only outside the work setting (McGregor, 1960). That is, a paycheck does little good while the worker is still standing next to the drill press or sewing machine. External rewards can increase satisfaction and produc-tivity and can spark innovative behavior. However, as we shall soon see, money is not a magic cure-all. For example, two salespersons operating on a commission basis may in the course of competing for a specific client lose a sale for the firm.

Self-determination and self-expression is a third motivational pattern. That is, satisfactions can be derived from exercising autonomy and using ability. When these satisfactions are present, absenteeism is likely to be low and production is likely to be high.

Finally, behavior necessary for productive organizational functioning is also encouraged when there is an **internalization of organizational values** so that the individual's values and the organization's values be-come one. This pattern is encouraged when the organization's goals re-flect general cultural values (social responsibility or success), when the organization's mission is dangerous or dramatic (such as combating crime), and when leaders inspire identification. Such internalization leads to low turnover and absenteeism and is the pattern most likely to produce innovation and activities that are above and beyond the call of duty.

The first two motivational patterns can be combined on the grounds that they are *extrinsic* (external) to the performance itself. For example, reliably stamping out hubcaps or keeping the sewing machines humming is a form of legal compliance that protects the worker from being fired and eventually yields a paycheck that can be spent during off-duty hours. The second two patterns involve inducements that are *intrinsic* (internal) to the job performance itself. Self-fulfillment and the expression of organization-related values occur in the actual process of working. For example, a person who likes athletics should enjoy the hours spent work-ing as a coach. The distinction between extrinsic and intrinsic rewards has been made repeatedly. Although we'll consider each type in turn, we should keep in mind that, from the worker's perspective, both a full belly and self-fulfillment are important.

EXTRINSIC REWARDS, SATISFACTION, AND PRODUCTIVITY

Although many extrinsic rewards are used to induce people to fill organizational roles (travel, the use of a company car, company-sponsored recreational facilities), pay remains the most important. In a national study of mental health, it was found that Americans worry a great deal about money and place considerable emphasis on material and economic considerations (Gurin, Veroff, & Feld, 1960). Almost all studies have shown that better pay is associated with more favorable attitudes toward occupational roles (Vroom, 1969; Lawler, 1973). A leading expert on monetary compensation notes that, when people are asked to list what they like or dislike about their jobs, salary is usually listed first and is almost invariably in the top three responses (Lawler, 1973). Pay has symbolic as well as material value; that is, it not only can purchase material goods, but it can raise social status and self-esteem.

External rewards can be divided into two types: **individual rewards,** which recognize individual achievement, and **group rewards** (also known as systems rewards), which are given or promised to all the members of the work group or system. Commissions and bonuses are good examples of individual rewards, and fringe benefits and across-the-board pay hikes are good examples of group rewards. For the most part, increases in both individual and group rewards lead to greater satisfaction. Increases in individual and group rewards may or may not lead to greater productivity.

Individual Rewards

Individual incentive plans are based on the assumption that people are motivated by the desire for money; thus, if the amount of money they receive is made dependent on their performance, that performance will improve. However, for this easy-to-understand procedure to work in practice, several conditions must be met (Vroom, 1969). First, individual performance must be easily measurable by some objective standard (such as the number of relays assembled), and the production data must not be easily distorted by the worker. Second, individual workers must have complete control over their own rate of performance. For example, a worker cannot show improved performance on an assembly line if the other workers move at a slow pace. Third, the inducements must be sufficiently large to justify the efforts. Fourth, there must be no conflict between short-term rewards (such as a bigger paycheck this week) and long-term costs (such as a layoff next week). To these conditions mentioned by Vroom, we might add that the incentive system must be considered equitable by the work group—including those workers who will not qualify for the bonuses (Katz & Kahn, 1966). Otherwise, informal norms will develop that prevent heroic individual efforts.

Not all of these conditions can be met in all work situations, and the absence of any one can wreck a plan to increase output through individual incentives. However, when all these conditions are met, tying pay to performance usually improves performance (Lawler, 1971, 1973). For example, Figure 11–2 shows rather unambiguously what happened during the course of a plan that gave cash bonuses to workers who showed up regularly for work (Lawler & Hackman, 1969; Scheflen, Lawler, & Hackman, 1971). Summarizing the evidence from old and new studies of all degrees of quality, Lawler (1973, p. 11) concludes that "Even the most conservative results suggest that individual incentive plans can increase productivity by 10 to 20 per cent."

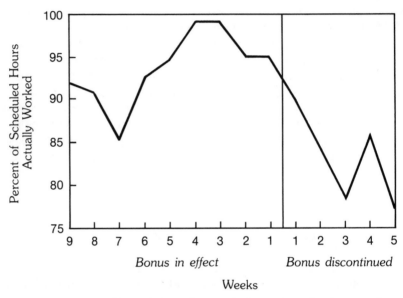

Figure 11-2. The effect on attendance of eliminating the bonus plan. (From "Long Term Impact of Employee Participation in the Development of Pay Incentive Plans: A Field Experiment Revisited," by K. D. Scheflen, E. E. Lawler, and J. R. Hackman, *Journal of Applied Psychology,* 1971, *55,* 184. Copyright 1971 by the American Psychological Association. Reprinted by permission.)

Group Rewards

Perhaps the two major obstacles that often render individual incentive plans ineffective are, first, that the individual does not have complete control over his or her own performance (as in the case of the assembly-line worker who is held up by workers at an earlier station) and, second, that the plans are often counteracted by group norms. In acknowledgement of the high degree of interdependency in many work settings, organizations frequently offer inducements in the form of promised benefits for the whole work group or company. In theory, this approach promotes a high degree of cooperation; since everyone stands to gain, the informal norms of the work group will foster a high level of productivity.

A proliferation of profit-sharing schemes has been based on this rationale. One of the most famous is the **Scanlon plan** (Scanlon, 1948), which operates as follows. First, through labor-management negotiations a certain minimum wage is set. This wage guarantees the workers a reasonable amount and alleviates fears that better performances today will lead to stricter standards tomorrow. Next, the product—a lamp, for instance—is evaluated in terms of the amount of money put into the labor that produces it. To use some handy figures that will not overburden my pocket calculator, let's say that the lamp, which is wholesaled for $12, costs the firm $10 to produce: $5 for the raw materials and $5 for the labor. Also for simplicity, let's say that this $5 labor cost represents two hours of work. If greater employee efforts can cut this two hours of labor to one hour, the labor cost will be reduced to $2.50. However, the lamp will still wholesale for $12. Normally, the $2.50 savings would go into the company coffers, but under the Scanlon plan the savings (or an agreed-upon high percentage) is distributed among the workers. Management's and stockholders' rewards come from having twice as many lamps to sell (using our optimistic figures), since each lamp now takes only half as long to produce. In a review of the outcome of the Scanlon plan in nine settings, Puckett (1958) reported an average increase in productivity of 22.5%.

Unfortunately, it is not clear that all such increases in performance can be attributed to the plan as outlined above. In some cases the plan was introduced as a "last resort" and was accompanied by many other measures to raise worker satisfaction and performance. Also, there is some suspicion that the dynamic personality of the plan's founder accounted for some of the spectacular results (Katz & Kahn, 1966).

In sum, considerable evidence suggests that extrinsic rewards can increase satisfaction and, under some conditions, productivity. However, other recent results suggest that under certain conditions large extrinsic rewards might have an *adverse* effect on motivation (Greene & Lepper, 1974). This finding is understandable within the framework of self-attribution or self-perception theory (Chapters 3 and 5). People who work hard for little or nothing in the way of extrinsic rewards may infer that they are doing so because the task itself is pleasant and enjoyable. As a result of self-perception, they define their work as intrinsically satisfying. People who work hard and receive large extrinsic rewards may infer that they are doing so only because of the paycheck, bonus, or commission. As a result of self-perception, they define their work as not intrinsically satisfying. In this latter case, when the extrinsic rewards are removed, there will no longer be any motivation to continue. Offering large extrinsic rewards for work that a person finds intrinsically satisfying could rob that work of its intrinsic satisfactions. Consider, for example, a person who makes stained-glass windows for the fun of it. People start buying the finished product. As a result of self-perception, the artisan may come to feel that he or she is constructing the windows only to make money. Then, when customers disappear, so also will the motivation to work with stained glass.

INTRINSIC REWARDS, SATISFACTION, AND PRODUCTIVITY

A number of theorists have emphasized the motivational advantages of tasks and jobs that are intrinsically rewarding. These theorists are humanistic in that they emphasize people's positive, striving nature. Most of these writers are indebted, in one way or another, to Abraham Maslow (1943, 1954, 1970).

According to Maslow's theory of motivation, people have a **need hierarchy.** Each need within the hierarchy becomes important only after the needs below it have been satisfied. At the lowest level, before all else, are the **physiological needs** for air, food, and water. At the second level are **safety needs** for security and a stable environment. **Belongingness and love needs** become dominant after the safety needs are met. **Esteem needs**—the needs to feel worthwhile and successful—are at the fourth level. At the pinnacle of the hierarchy is the need for **self-actualization,** which refers to the positive, striving process of using one's abilities to the fullest or realizing one's potential.

Most of these needs are deficit needs, but self-actualization is a growth need. **Deficit needs** are for things that are lacking, such as nourishment, comfort, and safety. **Growth needs** are positive needs to break the shackles of mediocrity and develop one's unique potentials. According to Maslow, only after deficit needs are satisfied will people seek personal growth. In other words, a person who is hungry or wearing wet sox cannot be expected to find fulfillment constructing a violin.

Research on the hierarchy of needs suggests that Maslow's scheme may be a little too ornate. Lawler and Suttle (1972) found that needs could be organized into a two-level hierarchy, with basic biological needs at the lower level and all other needs at the top. However, it would appear to remain true that, once people have staved off hunger, cold, and disease, their interests turn to such considerations as belonging, self-esteem, and self-actualization. Proponents of the view that self-actualization or personal growth can take place on the job are McGregor (1960) and

Herzberg and his associates (Herzberg, Mausner, & Snyderman, 1959; Herzberg, 1966).

Theory X and Theory Y

According to McGregor (1960), managers usually develop one of two theories about people and what motivates them in the organizational setting. One of these theories, **Theory X,** represents the traditional managerial view of motivation. Workers are seen as wanting, lacking creatures who are continually fighting for food, shelter, and a sense of security; they hate their jobs, viewing them merely as the lesser of two evils (the greater evil being starvation). From the Theory-X point of view, orders and threats are necessary and judicious application of rewards and punishments is required to keep the assembly line moving. Theory-X managers thus view workers as motivated by extrinsic rewards.

Theory-Y managers have a more humanistic view. They see workers' expenditure of physical and mental efforts as natural and recognize that the exercise of abilities and responsibilities can be inherently rewarding. From the perspective of Theory Y, individual needs and organizational goals can be compatible. The best managerial strategy is to organize tasks so that workers, while striving toward their own personal goals, contribute to the overall success of the organization. Theory-Y managers thus recognize that workers may be motivated by intrinsic rewards.

In many settings, suggests McGregor, the traditional Theory-X managerial practices prevail, and workers' needs for food, shelter, and security are satisfied. However, after these low-level needs are satisfied, extrinsic rewards no longer serve as good inducements for better performance. Higher-level needs for friendly social relations, esteem, and self-actualization will remain good motivators, but Theory-X managers do not recognize the importance of these factors and thus do not offer such intrinsic rewards. Passivity and marginal performance result.

Hygienic Factors and Motivators

Herzberg and his associates also argue that people will not be completely happy with their organizational roles unless those roles provide intrinsic satisfactions (Herzberg, Mausner, & Snyderman, 1959; Herzberg, 1966). These authors make a distinction between hygienic factors and motivators. **Hygienic factors** are those elements that must be present to *prevent dissatisfaction*. These factors are, for the most part, extrinsic, in that they *surround* the job. Good hygiene requires that the quality of pay, company policies, and supervision exceed given minimum levels. **Motivators** are factors that *produce satisfaction*. Most motivators are intrinsic to the performance of the job, such as recognition, achievement, autonomy, and the utilization of one's abilities.

An interesting implication of this theorizing is that the worker can at once be dissatisfied and satisfied. Failures in management may result from manipulation of hygienic factors such as pay when motivators such as recognition and autonomy are what is required. Tests of this two-factor theory involve relating hygienic factors and motivators to dissatisfaction and satisfaction.

Original support for the theory came from Herzberg et al. (1959), who asked workers to describe specific instances that made them feel exceptionally good or exceptionally bad about their jobs. An analysis of the responses suggested that extrinsic factors made them feel bad and intrinsic factors made them feel good. However, this distinction has not withstood the test of time. It has too often been found that, contrary to prediction, extrinsic or "hygienic" factors seem to affect satisfaction as well as dissatisfaction, and "motivators" seem to affect dissatisfaction as well as satisfaction (Kaplan, Tausky, & Bolaria, 1969; Evans, 1970; King, 1970).[1]

[1]One of the difficulties in testing Herzberg's theory has been that the usual scaling techniques do not make it easy to disentangle satisfactions from dissatisfactions. If person A likes the job better than person B, is it because A is more satisfied or because A is less dissatisfied? A new scaling technique proposed by Kaplan (1972) might be useful for future tests of Herzberg's theory.

Sources of Intrinsic Satisfaction

Why is it that some people find their jobs intrinsically rewarding whereas other people do not? In a sense, there are as many answers to this question as there are different people. For example, Murray (1938) has identified about 20 personality-based motives, most of which can be satisfied in an organizational setting. Different people have different patterns of needs. To the extent that a person's combination of needs is satisfied on the job, we would expect him or her to find that job intrinsically satisfying. For example, a person who seeks to be independent and free might find satisfaction working as a forest ranger, and a person who has a preference for being with others might enjoy being a public-relations director. Because people differ in their personality-based motives, not everyone should find the same job rewarding. The rationale behind vocational counseling and various personnel-selection procedures is to match the abilities, interests, and personality characteristics of the employee on the one hand to the demands of the job on the other (Dunnette, 1966; Super & Bohn, 1970). If a good match is made, the person should be happy and should prove to be an effective contributor to the organization.

It is also possible to make some generalizations about the kinds of jobs most people will find attractive. In Chapter 6 we saw that prolonged periods of lack of stimulation are aversive, leading to irritability and a decline in performance. In our earlier discussion of humanistic psychology, we saw that the fulfillment of one's potentials is, in and of itself, gratifying. In accordance with these findings, considerable evidence suggests that complex, varied, and challenging jobs generate more satisfaction than do simple, repetitive, and nonchallenging jobs. Walker and Guest (1952), for example, found greater satisfaction among assembly-line workers who had several different operations to perform than among assembly-line workers who had only a few operations to perform. In their study of mental health, Gurin et al. found the greatest satisfaction among managers, professionals, and high-level personnel who had a variety of duties; intermediate satisfaction among clerical, sales, and skilled workers who had some variety in their work; and the least satisfaction among unskilled workers assigned repetitive tasks.

Although survey results are in close accord, they can be difficult to interpret, since in many settings people with stimulating, challenging jobs are usually in "responsible" positions, which means that they are likely to be handsomely rewarded with money or status. However, additional evidence has come from investigations in which jobs have been rearranged to provide more variety. Studies reported by Trist and Bamforth (1951) and by Trist, Higgin, Murray, and Pollock (1963) have shown the effects of increased job variety in two very different settings: coal mines and textile mills.

In both settings there was maximal role differentiation. For example, in the coal mine one worker only chipped away at the coal, another only loaded the coal onto a cart, and a third only pushed the cart. Under these conditions absenteeism was high, and both morale and production were low. Having each worker do a little of everything by taking turns at all the tasks reversed these unfortunate conditions. It should be noted that in this particular study the changes also had the beneficial effect of breaking down status distinctions, which had been a major source of resentment. (The "chippers" were of higher status than the other workers.)

More recently an electronics firm plagued by absenteeism, turnover, and production problems switched from a system whereby each worker made only one part of an instrument to a system whereby the worker had responsibility for the whole instrument (Kuriloff, 1966). After this system was instituted, the workers had to learn the new jobs, so there was an initial drop in productivity. However, over time, satisfaction increased, absenteeism and turnover decreased, and both the quantity and the quality of production rose. One recent review of the literature indicates that, in six out of ten studies in which job variety was introduced, there was an increase in the quantity of output, and in all ten cases there was an increase in the quality of the output (Lawler, 1973).

Humanizing the Job

The preceding discussion suggests that organizations can make work more rewarding by rearranging jobs to provide increased variety and challenge and to draw more heavily on the individual worker's skills and abilities. This approach is called **job expansion.** A distinction can be made between horizontal and vertical expansion. **Horizontal expansion** involves increasing the number of tasks or lengthening the cycle of activity, as in the studies just discussed. **Vertical expansion** involves increasing the job holder's autonomy and responsibility. For example, workers may be given a voice in the decision-making process, the authority to depart from established work procedures, and some flexibility in work hours. Both horizontal and vertical expansion have been related to increased job satisfaction. If the expansion is sufficient to allow the worker to tap valued skills, it will increase productivity as well.

According to Robert Kahn (1973), workers will be happiest when they can mold their own jobs to meet their individual interests, skills, and needs for challenge and variety. He suggests that, to humanize jobs, we begin by determining the shortest length of time that is economically feasible and psychologically meaningful for working at a given task, such as typing, operating a switchboard, selling, stamping out hubcaps, sewing garments, and so forth. For purposes of illustration he assumes this unit of time to be two hours. Time-task units (for example, two hours of typing) are referred to as **work modules.** From the perspective of an organization, a workweek might consist of thousands or tens of thousands of modules involving hundreds of workers and dozens or hundreds of tasks. From the perspective of the individual worker, the workweek as we now know it consists of 20 two-hour modules, each of which involves doing pretty much the same thing (for example, typing). The conventional worker is saddled with four identical modules, five days a week.

Kahn proposes that individual workers be allowed to qualify for several different tasks (for example, typing, operating a switchboard, and selling) and then construct their own jobs using the requisite number of modules. For example, one worker might choose two modules of typing, one module of operating the switchboard, and one module of standing by the cash register each day. Another person might prefer to spend all four modules each day typing or handling the switchboard. Still another might rotate his or her job content depending on the day of the week. Moreover, Kahn proposes that the worker be given the additional opportunity to vary the way he or she distributes work time in the course of a week, month, or year. For example, rather than putting in four modules five days a week, an employee might choose to work five modules Monday through Thursday but stay home on Friday. Thus, within the limits established by the individual's ability, motivation, and stamina (most hospital orderlies cannot perform surgery) and the organization's needs (someone in the hospital will still have to empty the bedpans), the employee could be given the freedom to construct his or her own job. From the grand perspective of the organization, the workweek will still consist of thousands or tens of thousands of modules involving dozens or hundreds of tasks. However, the work will be done without forcing each individual to do the same thing eight hours a day, five days a week.

COMPARISON, SATISFACTION, AND PERFORMANCE

There are no absolute standards for defining what is "satisfying" or "unsatisfying" to a worker. Rather, the individual's assessment of his or her outcomes is usually based on social-comparison processes (Chapter 6). For example, Lawler and Porter (1963) found that relatively low-level supervisors who were making $12,000 a year were more satisfied than high-level managers who were making $49,000 a year. Whereas the supervisors were doing well by the standards of other supervisors, the highly paid managers were not doing well by the standards of their highly affluent reference group.

Two theories deal specifically with how people evaluate the costs or inputs they put into their jobs (effort, training, skill, intellect, and so forth) and the outcomes they receive from them. According to *discrepancy theory*, the comparison is between what one has been led to expect and what one in fact receives. According to *equity theory*, the comparison is between one's own outcomes and the outcomes obtained by others.

Discrepancy Theory

Although **discrepancy theory** can be made to appear rather elaborate, the basic idea is fairly simple. People will expect a certain level of input to yield a certain level of outcome. "Discrepancy" refers to the difference between the expected and the perceived outcomes. If the perceived outcome is less than the expected outcome, the person feels cheated and dissatisfied. If the perceived outcome is equal to the expected outcome, the person feels satisfied. If the perceived outcome exceeds the expected outcome, there is greater satisfaction yet. All these predictions were supported in an experiment by Spector (1956).

Male subjects, who were told that they were participating in a study of "teamwork in military intelligence," worked at decoding messages. They all began as "corporals" and were told that, after the first message was decoded, some men would be promoted to the rank of top sergeant. In one condition promotion was made to appear probable, whereas in another condition it was made to appear improbable. Within each of these two conditions, some subjects actually were promoted but others were not. Measures of satisfaction and morale showed that subjects who had expected promotions but were frustrated were the least satisfied, whereas subjects who had not expected promotions but were granted them were the most satisfied.

Discrepancy theory has two interesting implications. First, the promise of big rewards that cannot be delivered should have a very bad effect on morale. Second, "surprise" bonuses or other unanticipated rewards should have a very good effect on morale. As we shall soon see, unanticipated rewards may increase productivity as well as satisfaction, because people often feel compelled to deliver a "fair day's work" for their "fair day's pay."

Equity Theory

Equity theory, originally formulated by Adams (1963, 1965) and recently extended by Walster, Berscheid, and Walster (1973), also suggests that people compare expected and obtained outcomes. The comparison here is social and involves reference to other people's outcomes. What a person expects in return for his or her inputs is determined by observation of what other people get in return for their inputs. If you feel that you are getting as good a return on your "investments" as other people are, there is equity. If you believe that you are getting either less favorable returns or more favorable returns than other people are, there is inequity. If you do worse than what you see as equitable, you are said to be **undercompensated;** if you do better than seems fair, you are said to be **overcompensated.** Equity theory is typically regarded as an offshoot of dissonance theory. Perceived equity is analogous to consonance, and inequity (which arises as a result of under- or overcompensation) is analogous to dissonance. Thus people try to avoid or reduce inequity. If they cannot adjust their outcomes to suit their efforts, they adjust their efforts to suit their outcomes.

This means, reasonably enough, that if people feel undercompensated they will reduce the quantity or quality of their work. Kessler and Wiener (1972) found that undercompensated subjects were less productive than were equitably paid controls. Equity theory also implies, however, that overcompensation is similarly discomforting. Yuchtman (1972) found that managers of Israeli kibbutzim, although enjoying greater extrinsic and intrinsic rewards than the rank-and-file members, were less happy because they felt that, compared with the average kibbutz member, they got too much out of their job for what they put into it. Schmitt and Marwell (1972) found that subjects paid two, three, or five times as much as their partners for cooperating in an experimental game would forego rewards in order to avoid inequity. When overpaid, subjects would transfer some of their winnings to their undercompensated partner.

As noted earlier, under some conditions, overcompensated workers may increase their effort expenditure and other inputs in order to return a "fair day's work" for their pay. Adams and Rosenbaum (1962) paid students $3.50 an hour for collecting interviews. Some students were led to believe that this level of pay was excessive given their limited backgrounds (although it would nevertheless be paid because it had been publicly advertised), whereas other subjects were led to believe that, since they were "bright" and "educated," this compensation was "about right." Subjects who thought they were overcompensated collected more interviews.

Matters become a bit more complicated when the employee is paid on a piecework basis (Vroom, 1969; Garland, 1973). To adjust for undercompensation on a piece-rate basis, the person must work *faster* to get more money. Coupled with this burst of speed, however, is a decline in the *quality* of the performance. In other words, we might expect a worker paid a set but very small amount for each shirt sewed to sew a great many shirts but to do a very sloppy job (missing buttons, uneven seams, and so forth). To adjust for overcompensation on a piece-rate basis, people must slow down to get less money. However, they are likely to become more careful about the quality of their work.

Yet overcompensation is not a magic cure-all for shoddy goods and services. For one thing, increased performance as a result of overcompensation is likely to be short lived (Lawler, Koplan, Young, & Fadem, 1968). Moreover, overcompensated workers may find ways to reduce inequity that do not require harder or better work (Vroom, 1964, 1969; Moore & Baron, 1973). For example, they may raise their evaluation of their intangible inputs, such as "character" or "native ability." In this case a high level of effort expenditure and diligence would no longer be required for them to feel that they are maintaining an appropriate level of inputs.

This text has repeatedly stated that people try to maximize their rewards while minimizing their costs. In a sense, equity results showing that people may increase their inputs to be fair to their employer seem to conflict with the idea that people seek the most for the least. However, according to Walster, Berscheid, and Walster (1973), equity theory, too, assumes that people are selfish. People do try to maximize their outcomes, but, if everyone proceeded without restraints toward selfish ends, there would be perpetual rivalry; as each person tried to monopolize all the resources, everyone would suffer. Only by working out compromises can a group avoid internal conflicts and ensure that the group as a whole will secure generally favorable outcomes. Therefore groups will evolve systems for "equitably" distributing costs and rewards. Members who treat one another fairly will be rewarded, and those who treat one another unfairly will be punished. Thus, associated with overcompensation are costs in the form of criticism and rejection (consider, for example, usury laws that prohibit the charging of "unreasonably" high interest).

PART SUMMARY

All organizations must be concerned with problems of human motivation, for they cannot survive without attracting members and ensuring dependable performance. The interrelationships among motives, satisfactions, and productivity are complex, since the motivational conditions leading to satisfaction are not necessarily the same as those leading to productivity in terms of units of output per hour. However, worker satisfaction can reduce absenteeism and turnover and in this way help to reduce organizational costs.

Katz has identified four motivational patterns that, collectively, ensure all the behaviors necessary for an organization to survive. Legal compliance, which refers to the acceptance of organizational roles and directives because they are legitimate, guarantees a minimal amount of marginally acceptable work. Extrinsic rewards include wages, salaries, and fringe benefits; they may raise productivity. Satisfaction of needs for self-determination and self-expression can reduce absenteeism and raise productivity. Finally, if a member of the organization internalizes organizational goals, he or she is likely to engage in behavior that is innovative and above and beyond the call of duty.

Many writers have made a distinction between extrinsic job rewards and satisfactions (such as pay) and intrinsic rewards and satisfactions (such as challenge, responsibility, and the opportunity to exercise valued skills). Studies of extrinsic rewards have found that pay is an important determinant of satisfaction and productivity. Individual incentive plans can increase performance, but only if the performance can be easily assessed by an objective standard, if the worker has complete control over his or her output, if inducements are generous, if there are no conflicts between long-term and short-term goals, and if informal work-group norms do not conflict with heroic performance. Group incentive plans may help to overcome some of the limitations of individual incentive plans.

Maslow's hierarchy of needs has been influential in theories of worker motivation and satisfaction. According to Maslow, people have deficit needs (such as to ward off hunger and illness) and growth needs (such as to utilize their potentials). McGregor has made a distinction between Theory-X managers, who adopt the traditional, deficit view of motivation in organizations, and Theory-Y managers, who view people as seeking to self-actualize. Herzberg and others make a distinction between hygienic factors, which are external to the job, and motivators, which are intrinsic to the job. Although both external and internal factors affect the way a person will feel about his or her organizational role, the preponderance of data would not seem to support Herzberg's suggestion that external factors affect dissatisfaction but not satisfaction, whereas internal factors affect satisfaction but not dissatisfaction.

Among the intrinsic satisfactions of participating in an organization are the fulfillment of personal motives and the satisfaction of needs for self-expression and the utilization of potential. Most of the evidence suggests that complex, varied, and challenging tasks lead to more satisfaction and productivity than do simple, repetitive, and nonchallenging tasks. Often jobs can be made more attractive by increasing the number of operations, lengthening the cycle of activity, and granting individual workers greater autonomy. Kahn has suggested that people should be allowed to construct their own jobs by picking and choosing their own task-time modules. Within the limits established by their own abilities and by the needs of the organization, workers should be given control over both the content of their jobs and the distribution of their effort over time.

No absolute standards establish what is "satisfying" to a given organizational member. Satisfactions are relative to subjective standards. According to discrepancy theory, when outcomes fall below the anticipated level, dissatisfaction will result. According to equity theory, people compare their inputs and outcomes with the inputs and outcomes of others. If they feel that they are undercompensated relative to others, they will decrease their inputs; if they feel that they are overcompensated, they will increase their inputs. Leading people to believe that they are being overcompensated is likely to result in only a temporary spurt in actual performance.

LEADERSHIP IN THE ORGANIZATIONAL SETTING

Social structure, in the form of well-defined roles and established procedures, can help an organization to run itself (Perrow, 1970). No matter how carefully devised, however, social structure cannot guarantee that an organization will successfully adapt to internal stress and to external strain. There are at least three reasons for the limited effectiveness of social structure (Katz & Kahn, 1966). First, any structure will be imperfect and incomplete. Even if the role prescriptions are intricate and the rule book is fat, unanticipated situations will arise. Second, since environmental conditions change in sometimes unpredictable ways, inflexible procedures will not be adequate to handle the future. Finally, members of organizations have unique personalities. Individual decisions and personal influence are important for getting these unique personalities to cooperate and produce. In other words, an organization's survival requires a certain amount of built-in flexibility in the social structure so that people in influential positions can exercise their decision-making and human-relations skills. Such skills cannot be structurally imposed; people either bring them with them into the organization or acquire them in the course of job performance.

LEVELS OF LEADERSHIP

Leadership requires taking the initiative, planning and organizing action, and evoking cooperation in pursuit of a common goal. This process involves an interplay of the skills and abilities of the leader on the one hand and the demands of the situation on the other. For example, the same skills that might make one a good police captain would not necessarily make one a good encounter-group leader (and vice versa).

Within a large, complex organization there are many different positions, ranging from head of the board to low-level work supervisors, whose occupants are required to take the initiative, make decisions, and evoke cooperation. The demands of leadership vary with each level and involve different patterns of intellectual and emotional skills (Katz & Kahn, 1966). As Table 11-1 shows, leaders at the highest levels must have some of the same skills as leaders at the lower levels, but lower-level leaders can get by without higher-level skills. When there is a conflict of demands (for example, between administering pre-existing rules or formulating new ones), it is necessary for the higher-level leaders to follow the higher-level practices.

Low-level leaders are administrators who make sure that individual workers fulfill their obligations and receive their rewards. These leaders must have technical skills (for example, know how to use the tools or how to go about the secretarial procedures) and must understand all the organizational rules and directives so that they can apply them fairly. These leaders should show subordinates that they are concerned with fairness and equity and take into account the "spirit" as well as the letter of the laws.

Intermediate-level leaders also operate within the framework of pre-existing rules, but they are expected to improvise within this framework. They are required to supplement rules to handle unanticipated cases, interpret conflicting rules, and, when necessary, "read between the lines." Intellectually, they must have a two-way orientation—that is, be able to simultaneously understand and deal with the needs of subordinates and the demands of superiors. For example, the intermediate-level leader might present workers' demands to higher management and then explain higher management's responses to the workers. This function requires adeptness at integrating role requirements and human-relations skills.

High-level leaders change old policies and create new ones. This behavior requires a "systems perspective"; that is, top-level leaders must be alert to all the requirements of subsystems (for example, sales, personnel, research, and design), aware of the changing environment (the depletion of resources, new legislation), and sensitive to the future. Often such leaders display **charisma,** a magnetic personal quality that generates confidence and inspires identification. Selznik (1957) likens movement into a top-level position to a movement from councilman (or councilwoman) to statesman (or stateswoman).

For the most part, empirical studies of leadership have dealt with lower-level leaders. For one thing, there are more leaders at the lower

Table 11-1. Leadership patterns, their locus in the organization, and their skill requirements

Type of Leadership Process	Appropriate Organizational Level	Abilities and Skills	
		Cognitive	Affective
Origination: change, creation, and elimination of structure	Top echelons	Systems perspective	Charisma
Interpolation: supplementing and piecing out of structure	Intermediate levels: pivotal roles	Subsystem perspective: two-way orientation	Integration of primary and secondary relations: human-relations skills
Administration: use of existing structure	Lower levels	Technical knowledge and understanding of system of rules.	Concern with equity in use of rewards and sanctions

From The Social Psychology of Organizations, by D. Katz and R. Kahn. Copyright 1966 by John Wiley & Sons, Inc. Reprinted by permission.

levels. For another, manipulation of lower-level leaders is relatively easy because the top-level leaders who are sponsoring the research will tell them what to do. In general, top management seems more willing to effect changes in the basement than changes in the penthouse. Studies of leadership in the organizational setting thus usually focus on supervisors of small work groups.

DIMENSIONS OF LEADERSHIP BEHAVIOR

The distinction between task and socioemotional leaders encountered in Chapter 9 has been made repeatedly by social psychologists studying performance and satisfaction in organizations. For example, the two types of leadership behavior identified by Halpin (1954) involved **initiating structure,** or organizing the group to move toward its goal, and **showing consideration,** or being sensitive and responsive to the needs of group members. Blake and Mouton (1964) have made a distinction between managers who show **concern for production** and those who show **concern for people.** Although there are some differences in these formulations, for simplicity we'll stick with the terms that were introduced earlier and phrase our discussion in terms of task-oriented and socioemotional leadership behaviors.

As we saw in Chapter 9, in informal groups, task-oriented activity is not necessarily seen as legitimate by group members; as a result, task-oriented and socioemotional leadership behaviors may conflict (Burke, 1972). In the organizational setting, task activity is legitimate, and task-oriented and socioemotional behaviors are often treated as compatible but independent dimensions. That is, a leader may score high or low on *both* task activity and socioemotional activity or high on one of these activities but low on the other. The importance of both kinds of behaviors was shown in an early study by Halpin (1954), who made a comparison of Korean War bomber crews. Of the most effective crews, eight had commanders who scored above average on both "initiating structure" and "showing consideration," whereas only one of the most effective crews had a leader who scored below average on both of these dimensions.

Closeness of Supervision, Satisfaction, and Performance

One task-oriented activity that we expect from leaders is the monitoring of the performance of individual members of the organization. An interesting variable here is the closeness of this supervision. On the one hand, our instincts might tell us that "when the cat's away, the rat will play." On the other hand, Brehm's theory of reactance (Chapter 8)

and our discussion of the benefits of allowing people to proceed independently might suggest that close supervision would have an adverse effect on satisfaction and performance.

Generally, research evidence has shown that close supervision leads to dissatisfaction. In an early review, Katz and Kahn (1952) reported that, compared with workers who were not under close supervision, closely watched insurance-company employees were less satisfied with their supervisor's ability and expectations and less accepting of the rules she tried to enforce. In some settings, close supervision led to hostile attitudes toward management. Although aggressive feelings toward close supervisors are typically interpreted in terms of the frustration-aggression hypothesis, an alternative explanation is that close supervision is perceived as punitive and elicits hostile evaluations in return.

Close supervision can also have an adverse effect on productivity, whether or not the supervisor is seen as punitive. Day and Hamblin (1964) had groups of four women assemble models of molecules using blueprints for guidance. A fifth woman (a confederate) served as the supervisor. There were four conditions. Under close-supervision conditions, the supervisor watched closely, hovered around the workers, and gave 40 separate instructions that she kept repeating. Under general-supervision conditions, only the eight most important instructions were given, and the supervisor stood back from the group. Within each supervision condition half the groups had a punitive supervisor and the other half had a nonpunitive supervisor. The punitive supervisor made 40 sarcastic, negative, status-deflating remarks about the workers, whereas the nonpunitive supervisor withheld hostile criticism. After the task was finished, measures of overt aggression, performance, and attitudes were taken.

Both close supervision and a punitive attitude increased hostile feelings toward the supervisor and, to a lesser extent, toward coworkers. Given close and punitive supervision, the women were openly hostile. Most interesting, however, were the effects on productivity. Whether the punitive supervisor provided close or general supervision, a low level of production was maintained. In the case of a nonpunitive supervisor, closely watched workers completed an average of about 24 fewer units than did less closely watched workers. In other words, the relatively considerate supervisor lost her advantage when she supervised very closely.

A study by Strickland (1958) revealed some of the conditions under which supervisors felt that they had to closely monitor workers' performance. In this experiment, subjects supervised two workers. It was arranged that one supervisee's work was continually monitored, whereas the other's was only occasionally monitored. Later the subject was asked to choose which of the two workers to place under surveillance. Subjects tended to continue to monitor the worker who had been under close surveillance during the first part of the experiment. Here again we see the operation of the discounting principle, which was described in our discussion of attribution (Chapter 3). The good performance of the supervisee who had been under surveillance in the first part of the experiment could have reflected either diligence and ability or the high degree of supervision. The good performance of the less closely monitored worker was necessarily a result of diligence and skill. To play it safe, the subjects continued to monitor the unproven worker.

Consideration as a Determinant of Satisfaction and Performance

It should come as no surprise that people generally like nice, easygoing, friendly leaders who show a personal interest in their followers. Likert (1961) has amassed considerable evidence to this effect. As Figure 11-3 shows, supervisors of groups that had favorable attitudes on job-related matters did not differ from supervisors of groups that had unfavorable attitudes in terms of such task-oriented activities as enforcing rules, arranging work, and supplying tools and materials. However, compared with leaders of groups with unfavorable attitudes, leaders of groups with favorable attitudes were more likely to listen sympathetically to workers, to "go to bat" for them, and in general to treat them as worthwhile human beings.

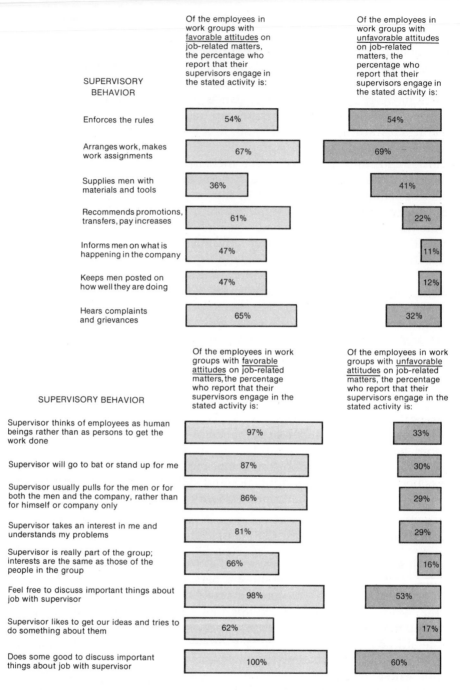

Figure 11-3. Relationship between supervisory behavior and the attitudes of workers on job-related matters. (From *New Patterns of Management,* by R. Likert. Copyright 1961 by McGraw-Hill Book Company. Reprinted by permission.)

Leaders' socioemotional activities are also related to measures of performance and productivity. In a comparison of productive and unproductive work groups, Likert (1961) found that, whereas about 75% of the productive groups had considerate supervisors, only about 30% of the unproductive groups had considerate supervisors. Compared with the supervisors of the unproductive groups, the supervisors of the productive groups were more likely to give general rather than close supervision, to respond to poor performance with helpful advice rather than with caustic criticism, to treat their supervisees as equals rather than as inferiors, and to put the group's interests ahead of their own personal interests. As Likert notes, because tasks and work groups differ, no one managerial strategy will invariably be "best"; it will always be necessary for a manager or supervisor to take workers' expectations, values, and skills into account. However, Likert's findings suggest that, in many industrial settings, consideration can yield dividends in terms of performance.

Of course, an analysis of the likely effects of warm and supportive treatment can be derived from our discussion of social reinforcement (Chapter 4). Lawler (1973) has suggested that consideration is most likely to improve workers' future performance when it is made contingent on good performance in the present. If consideration is shown following poor performance, ineptitude will be reinforced and there will be an adverse effect on productivity.

The Contingency Model

According to Fiedler (1964, 1967, 1971), different leaders have different styles for dealing with subordinates. These styles will interact with situational factors to determine group performance. The two independent variables in Fiedler's **contingency theory** of leadership are *leadership style* and *situational favorableness*. The dependent variable is *leadership effectiveness.*

Leadership style is determined in the following way. Leaders are asked to think of all the people with whom they have ever worked and to pick the person whom they liked the least as a coworker. This person is called the **LPC** (least-preferred coworker). Next, leaders are asked to rate this person on a number of evaluative scales, such as "Friendly——Unfriendly" and "Agreeable——Disagreeable." Rating the LPC in an unfavorable, harsh, rejecting way yields a low-LPC score and earns the rater the classification of a **low-LPC leader.** A favorable rating for this worst-possible coworker yields a high-LPC score and earns the rater a classification as a **high-LPC leader.**

Fiedler's (1971) interpretation of LPC scores is that they reflect two factors: the leader's motivation and the way in which he or she regards the world. Low-LPC leaders have a task orientation and want to get things done. They have a view of the world that is complex and incorporates many variables. High-LPC leaders have a more socioemotional orientation. They prefer warm, close relationships with others in the group and receive some satisfaction from seeing group members happy, even if some efficiency is lost in the process.

The second independent variable in Fiedler's theory, **situational favorableness,** is defined as the degree to which the situation provides the leader with influence over the group and hence makes it "easy" to lead. This variable depends, in turn, on three factors. First, a leader who is *accepted by his or her group and is held in high regard* is in a more favorable situation than is a leader who is distrusted or rejected. Second, *when the task and goals confronting the group are clear and structured,* the situation is more favorable than when the task and goals are vague or ambiguous. Finally, a situation is favorable to the extent that the leader is *vested with power* to reward and punish the group members through promotions, demotions, bonuses, fines, firings, and so forth. In other words, situational favorableness implies that the social structure is handling some of the functions of leadership (Katz & Kahn, 1966).

The dependent variable in contingency theory is **leadership effectiveness,** which is defined in terms of how well the job is done (the number of pies baked, the number of missions accomplished, the monthly sales figures, and so forth). It does not depend on whether the group members are happy; Fiedler considers member satisfaction to be a separate issue.

According to contingency theory, under conditions of both *very high* and *very low* situational favorableness, the best group performance should require the strong hand of a task-oriented low-LPC leader. In the first instance the group respects the leader, the task is clear, and the leader has power; thus the group needs only the leader's command to spring into action. In the second instance the group members and the leader dislike one another, they are all confronted with vague and ambiguous tasks, and the leader has no power to reward and punish; thus firm and decisive actions are the only ones with any hope of success. As Jacobs (1971) puts it, the leader can *afford* to be firm under conditions of great favorableness and *must* be firm under conditions of very low favorableness. However, under conditions of intermediate situational favorableness— that is, when the group is characterized by some sense of purpose but performance is impaired by conflicts and dissatisfactions—the socioemotional skills of the high-LPC leader should result in the best performance. In this instance the high-LPC leader would have the ability to help the group work through its moderately troubled relations and proceed onward toward the goal.

Tests of contingency theory involve (1) assessing LPC, (2) varying one or more of the factors that contribute to situational favorableness, and

(3) evaluating leadership effectiveness. The prediction has been that under conditions of very high and very low situational favorableness there will be negative correlations between leaders' LPC scores and leader effectiveness, whereas under conditions of intermediate situational favorableness there will be positive correlations between leaders' LPC scores and leader effectiveness. Contingency theory has been applied to many different kinds of groups, including aircraft crews, infantry squads, ball teams, crews of sailors, church groups, and sales groups. Leadership effectiveness has been measured in terms of originality and accuracy, as well as the more obvious number of sales or units of output per unit of time. Although the correlations have been low, reviews by Fiedler (1964, 1971, 1973) show that, for the most part, they are in the direction predicted by contingency theory.

A recent study by Chemers and Skrzypek (1972), for example, provides strong support for contingency theory. In this study, a comparison was made of 32 four-man groups of West Point cadets who were led by high-LPC or low-LPC leaders. There were eight degrees of situational favorableness, created by arranging all possible combinations of good and bad leader-member relations, structured and unstructured tasks (designing a barracks versus planning how to educate the troops), and high and low power. In accordance with Fiedler's hypothesis, Chemers and Skrzypek found that, under conditions of extreme situational favorableness and under conditions of extreme situational unfavorableness, there was a negative relationship between LPC scores and leader effectiveness; under conditions of moderate situational favorableness, there was a positive correlation between LPC scores and "getting things done."

As usual, not all results are in accord, and the contingency model of leadership has had some rather fierce critics. One commonly noted problem is that the generally low and sometimes insignificant correlations between LPC scores and leadership effectiveness suggest that the theory at best accounts for only a very small amount of the variability found in group performance (Graen, Alvares, Orris, & Martella, 1970; Ashour, 1973a, 1973b). The correlations are indeed often low, but in support of contingency theory it should be noted that (1) more often than not they are in the predicted direction (Fiedler, 1971, 1973), and (2) when situational favorableness is carefully specified, there is some predictive validity to the model (Chemers & Skrzypek, 1972). Less commonly harped upon, but possibly more of a problem in the long run, is the presentation of leadership styles as pretty well ingrained. That is, according to the theory, to increase a group's productivity, one must engineer the situation to fit the leader's style or choose a leader to fit the situation. Leadership styles may not be this inflexible (Hill, 1973; Larson & Rowland, 1973; Crowe, Bochner, & Clark, 1972). For example, in some situations low-LPC leaders will engage in socioemotional behaviors, and in some other situations high-LPC leaders will engage in task-oriented behaviors (Larson & Rowland, 1973). Ultimately, we will probably need more than a knowledge of LPC scores on the one hand and situational favorableness on the other to predict leader effectiveness. However, the contingency model represents a major attempt to account for the co-effects of personality variables and situational variables on measures of leaders' performance.

PARTICIPATIVE DECISION MAKING

An escapee from Nazi Germany, psychologist Kurt Lewin admired American democracy. In collaboration with Lippitt and White, Lewin conducted a major comparison of three leadership "climates" (Lewin, Lippitt, & White, 1939; White & Lippitt, 1960). Subjects in the study consisted of groups of five 10-year-old boys and one adult male. The groups played games and worked on crafts and projects over a several-week period. In the **autocratic climate** the adult laid down the policies, dictated activities step by step, assigned work partners, and remained cold and aloof. In the **democratic climate** all policies and procedures evolved from group discussions. The boys chose their own work partners, and the adult served as a resource person. In the **laissez-faire climate** the adult simply didn't participate.

Slightly more work was done in the autocratic climate than in the democratic climate. However, the autocracy created aggression, hostility, scapegoatism, and a certain amount of absenteeism and turnover. In the democratic climate the boys were more satisfied. They were more group minded and friendly toward one another. Moreover, motivation was stronger, and there was a higher level of originality and innovation. In the laissez-faire climate the boys had fun clowning around. Little was done, and what was accomplished was of poor quality.

As this study suggests, participating in the decision-making process can affect both attitudes and performance. Because there is some faith that the effects of participation are beneficial, many organizations have given up traditional autocratic decision-making procedures in favor of various kinds of **participative decision-making** practices, which give the rank and file inputs into the decision-making process. These arrangements may be referred to as **democratic decision making** (whereby members actually cast votes) or **consultative decision making** (whereby members do not vote but are encouraged to suggest or evaluate various alternatives).

Studies of participative decision making are hard to interpret, because what constitutes the "democratic" condition in one study may approach the "autocratic" condition in another. Furthermore, whole-hearted participative schemes are rare, since management is often very reluctant to relinquish all power to the rank and file. Another consideration is that not every member of the rank and file will greet the new power with enthusiasm, for people high in authoritarianism may prefer an autocracy in which someone tells them what to do (Vroom, 1964, 1969). Accordingly, managers may act democratically when dealing with democratic subordinates and autocratically when dealing with authoritarian or autocratic subordinates (Crowe et al., 1972). Nevertheless, despite these qualifications, the available evidence suggests that: (1) participative decision making can increase satisfaction, (2) decisions that are reached by a group may be accepted by the members as more binding than decisions imposed from above, and (3) participation in decision making can result in improved worker performance.

In a laboratory study using five-person groups, Scontrino (1972) found that groups given a democratic leader had more positive attitudes than groups given authoritarian leaders. Attitudes were particularly exaggerated or polarized when groups had been promised one kind of leader but given the other. Siegel and Ruh (1973) conducted a correlational field study of six manufacturing concerns and reported that participation in decision making correlated with job involvement—but did not correlate with measures of performance or absenteeism. In another field experiment, Morse and Reimer (1956) studied female clerical workers in a large insurance firm. Measures of satisfaction and productivity were taken before and after new decision-making systems were implemented. In one condition management gave workers greater decision-making power (autonomy), but in the other condition managers assumed more power for themselves. Greater autonomy led to improved attitudes. Compared with the women given less decision-making power, the women granted autonomy were more self-satisfied, liked both their superiors and the company better, and were happier with the experimental program. However, performance and efficiency increased in *both* groups. Perhaps, although the women given a voice did better because they *wanted* to, the women placed under conditions of decreased autonomy did better because they *had* to. Likert (1961) suggests that, if this study had continued for a longer period of time, the improved performance on the part of the women given increased autonomy would have continued, but the improved performance on the part of the women who had been given decreased autonomy would have deteriorated.

In accordance with theorizing by Lewin, an early study by Coch and French (1948) suggested that members of a group are more likely to accept a decision as binding when they have contributed to it than when it is imposed from above. The reason is that the informal, small-group norms should support, rather than conflict with, the decision. In this study the investigators compared three techniques for getting workers in a pajama factory to accept frequent changes in products and methods. In the control group, management told the workers what to do. In one experimental group, selected workers met with experts and with managers to plan the changes. In another experimental group, all the workers from a given unit were allowed to participate in the decisions. Although workers who were told what to do resisted the new methods, those who entered into the decision-making process readily accepted them, and this acceptance was reflected in improved performance. In the control group output decreased following the introduction of the new methods, but in the two experimental groups output increased (very slightly more so when everyone in the group had been allowed to enter into the decision-making process than when only selected employees participated). A number of other studies have also suggested that changes are more likely to yield improved performance when they are decided upon by the work group than when they are imposed from above (Marrow, Bowers, & Seashore, 1967; Lawler & Hackman, 1969).

There would not seem to be a one-to-one relationship between the degree of participation and the speed and quality of the decisions. This relationship is modified by the number and quality of the individual inputs, the degree of coordination among the group's members, the nature of the task, and other variables. (These factors were discussed separately in the preceding chapter.)

PART SUMMARY

Organizations require leaders because organizational structure is imperfect and incomplete, because changing environmental conditions give rise to unanticipated challenges, and because the organization's members have unique needs and personalities that must be coordinated if the organization is to achieve its goals. Katz and Kahn suggested that leaders at different levels in the organizational hierarchy must have different skills to perform different tasks. At the lowest levels, leaders must understand the organization's rules and administer them impartially. At the middle levels, leaders must have a two-way perspective as they improvise within the framework of pre-existing rules. At the highest levels, leaders must adopt a systems perspective as they formulate new policies. Top leaders are more statesmen or stateswomen than administrators, and the ability to instill confidence and inspire identification is necessary for their success.

The two dimensions of leadership behavior are task-oriented and socioemotional activity. Task-oriented leadership behavior is "no-nonsense" activity that helps the group reach its goal. Socioemotional leadership behavior involves a sensitivity and responsiveness to the individual needs of subordinates. In the organizational setting, where task activity is legitimate, task-oriented and socioemotional leadership activity are not necessarily mutually exclusive. People do not like close supervision, and close or punitive supervisors may cause a decline in productivity. Supervisors are most likely to monitor employees who have been under close surveillance in the past and have not had the opportunity to demonstrate their skill and motivation under conditions of autonomy. People like considerate leaders, and a number of studies suggest that considerate leaders are likely to inspire good performance.

Fiedler's contingency theory of leadership relates three variables. The first, leadership style, reflects in part a relative interest in task as compared with socioemotional activity. The second variable, situational favorableness, refers to the extent to which structural factors ease the burden of leadership. The third variable is leader effectiveness, which refers to the objective accomplishments coaxed from the group. The task-oriented or low-LPC leaders are expected to be more effective under conditions of very low or very high situational favorableness, and socio-emotionally oriented or high-LPC leaders are expected to be more effective under conditions of intermediate situational favorableness. Although the data are generally supportive of the contingency model, leadership style and situational favorableness account for only part of the variability in group productivity. Leaders seem to be capable of varying their styles to meet the demands of the situation.

Early studies suggested that democratic decision-making procedures led to greater satisfaction and to a better quality of performance than did autocratic or laissez-faire procedures. Subsequent research has shown that, although personality factors affect workers' responses to different kinds of leadership practices, there does seem to be a modest positive relationship between participative decision making and member satisfaction. There is some evidence that group decisions may be accepted as more binding by the members than are decisions that are hierarchically imposed from above. Participative decision making can result in the ready acceptance of new procedures designed to increase productivity.

ORGANIZATIONAL ADAPTATION AND CHANGE

All organizations must confront conflicts from within and challenges from without. For example, in a firm that manufactures computers and information-storage and -retrieval devices, the production department may be turning out more units than the sales staff can sell, or the sales staff may be selling more units than the assembly line can produce. Competition in the marketplace may force radical changes in the production system (as when a competitor markets a new generation of computers), and new legislation may threaten to render all or part of the organization's function obsolete (as when new legislation outlaws secret data banks). The world is ever changing, and an organization's survival depends on its ability to adapt. After considering some of the ways in which organizations respond to internal conflicts and to external demands, we'll discuss plans for effecting organizational change and for restructuring to meet the demands of the future.

INTERNAL CONFLICT

Frictions and conflicts within an organization reduce the members' motivation, create opposition to the organization, and decrease the amount of control exerted by the organization's leaders. One reason for internal conflict is an incompatibility of goals. Although there are a few formal, publicly stated goals that justify the organization's existence, there are also other, less formal and less freely acknowledged goals that provide special incentives for individuals and for subsystems within the organization. Conflict arises when the behavior required for achieving special-interest goals is incompatible with that required for achieving the overall goals of the organization. For example, to help preserve the squadron, a fighter pilot might have to remain in formation. But instead of pursuing this organizational goal, he may be tempted to seek personal glory by breaking formation to do combat with a fleeing enemy plane. Internal conflict can represent an incompatibility between the goals of the individual and the goals of the organization, the different goals of two subsystems, or the goals of a subsystem and those of the larger organization.

Conflict stemming from an incompatibility between an individual's and an organization's goals is, relatively speaking, easy to resolve. People who seem as if they might present problems can be denied admittance to the organization, or individuals with idiosyncrasies and quirks can be sent to departments where they are least likely to do damage. Counseling and other individual-change techniques may rectify the situation, and, if not, the individual can be fired.

Conflict between subsystems and between subsystems and the organization is less easily resolved. Consider, for example, an automobile-manufacturing firm with the easily understandable goal of maximizing profit through producing highly salable cars. Conflict could arise if the styling department insisted on a car so low and slinky that no known engine could fit under the hood, whereas the engineering department had just created an engine so reliable and powerful that it could only fit under the hood of a vehicle with the esthetic appeal of a cement mixer. This conflict would have repercussive effects in all the other subsystems of the organization. For instance, the assembly line would have to grind to a halt awaiting new production orders, and the sales department would have nothing to sell. Problems such as this cannot be solved through individual counseling, because each stylist's and engineer's values are supported by strong group norms. Since each subsystem is a necessary component of the overall system, firing a whole department is not a solution either.

There is, of course, no single, surefire technique for preventing or eliminating conflict among subsystems or between subsystems and the organization as a whole. However, the likelihood of such conflicts occurring (and the speed with which they are resolved once they do occur) may be influenced by the pattern of communication within the organization. In many traditional corporations there are barriers to communication that can handicap the organization as a whole (Likert, 1961; Katz & Kahn, 1966).

Organizations can be viewed as having both vertical and horizontal dimensions. The vertical dimension represents the hierarchical structure, ranging from errand runner to head of the board. Along the horizontal dimension are members who have equivalent authority and status but may engage in different tasks. For example, in an automobile company the janitor and file clerk may share the lowest vertical level but be at different horizontal locations. The stylist and the engineer would both be at a higher vertical level, but again at different horizontal locations. The various assistant vice-presidents in charge of different subsystems would share a higher vertical level yet still be at different horizontal locations.

According to classical models of organization, information flows along vertical channels. Each person communicates with the supervisor above and the supervisee below. For the most part, this flow is downward; that is, more information goes from supervisor to supervisee than from supervisee to supervisor. (Thus, within a traditional organization, people may be only dimly aware of what is going on at the next level down.) Good, although informal, horizontal communication exists within a subsystem (for instance, the stylists are continually interacting with one another), but there may be little communication among the various subsystems on a given horizontal plane (the stylists may seldom talk to the engineers). In the classical model there is thus a decentralized net, with people in the higher levels serving as clearinghouses for messages among the people below. This situation is shown in Figure 11-4(a), which is highly simplified for purposes of illustration. A real organization would have far more horizontal and vertical components.

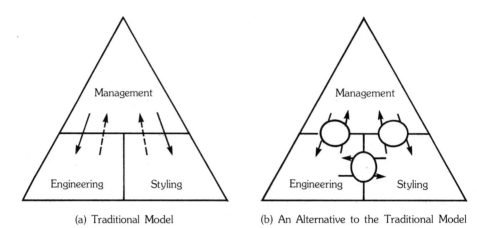

(a) Traditional Model   (b) An Alternative to the Traditional Model

Figure 11-4. Models of communication flow within the organization. Arrows indicate direction of flow. Solid arrows indicate a high rate of flow; dotted arrows indicate a low rate of flow. Circles indicate people serving horizontal and vertical "linking-pin" functions.

There are several problems with this classical arrangement. First, because of the power differential, people at Level 1 might withhold crucial information because of a fear of appearing incompetent to people at Level 2. Second, because people at different levels have different needs and receive different rewards, they are likely to see one another as having different values and being unsympathetic. This can cause serious communications problems. Third, as already noted, for one department (design) to communicate with another (engineering), the message must go up to Level 2 and then back down to Level 1. This sequence requires three steps instead of one, and at each stage of transmission parts of the message may be distorted or lost.

Some of these difficulties would be overcome if both vertical and horizontal barriers were reduced. Of course, completely unrestricted communication flow means pandemonium, and, if all structure were removed, it would be difficult to think of "an organization." However, barriers can be minimized by giving certain individuals dual membership in neighboring groups. People whose membership overlaps two or more groups are said to serve a **linking-pin function** (Likert, 1961; Wager, 1972). The linking-pin concept has usually been applied to the vertical or hierarchical dimension. Thus a person said to be in a linking-pin role is usually one who has gained membership in groups at two different vertical levels and is hence in a position to fairly represent superordinates and subordinates to one another. Yet a two-way perspective can apply to horizontal, as well as vertical, vision. People can also belong to more than one group at the horizontal level. If an individual has membership in two groups at different locations on the horizontal dimension, he or she can fairly represent each of these two groups to the other. In our present example, having someone belong to both styling and engineering departments might reduce the likelihood that a conflict will erupt. According to Likert, giving people membership in two or more groups within an organization will help speed the organization toward its overall goals.

ENVIRONMENTAL CHALLENGE AND ORGANIZATIONAL RESPONSE

Organizations draw resources from the larger environment and have an impact on it in return. According to Cyert and McCrimmon (1969), the interplay between organization and environment takes place at three levels: the *individual level*, the *intermediate level*, and the *aggregate level.*

At the **individual level** the organization deals with and has an impact on customers, clients, and potential employees. Except under very unusual conditions (as when a billionaire buys and then disbands an airline whose service has displeased him), the individual is unlikely to have much of an effect on the organization in return.

At the **intermediate level** the organization interacts with other organizations, which might be complementary or rivalrous. Examples of complementary organizations would be the automobile, rubber, and oil industries. Rivalrous organizations are, of course, those that compete for scarce resources. At the intermediate level, influence tends to be mutual and reciprocal.

At the **aggregate level** the organization interacts with the entire society. Organizations exist only because they offer solutions to certain problems. They are forced to operate within a series of economic, political, and legal restraints. At the aggregate level most organizations are influenced more than they influence in return, although lobbyists, political contributions, and clever advertising campaigns may sometimes reduce this imbalance.

Coping with Input Overload

As noted earlier, material and resources that enter an organization or system are called inputs, whereas the processed information or materials that are discharged from the system are called outputs. For the most part the level of inputs and outputs closely corresponds, although some of the inputs are retained for purposes of organizational growth. However, it is possible for inputs to increase beyond the system's capacity for ready processing (Miller, 1960). When such **input overload** occurs, efficiency and performance decrease and wear and tear increase. Let's consider some of the mechanisms that systems have for coping with input overload. For purposes of illustration, I'll show how these mechanisms might work in a "thing"-processing system (an appliance factory trying to respond to seasonal demands) and in a "person"-processing system (a college trying to respond to a glut of applicants).

One common technique of adjustment is to lower standards of performance and accept **error.** For example, appliances might be manufactured without the usual standards of excellence, and final inspection might be slipshod. When there are too many enrollment applications, a college might process them very quickly, accepting some people who are of substandard quality and overlooking some applicants who show exceptional promise.

A second mechanism is delaying or **queuing,** in which all inputs are processed, but over more than the usual amount of time. Orders for refrigerators may backlog, and applicants for college admission may have to wait longer than usual for a decision.

Filtering involves the processing of some, but not all, awaiting input. For example, the appliance firm might give priority to long-term customers, and the college admissions officer might show a preference to the offspring of former graduates. Such "filtering" on the part of a college could result in racial discrimination if earlier graduates all came from the same racial or ethnic group.

A fourth technique for coping with input overload is **omission,** or the nonprocessing of information. For example, the appliance firm may cease production on garbage compacters until refrigerator orders are filled, and the college might throw one out of four application forms into a wastebasket without looking at them. (Although this latter procedure has never been documented, I have some suspicions.)

Finally, **opening new channels** for processing can help to alleviate input overload. If the appliance firm believes that the deluge of orders is not merely temporary, it might decide to build new assembly lines. In those rare cases in which finances permit, the college might add to its faculty and staff to accommodate more applicants. All of these mechanisms may result in inefficiencies or in a decline in the quality of the output, but they also prevent the temporary breakdown or even death of the system (Miller, 1960).

Systems Research

One of the functions of the adaptive subsystem is to detect changes in environmental conditions and prepare solutions for problems that may arise. An effective adaptive system must go beyond an assessment of short-term feedback (for example, the number of cars sold last month) and attempt to research long-range environmental trends (for example, a growing need for cars with economical gas mileage).

Because long-term systems research offers little in the way of an immediate and visible payoff, resources to support this type of exploration may be skimpy. However, a failure to conduct such research can be very expensive. In 1955, the Ford Motor Company began to develop its Edsel, which was the epitome of the big, gaudy, high-powered American automobile of the era. Unfortunately for the manufacturer, the model was introduced very late in 1957, at which time, the country was ready for compacts, such as the then soon-to-be-successful Ford Falcon and Mustang. The failure of the Edsel, and Ford's net loss of 350 million dollars, is usually attributed to design, but it was really a failure to read the future (Brooks, 1971).

Long-range research is necessary to ensure a sufficient influx of raw materials, personnel, and money into the system. One problem that must be forestalled is the organization's consumption of its own resources. For example, the petroleum industry will eventually use up its raw materials, and, as indicated earlier, long-range company survival requires the development of alternative resources. Lumber firms replant the forests they chop down; this action not only is in the public interest, but it gives them more trees to cut in the future.

Another problem worthy of thought is that of preventing the dissolution of the organization following the attainment of its goals. For example, an organization dedicated to stamping out this or that illness or disease has to be ready to shift to a new goal if the vaccine or cure is attained; otherwise, there will be no more money and no more staff. Special problems can arise when the organization needs an outside agency for funding. Police departments, for instance, have to produce statistics showing that, on the one hand, they have been successful in reducing crime but, on the other hand, conditions are still so bad that more money for expansion is needed.

Adaptive subsystems must also be able to anticipate possible changes in societal values and norms that would render present operations obsolete. Rumor has long circulated that the liquor industry has blocked legislation to legalize marijuana but, "in light of the inevitable," secretly holds title to "prime marijuana farmland." Predicting changes in norms is also important for maintaining an adequate level of human resources. If the society's values change in such a way that the organization is left behind, there is likely to be turnover without replacement. For example, after the repeal of Prohibition, various temperance societies were left with dwindling membership rolls and few prospects for new recruits. To combat this type of problem, organizations could make their goals somewhat broad and vaguely defined. A "league of decency" could remain in action long after it was clear that the battle with alcohol was lost.

This discussion is not meant to provide an exhaustive catalog of all the problems organizations need to be able to foresee. In addition to difficulties arising from the consumption of resources, the attainment of goals, and changes in societal norms, external challenges can take the form of natural disaster, revolution, and threatened absorption by a competitor. The point is simply that organizational survival requires a competent intelligence service to maintain adaptation to an ever-changing world.

INDUCING ORGANIZATIONAL CHANGE

A recurrent and dismaying discovery is that organizations have a certain inertia and are very difficult to change (Katz & Kahn, 1966; Seashore & Bowers, 1970). There seems to be a certain amount of built-in equilibrium, so that changes in one part of the organization are compensated for by changes in another. For example, a potentially successful new design may fail to save a firm from bankruptcy because the production line can't quite put it together right; the liberal arm of a church may attempt to ordain a woman but be blocked by the formidable counterweight of the conservative arm; or Congress may propose exciting new

legislation that the President promptly vetoes. Established procedures become ends in and of themselves, and people with vested interests are reluctant to lose their advantages. Because of such considerations, new problems are sometimes better handled by new organizations than by pre-established organizations. For instance, a number of bureaucracies sprang up in Washington during both world wars. In theory, pre-existing bureaucracies could have been expanded to handle many of the war-related functions, but expected resistance to change led to the creation of new, unencumbered agencies (Katz & Kahn, 1966).

Models of Organizational Change

Several models have been used for specifying the conditions under which organizational change will occur. These models attempt to describe both the ways in which the organization gets the information it needs for solving its problems and improving its performance and the circumstances under which this important information will be acted upon. These models are the (1) *research-development-and-diffusion model*, (2) *the social-interaction-and-diffusion model*, (3) *the intervention model*, (4) *the planned-change model*, and (5) *the action-research model* (Sashkin, Morris, & Horst, 1973).

The **research-development-and-diffusion model** suggests that a change agent (who may be an outside consultant or a member of the organization) will identify relevant information in technical journals, texts, and so forth and then straightforwardly present this information to the organization's decision makers. It is assumed that, if the agent identifies the right information, it will be automatically accepted and acted upon. For example, an engineering consultant may note that certain plastics look as good and are as tough as chromium-plated metal and may then suggest that Rolls Royce pare its costs by switching from metal to plastic grills. The difficulty with this simple model is that it places too much faith on the rationality of people within the organization and ignores the problem that a simple statement of facts is likely to be insufficient in the face of proud heritages and established traditions.

The **social-interaction-and-diffusion model** focuses more on the way the change agent brings the information into the system. It suggests that the agent must identify people who hold key organizational roles—that is, people to whom others within the organization look for guidance. The trick is to get these "opinion leaders" or "gatekeepers of knowledge" to adopt the information, after which everyone else will fall into line. For example, if the advocate of change can get the most venerated wine taster and the union leaders enthusiastic about replacing natural fermentation processes with CO_2 cartridges, other organizational members may also become enthusiastic about this procedure, and champagne production might double. Of course, key people are not always that easy to identify or reach.

According to the **intervention model** of Argyris (1969), the basic information for solving problems usually already exists within the organization. The problem is that inadequate communication within the system (due to a lack of proper channels or the existence of blockages) prevents the information from being utilized. For example, an employee of one of a chain of delicatessens may discover that upping the percentage of soybean powder and water in the caviar does not alter perception of the caviar's taste, but this million-dollar discovery may remain covered with dust if there is no visible suggestion box outside management's door. The "interventionist" thus attempts to remove communications blockages and open up channels of communication flow. He or she is called an "interventionist" instead of a change agent because, rather than trying to implement specific changes, this person is trying to alter existing processes within the organization.

The **planned-change model** of Lippitt, Watson, and Westley (1958) assumes that the relevant information may be either brought in from outside the system or generated from within. The change agent is a consultant who is appointed to oversee a cycle of activities, including (1) data gathering, (2) action planning, (3) implementation, and (4) evaluation. These agents are also responsible for "stabilizing" changes—that is, ensuring that, once they leave or direct their efforts elsewhere, the organization's members do not revert to the former practices. This model draws heavily on the human-relations approach; for example, stabilization might be encouraged through participative techniques.

The fifth, or **action-research model,** is essentially a variation of the planned-change model. Whereas emphasis in the planned-change model is on solving specific problems and inducing specific changes, emphasis in the action-research model is on the *process* of problem solving. The intent of the action-research model is to help the client organization develop adaptive systems to research and solve its own problems after the consultants have departed.

Sashkin et al. (1973) suggest that each of the models probably works in some situations. Sometimes information needs to be brought into the system; at other times it is present but unutilized. Change agents can serve several useful functions: they can generate information through research, locate and introduce pre-existing information, train people within the organization to implement and evaluate new procedures, and so forth. Models such as the interventionist and action-research models, which emphasize changing processes within the organization, would seem to have an edge. If a specific "content" change is made (for example, switching from metal to plastic grills), subsequent content changes will probably involve just as much difficulty and resistance. If a "process" change is made (for example, instituting participative techniques to improve organizational practices), further changes should flow smoothly. That is, changes that help the organization to make subsequent changes are more valuable than those that do not promote subsequent adaptive responses.

THE CHALLENGE OF THE FUTURE

According to Alvin Toffler's book *Future Shock* (1970), people alive today are witnessing more technological and social change than has been seen in all preceding lifetimes put together. Contemporary Americans are confronted by a fleeting kaleidoscope of things, people, and situations. More and more things are built to be discarded or traded in, rather than kept, and are rented or leased, rather than purchased. People pass through our lives in an endless flow, and, whereas we may have more acquaintances than did our parents or grandparents, our relationships with each one are likely to lack depth and breadth (Chapter 8). Situations are also fleeting: jobs and neighborhoods change, marriages come and go, and yesterday's hobby lacks interest today.

Toffler heralds our era as the beginning of a second industrial revolution. During the first revolution, technology made it possible to cheaply produce large numbers of identical objects. During the present revolution, computer technology and flexible new machines make it possible to cheaply produce a variety of objects. For example, whereas in 1920 you could buy a Model-T Ford in any color you wanted as long as it was black, in 1970 the Ford Mustang was marketed as "the car you design yourself." Customers were given a choice of three bodies, four engines, three transmissions, and assorted variations in color, upholstery, and optional equipment. Toffler argues that it will be as cheap and as easy to turn out one million different items as one million identical items when computerized production becomes fully perfected.

This diversity in the material environment, Toffler suggests, is leading to diversity in the social environment. The increased variety of objects increases the number of differences in the ways people actually live. We are moving toward fragmentation and diversification in art, education, mass culture, and literature. People are immersing themselves in hobbies and activities of many different types, and more life-styles (such as those involving homosexuality and communal marriages) are becoming accepted by more and more people.

The organization of yesterday was successfully built around standardization and conformity. The organization of tomorrow will have to be built around destandardization and diversity. A particularly likely victim of this evolution is the bureaucracy. Since roles will have to continually shift and change to meet changing conditions, rigid, hierarchical structures will break down. Work groups, subsystems, and, perhaps, organizations themselves will be above all else temporary. More and more time will be devoted to the "nonroutine," so that the nonroutine will become routine. Toffler predicts the rise of the **adhocracy**—that is, groups of professionals and workers who assemble to tackle a given problem or task and who then disband to form other task forces of a different composition.

Ironically, one of society's major adaptive systems—its schools and colleges—is among the last to be aware of these coming conditions. Despite their avowed interest in the future, they prepare people for the past. Toffler argues that, to meet the needs of future society, our educational institutions will have to recognize a greater variety of individual interests. Traditional academic boundaries must be torn down and the number of optional and experimental course offerings increased. Curricula will have to be continually reassessed. Less emphasis should be placed on learning facts, and more emphasis on learning skills that help one to cope with change. These skills should include (1) learning how to learn—that is, how to absorb tomorrow's ideas and, if necessary, unlearn today's; (2) learning how to relate—that is, how to form rewarding and meaningful relationships in a world where human relationships are temporary; and (3) learning how to make choices in a society that offers a superabundance of things, activities, and life-styles.

Toffler's provocative book is necessarily tentative and speculative. The idea of flexible, ever-changing organizations is in some ways hard to grasp. At some point an organization may become so fluid and amorphous that it no longer makes sense to speak of it as an organization. However, Toffler's message is clear. Rather than conceiving of an organization as having a brittle and unbending structure, we should envision it as made out of bendable plastic and held together with rubber bands! The successful organization of tomorrow will be the one that adapts itself to the changing needs of society. In the next few decades we can expect to see tremendous changes in organizational practices (Toffler, 1970; Dunnette, 1973).

PART SUMMARY

To survive, organizations must resolve internal conflicts and adapt to external change. Internal strains may result from incompatibilities among the goals of individuals, the goals of subsystems, and the goals of the organization. Conflict between individual interests and organizational goals may be reduced through counseling or through changes in the individual's relationship to the organization. Conflict among subsystems may be minimized by increasing communication among these subsystems through such means as giving some people membership in two or more subsystems.

Organizations interact with the external environment on several different levels. They must deal with individual customers or clients, complementary and competing organizations, and society as a whole. Organizations need inputs in the form of materials, people, and money. Organizations can flounder and dissolve because of excessive or inadequate inputs. Techniques for coping with input overload include acceptance of error, queuing, filtering, omission, and the opening of new channels.

Forming a good intelligence system is the first step in adapting to environmental change. Problems that must be anticipated include a complete consumption of raw materials, a loss of enthusiasm once initial organizational goals have been attained, and changes in societal norms.

Because it is often difficult to change established procedures within organizations, we are often tempted to create new organizations rather than modify existing ones. Models of organizational change include (1) research development and diffusion, (2) social interaction and diffusion, (3) intervention, (4) planned change, and (5) action research. These models differ in terms of what activities they envision for change agents and consultants and whether they are directed toward content or process changes.

Toffler has stated that staggering technological and social changes have occurred in our lifetime. A new industrial revolution is introducing heterogeneity into objects and into life-styles. To adapt to this unending stream of variability, organizations must be based not on standardization and conformity but on destandardization and diversity. Toffler envisions continually shifting organizational roles, a breakdown of the hierarchical structure, and a new transience of work groups. Schools and colleges, which should be highly sensitive to these new conditions, may be among the least responsive organizations. Toffler argues that schools must allow for greater variability and must supplement the teaching of facts with the teaching of very general skills. Meeting the challenges of tomorrow will require incorporating great amounts of flexibility into organizational structures.

12

Intergroup Relations

HARMONY AND CONFLICT IN INTERGROUP RELATIONS

INTERGROUP CONFLICT

Functions of Conflict
Functions of Conflict Resolution

REWARD DISTRIBUTION AND CONFLICT: A PROTOTYPICAL STUDY

Group Formation
Intergroup Conflict
Conflict Resolution

RECURRENT THEMES

Win/Lose Situations
Own-Group Bias
Superordinate Goals

PART SUMMARY

CONFLICTS WITHIN SOCIETY

PREJUDICE

Dimensions of Prejudice
Ethnic Stereotypes
Discrimination
Prejudice and Discrimination as Self-Perpetuating

CONFLICT RESOLUTION

The Interracial-Contact Hypothesis
Planned Strategies for Conflict Resolution

PART SUMMARY

CONFLICT BETWEEN SOCIETIES

WHO RELATES IN INTERNATIONAL RELATIONS?

OWN-GROUP BIAS

The Mirror-Image Phenomenon
Dangerous Perceptions

COMPETITIVE STRATEGIES

Threat of Force
The Big Bluff
Limited Warfare

COOPERATIVE SOLUTIONS

Unilateral Disarmament
GRIT

PART SUMMARY

As a young boy, Nikos Kazantzakis was constantly reminded by his father that, since he was a Greek, it was his eternal duty to fight against the Turks. Later, as an adolescent, Kazantzakis and other Greek youths on Crete formed a "Friendly Society":

> We held sessions in secret, took and received oaths, . . . gave our lives a goal: to make uncompromising war on falsehood, servitude, and injustice . . . we did what we could to remain faithful to our vows. We never told lies, we beat up all the Turkish children we happened to meet in outlying lanes, and we replaced our collars and ties with undershirts striped white and blue, the colors of the Greek flag [Kazantzakis, 1965, p. 111].*

As Stagner (1967) points out, such mixtures of idealism and brutality are by no means limited to bands of adolescent Greeks; they are symptomatic of both sides in many intergroup conflicts. For example, within our society both white racists and black supremacists have vowed to uphold the word of God—and put each other in their place.

In this chapter we will discuss relations among groups, with a focus on the forces that generate or reduce tensions and conflicts. After defining intergroup conflict, we'll consider whether conflict serves some useful

---

*From *Report to Greco.* Copyright 1961 by Helen N. Kazantzakis, © 1965 by Simon & Schuster, Inc. Reprinted by permission.

functions or whether it is invariably harmful and should always be eliminated. We will then turn to an examination of a series of classic experiments that serve as models for understanding the origin and reduction of
intergroup conflict. We'll then probe, in turn, conflicts among groups
within our society and conflicts between our society and other societies.

HARMONY AND CONFLICT IN INTERGROUP RELATIONS

Two or more groups, like two or more individuals, can coordinate
their activities for mutual gain. In this case there is likely to be an atmosphere of acceptance and good will. We can find such harmonious relations at all levels, ranging from two couples on a double date to two
nations engaging in cultural exchange.

Two or more groups, like two or more individuals, can also compete
for scarce resources. In this case they are likely to generate an atmosphere
of ill will, mistrust, and suspicion. This type of relationship can also be
identified at all levels, from feuding families to nations at war.

INTERGROUP CONFLICT

Definitions of conflict usually involve an element of competition
and an element of aggression (Coser, 1956; Brickman, 1974). Let's define
intergroup conflict as the state existing between two or more groups that
are competing over scarce resources when one of the aims of the competition is to neutralize, injure, or eliminate the competitor. The resources
under dispute may be physical (a good home, farmland, oil fields), economic (money, good jobs, bright prospects), psychological (self-esteem,
self-actualization), social (prestige, influence), or any combination thereof.
By referring to these resources as scarce, I mean that each contending
group considers them inadequate to fulfill everyone's needs.

In some ways, conflict between two or more groups is analogous
to conflict between two or more people. In both intergroup conflict and
interpersonal conflict, *own-gain* and *relative-gain* motivation overpower
joint-gain motivation, although in the case of intergroup conflict we must
refer to "team" rather than "individual" interests. However, intergroup
conflicts have at least three very special properties that distinguish them
from interpersonal conflicts.

First, the death of one of the participants ends an interpersonal
conflict. The death of one participant does not end an intergroup conflict.

Because new contestants arise to take the place of the fallen, intergroup conflict can persist over generations. The conflict may even gain the status of a tradition. For the person born into a long-warring group, knowledge of the conflict will become one of the earliest memories, and constructive alternatives will be very hard to imagine.

Second, intergroup conflict is not governed by the same norms that govern interpersonal conflicts. Whereas norms may discourage all violence within a group, they may systematize and organize violence between groups. An isolated murder represents **social disorganization,** or a failure of norms to regulate individual conduct. The near-annihilation of an enemy in warfare reflects **social organization,** or a success of norms to regulate individual conduct. Organization and conformity are required, for example, to quickly mobilize an army and send it dashing off across the border.

A third factor that distinguishes individual and group conflict is that intergroup conflict is often accompanied by intragroup (within-group) cooperation. People will pull together to subdue the enemy. This intragroup cooperation can maintain the conflict, since it may provide some rewards that offset poor outcomes from the competition itself. For example, fighting units may develop a strong feeling of camaraderie, and warfare between societies may mend, or at least temporarily alleviate, conflicts within societies.

Functions of Conflict

Most of the social-psychological literature on intergroup conflict is based on the premise that conflict is harmful to all participants and must be eliminated. However, not all writers are reformers, and some have claimed that intergroup conflict serves important adaptive and maintenance functions for the group. Obviously, warfare can be instrumental if it gains for the group the strip of land, the resources, or the freedom that it seeks. (Curiously, the plum of victory has been given scant attention in social psychology.) Coser (1956) has listed a number of other functions or uses of intergroup conflict; here we will consider three of the major arguments.

First, conflict prevents the stagnation and decay of the social system by stimulating innovation and creativity. Conflict may lead to new social norms and reforms. According to Hare (1969), for example, black rebellion did more to reduce social inequalities in academia than did decades of "whimpering for integration." Conflict can also spur the economy and technology. World War II ended the Great Depression and triggered rapid developments in such different fields as pesticides, medicine, electronics, aviation, nuclear engineering, and the manufacture of rayon stockings. Such expensive inventions become likely when there are serious challenges to strong vested interests.

Second, conflict between groups may increase cohesiveness within groups. For example, Ziv, Kruglanski, and Shulman (1974) found that Israeli children who had been shelled by the Arabs showed greater patriotism than did children who had not been shelled. Bombardees also were more likely than nonbombardees to believe that the people where they lived were nicer than people elsewhere and to indicate an interest in remaining at their present place of residence. There are several reasons why intergroup conflict raises intragroup cohesiveness. One explanation, noted earlier, is that intergroup conflict may be accompanied by satisfying intragroup cooperation. A second possibility is that under conditions of conflict the group becomes a new source of safety and refuge (consider the relationship between fear and affiliation). A third reason is that, since being placed on rations and being placed in physical jeopardy are expensive membership dues, people may reduce the dissonance induced by the high cost of membership in a beleagured group by increasing their liking for the group. Fourth, we might note that the process of tightening group boundaries to keep the enemy out keeps one's own people in. Finally, according to both the ethological and frustration-aggression explanations of aggression, intergroup conflict should drain off intragroup tensions. Coser suggests that warfare with other societies may be the last chance for the survival of a society riddled with internal conflicts.

A third beneficial effect of conflict is that it can lead to the formation of associations and alliances. Two groups that have previously been indifferent or even antagonistic toward each other may join together to subjugate a third. The boundaries between the allies loosen, and common values emerge. Conflict can thus lead to the unification of otherwise isolated peoples.

Of course, technological advancement, esprit de corps, and the making of new friends would seem to be rather paltry gains if the ultimate result is annihilation of the society. However, Coser believes that, for three reasons, conflicts will be self-limiting. First, conflict sometimes binds the contending groups together. In the process of conflict, two previously unrelated groups form a negative relationship, out of which a positive relationship can evolve. For example, in an effort to head off war, two nations may discover a mutually advantageous course of action (such as splitting a contested weak nation down the middle). Second, conflict at a low level of intensity may establish and maintain a balance of power. Paradoxically, conflict on a small scale may be one of the most effective deterrents to conflict on a large scale, since small-scale conflict allows each side to show strength and resolve, which deters the other side from escalating the conflict. Finally, when a war becomes large enough so that other nations enter in, shifting coalitions and alliances may prevent the conflict from becoming an all-out war of annihilation. Etzioni (1969) suggests that this type of stability would require about five contenders. In the case of three groups, two are likely to gang up on the third; in the case of five, there is likely to be enough vacillation to make a permanent three-against-two alliance unlikely.

Coser does not argue that all kinds of intergroup conflict will benefit all groups. He merely suggests that intergroup conflict may serve some positive group-maintenance and adaptive functions. In passing, we might note that Simmel, Sorel, Park, and other sociological writers upon whose theories Coser based many of his arguments did their theorizing in the 1920s. It is doubtful that any of them ever envisioned hydrogen or atomic bombs.

Functions of Conflict Resolution

Most writers who have dealt with intergroup relations have emphasized the negative consequences of conflict. Whether we are dealing with a battlefield littered with dead or "merely" with the systematic blocking of alternatives (as in the case of racial discrimination), conflict involves personal suffering and social loss. This loss is measurable not only in terms of material and money but also in terms of wasted human potential. Dead soldiers do not compose symphonies or write novels, and blacks and other minorities who are kept out of universities will never exercise talents as engineers, historians, or physicians.

Certainly most of the positive effects of intergroup conflict can be achieved in peaceful ways as well. Negotiation and bargaining can lead to a favorable allocation of resources. Technological advancements do not depend on warfare. For example, the space program led to rapid technological developments in electronics, plastics, nutrition, and computers, and nobody was deliberately killed in the process. Cohesiveness and solidarity might be brought about through increased rewards within the society as well as through external threat. Thus wars on poverty, famine, and disease, like wars on neighbors, can raise society's cohesiveness. Finally, international alliances may be based on trade or cultural exchange rather than on a pact of "mutual defense" against some third party.

Most writers who have dealt with intergroup conflict do not attempt to maintain a stance of ethical neutrality. They openly abhor intergroup prejudice, discrimination, and violence. This value orientation is clear in the discussion that follows.

REWARD DISTRIBUTION AND CONFLICT: A PROTOTYPICAL STUDY

A rewards/costs analysis of conflict would suggest that the distribution of resources is the major determinant of intergroup harmony or conflict. Specifically, if, from the standpoint of each group, the best allocation of physical, economic, psychological, and social resources is obtained through intergroup cooperation, then harmonious intergroup relations will prevail. If, on the other hand, these resources are perceived as distributed in such a way that, what one group gains the other group loses, then the relationship is likely to be characterized by rough-and-tumble competition.

A classic research program by Sherif, which examined the effects of the distribution of resources or rewards on intergroup relations, was briefly previewed in Chapter 1. These experiments involved preadolescent boys who were formed into warring factions while attending a summer camp. Sherif's studies are important in the present context not because they shed some light on juvenile gangs but because they may help us to understand labor-management disputes, interracial frictions, and even international tensions. Thus the Sherif experiments would seem to be useful models or **prototypes** for understanding the origin and reduction of intergroup conflict.

The "camp studies" involved three sets of experiments. Although they were similar in many ways, they were conducted with different groups, at different locations, and in different years, and they varied somewhat in the number and types of manipulations. Here we will consider the "Robbers' Cave" experiment, which involved three phases: the formation of cohesive groups, the creation of intergroup conflict, and the resolution of intergroup conflict (Sherif, Harvey, White, Hood, & Sherif, 1961; Sherif, 1967; Sherif & Sherif, 1969).

Subjects were 11- and 12-year-old boys from white, Protestant, middle-class families. They were of average intelligence, and none had behavior problems. Selection of a homogeneous sample such as this eliminated the possibility that personality factors, such as psychopathic tendencies, would account for the results. Prior to the experiment, all boys were strangers to one another. Initially unacquainted boys were used so that it would be possible to observe the whole process of group formation. The experimental manipulations were made to appear to be a normal part of camp activity, and the boys were not told that they were taking part in an experiment.

Group Formation

First, subjects were divided into two groups, which were equated as much as possible in terms of individual skills and abilities. These two groups were taken to the camp on separate buses and located in cabins far enough apart so that they would not contact each other until the experimenter arranged it.

Group formation was accomplished by distributing rewards so that *the best pattern of outcomes could come only from intragroup cooperation.* That is, the boys participated in cookouts, overnight camping excursions, and other "fun" activities that required a close coordination of efforts. Meanwhile the boys began to express interest in and friendship for other members of their group. Leaders emerged, and norms developed and were enforced. A strong group feeling was indicated by the selection of snappy names for the groups (such as "Rattlers" and "Eagles"), the development of jargon and rituals, and the choice of special locations for group activities. These behavior patterns, of course, were consistent with earlier-cited studies suggesting that the satisfaction associated with group participation is a major determinant of cohesiveness.

Intergroup Conflict

After achieving group formation by making rewards contingent on intragroup cooperation, the experimenters created conflict by establishing a "win/lose" situation such that *the best pattern of outcomes could come only from intergroup competition.* This situation was produced by offering points and prizes to the winners of a tournament of contests and games. In the course of the competition, initial good sportsmanship rapidly disappeared as the equally matched teams vied for the points. An important finding was that the competition had an important effect on the attitudes of the contenders. Each group tended to *overestimate* its own abilities and performances and to *underestimate* the abilities and performances of the opposition.

During the conflict stage each group behaved in destructive ways toward the other. Raids were staged, enemy flags seized, enemy food consumed, and enemy territory littered. Some behavior (such as the stockpiling of hard apples for ammunition) was reminiscent of "cold-war" activity. Most of the boys seemed to want to continue the hostilities, and the few "pacifists" risked censure. Moreover, the evaluation and treatment of individuals were based entirely on group membership, not on individual merit. That is, everyone in one's own group was a "good guy" and was to be treated well, whereas everyone in the other group was a "bad guy" who was to be treated poorly.

Conflict Resolution

The third, or conflict-resolution, phase involved establishing conditions such that *the best pattern of rewards could come only from intergroup cooperation.* The experimenters did so by creating **superordinate goals**—that is, goals that were compelling for both groups but that could not be attained through the efforts of one group alone. For example, since the water supply was important to both groups, they worked together to locate the breakage point when the system failed. In another instance the two sides were forced to chip in to have a movie shown in camp. In a third situation the experimenter removed the starter from a truck bringing food into camp, and, after attaching a towline, the two groups literally pulled together for their supper.

Cooperation to attain one or two superordinate goals did not reduce the tensions, but cooperation at a series of such tasks resulted in a clear change in intergroup relations. Friendships formed between groups, there was a marked reduction in the tendency to rate outsiders unfavorably, and the boys from the two groups began cooperating in the absence of problems posed by the experimenters.

RECURRENT THEMES

The frictions that occurred between Sherif's Rattlers and Eagles are similar, but not identical, to those that are evident in interracial and international conflicts. Adult groups differ in many ways from Sherif's groups of preadolescents, and these differences can affect the course of their relationships. There are, however, certain themes in the camp studies that keep popping up in discussions of other intergroup relations. These recurrent themes are like Wagnerian *Leitmotiven,* played now on a piccolo, then on a pipe organ, and then again by the whole orchestra. Three such themes are as follows: (1) win/lose situations spark a form of aggressive competition that is characterized by attempts to neutralize, harm, and eliminate the competing group; (2) win/lose situations contribute to **own-group bias**—that is, cause group members to raise their evaluation of their own group and lower their evaluation of the opposing group; (3) if it were only possible to get two groups to pursue common (rather than mutually exclusive) goals, conflict would be eliminated.

Win/Lose Situations

Win/lose situations make the headlines and the history books. Historically, a major source of intergroup antagonism has been employment (Simpson & Yinger, 1958; Bonacich, 1972). Southern blacks emigrating north got a hostile reception from unskilled white laborers who felt that their jobs might be in jeopardy. Pressures to exclude foreigners from our shores may also have represented an attempt to protect jobs, and there is some speculation that, when Japanese Americans were stripped of their property and forced into concentration camps during World War II, this action was motivated by selfish economic considerations as well as by concern for "national security" (Simpson & Yinger, 1958). Class struggles and bloody battles between workers and management are essentially conflicts between the "haves" and the "have nots," and, whereas wars may be waged for "the hearts" of people, it is amazing how often rubber, oil, tin, and land are at least peripherally involved. Among the more recent prizes that contenders have seen as indivisible are Palestine, Cyprus, and the oil wells of the Middle East.

Of course, not every resource will be disputed. For example, although the Chamber of Commerce of Niagara Falls, New York, might like to have the scenic Canadian side of the falls incorporated into the United States, one hears little discussion these days about the annexation of Canada. For a win/lose situation to develop, each side must feel that it has a claim on the resource in question. Furthermore, not all disputed resources will spark open conflict. The lure of specific relative-gain goals

such as southern Ontario may be offset by a recognition that, for the most part, the two groups have had a cooperative relationship that has yielded a high level of mutual gains. Besides, the anticipated rewards of victory may be offset by the anticipated costs of the conflict. In many cases, both parties recognize that negotiated solutions provide the best outcomes.

A particular kind of win/lose situation is the **exploitative relationship,** in which one side does all the winning and the other side does all the losing. According to Blauner's (1970) controversial theory of **internal colonialism,** discord between blacks and whites in the United States is caused by an exploitative relationship in which whites control all the resources. Traditionally, colonialism refers to conditions whereby one country exerts economic and political domination over another country, which is populated by people of a different race or culture. The colonizers exploit the land, the natural resources, and, above all, the people.

According to Blauner, the black ghettos in our cities are ruthlessly exploited colonies within our national boundaries. Many groups of immigrants have settled into ghettos in the United States, but three features give black ghettos colonial status. First, whereas most other ghettos were voluntarily formed, black ghettos were enforced. Second, whereas most ghettos represented for the occupants a stopping point on the way to becoming one more indistinguishable mineral in the big melting pot, black ghettos have persisted over generations and have provided dead-end streets for many black families. Third, and most important, although in most ghettos it took only a brief time for ghetto dwellers to become landlords, merchants, and entrepreneurs within the ghetto, this was not true in the case of blacks. Greek Americans, Chinese Americans, and Polish Americans came to own their own laundries, banks, and restaurants, but the ghetto black has remained a captive patron of white-dominated businesses.

The subjugation of ghetto blacks is evidenced, says Blauner, not only in the fact that they are forced to pay high prices for shoddy goods and services but also in the fact that they lack political power. Within a relatively short span of time following their influx to America's shores, Italian Americans, Irish Americans, and others had a sizable amount of political power within the larger American community. Afro-Americans, who have been here for centuries, are still underrepresented among society's decision makers. Heavy police activity within the ghetto has limited the power of the blacks either to break out of the ghetto or to retaliate against the whites.

Blauner has offered an interesting interpretation of the riots that rocked black ghettos in Watts, Detroit, Newark, and other cities in the 1960s. The conventional view was voiced by the Kerner Commission report (1968), which suggested that there was an "explosive mixture" in the ghettos that was based on discrimination, crowding, frustrated hopes, un-employment, and poverty. Thus the riots were acts of desperation. How-ever, from the perspective of Blauner's theory of internal colonialism, these riots could have represented an act of strength motivated by hope rather than by despair. Feelings of powerlessness are a component of desperation and a symptom of alienation, but feelings of powerlessness were not common among ghetto rioters. Forward and Williams (1970) found that, compared with nonparticipants, participants in the Detroit riots were more likely to feel that they had the power to control their des-tinies and influence society.

According to the model of internal colonialism, the ghetto riots were not a simple outpouring of frustration or an attempt to gain middle-class life by stealing middle-class artifacts. They were, instead, attempts at a revolution. Blauner suggests that the violence and looting represented a determination on the part of blacks to "gain control over their own turf, to stake out a sphere of control, and to destroy symbols of oppression." He goes on to state that violence might be eliminated from the decolonial-ization process if the white community would (1) withdraw police and other "troops" from the ghettos and (2) offer technical assistance to the ghettos to help blacks gain autonomy.

Own-Group Bias

The attitudinal effects of win/lose competition noted in the Sherif camp studies have also been repeatedly noted in groups of conflicting adults. Specifically, there have been numerous reports of an own-group bias such that everyone within one's own group is favorably evaluated and everyone in the other group is unfavorably evaluated. A number of recent experimental studies have been aimed at pinpointing the causes of own-group bias (Rabbie & Horwitz, 1969; Kahn & Ryen, 1972; Gerard & Hoyt, 1974; Rabbie, Benoist, Oosterbaan, & Visser, 1974; Tajfel & Billig, 1974).

To begin with, it would appear that the simple act of being catego-rized as a member of a group is sufficient to produce some ingroup bias. Gerard and Hoyt (1974) told subjects that they belonged to a group of people with distinctive psychological characteristics. The size of this dis-tinctive group was said to be two, five, or eight. Next, after all subjects wrote essays, they were given the task of evaluating two other subjects' essays and their writers. One of these essays was written by an "in-grouper" and the other by an "outgrouper." Even though competition was not involved, own-group bias was revealed in the ratings of the two essayists. The more distinctive (that is, smaller) the ingroup, the greater the bias.

A second major finding has been that the *expectation* of competition can increase own-group bias. Rabbie et al. (1974) led groups to anticipate cooperating or competing with other groups. Some groups were led to believe that they would do well by cooperating or competing, but other groups were led to believe that they would not do well. Groups expecting to compete showed greater own-group bias than did groups expecting to cooperate—but only if they expected to do well in the competition. When they thought they were sure to lose, groups expecting to compete were demoralized in comparison with groups expecting to cooperate. Thus the anticipation of competition can increase own-group bias, but only if victory is in sight! Of course, if we were to interview troops at the beginning of hostilities, we would find no losing armies marching off to war.

Finally, studies that have investigated the effects of actual competition have found greater own-group bias in groups in win/lose situations than in groups not in such situations. Rabbie and Horwitz (1969) formed two groups of college students, the Greens and the Blues. In each four-person group, identification with the group was encouraged by having the subjects wear green (or blue) identification cards, write with green pens on green forms, call one another "Greens," and so forth. In one condition, subjects were told that the experimenter would flip a coin to determine which group would win transistor radios. This was done, and one group won and the other group lost. Compared with control subjects who were not placed in a win/lose situation, both winning and losing experimental subjects made more favorable ratings of their own group and less favorable ratings of the other group. Other research (Kahn & Ryen, 1972) has revealed that, when the competitors themselves determine who wins and who loses, the victors are likely to show more own-group bias than the vanquished.

There are several reasons why win/lose situations might enhance own-group bias. First, the winners' high rating of their own group may reflect their satisfaction, whereas the losers' low rating of the other group may reflect resentment. Second, differential ratings could reflect the feeling that it would be easier to interact with members of one's own group. For winners and losers to cordially interact, winners would have to hide their delight at winning (which implies satisfaction with the others' loss) and losers would have to hide their dissatisfaction at losing (which implies resentment of the others' win). Third, a balance-theory interpretation is possible. That is, people within the group have shared experiences that make them similar to one another but dissimilar to all the people in the other group. When we turn from a win/lose situation that is decided by chance or fate (as in the Horwitz and Rabbie experiment) to one that is decided by vigorous competitive activities, we can find additional reasons for own-group bias. For example, own-group bias might be an ego-defensive attitude (Chapter 5) through which one can rationalize attempts to injure, neutralize, or eliminate the competition.

Own-group bias among black Americans deserves a special comment. Historically, the attitude that "we are good and they are bad" has not been pronounced among American blacks. Three and a half decades ago, Bayton (1943) found that the negative images of blacks maintained by prejudiced whites were to a large extent accepted as true by black people themselves. Other early studies suggested that many blacks, especially black children, tended to identify with white people and to express shame over their ethnicity (Harding, Proshansky, Kutner, & Chein, 1969). Coles (1967), for example, has interpreted black children's drawings of blacks and of whites as expressing feelings of racial inferiority. In these pictures the black figures were small and incomplete compared with the white figures.

There are two possible explanations for a seeming lack of own-group bias among the American blacks of a generation ago. First, since blacks are embedded in white culture, they are exposed to white values and prejudices in the white-controlled television, newspapers, and magazines. The same modeling processes that resulted in whites' negative attitudes toward blacks could thus result in blacks' negative attitudes toward blacks. Second, blacks may simply have been more careful about expressing pride and independence, since such attitudes might have angered whites and triggered swift retaliation. "Uncle Tomism" was a tactic of ingratiation that reduced the inequality of power in interracial confrontations. For example, the "Uncle Tom" who sang the praises of white ways and was very humble and self-effacing protected himself against punishment. **Adaptive inferiority** refers to attitudes and activities that made blacks seem humble and childlike and provided some protection against the more powerful whites.

However, this situation appears to be changing. Surveys are uncovering a new sense of black pride (Kerner Commission, 1968), and psychologists are commenting on the abandonment of adaptive inferiority for a sense of self-esteem and autonomy (Pugh, 1972). Perhaps two simple studies, conducted 30 years apart, best illustrate this shift in attitudes. In 1939 Clark and Clark (1947) showed children two black and two white dolls. The children were asked to indicate which one was "nice," which one they "wanted to play with," and so forth. The majority of the black children preferred the white doll, although this preference decreased with age. In a 1969 sample in the same Midwestern city, Hraba and Grant (1970) found that black children preferred the black doll, and this preference increased with age.

Pugh (1972) traces the crystallization of a sense of black pride and unity to the civil-rights movements of the last 25 years or so. Since the 1954 decision by the Supreme Court that schools must desegregate, and since the 1957 decision by Rosa Parks not to step to the back of the bus, blacks have become increasingly unified for full and immediate citizenship. To express this change in terms of our prototypical study, intragroup cooperation to achieve economic, psychological, and social goals welded a loose-knit and demoralized aggregate into a cohesive group.

Superordinate Goals

A third theme in the camp studies that recurs in discussions of intergroup conflict is that, if by the imposition of superordinate goals a win/lose situation can be transformed into a situation in which both groups can win, conflict will be reduced or eliminated. For example, in the organizational setting superordinate goals have been used to resolve internal conflicts (Blake & Mouton, 1962; Blake, Shepard, & Mouton, 1964). In workshop settings, where small groups were encouraged to come up with better solutions than those offered in competing groups, there was evidence of intergroup antagonism. When common interests were highlighted and the groups were encouraged to work together for the good of the organization, intergroup hostilities were overcome.

Inspecting the history of international relations, one can find numerous illustrations of superordinate goals reducing intergroup tensions. Unfortunately, the superordinate goal in these cases usually involves the vanquishing of some third group. For example, during the 1930s many Americans considered both the Russian Communists and the German Nazis threatening and loathsome, but, despite the Communists' initial edge, the Nazis eventually proved the more hateful of the two. With the superordinate goal of defeating the Axis powers, the United States and the U. S. S. R. became allies—at least until that superordinate goal was reached. Although this kind of historical event certainly conforms with Sherif's theory, it does little to help us with the problem of conflict resolution, since, as Sherif points out, such alliances usually result in a widening of the conflict.

Nonetheless, it may still be possible to discover superordinate goals (other than the subjugation of some third party) that could reduce the antagonisms between traditionally conflicting social groups. This is no easy job, for glib pronouncements such as "Let's pull together for peace" will not work. According to Sherif and Sherif (1969), a superordinate goal *must* require cooperation, *cannot* be based on words alone, and *may not* be imposed by one group on another.

PART SUMMARY

Intergroup conflict involves an aggressive competition for scarce resources. There are some important differences between intergroup and interpersonal conflict. Intergroup conflicts often persist over generations, are governed by different social norms, and are maintained by intragroup cooperation.

A few theorists have suggested that intergroup conflict serves useful maintenance and adaptive functions for the society. According to these theorists, conflict prevents stagnation and decay, promotes technological and social change, increases cohesiveness within groups, and leads to the formation of rewarding associations and alliances. Conflicts may become self-limiting when the conflicting groups bind together, when a balance of power is established, and when shifts in coalitions and alliances occur. Most theorists suggest that intergroup conflict yields poor outcomes, is morally wrong, and should be eliminated. According to these people, the so-called benefits of conflict can be derived through peaceful means.

Sherif's research with preadolescent boys has shown that the distribution of rewards affects intergroup relations. When intragroup cooperation was required to reach goals, a cohesive group was formed. When intergroup competition was required to reach goals that were attractive to both groups but attainable by only one, conflict occurred. This conflict was reduced when intergroup cooperation was required to reach goals that were attractive to both groups. Sherif's observations concerning preadolescent groups are in many ways similar to some of the observations made concerning large-scale intergroup conflict among adults. First, win/lose situations seem conducive to rough-and-tumble activity. Second, although group membership alone is sufficient to induce own-group bias, competitive win/lose orientations would seem to intensify liking for one's own group and disliking for contending groups. Finally, it is commonly suggested that the imposition of superordinate goals would alleviate intrasocietal and intersocietal conflicts.

CONFLICTS WITHIN SOCIETY

Let's move up the scale from the small groups studied by Sherif and consider relationships among groups that constitute large identifiable segments of the U. S. population. An **ethnic group** is a collection of people who are considered by themselves and by others to have a common racial origin (as revealed by physical factors such as skin tone and facial features), a common national origin, a common language and cultural tradition, or some combination of these factors (Harding et al., 1969). Although reference will be made to several different ethnic groups, attention will focus on the conflict between black and white Americans, because this conflict has been one of the most serious and also one of the most carefully studied. A discussion of intergroup relations forces the use of generalities. However, this should not obscure the fact that within any given ethnic group it is possible to find represented a wide spectrum of attitudes and behaviors toward the members of other ethnic groups.

This section begins with a discussion of prejudice, that particular form of ingroup bias characterized by strong negative views of the outgroup. We will then consider the functions of discriminatory activity and will see that prejudice and discrimination tend to be self-perpetuating. Finally, we will look at two views concerning the best way to ensure good outcomes for one's own ethnic group.

PREJUDICE

Prejudicial attitudes are negative feelings that, according to Harding et al. (1969), depart from one or more of three ideal norms: the norm of rationality, the norm of justice, and the norm of human heartedness. The **norm of rationality** suggests that we should be accurate and factually correct, logical in our reasoning, and cautious when making judgments. A prejudiced attitude is likely to be inaccurate, incorrect, and illogical. The **norm of justice** suggests that all people should be treated equally, except with respect to their objective abilities. A prejudiced attitude includes the belief that differential treatment should be based on group membership, rather than on individual ability. The **norm of human heartedness** prescribes tolerance and compassion. A prejudiced attitude often advocates kicking, rather than rooting for, the underdog. A fully prejudiced attitude, then, is one that is irrational, unjust, and cold hearted.

Prejudicial attitudes presumably are acquired in many different ways—for example, as a result of modeling and social reinforcement (Chapter 4), as a result of persuasive communications, interpersonal influence, and conformity (Chapters 5, 8, and 9), and as a result of attempts to impose consistency on the world and see it as orderly and just (Chapters 3, 5, and 7). Moreover, prejudicial attitudes can serve any or all of the four functions identified by Katz (Chapter 5). For example, prejudice against blacks that might be prevalent in an urban neighborhood populated by poorly educated, lower-class whites who are in socially and economically insecure positions can simultaneously serve utilitarian, ego-defensive, value-expressive, and knowledge functions. Let's consider each of these functions in turn.

First, the arrival of a group of unskilled blacks raises the possibility that there will be more workers than jobs and thus can result in lowered wages and less job security for the equally unskilled white. Prejudicial activity aimed at preventing the blacks from obtaining jobs can have the utilitarian function of increasing the whites' job security. Second, the "I am better than you" attitude can serve the ego-defensive function of giving people with little going for them a sense of superiority. Third, prejudice against blacks can serve the value-expressive function for any person who has been indoctrinated in a heritage of white supremacy. Finally, the whites can make some sense out of their observation that blacks are treated shabbily if they draw the conclusion that "They must be bad to deserve this treatment." In this way prejudicial attitudes can serve the knowledge function.

Dimensions of Prejudice

Campbell (1947) sought to determine whether prejudice is a general attitude or factor (such that different measures of prejudice would inter-correlate highly) or whether it is actually a number of independent attitudes that are only loosely related. In the former case we would expect that, if an individual believed that Croatians were immoral, he or she would also believe that Croatians were lazy. In the latter case it would not be possible to predict ratings of industriousness given ratings of morality.

Campbell's study involved five "subtopics" of prejudice: (1) liking or disliking of a particular group, (2) beliefs about the degree of blame that should be accorded the group, (3) beliefs about the extent to which the group should be avoided, (4) beliefs about the intelligence of the group, and (5) beliefs about the morality of the group. Five-item scales were prepared dealing with each of these subtopics, and subjects rated five ethnic groups on each of the five scales. College students and high school students completed the scales, and intercorrelations were computed. The average interscale correlations for a given ethnic group were in the mid-.50s, which suggests a certain generality of prejudice. That is, if an ethnic group was disliked, it was also likely to be seen as blame-worthy, unintelligent, and immoral, and its representatives were likely to be avoided.

In a later series of three studies aimed at understanding prejudice toward blacks, Woodmansee and Cook (1967) found evidence that different facets of prejudice are to some extent independent. They identified 11 dimensions of prejudice toward blacks:

1. position on segregation and integration
2. acceptance of blacks in intimate relationships
3. belief in the inferiority of blacks
4. belief in the superiority of blacks
5. feelings of ease in interracial situations
6. expression of "derogatory beliefs" about blacks, such as "Blacks are educationally backward" or "Some blacks are so touchy about their rights that they are difficult to get along with"
7. position on the role of local autonomy in desegregation and civil-rights legislation
8. position on the role of individual choice in doing business with blacks or renting to blacks
9. acceptance of blacks as status superiors (such as a boss or as a teacher)
10. sympathy for victimized blacks
11. position on how quickly desegregation should take place

Evidence for these 11 dimensions of prejudice does not necessarily contradict the earlier findings of Campbell (Harding et al., 1969). In several cases the correlations among Woodmansee and Cook's "different" dimensions approached .70. Thus some of their interscale correlations exceeded Campbell's. (Woodmansee and Cook could argue that they found separate dimensions because their intrascale correlations were higher than their interscale correlations.) Thus prejudice would seem to have a certain amount of generality and a certain amount of specificity. For example, persons A and B might be more prejudiced against Croatians than person C, but A might be vocal about the group's intellectual inferiority, whereas B adamantly maintains that the integration of Croatians "should not be rushed."

Ethnic Stereotypes

A **stereotype** is a fixed attitude about the psychological and social attributes of the members of a given group. Once these generalizations have been formed, representatives of the group are automatically ascribed with these qualities. Stereotypes often involve negative evaluations, but they are not necessarily uncomplimentary to the group or its representative (Brigham, 1971). For example, the favorable view that all Italians are warm and friendly can be as much of a stereotype as the unfavorable view that all Scandinavians are cold and distant. Nonetheless, such blanket generalizations can be regarded as prejudicial in that they violate the norm of rationality (there is no factual basis for the stereotype) and the norm of justice (these generalizations are applied to people on the basis of group membership and without regard to their individuality). Although there is a certain ambiguity in the use of the term *stereotype* (Brigham, 1971), many psychologists still agree with Katz and Braly's (1935, p. 181) view that a stereotype is a "fixed impression which conforms very little to the facts it intends to represent, and results from our defining first and observing second."

Within our society there seems to be some long-standing agreement about the qualities that characterize different ethnic groups. On the basis of a literature search and interviews with a number of students, Katz and Braly (1933) assembled a list of 84 traits that people thought characteristic of several ethnic groups, including Jews, Chinese, Germans, Turks, blacks, and white Americans. Next the experimenters asked 100 subjects to select from this list the five traits they considered most applicable to each ethnic group. Despite the fact that there were 84 traits to choose from, more than half the choices used to characterize blacks involved only five different traits. The "Negro" was characterized as lazy, musical, ignorant, superstitious, and happy-go-lucky. Jews, it was agreed, were shrewd, mercenary, and ambitious, and Germans were industrious, methodical, and scientific.

About 20 years later, Gilbert (1951) repeated the Katz and Braly study. Although the same general picture emerged, there was a little less consensus among the respondents' choices. The "fading" of stereotypes suggested by this finding raised three heartening possibilities. First, the student body of 1950 might have contained larger proportions of minorities, with the result that students had learned through firsthand experience that the earlier characterizations were inaccurate. Second, social scientists' pronouncements on the evils of stereotyping could have been filtering down to the public at large. Third, the movies and other mass media might have stopped casting blacks in the roles of butler, maid, and musical chicken thief.

About 20 years later yet, Karlins, Coffman, and Walters (1969) found that, although some of the "traditional" stereotypes had been abandoned, new ones had sprung up to take their place. There was, however, another encouraging sign. The traits chosen to characterize the different ethnic groups were less polarized and more moderate. There was a sharp decrease, for example, in the unfavorability of the traits selected as "typifying" blacks.

Results of a still more recent study raise the possibility that it is not so much the negative stereotypes that have been fading as people's willingness to express them. In an experiment involving the bogus-pipeline technique (Chapter 2), Sigall and Page (1971) had 30 subjects indicate how characteristic they felt certain traits were of "Americans," whereas another 30 subjects indicated the extent to which they felt that these characteristics applied to "Negroes." Experimental or "pipeline" subjects were led to believe that lie-detector-like gadgetry made possible a direct physiological measure of their attitudes. As indicated earlier, "pipeline" subjects are presumed to give honest answers to avoid being second-guessed by the machine.

When the pipeline was not used, the stereotyped views of "Americans" (mean desirability = .53) and of "Negroes" (mean desirability = .49) were about the same. However, when the pipeline was used, the stereotyped view of "Americans" was much more favorable (mean rating = .84) than that of "Negroes" (mean rating = −.03). What these findings imply is that college students have learned that it is considered unintelligent, boorish, and undemocratic to adhere to negative stereotypes about blacks or other minorities. They may thus be reluctant to express such views, except under unusual conditions, such as when they run the risk of being unmasked as a liar by a machine.

Discrimination

Discriminatory behavior occurs whenever resources, conveniences, and comforts (such as good jobs, comfortable homes, membership in social clubs, and credit at a low interest rate) are controlled by one group and made inaccessible to another group. Although it is tempting to dismiss discriminatory acts as whimsical nastiness, they may serve a useful purpose for a group that is locked into a win/lose situation. Discriminatory behavior represents intragroup cooperation aimed at helping one's own group to do well in the overall intergroup competition. For example, keeping blacks out of good schools, good jobs, and good neighborhoods would mean that all these good things would remain in the hands of whites. Discriminatory behaviors, of course, are consonant with prejudicial beliefs.

Although (in theory at least) open attempts to discriminate through such means as posting "No Negroes Allowed" or "Orientals Need Not Apply" signs are relics of the past, less obvious procedures are still in use for penalizing members of different ethnic groups. For example, Johnson, Porter, and Mateljan (1971) had Mexican-American, black, and Caucasian couples visit apartment houses in a southern California city and ask about apartment availability and miscellaneous fees. About three-quarters of the managers showed some evidence of discrimination. Fewer apartments were available to the blacks and the Mexican Americans than to the Caucasians, and the fees cited blacks were higher than the fees cited Caucasians. Blacks were clearly less welcome than the Mexican Ameri-

cans; the Mexican Americans, in turn, were less welcome than the Caucasians.

To be discriminated against is to be exposed to special inconveniences, discourtesies, and frustrations. For example, at least two studies suggest that blacks are less likely than whites to be beneficiaries of white altruism. Gaertner and Bickman (1972) had a staff of male callers telephone more than 1100 subjects, about half of whom were black and half of whom were white. Half the callers gave the impression that they were white by speaking in standard English, whereas the other half gave the impression that they were black by talking in black dialect. As soon as someone answered the phone, the caller immediately indicated that he thought he had reached "Ralph's Garage" and said he needed emergency towing service. When informed that he had reached a wrong number, the caller expressed dismay over having wasted his only dime on the pay phone. He then implored the subject to dial Ralph's Garage for him. Whereas 65% of the white subjects did call Ralph's Garage for the white victim, only 53% did so for the black victim. The black subjects, however, were about equally likely to help a white victim as a black victim.

In a later study using similar "wrong-number" procedures, Gaertner (1973) found that registered members of both a "conservative" and a "liberal" political party were less likely to help a black victim than a white one. Whereas, for the most part, the conservatives' discriminatory behavior consisted of an outright refusal to help the black, the liberals' discriminatory behavior involved hanging up the phone before the black could finish making the request. Again, however, we should note that within any group there is a diversity of attitudes and opinions. In this experiment more than half of the "conservatives" and "liberals" did offer to help.

In some cases, people may be more likely to help a person of another race than a person of their own race. According to Dutton and Lake's (1973) **theory of reverse discrimination,** if people who consider themselves to be unprejudiced find something in their attitudes or behavior to suggest that they might be harboring prejudicial attitudes toward a minority group, they will give preferential treatment to members of that group, as if to prove to themselves that they are not prejudiced. In one test of this theory, subjects were Canadian college students who evaluated themselves as unprejudiced and who advocated equal treatment for all groups. After arriving for the experiment, they were connected to an apparatus that supposedly revealed their emotional responses. They were then shown a number of slides, including four group pictures of blacks and whites. The experimenters controlled the apparatus and in this way led some subjects to believe that they were emotionally upset by the interracial scenes. Other subjects were not led to believe that they might be prejudiced; instead, they were led to think that they were upset by pictures of riots and of sexual intercourse. As subjects left the lab, they were panhandled by either a black or a white confederate. In support of the theory of reverse discrimination, subjects who had been led to doubt their lack of prejudice gave more money to the black panhandler than did subjects who had no cause to doubt their impartiality. There was no comparable difference in the amount of money given to the white panhandler by subjects in the two conditions (Dutton & Lake, 1973).

Perhaps we have come a long way from the mid-1940s, when a man ran for governor of a Southern state with the promise that, if elected, all "Niggers" entering the state by train would be taken out of the first-class Pullman cars and forced to ride coach. Nonetheless, we can still find many practices that discriminate against people on the basis of their group membership. For example, chaining blacks, Indians, or Chicanos to menial jobs (with the rationalization that they are unqualified for better ones) effectively bars them from expensive neighborhoods, clubs, and resorts; introducing even nominal tuition fees makes a state university less accessible to the poor, thus ensuring that groups close to the poverty level will not be able to "better their lot."

Prejudice and Discrimination as Self-Perpetuating

Prejudicial attitudes may lead to discriminatory behavior. Discrimination, in turn, may bring about behaviors on the part of the victim that serve to justify or support the original prejudices. That is, if we expect another person to display certain behavior, we may act in such a way as to bring about the anticipated performance. This phenomenon is referred to as a **self-fulfilling prophecy.** As we smugly note that the other person acted as we expected, we minimize our own role in bringing it about.

For example, in a pilot study of a large metropolitan police force, Pamela Placencia, a graduate student at the University of California at Davis, discovered that police officers have different expectations and hence react quite differently when they stop cars in middle-class and in ghetto neighborhoods. In the middle-class neighborhood, no trouble is expected. The officer stops the car, questions the driver, and perhaps issues a citation. In the ghetto neighborhood, trouble is expected. Therefore a second prowl car is usually summoned before the suspect is approached. Walking up to the suspect, the officer is likely to unfasten the snap locking his pistol in its holster. The suspect, incensed by the display of power, may become angry and difficult to handle, with the consequence that there is indeed trouble, and an arrest is made. The episode strengthens the officer's expectation of trouble in the ghetto and the ghetto resident's expectation of harassment by the police.

Recently, Word, Zanna, and Cooper (1974) studied self-fulfilling prophecies in an interracial job-interview setting. In the first study, subjects interviewed applicants for a team that would be planning a marketing campaign. Some subjects interviewed a black and then a white candidate, whereas other subjects interviewed a white and then a black applicant. In point of fact, all applicants were confederates who had been carefully coached to act in a standard way with all interviewers. It was found that interviewers were more distant and aloof, made more speech errors, and allowed less time for the interview when examining the black candidate. In other words, for the black applicants the interview situation was made more uncomfortable, and they were given less of a chance to prove themselves. In a second study, Word and his associates attempted to discover the effects of the different treatments accorded the black and white applicants in the previous experiment. In this study the experimenters interviewed white applicants and varied distance, speech errors, and time. As expected, the subjects treated as the black applicants had been treated in the first experiment did not perform as well as the subjects treated as the white applicants had been treated in the first experiment.

Self-fulfilling prophecies can also affect academic performance. For example, a teacher might expect a Chicano (Mexican American) child to do poorly in class. He or she then decides that helping this student would be a waste of time, whereas helping a middle-class white student would pay rich dividends in the form of intellectual growth for the child. The teacher thus encourages the middle-class student but discourages the

Chicano. Then, when the Chicano student fails and the middle-class white student flourishes, the teacher's expectations are strengthened. This kind of thing can happen even if the two students are equal in motivation and ability. Rosenthal and Jacobsen (1968) led teachers to expect that certain students would show unusually little intellectual development, whereas others would show unusually great improvement, in the course of an academic year. In fact, these two groups of students were of equivalent promise and ability. Yet the group that the teachers expected to improve showed a leap in performance that the other group did not match.

Several subsequent studies have sought to uncover the different ways teachers act when they have high as compared with low expectations concerning a student's improvement. In general, teachers are more positive toward those students whom they expect to do well. Rubovits and Maehr (1973) found that students who were expected to do well were called upon and praised more often than were students who were expected to do poorly. Chaikin, Sigler, and Derlega (1974) found that, compared with subjects tutoring a 12-year-old boy who had been described as "dull," subjects tutoring a boy described as "bright" were more likely to smile, maintain eye contact, lean forward, and vigorously nod their heads in agreement. Thus students who were expected to do well were given more opportunity to exercise and develop their intellectual skills and received more encouragement and approval for doing so. For the most part, black students are not shown as much of this kind of encouragement as white students are (Rubovits & Maehr, 1973).

Teachers may expect blacks, Chicanos, Indians, and other minorities to do poorly because of low scores on intelligence tests. However, these scores may be misleading (Jorgensen, 1973, 1974). Although IQ tests are supposed to measure raw potential, they in fact assess vocabulary ("What is an envelope?"), quantitative skills ("If 12 pencils cost 60¢, how much would one pencil cost?"), and the extent to which one has acquired middle-class social values ("What do you do if you find an addressed, stamped envelope?"). These tests thus presume that the respondent is both familiar with the customs, artifacts, and values of white middle-class society and motivated to do as well on the test as possible.

Many blacks, Chicanos, Indians, and children of other minority groups are not familiar with white middle-class ways and do not share white middle-class children's zeal for test taking. Consequently, the test performance of minorities may lead to an underestimation of their abilities. On the basis of this underestimation, expectations may be formed that set self-fulfilling prophecies in motion. According to Jorgenson, because our present IQ tests do not fairly assess the intelligence of minorities, it is inappropriate to label certain blacks or other minorities as "dull" or "retarded" on the basis of their IQ scores. A more equitable test might establish that their intelligence is well within the range of the normal.

CONFLICT RESOLUTION

There seems to be an endless list of proposals for eliminating inter-group conflict within our society. In one group we find people who favor conflict resolution through defeat of one side by the other. In another group we find those who advocate some kind of mixture of competitive and cooperative activities. Many "black power" writers, for example, suggest that blacks should develop, through competitive and, if necessary, aggressive activities, a position of strength, which can then be used to induce cooperation and, ultimately, full integration (McEvoy & Miller, 1969). In a third group we could find people who favor purely cooperative means for reducing intergroup tensions and merging the conflicting groups into a larger, cohesive entity. This third group, which operates on the assumption that it is possible to move directly from intergroup conflict to intergroup cooperation, would seem to include nine out of ten social psychologists!

The Interracial-Contact Hypothesis

In our discussions of the mere-exposure effect in Chapter 3 and of propinquity and friendship in Chapter 6, we saw that contact between two individuals is likely to lead to their developing liking for each other. Considerable evidence suggests that intergroup contact often reduces interracial prejudices and leads to intergroup liking (Amir, 1969; Harding et al., 1969; Pettigrew, 1971). This result has been shown in the school, on the job, and in the community. Horowitz (1936) found a greater preference for interracial contact among students attending an integrated school than among students attending nonintegrated schools. Brophy (1945) reported that, the more times a white sailor had shipped with a black, the less prejudice he showed. Wilner, Walkley, and Cook (1952, 1955) indicated that whites who lived in integrated housing units (and who thus had considerable contact with blacks) were less prejudiced than those who lived in segregated housing. Williams (1964) reported that interracial contact within small towns was associated with a low level of prejudice, and Hyman and Sheatsley (1964) found reductions in prejudice in settings where desegregation had already taken place.

Some of these studies are difficult to interpret, since initial low levels of prejudice might have been responsible for the interracial contact. Harding et al. point out that, in Brophy's study, for example, the merchant seamen who shipped more than once with blacks almost all belonged to a union with a militant antidiscrimination policy. Yet in some studies it is clear that the contact was the cause and the more favorable attitudes the effect. For example, Mann (1959) assigned blacks and whites to six-person discussion groups and found that over successive meetings members of these groups became less sensitive to racial barriers.

However, despite these encouraging findings, interracial contact by itself cannot be expected to resolve interethnic conflicts. There are important limitations to the **interracial-contact hypothesis.**

To begin with, intergroup contacts can take place in many different settings, such as on the job, at school, or in the neighborhood. Whereas contact within a particular setting can reduce prejudice in that setting, it does not necessarily result in lesser prejudice in other settings. Thus, thrown together to combat a common enemy, white and black soldiers may develop respect for each other as fighters but still avoid each other at base or home on leave. Harding and Hogrefe (1952), in a study of integrated department stores, reported that whites showed little prejudice against their black coworkers on the job but retained their prejudices when off the job. Minard (1952) found that, even though blacks and whites worked well side by side in coal mines, they maintained separate lives during off-duty hours.

Moreover, for intergroup contact to lead to a reduction of prejudice, certain conditions must be met. In one of Sherif's camp studies, an attempt was made to reduce conflict by bringing the boys together to set off fireworks. Once assembled, however, the boys segregated themselves into two separate groups and exploded their fireworks some yards away from each other. At the interracial level, the slave owners of the Old South certainly had considerable contact with blacks, yet they were less favorable toward blacks than were Northern abolitionists, some of whom had never seen a black. To take a more recent example, we would not expect interracial contact in the course of a ghetto uprising to lead to a reduction of prejudice.

Allport (1954b) has discussed four conditions under which interaction is likely to lead to a decrease in prejudice. First, equality of status is important. If a high-status white interacts with a low-status black, reduction of prejudice is unlikely. MacKenzie (1948) found that, among American war veterans, only 5% of those who had contact with unskilled, low-status blacks had favorable interracial attitudes, whereas 64% of the veterans who had contact with skilled, professional, high-status blacks expressed favorable interracial attitudes. Second, Allport suggests that intergroup contact will lead to a reduction of prejudice if the representatives of the two groups are seeking common goals. Third, a decrease in prejudice is likely if the representatives of the two groups are cooperating to reach these common goals. (These second and third conditions, of course, involve superordinate goals.) Finally, interracial contact is likely to lead to a reduction in prejudice if that contact is consistent with prevailing laws, customs, and traditions.

Thus we would *not* expect intergroup contact to reduce prejudice if the groups were of unequal status, pursuing different or separatist goals, competing over scarce resources, or discouraged by law, customs, and etiquette from friendly interaction. Pettigrew (1971) suggests that Allport's four conditions lead to a decrease in prejudice because they bring out the *similarities* between the two groups.

Planned Strategies for Conflict Resolution

A number of strategies have been offered for reducing intergroup prejudices and putting avowed principles of equality into action. These change techniques have been aimed at the individual, at the small group, and at the entire "system," or society at large. Yet to those who remain disadvantaged, discouragingly little progress seems evident (McEvoy & Miller, 1969).

Attempts have been made to apply the attitude-change procedures discussed in Chapter 5 to reduce prejudice on the part of individual attitude holders. For example, Culbertson (1957) found that inducing white subjects to play the role of an integrationist reduced their segregationist leanings, and the original experiment supporting Kelman's (1958) three processes of attitude change manipulated blacks' attitudes about the integration of black colleges. Katz, Sarnoff, and McClintock's (1956) tests of the functional theory of attitude change showed that prejudices serving the ego-defensive function could not be eliminated by straightforward informational appeals. Instead, it was necessary to help the person understand the irrational nature of the attitudes and "work through" the associated negative feelings.

Of course, 200 million Americans cannot be run through the laboratory one by one, but repeated attempts have been made to use the mass media (such as radio, television, and the movies) to improve attitudes toward particular minority groups. However, special propaganda programs may not reach the intended audience, whose prejudices direct them to tune in other stations. Instead, these shows are more likely to be enthusiastically heard or viewed by members of the minority group itself (Lazarsfeld, 1940).

Nevertheless, people are affected by what they see in movies and on TV, particularly if the same theme is repeated over time (Weiss, 1969). For example, children in a town where there were no blacks became antiblack after seeing *Birth of a Nation,* which glorified the Ku Klux Klan (Peterson & Thurstone, 1933), and some viewers became less anti-Semitic after seeing *Gentleman's Agreement,* which was sympathetic toward Jews (Rosen, 1948). There have been many changes in the content of films and TV programs over the last few decades, and from our discussion of modeling we have every reason to believe that these changes should help reduce prejudice. The stereotypes evident in the movies of the 1930s and 1940s are no longer perpetuated in movies or on television today. Now, for example, blacks are likely to have lead roles and are hired as authoritative TV spokespersons for various commercial products. Today's comedies involving blacks are written to encourage white audiences to laugh with blacks, rather than at them.

Group-oriented change procedures have involved interracial conferences and encounter groups (Cobbs, 1972). Although there is likely to be a self-selection factor such that people who are already low in prejudice are the most likely to be in attendance, new organizational role prescriptions may force interracial contact among people high in prejudice. For example, an industrial firm may expect all employees at a given level to participate in a laboratory-training group, and, if the firm is truly integrated, interracial contact would automatically follow. Racial tensions may become a direct focus of the group. One exercise intended to encourage understanding and develop a "feel" for the other side is to have blacks wear white masks and whites wear black masks.

To study the effects of interracial interaction on prejudice, Cook (1970) has devised an experimental task on which two whites interact with one black under carefully controlled conditions. One white is the subject, who is known to be highly prejudiced against blacks; the other white and the black are carefully trained confederates. The trio is confronted with the task of operating a mock railroad, which involves using the railroad's limited equipment to make as many shipments to as many cities as possible in a limited period of time. By careful manipulation of roles and activities, Cook and his associates can explore the conditions under which black-white interaction leads to a reduction of prejudice. In an early study, interaction took place under five conditions, which Cook saw as essential for reducing prejudice: (1) equality of status, (2) a cooperative task, (3) norms favoring interracial interaction, (4) an intimate setting in which the black engaged in self-disclosure, and (5) deliberate attempts on the part of the black to behave in ways that contradicted prevalent stereotypes. For example, the black was given a highly responsible position in the organization, all three participants had to cooperate to run the railroad, and the black revealed personal information. After a number of sessions, about 40% of the subjects had become less prejudiced.

Subsequent research using the "railroad game" has varied group success and failure (Blanchard, Adelman, & Cook, 1975) and the perceived competence of the black (Blanchard, Weigl, & Cook, 1975). Only the latter of these two variables has turned out to be highly important.

The competence of the white work partners had little effect on ratings of their attractiveness. However, the less competently the black stimulus persons performed, the lower the attractiveness ratings they received. Blanchard et al. suggest that poor performance on the part of the black triggers negative stereotypes not associated with whites. That is, incompetent behavior calls forth the prejudiced person's "customary" dislike and disrespect for blacks. The authors point out that, in many cases, blacks have not been taught the skills necessary to do well in newly desegregated task-oriented situations. The initially lower level of task competence shown by some minority-group members could thus prevent the reduction of prejudice in a cooperative interracial work group.

Systems change involves legislative action. At first it may seem that intergroup harmony cannot be enacted by law. However, there are at least three ways in which equal-rights legislation can help to reduce conflicts. First, legislation has an important symbolic effect, and many people accept it simply because it is the "law of the land." Second, legislation may lead to intergroup contact under conditions favorable to the reduction of prejudice. Third, legislation may prevent discrimination, which has two beneficial effects. One is that, in accordance with dissonance theory, people who are prevented by threat of fine from discriminatory acts may change their attitudes to be in line with their new egalitarian practices (provided that the fine is not so heavy that it provides sufficient external justification for the nondiscriminatory behavior!). The other is that antidiscrimination laws can destroy self-fulfilling prophecies. For example, new educational and employment options can give a minority group the opportunity to achieve and to smash the stereotypes that may have blocked these options in the first place.

We are a long way from a society in which members of different ethnic groups can claim equal autonomy and equal political influence. No one technique seems certain to reduce interethnic conflict. Hopefully, an awareness of the problem and the use of a combination of procedures will make some headway toward the elimination of prejudice, discrimination, and interethnic violence.

PART SUMMARY

Prejudicial attitudes violate the norms of rationality, justice, and human heartedness. Different components or facets of prejudice are moderately intercorrelated. Once a person has been identified as a member of an ethnic group, the perceiver may automatically ascribe that person with a number of personality characteristics. Stereotypes refer to fixed impressions of the qualities of the members of a given group. Stereotypes violate the norms of rationality and justice. Research between the early 1930s and the late 1960s suggested that stereotypes were fading, in that there was less consensus about the traits that characterized a given ethnic group and in that the traits selected were less and less polarized. An implication of a relatively recent study, however, is that some of this "fading" may merely represent an unwillingness to publicly admit to holding stereotyped views.

Discrimination occurs whenever the resources, conveniences, and comforts under the control of one•group are made inaccessible to members of another group. Although strong legislation discourages open discrimination, it does not eliminate differential treatment that may make schooling or good jobs less accessible to certain segments of our population. Recent research suggests that, if people who consider themselves unprejudiced toward a minority group are given reason to doubt their lack of prejudice, they may respond by showing preferential treatment toward that minority group. This behavior is known as reverse discrimination.

Prejudicial attitudes and discriminatory behaviors are likely to be self-perpetuating. If we expect another person to do poorly, we may act in such a way as to bring about the expected poor performance. This effect is called a self-fulfilling prophecy. The poor performance is likely to strengthen the initial prejudice, leading to more militant discrimination and even poorer performances on the part of the victim.

Many suggestions have been offered for eliminating intergroup conflict in our society. Most social psychologists have offered "cooperative" solutions that involve merging conflicting groups into a larger, cohesive entity. According to the interracial-contact hypothesis, contact between conflicting ethnic groups should lead to a lessening of prejudice and the development of harmony and good will. Contact sometimes does reduce prejudice, but there are many important qualifications to the interracial-contact hypothesis. Contact in one setting does not necessarily lead to lessened prejudice in another setting. Contact will not reduce prejudice when the representatives of the two groups are of unequal status, are pursuing different or separatist goals, are competing over scarce resources, or are discouraged from friendly interaction by law or custom.

Attempts to reduce prejudice and conflict have been aimed at the individual, at the small group, and at the society as a whole. Procedures directed toward the individual have included role playing, persuasive appeals, and other attitude-change techniques. Attempts at eliminating prejudice in small groups have involved encouraging interethnic interaction under conditions believed likely to generate good will and harmony. At the societal or systems level, legislation has been aimed at reducing prejudice and conflict. At present no single change procedure promises to eliminate the conflicts within our society.

CONFLICT BETWEEN SOCIETIES

Nobody ever seems to want war. Even Adolf Hitler found it inopportune to openly advocate war; to justify his invasion of Poland as "retaliatory," he staged a raid on one of his own radio stations and made it appear that the "enemy" was responsible. Yet the last century has been one of almost unending warfare, and a "lesson of history" is that war is inevitable. Yet, is armed conflict really unavoidable, or is it sometimes a matter of compounded errors of judgment? Discussing the origin of World War I, the British historian A. J. P. Taylor said:

> Men are reluctant to believe that great events have small causes. Therefore, once the Great War started, they were convinced that it was the result of profound forces. It is hard to discover these when we examine the details. Nowhere was there conscious determination to provoke a war. Statesmen miscalculated. They used the instruments of bluff and threat which had proved effective on previous occasions. This time, things went wrong. The deterrent on which they relied failed to deter; the statesmen became the prisoners of their own weapons. The great armies accumulated to provide security and preserve the peace carried the nations to war by their own weight [1964, p. 13].

WHO RELATES IN INTERNATIONAL RELATIONS?

Newspapers sometimes describe whole nations as if they were individuals. It is easy to visualize, say, Uncle Sam and a bear branded with a hammer and sickle dancing on the edge of a cliff inscribed *"nuclear disaster."* Yet such descriptions obscure the complexity of international relations. Two nations are not the same as two people dressed up for a Halloween party.

International relations can be analyzed at three levels: the *personal,* the *microscopic social,* and the *macroscopic social* (Etzioni, 1969). The levels chosen have an effect on the remedies proposed for reducing international tensions.

At the **personal level,** international conduct can be viewed as an interaction between two leaders. For example, some of the origins of World War I might be sought in private discussions between the German Kaiser and his cousins, the Czar of Russia and the King of England; the

origins of World War II in various concessions that British Prime Minister Chamberlain granted to Adolf Hitler; and the origins of the Vietnam War in relations between a number of American Presidents and North Vietnamese leader Ho Chi Minh. Ensuring peace at this level would require preventing a "maniac" from gaining the helm or finding techniques to help individual leaders to develop faith and trust in each other as human beings.

At the **microscopic social level,** international relations are viewed as interaction between select and relatively small segments of the different societies. These segments or groups are the **elite**—that is, those members of society who have power and privilege, such as high government officials, top military brass, rich industrialists, and a sprinkling of scientists and professors. Staving off a war at this level would require directing appeals toward the privileged or powerful segments of the population.

At the **macroscopic social level,** international relations are viewed as interaction between whole societies or entire populations. This does not necessarily mean that individuals from the two societies actually interact with each other (when was the last time you interacted with a Russian, a Red Chinese, or a Cuban?). However, through the mass media, word of mouth, and occasional limited contacts, each side forms an image of the other. By voting "hawk" or "dove" and by vociferously expressing opinions, very large segments in each society might determine the course of international affairs. At this level, preventing a war might involve an appeal to the two populations involved. Exchange programs might be encouraged, international endeavors supported, and massive propaganda campaigns launched to convince each side of the good intentions of the other.

Etzioni's own view is that international conduct is a mixture of personal, microscopic social, and macroscopic social variables. He suggests that public opinion forms a framework that sets significant limits on the alternatives open to top leaders and affects their range of maneuverability. Public opinion, in turn, is not a simple product or summation of the attitudes of each person in the society; the educated and the politically active contribute more to it than the uneducated and the politically inactive. The framework within which the top decision makers must maneuver is, in effect, based on broad and vague ideas about such concepts as "colonialism," "appeasement," or "the American way of life."

OWN-GROUP BIAS

Earlier I noted that, during the phase of intergroup conflict, Sherif's Rattlers and Eagles developed pronounced "we-are-good-and-they-are-bad" attitudes. Own-group bias has been repeatedly noted during times of tense international relations. Such bias usually involves some distortion, for it is not possible to have two groups, each of which is objectively better than the other!

The Mirror-Image Phenomenon

During the "heat" of the cold war of the 1950s, an American psychologist, Urie Bronfenbrenner (1961), noted an interesting symmetry between Americans' views of Russians and Russians' views of Americans. He discovered that the people of both nations were genuinely satisfied with their way of life and considered themselves to be a peace-loving people led by well-intentioned leaders. He also found that each side thought the other side was led by wicked leaders who lied to and exploited their people and pursued foolish and insane policies that would force the world into war. By choosing illustrations carefully, each side could find examples to support its views. The discovery that the Russians saw themselves as we saw ourselves and saw us as we saw them was labeled the **mirror-image phenomenon.**

The mirror-image phenomenon appears in the judgments we make of each other's actions. Since behavior is in some ways objective (during the cold war both the United States and the Soviet Union sent troops into other countries), the differences in judgments are likely to appear in such factors as the suspected motive for the behavior. Thus, if we invade Wallonia, we are doing so to preserve the peace; if the Russians invade the same country, it is but one more example of their shameless intent to overrun the world.

To study this phenomenon, Oskamp (1965) identified 50 actions, both friendly and hostile, that had been taken in recent years by *both* the United States and Russia. The items were listed in two different questionnaires; in one they were attributed to the United States and in the other to Russia. American college students then evaluated the actions. The same actions were far more likely to be rated favorably when the United States was presented as the instigator than when Russia was presented as the instigator.

Dangerous Perceptions

According to White (1966), own-group bias is a major factor in the outbreak of war. Such views contribute to a feeling that war is necessary and that one will emerge the victor. White suggests that six similar perceptions and attitudes could be noted among the Austrians prior to their movement against Serbia (and the commencement of World War I) and among the Germans prior to their movement against Poland (and the commencement of World War II). These six common perceptions and attitudes were a *diabolical enemy image*, a *virile self-image*, a *moral self-image*, *selective inattention*, an *absence of empathy*, and *military overconfidence*.

The **diabolical enemy image** is the perception that the other group is evil and does not live up to the minimal standards for human decency. For example, the Austrians saw the Serbians as criminal assassins, and Hitler saw the Russians, Jews, and people of Central Europe as evil incarnate.

The **virile self-image** is a preoccupation with one's own power and prestige. According to this attitude, backing down before another nation would be an intolerable humiliation that would weaken one's hand in other international bargaining situations. In our own history, a virile self-image is reflected in such ringing slogans as "Millions for defense, but not one cent for tribute."

The **moral self-image** refers to the view of oneself as completely just and right. This self-image endows the status of a holy crusader or an avenging angel spurred on by the hurrahs of the heavenly hosts. Once war has begun, groups with moral self-images usually do not think of themselves as having started the trouble; if it is clear that they opened fire first, they can explain in great deal why they "had" to do so.

Selective inattention refers to an inability to see all sides of an issue. It also implies a highly faulty assessment of the various alternatives. For example, Austria did not stop to think about the differences between punishing Serbian nationals within the Austrian borders and sending a military expedition to punish Serbians within Serbia. Inattentiveness is likely to be greatest toward those details that might lead to military defeat.

An **absence of empathy** refers to a failure to understand the other side's point of view. For example, it is difficult for an invader who sends a "courageous force" across the border to see that the other side might view the action as "naked aggression" or that a forceful proclamation might be viewed by the other side as a painful humiliation.

Finally, **military overconfidence** is an attitude that can take three major forms: (1) a failure to carefully weigh the possibility that other countries will intervene on behalf of one's enemy; (2) an underestimation of the stiff resistance likely from an aroused enemy fighting on its own soil; and (3) a false hope that the enemy people (as compared with the enemy leaders) are really on one's own side and, once the war has begun, will overthrow their evil leaders and quickly change sides. Military overconfidence lowers the perceived costs of conflict.

Prejudicial attitudes and distorted perceptions such as these can increase the probability of warfare. They fan animosities, prevent a clear-headed and realistic assessment of the situation, and make intergroup communication and negotiation very difficult. Perhaps an awareness of the possibility of such attitudes may lessen the likelihood that we will be caught up in them during times of international crisis.

COMPETITIVE STRATEGIES

Each side in an international dispute seeks to protect its own interests. Various types of competitive strategies have been proposed for doing so. Most of these strategies involve marshaling (and, if necessary, using) economic, military, and other forms of power in an effort to do well in the competition.

Threat of Force

Judging by the huge military budgets of many countries, an expensive war machine is considered very useful for the conduct of international affairs. A military machine need not be put into action to serve its sponsor's interests; the mere threat that it could be used is often sufficient to accomplish this end. The reasoning underlying the threat of force is that, if the other side can be made to see that a failure to comply will be *too costly*, then one's demands are likely to be met.

Of course, many Americans feel that only "bad guys" would use threat to take advantage of another nation. However, the fact that we are "good guys" does not allow us to relax and channel our military expenditures into other areas. As "good guys" we, too, must maintain an expensive military—not to take things from other countries, but to keep other countries from taking things from us or from our friends. The idea is that, if the "bad guys" can be convinced that it is dangerous to continue pursuing their reckless course, they will show some restraint. **Deterrence** refers to the use of threat defensively—that is, to prevent an opposing group from becoming too aggressive or too greedy. Many of our military expenditures are based on the strategy of deterrence. The value of a nuclear warhead is not realized when it disintegrates an enemy city; it is realized when the enemy recognizes that it *could* disintegrate one of its cities. The motto of the people who are responsible for delivering our nuclear bombs—"Peace is our profession"—is not intended to be hypocritical.

The Big Bluff

Financing a large military machine is only one part of creating a position of strength. It is also necessary that the other side *see* this force and understand that one is *resolved to use it.* Schelling (1960) suggests that flaunting one's military strength (for example, having the army parade around an enemy's borders or stationing the navy just outside the enemy's territorial waters) and freely and openly issuing challenges and threats can be a good way of getting what you want. According to Schelling's line of reasoning, in a dispute the side that appears more irrational, desperate, or crazy will have a definite advantage. The other side, being rational, will capitulate on the grounds that holding out simply isn't worth the risk. For example, if you see a driver racing onto a one-lane bridge at such a high rate of speed that it is questionable whether he or she could stop, you would most likely yield the right of way.

The same kind of strategy used by the road hog has been successfully employed in international relations. Following World War I, Germany was forced to demilitarize the Rhineland. In 1936 the Nazis did not bargain with France to reoccupy the Rhineland; they simply marched in. France, having the choice of going to war or grudgingly accepting the situation, chose the latter. Yet the occupation of the Rhineland was an act of bravado on Hitler's part. Despite an appearance of strength, the German army was very weak at that time and was under orders to retreat if the French army showed signs of resistance.

Two sides, of course, can use threat and bluff, and, according to Schelling, the side that makes the larger threats and the bigger bluffs is likely to win. Schelling discusses an example of a group of strikers and a railroad engineer. The strikers block the path of the train, leaving it up to the engineer to stop. Next, the engineer sets the throttle on low, jumps out of the cab, and walks alongside the train, leaving it up to the strikers to get out of the way. Then the strikers chain themselves to the track and, with a flourish, throw away the key, leaving it up to the engineer to jump back into the cab and stop the train. Quite likely, at this point, if the engineer sees this last maneuver and can get back into the train fast enough, the issue will be resolved in favor of the strikers.

Schelling has some interesting ideas concerning who makes a "good" negotiator. According to the traditional view, the negotiator is given the power to make concessions, with the hope that he or she will use this power wisely. Schelling's alternative view recommends sending in a handicapped negotiator whose "hands are tied" in that he or she does not have the power to accede to the other side's demands. This negotiator can, however, cheerfully accept concessions from the other side.

Very often, says Schelling, making big threats and playing with fire just require acting ability. Underneath the front of a homicidal or suicidal maniac is a highly rational individual who is cooly calculating the other side's reactions. Here's hoping that the people doing the calculating never make mistakes! Suppose, for example, the strikers were to underestimate how long it would take the engineer to scurry back up into his cab and stop the train. There is always the possibility that an error will be made or that the other side will call the bluff. Threat and bluff have gotten good results, but for many of us the element of risk makes "coming across like gangbusters" an unacceptable strategy.

Limited Warfare

Hermann Kahn (1960, 1965, 1966) notes that threat and force, when used, should be carefully gauged to meet the needs of each specific situation. Let's say you decide that a military strike is required against some foe. If your opponent retaliates or makes a countermove, you should increase your level of military activity. Repeatedly proving that you are a little tougher and a little more resolute than your opponent will cause that opponent to conclude that further resistance will be too expensive, so it is best to concede right now.

Kahn believes that warfare on a limited scale can prevent all-out nuclear holocaust. He has devised an "escalation ladder" with rungs indicating the degree of conflict. His fanciest ladder contains no fewer than 44 graduated steps and 6 major thresholds (Kahn, 1965). At the bottom are half-hearted threat (rung 1) and political, economic, and diplomatic gestures (rung 2). At rung 5 comes a show of force, at rung 12 a large "conventional" war, and at rung 21 a "local" nuclear war. The next 22 rungs involve increasing use of atomic weapons, culminating in "spasm or insensate war" at rung 44. Following initial disagreement, the major thresholds of conflict are (1) boat rocking, (2) nuclear threat, (3) battlefield use of nuclear weapons, (4) exemplary use of nuclear weapons against the enemy homeland, (5) destruction of enemy bases within the homeland, and (6) destruction of enemy population centers. Maintaining the peace, suggests Kahn, requires a good defensive system (including fallout shelters, evacuation plans, and so forth), which reduces the effectiveness of the other side's weapons, and a good offensive system, which our enemies believe we are ready and willing to use.

Kahn discusses arms races and warfare of different grades much as one might discuss a board game such as Uncle Wiggily. Land on the wrong rung of the escalation ladder, and you have to go home. (At any rung one side will have an advantage over the other, but the advantage may shift from rung to rung.) A criticism of Kahn is that his coldly intellectual arguments obscure the incredible cost of warfare and encourage "thinking about the unthinkable" (namely, a nuclear holocaust). Kahn responds that unemotional discussion is exactly what is required for dealing with life-or-death issues. Don't we expect a certain amount of detachment on the part of surgeons? Kahn further argues that thinking about the unthinkable is what we need to do. After all, ignoring the nuclear monster does not mean that it isn't there. Indeed, we must deliberately try to avoid wishful and unrealistic thinking. *One week* before World War II began, 10 out of 12 European newspapers surveyed responded that there would be "no war this year" (Kahn, 1966).

For controlled escalation to protect national interests and prevent nuclear disaster, the nation's decision makers must: (1) have clear knowledge of the situation, (2) be able to assess probable countermoves that would follow various actions on their part, and (3) have complete control over their own forces. In other words, they must be able to exercise conscious, rational, and deliberate control over the escalation. And herein lies the flaw. The situation can easily get out of hand and the process of escalation career forward without restraint, as seemed to happen in World War I. Approximately 27.5 million people died in World War I, and more than 55 million people died in World War II. We can only speculate on the number of casualties that would result from the use of nuclear weapons and sophisticated delivery systems such as are ready for World War III.

There are at least three reasons why after the first few steps up the escalation ladder matters might get out of control (Osgood, 1965; Etzioni, 1969). First, the two sides may have different perceptions about the magnitude of a given step. One side may take what it considers to be a minor step, but the other side interprets it as a major step and retaliates accordingly. Second, a forceful action may show the enemy one's own resolve but also strengthen the enemy's resolve. It is generally felt that the bombing of German civilians in World War II did more to stiffen resistance than to break morale. Finally, a vicious pattern of rewards and frustrations is likely to keep increasing the escalation. Following each step up, one side is sure to be rewarded and the other side frustrated. The rewarded side is reinforced for violence, and the frustrated side is spurred on to greater efforts. Certainly, wars can be contained, as has been proven in Korea and Vietnam. However, Kahn's proposals, like Schelling's, involve an element of risk that many of us would find unacceptable.

COOPERATIVE SOLUTIONS

Many social scientists reject power-oriented solutions to international conflicts because they feel it is too likely that something will go dreadfully wrong and because strong-arm tactics do not fit in with their humanitarian values. They point instead to alternatives that seek to decrease the level of armaments and reduce international tensions.

Unilateral Disarmament

One strategy that has repeatedly been proposed as a solution to international conflict is that we disarm ourselves (unilateral disarmament). Since the end of World War II a number of writers have suggested that, if we initiate unilateral disarmament, Russia and the other world powers will follow suit. The idea is that, after we render ourselves defenseless, Russia will be nice to us, since we will finally have proven that we are peace loving and trustworthy. According to the more outspoken proponents of this approach, even if our enemies take advantage of us after we're disarmed, "Better red than dead."

Proposals for unilateral disarmament show more in the way of heart than in the way of sensitivity to the demands of reality. Effecting unconditional unilateral disarmament is the same as granting an enemy absolute victory. In fact, the famous Prussian strategist Karl von Clausewitz defined absolute victory as disarmament of the enemy, for, "When an enemy is disarmed, it is possible to impose any condition one wishes, including total annihilation" (Aron, 1966). For this reason, advocates of unilateral disarmament have been decried as Communists and traitors. Whatever their intentions, there is no guarantee that, if we disarmed, other nations would respect our interests and rights and refrain from taking advantage of us (Osgood, 1962). At the risk of incurring the wrath of my colleagues, I would like to suggest that viewing the world through rose-colored glasses can yield perceptions as distorted as those discussed by Bronfenbrenner and White. Whether or not unilateral disarmament would work, it will not come about, because the kinds of risks involved would not be tolerated by major factions within our society.

GRIT

An alternative to unilateral disarmament has been offered by Osgood (1962), who proposes an "arms race in reverse." The name of his plan is *Graduated Reciprocation in Tension Reduction,* or **GRIT** for short. This plan should work between any two belligerents. However, for purposes of illustration, we'll consider it in the context in which it was developed: as pertaining to the relationship between the United States and Russia during an intense phase of the cold war.

International tensions build up slowly, over time, and as a result of repeated incidents involving the threat or use of force. Osgood suggests that this pattern provides a model for its own reversal. That is, it should be possible to throw the arms race into "reverse gear." This feat can be accomplished by initiating and responding to actions that *reduce* tensions rather than induce them. Actions, not just words, are required, because words no longer have credibility. The series of moves aimed at eliminating tensions must be both *graduated* and *reciprocated.* This feature distinguishes Osgood's approach from unilateral disarmament.

By "graduated," Osgood means that the initial steps should be small ones involving very minor risks, although later steps can be more dramatic and pronounced. By "reciprocated," he means that each time one side makes a move toward peace, the other side must respond in kind. This reciprocation is a precondition for the first side's taking another step.

Applying this model to U. S.-U. S. S. R. relations, Osgood suggested that we should take the initial step. The process would begin with the announcement of a few "low-risk" moves—that is, actions that could not be taken advantage of in such a way that our national security or international commitments would be endangered. Whereas most disarmers would throw nuclear weapons into the sea first and then relinquish the smaller weapons, Osgood argues that the "popguns" should be the first to go.

Examples of low-risk actions would include closing useless but visible military bases, sharing information gained in space, and loosening restrictions on travel and trade. The steps must be well publicized, real, and verifiable, and the reasons why they are being taken must be made clear. Once the initiative has been taken, it is imperative that the other side respond in kind. Only then are more dramatic steps possible. There must always be defense against attack, and the speed, number, and size of the peace moves should be gauged on the basis of the other side's responses.

Osgood admits that GRIT is difficult to implement, since it has to be sold not only to the other side but to those within each society who would interpret the necessary friendly acts as concessions or signs of weakness. Yet he argues that the only way to ensure peace is for one side to take the initiative and make conciliatory gestures while maintaining its own security. His plan has received some testing, both in the laboratory (Pilisuk & Skolnick, 1968; Tedeschi, Lindskold, Horai, & Gahagan, 1969) and in the field (Etzioni, 1967, 1969).

Pilisuk and Skolnick (1968) devised an experimental game to test GRIT. It was modeled after the Prisoner's Dilemma Game in that it involved two responses, one cooperative or conciliatory and the other competitive or nonconciliatory. Male subjects were seated before a board that contained five levers. These levers could be thrown either toward a factory or toward a missile. At the beginning of each trial, five missiles showed. Within the trial the subject had the opportunity to make five moves: on each move he could maintain his present number of missiles, shift a lever from a factory to a missile, or shift a lever from a missile to a factory (disarmament). After the five moves the subject discovered how many missiles his opponent had. At the end of each trial, points were awarded: +1 point for each factory, +2 points for each missile more than the opponent had, and −2 points for each missile less than the opponent had.

In one condition, called the "natural" condition, two subjects played against each other. In two other conditions, subjects played against a simulated other. In the matched-strategy condition, it was arranged that the simulated opponent showed the same number of missiles and factories as had the subject on the preceding trial. In the conciliatory-strategy condition, it was arranged that the simulated opponent showed one missile less than the real player had on the preceding trial. Within each of these conditions there were two subconditions. Under inspection conditions the subject was shown the real or simulated partner's number of missiles and factories after the third move within a five-move trial. Under no-inspection conditions the subject did not know the other's moves until all five moves within the trial had been completed. In the simulated-other conditions the inspection was "honest," in that on the inspection trial the simulated other displayed the number of missiles or factories that he would have at the end of the five full moves. Inspection thus served an important communicative function.

Results indicated that both the matched and the conciliatory strategies increased cooperation. That is, either reciprocation or the initiation of cooperation facilitated disarmament in the form of trading missiles for factories. Also, it was found that, in the natural groups, communication was often used deceptively. Each side would try to convince the other on the inspection trials that it was disarming but then would rapidly add missiles on the remaining moves within the trial. However, when communication was used honestly (in the inspection conditions of the matched and conciliatory conditions), inspection tended to reduce the level of armament. The greatest cooperation was found under conditions of a conciliatory strategy coupled with inspection. Thus the results supported Osgood's hypothesis that conciliatory moves coupled with a clear indication of intent would lead to tension reduction and cooperation.

The question remains, of course, whether Osgood's plan would work outside the laboratory. Although there is no way to take two sets of nations consisting of two large powers armed to the teeth and a number of smaller powers serving as pawns and then randomly assign them to either experimental or control conditions, a *partial* test of Osgood's GRIT proposal took place between June 10 and November 22, 1963, and has been referred to as the "Kennedy Experiment" (Etzioni, 1967, 1969).

In a speech delivered at the American University, President Kennedy reminded the nation of the emotional and financial damage being done by the sad state of American-Russian relations. He then indicated a willingness to improve these relations. He announced that, as a first step, nuclear tests in the atmosphere had been discontinued and would not be resumed unless other nations did so first. Although this decision was a clear move toward lessening international tensions, it was also a low-risk action. A nuclear test ban does not undermine national security when one's nuclear arsenal already contains as much explosive force as would be provided by an ankle-deep layer of dynamite spread over the surface of the entire country (see Osgood, 1962, for some interesting figures on our state of preparedness at that time).

A possible weak point in GRIT is the assumption that the Russians would respond in kind to our gestures. However, Russia did react favorably to Kennedy's announcement. The day after Kennedy's speech appeared in full in the Russian newspaper *Izvestia* (in itself a rare event, according to Etzioni), the U. S. S. R. agreed to our request to send U. N. observers to war-ravaged Yemen.

Next, the United States ended a lengthy dispute by agreeing to seat the Hungarian delegation to the United Nations. Khrushchev subsequently announced that he would halt the production of strategic bombers. Limited bans on nuclear tests were put into effect, discussions on joint exploration of space began, new East-West trade agreements were considered, and proposals were offered for the establishment of new consulates and the removal of travel restrictions within each country.

Thus, when procedures were tested that sounded very much like those of GRIT, the Russians responded to American initiatives and the Americans to Russian initiatives. A cycle of actions leading to a lessening of international tensions began to replace the cycle that had led to increased tensions. The Kennedy Experiment ended before all conflicts were resolved. We don't know what would have happened if it had not been "slowed down with the approach of an election year, halted with the assassination of President Kennedy, and undermined by the escalation of the Vietnam War" (Etzioni, 1969, p. 551). On the whole, however, the available evidence from both the laboratory and the field suggests that honest conciliatory moves will reduce international tensions.

PART SUMMARY

International relations can be analyzed in terms of personal variables, microscopic social variables, and macroscopic social variables. Each level of analysis proposes different remedies for international conflicts. Etzioni suggests that international conduct is a mixture of all these variables. Public opinion provides a framework or context that limits the range of options available to national leaders.

Own-group bias is a common correlate of international conflict. Bronfenbrenner found that Russians had the same flattering views of themselves that we have of ourselves and the same unflattering views of us that we have of them. White has identified a number of perceptions or attributes that preceded the outbreak of both world wars. These include the diabolical enemy image, the virile self-image, the moral self-image, selective inattention, the absence of empathy, and military overconfidence.

Competitive solutions to international disputes emphasize the role of threat as a tool for bargaining and for deterring potential aggressors. Schelling suggests that the side that appears to be more reckless, irrational, and desperate will have an advantage, since the opposing side is likely to give in. The element of risk and the renunciation of humanitarian values make this solution unacceptable to many Americans. Kahn argues that the show and application of force should be carefully gauged to meet the situation and should be just sufficient to show that one's resolve exceeds that of the other side. By means of controlled escalation, it should be possible to serve the national interest and prevent an all-out war. A major difficulty is that escalation can easily get out of hand. The two sides may have differing interpretations of the magnitude of an escalatory step; a show of resolve on one nation's part may strengthen resolve on the other nation's part; and, once the escalation has begun, the pattern of rewards and frustrations may encourage further escalation. As in the case of Schelling, Kahn's ideas have been criticized on the basis of risk and of ethicality.

Tension-reduction responses to international conflicts involve decreasing levels of armament and threat. Unilateral disarmament is unworkable, because it is tantamount to surrender and is not supported by public opinion. An alternative is Osgood's plan of GRIT. Osgood suggests that one side initiate peace moves and then wait until the other side reciprocates before new moves are taken. These moves are graduated in that the first ones represent minor steps toward peace, whereas the later ones represent major moves. Laboratory experimentation and relatively recent history suggest that conciliatory moves coupled with honest communication are likely to be reciprocated.

Glossary

Absence of empathy. A failure to understand another's feelings and point of view.

ABX system. A form of balance theory that involves the relationship between two people, *A* and *B*, and their attitudes toward an attitude object, *X*.

Accentuation hypothesis. The hypothesis that the perceived dimensions or prominence of a stimulus are positively correlated with that stimulus' relevance to the perceiver's needs and motives.

Acceptance. An unconditional positive regard for a person as a worthwhile human being. This is to be distinguished from approval, which is a positive reaction to or endorsement of a specific act.

Achievement imagery. The extent to which the central characters in a story endorse standards of excellence and strive to do tasks well.

Achievement motive. A concern with excellence and a preference for engaging in success-related activities.

Acquiescence. A response bias to agree with a statement or question no matter what its nature.

Action conformity. Following courses of action that are prescribed by the group.

Action-research model. A model of organizational adaptation and change that is very similar to the planned-change model (*see* Planned-change model), except that in addition a consultant helps the client organization develop new adaptive systems in order to research and solve its own new problems as they arise.

Adaptive inferiority. Self-effacing and ingratiating behaviors on the part of blacks that made it possible for them to survive in a white-dominated society.

Adaptive organizations. Organizations that create knowledge and help a society plan for its future.

Adaptive systems. Systems that analyze feedback and are concerned with research and development.

Adaptors. Gestures that help a person cope or deal with a tense situation by draining off tensions.

Adhocracy. An organizational form consisting of a group of people who have been assembled to work on a specific problem or task and who will then disband to form other task forces of different composition.

Adjustive function. In Katz' theory of attitudes, the use of an attitude to maximize rewards and to minimize punishments.

Affective component. The emotional or "feeling" component of an attitude.

Affective support. Encounter-group leadership behavior that involves offering approval, praise, and encouragement and protecting members who are under attack.

Affiliation. The most general process of seeking out and being with others.

Affiliative and dependent need. According to Rubin (1973), a component of romantic love. The affiliative and dependent need is reflected in the person's desire to be with and dependent upon the partner.

Agentic shift. Transition from the autonomous state, in which one is under self-control, to the agentic state, in which one is under the control of an authority.

Agentic state. A condition in which a person is controlled by a superior in a social hierarchy and sees himself or herself as an "agent" of another person, an organization, or a society.

Aggregate level. In organizational psychology, an organization's interaction with the entire society.

Aggression. Any activity, either physical or verbal, that has as a goal the infliction of harm or damage on someone or something.

Aggressive drive. In ethological theories of aggression, self-generating motivation to aggress that builds up over time and without external provocation.

Agonistic display. A frightening or threatening grimace or gesture.

Alienation. A state of "normlessness" in a community or a society. In the individual, alienation is symptomatized by feelings of isolation, indifference, and powerlessness and by a fear that life is meaningless.

Altruism. *See* Altruistic behavior.

Altruistic behavior. Voluntary acts that benefit other people and are not easily explained in terms of personal gain.

Androgynous. A term describing individuals who are able to engage in either masculine or feminine role behaviors depending on situation and mood.

Anticonformity. Endorsing attitudes and behaving in ways that are antithetical to those prescribed by one's group.

Antisocial behavior. Behavior that is harmful to other people or threatens the established social order.

Anxiety. Vague feelings of apprehension and dread that are of unspecific origin or that have their origin in objectively harmless conditions.

Approval. A positive reaction to or endorsement of a specific act. (*Compare with* Acceptance.)

Arbitrary frustration. A frustration that is perceived as deliberately or willfully imposed.

AR Scale (Ascription of Responsibility Scale). A paper-and-pencil test that assesses the extent to which respondents are aware that their actions have consequences for others.

Artificial task. A task that is recognizable as having been set up by a researcher.

Ascription of Responsibility Scale. *See* AR scale.

Assertion constant. In congruity theory, the finding that attitudes toward the source of an assertion change slightly less than do attitudes toward the object of the assertion.

Assimilation effect. Assuming or accentuating the similarities between two or more stimuli.

Associative bond. In congruity theory, a positive relationship (goes with, likes, endorses, and so forth).

Assumed desirability of effects. In the attribution process, the assumption that the person's behavior was motivated by its desirable rather than by its undesirable consequences.

Attention focusing. Encounter-group leadership behaviors that direct attention toward specific people or issues within the group.

Attitude holder. A person who holds or maintains an attitude.

Attitude object. The person, thing, or event about which an attitude is held.

Attitudes. Learned emotional, intellectual, and behavioral responses to a person, thing, or event.

Attribution. The process of inferring the cause of a person's behavior.

Attribution theory. A theory concerning the procedures through which the average individual infers the causes of behavior.

Audience effects. The energizing effects of passive spectators on performance.

Audience studies. Studies that compare solitary performances with performances in the presence of passive spectators.

Authoritarianism. A term used to indicate the extent to which a person shows a constellation of attitudes, including: (1) deference toward superiors but intolerance of inferiors, (2) an emphasis on power and toughness in social relations, (3) prejudice, and (4) adherence to conventional morality.

Autocratic climate. The atmosphere prevailing when one person is delegated or assumes a leadership position and tells others in the group what to do.

Autokinetic effect. Apparent motion of a stationary pinpoint of light.

Autonomous control. A managerial technique under which workers are given a significant voice in the decisions that affect their daily lives.

Autonomous state. A condition in which a person is controlled by internal regulators of behavior, such as the conscience.

Averaging model. A rule suggesting that our overall impression of the favorability of a person represents the average or arithmetic mean of the favorability values associated with each item of information that we have about that person.

Balanced relationships. In attitude theory, relationships between two or more elements that are consistent, stable, and unlikely to change.

Balance theory. A consistency theory of attitudes suggesting that there is an assumed "normal state" among attitudes or cognitions and that, when conditions depart from this normal state, there will be a tendency to return to them.

Behavioral component. The "action" component of an attitude.

Behavioral dependence. "A relation among the behaviors of a number of individuals, such that a given behavior of one or more individuals is a cause or an occasion for a change in the behavior of one or more other individuals" (Zajonc, 1966, p. 1).

Behavioral tests. Specific tasks or situations set up in such a way as to allow easy observation and recording of responses.

Behavior control. The ability to make it likely that another person will choose a certain response by varying one's own behavior in such a way that the response in question will yield the other person the most favorable outcome.

Behavioristic model. A conception of the individual as a collection of learned habits.

Belief congruence. A theory suggesting that people reject one another not because of their race but because they believe that people of other races have attitudes, values, and beliefs that are different from their own.

Belongingness and love needs. Needs to receive acceptance, affection, and respect. These needs are at the third level in Maslow's need hierarchy.

Biased scanning. During counterattitudinal role playing, concentration on the positive features of the counteropinion and on the negative features of the privately held belief.

Binocular rivalry. An experimental technique that involves presenting two different pictures, one to each eye, and assessing which of the two is most clearly seen.

Bogus pipeline. A procedure for obtaining truthful answers from subjects by convincing them that an elaborate (but fake) piece of electronic apparatus will reveal their true attitudes when they are asked a question. To avoid being second-guessed by a machine, subjects supposedly answer honestly and candidly.

Bond. In consistency theories of attitudes, a relationship between any two elements.

Boundary. A visible or invisible line that separates a system from the surrounding environment.

Boundary organizations. Customs and immigration services, which help a society maintain its boundaries.

Boundary systems. Systems that separate an organization from other organizations and from the environment.

Brainstorming. A procedure intended to overcome the inhibiting pressures of group membership on the offering of new and novel solutions by encouraging group members to offer all suggestions, no matter how seemingly unworkable, zany, or bizarre.

Breadth dimension. The dimension of a relationship that expresses the number of the participants' needs or "parts of their lives" that enter into the relationship.

Bureaucracy. A form of organization in which rationality and impersonality are developed to the highest degree.

Bystander effect. The finding that, as the number of witnesses to an emergency increases, the probability of any specific individual's intervening decreases.

Catharsis. The release of pent-up emotions.

CDQ. *See* Choice-Dilemma Questionnaire.

Centrality. In communications nets research, the location of a position with respect to all the other positions within the net. A position is central to the extent that a large number of messages must pass through it.

Central trait. A trait that can cause changes in the perception of other traits and hence contributes disproportionately to overall impressions.

Chain. In communications-network research, a net of intermediate centrality.

Charisma. A personal quality of some leaders that generates confidence and inspires identification.

Choice-Dilemma Questionnaire (CDQ). A device for measuring risk taking, this questionnaire presents 12 hypothetical situations, involving the choice between a more certain, less attractive alternative and a less certain, more attractive alternative. Subjects indicate the minimum odds that they would find acceptable for recommending pursuit of the more attractive alternative.

Circle. In communications-network research, a net in which each person may communicate only with persons in immediately adjacent positions.

CL. *See* Comparison level.

CLalt. *See* Comparison level for alternatives.

Classical conditioning. A learning process whereby the pairing of an initially neutral stimulus with one that reliably elicits a response results in the initially neutral stimulus' eventually eliciting an identical or similar response.

Closed-ended measures. Questionnaires and rating devices that force the respondent to choose one of a limited number of answers provided by the researcher.

Coaction. Two or more members of the same species engaging in independent tasks in the presence of each other.

Coding systems. Rules for classifying or categorizing observed behavior.

Coefficient of correlation. *See* Correlation.

Cognition. (1) Any thought, mental image, or item of information; (2) the act of thinking.

Cognitive. Of or having to do with the process of thinking.

Cognitive clarity. An understanding of what has happened and what is likely to happen next. The search for cognitive clarity often involves gossip, rumor, and the comparison of notes and impressions.

Cognitive component. The intellectual or "belief" component of an attitude.

Cognitive-consistency theories. Dissonance, balance, and other attitude theories suggesting that attitudes are best viewed as packages of interrelated elements. According to these theories, certain "packages" or arrangements of elements are consistent, stable, and unlikely to change, whereas others are inconsistent, unstable, and likely to change.

Cognitive consonance. *See* Consonance.

Cognitive dissonance. *See* Dissonance.

Cognitive-dissonance theory. *See* Dissonance theory.

Cognitive tuning. Establishing a mental set to receive and organize information in such a way as to make it useful for future purposes.

Cognitizing. A form of encounter-group leadership behavior involving teaching and instructional activities.

Cohesiveness. (1) The "groupiness" of a group. (2) The degree of unification and solidarity of the members of a group.

Comcon. In communications-network research, a "completely connected" network, in which each group member may communicate directly with any other member.

Command stimulation. Encounter-group leadership behavior involving attempts to get responses through invitations, questions, and suggestions.

Communication. The transmission of information and affect from one person to another.

Communications approach. An approach to attitude formation and change that simultaneously considers the source, the content, and the recipient of the message.

Communications net. *See* Net.

Comparative reference group. A reference group that provides standards for comparison and for self-appraisal.

Comparison group. In reference-group research, a group believed to be rivalrous with the designated reference group.

Comparison level. The level of outcomes that the person feels he or she has "earned" or otherwise "deserves."

Comparison level for alternatives. The lowest level of outcomes a person will accept without terminating the interaction or breaking off the relationship.

Competence hierarchies. Rankings of people in terms of abilities, skills, and knowledge.

Competition. Striving for gains at another's expense.

Complementarity hypothesis. The hypothesis that certain different-appearing characteristics of two people will fit together in such a way as to make an association mutually rewarding.

Completion principle. The principle that one person will like another if that other person has characteristics that the first person would like to possess.

Compliance-based attitude. In Kelman's theory of attitudes, an attitude that is adopted because it secures favorable reactions from others.

Compresence. Two or more organisms of the same species that are in the presence of each other.

Conceptual replication. A replication in which the experimenter does not attempt to follow the earlier procedures as closely as possible but uses different operations and perhaps different kinds of subjects as well.

Conceptual variables. Abstract classes or categories that tie together or denote a number of different elements.

Concern for people. Leadership behaviors directed toward ensuring good human relations within the group.

Concern for production. Leadership behaviors directed toward accomplishing the objective task at hand.

Conditioned response (CR). In classical conditioning, the learned response.

Conditioned stimulus (CS). In classical conditioning, a stimulus that does not reliably elicit the response to be learned at the beginning of the learning procedures.

Conformity. Socially caused uniformities in the attitudes or behaviors of people in a group.

Confrontation. In encounter groups, a special kind of feedback whereby one person points out to another some sort of discrepancy or inconsistency in his or her statements or behavior.

Congruity. Conditions of consistency and stability in congruity theory.

Congruity theory. A consistency theory of attitudes suggesting that stimuli can be placed on a scale ranging from -3 to $+3$. According to this theory, a perceiver's attitudes toward the two stimuli on this scale will be determined by the two stimuli's relationship to each other.

Conscience. Society's rules as embodied in the individual. Conscience is reflected in judgments of right and wrong, self-control, and feelings of unworthiness or guilt after succumbing to temptation.

Consensus. (1) Agreement within a group. (2) In attribution theory, one criterion for making a dispositional inference. In this latter context, consensus refers to the extent to which different observers report similar experiences with the target person.

Conservative shift. Following individual risk taking, lesser risk taking under group-membership conditions.

Consistency over modality. In attribution theory, one criterion for making a dispositional inference. The term refers to the extent to which the entity or target is associated with similar phenomena under differing conditions.

Consistency over time. In attribution theory, one criterion for making a dispositional inference. The term refers to the extent to which the phenomenon is observed each time the entity or target is present.

Consistency theories. *See* Cognitive-consistency theories.

Consonance. In dissonance theory, a case involving two (or more) interrelated cognitions that are compatible such that one logically follows from or is implied by the other.

Conspecifics. Members of the same species.

Construct validity. Validity arising from a complex web of evidence that events happen in ways one would expect if the construct or the measure of the construct is useful.

Consultative decision making. A form of participative decision making in which the organization's rank and file do not cast votes but are encouraged to suggest or appraise the various alternatives.

Content validity. In tests and measurements, a form of validity that indicates the extent to which the items included on a test faithfully represent all the possible items that could be included.

Content variables. In attitude theory and research, *what* is said in an attitude-change appeal.

Contingency table. A table that shows how closely variables are related by expressing the number of cases that fall into various combinations of categories. Or, more formally, a multidimensional tabular presentation of frequencies by categories.

Contingency theory. A theory of leadership suggesting that a dispositional variable (leadership style) and a situational variable (situational favorableness) combine to determine leadership effectiveness.

Contrast effect. The accentuation of the differences between two stimuli that results from their appearing close together.

Contrived task. A task that is deliberately set up by a researcher.

Control. The process of altering or changing the course of events.

Control conditions. In an experiment, conditions under which a designated experimental treatment is not applied.

Control group. In an experiment, subjects who are treated in the same way as the experimental subjects except that the experimental manipulation or treatment is not applied.

Controlled escalation. Deliberately and calculatingly intensifying a conflict in such a way that the enemy backs down before an all-out war results. Controlled escalation may be more likely to lead to an all-out war than to prevent it.

Controls. Procedures for ruling out alternative explanations of the results of an experiment.

Cooperation. The coordination of activities for mutual rewards.

Copying. A form of imitation that differs from matched-dependent behavior in that the learner or imitator responds to cues of sameness and difference of results when comparing his or her behavior with the behavior of the model.

Correction for incredulity. In congruity theory, a correction factor dealing with the problem that people do not necessarily believe the assertion that associates S and O.

Correlation. A relationship between two variables such that, given the value of one variable, it is possible to make a guess concerning the value of the associated variable.

Correlational studies. Research procedures that involve discovering the extent to which two or more variables naturally covary. Correlational studies differ from experimental studies in that there is no attempt to actively manipulate the variables under inspection.

Costs. In Thibaut and Kelley's theory, all the negative aspects of an outcome (effort expenditure, embarrassment, and so forth).

Counterattitudinal role playing. Expression of an attitudinal position that is discrepant with one's privately held position. The person does not simply state the discrepant attitude but attempts to adopt the discrepant point of view and provide arguments to support it.

Credibility. The believability of a person who is making a statement. Credibility has two components: expertise and trustworthiness.

Criterion measures. Accepted indicators of people's attitudes or behaviors. These measures provide yardsticks for gauging the success of tests or questionnaires. For example, the number of times a person is asked for a date in a month could be a criterion measure for validating a paper-and-pencil test of popularity.

Cues. (1) Stimuli that allow the perceiver to distinguish a situation from other situations. (2) Parts of a stimulus or stimulus pattern that contribute a disproportionately large amount to a perception.

Defensive-avoidance hypothesis. The hypothesis that an audience will reject an attitude-change appeal that incorporates highly threatening and frightening arguments because these arguments will be too painful to listen to.

Deficit needs. In Maslow's theorizing, needs for nourishment, comfort, and safety. The satisfaction of deficit needs involves overcoming lackings and shortcomings. Deficit needs are to be distinguished from growth needs.

Deindividuation. A state of affairs within a group such that the individual member is not seen or paid attention to as an individual but is instead "submerged" in the group.

Deintensification. The process of "toning down" a facial reaction to convey the impression that one's feelings are less intense than they really are.

Delay orientation. In social-learning theory, a preference for a large reward in the future over a small reward in the present.

Demand characteristics. Explicit and implicit cues in the laboratory setting that elicit behavior masking or obscuring the behavior of interest.

Democratic climate. Conditions under which group goals and procedures evolve from a discussion involving all members of the group.

Democratic decision making. A form of participative decision making in which the organization's rank and file are allowed to cast votes.

Dependent variable. (1) That which varies or changes as a result of changes in the independent variable. (2) In an experiment, the behavior assessed by the experimenter.

Depth dimension. The dimension of a relationship that expresses the extent to which the people are willing to share intimate personal experiences.

Description. A set of statements telling what has already happened.

Deterrence. In international relations, the use of threat for preventing another nation from acting against one's best interests.

Diabolical enemy image. In intergroup conflict, the attitude that the opposing group is evil and fails to live up to the minimum standards of human decency.

Diffusion of responsibility. A process whereby personal feelings of accountability are diluted when others are present or involved.

Diffusion-of-responsibility theory. An interpretation of extremity shifts suggesting that people are most likely to choose extreme alternatives in a group setting, because they feel less personally responsible for the negative consequences that might flow from their decisions.

Direct punishment. Harsh punishment consisting of beatings, strong verbal assaults, deprecations, and screaming.

Discounting principle. In attribution theory, the rule that, to the extent that there are a number of viable explanations of a given act, we tend to have less confidence in any one of them.

Discrepancy theory. A theory that people will expect a certain level of input to yield a certain level of outcome. To the extent that the expected outcome exceeds the obtained outcome, the person is dissatisfied. To the extent that the obtained outcome equals or exceeds the expected outcome, the person is satisfied.

Discriminant validity. A form of validity showing that one measure or test (such as a liking scale) does not assess the same quality or dimension that is assessed by another test (such as a love scale).

Discrimination. In perception, the process of distinguishing one stimulus from another.

Discrimination learning. Learning to distinguish among and respond differentially to different cues.

Discriminatory behavior. Behavior that makes the resources, conveniences, and comforts of one group difficult to obtain or even inaccessible to members of another group.

Disinhibition. The removal of forces that prevent the performance of a response.

Displaced aggression. Aggression that is directed toward a safer target than the person who infuriated the aggressor.

Display rules. Socially learned strategies for managing and controlling facial reactions.

Dispositional inference. In attribution theory, attributing an act to a quality or characteristic of the person (as compared with a quality or characteristic of the situation).

Dispositional variables. Those forces contributing to behavior that have their origin inside the organism.

Dissociative bond. In congruity theory, a negative relationship (dislikes, disavows, leaves, and so forth).

Dissonance. In dissonance theory, the case of two (or more) interrelated cognitions that are incompatible with each other such that one cognition is the opposite of what would be expected given knowledge of the other.

Dissonance theory. A consistency approach to attitudes suggesting that the coexistence of two or more incompatible (dissonant) cognitions will produce an unpleasant tension state that the individual will seek to reduce by changing one or more of the cognitions or by redefining their relationship to each other.

Distance. In communications-nets research, the number of people a message must pass through to get from one person to another by the shortest route.

Distinctiveness. In attribution theory, a criterion for making a dispositional inference. The term refers to the extent to which a phenomenon is observed when the entity or target is present but is not observed in its absence.

Distraction hypothesis. The hypothesis that an audience distracted at the time an attitude-change appeal is made will show more attitude change than will an audience that is not distracted.

Division of labor. The assignment of different tasks to different people. The resulting conditions of mutual dependency impart feelings of solidarity and belonging.

Dominant response. The response most likely to occur under stated conditions.

Drive. A broad motivational state that energizes behavior.

Duplication theorem. Toman's principle that the relationship between two adults will be satisfactory to the extent that both can re-enact within the relationship roles that they learned in their families in childhood.

Dyad. A two-person group.

Dyadic relationships. In balance theory, relationships involving two elements.

Effect dependence. Conditions under which the person is reliant on others for rewards and gratifications.

Ego defenses. Mechanisms that protect the person from full awareness of unpleasant conditions or threatening circumstances.

Ego-defensive function. In Katz' theory of attitudes, the use of an attitude to protect the attitude holder from a full recognition of harsh circumstances or unpleasant conditions.

Elite. Individuals or groups who have special power and privileges.

Emblems. Gestures that substitute for a verbal communication.

Empathy. The ability to understand another's views and feelings.

Empirical observation. An observation made through the use of the senses.

Empiricism. The doctrine stating that the gateway to knowledge is through the evidence confronting our senses.

Encounter group. A particular kind of laboratory-training group in which personal and interpersonal issues are the direct focus of the group.

Endogamous choice. The choice of a romantic or marriage partner from one's own group, class, or kind.

Equity theory. A theory suggesting that people compare what they put into a task or job and what they get out of it with what others put into and get out of their tasks or jobs. People then attempt to adjust their inputs and outcomes so that they do about as well as others.

Error. In open-systems theory, faulty or incorrect processing in response to input overload.

Escalation ladder. A rank ordering of actions in terms of the threat and application of force. The lower "rungs" represent minor threats or military actions, and the higher rungs represent nuclear war.

Esteem need. The need to feel worthwhile, competent, and successful. This need represents the fourth level in Maslow's hierarchy of needs.

Ethnic group. A collection of people who are considered by themselves and by others to have a common religion, racial origin, national origin, language and cultural tradition, or some combination of these factors.

Ethnic stereotypes. Preconceived ideas about the abilities, skills, and traits likely to be possessed by a member of a given ethnic group.

Ethological theories. Theories of behavior that draw heavily on the concepts of evolution and instinct.

Evaluation-apprehension hypothesis. In social-facilitation theorizing, the hypothesis that anxiety generated by the knowledge that one is being evaluated creates drive or arousal, which is responsible for social-facilitation effects.

Evoking stimuli. Stimuli that elicit or trigger an emotional reaction such as fear or disgust.

Exact replication. A replication in which the experimenter attempts to follow the earlier procedures as closely as possible.

Exchange theories. Economic theories of social behavior suggesting that the initiation, process, and termination of social interaction are determined by the patterns of rewards and costs associated with the interaction.

Exclusiveness and absorption. According to Rubin (1973), a component of romantic love. This component is reflected in the extent to which the person emphasizes the relationship at hand at the expense of other relationships.

Exogamous choice. The selection of a romantic or marriage partner who is not from one's own group, class, or kind.

Expectancy. An anticipation that an action will lead to a certain outcome.

Experiment. An attempt to arrange a sequence of events in order to see what led to what. The two defining characteristics of the experimental method are manipulation and control.

Experimental conditions. In an experiment, conditions under which a designated treatment or manipulation is present or applied.

Experimental games. Based on exchange theory, experimental games provide a research technique for the study of social interaction. Each of two or more players has available two or more response alternatives, and, on the basis of their mutual choices, each player incurs various wins and losses.

Experimental group. In an experiment, those subjects who receive an experimental treatment or manipulation.

Experimenter bias. (1) A tendency on the part of an experimenter to "see" his or her subjects as behaving in the desired ways. (2) Unintentional behavior on the part of the experimenter that encourages the subject to perform in a way that proves satisfactory to the experimenter.

Exploitative relationship. A relationship in which one party uses and takes advantage of the other party.

Expressive role. The socioemotionally oriented or "feminine role," which involves nurturance, the expression of emotion, and passive dependency.

External justifications. Rationalizations, excuses, or conditions that make people feel that they are not responsible for having engaged in public behavior that violates their private beliefs. External justifications lower the likelihood of attitude change in the direction of the public behavior.

External rewards. In organizational psychology, external rewards include wages, promotions, and fringe benefits, which have value only outside the work setting.

External validity. The extent to which laboratory results can be extended beyond the laboratory or generalized to different populations and settings.

Extinction. The weakening or disappearance of a learned response.

Extremity shifts. Following individual risk taking, greater or lesser risk taking as a result of participation in a group discussion.

Extrinsic rewards. Rewards and satisfactions that follow a performance. These are to be distinguished from intrinsic rewards, which are associated with the performance itself.

Face validity. In psychological testing, a quality of a test such that it appears to measure that which it was designed to measure.

Factor. An inferred construct that underlies or ties together clusters of intercorrelated attitudes, traits, or behaviors.

Factor analysis. Correlational techniques that make it possible to identify factors.

Faking. Responding to a test or questionnaire in such a way as to present a distorted view of oneself.

False majority. In conformity experiments, a group of confederates coached to agree on a wrong judgment or answer.

Familiarization theory. An interpretation of risky shifts suggesting that discussing choice dilemmas in the group setting results in a new familiarity with the problems, which lessens people's fears of the riskier alternatives.

Fate control. The ability to affect another person's outcomes no matter what that other person does.

Fear. A response to confrontation with an object or event that is dangerous and likely to produce pain.

Feedback. (1) Information concerning the results of an action. (2) In open-systems theory, environmental reactions to the system's output.

Field. The natural environment or habitat.

Field experiment. An experimental study in which the experimenter creates the conditions of interest outside the laboratory setting.

Field study. A study that investigates the effects of conditions as they are found outside the laboratory.

Filtering. In open-systems theory, a technique for coping with information overload by means of neglecting some, but not all, input awaiting processing.

Filmed model. In contemporary social-learning theory, a model presented by means of a motion-picture or videotape recording.

Foot-in-the-door hypothesis. The hypothesis that a large request is more likely to be granted if it has been preceded by a small request.

Forced compliance. A condition under which a person is induced to say or do something that conflicts with a private attitude or belief.

Forewarning. Advising an audience that a speaker will attempt to change its attitudes.

Frame of reference. The product of past experiences, present needs, and social pressures that allows the person to interpret or order new stimuli.

Free behaviors. Responses that the individual feels he or she can choose to perform.

Free-choice situation. A situation in which a person is confronted with selecting one of two or more alternatives.

Frustration. The blocking of goal-directed behavior.

Frustration-aggression hypothesis. The hypothesis that aggression is a natural and inevitable consequence of frustration.

Functional theories. Any theory that explains attitudes or behavior in terms of the uses or purposes these have for the individual.

Generalization. Following the learning of a response, the emission of that response in the presence of cues that are similar, but not identical, to the cues that were present when the response was learned.

Generalized tendency to imitate. A tendency, after learning to imitate one model in one situation, to imitate other models in other situations.

Goal. A sought-after end state.

GRIT. A plan suggesting that intergroup tensions can be reduced if one side initiates a few "low-risk," friendly actions. The other side will reciprocate, and then the first side can make additional overtures for peace, starting an upward spiral of improved relations.

Group. A collection of individuals who have some sort of specified relationship to one another. Typically, members of a group are bound together by interaction and interdependence.

Group dynamics. (1) Processes within small groups. (2) The study of processes within small groups. (3) Techniques for influencing people in groups.

Group mind. A superindividual consciousness that represents more than the sum of the minds of the members of the group. The now-abandoned concept of the group mind was the ultimate expression of the view that "groups are real."

Group rewards. Also known as systems rewards, group rewards are fringe benefits, cost-of-living pay hikes, and other rewards that are given to all the members of a work group or organization.

Group-size effect. *See* Bystander effect.

Groupthink. In group decision making and problem solving, a mode of thinking in which innovation, objectivity, and careful analysis are undermined by loyalty to the group and the seeking of agreement.

Growth needs. In Maslow's theorizing, the need to overcome mediocrity, grow psychologically, and self-actualize.

Guidance. In social-learning theory, directions, instructions, and physical assists.

Hawthorne effect. An increase in group productivity as a result of an expression of interest by management; brought about by establishing a friendly atmosphere and relaxing formal rules and procedures.

Hedonic relevance. In attribution theory, the extent to which the target's acts are in the interests of the perceiver.

Helping behavior. Voluntary acts that benefit other people.

Hierarchical control. A managerial technique under which workers carry out decisions that were made at a higher level in the organization.

Hierarchical structure. An unequal distribution of power within a group or organization. Members with more power are said to be higher in the structure.

Hierarchy of needs. *See* Need hierarchy.

High-level leaders. Leaders who change old policies and create new ones.

High-LPC leader. In the contingency theory of leadership, a leader with an interest in maintaining cordial relations within the group.

High-talking seat. At a table, a position whose occupant issues more than the average number of communications in the course of the group discussion.

Homeostasis. The tendency of a system to be self-regulating so that, following disruption, it will return to its normal state.

Horizontal expansion. A form of job expansion that involves increasing the individual worker's number of tasks or lengthening the cycle of activity.

Humanistic model. A view of people as conscious, free, whole beings who set goals and then actively strive to attain them.

Human-relations perspective. In organizational theory and research, the view that the personal and social needs of organizational members and dynamics within informal work groups are highly important.

Hygienic factors. In Herzberg's theory of motivation, those factors that must be present in a work setting to prevent dissatisfaction (as compared with those that produce satisfaction).

Hypothesis. An expected or tentatively identified relationship between variables.

Hypothetical constructs. A useful idea or intellectual tool; an inference that serves to account for the relationship between two or more variables.

Ideal type. An intellectual tool produced by abstracting and distilling the characteristics of people (or groups) and forging these qualities into a unified, coherent construct.

Identification. The process of assuming or "taking on" the attributes or qualities of another person.

Identification-based attitude. In Kelman's theory, an attitude that is adopted because it serves to establish or maintain an intrinsically satisfying relationship with another person or group.

Idiosyncrasy credits. Favorable impressions of an individual that are accumulated within a group. Earned by demonstrations of competence and conformity, these credits may be traded for freedom to engage in nonconforming activities.

Illustrators. Hand and arm gestures that complement or supplement a verbal communication.

Imbalanced relationships. In attitude theory, relationships between two or more elements that are inconsistent, unstable, and likely to change.

Immediate orientation. In social-learning theory, a person's preference for a small but immediate reward over a large but delayed reward.

Implicit theories of personality. Informal, impressionistic theories of personality that each of us develops. These theories suggest the kinds of qualities or traits that "go together" and hence allow us to form overall impressions of another on the basis of only minimal evidence.

Impression formation. The process of integrating various items of information about a person to form an overall picture.

Incentive. (1) An inducement to act. (2) The value accorded the consequences of an action.

Incentive theory. A theory suggesting that, the larger the incentive for counterattitudinal role playing, the greater the attitude change. This hypothesis contrasts with dissonance theory's prediction of a negative relationship between the magnitude of the incentive and attitude change.

Incongruity. Conditions of inconsistency and instability in congruity theory.

Independence. An alternative to conformity or anticonformity characterized by an awareness of group norms rather than an automatic acceptance or rejection of the norms.

Independent variable. (1) A suspected antecedent or "cause." (2) A change in the environment that contributes to or causes a change in behavior. (3) A variable that is deliberately manipulated or changed for purposes of an experiment.

Individual level. In organizational psychology, the organization's transactions with individual customers, clients, and potential employees.

Individual reward. In organizational psychology, a bonus, commission, or other reward that is given to an individual in recognition of personal achievement or merit.

Informational social influence. Conditions under which an individual accepts information provided by others as evidence of reality.

Information dependence. Conditions under which the individual depends on others for understanding or interpreting reality.

Information-exchange theory. An interpretation of extremity shifts suggesting that the occurrence and direction of extremity shifts depend on the number and type of arguments brought out in the group discussion.

Information overload. Bombardment of a system by more stimulation or input than can be adequately coded or processed.

Ingratiation. Any activities aimed at putting oneself in the good graces of another.

Inhibition. In frustration-aggression theorizing, the learned suppression of aggressive responses.

Initiating structure. Leadership behavior that helps to move the group toward its goal.

Inoculation theory. In attitudes, a theory suggesting that exposing an audience to some mild arguments against the advocated position will make the audience resistant to subsequent strong arguments against that advocated position.

Input. In open-systems theory, the information or material entered into the system for processing.

Input overload. Conditions under which the information or material coming into a system is more than the system can efficiently process.

Insight problem. A problem whose solution requires viewing things in a new or different way. Such problems require few steps for solution and, when the solution is found, provide an "Aha!" experience.

Instigation. In frustration-aggression theorizing, the motivation to aggress. The strength of the instigation depends on the strength of the blocked behavior, the extent of the frustration, and the total number of blocked responses.

Instinct. An inherited disposition to respond in a preprogrammed way.

Instrumental role. The task-oriented, "masculine" role, which involves "getting things done."

Intelligence. An ability to read environmental cues, reason, and identify or improvise solutions to problems.

Intensification. The process of exaggerating a facial reaction to convey the impression that one's feelings are more intense than they really are.

Interaction Process Analysis. A coding system of 12 categories that is used for quantifying and analyzing the natural flow of communication within a small group.

Intergroup conflict. The state existing between two or more groups that are competing over scarce resources when one of the aims of the competition is to neutralize, injure, or eliminate the competitor.

Intergroup relations. Relations between groups.

Intermediate level. In organizational psychology, the interaction between an organization and complementary or rivalrous organizations.

Intermediate-level leaders. At a middle level in the organizational hierarchy, middle-level leaders improvise within the framework of pre-existing rules.

Intermittent reinforcement. Reinforcement following some, but not all, emissions of a "correct" response.

Internal colonialism. Blauner's theory that black ghettos represent colonies within the United States. According to Blauner, the land, resources, and people of the ghettos are exploited by whites.

Internal consistency. A form of reliability that expresses the extent to which the parts of a test of the same attribute intercorrelate. To the extent that a test is internally consistent, it is believed to assess one psychological attribute in a systematic way rather than a number of different attributes haphazardly.

Internalization. The process of incorporating social standards and rules into one's personality.

Internalization-based attitude. In Kelman's functional theory of attitudes, an attitude that is adopted because it is compatible or consistent with one's underlying values.

Internalization of organizational values. In organizational psychology, the merging of individual and organizational goals, usually resulting in behavior that is "above and beyond the call of duty."

Internal validity. The extent to which experimental manipulations affect the subjects' behavior within the experiment.

Internationalists. People who tend to favor cooperative international endeavors, the easy flow of communications among nations, and friendly, negotiated solutions to international disputes.

Interpersonal attraction. The drawing of one person to another; includes affiliation, liking, and love.

Interpersonal influence. Any means by which one person induces another to grant a favor or comply with a request.

Interracial-contact hypothesis. The hypothesis that contact among members of conflicting racial or ethnic groups will lead to a reduction of prejudice and to mutual liking.

Intervention model. A model of organizational adaptation and change suggesting that the basic information for solving organizational problems already exists within the organization but remains unutilized because of inadequate communication within the system. The role of the consultant is to open up channels of communication within the organization so that the information can be utilized.

Intimate distance. The closest of the four zones that, according to Hall, reflect how people are feeling about each other. This "distance of mattresses and wrestling mats" extends from skin contact to about 18 inches.

Intragroup relations. Relations within groups.

Intrinsic rewards. Rewards and satisfactions, such as the utilization of skills and the exercise of autonomy, that are associated with the performance of the task itself. These are to be distinguished from extrinsic rewards, such as a paycheck, which follow the performance or activity.

Intrusive modeling. Encounter-group leadership behavior that involves eliciting responses from members by issuing direct demands and exhortations and by serving as an exemplary or model group member.

IPA. *See* Interaction Process Analysis.

Isolationists. People who tend to distrust those of other nationalities, who favor restricting the flow of international commerce, and who advocate military solutions to international disputes.

Job expansion. Rearrangement of a job to provide increased variety and challenge for the job holder. (*See* Horizontal expansion; Vertical expansion.)

Joint gain. The motivation to ensure that other people, as well as oneself, secure good outcomes.

Just-world hypothesis. The hypothesis that people see themselves or others as getting what they deserve in life.

Kinesic communication. The transmission of information and affect through motions of the body and limbs.

Knowledge function. In Katz' theory of attitudes, the use of an attitude for explaining conditions or making sense out of the world.

Laboratory-training group. A small group used for (1) increasing self-awareness, (2) increasing sensitivity to others, (3) increasing sensitivity to small-group processes, (4) improving skills at diagnosing problems in human relations, and (5) improving leadership skills on both task and socioemotional dimensions.

Laissez-faire climate. Conditions under which a group is left to run its own course, without leadership influence being exerted.

Leadership. The exercise of an ability to get things done—to organize and coordinate people in pursuit of a common goal.

Leadership effectiveness. In the contingency theory of leadership, the extent to which the group efficiently accomplishes the task at hand.

Leadership style. In the contingency theory of leadership, the extent to which the leader favors efficiency and task accomplishment over cordial leader-follower relations.

Learning. A change or modification of behavior as a result of experience.

Least-preferred coworker. *See* LPC.

Legal compliance. The acceptance of organizational role prescriptions as stemming from a higher power or authority.

Liking scale. A paper-and-pencil test used to measure liking (as compared with love).

Linking-pin function. In an organization, a person who belongs to two or more different groups and hence helps to coordinate these groups.

Love-oriented punishment. Psychological (as compared to physical) punishment involving the withdrawal of affection and mild forms of disapproval coupled with explanations of the reasons for the disapproval.

Love scale. A paper-and-pencil test designed to measure love (as compared with liking).

Low-level leaders. Low-level leaders are administrators who make sure that individual organizational members fulfill their obligations and receive their rewards. They are relatively low in the hierarchy.

Low-LPC leader. In the contingency model of leadership, a task-oriented leader who wants to get things done.

Low-talking seat. At a table, a position whose occupant issues fewer than the average number of communications in the course of a group discussion.

LPC (least-preferred coworker). A measure of leadership style. On this scale, respondents rate their least-liked working companion. Favorable ratings yield a high-LPC score and unfavorable ratings a low-LPC score. (*See* High-LPC leader; Low-LPC leader.)

Machiavellianism. The use of deceit, cunning, and opportunism in interpersonal relations.

Mach scales. Questionnaires that assess Machiavellianism.

Macrocosm. In social psychology, a large social system, such as a society.

Macroscopic social level. In international relations, the viewpoint that international conduct is determined by the entire populations of the nations involved.

Maintenance organizations. Organizations that socialize people for their roles in society.

Maintenance systems. Systems that bring people into an organization, ensure reliable performance, and handle problems of absenteeism and turnover.

Managerial organizations. Organizations that coordinate and control people and resources.

Managerial systems. Authority systems that provide synchronization and control.

Managing. Encounter-group leadership behavior that involves establishing ground rules, helping the group to set goals, starting and stopping sessions, and other "house-keeping" duties.

Manipulation check. A measure intended to verify that the subject in an experiment perceived conditions in the ways intended by the experimenter.

Markers. Devices used to "stake out" a territorial area that is to remain private.

Masking. The process of substituting one facial reaction for another and hence conveying a false impression about one's feelings.

Matched-dependent behavior. An action that matches or duplicates the behavior of another person and is contingent on cues emitted by the other.

Matrix. (1) A mathematical table depicting interrelated numbers. (2) In exchange theory, a table showing the various response alternatives available to the participants and the outcomes associated with the various combinations of responses.

Maximization principle. In the open-systems approach to organizations, the rule of thumb that systems strive to become larger and more powerful and to increase the number of resources under their control.

Maximizing Difference Game (MDG). A form of experimental game in which each of two players is allowed to make a cooperative response or a response that yields fewer points in the absolute sense but that provides a relative advantage in points over the opponent.

MDG. *See* Maximizing Difference Game.

Media. The agencies or means for presenting a message.

Mere-exposure hypothesis. The hypothesis that the mere repeated exposure of an individual to a stimulus is a sufficient condition for enhancing his or her attitude toward that stimulus.

Mere-presence hypothesis. In social facilitation, the hypothesis that the presence of a conspecific is a sufficient condition for increasing drive or arousal.

Microcosm. In social psychology, a small social system, such as a dyad.

Microculture. A simplified, miniature laboratory society believed to function along the same general lines as the larger society, allowing the study of society under controlled conditions.

Microscopic social level. In international relations, the viewpoint that international conduct is determined by select and relatively small segments within each nation.

Midrange theories. Theories that are general enough to provide some scope but restricted enough to offer some specific predictions.

Military overconfidence. Unrealistic assessment of one's own army as having a major advantage over the enemy's army. This factor often involves (1) a failure to weigh the possibility that other countries will intervene in the enemy's behalf, (2) an underestimation of stiff resistance on the part of the enemy, and (3) false beliefs that many of the enemy people are really on one's own side.

Mirror-image phenomenon. A tendency of the members of two conflicting social groupings to describe the members of their own group as friendly, sincere, and trustworthy and the members of the other group as unfriendly, insincere, and deceitful.

Mirroring. Encounter-group leadership behavior that involves reflecting occurrences within the group by summarizing events and reminding the group of its decisions and goals.

Model. An original learner or performer whose behavior is learned or imitated by an observer. The model's behavior may be live, filmed, or verbally described.

Modeling. A process that occurs whenever an observer adopts the live, filmed, or verbally described behavior of another person.

Modular man. An individual who interacts with a large number of people, but only on a limited basis with each one; that is, each single relationship lacks breadth.

Moral self-image. The conviction that oneself or one's own group is morally and ethically correct.

Mores. Strong social norms regarding morally and ethically acceptable and unacceptable behavior.

Motivational patterns. In organizational psychology, sources of satisfaction that draw members to organizations and ensure all the behaviors required for effective organizational functioning. These patterns include (1) legal compliance, (2) external rewards, (3) self-determination and self-expression, and (4) the internalization of organizational goals.

Motivators. Factors that must be present in a work setting to produce satisfaction (as compared with those that prevent dissatisfaction).

Motives. Preferences for broad classes of activities.

Naïve empiricism. Observation made by use of the senses but without using procedures that safeguard against expectancies, prejudices, and other human frailties.

Nay-saying. A response bias to disagree with a statement no matter what its nature.

Need for affiliation. A preference for activities that involve being with others.

Need for autonomy. A preference for being independent and free.

Need hierarchy. An ordering of needs such that the lower needs (such as for air, water, and food) must be satisfied before the higher needs (feeling loved, feeling worth-while, and self-actualizing) can be satisfied.

Needs. Biological or psychological deficits.

Negative bond. In consistency theories of attitudes, a state of dissociation or disavowal.

Negative correlation. A relationship between two variables such that, as the magnitude of one variable increases, the magnitude of the associated variable decreases.

Negative reference groups. Reference groups providing standards that the individual disavows or opposes.

Negative reinforcer. A reinforcer whose withdrawal increases the likelihood of the response that it follows.

Negative social reinforcers. Disapproval, disagreement, disliking, frowns, and other signs of disregard or rejection.

Negative-state relief hypothesis. The hypothesis that, when a person begins to feel bad about having harmed or injured someone, he or she will try to be helpful in order to restore a feeling of comfort and well-being.

Net. A communication network that requires messages to flow along prescribed channels.

Neutralization. The process of inhibiting a facial reaction to hide one's feelings.

Nominal group. In research on group productivity and problem solving, a collection of noninteracting people whose collective performance is compared with the collective performance of a real group in which members interact.

Nonarbitrary frustration. A frustration that is perceived as accidental or unintended.

Nonreactive measures. Measures of behavior that leave subjects unaware that they are under scrutiny.

Nonsense words. Made-up words that are used for experimental purposes.

Nonverbal communication. The transmission of information and affect through all means other than using actual words. Major forms include proxemic, kinesic, and paralinguistic.

Normative altruism. Altruistic behavior that is not internally caused but is the result of normative social influence. (*Contrast with* Autonomous altruism.)

Normative reference groups. Reference groups that provide standards and values for defining what is right and proper.

Normative social influence. The pressure to live up to the expectations of the group in order to secure rewards and avoid punishment.

Norm of human heartedness. A societal norm prescribing that people should be treated with tolerance and compassion.

Norm of justice. A societal norm prescribing that people should be treated equally, except with respect to their objective abilities.

Norm of rationality. A societal norm prescribing that people should be accurate and factually correct, logical in their reasoning, and cautious when making judgments.

Norm of reciprocity. A social rule prescribing that one person should feel about and do to another person as this other person feels about and does to him or her.

Norm of social responsibility. A societal norm prescribing that people should help those who need help and that goodness is its own reward.

Norms. Socially devised standards that provide a framework for interpreting and evaluating behavior and that define degrees of acceptability and unacceptability.

Obedience. Compliance with the express demands of another.

Objective-responsibility orientation. A moral perspective that involves interpreting the seriousness of a transgression in terms of the objective damage done.

Observational learning. Learning through observing the behavior of another person.

Omission. In open-systems theory, a technique for coping with information overload by neglecting to process some of the potential input.

One-sided presentation. An appeal in which the source does not acknowledge or discuss the opposition's views or arguments.

Open-ended measures. Questionnaires and rating devices that allow the respondent to answer in his or her own words.

Opening new channels. In open-systems theory, the process of readjusting the system to cope with information overload by means of establishing new production lines for processing additional input.

Open-systems perspective. In organizational theory and research, the view that organizations are analogous to computers.

Open-systems theory. The theory that there are certain principles that hold true for groups of varying sizes—each one of which is a system.

Operations. Procedures followed to manipulate or define variables.

Organization. A system having a complex hierarchical structure that operates within an amorphous environment. Less formally, organizations may be considered large, complex groups that are oriented toward the attainment of specific goals.

Organizational roles. Patterns of behavior prescribed for individuals who occupy designated positions within an organization. (*See* Roles.)

Outcomes. (1) The consequences or results of a choice or an action. (2) Consequences for the participants of a social-interaction sequence.

Output. In open-systems theory, information or material transmitted from the system after processing.

Overcompensation. In equity theory, receiving more than you feel you deserve given your investment of time and energy.

Own gain. The motivation to do as well as one can for oneself, regardless of the outcomes experienced by others.

Own-group bias. Unrealistically high evaluations of the skills, abilities, customs, and traditions of one's own group and unrealistically low evaluations of the skills, abilities, customs, and traditions of other (especially competing) groups.

Paralinguistic communication. The transmission of information and affect through manner of speaking.

Parental Interference Scale. A questionnaire designed to assess the extent to which the respondent's parents tried to meddle in and exert a bad influence on the respondent's relationship with a romantic partner.

Parsimony. Use of the smallest possible number of terms and principles to provide an adequate explanation for a phenomenon.

Participative decision making. Managerial practices that allow workers to have inputs into the decision-making process.

Passive-dependent role. A role involving meekness, submissiveness, indecisiveness, and reliance on others.

PDG. *See* Prisoner's Dilemma Game.

Peer group. A group of individuals of similar ages and interests and with similar rights and obligations.

Perceiver variables. In perception, the private or "subjective" determinants of perception, such as moods, motives, and expectancies.

Perception. Processes by which the individual receives, structures, and interprets information from the environment.

Perceptual-accentuation hypothesis. The hypothesis that, when stimuli are related to the satisfaction of the individual's needs or motives, they will appear bigger, brighter, heavier, or more intense than when they are irrelevant to the perceiver's needs and motives.

Perceptual-defense hypothesis. The hypothesis that people have an inability to perceive obnoxious, threatening, or unpleasant stimuli.

Peripheral trait. A trait that does not precipitate changes in the perception of other traits.

Personal consequences. Habits, attitudes, personality, and other individual characteristics that result from the social-influence process.

Personal distance. The second closest of the four zones that, according to Hall, reflect how people are feeling about each other. This distance typifies close relationships and ranges from about 18 inches to 4 feet.

Personal growth. In humanistic theorizing, the utilization of one's human potential, including development of: (1) faith and trust in other people, (2) communication skills, (3) self-determination and responsibility, and (4) a sense of interdependence with others without surrendering personal freedom.

Personalism. In attribution theory, the extent to which a perceiver believes a target's act was somehow caused or occasioned by his or her presence.

Personality. The sum and total of the dispositional variables that provide individuality and consistency in a person's behavior.

Personal level. In international relations, the viewpoint that the course of international conduct is determined by the personalities of the nation's top leaders.

Phantom-other procedures. Experimental procedures whereby a subject is purportedly shown the attitudes of another person. In actuality, there is no other person, and the questionnaire has been prepared so that the attitudes coincide to a specified extent with the attitudes of the subject.

Phobia. A strong, irrational fear.

Physiological needs. Needs for air, food, water, and other necessities for life. These needs are at the lowest level of Maslow's need hierarchy.

Planned-change model. A model of organizational adaptation and change in which a change agent or consultant oversees a cycle of activities, including (1) data gathering, (2) action planning, (3) implementation, and (4) evaluation.

PONS (Profile on Nonverbal Sensitivity). A test of people's abilities to decode nonverbal messages.

Population. The entire group of people who could be questioned or studied. For example, in a Presidential poll, all registered voters would constitute a population.

Positive bond. In consistency theories of attitudes, a state of association or connectedness between two elements.

Positive correlation. A relationship between two variables such that, as the magnitude of one variable increases, the magnitude of the associated variable also increases.

Positive habituation. A reduction of uncertainty and conflict as a result of increasing familiarity.

Positive reference groups. Reference groups providing standards that the individual endorses.

Positive reinforcer. A reinforcer whose application increases the probability of the response that it follows.

Positive social reinforcers. Approval, agreement, liking, smiles, nods, and other signs of regard, esteem, and acceptance.

Postdecisional dissonance. Following a choice, dissonance arising from the attractive features of the rejected alternative and from the unattractive features of the selected alternative.

Precise. Definite or exact. A precise measure is one that makes possible accurate or exact observations. Precision contributes to reliability.

Prediction. A set of statements concerning what is likely to happen in the future.

Predisposition to help. One of the three components of love; reflected in a display of kindness and consideration toward the partner.

Prejudicial attitudes. Attitudes that depart from one or more of three ideal norms: the norm of rationality, the norm of justice, and the norm of human heartedness.

Presentation variables. Variables associated with the way an attitude-change appeal is made.

Primacy effect. Assignment of more weight to information given early in a sequence than to information given late in a sequence.

Primary group. A group in which people respond to one another as distinct personalities with unique strengths, weaknesses, and needs.

Prisoner's Dilemma Game (PDG). A form of experimental game in which each of two players is allowed to make a cooperative or a competitive response.

Proactive inhibition. Interference with the learning of new material by earlier-learned, conflicting material.

Production organizations. Organizations whose function is to create wealth, manufacture goods, and provide services.

Production systems. Systems that deal with central productive processes, such as turning out automobiles, friars, or advertising slogans.

Propinquity. Nearness or closeness in space.

Prosocial behavior. Behavior that is helpful to others.

Prototypes. Models or exemplary cases that provide a basis for generalizations about a whole class of instances or cases.

Proxemic communication. The transmission of information and affect through spatial arrangement.

Pseudorecognition trials. Trials on which subjects are asked to "guess" what stimulus word has been flashed on a screen when, in actuality, only a brief flash of light (and no word) has been presented.

Psychoanalytic model. A conception of the individual as buffeted about by unconscious mental forces.

Psychology. The study of the thoughts, feelings, and actions of the individual.

Public distance. The least intimate of the four zones that, according to Hall, reflect how people are feeling about each other. This is the distance "of presidents and princes" and extends from 12 feet onward.

Queuing. In open-systems theory, a technique for coping with information overload by means of delaying the processing of information.

Rational perspective. In organizational psychology, the view that organizations are analogous to machines.

Reactance. An aversive state that results when a free behavior is eliminated or is threatened with elimination. The result of reactance is that the threatened or eliminated alternative gains in importance and the person becomes highly motivated to perform the threatened response.

Real group. In research on group productivity and problem solving, a group in which members interact while solving the problem or accomplishing the task. Their collective performance is compared with the collective performance of a nominal group, in which members do not interact.

Recency effect. The assignment of more weight to information given late in a sequence than to information given early in the sequence.

Reciprocity. *See* Norm of reciprocity.

Recognition threshold. The minimum amount of stimulation required for a word or other stimulus to be recognized.

Reference group. A group that provides us with standards for evaluating our own or others' attitudes or behaviors.

Regression. Reversion to a childish or infantile mode of behavior.

Regression equations. Mathematical formulas that allow the determination of the value of one variable given the value of a correlated variable.

Reinforcers. Things or events that follow a response and affect the response's subsequent probability.

Relative gain. The motivation to secure outcomes that are better than those secured by others.

Releaser. In ethological theories of behavior, a stimulus that elicits an instinctive or biologically preprogrammed behavior or series of behaviors.

Reliability. A desirable quality of observations and measurements that is roughly equivalent to "repeatability" or "verifiability." An observation or measurement is reliable to the extent that it is the same when made by different people or on different occasions.

Replication. A duplication of procedures or results by a different experimenter or by the same experimenter at a later point in time.

Repression. A process through which emotionally painful or threatening material is blotted from awareness.

Research-development-and-diffusion model. A model of organizational change suggesting that inducing change requires only that the consultant discover the relevant information in technical journals, texts, and so forth and then simply present it in a straightforward way to the organization's decision makers.

Resistance to extinction. The durability of a learned response (1) after the withdrawal of reinforcement following emission of the response, or (2) in the absence of additional unconditioned stimulus/conditioned stimulus pairings.

Response alternatives. Various responses or courses of action available to each participant in a social interaction.

Response facilitation. In modern social-learning theory, the prompting of an already learned response through observing that response performed by others.

Response-facilitation effects. In modern social-learning theory, performance of an already learned and socially acceptable response after having observed its performance by a model.

Response sets. Predispositions to respond to psychological test questions in a certain way independent of the content of the questions.

Rewards. (1) Gratifications or pleasures. (2) In Thibaut and Kelley's theory, all the positive aspects of an outcome.

Risk. The probability of securing a favorable outcome under stated conditions.

Risky shift. Following individual risk taking, greater risk taking under group-membership conditions.

Role. (1) A set of expectations concerning what a person in a given position must, must not, or may do. (2) The actual behavior of a person who occupies a position.

Role-complementarity hypothesis. The hypothesis that a person who occupies a role will find attractive a person who occupies an interlocking role.

Role theory. A theory suggesting that a person's position within a group contributes heavily to his or her behavior and to how he or she will act toward others in the group.

Romeo and Juliet effect. Intensified feelings of attraction toward a romantic partner following parental attempts to meddle in the relationship.

Safety needs. Needs for security and a stable environment. These needs are at the second lowest level in Maslow's need hierarchy.

Same behavior. Uniformities in the behavior of different people that represent independent responding to similar or identical conditions.

Sample. A relatively small group of people singled out from a larger group for study or assessment.

Scanlon plan. A management-labor profit-sharing scheme that protects workers by guaranteeing a minimum wage.

Science. A set of rules of inquiry for understanding regularities in the world.

Scientific management. A plan for improving organizational efficiency through a combination of (1) time and motion analyses, (2) large incentives, and (3) a strict hierarchical structure.

Secondary group. A group in which people respond to one another as occupants of interlocking roles rather than as unique individuals.

Selective inattention. Failure to attend to facts or arguments that support the opposition in a controversy.

Selective perception. Perceiving or emphasizing those aspects of a situation that fulfill wishes or expectations while not perceiving those aspects of a situation that disconfirm expectations or add to frustration or misery.

Self-actualization. The process of utilizing abilities in such a way as to best realize one's potential.

Self-actualization need. The need to use one's potential, exercise one's freedom, and grow psychologically. This need is at the top of Maslow's need hierarchy.

Self-control mechanisms. Conscience and other regulators of behavior that are internal to or a part of the behaving individual and that prevent the expression of some impulses and limit the expression of others.

Self-determination and self-expression. A motivational base for performing organizational roles. The rewards come from the exercise of ability while on the job.

Self-disclosure. The process of revealing information about oneself.

Self-esteem. A person's sense of being powerful, significant, virtuous, and competent.

Self-fulfilling prophecy. Predicting an event and then behaving in such a way as to make that event come about.

Self-perception theory. The theory that people infer their own attitudes from knowledge of their behavior.

Self-report measures. Questionnaires, rating scales, and other devices that allow the respondent to indicate feelings, beliefs, and intentions.

Sensitivity group. *See* Encounter group.

Sensitivity to individual differences. In social perception, a perceiver's ability to identify the ways in which individuals differ from one another and from the average member of their group.

Sensitivity to the generalized other. In social perception, a perceiver's awareness of the typical characteristics or responses of a large class or group of people.

Sensory deprivation. A condition of highly reduced stimulation that generally results in irritability, confusion, and a decline in test performance.

Sex typing. Socialization processes through which people develop the emotional responses, personality, attitudes, and beliefs that are defined as appropriate for their sex and in their culture.

Shaping. In learning, a procedure whereby successively close approximations of the desired response are reinforced.

Showing consideration. Leadership behavior that involves being sensitive and responsive to human needs.

Signal conformity. Accepting a group's judgments as cues for rendering similar judgments. Distinguished from action conformity, in which the group's norms are translated into overt actions (as in the case of obedience).

Simple sovereign theories. Theories that offer a single principle or concept as a key for explaining all social behavior.

Simulated others. In laboratory studies of social interaction (particularly studies involving experimental games), fake partners preprogrammed to "behave" in specified ways. Although the subjects believe that through pushing buttons and so forth they are interacting with other subjects, their outcomes in fact are a result of their response choices and the selections are carefully controlled by the experimenter.

Situational favorableness. In the contingency theory of leadership, the extent to which the leader has power and influence over the group.

Situational variables. Those forces contributing to behavior that are the product of the immediate environment, setting, or situation in which the behavior occurs.

Sleeper effect. Attitude change that does not appear until some time after the attitude-change appeal has been made. Serious doubt has been cast upon the sleeper effect by recent research.

Small group. A group in which each member has the opportunity for face-to-face interaction with each and every other member.

Social anchorage. In Kelman's theory of attitudes, the perceived attitudes of the person with whom the attitude holder identifies.

Social-comparison theory. A theory suggesting that people are motivated to evaluate their abilities, feelings, and opinions by comparing them with the abilities, feelings, and opinions of others.

Social consequences. The effects of the individual's habits, attitudes, and personality on the group or society.

Social control. Preventing the expression of some impulses and limiting the expression of others by means of surveillance or surveillance agencies (such as the police). The defining characteristic is that the individual's behavior is regulated by external mechanisms.

Social depenetration. The processes through which people deintensify their relationship and become less involved with each other.

Social desirability. (1) The extent to which behavior or attitudes are evaluated as good, favorable, or positive. (2) As a response bias, a tendency to choose answers that present oneself in a favorable light.

Social differentiation. The process through which the different members of a group make themselves distinguishable from one another.

Social disorganization. A failure of norms to regulate individual conduct.

Social distance. (1) The degree to which people are willing to interact in situations that are ordered in terms of intimacy. (2) The third closest of the four zones that, according to Hall, reflect how people are feeling about each other. This distance typifies non-casual relationships and extends from about 4 to 12 feet.

Social effect. In Kelman's theory of attitudes, the approval or disapproval a person receives for expressing a given attitude.

Social facilitation. The energizing effects of passive spectators or of coactors on individual performance.

Social interaction. Mutual and reciprocal social-influence processes that occur within groups.

Social-interaction-and-diffusion model. A model of organizational change suggesting that, once the consultant has decided upon desirable new practices, putting them into action requires identifying and then persuading those people within the organization whom others seek for guidance.

Socialization. The processes that transform individuals into functioning members of society.

Social learning. A change or modification of behavior as a result, in part, of the actions, reactions, or observed fate of another person.

Social motives. The personal needs that are satisfied by overt social responses or "social strategies" (*see* Joint gain; Own gain; Relative gain).

Social norms. Socially devised standards that provide a framework for interpreting and evaluating behavior and that define degrees of acceptability and unacceptability.

Social organization. The regulation of individual and group conduct by means of social norms.

Social penetration. The process through which two people get to know and develop a relationship with each other.

Social perception. (1) Processes by which the individual receives, structures, and interprets the environment when such processes are affected by the presence or actions of others. (2) The perception of people.

Social psychology. An attempt to understand the ways in which the thoughts, feelings, and actions of one person (or group of people) are affected by the actual, imagined, or implied presence or actions of another person (or group of people).

Social reinforcement. Altering the subsequent probability of another person's response by showing approval (smiles, nods, agreement, and so forth) or disapproval (frowns, grimaces, disagreement, and so forth) following the emission of that response.

Social reinforcers. Reinforcers, such as approval and rejection, that are dispensed by other people.

Social strategies. In experimental games, overt responses such as the cooperative or competitive choices on the PDG.

Society. A large social grouping that attempts to coordinate all the people with varied interests who are considered members.

Socioemotional acts. In social interaction, behaviors that express positive or negative emotional reactions to others in the group.

Socioemotional leader. The member of the group who assumes responsibility for maintaining cordial relations within the group.

Sociofugal environments. Environments that seem to keep or drive people apart and prevent intimacy.

Sociology. The study of relationships among people that exist independent of any individual.

Sociopetal environments. Environments that seem to draw people together and encourage intimacy.

Sophisticated empiricism. Observation made in such a way as to provide safeguards against prejudices, biases, and other frailties of individual observers.

Source. In the communications approach to attitude formation and change, the communicator or person who makes the attitude-change appeal.

Specialized subsystems. Parts of an organization that serve specialized functions to help the organization reach its overall goals. These subsystems include adaptive systems, boundary systems, maintenance systems, and managerial systems.

Statistically significant. A finding or result that is not easily and convincingly dismissed as due to chance alone.

Statisticized group. A judgment or estimate representing the arithmetical mean or average judgment of a number of noninteracting individuals.

Stereotype. A fixed impression of the psychological and social qualities and attributes of the members of a group. Stereotypes are blanket generalizations that violate the norms of rationality and justice.

Stereotyped responding. Senseless repetition of an act.

Stooge. A secret accomplice or confederate of the experimenter's.

Structure. Communication channels, lines of authority or influence, and all other social variables that reduce the number of behavioral options available to the individual.

Study of Values. A scale for measuring people's underlying interests or values.

Subjective-responsibility orientation. A moral perspective that involves interpreting the seriousness of a transgression in terms of the perpetrator's intent.

Summation model. A model of impression formation suggesting that our overall impressions of favorability of a person represent the sum of the favorability values associated with each item of information that we have about that person.

Superordinate goals. Goals that are of overriding importance to two or more conflicting groups and that require intergroup cooperation to attain.

Symbolic models. Models whose behavior is portrayed through oral or written descriptions.

Systems. Dynamic entities with a number of interdependent and functioning parts.

Tachistoscope. A device for presenting visual stimuli for brief periods of time (milliseconds) under conditions of controlled illumination.

Target. (1) In social perception, the person who is the focus of perceptual activity. (2) In attitude research, the person to whom the attitude-change appeal is made.

Task acts. In social interaction, emotionally neutral behaviors for completing the task confronting the group.

Task leader. The member of a group who assumes responsibility for directing group activities toward accomplishing the task at hand.

Tedium. A state of underarousal that makes conditions seem dull and boring.

Tension-reduction strategies. Proposed responses to intergroup conflict that involve de-emphasizing the differences between groups and attempting to induce intergroup cooperation.

Territorial defense. Techniques used to keep other people at a comfortable distance.

Test-retest stability. An estimate of reliability expressed as the correlations of the scores of successive administrations of a test.

t-group. *See* Laboratory-training group.

Theory. A set of statements intended to logically and convincingly capture or express some aspect of reality.

Theory of reverse discrimination. A theory suggesting that, if people who consider themselves unprejudiced toward a given group are given reason to doubt their lack of prejudice, they may respond by showing preferential treatment toward members of that group.

Theory X. The traditional managerial view that workers hold jobs only because work is a lesser evil than starvation and that workers must be continually prodded and closely supervised.

Theory Y. The humanistic managerial view that workers want to exercise their abilities and shoulder responsibilities.

Throughput. In open-systems theory, information or material as it is being processed.

Top-level leaders. Those at the pinnacle of the organizational hierarchy who formulate new policy.

Tracking. A procedure whereby school students are grouped according to their perceived abilities and then given curricula that will send them on their way to seemingly appropriate life goals.

Trait. An inferred, relatively enduring characteristic or attribute of an individual that hypothetically shows itself in a variety of situations and under differing conditions.

Triadic relationships. In balance theory, relationships involving three elements.

Trucking Game. An experimental game in which each of two players attempts to move trucks toward a destination. To avoid costly delays, the subjects must cooperate.

Turnover. (1) In organizational psychology, the loss and replacement of organizational members. (2) A small pielike pastry.

Two-sided presentation. An appeal in which the source acknowledges and discusses opposition views and arguments.

Two-way orientation. An ability on the part of middle-level leaders to simultaneously understand and deal with the needs of subordinates and the demands of superiors.

Unbalanced relationships. In balance theory, "incomplete" relationships in which one or more of the bonds is missing.

Uncommon effects. In attribution theory, the consequences of an act that are unique in that they would not follow from alternative acts. Such unique consequences are seen as highly revealing of motives and intent.

Unconditioned response (UCR). In the classical-conditioning process, a response reliably elicited by the unconditioned stimulus at the beginning of the conditioning procedures.

Unconditioned stimulus (UCS). In the classical-conditioning process, a stimulus that reliably elicits a specific response at the beginning of the conditioning procedures.

Undercompensation. In equity theory, receiving inadequate outcomes for investments of time and energy.

Understanding. A plausible and convincing explanation of a phenomenon.

Unilateral disarmament. Disarming on the part of one nation without regard to whether or not potential enemies will also disarm.

Validity. The degree to which an observation is considered "truthful" or "an instance of that which it is supposed to be."

Value congruence. In Kelman's theory of attitudes, the extent to which an attitude is consistent with the attitude holder's underlying system of values.

Value-expressive function. In Katz' theory of attitudes, the use of an attitude to reveal one's deepest values and to proclaim to the world the kind of person one considers oneself to be.

Values. Judgments of attractiveness, desirability, and worth that are based on abstract concepts and broad classifications.

Value theory. An interpretation of extremity shifts (particularly the risky shift) suggesting that risk taking is valued in our culture and that this value becomes particularly salient in a group setting.

Variable. Anything that varies or changes.

Verbal communication. Communication through words.

Verbal conditioning. Changes in the rate and type of verbal response as a result of the manipulation of social reinforcement.

Veridicality. The accuracy or validity of a perception.

Vertical expansion. A form of job expansion that involves increasing the job holder's autonomy and responsibility.

Virile self-image. Within a group, a preoccupation with the group's power and prestige.

Warm-glow hypothesis. The hypothesis that a person who is put in a good mood (such as by learning of success or good fortune) will be likely to help out other people.

Wheel. A communications network in which all messages must pass through one person, who occupies a "clearinghouse" role.

Work modules. In organizational psychology, time-task units (for example, two hours of stamping out hubcaps).

XYY genotype. A chromosomal aberration that can occur only in men and that is associated with violent, antisocial behavior.

Y. In communications-network research, the second most centralized net (the first being the wheel).

References

Acock, A. C., & DeFleur, M. L. A configurational approach to contingent consistency in the attitude-behavior relationship. *American Sociological Review*, 1972, 37, 714–726.

Adair, J. G. *The human subject: The social psychology of the psychological experiment.* Boston: Little, Brown, 1973.

Adair, J. G., & Schachter, B. S. To cooperate or look good? The subjects' and experimenters' perceptions of each other's intentions. *Journal of Experimental Social Psychology*, 1972, 8, 74–85.

Adams, J. S. Toward an understanding of inequity. *Journal of Abnormal and Social Psychology*, 1963, 67, 422–436.

Adams, J. S. Inequity in social exchange. In L. Berkowitz (Ed.), *Advances in experimental social psychology* (Vol. 2). New York: Academic Press, 1965. Pp. 267–299.

Adams, J. S., & Hoffman, D. The frequency of self-reference statements as a function of generalized reinforcement. *Journal of Abnormal and Social Psychology*, 1960, 6, 384–389.

Adams, J. S., & Jacobsen, P. Effects of wage inequities on work quality. *Journal of Abnormal and Social Psychology*, 1964, 69, 19–25.

Adams, J. S., & Rosenbaum, W. B. The relationship of worker productivity to cognitive dissonance about wage inequities. *Journal of Applied Psychology*, 1962, 46, 161–164.

Aderman, D. Effects of anticipating future interaction on the preference for balanced states. *Journal of Personality and Social Psychology*, 1969, 11, 214–219.

Adorno, T., Frenkel-Brunswik, E., Levinson, D., & Sanford, R. *The authoritarian personality.* New York: Harper & Row, 1950.

Ajzen, I., & Fishbein, M. Attitudinal and normative variables as predictors of specific behaviors. *Journal of Personality and Social Psychology*, 1973, 27, 41–57.

Aldrich, H. Organizational boundaries and inter-organizational conflict. *Human Relations*, 1971, 24, 279–293.

Allen, H. Bystander intervention and helping on the subway. In L. Bickman & T. Henchy (Eds.), *Beyond the laboratory: Field research in social psychology.* New York: McGraw-Hill, 1972. Pp. 22–33.

Allen, V. L., & Levine, J. M. Consensus and conformity. *Journal of Experimental Social Psychology*, 1969, 5, 383–399.

Allen, V. L., & Newtson, D. Development of conformity and independence. *Journal of Personality and Social Psychology*, 1972, 22, 18–30.

Allgeier, A. R., & Byrne, D. Attraction toward the opposite sex as a determinant of physical proximity. *Journal of Social Psychology*. 1973, 90, 213–219.

Allport, F. H. *Social psychology.* Cambridge, Mass.: Riverside Press, 1924.

Allport, F. H. *Theories of perception and the concept of structure.* New York: Wiley, 1955.

Allport, G. W. The historical background of modern social psychology. In G. Lindzey (Ed.), *Handbook of social psychology* (Vol. 1). Reading, Mass.: Addison-Wesley, 1954a.

Allport, G. W. *The nature of prejudice.* Reading, Mass.: Addison-Wesley, 1954b.

Allport, G. W. *Pattern and growth in personality.* New York: Holt, Rinehart and Winston, 1961.

Allport, G. W., & Odbert, H. S. Trait-names: A psycholexical study. *Psychological Monographs,* 1936, *47,* (Whole No. 211), 1–171.

Allport, G. W., Vernon, P. E., & Lindzey, G. *A study of values* (3rd ed.). Boston: Houghton Mifflin, 1960.

Altman, D., Levine, M., Nadien, M., & Villena, J. Trust of the stranger in the city and the small town. Unpublished research, Graduate Center, City University of New York, 1969. Cited in S. Milgram, The experience of living in cities. *Science,* 1969, *167,* 1461–1468.

Altman, I., & Taylor, D. *Social penetration: The development of interpersonal relationships.* New York: Holt, Rinehart and Winston, 1973.

American Psychological Association. *Ethical principles in the conduct of research with human participants.* Washington, D. C.: Author, 1973.

Amir, Y. Contact hypothesis in ethnic relations. *Psychological Bulletin,* 1969, *71,* 319–342.

Amoroso, D. M., & Walters, R. H. Effects of anxiety and socially mediated anxiety reduction on paired-associate learning. *Journal of Personality and Social Psychology,* 1969, *11,* 388–396.

Anderson, N. H. Adding versus averaging as a stimulus combination rule in impression formation. *Journal of Experimental Psychology,* 1965, *70,* 394–400.

Anderson, N. H. Component ratings in impression formation. *Psychonomic Science,* 1966, *6,* 279–280.

Anderson, N. H. A simple model for information integration. In R. Abelson, E. Aronson, W. McGuire, T. Newcomb, M. Rosenberg, & P. Tannenbaum (Eds.), *Theories of cognitive consistency: A sourcebook.* Chicago: Rand McNally, 1968a. Pp. 731–743.

Anderson, N. H. Likeableness ratings of 555 personality-trait words. *Journal of Personality and Social Psychology,* 1968b, *9,* 272–279.

Anderson, N. H. Integration theory and attitude change. *Psychological Review,* 1971, *78,* 171–206.

Anderson, N. H., Lindner, R., & Lopes, L. L. Integration theory applied to judgments of group attractiveness. *Journal of Personality and Social Psychology,* 1973, *26,* 400–408.

Andreoli, V. A., Worchel, S., & Folger, R. Implied threat to behavioral freedom. *Journal of Personality and Social Psychology,* 1974, *30,* 765–771.

Ardrey, R. *African genesis.* New York: Atheneum, 1961.

Ardrey, R. *The territorial imperative.* New York: Atheneum, 1966.

Argyle, M., & Dean, J. Eye-contact, distance, and affiliation. *Sociometry,* 1965, *28,* 289–304.

Argyris, C. *Intervention theory and method.* Reading, Mass.: Addison-Wesley, 1969.

Aron, R. Introduction. In H. Kahn, *Thinking about the unthinkable.* New York: Avon, 1966.

Aronfreed, J. The nature, variety, and social patterning of moral responses to transgression. *Journal of Abnormal and Social Psychology,* 1961, *63,* 233–240.

Aronfreed, J. The effects of experimental socialization paradigms upon two moral responses to transgression. *Journal of Abnormal and Social Psychology,* 1963, *66,* 437–448.

Aronfreed, J. The origin of self-criticism. *Psychological Review,* 1964, *71,* 193–218.

Aronfreed, J. The concept of internalization. In D. A. Goslin (Ed.), *Handbook of socialization theory and research.* Chicago: Rand McNally, 1969. Pp. 263–324.

Aronfreed, J., & Reber, A. Internalized behavioral suppression and the timing of social punishment. *Journal of Personality and Social Psychology,* 1965, *1,* 3–16.

Aronoff, J., & Messé, L. A. Motivational determinants of small group structure. *Journal of Personality and Social Psychology,* 1971, *17,* 319–324.

Aronson, E. Dissonance theory: Progress and problems. In R. P. Abelson, E. Aronson, W. J. McGuire, T. M. Newcomb, M. J. Rosenberg, & P. H. Tannenbaum (Eds.), *Theories of cognitive consistency: A sourcebook.* Chicago: Rand McNally, 1968.

Aronson, E., & Carlsmith, J. M. The effect of the severity of threat on the devaluation of forbidden behavior. *Journal of Abnormal and Social Psychology, 1963, 66,* 584–588.

Aronson, E., & Cope, V. My enemy's enemy is my friend. *Journal of Personality and Social Psychology, 1968, 8,* 8–12.

Aronson, E., & Linder, D. Gain and loss of esteem as determinants of interpersonal attractiveness. *Journal of Experimental Social Psychology, 1965, 1,* 156–171.

Aronson, E., & Mills, J. The effect of severity of initiation on liking for a group. *Journal of Abnormal and Social Psychology, 1959, 59,* 177–181.

Aronson, E., Willerman, B., & Floyd, J. The effect of a pratfall on increasing interpersonal attractiveness. *Psychonomic Science, 1966, 4,* 227–228.

Asch, S. Forming impressions of personality. *Journal of Abnormal and Social Psychology, 1946, 41,* 258–290.

Asch, S. *Social psychology.* Englewood Cliffs, N. J.: Prentice-Hall, 1952.

Asch, S. Studies of independence and conformity: A minority of one against a unanimous majority. *Psychological Monographs, 1956, 70,* No. 9 (Whole No. 416).

Ashour, A. S. The contingency model of leadership effectiveness: An evaluation. *Organizational Behavior and Human Performance, 1973a, 9,* 339–355.

Ashour, A. S. Further discussion of Fielder's contingency model of leadership effectiveness. *Organizational Behavior and Human Performance, 1973b, 9,* 369–376.

Azrin, N. H., Hutchinson, R. R., & Hake, D. F. Extinction of induced aggression. *Journal of the Experimental Analysis of Behavior, 1966, 9,* 191–204.

Back, K. Influence through social communication. *Journal of Abnormal and Social Psychology, 1951, 46,* 9–23.

Backman, C. W., & Secord, P. F. The effect of perceived liking on interpersonal attraction. *Human Relations, 1959, 12,* 379–384.

Bagby, J. W. A cross-cultural study of perceptual predominance in binocular rivalry. *Journal of Abnormal and Social Psychology, 1957, 54,* 331–334.

Bales, R. F. *Interaction process analysis: A method for the study of small groups.* Reading, Mass.: Addison-Wesley, 1950a.

Bales, R. F. A set of categories for the analysis of small group interaction. *American Sociological Review, 1950b, 15,* 257–263.

Bales, R. F. The equilibrium problem in small groups. In T. Parsons, R. F. Bales, & E. A. Shils (Eds.), *Working papers in the theory of action.* New York: Free Press, 1953. Pp. 111–161.

Bales, R. F. Task status and likeability as a function of talking and listening in decision-making groups. In L. D. White (Ed.), *The state of the social sciences.* Chicago: University of Chicago Press, 1956. Pp. 148–161.

Bales, R. F. Task roles and social roles in problem solving groups. In E. Maccoby, T. M. Newcomb, & E. Hartley (Eds.), *Readings in social psychology.* New York: Holt, Rinehart and Winston, 1958. Pp. 437–443.

Bales, R. F. *Personality and interpersonal behavior.* New York: Holt, Rinehart and Winston, 1970.

Bales, R. F., & Slater, P. E. Role differentiation in small decision making groups. In T. Parsons (Ed.), *Family socialization and interaction process.* New York: Free Press, 1955. Pp. 259–306.

Bales, R. F., & Strodtbeck, F. L. Phases in group problem solving. *Journal of Abnormal and Social Psychology, 1951, 46,* 485–495.

Ball-Rokeach, S. J. Review of *Television and aggression,* by S. Feshbach & R. D. Singer. *Public Opinion Quarterly, 1971, 35,* 501–504.

Bandura, A. Social learning through imitation. In M. R. Jones (Ed.), *Nebraska symposium on motivation, 1962.* Lincoln: University of Nebraska Press, 1962.

Bandura, A. Influence of model's reinforcement contingencies on the acquisition of imitative responses. *Journal of Personality and Social Psychology, 1965a, 1,* 589–595.

Bandura, A. Vicarious processes: A case of no-trial learning. In L. Berkowitz (Ed.), *Advances in experimental social psychology* (Vol. 2). New York: Academic Press, 1965b. Pp. 1–55.

Bandura, A. *Principles of behavior modification.* New York: Holt, Rinehart and Winston, 1969.

Bandura, A. Psychotherapy based upon modeling principles. In A. E. Bergin & S. L. Garfield (Eds.), *Handbook of psychotherapy and behavior change.* New York: Wiley, 1971a. Pp. 653–708.

Bandura, A. (Ed.). *Psychological modeling.* Chicago: Aldine-Atherton, 1971b.

Bandura, A. *Aggression: A social learning analysis.* New York: Holt, Rinehart and Winston, 1973.

Bandura, A., Blanchard, E., & Ritter, B. Relative efficacy of desensitization and modeling approaches for inducing behavioral, affective, and attitudinal changes. *Journal of Personality and Social Psychology,* 1969, *13*, 173–200.

Bandura, A., Grusec, J. E., & Menlove, F. L. Observational learning as a function of symbolization and incentive set. *Child Development,* 1966, *37*, 499–506.

Bandura, A., & Huston, A. C. Identification as a process of incidental learning. *Journal of Abnormal and Social Psychology,* 1961, *63*, 311–318.

Bandura, A., & Jeffery, R. W. Role of symbolic coding and rehearsal processes in observational learning. *Journal of Personality and Social Psychology,* 1973, *26*, 122–130.

Bandura, A., & McDonald, F. J. The influence of social reinforcement and the behavior of models in shaping children's moral judgments. *Journal of Abnormal and Social Psychology,* 1963, *67*, 271–284.

Bandura, A., & Menlove, F. L. Factors determining vicarious extinction of avoidance behaviors through symbolic modeling. *Journal of Personality and Social Psychology,* 1968, *8*, 99–108.

Bandura, A., & Mischel, W. Modification of self-imposed delay of reward through exposure to live and symbolic models. *Journal of Personality and Social Psychology,* 1965, *2*, 698–705.

Bandura, A., Ross, D., & Ross, S. A. Imitation of film-mediated aggressive models. *Journal of Abnormal and Social Psychology,* 1963a, *66*, 3–11.

Bandura, A., Ross, D., & Ross, S. A comparative test of the status envy, social power, and secondary reinforcement theories of identificatory learning. *Journal of Abnormal and Social Psychology,* 1963b, *66*, 527–534.

Bandura, A., & Walters, R. H. *Adolescent aggression.* New York: Ronald Press, 1959.

Bandura, A., & Walters, R. H. *Social learning and personality development.* New York: Holt, Rinehart and Winston, 1963.

Barber, T. X., & Silver, M. J. Pitfalls in data analysis and interpretation: A reply to Rosenthal. *Psychological Bulletin Monograph Supplement,* 1968, *70*, 48–62.

Baron, J. S. Is experimental psychology relevant? *American Psychologist,* 1971, *26*, 685–695.

Baron, R. A., & Kepner, C. R. Model's behavior and attraction toward the model as determinants of adult aggressive behavior. *Journal of Personality and Social Psychology,* 1970, *14*, 335–344.

Baron, R. A., & Liebert, R. M. (Eds.). *Human social behavior: A contemporary view of experimental research.* Homewood, Ill.: Dorsey Press, 1971.

Baron, R. S., Baron, P. H., & Miller, N. The relation between distraction and persuasion. *Psychological Bulletin,* 1973, *80*, 310–323.

Baron, R. S., Monson, T. C., & Baron, P. H. Conformity pressure as a determinant of risk taking: Replication and extension. *Journal of Personality and Social Psychology,* 1973, *28*, 406–413.

Baron, R. S., Roper, G., & Baron, P. H. Group discussion and the stingy shift. *Journal of Personality and Social Psychology,* 1974, *30*, 538–545.

Barry, W. A. Marriage research and conflict: An integrative review. *Psychological Bulletin,* 1970, *73*, 41–54.

Bateson, N. Familiarization, group discussion, and risk-taking. *Journal of Experimental Social Psychology,* 1966, *2,* 119–129.

Bavelas, A. Communication patterns in task-oriented groups. *Journal of the Acoustical Society of America,* 1950, *22,* 725–730.

Bavelas, A., Hastorf, A. H., Gross, A. E., & Kite, W. R. Experiments in the alteration of group structure. *Journal of Experimental Social Psychology,* 1965, *1,* 55–71.

Baxter, G. W., Jr. Personality and attitudinal characteristics and cooperation in two person games: A review. In L. S. Wrightsman, J. O'Connor, & N. J. Baker (Eds.), *Cooperation and competition: Readings on mixed-motive games.* Monterey, Calif.: Brooks/Cole, 1972.

Bayton, J. A. The racial stereotypes of Negro college students. *Journal of Abnormal and Social Psychology,* 1943, *38,* 525–531.

Bebout, J., & Gordon, B. The value of encounter. In L. Solomon & B. Berzon (Eds.), *New perspectives on encounter groups.* San Francisco: Jossey-Bass, 1972. Pp. 83–118.

Becker, F. D. Study of spatial markers. *Journal of Personality and Social Psychology,* 1973, *26,* 439–445.

Bem, D. J. Self perception: An alternative interpretation of cognitive dissonance phenomena. *Psychological Review,* 1967, *74,* 183–200.

Bem, D. J. *Beliefs, attitudes, and human affairs.* Monterey, Calif.: Brooks/Cole, 1970.

Bem, D. J. Self-perception theory. In L. Berkowitz (Ed.), *Advances in experimental social psychology* (Vol. 6). New York: Academic Press, 1972. Pp. 1–62.

Bem, D. J., & Allen, A. On predicting some of the people some of the time. *Psychological Review,* 1974, *81,* 506–520.

Bem, D. J., & McConnell, H. K. Testing the self-perception explanation of dissonance phenomena: On the salience of premanipulation attitudes. *Journal of Personality and Social Psychology,* 1970, *14,* 23–31.

Bem, D. J., Wallach, M. A., & Kogan, N. Group decision making under risk of aversive consequences. *Journal of Personality and Social Psychology,* 1965, *1,* 453–460.

Bem, S. L. Psychology looks at sex roles: Where have all the androgynous people gone? Paper presented at U. C. L. A. Symposium on Women, May 1972.

Bem, S. L. The measurement of psychological androgyny. *Journal of Consulting and Clinical Psychology,* 1974, *42,* 155–162.

Bem, S. L. Sex-role adaptability: One consequence of psychological androgyny. *Journal of Personality and Social Psychology,* 1975, in press.

Bem, S. L., & Bem, D. J. Case study of a nonconscious ideology: Training the woman to know her place. In D. J. Bem, *Beliefs, attitudes, and human affairs.* Monterey, Calif.: Brooks/Cole, 1970.

Bem, S. L., & Bem, D. J. Homogenizing the American woman: The power of a nonconscious ideology. In P. Zimbardo & C. Maslach (Eds.), *Psychology for our times: Readings.* Glenview, Ill.: Scott, Foresman, 1973a.

Bem, S. L., & Bem, D. J. Sex-segregated want ads: Do they discourage female job applicants? In J. H. Hamsher & H. Sigall (Eds.), *Psychology and social issues.* New York: Macmillan, 1973b. Pp. 261–265.

Berger, S. M. Conditioning through vicarious instigation. *Psychological Review,* 1962, *69,* 450–466.

Berger, S. M. Observer perseverance as related to a model's success: A social comparison analysis. *Journal of Personality and Social Psychology,* 1971, *19,* 341–350.

Berkowitz, L. Group standards, cohesiveness, and productivity. *Human Relations,* 1954, *7,* 509–519.

Berkowitz, L. Responsibility, reciprocity, and social distance in help giving: An experimental investigation of English social class differences. *Journal of Experimental Social Psychology,* 1968, *4,* 46–63.

Berkowitz, L. *Roots of aggression: A re-examination of the frustration-aggression hypothesis.* New York: Atherton Press, 1969a.

Berkowitz, L. Simple views of aggression: An essay review. *American Scientist,* 1969b, *57,* 372–383.

Berkowitz, L. Aggressive humor as a stimulus to aggressive response. *Journal of Personality and Social Psychology,* 1970a, *16,* 710–717.

Berkowitz, L. The contagion of violence: An S-R mediational analysis of some effects of observed aggression. In W. J. Arnold & M. M. Page (Eds.), *Nebraska Symposium on Motivation.* Lincoln: University of Nebraska Press, 1970b. Pp. 95–135.

Berkowitz, L. Some determinants of impulsive aggression: Role of mediated associations with reinforcements for aggression. *Psychological Review,* 1974, *81,* 165–176.

Berkowitz, L., & Alioto, J. T. The meaning of an observed event as a determinant of its aggressive consequences. *Journal of Personality and Social Psychology,* 1973, *28,* 206–217.

Berkowitz, L., & Daniels, L. Responsibility and dependency. *Journal of Abnormal and Social Psychology,* 1963, *66,* 429–436.

Berkowitz, L., & Daniels, L. Affecting the salience of the social responsibility norm: Effects of past help on the response to dependency relationships. *Journal of Abnormal and Social Psychology,* 1964, *68,* 275–281.

Berkowitz, L., & Geen, R. G. Film violence and cue properties of available targets. *Journal of Personality and Social Psychology,* 1966, *3,* 525–530.

Berkowitz, L., & Knurek, D. Label-mediated hostility and generalization. *Journal of Personality and Social Psychology,* 1969, *13,* 200–206.

Berkowitz, L., & LePage, A. Weapons as aggression-eliciting stimuli. *Journal of Personality and Social Psychology,* 1967, *7,* 202–207.

Berlyne, D. E. The influence of complexity and novelty in visual figures on orienting responses. *Journal of Experimental Psychology,* 1958, *55,* 289–296.

Berlyne, D. E. *Conflict, arousal, and curiosity.* New York: McGraw-Hill, 1960.

Berlyne, D. E. Curiosity and exploration. *Science,* 1966, *153,* 23–33.

Berlyne, D. E. Novelty, complexity, and hedonic value. *Perception and Psychophysics,* 1970, *8,* 279–286.

Berlyne, D. E. *Aesthetics and psychobiology.* New York: Appleton-Century-Crofts, 1972.

Bermann, E., & Miller, D. R. The matching of mates. In R. Jessor & S. Feshbach (Eds.), *Cognition, personality, and clinical psychology.* San Francisco: Jossey-Bass, 1967. Pp. 90–111.

Berne, E. *Games people play: The psychology of human relationships.* New York: Grove Press, 1964.

Berscheid, E., Dion, K., Walster, E., & Walster, G. Physical attractiveness and dating choice: A test of the matching hypothesis. *Journal of Experimental Social Psychology,* 1971, *7,* 173–189.

Berscheid, E., & Walster, E. When does a harmdoer compensate a victim? *Journal of Personality and Social Psychology,* 1967, *6,* 435–441.

Berscheid, E., & Walster, E. *Interpersonal attraction.* Reading, Mass.: Addison-Wesley, 1969.

Berscheid, E., & Walster, E. Beauty and the best. *Psychology Today,* 1972, *5* (Oct.), 42–46.

Bickman, L. The effect of another bystander's ability to help on bystander intervention in an emergency. *Journal of Experimental Social Psychology,* 1971, *7,* 367–369.

Bickman, L. Social influence and diffusion of responsibility in an emergency. *Journal of Experimental Social Psychology,* 1972, *8,* 438–445.

Bickman, L., & Kamzan, M. The effect of race and need on helping behavior. *Journal of Social Psychology,* 1973, *89,* 73–77.

Biddle, B. J., & Thomas, E. (Eds.). *Role theory: Concepts and research.* New York: Wiley, 1965.

Birdwhistell, R. L. *Kinesics and context: Essays on body motion communication.* Philadelphia: University of Pennsylvania Press, 1970.

Birnbaum, M. Morality judgments: Tests of an averaging model. *Journal of Experimental Psychology,* 1972, *93,* 35–42.

Bixenstine, V. E., Potash, H. M., & Wilson, K. V. Effects of level of cooperative choice by the other player on choices in a prisoner's dilemma game. *Journal of Abnormal and Social Psychology,* 1963, *66,* 308–313.

Blake, R. R., & Mouton, J. S. The intergroup dynamics of win-lose conflict and problem solving in union-management relations. In M. Sherif (Ed.), *Intergroup relations and leadership.* New York: Wiley, 1962.

Blake, R. R., & Mouton, J. S. *The managerial grid.* Houston: Gulf, 1964.

Blake, R. R., Shepard, H. A., & Mouton, J. S. *Managing intergroup conflict in industry.* Houston: Gulf, 1964.

Blanchard, F. A., Adelman, L., & Cook, S. W. The effect of group success and failure upon interpersonal attraction in cooperating interracial groups. *Journal of Personality and Social Psychology,* 1975, *31,* 1020–1030.

Blanchard, F. A., Weigl, R. H., & Cook, S. W. The effect of relative competence of group members upon interpersonal attraction in cooperating interracial groups. *Journal of Personality and Social Psychology,* 1975, *32,* 519–530.

Blauner, R. Internal colonialism and ghetto revolt. In M. Wertheimer (Ed.), *Confrontation: Psychology and the problems of today.* Glenview, Ill.: Scott, Foresman, 1970. Pp. 122–129.

Bochner, S., & Insko, C. Communicator discrepancy, source credibility, and influence. *Journal of Personality and Social Psychology,* 1966, *4,* 614–621.

Bolles, R. C. Reinforcement, expectancy, and learning. *Psychological Review,* 1972, *79,* 394–409.

Bonacich, E. A theory of ethnic antagonism: The split labor market. *American Sociological Review,* 1972, *37,* 547–559.

Bowers, K. S. Situationism· in psychology: An analysis and a critique. *Psychological Review,* 1973, *80,* 307–336.

Braginsky, B., & Braginsky, D. *Mainstream psychology: A critique.* New York: Holt, Rinehart and Winston, 1974.

Braginsky, D. Machiavellianism and manipulative interpersonal behavior in children. *Journal of Experimental Social Psychology,* 1970, *6,* 77–99.

Brehm, J. W. Postdecision changes in the desirability of alternatives. *Journal of Abnormal and Social Psychology,* 1956, *52,* 384–389.

Brehm, J. W. *A theory of psychological reactance.* New York: Academic Press, 1966.

Brehm, J. W., & Cohen, A. R. Choice and chance relative deprivations as determinants of cognitive dissonance. *Journal of Abnormal and Social Psychology,* 1959, *58,* 383–387.

Brehm, J. W., & Cohen, A. R. *Explorations in cognitive dissonance.* New York: Wiley, 1962.

Brehm, J. W., & Cole, A. Effect of a favor which reduces freedom. *Journal of Personality and Social Psychology,* 1966, *3,* 420–426.

Brickman, P. *Social conflict: Readings in rule structures and conflict relationships.* Lexington, Mass.: D. C. Heath, 1974.

Brickman, P., & Horn, C. Balance theory and interpersonal coping in triads. *Journal of Personality and Social Psychology,* 1973, *26,* 347–385.

Brigham, J. C. Ethnic stereotypes. *Psychological Bulletin,* 1971, *76,* 15–38.

Brigham, J. C., Bloom, L. M., Gunn, S. P., & Torok, T. Attitude measurement via the bogus pipeline: A dry well? *Representative Research in Social Psychology,* 1974, *5,* 97–114.

Broadbent, D. E. Word-frequency effect and response bias. *Psychological Review,* 1967, *74,* 1–15.

Brock, T. C. Effects of prior dishonesty on post-decision dissonance. *Journal of Abnormal and Social Psychology,* 1963, *66,* 325–332.

Brock, T. C., & Fromkin, H. L. Receptivity to discrepant information. *Journal of Personality,* 1968, *36,* 108–125.

Bronfenbrenner, U. The mirror-image in Soviet-American relations—a social psychologists report. *Journal of Social Issues,* 1961, *17,* 45–56.

Bronfenbrenner, U., Harding, J., & Gallwey, M. O. The measurement of skill in social perception. In A. L. Baldwin (Ed.), *Talent and society*. Princeton, N.J.: Van Nostrand, 1958.

Brooks, J. A net loss of $350 million: The fate of the Edsel. In I. Barmash (Ed.), *Great business disasters*. New York: Ballantine, 1971. Pp. 84–141.

Brophy, I. N. The luxury of anti-Negro prejudice. *Public Opinion Quarterly*, 1945, 9, 456–466.

Broverman, I. K., Vogel, S. R., Broverman, D. M., Clarkson, F. E., & Rosenkrantz, P. S. Sex-role stereotypes: A current appraisal. *Journal of Social Issues*, 1972, 28, 59–78.

Brown, R. *Social psychology*. New York: Free Press, 1965.

Brüel, O. A moving picture as a psychopathogenic factor: A paper on primary psychotraumatic neurosis. *Character and Personality*, 1938, 7, 68–76.

Bruner, J. S., & Goodman, C. D. Value and need as organizing factors in perception. *Journal of Abnormal and Social Psychology*, 1947, 42, 33–44.

Bruner, J. S., & Postman, L. J. On the perception of incongruity: A paradigm. *Journal of Personality*, 1949, 18, 206–223.

Bruner, J. S., & Taguiri, R. The perception of people. In G. Lindzey (Ed.), *Handbook of social psychology*. Reading, Mass.: Addison-Wesley, 1954. Pp. 634–654.

Bruno, J., & Greenfield, J. *The advance man*. New York: Bantam Books, 1972.

Bryan, J. H., & London, P. Altruistic behavior by children. *Psychological Bulletin*, 1970, 73, 200–211.

Bryan, J. H., & Test, M. A. Models and helping: Naturalistic studies in aiding behavior. *Journal of Personality and Social Psychology*, 1967, 6, 400–407.

Buchwald, A. M. Effects of "right" and "wrong" on subsequent behavior: A new interpretation. *Psychological Review*, 1969, 76, 132–143.

Buck, R., Miller, R. E., & Caul, W. F. Sex, personality, and physiological variables in the communication of affect via facial expression. *Journal of Personality and Social Psychology*, 1974, 30, 587–596.

Buck, R. W., & Parke, R. D. Behavioral and physiological response to the presence of a friendly or neutral person in two types of stressful situations. *Journal of Personality and Social Psychology*, 1972, 26, 143–153.

Buck, R. W., Savin, V. J., Miller, R. E., & Caul, W. F. Communication of affect through facial expressions in humans. *Journal of Personality and Social Psychology*, 1972, 23, 362–371.

Buckley, W. *Sociology and modern systems theory*. Englewood Cliffs, N.J.: Prentice-Hall, 1967.

Buckley, W. (Ed.). *Modern systems research for the behavioral scientist*. Chicago: Aldine, 1968.

Bugental, D. E., Love, L. R., & Gianetto, R. M. Perfidious feminine faces. *Journal of Personality and Social Psychology*, 1971, 17, 317–318.

Burdick, H. A., & Burnes, A. J. A test of "strain towards symmetry" theories. *Journal of Abnormal and Social Psychology*, 1958, 57, 367–370.

Burgess, T. D. G. II, & Sales, S. M. Attitudinal effects of "mere exposure": A re-evaluation. *Journal of Experimental Social Psychology*, 1971, 7, 461–472.

Burke, P. J. Role differentiation and the legitimation of task activity. *Sociometry*, 1968, 31, 404–411.

Burke, P. J. Leadership role differentiation. In C. G. McClintock (Ed.), *Experimental social psychology*. New York: Holt, Rinehart and Winston, 1972. Pp. 514–546.

Burnstein, E., & Vinokur, A. Testing two classes of theories about group-induced shifts in individual choice. *Journal of Experimental Social Psychology*, 1973, 9, 123–137.

Burnstein, E., Vinokur, A., & Pichevin, M. F. What do differences between own, admired, and attributed choices have to do with group induced shifts in choice? *Journal of Experimental Social Psychology*, 1974, 10, 428–443.

Burnstein, E., Vinokur, A., & Trope, Y. Interpersonal comparison versus persuasive argumentation: A more direct test of alternative explanations for group-induced shifts in individual choice. *Journal of Experimental Social Psychology*, 1973, *9*, 236–245.

Burnstein, E., & Worchel, P. Arbitrariness of frustration and its consequences for aggression in a social situation. *Journal of Personality*, 1962, *30*, 528–540.

Buss, A. *The psychology of aggression*. New York: Wiley, 1961.

Buss, A., Booker, A., & Buss, E. Firing a weapon and aggression. *Journal of Personality and Social Psychology*, 1972, *27*, 296–302.

Buss, A., & Portnoy, N. W. Pain tolerance and group identification. *Journal of Personality and Social Psychology*, 1967, *6*, 106–118.

Byrne, D. The influence of propinquity and opportunities for interaction on classroom relationships. *Human Relations*, 1961, *14*, 63–69.

Byrne, D., Baskett, G. D., & Hodges, L. Behavioral indicators of interpersonal attraction. *Journal of Applied Social Psychology*, 1971, *1*, 137–149.

Byrne, D., & Blaylock, B. Similarity and assumed similarity of attitudes between husbands and wives. *Journal of Abnormal and Social Psychology*, 1963, *67*, 636–640.

Byrne, D., Gouaux, C., Griffitt, W., Lamberth, J., Murakawa, N., Prasad, M., Prasad, A., & Ramirez, M. III. The ubiquitous relationship: Attitude similarity and attraction. *Human Relations*, 1971, *24*, 201–207.

Byrne, D., Lamberth, J., Palmer, J., & London, O. Sequential effects as a function of explicit and implicit interpolated attraction responses. *Journal of Personality and Social Psychology*, 1969, *13*, 70–78.

Byrne, D., & McGraw, D. Interpersonal attraction towards Negroes. *Human Relations*, 1964, *17*, 201–213.

Byrne, D., & Nelson, D. Attraction as a linear function of proportion of positive reinforcements. *Journal of Personality and Social Psychology*, 1965, *1*, 659–663.

Campbell, D. T. *The generality of social attitude*. Unpublished doctoral dissertation, University of California, Berkeley, 1947.

Campbell, D. T. On the genetics of altruism and the counterhedonic components in human culture. *Journal of Social Issues*, 1972, *28*, 21–38.

Campbell, E. Q. Adolescent socialization. In D. A. Goslin (Ed.), *Handbook of socialization theory and research*. Chicago: Rand McNally, 1969.

Campbell, J., & Dunnette, M. Effectiveness of T-group experiences in managerial training and development. *Psychological Bulletin*, 1968, *70*, 73–104.

Cannavale, F. J., Scarr, H. A., & Pepitone, A. Deindividuation in the small group: Further evidence. *Journal of Personality and Social Psychology*, 1970, *16*, 141–147.

Caplan, N., & Nelson, S. D. On being useful: The nature and consequences of psychological research on social problems. *American Psychologist*, 1973, *28*, 199–212.

Carlsmith, J. M., Collins, B. E., & Helmreich, R. L. The effect of pressure for compliance on attitude change. *Journal of Personality and Social Psychology*, 1966, *4*, 1–13.

Carlsmith, J. M., & Gross, A. Some effects of guilt on compliance. *Journal of Personality and Social Psychology*, 1969, *11*, 232–240.

Cartwright, D. The nature of group cohesiveness. In D. Cartwright & A. Zander (Eds.), *Group dynamics: Research and theory* (3rd ed.). New York: Harper & Row, 1968.

Cartwright, D. Risk-taking by individuals and groups: An assessment of research involving choice dilemmas. *Journal of Personality and Social Psychology*, 1971, *20*, 361–378.

Cartwright, D., & Harary, F. Structural balance: A generalization of Heider's theory. *Psychological Review*, 1956, *63*, 277–293.

Cartwright, D., & Zander, A. (Eds.). *Group dynamics: Research and theory* (3rd ed.). New York: Harper & Row, 1968.

Cates, J. N. Sex and salary. *American Psychologist*, 1973, *28*, 929–930.

Cattell, R. B. Friends and enemies: A psychological study of character and temperament. *Character and Personality*, 1934, *3*, 54–63.

Cattell, R. B., & Nesselroade, J. R. Likeness and completeness theories examined by sixteen personality factor measures on stably and unstably married couples. *Journal of Personality and Social Psychology*, 1967, *7*, 351–361.

Centers, R. A laboratory adaptation of the controversial procedure for the conditioning of verbal operants. *Journal of Abnormal and Social Psychology*, 1963, *67*, 334–339.

Chaikin, A. I., & Cooper, J. Evaluation as a function of correspondence and hedonic relevance. *Journal of Experimental Social Psychology*, 1973, *9*, 257–264.

Chaikin, A. L., Sigler, E., & Derlega, V. J. Nonverbal mediation of teacher expectancy effects. *Journal of Personality and Social Psychology*, 1974, *30*, 144–149.

Chapanis, A. *Man-machine engineering*. Belmont, Calif.: Wadsworth, 1965.

Chapanis, A. Prelude to 2001: Explorations in human communication. *American Psychologist*, 1971, *26*, 949–961.

Chapanis, A. The communication of factual information through various channels. *Information Storage and Retrieval*, 1973, *9*, 215–231.

Chapman, A. J. Social facilitation of laughter in children. *Journal of Experimental Social Psychology*, 1973, *9*, 528–541.

Chemers, M. M., & Skrzypek, G. J. Experimental test of the contingency model of leadership effectiveness. *Journal of Personality and Social Psychology*, 1972, *24*, 172–177.

Chen, S. C. Social modification of activity of ants in nest building. *Physiological Zoology*, 1937, *10*, 420–436.

Child, I. L., Potter, E. H., & Levin, E. M. Children's textbooks and personality development: An exploration in the social psychology of education. *Psychological Monographs*, 1946, *60* (Whole No. 279).

Christie, R., & Geis, F. Some consequences of taking Machiavelli seriously. In E. F. Borgatta & W. W. Lambert (Eds.), *Handbook of personality theory and research*. Chicago: Rand McNally, 1968.

Christie, R., & Geis, F. (Eds.). *Studies in Machiavellianism*. New York: Academic Press, 1970a.

Christie, R., & Geis, F. The ten dollar game. In R. Christie & F. Geis (Eds.), *Studies in Machiavellianism*. New York: Academic Press, 1970b. Pp. 161–172.

Cialdini, R. B. Attitudinal advocacy in the verbal conditioner. *Journal of Personality and Social Psychology*, 1971, *17*, 350–358.

Cialdini, R. B., Braver, S. L., & Lewis, S. K. Attributional bias and the easily persuaded other. *Journal of Personality and Social Psychology*, 1974, *30*, 631–637.

Cialdini, R. B., Darby, B. L., & Vincent, J. E. Transgression and altruism: A case for hedonism. *Journal of Experimental Social Psychology*, 1973, *9*, 502–516.

Cialdini, R. B., & Insko, C. A. Attitudinal verbal reinforcement as a function of informational consistency: A further test of two factor theory. *Journal of Personality and Social Psychology*, 1969, *12*, 342–350.

Cialdini, R. B., Levy, A., Herman, P., & Evenbeck, S. Attitudinal politics: The strategy of moderation. *Journal of Personality and Social Psychology*, 1973, *25*, 100–108.

Cialdini, R. B., Vincent, J. E., Lewis, S. K., Catalan, J., Wheeler, D., & Darby, B. L. A reciprocal concessions procedure for inducing compliance: The door-in-the-face technique. *Journal of Personality and Social Psychology*, 1975, *31*, 206–215.

Clark, K. B., & Clark, M. K. Racial identification and preference in Negro children. In T. Newcomb & E. Hartley (Eds.), *Readings in social psychology*. New York: Holt, Rinehart and Winston, 1947.

Clark, R. D. Group-induced shift towards risk: A critical appraisal. *Psychological Bulletin*, 1971, *76*, 251–270.

Clark, R. D. Effects of sex and race on helping behavior in a nonreactive setting. *Representative Research in Social Psychology*, 1974, *5*, 1–6.

Clark, R. D., & Willems, E. P. Two interpretations of Brown's hypothesis for the risky shift. *Psychological Bulletin*, 1972, *78*, 62–73.

Clark, R. D., & Word, L. Why don't bystanders help? Because of ambiguity? *Journal of Personality and Social Psychology*, 1972, *24*, 392–400.

Cline, M. The influence of social context on the perception of faces. *Journal of Personality*, 1956, *24*, 142–158.

Cline, V. B., & Richards, J. M., Jr. Accuracy in interpersonal perception—A general trait? *Journal of Abnormal and Social Psychology*, 1960, *60*, 1–7.

Clore, G. L., & Baldridge, B. Interpersonal attraction: The role of agreement and topic interest. *Journal of Personality and Social Psychology*, 1968, *9*, 340–346.

Clore, G. L., & Jeffery, K. Emotional role playing, attitude change, and attraction toward a disabled person. *Journal of Personality and Social Psychology*, 1972, *23*, 105–111.

Cobbs, P. M. Ethnotherapy in groups. In L. Solomon & B. Berzon (Eds.), *New perspectives on encounter groups*. San Francisco: Jossey-Bass, 1972. Pp. 383–403.

Coch, L., & French, J. R. P., Jr. Overcoming resistance to change. *Human Relations*, 1948, *1*, 512–532.

Cohen, A. A., & Harrison, R. P. Intentionality in the use of hand illustrators in face-to-face communication situations. *Journal of Personality and Social Psychology*, 1973, *28*, 276–279.

Cohen, A. M., Bennis, W. G., & Wolkon, G. H. The effects of changes in communication networks on the behaviors of problem solving groups. *Sociometry*, 1962, *25*, 177–196.

Cohen, A. R. Upward communication in experimentally-created hierarchies. *Human Relations*, 1958, *11*, 41–53.

Cohen, A. R. Cognitive tuning as a factor affecting impression formation. *Journal of Personality*, 1961, *29*, 235–245.

Cohen, J. L., & Davis, J. H. Effects of audience status, evaluation, and time of action on performance with hidden word problems. *Journal of Personality and Social Psychology*, 1973, *27*, 74–83.

Coles, R. *Children of crisis: A study of courage and fear*. Boston: Little, Brown, 1967.

Collins, B. E., Ashmore, R. D., Hornbeck, F. W., & Whitney, R. E. Studies in forced compliance: XIII and XV. In search of a dissonance-producing forced-compliance paradigm. *Representative Research in Social Psychology*, 1970, *1*, 24–28.

Collins, B. E., & Hoyt, M. F. Personal responsibility for consequences: An integration and extension of the "forced compliance" literature. *Journal of Experimental Social Psychology*, 1972, *8*, 558–593.

Collins, B. E., & Raven, B. Psychological aspects of structure in the small group: Interpersonal attraction, coalitions, communication, and power. In G. Lindzey & E. Aronson (Eds.), *Handbook of social psychology* (2nd ed.), Vol. 4. Reading, Mass.: Addison-Wesley, 1969. Pp. 102–204.

Conolley, E. S. The attitudinal effects of commitment to discrepant behavior. *Proceedings of the 78th Annual Convention of the American Psychological Association*, 1970, *5*, 389–390.

Constanzo, P. R. Conformity development as a function of selfblame. *Journal of Personality and Social Psychology*, 1970, *14*, 366–374.

Cook, S. W. A preliminary study of attitude change. In M. Wertheimer (Ed.), *Confrontation: Psychology and the problems of today*. Glenview, Ill.: Scott, Foresman, 1970. Pp. 130–135.

Cooper, J., Darley, J. M., & Henderson, J. E. On the effectiveness of deviant and conventional appearing communicators: A field experiment. *Journal of Personality and Social Psychology*, 1974, *29*, 752–757.

Cooper, J., & Jones, R. A. Self-esteem and consistency as determinants of anticipatory attitude change. *Journal of Personality and Social Psychology,* 1970, *14,* 312–320.

Coser, L. A. *The functions of social conflict.* Glencoe, Ill.: Free Press, 1956.

Coss, R. G. The cut-off hypothesis: Its relevance to the design of public places. *Man-Environment Systems,* 1973, *3,* 417–440.

Coss, R. G., Jacobs, L. S., & Allerton, M. W. Changes of stereotypical and nonstereotypical motor activity of subjects in free-field settings during intrusions of personal space by unfamiliar people. Paper presented at the Human Ethology Meeting of the Animal Behavior Society, May 22–26, 1975, University of North Carolina.

Cottrell, N. B. Social facilitation. In C. G. McClintock (Ed.), *Experimental social psychology.* New York: Holt, Rinehart and Winston, 1972. Pp. 185–236.

Cottrell, N. B. Heider's structural balance principle as a conceptual rule. *Journal of Personality and Social Psychology,* 1975, *31,* 713–720.

Cottrell, N. B., Wack, D. L., Sekerak, G. J., & Rittle, R. H. Social facilitation of dominant responses by the presence of an audience and the mere exposure of others. *Journal of Personality and Social Psychology,* 1968, *9,* 245–250.

Cowan, P. A., & Walters, R. H. Studies of reinforcement of aggression: 1. Effects of scheduling. *Child Development,* 1963, *34,* 543–551.

Crandall, R. Social facilitation. In A. A. Harrison (Ed.), *Explorations in psychology.* Monterey, Calif.: Brooks/Cole, 1974.

Crano, W. D., & Brewer, M. B. *Principles of research in social psychology.* New York: McGraw-Hill, 1973.

Crano, W. D., & Cooper, R. E. Examination of Newcomb's extension of structural balance theory. *Journal of Personality and Social Psychology,* 1973, *27,* 344–353.

Crisci, R., & Kassinove, H. Effect of perceived expertise, strength of advice, and environmental setting on parental compliance. *Journal of Social Psychology,* 1973, *84,* 245–250.

Crockett, W. H. Balance, agreement, and subjective evaluations of the P-O-X triads. *Journal of Personality and Social Psychology,* 1974, *29,* 102–110.

Cronbach, L. J. *Essentials of psychological testing* (3rd ed.). New York: Harper & Row, 1969.

Cronbach, L. J., & Meehl, P. E. Construct validity in psychological tests. *Psychological Bulletin,* 1955, *52,* 281–302.

Cross, H. A., Halcomb, C. G., & Matter, W. W. Imprinting or exposure learning in rats given early auditory stimulation. *Psychonomic Science,* 1967, *10,* 233–234.

Crow, J. W. The effect of training upon accuracy and variability in interpersonal perception. *Journal of Abnormal and Social Psychology,* 1957, *55,* 355–359.

Crowe, B. J., Bochner, S., & Clark, A. W. The effects of subordinate's behavior on managerial style. *Human Relations,* 1972, *25,* 215–237.

Crutchfield, R. S. Conformity and character. *American Psychologist,* 1955, *10,* 191–198.

Culbertson, F. Modification of an emotionally held attitude through role playing. *Journal of Abnormal and Social Psychology,* 1957, *54,* 230–234.

Cvetkovich, G., & Baumgardner, S. R. Attitude polarization: The relative influence of discussion group structure and reference group norms. *Journal of Personality and Social Psychology,* 1973, *28,* 159–165.

Cyert, R. M., & MacCrimmon, K. R. Organizations. In G. Lindzey & E. Aronson (Eds.), *Handbook of social psychology* (2nd ed.) Vol. 1. Reading, Mass.: Addison-Wesley, 1968. Pp. 568–614.

Dabbs, J. M., & Janis, I. L. Why does eating while reading facilitate opinion change? An experimental inquiry. *Journal of Experimental Social Psychology,* 1965, *1,* 133–144.

Dannenmaier, W. V., & Thumin, F. J. Authority status as a factor in the perception of size. *Journal of Social Psychology,* 1964, *63,* 361–365.

Darley, J. M. Fear and social comparison as determinants of conformity behavior. *Journal of Personality and Social Psychology,* 1966, *4,* 73–78.

Darley, J., & Aronson, E. Self-evaluation vs. direct anxiety reduction as determinants of the fear-affiliation relationship. *Journal of Experimental Social Psychology Monograph Supplement,* 1966, *1,* 66–79.

Darley, J. M., & Batson, C. D. From Jerusalem to Jericho: A study of situational and dispositional variables in helping behavior. *Journal of Personality and Social Psychology,* 1973, *27,* 100–108.

Darley, J. M., & Cooper, J. The "Clean for Gene" phenomenon: The effect of students' appearance on political campaigning. *Journal of Applied Social Psychology,* 1972, *2,* 24–33.

Darley, J., & Latané, B. Bystander intervention in emergencies: Diffusion of responsibility. *Journal of Personality and Social Psychology,* 1968, *8,* 377–383.

Darley, J. M., & Latané, B. Norms and normative behavior: Field studies of normative interdependence. In J. Macaulay & L. Berkowitz (Eds.), *Altruism and helping behavior.* New York: Academic Press, 1970.

Darley, J. M., Teger, A. I., & Lewis, L. D. Do groups always inhibit individual's responses to potential emergencies? *Journal of Personality and Social Psychology,* 1973, *26,* 395–399.

Darley, S. A., & Cooper, J. Cognitive consequences of forced noncompliance. *Journal of Personality and Social Psychology,* 1972, *24,* 321–326.

Davis, J. D., & Skinner, A. E. G. Reciprocity of self-disclosure in interviews: Modeling or social exchange? *Journal of Personality and Social Psychology,* 1974, *29,* 779–784.

Davitz, J. R. The effects of previous training on post-frustrative behavior. *Journal of Abnormal and Social Psychology,* 1952, *47,* 309–315.

Davitz, J. R., & Davitz, L. J. The communication of feelings by content-free speech. *Journal of Communication,* 1959, *9,* 6–13.

Davitz, J. R., & Mason, D. J. Socially facilitated reduction of a fear response in rats. *Journal of Comparative and Physiological Psychology,* 1955, *48,* 149–151.

Day, R., & Hamblin, R. Some effects of close and punitive styles of supervision. *American Journal of Sociology,* 1964, *69,* 499–510.

Dean, R. B., Austin, J. A., & Watts, W. A. Forewarning effects in persuasion: Field and classroom experiments. *Journal of Personality and Social Psychology,* 1971, *18,* 210–221.

Deaux, K. To err is humanizing: But sex makes the difference. *Representative Research in Social Psychology,* 1972, *3,* 20–27.

Deaux, K., & Emswiller, T. Explanations of successful performance on sex-linked tasks: What is skill for the male is luck for the female. *Journal of Personality and Social Psychology,* 1974, *29,* 80–85.

DeLamater, J. Intimacy in a coeducational community. In A. A. Harrison (Ed.), *Explorations in psychology.* Monterey, Calif.: Brooks/Cole, 1974.

DeNike, L. D. The temporal relationship between awareness and performance in verbal conditioning. *Journal of Experimental Psychology,* 1964, *68,* 521–529.

Derlega, V. I., Harris, M. S., & Chaikin, A. L. Self-disclosure, reciprocity, liking, and the deviant. *Journal of Experimental Social Psychology,* 1973, *9,* 277–284.

Dermer, M., & Thiel, D. L. When beauty may fail. *Journal of Personality and Social Psychology,* 1975, in press.

Deutsch, M. Trust, trustworthiness, and the F scale. *Journal of Abnormal and Social Psychology,* 1960, *61,* 138–140.

Deutsch, M. Socially relevant science: Reflections on some studies of conflict. *American Psychologist,* 1969, *24,* 1076–1092.

Deutsch, M., & Gerard, H. B. A study of normative and informational social influences upon individual judgment. *Journal of Abnormal and Social Psychology, 1955, 51,* 629–636.

Deutsch, M., & Krauss, R. M. The effect of threat upon interpersonal bargaining. *Journal of Abnormal and Social Psychology, 1960, 61,* 181–189.

Deutsch, M., & Krauss, R. M. Studies of interpersonal bargaining. *Journal of Conflict Resolution, 1962, 4,* 52–76.

Deutsch, M., & Solomon, L. Reactions to evaluations of others as influenced by self-evaluations. *Sociometry, 1959, 22,* 93–112.

Dickoff, H. Reactions to evaluations by another person as a function of self-evaluation and the interaction context. Unpublished doctoral dissertation, Duke University, 1961.

Diener, E., Dineen, J., Endresen, K., Beaman, A. L., & Fraser, S. C. Effects of altered responsibility, cognitive set, and modeling on physical aggression and deindividuation. *Journal of Personality and Social Psychology, 1975, 31,* 328–337.

Diener, E., Westford, K. L., Diener, C., & Beaman, A. L. Deindividuating effects of group presence and arousal on stealing by Halloween trick-or-treaters. *Proceedings of the 81st Annual Convention of the American Psychological Association, 1973, 8,* 219–220.

Diener, E., Westford, K. L., Dineen, J., & Fraser, S. C. Beat the pacifist: The deindividuating effects of anonymity and group presence. *Proceedings of the 81st Annual Convention of the American Psychological Association, 1973, 8,* 221–222.

Dion, K. Physical attractiveness and evaluations of children's transgressions. *Journal of Personality and Social Psychology, 1972, 24,* 207–215.

Dion, K., Berscheid, E., & Walster, E. What is beautiful is good. *Journal of Personality and Social Psychology, 1972, 24,* 285–290.

Dollard, J., Doob, L., Miller, N., Mowrer, O., & Sears, R. *Frustration and aggression.* New Haven, Conn.: Yale University Press, 1939.

Dollard, J., & Miller, N. *Personality and psychotherapy: An analysis in terms of learning, thinking, and culture.* New York: McGraw-Hill, 1950.

Doob, A. N. Catharsis and aggression: The effect of hurting one's enemy. *Journal of Experimental Research in Personality, 1970, 4,* 291–296.

Doob, A. N., Carlsmith, J., Freedman, J., Landauer, T., & Tom, S. Effects of initial selling price on subsequent sales. *Journal of Personality and Social Psychology, 1969, 11,* 345–350.

Doob, A. N., & Gross, A. E. Status of frustrator as an inhibitor of horn-honking responses. *Journal of Social Psychology, 1968, 76,* 213–218.

Doob, A. N., & Wood, L. Catharsis and aggression: The effects of annoyance and retaliation on aggressive behavior. *Journal of Personality and Social Psychology, 1972, 22,* 156–172.

Dorfman, D. D., & Zajonc, R. B. Some effects of sound, background brightness, and economic status on the perceived size of coins and discs. *Journal of Abnormal and Social Psychology, 1963, 66,* 87–90.

Dorris, J. W. Reactions to unconditional cooperation: A field study emphasizing variables neglected in laboratory research. *Journal of Personality and Social Psychology, 1972, 22,* 387–397.

Douvan, E., & Adelson, J. *The adolescent experience.* New York: Wiley, 1966.

Driscoll, R., Davis, K. E., & Lipetz, M. Parental interference and romantic love. *Journal of Personality and Social Psychology, 1972, 24,* 1–10.

Duncan, S., Jr. Nonverbal communication. *Psychological Bulletin, 1969, 72,* 118–138.

Duncan, S., Jr. Some signals and rules for speaking turns in conversations. *Journal of Personality and Social Psychology, 1972, 23,* 283–392.

Duncan, S., Jr., & Niederehe, G. On signaling that it's your turn to speak. *Journal of Experimental Social Psychology,* 1974, *10,* 234–247.

Dunnette, M. D. *Personnel selection and placement.* Monterey, Calif.: Brooks/Cole, 1966.

Dunnette, M. D. *Work and nonwork in the year 2001.* Monterey, Calif.: Brooks/Cole, 1973.

Dunnette, M. D., Campbell, J., & Jaastad, L. The effect of group participation on problem solving. *Journal of Applied Psychology,* 1963, *47,* 30–37.

Durkheim, E. *Le suicide.* Paris: F. Alcan, 1897.

Durkheim, E. *De la division du travail social.* Paris: F. Alcan, 1902.

Dutton, D. G. Effect of feedback parameters on congruency versus positivity effects in reactions to personal evaluations. *Journal of Personality and Social Psychology,* 1972, *24,* 366–371.

Dutton, D. G., & Aron, A. P. Some evidence for heightened sexual attraction under conditions of high anxiety. *Journal of Personality and Social Psychology,* 1974, *30,* 510–517.

Dutton, D. G., & Arrowood, A. J. Situational factors in evaluation congruency and interpersonal attraction. *Journal of Personality and Social Psychology,* 1971, *18,* 222–229.

Dutton, D. G., & Lake, R. A. Threat of own prejudice and reverse discrimination in interracial situations. *Journal of Personality and Social Psychology,* 1973, *28,* 94–100.

Duval, S., & Wicklund, R. A. Effects of objective self-awareness on attribution of causality. *Journal of Experimental Social Psychology,* 1973, *9,* 17–31.

Efran, M. G., & Cheyn, J. A. Affective concomitants of the invasion of shared space: Behavioral, physiological, and verbal indicators. *Journal of Personality and Social Psychology,* 1974, *29,* 219–226.

Egan, G. *Encounter: Group processes for interpersonal growth.* Monterey, Calif.: Brooks/Cole, 1970.

Egan, G. (Ed.). *Encounter groups: Basic readings.* Monterey, Calif.: Brooks/Cole, 1971.

Eisenberger, R. Explanation of rewards that do not reduce tissue needs. *Psychological Bulletin,* 1972, *77,* 319–339.

Eisner, W. *Incredible facts, amazing statistics, and monumental trivia.* New York: Poorhouse Press, 1974.

Ekehammar, B. Interactionism in personality from a historical perspective. *Psychological Bulletin,* 1974, *81,* 1026–1048.

Ekman, P. Body position, facial expression, and verbal behavior during interviews. *Journal of Abnormal and Social Psychology,* 1964, *68,* 295–301.

Ekman, P. Differential communication of affect by head and body cues. *Journal of Personality and Social Psychology,* 1965, *2,* 726–735.

Ekman, P. Universal facial expressions of emotion. *California Mental Health Research Digest,* 1970, *8,* 151–158.

Ekman, P. Universals and cultural differences in facial expressions of emotion. In *Nebraska symposium on motivation.* Lincoln: University of Nebraska Press, 1972.

Ekman, P. (Ed.). *Darwin and facial expression: A century of research in review.* New York: Academic Press, 1973.

Ekman, P., & Friesen, W. V. Nonverbal leakage and clues to deception. *Psychiatry,* 1969, *32,* 88–106.

Ekman, P., & Friesen, W. V. Constants across cultures in the face and emotion. *Journal of Personality and Social Psychology,* 1971, *17,* 124–129.

Ekman, P., & Friesen, W. V. Hand movements. *The Journal of Communication,* 1972, *22,* 353–374.

Ekman, P., Friesen, W., & Ellsworth, P. *Emotion in the human face: Guidelines for research and an integration of findings.* New York: Pergamon Press, 1972.

Ekman, P., Friesen, W. V., & Tomkins, S. Facial affect scoring technique: A first validity study. *Semiotica,* 1971, *3,* 37–58.

Ellsworth, P., Carlsmith, J. M., & Henson, A. The stare as a stimulus to flight in human subjects: A series of field experiments. *Journal of Personality and Social Psychology,* 1972, *21,* 302–311.

Elms, A. C. *Role playing, reward, and attitude change.* New York: Van Nostrand-Reinhold, 1969.

Elms, A. C. *Social psychology and social relevance.* Boston: Little, Brown, 1972.

Elms, A. C., & Janis, I. Counter-norm attitudes induced by consonant versus dissonant conditions of role playing. *Journal of Experimental Research in Personality,* 1965, *1,* 50–60.

Emrich, D. *The folklore of love and courtship: The charms and divinations, superstitions and beliefs, signs and prospects of love, sweet love.* New York: American Heritage Press, 1970.

Emswiller, T., Deaux, K., & Willits, J. E. Similarity, sex, and requests for small favors. *Journal of Applied Social Psychology,* 1971, *1,* 284–291.

Endler, N. S. The effects of verbal reinforcement on conformity and social pressure. *Journal of Social Psychology,* 1965, *66,* 147–154.

Endler, N. S. Conformity as a function of different reinforcement schedules. *Journal of Personality and Social Psychology,* 1966, *4,* 175–180.

Epley, S. W. *The effects of the presence of a companion upon the speed of escape from electric shock.* Unpublished doctoral dissertation, University of Iowa, 1973.

Epley, S. W. Reduction of the behavioral effects of aversive stimulation by the presence of companions. *Psychological Bulletin,* 1974, *81,* 271–281.

Eron, L. D., Huesmann, L. R., Lefkowitz, M. M., & Walder, D. O. Does television violence cause aggression? *American Psychologist,* 1972, *27,* 253–263.

Ettinger, R. F., Marino, C. J., Endler, N. S., Geller, S. H., & Natziuk, T. Effects of agreement and correctness on relative competence and conformity. *Journal of Personality and Social Psychology,* 1971, *19,* 204–212.

Etzioni, A. Nonconventional uses of sociology as illustrated by peace research. In P. R. Lazarsfeld, W. H. Sewell, & H. L. Wilensky (Eds.), *The uses of sociology.* New York: Basic Books, 1967. Pp. 806–838.

Etzioni, A. Social psychological aspects of international relations. In G. Lindzey & E. Aronson (Eds.), *Handbook of social psychology* (2nd ed.) Vol. 5. Reading, Mass.: Addison-Wesley, 1969. Pp. 538–601.

Evans, N. G. Herzberg's two-factor theory of motivation: Some problems and a suggested test. *Personnel Journal,* 1970, *49,* 32–35.

Exline, R. V., Thibaut, J., Hickey, C. B., & Gumpert, P. Visual interaction in relation to Machiavellianism and an unethical act. In R. Christie & F. Geis (Eds.), *Studies in Machiavellianism.* New York: Academic Press, 1970. Pp. 53–75.

Faust, W. L. Group versus individual problem solving. *Journal of Abnormal and Social Psychology,* 1959, *59,* 68–72.

Fechner, G. T. *Vorschule der Aesthetik.* Leipzig: Breitkopf und Härtel, 1876.

Feldman, R. Response to compatriots and foreigners who seek assistance. *Journal of Personality and Social Psychology,* 1968, *10,* 202–214.

Feldman, S. Motivational aspects of attitudinal elements and their place in cognitive interaction. In S. Feldman (Ed.), *Cognitive consistency.* New York: Academic Press, 1966.

Feldman-Summers, S., & Kiesler, S. B. Those who are number two try harder: The effect of sex on attributions of causality. *Journal of Personality and Social Psychology,* 1974, *30,* 846–855.

Felipe-Russo, N., & Sommer, R. Invasions of personal space. *Social Problems,* 1966, *14,* 206–214.

Ferguson, G. A. *Statistical analysis in psychology and education* (3rd ed.). New York: McGraw-Hill, 1971.

Feshbach, S., & Singer, R. *Television and aggression.* San Francisco: Jossey-Bass, 1971.

Festinger, L. A theory of social comparison processes. *Human Relations,* 1954, *7,* 117–140.

Festinger, L. *A theory of cognitive dissonance.* New York: Harper & Row, 1957.

Festinger, L., & Carlsmith, J. M. Cognitive consequences of forced compliance. *Journal of Abnormal and Social Psychology,* 1959, *58,* 203–211.

Festinger, L., & Maccoby, N. On resistance to persuasive communications. *Journal of Abnormal and Social Psychology,* 1964, *68,* 359–366.

Festinger, L., Pepitone, A., & Newcomb, T. M. Some consequences of deindividuation in a group. *Journal of Abnormal and Social Psychology,* 1952, *47,* 382–389.

Festinger, L., Schachter, S., & Back, K. *Social pressures in informal groups: A study of human factors in housing.* New York: Harper & Row, 1950.

Fidell, L. Unpublished research reported in *Behavior Today.* 1970, *1*(4), 4.

Fiedler, F. E. A contingency model of leader effectiveness. In L. Berkowitz (Ed.), *Advances in Experimental Social Psychology* (Vol. 1). New York: Academic Press, 1964.

Fiedler, F. E. *A theory of leadership effectiveness.* New York: McGraw-Hill, 1967.

Fiedler, F. E. Validation and extension of the contingency model of leadership effectiveness: A review of empirical findings. *Psychological Bulletin,* 1971, *76,* 128–148.

Fiedler, F. E. The contingency model—A reply to Ashour. *Organizational Behavior and Human Performance,* 1973, *9,* 356–368.

Firestone, I. J., Kaplan, K. J., & Moore, M. The attitude-gradient model. In A. A. Harrison (Ed.), *Explorations in psychology.* Monterey, Calif.: Brooks/Cole, 1974.

Firestone, I. J., Kaplan, K. J., & Russell, J. C. Anxiety, fear, and affiliation with similar state versus dissimilar state others: Misery sometimes loves nonmiserable company. *Journal of Personality and Social Psychology,* 1973, *26,* 409–414.

Fishbein, M. Attitude and the prediction of behavior. In M. Fishbein (Ed.), *Readings in attitude theory and measurement.* New York: Wiley, 1967.

Fishbein, M., & Ajzen, I. Attitudes toward objects as predictors of single and multiple behavioral criteria. *Psychological Review,* 1974, *81,* 59–74.

Fisher, E. The second sex: Junior division. New York Times Book Review, May 1970.

Fisher, J. D., & Byrne, D. Too close for comfort: Sex differences in response to invasions of personal space. *Journal of Personality and Social Psychology,* 1975, in press.

Fiske, D. W. *Measuring concepts of personality.* Chicago: Aldine, 1971.

Flament, C. Influence sociale et perception. *Aneé Psychologie,* 1958, *58,* 378–400. (Cited in H. Tajfel, Social and cultural factors in perception. In G. Lindzey & E. Aronson (Eds.), *Handbook of social psychology* (2nd ed.), Vol. 3. Reading, Mass.: Addison-Wesley, 1969. Pp. 315–394.)

Flanders, J. P., & Thistlethwaite, D. L. Effects of familiarization and group discussion upon risk-taking. *Journal of Personality and Social Psychology,* 1967, *5,* 91–97.

Fleishman, E., & Harris, E. Patterns of leadership behavior related to employee grievances and turnover. *Personnel Psychology,* 1962, *15,* 43–56.

Forward, J. R., & Williams, J. R. Internal-external control and black militancy. *Journal of Social Issues,* 1970, *26,* 75–92.

Fraser, S. C., Kelem, R. T., Diener, E., & Beaman, A. L. The Halloween caper: The effects of deindividuation variables on stealing. *Journal of Personality and Social Psychology,* 1975, in press.

Freedman, J., & Fraser, S. Compliance without pressure: The foot-in-the-door technique. *Journal of Personality and Social Psychology,* 1966, *4,* 195–202.

Freedman, J. L., Wallington, S. A., & Bless, E. Compliance without pressure: The effect of guilt. *Journal of Personality and Social Psychology,* 1967, *7,* 117–124.

Fried, S. B., Gumpper, D. C., & Allen, J. C. Ten years of social psychology: Is there a growing commitment to field research? *American Psychologist,* 1973, *28,* 155–160.

Frijda, N. Recognition of emotion. In L. Berkowitz (Ed.), *Advances in experimental social psychology* (Vol. 4). New York: Academic Press, 1969. Pp. 167–223.

Gaddis, T. E., & Long, J. O. *Killer: A journal of murder*. New York: Macmillan, 1970.

Gaertner, S. L. Helping behavior and racial discrimination among liberals and conservatives. *Journal of Personality and Social Psychology*, 1973, 25, 335–341.

Gaertner, S., & Bickman, L. A nonreactive indicator of racial discrimination: The wrong number technique. In L. Bickman and T. Henchy (Eds.), *Beyond the laboratory: Field research in social psychology*. New York: McGraw-Hill, 1972. Pp. 162–170.

Galizio, M., & Hendrick, C. Effect of musical accompaniment on attitude: The guitar as a prop for persuasion. *Journal of Applied Social Psychology*, 1972, 2, 350–359.

Gallo, P. S. Effects of increased incentives upon the use of threat in bargaining. *Journal of Personality and Social Psychology*, 1966, 4, 14–20.

Gallo, P. S. Prisoners of our own dilemma? Paper presented at the Western Psychological Association convention, San Diego, 1968. (Reprinted in L. S. Wrightsman, J. O'Connor, & N. J. Baker (Eds.), *Cooperation and competition: Readings on mixed-motive games*. Monterey, Calif.: Brooks/Cole, 1972.)

Gallo, P. S., Funk, S., & Levine, J. Reward size, method of presentation, and number of alternatives in a prisoner's dilemma game. *Journal of Personality and Social Psychology*, 1969, 13, 239–244.

Gallo, P. S., & McClintock, C. G. Cooperative and competitive behavior in mixed-motive games. *Journal of Conflict Resolution*, 1965, 9, 68–78.

Gardin, H., Kaplan, K. J., Firestone, I. J., & Cowan, G. A. Proxemic effects on cooperation, attitude, and approach-avoidance in a prisoner's dilemma game. *Journal of Personality and Social Psychology*, 1973, 27, 13–18.

Gardner, R., & Heider, K. G. *Gardens of war: Life and death in the New Guinea stone age*. New York: Random House, 1969.

Garland, H. The effects of piece rate underpayment and overpayment on job performance: A test of equity theory with a new induction procedure. *Journal of Applied Social Psychology*, 1973, 3, 325–334.

Gates, M. G., & Allee, W. C. Conditioned behavior of isolated and grouped cockroaches in a simple maze. *Journal of Comparative Psychology*, 1933, 13, 331–358.

Geen, R. G. Effects of frustration, attack, and prior training in aggressiveness upon aggressive behavior. *Journal of Personality and Social Psychology*, 1968, 9, 316–321.

Geen, R. G., & O'Neal, E. C. Activation of cue-elicited aggression by general arousal. *Journal of Personality and Social Psychology*, 1969, 11, 289–292.

Geen, R. G., & Stonner, D. Effects of aggressiveness habit strength on behavior in the presence of aggression-related stimuli. *Journal of Personality and Social Psychology*, 1971, 17, 149–153.

Geis, F. L. The con game. In R. Christie & F. L. Geis (Eds.), *Studies in Machiavellianism*. New York: Academic Press, 1970. Pp. 106–130.

Geis, F. L., & Christie, R. Overview of experimental research. In R. Christie & F. L. Geis (Eds.), *Studies in Machiavellianism*. New York: Academic Press, 1970. Pp. 285–313.

Geis, F. L., Krupat, E., & Berger, D. Taking over in group discussion. Unpublished manuscript, New York University, 1965. (Cited in R. L. Christie & F. L. Geis (Eds.), *Studies in Machiavellianism*. New York: Academic Press, 1970.)

Gerard, H. B., & Conolley, E. S. Conformity. In C. G. McClintock (Ed.), *Experimental social psychology*. New York: Holt, Rinehart and Winston, 1972. Pp. 237–264.

Gerard, H. B., & Greenbaum, C. W. Attitudes toward an agent of uncertainty reduction. *Journal of Personality*, 1962, 30, 485–495.

Gerard, H. B., & Hoyt, M. F. Distinctiveness of social categorization and attitude toward ingroup members. *Journal of Personality and Social Psychology*, 1974, 29, 836–842.

Gerard, H. B., & Mathewson, G. C. The effect of severity of initiation on liking for a group: A replication. *Journal of Experimental Social Psychology*, 1966, 2, 278–287.

Gerard, H. B., & Rabbie, J. Fear and social comparisons. *Journal of Abnormal and Social Psychology,* 1961, *62,* 586–592.

Gerard, H. B., Wilhelmy, R., & Conolley, E. Conformity and group size. *Journal of Personality and Social Psychology,* 1968, *8,* 79–82.

Gergen, K. J. *The psychology of behavior exchange.* Reading, Mass.: Addison-Wesley, 1969.

Gergen, K. J. Social psychology as history. *Journal of Personality and Social Psychology,* 1973, *26,* 309–320.

Gergen, K. J., Gergen, M. M., & Meter, K. Individual orientations to prosocial behavior. *Journal of Social Issues,* 1972, *28,* 105–130.

Gerst, M. S. Symbolic coding processes in observational learning. *Journal of Personality and Social Psychology,* 1971, *19,* 7–17.

Ghiselli, E. E. *Theory of psychological measurement.* New York: McGraw-Hill, 1964.

Gibb, C. A. Leadership. In G. Lindzey & E. Aronson (Eds.), *The handbook of social psychology* (2nd ed.) Vol. 4. Reading, Mass.: Addison-Wesley, 1969. Pp. 205–282.

Gibb, J. R. Sensitivity training as a medium for personal growth and improved interpersonal relations. *Interpersonal Development,* 1970, *1,* 6–31.

Gibb, J. R. Effects of human relations training. In A. E. Bergin & S. L. Garfield (Eds.), *Handbook of psychotherapy and behavior change.* New York: Wiley, 1971.

Gibb, J. R. Meaning of the small group experience. In L. S. Solomon & B. Berzon (Eds.), *New perspectives in encounter groups.* San Francisco: Jossey-Bass, 1972. Pp. 1–12.

Gilbert, G. M. Stereotype persistence and change among college students. *Journal of Abnormal and Social Psychology,* 1951, *46,* 245–254.

Gillig, P. M., & Greenwald, A. G. Is it time to lay the sleeper effect to rest? *Journal of Personality and Social Psychology,* 1974, *29,* 132–139.

Gilliland, A. R., & Moore, H. T. The immediate and long-time effects of classical and popular phonograph selections. *Journal of Applied Psychology,* 1924, *8,* 309–323.

Glaser, B. G., & Strauss, A. L. *Time for dying.* Chicago: Aldine, 1968.

Godfrey, B. W., & Lowe, C. A. Devaluation of innocent victims: An attribution analysis within the just world paradigm. *Journal of Personality and Social Psychology,* 1975, *31,* 944–951.

Goethals, G. R., & Beckman, R. F. The perception of consistency in attitudes. *Journal of Experimental Social Psychology,* 1973, *3,* 491–501.

Goethals, G. R., & Cooper, J. Role of intention and postbehavioral consequence in the arousal of cognitive dissonance. *Journal of Personality and Social Psychology,* 1972, *23,* 293–304.

Goffman, E. On cooling the mark out: Some aspects of adaptation to failure. *Psychiatry,* 1952, *15,* 451–463.

Goffman, E. *The presentation of self in everyday life.* New York: Doubleday, 1959.

Goldberg, P. A. Are women prejudiced against women? *Trans-action,* April, 1968, pp. 28–30.

Goldstein, M., & Davis, E. E. Race and belief: A further analysis of the social determinants of behavioral intentions. *Journal of Personality and Social Psychology,* 1972, *22,* 346–355.

Goranson, R., & Berkowitz, L. Reciprocity and responsibility reactions to prior help. *Journal of Personality and Social Psychology,* 1966, *3,* 227–232.

Gordon, K. Group judgments in the field of lifted weights. *Journal of Experimental Psychology,* 1924, *7,* 389–400.

Gore, W. V., & Taylor, D. A. The nature of the audience as it affects social inhibition. *Representative Research in Social Psychology,* 1973, *4,* 18–27.

Grabitz-Gniech, G. Some restrictive conditions for the occurrence of psychological reactance. *Journal of Personality and Social Psychology,* 1971, *19,* 188–196.

Graen, G., Alvares, K., Orris, J. B., & Martella, J. A. Contingency model of leadership effectiveness: Antecedent and evidential results. *Psychological Bulletin*, 1970, *74*, 284–295.

Green, D. Dissonance and self-perception analyses of "forced compliance": When two theories make competing predictions. *Journal of Personality and Social Psychology*, 1974, *29*, 814–828.

Greenberg, M. S., & Frisch, D. M. Effect of intentionality on willingness to reciprocate a favor. *Journal of Experimental Social Psychology*, 1972, *8*, 99–111.

Greene, D., & Lepper, M. R. How to turn play into work. *Psychology Today*, September 1974. Pp. 49–54.

Greenspoon, T. The reinforcing effect of two spoken sounds on the frequency of two responses. *American Journal of Psychology*, 1955, *68*, 409–416.

Grider, G., & Sims, L. *War fish*. New York: Ballantine Books, 1973.

Gross, A. E., Schmidt, M. J., Keating, J. P., & Saks, M. J. Persuasion, surveillance, and voting behavior. *Journal of Experimental Social Psychology*, 1974, *10*, 451–460.

Grusec, J. E. Demand characteristics of the modeling experiment: Altruism as a function of age and aggression. *Journal of Personality and Social Psychology*, 1972, *22*, 139–148.

Gumpert, P., Deutsch, M., & Epstein, Y. Effect of incentive magnitude on cooperation in the prisoner's dilemma game. *Journal of Personality and Social Psychology*, 1969, *11*, 66–69.

Gurin, G., Veroff, J., & Feld, S. *Americans view their mental health*. New York: Basic Books, 1960.

Gutman, G. M., & Knox, R. E. Balance, agreement, and attraction in pleasantness, tension, and consistency ratings of hypothetical social situations. *Journal of Personality and Social Psychology*, 1972, *24*, 351–357.

Gutman, G. M., Knox, R. E., & Storm, T. F. Developmental study of balance, agreement, and attraction effects in the ratings of hypothetical social situations. *Journal of Personality and Social Psychology*, 1974, *29*, 201–211.

Hall, E. T. *The silent language*. New York: Fawcett, 1959.

Halpin, A. W. The leadership behavior and combat performance of airplane commanders. *Journal of Abnormal and Social Psychology*, 1954, *49*, 19–22.

Hamilton, D. L., Thompson, J. J., & White, A. M. Role of awareness and intentions in observational learning. *Journal of Personality and Social Psychology*, 1970, *16*, 689–694.

Hanratty, M. A., Liebert, R. M., Morris, E. W., & Fernandez, L. E. Imitation of film-mediated aggression against live and inanimate victims. *Proceedings of the 77th Annual Convention of the American Psychological Association*, 1969, *4*, 457–458.

Hanratty, M. A., O'Neal, E., & Sulzer, J. L. Effect of frustration upon the imitation of aggression. *Journal of Personality and Social Psychology*, 1972, *21*, 30–34.

Harding, J., & Hogrefe, R. Attitudes towards Negro co-workers in an eastern urban department store. *Journal of Social Issues*, 1952, *8*, 18–28.

Harding, J., Proshansky, H., Kutner, B., & Chein, I. Prejudice and ethnic relations. In G. Lindzey & E. Aronson (Eds.), *Handbook of social psychology* (2nd ed.) Vol. 5. Reading, Mass.: Addison-Wesley, 1969. Pp. 1–76.

Hardy, R. C. Effect of leadership style on the performance of small classroom groups: A test of the contingency model. *Journal of Personality and Social Psychology*, 1971, *19*, 367–374.

Hare, H. P., & Bales, R. F. Seating position and small group interaction. *Sociometry*, 1963, *4*, 480–486.

Hare, N. The case for separatism: Black perspective. In J. McEvoy & A. Miller (Eds.), *Black power and student rebellion: Conflict on the American campus*. Belmont, Calif.: Wadsworth, 1969.

Harford, T. C., & Solomon, L. The effects of game strategies upon interpersonal trust in paranoid schizophrenic samples. Paper presented at the Eastern Psychological Association Convention, 1965.

Harris, M. B., & Huang, L. C. Competence and helping. *Journal of Social Psychology*, 1973, *89*, 203–210.

Harris, T. M. Machiavellianism, judgment, independence, and attitudes toward teammate in a cooperative judgment task. Unpublished doctoral dissertation, Columbia University, 1966. (Cited in R. Christie & F. L. Geis (Eds.), *Studies in Machiavellianism*. New York: Academic Press, 1970.)

Harrison, A. A. Response competition, frequency, exploratory behavior, and liking. *Journal of Personality and Social Psychology*, 1968, *9*, 363–368.

Harrison, A. A. Exposure and popularity. *Journal of Personality*, 1969, *37*, 359–367.

Harrison, A. A., & Crandall, R. Heterogeneity-homogeneity of exposure sequence and the attitudinal effects of exposure. *Journal of Personality and Social Psychology*, 1972, *21*, 234–238.

Harrison, A. A., & Hines, P. The effects of frequency of exposure at three short exposure times on affective ratings and exploratory behavior. *Proceedings of the 78th Annual Convention of the American Psychological Association*, 1970. Pp. 391–392.

Harshberger, D. An investigation of a structural model of small group problem solving. *Human Relations*, 1971, *24*, 43–63.

Hartshorne, H., & May, M. A. Studies in the nature of character (Vol. 1). *Studies in deceit*. New York: Macmillan, 1928.

Hastorf, A. H., & Cantril, H. They saw a game: A case study. *Journal of Abnormal and Social Psychology*, 1954, *49*, 129–234.

Hastorf, A. H., Kite, W. R., Gross, A. E., & Wolfe, L. J. The perception and evaluation of behavior change. *Sociometry*, 1965, *28*, 400–410.

Hastorf, A. H., Schneider, D. J., & Polefka, J. *Person perception*. Reading, Mass.: Addison-Wesley, 1970.

Heider, F. Attitudes and cognitive organization. *Journal of Psychology*, 1946, *21*, 107–112.

Heider, F. *The psychology of interpersonal relations*. New York: Wiley, 1958.

Heingartner, A., & Hall, J. V. Affective consequences in adults and children of repeated exposure to auditory stimuli. *Journal of Personality and Social Psychology*, 1974, *29*, 719–723.

Heller, J. F., Pallak, M. S., & Picek, J. M. The interactive effects of intent and threat on boomerang attitude change. *Journal of Personality and Social Psychology*, 1973, *26*, 273–279.

Helm, B., Bonoma, T. V., & Tedeschi, J. T. Reciprocity for harm done. *Journal of Social Psychology*, 1972, *87*, 89–98.

Henchy, T., & Glass, D. C. Evaluation apprehension and the social facilitation of dominant and subordinate responses. *Journal of Personality and Social Psychology*, 1968, *10*, 446–454.

Hendrick, C., Bixenstine, V., & Hawkins, G. Race versus belief similarity as determinants of attraction: A search for a fair test. *Journal of Personality and Social Psychology*, 1971, *17*, 250–258.

Hendrick, C., & Jones, R. A. *The nature of theory and research in social psychology*. New York: Academic Press, 1972.

Heron, W. The pathology of boredom. *Scientific American*, 1957, *196*, 52–66.

Heron, W., Doane, B. K., & Scott, T. H. Visual disturbances after prolonged perceptual isolation. *Canadian Journal of Psychology*, 1956, *10*, 13–18.

Herzberg, F. *Work and the nature of man*. Cleveland: World, 1966.

Herzberg, F., Mausner, B., & Snyderman, B. *The motivation to work* (2nd ed.). New York: Wiley, 1959.

Higbee, K. L. Fifteen years of fear arousal: Research on threat appeals. *Psychological Bulletin*, 1969, *72*, 426–444.

Higgs, W. J., & Joseph, K. B. Effects of real and anticipated audiences on verbal learning and reproduction. *Journal of Social Psychology*, 1971, *85*, 41–49.

Hildum, D. C., & Brown, R. W. Verbal reinforcement and interviewer bias. *Journal of Abnormal and Social Psychology,* 1956, *53,* 108–111.

Hill, W. A. Leadership style: Rigid or flexible? *Organizational Behavior and Human Performance,* 1973, *9,* 35–47.

Hingston, R. W. G. Instinct and intelligence in insects. *Character and Personality,* 1932, *1,* 129–136.

Hodges, B. H. Adding and averaging models for information integration. *Psychological Review,* 1973, *80,* 80–84.

Hoffman, M. L. Altruistic behavior and the parent-child relationship. *Journal of Personality and Social Psychology,* 1975, *31,* 937–943.

Hollander, E. P. Conformity, status, and idiosyncrasy credit. *Psychological Review,* 1958, *65,* 117–127.

Hollander, E. P. Competence and conformity in the acceptance of influence. *Journal of Abnormal and Social Psychology,* 1960, *61,* 361–365.

Hollander, E. P. *Leaders, groups, and influence.* New York: Oxford University Press, 1964.

Hollander, E. P., & Willis, R. Some current issues in the psychology of conformity and nonconformity. *Psychological Bulletin,* 1967, *68,* 62–76.

Hollander, S. W. Effects of forewarning factors on pre- and post-communication attitude change. *Journal of Personality and Social Psychology,* 1974, *30,* 272–278.

Holmes, D. S., & Jorgensen, B. W. Do personality and social psychologists study men more than women? *Representative Research in Social Psychology,* 1971, *2,* 66–70.

Holmes, J. G., & Strickland, L. H. Choice freedom and confirmation of incentive expectancy as determinants of attitude change. *Journal of Personality and Social Psychology,* 1970, *14,* 39–45.

Homans, G. *The human group.* New York: Harcourt Brace Jovanovich, 1950.

Homans, G. *Social behavior: Its elementary forms.* New York: Harcourt Brace Jovanovich, 1961.

Hood, T., & Back, K. Self-disclosure and the volunteer: A source of bias in laboratory experiments. *Journal of Personality and Social Psychology,* 1971, *17,* 130–136.

Hood, W. R., & Sherif, M. Verbal report and judgment of an unstructured stimulus. *Journal of Psychology,* 1962, *54,* 121–130.

Hook, E. B. Behavioral implications of the human XYY genotype. *Science,* 1973, *179,* 139–150.

Hornstein, H. The influence of social models on helping. In J. Macaulay & L. Berkowitz (Eds.), *Altruism and helping behavior: Social psychological studies of some antecedents and consequences.* New York: Academic Press, 1970. Pp. 29–41.

Hornstein, H., Fisch, E., & Holmes, L. Influence of a model's feelings about his behavior and his relevance as a comparison on other observers' helping behavior. *Journal of Personality and Social Psychology,* 1968, *10,* 222–226.

Horowitz, E. L. The development of attitude toward the Negro. *Archives of Psychology in New York,* 1936, *194.* Cited in J. Harding, H. Proshansky, B. Kunter, & I. Chein, Prejudice and ethnic relations. In G. Lindzey & E. Aronson (Eds.), *Handbook of social psychology* (2nd ed.) Vol. 5. Reading, Mass.: Addison-Wesley, 1969. Pp. 1–76.

House, W. C., & Perney, V. Valence of expected and unexpected outcomes as a function of locus of goal and type of expectancy. *Journal of Personality and Social Psychology,* 1974, *29,* 454–463.

Hovland, C. I., Lumsdaine, A., & Sheffield, F. *Experiments on mass communication.* Princeton, N.J.: Princeton University Press, 1949.

Hovland, C. I., & Mandell, W. Is there a law of primacy in persuasion? In C. I. Hovland (Ed.), *The order of presentation in persuasion.* New Haven, Conn.: Yale University Press, 1957.

Hovland, C. I., & Rosenberg, M. J. (Eds.). *Attitude organization and change.* New Haven, Conn.: Yale University Press, 1960.

Howell, F. C. *Early man.* New York: Time-Life, 1965.

Howes, D. H., & Solomon, R. L. A note on McGinnies' "Emotionality and perceptual defense." *Psychological Review,* 1950, *57,* 229–234.

Howes, D. H., & Solomon, R. L. Visual duration threshold as a function of word probability. *Journal of Experimental Psychology,* 1951, *41,* 401–410.

Hraba, J., & Grant, G. Black is beautiful: A re-examination of racial preference and identification. *Journal of Personality and Social Psychology,* 1970, *16,* 398–402.

Hull, C. L. *Principles of behavior: An introduction to behavior theory.* New York: Appleton-Century-Crofts, 1943.

Hunt, P. J., & Hillery, J. M. Social facilitation in a coaction setting: An examination of the effects over learning trials. *Journal of Experimental Social Psychology,* 1973, *9,* 563–571.

Hurwitz, J. I., Zander, A., & Hymovitch, B. Some effects of power on the relations among group members. In D. Cartwright & A. Zander (Eds.), *Group dynamics: Research and theory* (2nd ed.). New York: Harper & Row, 1960.

Huston, T. L. Ambiguity of acceptance, social desirability, and dating choice. *Journal of Experimental Social Psychology,* 1973, *9,* 32–42.

Hyman, H. H., & Sheatsley, P. B. Attitudes toward desegregation. *Scientific American,* 1964, *211,* 16–23.

Insko, C. A. Verbal reinforcement of attitude. *Journal of Personality and Social Psychology,* 1965, *2,* 621–623.

Insko, C. A., & Schopler, J. *Experimental social psychology.* New York: Academic Press, 1972.

Insko, C. A., & Wetzel, C. Preacquaintance attraction as an interactive function of the proportion and number of similar attitudes. *Representative Research in Social Psychology,* 1974, *5,* 27–33.

Isen, A. M. Success, failure, attention, and reaction to others: The warm glow hypothesis. *Journal of Personality and Social Psychology,* 1970, *15,* 294–301.

Isen, A. M., Horn, N., & Rosenhan, D. L. Effects of success and failure on children's generosity. *Journal of Personality and Social Psychology,* 1973, *27,* 239–247.

Isen, A. M., & Levin, P. F. The effect of feeling good on helping: Cookies and kindness. *Journal of Personality and Social Psychology,* 1972, *21,* 384–388.

Jacobs, R. C., & Campbell, D. T. The perpetuation of an arbitrary tradition through several generations of a laboratory microculture. *Journal of Abnormal and Social Psychology,* 1961, *62,* 649–658.

Jacobs, T. O. *Leadership and exchange in formal organizations.* Alexandria, Va.: HUMRRO, 1971.

Jahoda, M. Conformity and independence—A psychological analysis. *Human Relations,* 1959, *12,* 99–120.

Janis, I. L. Effects of fear arousal on attitude change: Recent developments in theory and experimental research. In L. Berkowitz (Ed.), *Advances in experimental social psychology* (Vol. 3). New York: Academic Press, 1967. Pp. 167–224.

Janis, I. L. Groupthink. *Psychology Today,* 1971, *5* (No. 6), 43–46.

Janis, I. L. *Victims of groupthink.* Boston: Houghton-Mifflin, 1974.

Janis, I. L., & Feshbach, S. Effects of fear-arousing communications. *Journal of Abnormal and Social Psychology,* 1953, *48,* 78–92.

Janis, I. L., & Feshbach, S. Personality differences associated with responsiveness to fear-arousing communications. *Journal of Personality,* 1954, *23,* 154–166.

Janis, I. L., & Gilmore, J. B. The influence of incentive conditions on the success of role playing in modifying attitudes. *Journal of Personality and Social Psychology,* 1965, *1,* 17–27.

Janis, I. L., & Terwilliger, R. F. An experimental study of psychological resistances to fear-arousing communications. *Journal of Abnormal and Social Psychology*, 1962, *65*, 403–410.

Jecker, J. D. The cognitive effects of conflict and dissonance. In L. Festinger (Ed.), *Conflict, decision, and dissonance*. Stanford, Calif.: Stanford University Press, 1964. Pp. 21–30.

Jellison, J. M. Communicator credibility: A social comparison of abilities interpretation. In A. A. Harrison (Ed.), *Explorations in psychology*. Monterey, Calif.: Brooks/Cole, 1974. Pp. 165–171.

Jellison, J., Riskind, J., & Broll, L. Attribution of ability to others on skill and chance tasks as a function of level of risk. *Journal of Personality and Social Psychology*, 1972, *22*, 135–138.

Johnson, D. A., Porter, R. J., & Mateljan, P. L. Racial discrimination in apartment rentals. *Journal of Applied Social Psychology*, 1971, *4*, 364–377.

Johnson, D. W. Cooperativeness and social perspective taking. *Journal of Personality and Social Psychology*, 1975, *31*, 241–244.

Johnson, R. C., Thomson, C. W., & Frincke, G. Word values, word frequency, and visual duration threshold. *Psychological Review*, 1960, *67*, 332–342.

Jones, E. E. *Ingratiation: A social psychological analysis*. New York: Appleton-Century-Crofts, 1964.

Jones, E. E., & Davis, K. E. From acts to dispositions: The attribution process in person perception. In L. Berkowitz (Ed.), *Advances in experimental social psychology* (Vol. 2). New York: Academic Press, 1965.

Jones, E. E., Davis, K. E., & Gergen, K. J. Role playing variations and their informational value for person perception. *Journal of Abnormal and Social Psychology*, 1961, *63*, 302–310.

Jones, E. E., & Gerard, H. B. *Foundations of social psychology*. New York: Wiley, 1967.

Jones, E. E., Gergen, K. J., & Jones, R. G. Tactics of ingratiation among leaders and subordinates in a status hierarchy. *Psychological Monographs*, 1963, *77*(566).

Jones, E. E., & Goethals, G. R. Order effects in impression formation: Attribution context and the nature of the entity. In E. E. Jones, D. E. Kanouse, H. H. Kelley, R. E. Nisbett, S. Valins, & B. Weiner, *Attribution: Perceiving the causes of behavior*. Morristown, N.J.: General Learning Press, 1972.

Jones, E. E., & Gordon, E. M. Timing of self-disclosure and its effects on personal attraction. *Journal of Personality and Social Psychology*, 1972, *24*, 358–365.

Jones, E. E., Kanouse, D. E., Kelley, H. H., Nisbett, R. E., Valins, S., & Weiner, B. *Attribution: Perceiving the causes of behavior*. Morristown, N.J.: General Learning Press, 1972.

Jones, E. E., & Nisbett, R. E. The actor and the observer: Divergent perceptions of the causes of behavior. In E. E. Jones, D. E. Kanouse, H. H. Kelley, R. E. Nisbett, S. Valins, & B. Weiner, *Attribution: Perceiving the causes of behavior*. Morristown, N.J.: General Learning Press, 1972.

Jones, E. E., Rock, L., Shaver, K. G., Goethals, G. R., & Ward, L. M. Pattern of performance and ability attribution: An unexpected primacy effect. *Journal of Personality and Social Psychology*, 1968, *10*, 317–340.

Jones, E. E., & Sigall, H. The bogus pipeline: A new paradigm for measuring affect and attitude. *Psychological Bulletin*, 1971, *76*, 349–364.

Jones, E. E., & Sigall, H. Where there is *ignis* there may be fire. *Psychological Bulletin*, 1973, *79*, 260–262.

Jones, R. A., Linder, D. E., Kiesler, C. A., Zanna, M., & Brehm, J. W. Internal states or external stimuli: Observers' attitude judgments and the dissonance theory–self-perception controversy. *Journal of Experimental Social Psychology*, 1968, *4*, 247–269.

Jordan, N. Behavioral forces that are a function of the attitudes and of cognitive organization. *Human Relations*, 1953, *6*, 273–287.

Jorgensen, C. C. IQ tests and their educational supporters. *Journal of Social Issues*, 1973, *29*, 33–40.

Jorgensen, C. C. Racism in mental testing: The use of IQ tests to mislabel black children. In A. A. Harrison (Ed.), *Explorations in psychology.* Monterey, Calif.: Brooks/Cole, 1974.

Jourard, S. M. *Self disclosure.* New York: Wiley, 1971.

Kagan, J. The child's sex role classification of school objects. *Child Development,* 1964, *35*, 1051–1056.

Kahn, A., & Ryen, A. H. Factors influencing the bias towards one's own group. *International Journal of Group Tensions,* 1972, *2*, 33–50.

Kahn, A., & Tice, T. Returning a favor and retaliating harm: The effects of stated intentions and actual behavior. *Journal of Experimental Social Psychology*, 1973, *9*, 43–56.

Kahn, H. *On thermonuclear war.* Princeton: Princeton University Press, 1960.

Kahn, H. *On escalation: Metaphors and scenarios.* New York: Praeger, 1965.

Kahn, H. *Thinking about the unthinkable.* New York: Avon, 1966.

Kahn, R. L. The work module—a tonic for lunchpail lassitude. *Psychology Today,* February 1973, 35–40.

Kanfer, F. H. Verbal conditioning: A review of its current status. In T. R. Dixon & D. L. Horton (Eds.), *Verbal behavior and general behavior theory.* Englewood Cliffs, N.J.: Prentice-Hall, 1968. Pp. 245–290.

Kanouse, D. E., & Hanson, L. R. Negativity in evaluations. In E. E. Jones, D. E. Kanouse, H. H. Kelley, R. E. Nisbett, S. Valins, & B. Weiner, *Attribution: Perceiving the causes of behavior.* Morristown, N.J.: General Learning Press, 1972.

Kaplan, H. R., Tausky, C., & Bolaria, B. S. Job enrichment. *Personnel Journal,* 1969, *48*, 791–798.

Kaplan, K. J. On the ambivalence-indifference problem in attitude theory and measurement: A suggested modification of the semantic differential technique. *Psychological Bulletin,* 1972, *77*, 361–372.

Kaplan, K. J., Firestone, I. J., Moore, M., & Degnore, R. Attitudes toward interviewer as a function of question intimacy across three interview settings. *Proceedings of the 79th Annual Convention of the American Psychological Association,* 1971, p. 376.

Karaz, V., & Perlman, D. Attribution at the wire: Consistency and outcome finish strong. *Journal of Experimental Social Psychology,* 1975, in press.

Karlins, M., Coffman, T. L., & Walters, G. On the fading of social stereotypes: Studies on three generations of college students. *Journal of Personality and Social Psychology,* 1969, *13*, 1–16.

Kassarjian, H. Voting intentions and political perception. *Journal of Psychology,* 1963, *56*, 85–88.

Katz, D. The functional approach to the study of attitude change. *Public Opinion Quarterly,* 1960, *24*, 163–204.

Katz, D. The motivational basis of organizational behavior. *Behavioral Science,* 1964, *9*, 131–146.

Katz, D. Some final considerations about experimentation in social psychology. In C. G. McClintock (Ed.), *Experimental social psychology.* New York: Holt, Rinehart and Winston, 1972.

Katz, D., & Braly, K. Racial stereotypes in one hundred college students. *Journal of Abnormal and Social Psychology,* 1933, *28*, 280–290.

Katz, D., & Braly, K. Racial prejudice and racial stereotypes. *Journal of Abnormal and Social Psychology,* 1935, *30*, 175–193.

Katz, D., & Kahn, R. L. Some recent findings in human relations research in industry. In G. E. Swanson, T. M. Newcomb, & E. L. Hartley (Eds.), *Readings in social psychology* (2nd ed.). New York: Holt, Rinehart and Winston, 1952. Pp. 650–655.

Katz, D., & Kahn, R. L. *The social psychology of organizations.* New York: Wiley, 1966.

Katz, D., Sarnoff, I., & McClintock, C. G. Ego-defense and attitude change. *Human Relations,* 1956, *9,* 27–45.

Kazantzakis, N. *Report to Greco.* Translated by P. A. Bien. New York: Simon & Schuster, 1965.

Kazdin, A. E., & Bryan, J. H. Competence and volunteering. *Journal of Experimental Social Psychology,* 1971, *7,* 87–97.

Keasey, C. B., & Keasey, M. Social influence in a high-ego-involvement situation: A field study of petition signing. Paper presented at the 42nd Annual Meeting of the Eastern Psychological Association, New York, April 1971.

Kelley, H. H. The warm-cold variable in first impressions. *Journal of Personality,* 1950, *18,* 431–439.

Kelley, H. H. Communication in experimentally created hierarchies. *Human Relations,* 1951, *4,* 39–56.

Kelley, H. H. Attribution theory in social psychology. In D. Levine (Ed.), *Nebraska symposium on motivation, 1967.* Lincoln: University of Nebraska Press, 1967. Pp. 192–238.

Kelley, H. H. Attribution in social interaction. In E. E. Jones, D. E. Kanouse, H. H. Kelley, R. E. Nisbett, S. Valins, & B. Weiner. *Attribution: Perceiving the causes of behavior.* Morristown, N.J.: General Learning Press, 1972.

Kelley, H. H., & Lamb, T. W. Certainty of judgment and resistance to social influence. *Journal of Abnormal and Social Psychology,* 1957, *55,* 137–139.

Kelley, H. H., & Stahelski, A. J. Social interaction basis of cooperators' and competitors' beliefs about others. *Journal of Personality and Social Psychology,* 1970, *16,* 66–91.

Kelley, H. H., & Thibaut, J. W. Group problem solving. In G. Lindzey & E. Aronson (Eds.), *Handbook of social psychology* (2nd ed.), Vol. 4. Reading, Mass.: Addison-Wesley, 1969. Pp. 1–101.

Kelman, H. C. Compliance, identification, and internalization: Three processes of attitude change. *Journal of Conflict Resolution,* 1958, *2,* 51–60.

Kelman, H. C. Processes of opinion change. *Public Opinion Quarterly,* 1961, *25,* 57–78.

Kelman, H. C. Attitudes are alive and well and gainfully employed in the sphere of action. *American Psychologist,* 1974, *29,* 310–324.

Kepka, E. J., & Brickman, P. Consistency versus discrepancy as clues in the attribution of intelligence and motivation. *Journal of Personality and Social Psychology,* 1971, *20,* 323–329.

Kerckhoff, A., & Davis, K. E. Value consensus and need complementarity in mate selection. *American Sociological Review,* 1962, *27,* 295–303.

Kerner Commission. *Report of the U.S. National Advisory Commission on Civil Disorders.* Washington, D.C.: U.S. Government Printing Office, 1968.

Kessler, J. J., & Wiener, Y. Self-consistency and inequity dissonance as factors in under-compensation. *Organizational Behavior and Human Performance,* 1972, *8,* 456–466.

Kiesler, C., Collins, B., & Miller, N. *Attitude change: A critical analysis of theoretical approaches.* New York: Wiley, 1969.

Kilham, W., & Mann, L. Level of destructive obedience as a function of the transmitter and executant roles in the Milgram obedience paradigm. *Journal of Personality and Social Psychology,* 1974, *29,* 696–702.

Kinch, J. W. *Social psychology.* New York: McGraw-Hill, 1973.

King, N. Clarification and evaluation of the two-factor theory of job satisfaction. *Psychological Bulletin,* 1970, *74,* 18–32.

Kipnis, D., & Vanderveer, R. Ingratiation and the use of power. *Journal of Personality and Social Psychology,* 1971, *17,* 280–286.

Kleinke, C. L., Staneski, R. A., & Weaver, P. Evaluation of a person who uses another's name in ingratiating and noningratiating situations. *Journal of Experimental Social Psychology,* 1972, *8,* 457–466.

Klugman, S. F. Group and individual judgments for anticipated events. *Journal of Social Psychology*, 1945, *32*, 103–110.

Knight, H. C. *A comparison of the reliability of group and individual judgments.* Unpublished master's thesis, Columbia University, 1921. (Cited in I. Lorge, D. Fox, J. Davitz, & M. Brenner, A survey of studies contrasting the quality of group performance and individual performance: 1920–1957. *Psychological Bulletin, 1958, 55,* 337–372.)

Knowles, E. S. Boundaries around group interaction: The effect of group size and member status on boundary permeability. *Journal of Personality and Social Psychology*, 1973, *26*, 327–331.

Knox, R. E., & Douglas, R. L. Trivial incentives, marginal comprehension, and dubious generalizations from Prisoner's Dilemma research. *Journal of Personality and Social Psychology*, 1971, *20*, 160–165.

Knox, R. E., & Inkster, J. A. Post-decision dissonance at post time. *Journal of Personality and Social Psychology*, 1968, *4*, 319–323.

Koch, S. An implicit image of man. In L. Solomon & B. Berzon (Eds.), *New perspectives on encounter groups.* San Francisco: Jossey-Bass, 1974. Pp. 30–52.

Koeske, G., & Crano, W. The effect of congruous and incongruous source-statement combinations upon the judged credibility of a communication. *Journal of Experimental Social Psychology*, 1968, *4*, 384–399.

Kohlberg, L. Development of moral character and moral ideology. In M. L. Hoffman & L. W. Hoffman (Eds.), *Review of child development research* (Vol. 1). New York: Russel Sage Foundation, 1964. Pp. 383–431.

Kohlberg, L. The cognitive-developmental approach to socialization. In D. A. Goslin (Ed.), *Handbook of socialization theory and research.* Chicago: Rand McNally, 1969. Pp. 347–480.

Konečni, V. J. Some effects of guilt on compliance: A field replication. *Journal of Personality and Social Psychology*, 1972, *23*, 30–32.

Konečni, V. J., & Doob, A. N. Catharsis through the displacement of aggression. *Journal of Personality and Social Psychology*, 1972, *23*, 379–387.

Kothandapani, V. Validation of feeling, belief, and intention to act as three components of attitude and their contribution to prediction of contraceptive behavior. *Journal of Personality and Social Psychology*, 1971, *19*, 321–333.

Kranser, L., Knowles, J. P., & Ullman, L. P. Effect of verbal conditioning on subsequent motor performance. *Journal of Personality and Social Psychology*, 1965, *1*, 407–412.

Krebs, D. Altruism—An examination of the concept and a review of the literature. *Psychological Bulletin*, 1970, *73*, 258–302.

Krisher, H. P., Darley, S. A., & Darley, J. M. Fear-provoking recommendations, intentions to take preventive actions, and actual preventive actions. *Journal of Personality and Social Psychology*, 1973, *26*, 301–308.

Kruglanski, A. W. Much ado about the "volunteer artifacts." *Journal of Personality and Social Psychology*, 1973, *28*, 348–354.

Kruglanski, A. W., & Cohen, M. Attributed freedom and personal causation. *Journal of Personality and Social Psychology*, 1973, *26*, 245–250.

Krugman, H. E. Affective response to music as a function of familiarity. *Journal of Abnormal and Social Psychology*, 1943, *38*, 338–392.

Kuo, Z. Y. The genesis of the cat's responses to the rat. *Journal of Comparative Psychology*, 1930, *11*, 1–35.

Kuriloff, A. H. *Reality in management.* New York: McGraw-Hill, 1966.

Laird, J. D. Self-attribution of emotion: The effects of expressive behavior on the quality of emotional experience. *Journal of Personality and Social Psychology*, 1974, *29*, 475–486.

Lalljee, M., & Cook, M. Uncertainty in first encounters. *Journal of Personality and Social Psychology*, 1973, *26*, 137–141.

Lambert, B. G., Rothschild, B. F., Altland, R., & Green, L. B. *Adolescence: Transition from childhood to maturity.* Monterey, Calif.: Brooks/Cole, 1972.

Lamm, H. Will an isolated individual advise higher risk-taking after hearing a discussion of the decision problem? *Journal of Personality and Social Psychology,* 1967, 6, 467–471.

LaPiere, R. T. Attitudes and actions. *Social Forces,* 1934, 13, 230–237.

Larson, L. L., & Rowland, K. M. Leadership style, stress, and behavior in task performance. *Organizational Behavior and Human Performance,* 1973, 9, 407–420.

Latané, B., & Darley, J. M. Group inhibition of bystanders in emergencies. *Journal of Personality and Social Psychology,* 1968, 10, 215–221.

Latané, B., & Darley, J. Bystander "apathy." *American Scientist,* 1969, 57, 244–268.

Latané, B., & Glass, D. C. Social and nonsocial attraction in rats. *Journal of Personality and Social Psychology,* 1968, 9, 142–146.

Latané, B., & Rodin, J. A lady in distress: Inhibiting effects of friends and strangers on bystander intervention. *Journal of Experimental Social Psychology,* 1969, 5, 189–202.

Lave, L. B. Factors affecting cooperation in the Prisoner's Dilemma. *Behavioral Science,* 1965, 10, 26–38.

Lawler, E. E. *Pay and organizational effectiveness: A psychological view.* New York: McGraw-Hill, 1971.

Lawler, E. E. *Motivation in work organizations.* Monterey, Calif.: Brooks/Cole, 1973.

Lawler, E. E., & Hackman, R. The impact of employee participation in the development of pay incentive plans: A field experiment. *Journal of Applied Psychology,* 1969, 53, 467–471.

Lawler, E. E., Koplin, C. A., Young, T. F., & Fadem, J. A. Inequity reduction over time in an induced overpayment situation. *Organizational Behavior and Human Performance,* 1968, 3, 253–268.

Lawler, E. E., & Porter, L. W. Perceptions regarding management compensation. *Industrial Relations,* 1963, 3, 41–49.

Lawler, E. E., & Suttle, J. L. A causal correlation test of the need hierarchy concept. *Organizational Behavior and Human Performance,* 1972, 7, 265–287.

Lazarsfeld, P. F. *Radio and the printed page.* New York: Duell, Sloan, & Pearce, 1940.

Lazarus, R. S., Speisman, J. C., Mordkoff, A. M., & Davison, L. A. A laboratory study of psychological stress produced by a motion picture film. *Psychological Monographs,* 1962, 76 (Whole No. 553).

Leavitt, H. J. Some effects of certain communication patterns on group performance. *Journal of Abnormal and Social Psychology,* 1951, 46, 38–50.

Leeper, R. A study of a neglected portion of a field of learning—The development of sensory organization. *Journal of Genetic Psychology,* 1935, 46, 41–75.

Lefkowitz, M., Blake, R. R., & Mouton, J. S. Status factors in pedestrian violation of traffic signals. *Journal of Abnormal and Social Psychology,* 1955, 51, 704–706.

Lepper, M. R. Dissonance, self perception, and honesty in children. *Journal of Abnormal and Social Psychology,* 1973, 25, 65–74.

Lerner, L., & Weiss, R. L. Role of value of reward and model affective response in vicarious reinforcement. *Journal of Personality and Social Psychology,* 1972, 21, 93–100.

Lerner, M. J. The desire for justice and reaction to victims. In J. Macaulay & L. Berkowitz (Eds.), *Altruism and helping behavior: Social psychological studies of some antecedents and consequences.* New York: Academic Press, 1970. Pp. 205–229.

Lerner, M. J., & Matthews, G. Reactions to suffering of others under conditions of indirect responsibility. *Journal of Personality and Social Psychology,* 1967, 5, 319–325.

Lerner, M. J., & Simmons, C. H. Observer's reaction to the "innocent victim." *Journal of Personality and Social Psychology,* 1966, 4, 203–210.

Leventhal, H., & Niles, P. A field experiment on fear arousal with data on the validity of questionnaire measures. *Journal of Personality,* 1964, 32, 459–479.

Leventhal, H., & Singer, D. L. Cognitive complexity, impression formation, and impression change. *Journal of Personality*, 1964, *32*, 210–226.

Leventhal, H., Singer, R. P., & Jones, S. Effects of fear and specificity of recommendation upon attitudes and behavior. *Journal of Personality and Social Psychology*, 1965, *2*, 20–29.

Levinger, G., & Breedlove, J. Interpersonal attraction and agreement: A study of marriage partners. *Journal of Personality and Social Psychology*, 1966, *3*, 367–372.

Levinger, G., & Schneider, D. J. A test of the risk is a value hypothesis. *Journal of Personality and Social Psychology*, 1969, *11*, 165–169.

Levy, P., Lundgren, D., Ansel, M., Fell, D., Fink, B., & McGrath, J. E. Bystander effect in a demand-without-threat situation. *Journal of Personality and Social Psychology*, 1972, *24*, 166–171.

Lewin, K., Lippitt, R., & White, R. Patterns of aggressive behavior in experimentally created "social climates." *Journal of Social Psychology*, 1939, *10*, 271–299.

Lewis, M. Parents and children: Sex-role development. *The School Review*, 1972, *80*, 229–239.

Lieberman, M. A., Yalom, I. D., & Miles, M. *Encounter groups: First facts.* New York: Basic Books, 1973.

Lieberman, S. The effects of changes in roles on the attitudes of role occupants. *Human Relations*, 1956, *9*, 385–402.

Liebert, R. M., & Baron, R. A. Short-term effects of televised aggression on children's aggressive behavior. In J. P. Murray, E. A. Rubinstein, & G. A. Comstock (Eds.), *Television and social behavior.* Washington, D.C.: Government Printing Office, 1972. Pp. 181–201.

Likert, R. *New patterns of management.* New York: McGraw-Hill, 1961.

Linder, D. E., Cooper, J., & Jones, E. E. Decision freedom as a determinant of the role of incentive magnitude in attitude change. *Journal of Personality and Social Psychology*, 1967, *6*, 245–254.

Lindsay, J. S. B. On the number in a group. *Human Relations*, 1972, *25*, 47–64.

Lindzey, G., & Aronson, E. (Eds.). *The handbook of social psychology* (Vols. 1–5). Reading, Mass.: Addison-Wesley, 1968–1969.

Lindzey, G., & Byrne, D. Measurement of social choice and interpersonal attractiveness. In G. Lindzey and E. Aronson (Eds.), *Handbook of social psychology* (2nd ed.), Vol. 2. Reading, Mass.: Addison-Wesley, 1968.

Lippitt, R. An experimental study of authoritarian and democratic group atmospheres. *University of Iowa Studies in Child Welfare*, 1940, *16*(3), 43–195.

Lippitt, R., Watson, J., & Westley, B. *The dynamics of planned change.* New York: Harcourt Brace Jovanovich, 1958.

Lipset, S. M., & Ladd, E. C. . . . And what professors think. *Psychology Today*, 1970, *4*(6), 49–51.

Liska, A. E. Emergent issues in the attitude-behavior consistency controversy. *American Sociological Review*, 1974, *39*, 261–272.

Lockard, R. B. Reflection on the fall of comparative psychology: Is there a message for all of us? *American Psychologist*, 1971, *26*, 168–179.

Locke, E. A. Job satisfaction and job performance: A theoretical analysis. *Organizational Behavior and Human Performance*, 1970, *5*, 484–500.

Lombardo, J. P., Weiss, R. F., & Buchanan, W. Reinforcing and attracting functions of yielding. *Journal of Personality and Social Psychology*, 1972, *21*, 359–368.

London, H., McSeveny, D., & Tropper, R. Confidence, overconfidence, and persuasion. *Human Relations*, 1971, *24*, 359–369.

Lonergan, B. G., & McClintock, C. G. Effects of group membership on risk taking behavior. *Psychological Reports*, 1961, *8*, 447–455.

Lord, W. *The good years.* New York: Bantam Books, 1969.

Lorenz, K. *On aggression.* New York: Harcourt Brace Jovanovich, 1966.

Lorge, I., Fox, D., Davitz, J., & Brenner, M. A survey of studies contrasting the quality of group performance and individual performance: 1920–1957. *Psychological Bulletin,* 1958, *55,* 337–372.

Lott, A., & Lott, B. Group cohesiveness, communication level, and conformity. *Journal of Abnormal and Social Psychology,* 1961, *62,* 408–412.

Lott, A., & Lott, B. Group cohesiveness as interpersonal attraction: A review of the relationships with antecedent and consequent variables. *Psychological Bulletin,* 1965, *64,* 259–309.

Lott, A., Lott, B., & Crow, T. Use of descriptive words in measuring liking for persons. *Proceedings of the 77th Annual Convention of the American Psychological Association,* 1969. Pp. 407–408.

Lott, D. F., & Sommer, R. Seating arrangement and status. *Journal of Personality and Social Psychology,* 1967, *7,* 90–95.

Luce, R. D., & Raiffa, H. *Games and decisions.* New York: Wiley, 1957.

Lund, F. H. The psychology of belief: A study of its emotional and volitional determinants. *Journal of Abnormal and Social Psychology,* 1925, *20,* 174–196.

Lutzker, D. Internationalism as a predictor of cooperative behavior. *Journal of Conflict Resolution,* 1960, *4,* 426–435.

Lynn, D. B. Determinants of intellectual growth in women. *School Review,* 1972, *80,* 241–260.

Lyons, J., Walster, E., & Walster, G. W. Playing hard to get: An elusive phenomenon. University of Wisconsin, Madison. Unpublished manuscript. (Cited in E. Walster, G. W. Walster, J. Piliavin, & L. Schmidt, Playing hard to get: Understanding an elusive phenomenon. *Journal of Personality and Social Psychology,* 1973, *26,* 113–121.)

Macauley, J. R. A shill for charity. In J. Macauley & L. Berkowitz (Eds.), *Altruism and helping behavior.* New York: Academic Press, 1970. Pp. 43–60.

Maccoby, E. E. *The development of sex differences.* Stanford, Calif.: Stanford University Press, 1966.

MacDonald, A. P. Anxiety, affiliation, and social isolation. *Developmental Psychology,* 1970, *3,* 242–254.

MacDonald, A. P., & Majumder, R. K. On the resolution and tolerance of cognitive inconsistency in another naturally occuring event: Attitudes and beliefs following the Senator Eagleton incident. *Journal of Applied Social Psychology,* 1973, *3,* 132–143.

MacKenzie, B. K. The importance of contact in determining attitudes towards Negroes. *Journal of Abnormal and Social Psychology,* 1948, *43,* 417–441.

MacKinnon, D. W., & Dukes, W. F. Repression. In L. Postman (Ed.), *Psychology in the making.* New York: Knopf, 1962.

MacNeil, M. K. Norm change over subject generations as a function of arbitrariness of prescribed group norms. Unpublished master's thesis, University of Oklahoma, 1965. (Cited in M. Sherif & C. Sherif, *Social psychology.* New York: Harper & Row, 1969.)

Malof, M., & Lott, A. J. Ethnocentrism and the acceptance of Negro support in a group pressure situation. *Journal of Abnormal and Social Psychology,* 1962, *65,* 254–258.

Malpass, R. S., & Kravitz, J. Recognition for faces for own and other race. *Journal of Personality and Social Psychology,* 1969, *13,* 330–334.

Mann, J. H. The effects of interracial contact on sociometric choices and perceptions. *Journal of Social Psychology,* 1959, *50,* 143–152.

Mann, L., & Taylor, K. F. Queue counting: The effect of motives upon estimates of the number of people waiting in lines. *Journal of Personality and Social Psychology,* 1969, *12,* 95–103.

March, J. G., & Simon, H. A. *Organizations.* New York: Wiley, 1958.

Marlatt, G. A. A comparison of vicarious and direct reinforcement control of verbal behavior in an interview setting. *Journal of Personality and Social Psychology,* 1970, *16,* 695–703.

Marlatt, G. A. Task structure and the experimental modification of verbal behavior. *Psychological Bulletin,* 1972, *78,* 335–350.

Marrow, A. J., Bowers, D. G., & Seashore, S. E. *Management by participation.* New York: Harper & Row, 1967.

Martens, R. Effect of an audience on learning of a complex motor skill. *Journal of Personality and Social Psychology,* 1969, *12,* 252–260.

Martens, R., & Landers, D. M. Evaluation potential as a determinant of coaction effects. *Journal of Experimental Social Psychology,* 1972, *8,* 347–359.

Martin, J. B. *Break down the walls.* New York: Ballantine, 1954.

Mascaro, G. F., & Graves, W. Contrast effects of background factors on the similarity-attraction relationship. *Journal of Personality and Social Psychology,* 1973, *25,* 346–350.

Maslow, A. H. A theory of human motivation. *Psychological Review,* 1943, *50,* 370–396.

Maslow, A. H. *Motivation and personality.* New York: Harper & Row, 1954.

Maslow, A. H. Self-actualization and beyond. In J. F. T. Bugental (Ed.), *Challenges of humanistic psychology.* New York: McGraw-Hill, 1967. Pp. 279–286.

Maslow, A. H. *Motivation and personality* (2nd ed.). New York: Harper & Row, 1970.

Mason, H. N., Hornstein, H. A., & Tobin, T. A. Modeling, motivational interdependence, and helping. *Journal of Personality and Social Psychology,* 1973, *28,* 236–248.

Mathes, E. W., & Kahn, A. Diffusion of responsibility and extreme behavior. *Journal of Personality and Social Psychology,* 1975, *31,* 881–886.

Maurar, A. Corporal punishment. *American Psychologist,* 1974, *29,* 614–626.

Mayfield, E. C. The selection interview: A re-evaluation of published research. *Personnel Psychology,* 1964, *17,* 239–260.

Maykovich, M. K. Reciprocity in racial stereotypes: White, black, and yellow. *American Journal of Sociology,* 1972, *77,* 876–897.

Mazis, M. B. Cognitive tuning and receptivity to novel information. *Journal of Experimental Social Psychology,* 1973, *9,* 307–319.

Mazis, M. B. Anti-pollution measures and psychological reactance theory: A field experiment. *Journal of Personality and Social Psychology,* 1975, *31,* 654–660.

McArthur, L. A. The how and what of why: Some determinants and consequences of causal attribution. *Journal of Personality and Social Psychology,* 1972, *22,* 171–193.

McCain, G., & Segal, G. *The game of science* (2nd ed.). Monterey, Calif.: Brooks/Cole, 1973.

McCandless, B. R. Childhood socialization. In D. A. Goslin (Ed.), *Handbook of socialization theory and research.* Chicago: Rand McNally, 1969. Pp. 791–820.

McClelland, D. C. *The achieving society.* Princeton, N. J.: Van Nostrand, 1961.

McClintock, C. G. Personality syndromes and attitude change. *Journal of Personality,* 1958, *26,* 479–593.

McClintock, C. G. Game behavior and social motivation in interpersonal settings. In C. G. McClintock (Ed.), *Experimental social psychology.* New York: Holt, Rinehart and Winston, 1972.

McClintock, C. G., Gallo, P. S., & Harrison, A. A. Some effects of variations in the other's strategy upon cooperative game behavior. *Journal of Personality and Social Psychology,* 1965, *1,* 319–325.

McClintock, C. G., Harrison, A. A., Strand, S., & Gallo, P. G. Internationalism-isolationism, strategy of the other player, and two-person game behavior. *Journal of Abnormal and Social Psychology,* 1963, *67,* 631–635.

McClintock, C. G., & McNeel, S. P. Reward level and game playing behavior. *Journal of Conflict Resolution,* 1966, *10,* 98–102.

McClintock, C. G., & McNeel, S. P. Prior dyadic experience and monetary reward as determinants of cooperative behavior. *Journal of Personality and Social Psychology,* 1967, 5, 282–294.

McClintock, C. G., Nuttin, J., & McNeel, S. P. Sociometric choice, visual presence, and game playing behavior. *Behavioral Science,* 1970, 15, 124–131.

McDougall, W. *Introduction to social psychology.* London: Methuen, 1908.

McEvoy, J., & Miller, A. (Eds.). *Black power and student rebellion: Conflict on the American campus.* Belmont, Calif.: Wadsworth, 1969.

McGinnies, E. Emotionality and perceptual defense. *Psychological Review,* 1949, 56, 244–251.

McGregor, D. *The human side of enterprise.* New York: McGraw-Hill, 1960.

McGuire, W. J. Some impending reorientations in social psychology: Some thoughts provoked by Kenneth Ring. *Journal of Experimental Social Psychology,* 1967, 3, 124–139.

McGuire, W. J. The nature of attitudes and attitude change. In G. Lindzey & E. Aronson (Eds.), *Handbook of social psychology* (2nd ed.), Vol. 3. Reading, Mass.: Addison-Wesley, 1969. Pp. 136–314.

McGuire, W. J. The Yin and Yang of progress in social psychology. Seven koan. *Journal of Personality and Social Psychology,* 1973, 26, 446–456.

McNeil, E. B. *The concept of human development.* Belmont, Calif: Wadsworth, 1966.

McWhirter, N., & McWhirter, R. *Guinness book of world records: 1975 edition.* New York: Sterling, 1974.

Mead, M. *Sex and temperament in three primitive societies.* New York: Morrow, 1935.

Mehrabian, A. *Silent messages.* Belmont, Calif.: Wadsworth, 1971.

Mehrabian, A., & Diamond, S. G. Effects of furniture arrangements, props, and personality on social interaction. *Journal of Personality and Social Psychology,* 1971, 20, 18–30.

Meichenbaum, D. H. Examination of model characteristics in reducing avoidance behavior. *Journal of Personality and Social Psychology,* 1971, 17, 298–307.

Meltzer, L., Morris, W. N., & Hayes, D. P. Interruption outcomes and vocal amplitude: Explorations in social psychophysics. *Journal of Personality and Social Psychology,* 1971, 18, 392–402.

Menges, R. J. Openness and honesty versus coercion and deception in psychological research. *American Psychologist,* 1973, 28, 1030–1034.

Merton, R. K. Bureaucratic structure and personality. In R. K. Merton (Ed.), *Reader in bureaucracy.* Glencoe, Ill.: Free Press, 1952.

Merton, R. K. (Ed.). *Social theory and social structure.* New York: Free Press, 1957a.

Merton, R. K. Social structure and anomie *and* Continuities in the theory of social structure and anomie. In R. K. Merton (Ed.), *Social theory and social structure.* New York: Free Press, 1957b.

Meumann, E. Haus- und Schularbeit: Experimente an Kindern der Volkschule. *Die Deutsche Schule,* 1904, 8, 278–303; 337–359; 416–431. (Cited in R. B. Zajonc, *Social psychology: An experimental approach.* Monterey, Calif.: Brooks/Cole, 1966).

Meyer, M. Experimental studies in the psychology of music. *American Journal of Psychology,* 1903, 14, 456–476.

Michaelsen, L. K. Leader orientation, leader behavior, group effectiveness and situational favorability: An empirical extension of the contingency model. *Organizational Behavior and Human Performance,* 1973, 9, 226–245.

Milgram, S. Behavioral study of obedience. *Journal of Abnormal and Social Psychology,* 1963, 67, 371–378.

Milgram, S. Some conditions of obedience to authority. *Human Relations,* 1965a, 18, 57–76.

Milgram, S. Liberating effects of group pressure. *Journal of Personality and Social Psychology,* 1965b, 1, 127–134.

Milgram, S. The experience of living in cities. *Science,* 1970, 167, 1461–1468.

Milgram, S. *Obedience to authority.* New York: Harper & Row, 1974.

Miller, D. R. The study of social relationships. In S. Koch (Ed.), *Psychology: The study of a science* (Vol. 5). New York: McGraw-Hill, 1963. Pp. 639–737.

Miller, H., & Geller, D. Structural balance in dyads. *Journal of Personality and Social Psychology*, 1972, *21*, 135–138.

Miller, J. G. Toward a general theory for the behavioral sciences. *American Psychologist*, 1955, *10*, 513–531.

Miller, J. G. Information input overload and psychopathology. *American Journal of Psychiatry*, 1960, *116*, 695–704.

Miller, N., & Bugelski, R. Minor studies of aggression: II. The influence of frustrations imposed by the in-group on attitudes expressed toward the out-group. *Journal of Psychology*, 1948, *25*, 437–452.

Miller, N., & Campbell, D. T. Recency and primacy in persuasion as a function of the timing of speeches and measurements. *Journal of Abnormal and Social Psychology*, 1959, *59*, 1–9.

Miller, N., Campbell, C. T., Twedt, H., & O'Connell, E. Similarity, contrast, and complementarity in friendship choice. *Journal of Personality and Social Psychology*, 1966, *3*, 3–12.

Miller, N., & Dollard, J. *Social learning and imitation.* New Haven, Conn.: Yale University Press, 1941.

Mills, J. Comment on Bem's "Self perception: An alternative interpretation of cognitive dissonance phenomena." *Psychological Review*, 1967, *74*, 535.

Mills, J., & Harvey, J. Opinion change as a function of when information about the communicator is received and whether he is attractive or expert. *Journal of Personality and Social Psychology*, 1972, *21*, 52–55.

Mills, J., & Mintz, P. M. Effect of unexplained arousal on affiliation. *Journal of Personality and Social Psychology*, 1972, *24*, 11–13.

Milmoe, S., Novey, M. S., Kagan, J., & Rosenthal, R. The mother's voice: Postdictor of aspects of her baby's behavior. *Proceedings of the 76th Annual Convention of the American Psychological Association*, 1968. Pp. 463–464.

Milmoe, S., Rosenthal, R., Blane, H. T., Chafetz, M. E., & Wolf, I. The doctor's voice: Postdictor of successful referral of alcoholic patients. *Journal of Abnormal Psychology*, 1967, *72*, 78–84.

Minard, R. D. Race relations in the Pocahontas coal field. *Journal of Social Issues*, 1952, *8*, 29–44.

Mirels, H., & Mills, J. Perception of the pleasantness and competence of a partner. *Journal of Abnormal and Social Psychology*, 1964, *68*, 456–460.

Mischel, E., Ebbesen, E., & Zeiss, A. R. Cognitive and attentional mechanisms in delay of gratification. *Journal of Personality and Social Psychology*, 1972, *21*, 204–218.

Mischel, W. Preference for delayed reinforcement and social responsibility. *Journal of Abnormal and Social Psychology*, 1961, *62*, 1–7.

Mischel, W. *Personality and assessment.* New York: Wiley, 1968.

Mischel, W. Toward a cognitive social learning reconceptualization of personality. *Psychological Review*, 1973, *80*, 252–283.

Montagu, M. F. A. (Ed.). *Man and aggression.* New York: Oxford University Press, 1968.

Mooney, C. M. Petty paranoia. In R. D. Baker (Ed.), *Psychology in the wry.* Princeton, N. J.: Van Nostrand, 1963. Pp. 37–47.

Moore, H. T., & Gilliland, A. R. The immediate and long-term effects of classical and popular phonograph selections. *Journal of Applied Psychology*, 1924, *8*, 309–323.

Moore, L. M., & Baron, R. M. Effects of wage inequities on work attitudes and performance. *Journal of Experimental Social Psychology*, 1973, *9*, 1–16.

Moore, M. Forming impressions of others. In A. A. Harrison (Ed.), *Explorations in psychology.* Monterey, Calif.: Brooks/Cole, 1974.

Morgan, W. J. *The O. S. S. and I.* New York: Norton, 1957.

Morissette, J. An experimental study of the theory of structural balance. *Human Relations,* 1958, *11,* 239–254.

Morris, W. N. Manipulated attitude and interruption outcomes. *Journal of Personality and Social Psychology,* 1971, *20,* 319–331.

Morrison, B. J., & Hill, W. F. Socially facilitated reduction of the fear response in rats raised in groups or in isolation. *Journal of Comparative and Physiological Psychology,* 1967, *63,* 71–76.

Morse, N., & Reimer, E. The experimental change of a major organizational variable. *Journal of Abnormal and Social Psychology,* 1956, *52,* 120–129.

Moscovici, S., Lage, E., & Naffrechoux, M. Influence of a consistent minority on the responses of a majority in a color perception task. *Sociometry,* 1969, *32,* 365–380.

Moscovici, S., & Nemeth, C. Minority influence. In C. Nemeth (Ed.), *Social psychology: Classic and contemporary integrations.* Chicago: Rand McNally, 1974. Pp. 217–249.

Mosely, L. *On borrowed time.* New York: Pyramid Books, 1971.

Mull, H. K. The effect of repetition upon the enjoyment of modern music. *Journal of Psychology,* 1957, *43,* 155–162.

Murray, H. A. *Explorations in personality.* New York: Oxford University Press, 1938.

Murstein, B. A theory of marital choice and its applicability to marriage adjustment. In B. Murstein (Ed.), *Theories of attraction and love.* New York: Springer, 1971. Pp. 100–151.

Murstein, B. Physical attractiveness and marital choice. *Journal of Personality and Social Psychology,* 1972, *22,* 8–12.

Mussen, P. H. Early sex-role development. In D. A. Goslin (Ed.), *Handbook of socialization theory and research.* Chicago: Rand McNally, 1969.

Myers, A. Team competition, success, and the adjustment of group members. *Journal of Abnormal and Social Psychology,* 1962, *65,* 325–332.

Myrdal, G. How scientific are the social sciences? *Journal of Social Issues,* 1972, *28,* 151–170.

Nathanson, C. A., & Becker, M. H. Job satisfaction and job performance: An empirical test of some theoretical propositions. *Organizational Behavior and Human Performance,* 1973, *9,* 267–279.

National Training Laboratories. *Standards for the use of the laboratory method.* Washington, D. C., 1969.

Neale, J. M., & Liebert, R. M. *Science and behavior: An introduction to methods of research.* Englewood Cliffs, N. J.: Prentice-Hall, 1973.

Nelson, S. D. Nature/nurture revisited. I: A review of the biological bases of conflict. *Journal of Conflict Resolution,* 1974, *18,* 285–335.

Nemeth, C., & Wachtler, H. Consistency and modification of judgment. *Journal of Experimental Social Psychology,* 1973, *9,* 65–79.

Newberry, B. H. Truth telling in subjects with information about experiments: Who is being deceived? *Journal of Personality and Social Psychology,* 1973, *25,* 369–374.

Newcomb, T. M. *Personality and social change: Attitude formation in a student community.* New York: Holt, Rinehart and Winston, 1943.

Newcomb, T. M. An approach to the study of communicative acts. *Psychological Review,* 1953, *60,* 393–404.

Newcomb, T. M. *The acquaintance process.* New York: Holt, Rinehart and Winston, 1961.

Newcomb, T. M. Persistence and regression of changed attitudes: Long range studies. *Journal of Social Issues,* 1963, *19,* 3–14.

Newcomb, T. M. An approach to the study of communicative acts. In M. Fishbein (Ed.), *Readings in attitude theory and measurement.* New York: Wiley, 1967. Pp. 293–311.

Niles, P. *The relationships of susceptibility and anxiety to acceptance of fear-arousing communication.* Unpublished doctoral dissertation, Yale University, 1964. (Discussed in A. C. Elms, *Social psychology and social relevance.* Boston: Little, Brown, 1972.)

Nisbett, R. E., & Valins, S. Perceiving the causes of one's own behavior. In E. E. Jones,

D. E. Kanouse, H. H. Kelley, R. E. Nisbett, S. Valins, & B. Weiner, *Attribution: Perceiving the causes of behavior.* Morristown, N. J.: General Learning Press, 1972. Pp. 63–78.

Noel, R. C. Transgression-compliance: A failure to confirm. *Journal of Personality and Social Psychology.* 1973, *27*, 151–153.

Nosanchuk, T. A., & Lightstone, J. Canned laughter and public and private conformity. *Journal of Personality and Social Psychology,* 1974, *29*, 153–156.

Novak, D., & Lerner, M. Rejection as a consequence of perceived similarity. *Journal of Personality and Social Psychology,* 1968, *9*, 147–152.

O'Leary, V. E. Some attitudinal barriers to occupational aspirations in women. *Psychological Bulletin,* 1974, *81*, 809–826.

Orne, M. T. On the social psychology of the psychological experiment: With particular reference to demand characteristics and their implications. *American Psychologist,* 1962, *17*, 776–783.

Orne, M. T. Demand characteristics and the concept of quasi-controls. In R. Rosenthal & R. Rosnow (Eds.), *Artifacts in behavioral research.* New York: Academic Press, 1969. Pp. 143–179.

Osborn, A. F. *Applied imagination.* New York: Scribner's, 1957.

Osgood, C. E. *An alternative to war or surrender.* Urbana: University of Illinois Press, 1962.

Osgood, C. E. Escalation as a strategy. *War/Peace Reports,* 1965, *5*, 12–14.

Osgood, C. E., & Tannenbaum, P. H. The principle of congruity in the prediction of attitude change. *Psychological Review,* 1955, *62*, 42–55.

Oskamp, S. Attitudes towards U. S. and Russian actions: A double standard. *Psychological Reports,* 1965, *16*, 43–46.

Oskamp, S. Effect of preprogrammed strategies on cooperation in the Prisoner's Dilemma and other mixed-motive games. In L. S. Wrightsman, J. O'Connor, & N. J. Baker (Eds.), *Cooperation and competition: Readings on mixed-motive games.* Monterey, Calif.: Brooks/Cole, 1972. Pp. 147–188.

Oskamp, S., & Perlman, D. Factors affecting cooperation in a prisoner's dilemma game. *Journal of Conflict Resolution,* 1965, *9*, 359–374.

Oskamp, S., & Perlman, D. Effects of friendship and disliking on cooperation in a mixed-motive game. *Journal of Conflict Resolution,* 1966, *10*, 221–226.

Ostrom, T. M. The bogus pipeline: A new Ignis Fatuus? *Psychological Bulletin,* 1973, *79*, 252–259.

Owen, D. R. The 47, XYY male: A review. *Psychological Bulletin,* 1972, *78*, 209–233.

Page, M. M. Social psychology of a classical conditioning of attitudes experiment. *Journal of Personality and Social Psychology,* 1969, *11*, 177–186.

Page, M. M. Demand characteristics and the verbal operant conditioning experiment. *Journal of Personality and Social Psychology,* 1972, *23*, 372–378.

Page, M. M. Demand characteristics and the classical conditioning of attitudes experiment. *Journal of Personality and Social Psychology,* 1974, *30*, 468–476.

Pallak, M. S., & Pittman, T. S. General motivational effects of dissonance arousal. *Journal of Personality and Social Psychology,* 1972, *21*, 349–358.

Passini, F., & Norman, W. T. A universal conception of personality structure? *Journal of Personality and Social Psychology,* 1966, *4*, 44–49.

Pepitone, A. Review of *Aggression: A social learning analysis. Contemporary Psychology,* 1974, *19*, 769–771.

Pepitone, A., & Wilpizeski, C. Some consequences of experimental rejection. *Journal of Abnormal and Social Psychology,* 1960, *60*, 359–364.

Perlman, D., & Oskamp. S. The effects of picture content and exposure frequency on evaluations of Negroes and whites. *Journal of Experimental Social Psychology,* 1971, *7*, 503–515.

Perrow, C. *Organizational analysis: A sociological view.* Monterey, Calif.: Brooks/Cole, 1970.

Perry, P. Gallup poll election survey experience, 1950–1960. *Public Opinion Quarterly, 1962, 26,* 272–279.

Pessin, J. The comparative effects of social and mechanical stimulation on memorizing. *American Journal of Psychology, 1933, 45,* 263–270.

Peterson, R. C., & Thurstone, L. L. *Motion pictures and the social attitudes of children.* New York: Macmillan, 1933.

Pettigrew, T. F. *Racially separate or together?* New York: McGraw-Hill, 1971.

Pheterson, G. I., Kiesler, S. B., & Goldberg, P. A. Evaluation of the performance of women as a function of their sex, achievement, and personal history. *Journal of Personality and Social Psychology, 1971, 19,* 114–118.

Piaget, J. *The moral judgment of the child.* Glencoe, Ill.: Free Press, 1948.

Picek, J. S., Sherman, S. J., & Shiffrin, R. M. Cognitive organization and coding of social structures. *Journal of Personality and Social Psychology, 1975, 31,* 758–768.

Piliavin, I., Rodin, J., & Piliavin, J. Good Samaritanism: An underground phenomenon? *Journal of Personality and Social Psychology, 1969, 13,* 289–299.

Piliavin, J., & Piliavin, I. Effects of blood on reactions to a victim. *Journal of Personality and Social Psychology, 1972, 23,* 353–361.

Pilisuk, M., & Skolnick, P. Inducing trust: A test of the Osgood proposal. *Journal of Personality and Social Psychology, 1968, 8,* 121–133.

Pliner, P., Hart, H., Kohl, J., & Saari, D. Compliance without pressure: Some further data on the foot-in-the-door technique. *Journal of Experimental Social Psychology, 1974, 10,* 17–22.

Pomazal, R. J., & Clore, G. L. Helping on the highway: The effects of dependency and sex. *Journal of Applied Social Psychology, 1973, 3,* 150–164.

Porter, L. W., & Steers, R. M. Organizational, work, and personal factors in employee turnover and absenteeism. *Psychological Bulletin, 1973, 80,* 151–176.

Postman, L., Bruner, J. S., & McGinnies, E. Personal values as selective factors in perception. *Journal of Abnormal and Social Psychology, 1948, 43,* 142–154.

Potter, D. A. Personalism and interpersonal attraction. *Journal of Personality and Social Psychology, 1973, 28,* 192–198.

Price, K. O., Harburg, E., & Newcomb, T. M. Psychological balance in situations of negative interpersonal attitudes. *Journal of Personality and Social Psychology, 1966, 3,* 265–270.

Priest, R. F., & Sawyer, J. Proximity and peership: Bases of balance in interpersonal attraction. *American Journal of Sociology, 1967, 72,* 633–649.

Pruitt, D. G. Reward structure and cooperation: The decomposed Prisoner's Dilemma Game. *Journal of Personality and Social Psychology, 1967, 7,* 21–27.

Pruitt, D. G. Choice shifts in group discussion: An introductory review. *Journal of Personality and Social Psychology, 1971, 20,* 339–360.

Puckett, E. S. Productivity achievements—A measure of success. In F. G. Lesieur (Ed.), *The Scanlon plan.* Cambridge, Mass.: MIT Press, 1958.

Pugh, R. W. *Psychology and the black experience.* Monterey, Calif.: Brooks/Cole, 1972.

Quay, H. The effect of verbal reinforcement on the recall of early memories. *Journal of Abnormal and Social Psychology, 1959, 59,* 254–257.

Quey, R. L. Functions and dynamics of work groups. *American Psychologist, 1971, 26,* 1077–1082.

Rabbie, J. Differential preference for companionship under stress. *Journal of Abnormal and Social Psychology, 1963, 67,* 643–648.

Rabbie, J. M., Benoist, F., Oosterbaan, H., & Visser, L. Differential power and effects of expected competitive and cooperative intergroup interaction on intragroup and outgroup attitudes. *Journal of Personality and Social Psychology, 1974, 30,* 46–56.

Rabbie, J. M., & Horwitz, M. Arousal of ingroup-outgroup bias by chance win or loss. *Journal of Personality and Social Psychology, 1969, 13,* 269–277.

Rasmussen, E. E. Social facilitation in albino rats. *Acta Psychologica*, 1939, *4*, 275–294.

Reader, N., & English, H. B. Personality factors in adolescent female friendships. *Journal of Consulting Psychology*, 1947, *11*, 212–220.

Reddy, W. B. Screening and selection of participants. In L. Solomon & B. Berzon (Eds.), *New perspectives on encounter groups*. San Francisco: Jossey-Bass, 1972. Pp. 53–67.

Reeves, E. T. *The dynamics of group behavior*. New York: American Management Association, 1970.

Regan, D. T., & Cheng, J. B. Distraction and attitude change: A resolution. *Journal of Experimental Social Psychology*, 1973, *9*, 138–147.

Regan, D. T., Williams, M., & Sparling, S. Voluntary expiation of guilt: A field experiment. *Journal of Personality and Social Psychology*, 1972, *24*, 42–45.

Regan, J. W., & Brehm, J. W. Compliance in buying as a function of inducements that threaten freedom. In L. Bickman & T. Henchy (Eds.), *Beyond the laboratory: Field research in social psychology*. New York: McGraw-Hill, 1972. Pp. 269–274.

Riley, M., Cohn, W. R., Toby, J., & Riley, R. W., Jr. Interpersonal orientations in small groups: A consideration of the questionnaire approach. *American Sociological Review*, 1954, *19*, 715–724.

Rim, Y. Machiavellianism and decisions involving risks. *British Journal of Social and Clinical Psychology*, 1966, *5*, 36–50.

Ring, K. Experimental social psychology: Some sober questions about frivolous values. *Journal of Experimental Social Psychology*, 1967, *3*, 113–123.

Rodrigues, A. Effects of balance, positivity, and agreement in triadic social relations. *Journal of Personality and Social Psychology*, 1965, *5*, 472–476.

Roethlisberger, F., & Dickson, W. *Management and the worker*. Cambridge, Mass.: Harvard University Press, 1939.

Rogers, C. R. The process of the basic encounter group. In J. F. T. Bugental (Ed.), *Challenges of humanistic psychology*. New York: McGraw-Hill, 1967. Pp. 261–278.

Rogers, C. R. *On encounter groups*. New York: Harper & Row, 1970.

Rokeach, M., Smith, P. W., & Evans, R. I. Two kinds of prejudice or one? In M. Rokeach, *The open and closed mind*. New York: Basic Books, 1960. Pp. 196–210.

Rosen, I. C. The effects of the motion picture "Gentleman's Agreement" on attitudes towards Jews. *Journal of Psychology*, 1948, *26*, 525–536.

Rosen, S., Johnson, R. D., Johnson, M. J., & Tesser, A. Interactive effects of news valence and attraction on communicator behavior. *Journal of Personality and Social Psychology*, 1973, *28*, 298–300.

Rosenberg, M. When dissonance fails: On eliminating evaluation apprehension from attitude measurement. *Journal of Personality and Social Psychology*, 1965, *1*, 28–42.

Rosenberg, M. J., & Abelson, R. P. An analysis of cognitive balance. In C. I. Hovland & M. J. Rosenberg (Eds.), *Attitude organization and change*. New Haven, Conn.: Yale University Press, 1960.

Rosenberg, S., & Sedlak, A. Structural representations of implicit personality theory. In L. Berkowitz (Ed.), *Advances in experimental social psychology* (Vol. 6). New York: Academic Press, 1972.

Rosenhan, D. The natural socialization of altruistic autonomy. In J. Macauley & L. Berkowitz (Eds.), *Altruism and helping behavior: Social psychological studies of some antecedents and consequences*. New York: Academic Press, 1970. Pp. 251–268.

Rosenhan, D. Learning theory and prosocial behavior. *Journal of Social Issues*, 1972, *28*, 151–163.

Rosenthal, R. *Experimenter effects in behavioral research*. New York: Appleton-Century-Crofts, 1966.

Rosenthal, R., Archer, D., DiMatteo, M. R., Koivumaki, J. H., & Rogers, P. L. Body talk and tone of voice: The language without words. *Psychology Today*, 1974, *8*, 64–68.

Rosenthal, R., & Fode, K. The effect of experimental bias on the performance of the albino rat. *Behavioral Science, 1963, 8,* 183–189.

Rosenthal, R., & Jacobsen, L. *Pygmalion in the classroom: Teacher expectation and pupils' intellectual development.* New York: Holt, Rinehart and Winston, 1968.

Rosenthal, R., & Rosnow, R. (Eds.). *Artifact in behavioral research.* New York: Academic Press, 1969.

Rosnow, R. L., Goodstadt, B. E., Suls, J. M., & Gitter, A. G. More on the social psychology of the experiment: When compliance turns to self-defense. *Journal of Personality and Social Psychology, 1973, 27,* 337–343.

Rosnow, R., & Rosenthal, R. Volunteer effects in behavioral research. *New directions in psychology* (Vol. 4). New York: Holt, Rinehart and Winston, 1970. Pp. 213–277.

Ross, A. S. Effect of increased responsibility on bystander intervention: The presence of children. *Journal of Personality and Social Psychology, 1971, 19,* 306–310.

Ross, A. S., & Braband, J. Effect of increased responsibility on bystander intervention. II: The cue value of a blind person. *Journal of Personality and Social Psychology, 1973, 25,* 254–258.

Ross, E. A. *Social psychology.* New York: Macmillan, 1908.

Ross, I., & Zander, A. Need satisfaction and employee turnover. *Personnel Psychology, 1957, 10,* 327–338.

Ross, M., & Shulman, R. F. Increasing the salience of initial attitudes: Dissonance versus self-perception theory. *Journal of Personality and Social Psychology, 1973, 28,* 138–144.

Ross, S., & Kupferberg, H. A hero cop's own story: How he saved 25 hostages and 2 teenage bank robbers. *Parade Magazine,* July 14, 1974, pp. 10–15.

Rossi, A. Status of women in graduate departments of sociology. *American Sociologist, 1970, 5,* 1–12.

Rubin, Z. Measurement of romantic love. *Journal of Personality and Social Psychology, 1970, 16,* 265–273.

Rubin, Z. *Liking and loving: An invitation to social psychology.* New York: Holt, Rinehart and Winston, 1973.

Rubovits, P. C., & Maehr, M. L. Pygmalion black and white. *Journal of Personality and Social Psychology, 1973, 25,* 210–218.

Rump, E. E., & Delin, P. S. Differential accuracy in the status-height phenomenon and an experimenter effect. *Journal of Personality and Social Psychology, 1973, 28,* 343–347.

Runyan, D. L. The group risky-shift effect as a function of emotional bonds, actual consequences, and extent of responsibility. *Journal of Personality and Social Psychology, 1974, 29,* 670–676.

Saegert, S. C., & Jellison, J. Effects of initial level of response competition and frequency of exposure on liking and exploratory behavior. *Journal of Personality and Social Psychology, 1970, 16,* 553–558.

Saegert, S. C., Swap, W., & Zajonc, R. B. Exposure, context, and interpersonal attraction. *Journal of Personality and Social Psychology, 1973, 25,* 234–242.

Sales, S. Need for stimulation as a factor in social behavior. *Journal of Personality and Social Psychology, 1971, 19,* 124–134.

Sales, S. Economic threat as a determinant of conversion rates in authoritarian and non-authoritarian churches. *Journal of Personality and Social Psychology, 1972, 23,* 420–428.

Sales, S. Threat as a factor in authoritarianism. *Journal of Personality and Social Psychology, 1973, 28,* 44–57.

Sales, S., Guydosh, R. M., & Iacono, W. Relationship between "strength of the nervous system" and the "need for stimulation." *Journal of Personality and Social Psychology, 1974, 29,* 16–22.

Sarbin, T. R., & Allen, V. L. Increasing participation in a natural group setting: A preliminary report. *Psychological Record, 1968, 18,* 1–7.

Sarnoff, I., & Zimbardo, P. Anxiety, fear, and social affiliation. *Journal of Abnormal and Social Psychology*, 1961, *62*, 356–363.

Sasfy, J., & Okun, M. Form of evaluation and audience expertness as joint determinants of audience effects. *Journal of Experimental Social Psychology*, 1974, *10*, 461–467.

Sashkin, M., Morris, W. C., & Horst, L. A comparison of social and organizational change models: Information flow and data use processes. *Psychological Review*, 1973, *80*, 510–526.

Savicki, V. Outcomes of nonreciprocal self-disclosure strategies. *Journal of Personality and Social Psychology*, 1972, *23*, 271–276.

Scanlon, J. N. Profit sharing under collective bargaining: Three case studies. *Industrial and Labor Relations Review*, 1948, *2*, 58–75.

Schachter, S. Deviation, rejection, and communication. *Journal of Abnormal and Social Psychology*, 1951, *46*, 190–207.

Schachter, S. *The psychology of affiliation.* Stanford, Calif.: Stanford University Press, 1959.

Schachter, S. The interaction of cognitive and physiological determinants of emotional state. In L. Berkowitz (Ed.), *Advances in experimental social psychology* (Vol.1). New York: Academic Press, 1964. Pp. 49–80.

Schachter, S. Obesity and eating. *Science.* 1968, *161*, 751–756.

Schachter, S. Some extraordinary facts about obese humans and rats. *American Psychologist*, 1971, *26*, 129–144.

Schachter, S., & Burdick, H. A field experiment of rumor transmission and distortion. *Journal of Abnormal and Social Psychology*, 1955, *50*, 363–372.

Schachter, S., Ellertson, N., McBride, D., & Gregory, D. An experimental study of cohesiveness and productivity. *Human Relations*, 1951, *4*, 229–238.

Schachter, S., & Singer, J. Cognitive, social and physiological determinants of emotional state. *Psychological Review*, 1962, *69*, 379–399.

Schaps, E. Cost, dependency, and helping. *Journal of Personality and Social Psychology*, 1972, *21*, 74–78.

Scheflen, K. D., Lawler, E. E., & Hackman, J. R. Long-term impact of employee participation in the development of pay incentive plans: A field experiment revisited. *Journal of Applied Psychology*, 1971, *55*, 182–186.

Schein, E. H. The Chinese indoctrination program for prisoners of war: A study of attempted "brainwashing." In E. Maccoby, T. M. Newcomb, & E. L. Hartley (Eds.), *Reading in social psychology* (3rd ed.). New York: Holt, Rinehart and Winston, 1958.

Schelling, T. C. *The strategy of conflict.* Cambridge: Harvard University Press, 1960.

Schlenker, B. R. Social psychology and science. *Journal of Personality and Social Psychology*, 1974, *29*, 1–15.

Schmitt, D. R., & Marwell, G. Withdrawal and reward reallocation as responses to inequity. *Journal of Experimental Social Psychology*, 1972, *8*, 207–221.

Schneider, D. J. Implicit personality theory: A review. *Psychological Bulletin*, 1973, *79*, 294–309.

Schneider, D. J., & Eustis, A. C. Effects of ingratiation motivation, target positiveness, and revealingness of self-presentation. *Journal of Personality and Social Psychology*, 1972, *22*, 149–155.

Schultz, S. P. Panic in the military. In *The study of leadership* (Vol. 2). West Point, N.Y.: United States Military Academy, 1972. Pp. 21-2 through 21-12.

Schwartz, S. Words, deeds, and the perception of consequences and responsibility in action situations. *Journal of Personality and Social Psychology*, 1968, *10*, 232–242.

Schwartz, S. Normative explanations of helping behavior: A critique, proposal, and empirical test. *Journal of Experimental Social Psychology*, 1973, *9*, 349–364.

Schwartz, S., & Clausen, G. Responsibility, norms, and helping in an emergency. *Journal of Personality and Social Psychology*, 1970, *16*, 299–310.

Scontrino, M. P. The effects of fulfilling and violating group members' expectations about leadership style. *Organizational Behavior and Human Performance*, 1972, *8*, 118–138.

Scott, J. F. The American college sorority: Its role in class and ethnic endogamy. *American Sociological Review*, 1965, *30*, 514–527.

Scott, J. P. The social psychology of infrahuman animals. In G. Lindzey & E. Aronson (Eds.), *Handbook of social psychology* (2nd ed.), Vol. 4. Reading, Mass.: Addison-Wesley, 1969.

Scott, W. A. Attitude change by response reinforcement: Replication and extension. *Sociometry*, 1959, *22*, 328–335.

Sears, R. R., Hovland, C. I., & Miller, N. E. Minor studies of aggression: 1. Measurement of aggressive behavior. *Journal of Psychology*, 1940, *9*, 275–279.

Seashore, S. E. *Group cohesiveness in the industrial work group.* Ann Arbor: University of Michigan Press, 1954.

Seashore, S. E., & Bowers, D. G. Durability of organizational change. *American Psychologist*, 1970, *25*, 227–233.

Seaven, W. B. Effects of naturally induced teacher expectancies. *Journal of Personality and Social Psychology*, 1973, *28*, 333–342.

Segal, M. W. Alphabet and attraction: An unobtrusive measure of the effect of propinquity in a field setting. *Journal of Personality and Social Psychology*, 1974, *30*, 654–657.

Selznik, P. *Leadership in administration.* Evanston, Ill.: Row, Peterson, 1957.

Sensenig, J., & Brehm, J. W. Attitude change from an implied threat to attitudinal freedom. *Journal of Personality and Social Psychology*, 1968, *8*, 324–330.

Sermat, V. Is game behavior related to behavior in other situations? *Journal of Personality and Social Psychology*, 1970, *16*, 92–109.

Sermat, V., & Smyth, M. Content analysis of verbal communication in the development of a relationship. *Journal of Personality and Social Psychology*, 1973, *26*, 332–346.

Seyfried, B. A., & Hendrick, C. When do opposites attract? When they are opposite in sex-role attitudes. *Journal of Personality and Social Psychology*, 1973, *25*, 15–20.

Shaw, M. E. Some effects of problem complexity upon problem solution efficiency in different communications nets. *Journal of Experimental Psychology*, 1954, *48*, 211–217.

Shaw, M. E. Communication networks. In L. Berkowitz (Ed.), *Advances in experimental social psychology* (Vol. 1). New York: Academic Press, 1964. Pp. 111–147.

Shaw, M. E. *Group dynamics: The psychology of small group behavior.* New York: McGraw-Hill, 1971.

Shaw, M., & Costanzo, P. *Theories of social psychology.* New York: McGraw-Hill, 1970.

Sherif, M. *The psychology of group norms.* New York: Harper & Row, 1936.

Sherif, M. *Group conflict and co-operation: Their social psychology.* London: Routledge & Kegan Paul, Ltd., 1967.

Sherif, M., Harvey, O., White, B., Hood, W., & Sherif, C. *Intergroup conflict and cooperation: The robbers' cave experiment.* Norman, Okla.: Institute of Group Relations, University of Oklahoma, 1961.

Sherif, M., & Sherif, C. W. *Social psychology.* New York: Harper & Row, 1969.

Sherman, S. J. Effects of choice and incentive on attitude change in a discrepant behavior situation. *Journal of Personality and Social Psychology*, 1970, *15*, 245–252.

Sherwood, J. J., Baron, J. W., & Fitch, H. G. Cognitive dissonance: Theory and research. In R. V. Wagner & J. J. Sherwood (Eds.), *The study of attitude change.* Monterey, Calif.: Brooks/Cole, 1969. Pp. 56–86.

Shirer, W. L. *The collapse of the third republic.* New York: Pocket Books, 1971.

Shostrom, E. L. Group therapy: Let the buyer beware. *Psychology Today*, 1969, *4*, 37–40.

Siegal, A. E., & Siegal, S. Reference groups, membership groups, and attitude change. *Journal of Abnormal and Social Psychology*, 1957, *55*, 360–364.

Siegel, A. L., & Ruh, R. A. Job involvement, participation in decision making, personal background, and job behavior. *Organizational Behavior and Human Performance,* 1973, *9,* 318–327.

Sigall, H., & Aronson, E. Liking for an evaluator as a function of her physical attractiveness and nature of the evaluations. *Journal of Experimental Social Psychology,* 1969, *5,* 93–100.

Sigall, H., Arsonson, E., & VanHoose, T. The cooperative subject: Myth or reality? *Journal of Experimental Social Psychology,* 1970, *6,* 1–10.

Sigall, H., & Landy, D. Radiating beauty: Effects of having a physically attractive partner on person perception. *Journal of Personality and Social Psychology,* 1973, *28,* 218–224.

Sigall, H., & Page, R. Current stereotypes: A little fading, a little faking. *Journal of Personality and Social Psychology,* 1971, *18,* 247–255.

Silverman, B. I. Consequences, racial discrimination, and the principle of belief congruence. *Journal of Personality and Social Psychology,* 1974, *29,* 496–508.

Silverman, B. I., & Cochrane, R. Effect of the social context on the principle of belief congruence. *Journal of Personality and Social Psychology,* 1972, *22,* 259–268.

Silverman, I. On the resolution and tolerance of cognitive consistency in a natural-occurring event: Attitudes and beliefs following the Senator Edward M. Kennedy incident. *Journal of Personality and Social Psychology,* 1971, *17,* 171–178.

Simmons, C., & Lerner, M. Altruism as a search for justice. *Journal of Personality and Social Psychology,* 1968, *9,* 216–225.

Simpson, G. E., & Yinger, J. M. *Racial and cultural minorities: An analysis of prejudice and discrimination.* New York: Harper & Row, 1958.

Singer, J. E. The use of manipulative strategies: Machiavellianism and attractiveness. *Sociometry,* 1964, *27,* 128–150.

Singer, J. E., Brush, C. A., & Lublin, S. C. Some aspects of deindividuation: Identification and conformity. *Journal of Experimental Social Psychology,* 1965, *1,* 356–378.

Sistrunk, F., & McDavid, J. Sex variable in conforming behavior. *Journal of Personality and Social Psychology,* 1971, *17,* 200–207.

Skolnick, P. Reactions to personal evaluations: A failure to replicate. *Journal of Personality and Social Psychology,* 1971, *18,* 62–67.

Skousen, W. C. Chief, watch out for those T-group promoters! *Law and Order,* November 1967. Pp. 10–12; 70.

Slater, P. E. Role differentiation in small groups. *American Sociological Review,* 1955, *20,* 300–310.

Smith, E. E. The power of dissonance techniques to change attitudes. *Public Opinion Quarterly,* 1961, *25,* 626–639.

Smith, G. F., & Dorfman, D. D. The effect of stimulus uncertainty on the relationship between frequency of exposure and liking. *Journal of Personality and Social Psychology,* 1975, *31,* 150–156.

Smith, M. B., Bruner, J. S., & White, R. W. *Opinions and personality.* New York: Wiley, 1956.

Smith, R. E., Smythe, L., & Lien, D. Inhibition of helping behavior by a similar or dissimilar nonreactive fellow bystander. *Journal of Personality and Social Psychology,* 1972, *23,* 414–419.

Smoke, W., & Zajonc, R. B. On the reliability of group judgments and decisions. In J. Criswell, H. Solomon, & P. Suppes (Eds.), *Mathematical methods in small group processes.* Stanford, Calif.: Stanford University Press, 1962.

Solomon, L. The influence of some types of power relationships and game strategies upon the development of interpersonal trust. *Journal of Abnormal and Social Psychology,* 1960, *61,* 223–230.

Solomon, L. N. Inquiry through encounter. In B. Marshall (Ed.), *Experiences in being.* Monterey, Calif.: Brooks/Cole, 1971.

Solomon, L. N., & Berzon, B. *New perspectives on encounter groups.* San Francisco: Jossey-Bass, 1972.

Solomon, R. L., & Howes, D. H. Word frequency, personal values, and visual duration thresholds. *Psychological Review*, 1951, *58*, 256–270.

Sommer, R. Further studies of small group ecology. *Sociometry*, 1965, *28*, 237–248.

Sommer, R. Sociofugal space. *American Journal of Sociology*, 1967, *72*, 654–660.

Sommer, R. *Personal space.* Englewood Cliffs, N. J.: Prentice-Hall, 1969.

Sommer, R. *Tight spaces: Hard architecture and how to humanize it.* Englewood Cliffs, N.J.: Prentice-Hall, 1974.

Sommer, R., & Becker, F. D. Territorial defense and the good neighbor. *Journal of Personality and Social Psychology*, 1969, *11*, 85–92.

Sosis, R. H. Internal-external control and the perception of responsibility for an accident. *Journal of Personality and Social Psychology*, 1974, *30*, 393–399.

Spector, A. J. Fulfillment and morale. *Journal of Abnormal and Social Psychology*, 1956, *52*, 51–56.

Spielberger, C. D. The role of awareness in verbal conditioning. In C. W. Eriksen (Ed.), *Behavior and awareness.* Durham, N.C.: Duke University Press, 1962.

Spielberger, C. D., & DeNike, L. D. Descriptive behaviorism versus cognitive theory in verbal operant conditioning. *Psychological Review*, 1966, *73*, 306–326.

Stagner, R. *Psychological aspects of international conflict.* Monterey, Calif.: Brooks/Cole, 1967.

Stang, D. J. Conformity, ability, and self-esteem. *Representative Research in Social Psychology*, 1972, *3*, 97–103.

Stang, D. J. Effect of interaction rate on ratings of leadership and liking. *Journal of Personality and Social Psychology*, 1973a, *27*, 405–408.

Stang, D. J. Theories of novelty and affect: An empirical evaluation (Doctoral dissertation, University of Syracuse, 1973). Ann Arbor, Mich.: University Microfilms No. 74-8318, 1973b.

Stang, D. J. Methodological factors in mere exposure research. *Psychological Bulletin*, 1974, *81*, 1014–1025.

Staub, E., & Baer, R. S., Jr. Stimulus characteristics of a sufferer and difficulty of escape as determinants of helping. *Journal of Personality and Social Psychology*, 1974, *30*, 279–284.

Stein, D. D., Hardyck, J. E., & Smith, M. B. Race and belief: An open and shut case. *Journal of Personality and Social Psychology*, 1965, *1*, 281–289.

Stein, R. T., Geis, F. L., & Damarin, F. Perception of emergent leadership hierarchies in task groups. *Journal of Personality and Social Psychology*, 1973, *28*, 77–87.

Steiner, I. D. Whatever happened to the group in social psychology? *Journal of Experimental Social Psychology*, 1974, *10*, 94–108.

Steiner, I. D., & Johnson, H. Authoritarianism and "tolerance of trait inconsistency." *Journal of Abnormal and Social Psychology*, 1963, *67*, 388–391.

Steinzor, B. The spatial factor in face-to-face discussion groups. *Journal of Abnormal and Social Psychology*, 1950, *45*, 552–555.

Stephan, W., Berscheid, E., & Walster, E. Sexual arousal and heterosexual perception. *Journal of Personality and Social Psychology*, 1971, *20*, 93–101.

Stodgill, R. M. Group productivity, drive, and cohesiveness. *Organizational Behavior and Human Performance*, 1972, *8*, 26–43.

Stoner, J. A. F. *A comparison of individual and group decisions involving risk.* Unpublished master's thesis, M. I. T., Sloan School of Management, 1961.

Stricker, L. J., Jacobs, P. I., & Kogan, N. Trait interrelations in implicit personality theories and questionnaire data. *Journal of Personality and Social Psychology*, 1974, *30*, 198–207.

Stricker, L. J., Messick, S., & Jackson, D. N. Conformity, anticonformity, and independence: Their dimensionality and generality. *Journal of Personality and Social Psychology*, 1970, *16*, 494–507.

Strickland, L. Surveillance and trust. *Journal of Personality*, 1958, *26*, 200–215.

Strodtbeck, F. L. Husband-wife interaction over revealed differences. *American Sociological Review*, 1951, *16*, 468–473.

Stroebe, W., Insko, C. A., Thompson, V. D., & Layton, B. D. Effects of physical attractiveness, attitude similarity, and sex on various aspects of interpersonal attraction. *Journal of Personality and Social Psychology*, 1971, *18*, 79–91.

Stroop, J. B. Is the judgment of the group better than that of the average member of the group? *Journal of Experimental Psychology*, 1932, *15*, 550–560.

Stryker, P. How executives get jobs. *Fortune*, August 1953, p. 182. Cited in E. Goffman, *The presentation of self in everyday life*. New York: Anchor Books, 1953.

Stumphauzer, J. S. Increased delay of gratification in young prison inmates through imitation of high-delay peer models. *Journal of Personality and Social Psychology*, 1972, *21*, 10–17.

Super, D. E., & Bohn, J. *Occupational psychology*. Monterey, Calif.: Brooks/Cole, 1970.

Susman, G. I. Automation, alienation, and work group autonomy. *Human Relations*, 1972, *25*, 176–180.

Swingle, P. G., & Gillis, J. S. Effects of the emotional relations between protagonists in the Prisoner's Dilemma. *Journal of Personality and Social Psychology*, 1968, *8*, 160–165.

Tajfel, H. Social and cultural factors in perception. In G. Lindzey & E. Aronson (Eds.), *Handbook of social psychology* (2nd ed.), Vol. 3. Reading, Mass.: Addison-Wesley, 1969. Pp. 315–394.

Tajfel, H., & Billig, M. Familiarity and categorization in intergroup behavior. *Journal of Experimental Social Psychology*, 1974, *10*, 159–170.

Tajfel, H., & Cawasjee, S. D. Values and the accentuation of judged differences: A confirmation. *Journal of Abnormal and Social Psychology*, 1959, *59*, 436–439.

Tannenbaum, A. S. *Social psychology of the work organization*. Monterey, Calif.: Brooks/Cole, 1966.

Taylor, A. J. P. *Illustrated history of the first world war*. New York: G. P. Putnam's Sons, 1964.

Taylor, D. A. Self-disclosure as an exchange process: Reinforcement effects. Paper presented at a symposium on exchange theory and interpersonal relationships at the 81st Annual Convention of the American Psychological Association, Montreal, Canada, August 1973.

Taylor, D. A., & Altman, I. *Intimacy scaled stimuli for use in research of interpersonal exchange*. Bethesda, Md.: Naval Medical Research Institute, Technical Report No. 9, MF022.01.03-1002, May 1966.

Taylor, D. A., Altman, I., & Sorrentino, R. Interpersonal exchange as a function of rewards and costs and situational factors: Expectancy confirmation-disconfirmation. *Journal of Experimental Social Psychology*, 1969, *5*, 324–339.

Taylor, D. W., Berry, P. C., & Block, C. H. Does group participation when using brainstorming facilitate or inhibit creative thinking? *Administrative Science Quarterly*, 1958, *3*, 23–47.

Taylor, F. W. *Scientific management*. New York: Harper & Row, 1911.

Taylor, S., & Mettee, D. When similarity breeds contempt. *Journal of Personality and Social Psychology*, 1971, *20*, 75–81.

Tedeschi, J., Lindskold, S., Horai, J., & Gahagan, J. Social power and the credibility of promises. *Journal of Personality and Social Psychology*, 1969, *13*, 253–261.

Tedeschi, J. T., Smith, R. B. III, & Brown, R. C. A reinterpretation of research on aggression. *Psychological Bulletin*, 1974, *81*, 540–562.

Teichman, Y. Emotional arousal and affiliation. *Journal of Experimental Social Psychology*, 1973, *9*, 591–605.

Terhune, K. W. The effects of personality in cooperation and conflict. In P. Swingle (Ed.), *The structure of conflict*. New York: Academic Press, 1970. Pp. 193–234.

Thalhofer, N. N. Responsibility, reparation, and self-protection as reasons for three types of helping. *Journal of Personality and Social Psychology*, 1971, *19*, 144–151.

Tharp, R. G. Psychological patterning in marriage. *Psychological Bulletin*, 1963, *60*, 97–117.

Thelen, M. H., McGuire, D., Simmonds, D. W., & Akamatsu, T. J. Effect of model reward on the observer's recall of the modeled behavior. *Journal of Personality and Social Psychology*, 1974, *29*, 140–144.

Thibaut, J. W., & Kelley, H. H. *The social psychology of groups.* New York: Wiley, 1959.

Thomas, E. J., & Biddle, B. J. The nature and history of role theory. In B. J. Biddle & E. J. Thomas (Eds.), *Role theory: Concepts and research.* New York: Wiley, 1965.

Thomas, E. J., & Fink, C. Effects of group size. *Psychological Bulletin*, 1963, *60*, 371–384.

Thompson, D. F., & Meltzer, L. Communication of emotional intent by facial expression. *Journal of Abnormal and Social Psychology*, 1964, *68*, 129–135.

Thorndike, E. L., & Lorge, I. *The teacher's wordbook of 30,000 words.* New York: Teachers College, Columbia University Press, 1944.

Throm, E. L. *Popular Mechanic's picture history of American transportation.* New York: Simon & Schuster, 1952.

Toch, H. *Violent men: An inquiry into the psychology of violence.* Chicago: Aldine, 1969.

Toch, H. H., & Schulte, R. Readiness to perceive violence as a result of police training. *British Journal of Psychology*, 1961, *52*, 383–393.

Toffler, A. *Future shock.* New York: Bantam Books, 1970.

Toman, W. The duplication theorem of social relationships as tested in the general population. *Psychological Review*, 1971, *78*, 380–390.

Touhey, J. C. Attribution of person concepts by role accessibility and interaction outcomes. *Journal of Social Psychology*, 1972a, *87*, 269–272.

Touhey, J. C. Comparison of two dimensions of attitude similarity on heterosexual attraction. *Journal of Personality and Social Psychology*, 1972b, *23*, 8–10.

Travis, E. J. An investigation of the rational decision making, cooperation, greed, punishment, and withdrawal manifested by schizophrenics in several experimental conflict situations. *Dissertation Abstracts*, 1966, *26*, 7449.

Travis, L. E. The effects of a small audience upon hand-eye coordination. *Journal of Abnormal and Social Psychology*, 1925, *20*, 142–146.

Traylor, G. Joking in a bush camp. *Human Relations*, 1973, *26*, 479–486.

Triandis, H. C., & Fishbein, M. Cognitive interaction in person perception. *Journal of Abnormal and Social Psychology*, 1964, *78*, 469–478.

Triplett, N. The dynamogenic factors in pacemaking and competition. *American Journal of Psychology*, 1897, *9*, 507–553.

Trist, E. L., & Bamforth, K. W. Some social and psychological consequences of the longwall method of coal-getting. *Human Relations*, 1951, *4*, 3–38.

Trist, E. L., Higgins, G. W., Murray, H., & Pollock, A. B. *Organizational choice.* London: Tavistock, 1963.

Tuddenham, R. C. Correlates of yielding to a distorted group norm. *Journal of Personality*, 1959, *27*, 272–284.

Turner, C. W., & Simons, L. S. Effects of subject sophistication and evaluation apprehension on aggressive responses to weapons. *Journal of Personality and Social Psychology*, 1974, *30*, 341–348.

Uranowitz, S. W. Helping and self-attributions: A field experiment. *Journal of Personality and Social Psychology*, 1975, *31*, 852–854.

Valins, S. Cognitive effects of false heart-rate feedback. *Journal of Personality and Social Psychology*, 1966, *4*, 400–408.

Valins, S., & Ray, A. A. Effects of cognitive desensitization on avoidance behavior. *Journal of Personality and Social Psychology*, 1967, *7*, 345–350.

Venn, J. R., & Short, J. G. Vicarious classical conditioning of emotional responses in nursery school children. *Journal of Personality and Social Psychology*, 1973, *28*, 249–255.

Verveer, E. M., Barry, H., Jr., & Bousfield, W. A. Change in affectivity with repetition. *American Journal of Psychology*, 1933, *45*, 130–134.

Vinacke, W. E. Variables in experimental games: Toward a field theory. *Psychological Bulletin*, 1969, *71*, 293–318.

Vinokur, A. Review and theoretical analysis of the effects of group processes upon individual and group decisions involving risk. *Psychological Bulletin*, 1971a, *76*, 231–250.

Vinokur, A. Cognitive and affective processes influencing risk taking in groups: An expected utility approach. *Journal of Personality and Social Psychology*, 1971b, *20*, 472–486.

Voissem, N. H., & Sistrunk, F. Communication schedule and cooperative game behavior. *Journal of Personality and Social Psychology*, 1971, *19*, 160–167.

Vroom, V. *Work and motivation*. New York: Wiley, 1964.

Vroom, V. Industrial social psychology. In G. Lindzey & E. Aronson (Eds.), *Handbook of social psychology* (2nd ed.), Vol. 5. Reading, Mass.: Addison-Wesley, 1969. Pp. 196–268.

Vroom, V. H., Grant, L. D., & Cotton, T. S. The consequences of social interaction in group problem solving. *Organizational Behavior and Human Performance*, 1969, *4*, 77–95.

Wager, L. W. Organizational "linking pins": Hierarchical status and communicative roles in interlevel conferences. *Human Relations*, 1972, *25*, 307–326.

Wagner, C., & Wheeler, L. Model, need, and cost effects in helping behavior. *Journal of Personality and Social Psychology*, 1969, *12*, 111–116.

Wagner, R. V. Complementary needs, role expectations, interpersonal attraction, and the stability of working relationships. *Journal of Personality and Social Psychology*, 1975, *32*, 116–124.

Walker, C. R., & Guest, H. *The man on the assembly line*. Cambridge, Mass.: Harvard University Press, 1952.

Wallach, M. A., Kogan, N., & Bem, D. J. Group influence on individual risk taking. *Journal of Abnormal and Social Psychology*, 1962, *65*, 75–86.

Wallach, M. A., Kogan, N., & Bem, D. J. Diffusion of responsibility and level of risk taking in groups. *Journal of Abnormal and Social Psychology*, 1964, *68*, 263–274.

Wallington, S. A. Consequences of transgression: Self-punishment and depression. *Journal of Personality and Social Psychology*, 1973, *28*, 1–7.

Walster, E. Passionate love. In B. Murstein (Ed.), *Theories of attraction and love*. New York: Springer, 1971. Pp. 85–99.

Walster, E., Aronson, E., & Abrahams, D. On increasing the persuasiveness of a low prestige communicator. *Journal of Experimental Social Psychology*, 1966, *2*, 325–342.

Walster, E., Aronson, V., Abrams, D., & Rottman, L. Importance of physical attractiveness in dating behavior. *Journal of Personality and Social Psychology*, 1966, *4*, 508–516.

Walster, E., Berscheid, E., & Walster, G. W. New directions in equity research. *Journal of Personality and Social Psychology*, 1973, *25*, 151–176.

Walster, E., & Festinger, L. The effectiveness of "overheard" persuasive communications. *Journal of Abnormal and Social Psychology*, 1962, *65*, 395–402.

Walster, E., Walster, G. W., & Berscheid, E. The efficacy of playing hard-to-get. *Journal of Experimental Education*, 1971, *39*, 73–77.

Walster, E., Walster, G. W., & Lambert, P. Playing hard to get: A field study. University of Wisconsin, Madison. Unpublished report. (Cited in E. Walster, G. W. Walster, J. Piliavin, & L. Schmidt, Playing hard to get: Understanding an elusive phenomenon. *Journal of Personality and Social Psychology*, 1973, *26*, 113–121.)

Walster, E., Walster, G. W., Piliavin, J., & Schmidt, L. Playing hard to get: Understanding an elusive phenomenon. *Journal of Personality and Social Psychology*, 1973, *26*, 113–121.

Watson, S. G. Judgment of emotion from facial and contextual cue combinations. *Journal of Personality and Social Psychology*, 1922, *24*, 334–342.

Wattenberg, B. J. *The real America: A surprising examination of the state of the union*. New York: Doubleday, 1974.

Webb, E., Campbell, D., Schwartz, R., & Sechrest, L. *Unobtrusive measures: Nonreactive research in the social sciences.* Chicago: Rand McNally, 1966.

Weber, M. The essentials of bureaucratic organization: An ideal type construction. In R. K. Merton (Ed.), *Reader in bureaucracy.* Glencoe, Ill.: Free Press, 1952.

Weber, S. J., & Cook, T. D. Subject effects in laboratory research: An examination of subject roles, demand characteristics, and valid inference. *Psychological Bulletin, 1972, 77,* 273–295.

Webster, M. Psychological reductionism, methodological individualism, and large-scale problems. *American Sociological Review, 1973, 38,* 258–273.

Weick, K. E., & Gilfallan, D. P. Fate of arbitrary traditions in a laboratory microculture. *Journal of Personality and Social Psychology, 1971, 17,* 179–191.

Weiner, B., Frieze, I., Kukla, A., Reed, L., Rest, S., & Rosenbaum, R. M. Perceiving the causes of success and failure. In E. E. Jones, D. E. Kanouse, H. H. Kelley, R. E. Nisbett, S. Valins, & B. Weiner, *Attribution: Perceiving the causes of behavior.* Morristown, N.J.: General Learning Press, 1972. Pp. 95–120.

Weiss, J. H. Effect of professional training and amount and accuracy of information on behavioral prediction. *Journal of Consulting Psychology, 1963, 27,* 257–262.

Weiss, R. F., & Miller, F. G. The drive theory of social facilitation. *Psychological Review, 1971, 78,* 44–57.

Weiss, W. Effects of mass media of communication. In G. Lindzey & E. Aronson (Eds.), *Handbook of social psychology* (Vol. 5). Reading, Mass.: Addison-Wesley, 1969. Pp. 77–195.

Weitzman, L. J., Eiffler, D., Hokada, E., & Ross, C. Sex-role socialization in picture books for preschool children. *American Journal of Sociology, 1972, 77,* 1125–1150.

White, G. M. Immediate and deferred effects of model observation and guided and unguided rehearsal on donating and stealing. *Journal of Personality and Social Psychology, 1972, 21,* 139–148.

White, H. A., & Schumsky, D. A. Prior information and "awareness" in verbal conditioning. *Journal of Personality and Social Psychology, 1972, 24,* 162–165.

White, R. K. Misperception as a cause of two world wars. *Journal of Social Issues, 1966, 23,* 1–19.

White, R., & Lippit, R. *Autocracy and democracy.* New York: Harper & Row, 1960.

Whyte, W. *Street corner society.* Chicago: University of Chicago Press, 1943.

Wichman, H. Effects of isolation and communication on cooperation in a two-person game. *Journal of Personality and Social Psychology, 1970, 16,* 114–120.

Wicker, A. W. Attitudes vs. actions: The relationship of verbal and overt behavioral responses to attitude objects. *Journal of Social Issues, 1969, 25,* 41–78.

Wicker, A. W., & Pomazal, R. J. The relationship between attitudes and behavior as a function of specificity of attitude object and presence of a significant person during assessment conditions. *Representative Research in Social Psychology, 1971, 2,* 26–31.

Wiener, M., Devoe, S., Rubinow, S., & Geller, J. Nonverbal behavior and nonverbal communication. *Psychological Review, 1972, 79,* 185–214.

Wilhelmy, R. A., & Duncan, B. L. Cognitive reversibility in dissonance reduction. *Journal of Personality and Social Psychology, 1974, 29,* 806–811.

Wilkening, H. E. *The psychology almanac: A handbook for students.* Monterey, Calif.: Brooks/Cole, 1973.

Williams, R. M., Jr. *Strangers next door: Ethnic relations in American communities.* Englewood Cliffs, N. J.: Prentice-Hall, 1964.

Willis, R. H. Two dimensions of conformity-nonconformity. *Sociometry, 1963, 26,* 499–515.

Willis, R. H. Conformity, independence, and anti-conformity. *Human Relations, 1965, 18,* 373–388.

Willis, R. H., & Burgess, T. D. G., III. Cognitive and affective balance in sociometric dyads. *Journal of Personality and Social Psychology,* 1974, *29,* 145–152.

Wilner, D. M., Walkley, R. P., & Cook, S. W. Two studies of the effects of Negroes at varying distances from white neighbors in housing projects. *Journal of Social Issues,* 1952, *8,* 45–69.

Wilner, D. M., Walkley, R. P., & Cook, S. W. *Human relations in interracial housing.* Minneapolis: University of Minnesota Press, 1955.

Wilson, E. O. Competitive and aggressive behavior. In J. F. Eisenberg & W. S. Dillon (Eds.), *Man and beast: Comparative social behavior.* Washington, D.C.: Smithsonian Institution Press, 1969. Pp. 181–218.

Wilson, P. R. Perceptual distortion of height as a function of ascribed academic status. *Journal of Social Psychology,* 1968, *74,* 97–102.

Winch, R. F. *Mate selection: A study of complementary needs.* New York: Harper & Row, 1958.

Winch, R. F., Ktsanes, T., & Ktsanes, V. Empirical elaboration of the theory of complementary needs in mate selection. *Journal of Abnormal and Social Psychology,* 1955, *51,* 508–514.

Wishner, J. Reanalysis of "impressions of personality." *Psychological Review,* 1960, *67,* 96–112.

Wolosin, R., Sherman, S. J., & Mynatt, C. R. Perceived social influence in a conformity situation. *Journal of Personality and Social Psychology,* 1972, *23,* 184–191.

Woodmansee, J. J., & Cook, S. W. Dimensions of verbal racial attitudes: Their identification and measurement. *Journal of Personality and Social Psychology,* 1967, *7,* 240–250.

Worchel, S., & Arnold, S. E. The effects of censorship and attractiveness of the censor on attitude change. *Journal of Experimental Social Psychology,* 1973, *9,* 365–377.

Worchel, S., & Brehm, J. W. Direct and implied social restoration of freedom. *Journal of Personality and Social Psychology,* 1971, *18,* 294–304.

Worchel, S., Insko, C. A., Andreoli, V. A., & Drachman, D. Attribution of attitude as a function of behavioral direction and freedom: Reactance in the eye of the observer. *Journal of Experimental Social Psychology,* 1974, *10,* 399–414.

Word, C. O., Zanna, M. P., & Cooper, J. The nonverbal mediation of self-fulfilling prophecies in interracial interaction. *Journal of Experimental Social Psychology,* 1974, *10,* 100–120.

Wright, P. H., & Crawford, A. C. Agreement and friendship: A close look and some second thoughts. *Representative Research in Social Psychology,* 1971, *2,* 52–69.

Wrightsman, L. S. Effects of waiting with others on changes in level of felt anxiety. *Journal of Abnormal and Social Psychology,* 1960, *61,* 216–222.

Wrightsman, L. S. Personality and attitudinal correlates of trusting and trustworthy behaviors in a two-person game. *Journal of Personality and Social Psychology,* 1966, *4,* 328–332.

Wrightsman, L. S. Wallace supporters and adherence to "law and order." *Journal of Personality and Social Psychology,* 1969, *13,* 17–22.

Wrightsman, L. S. Review of *Obedience to authority: An experimental view. Contemporary Psychology,* 1974, *19,* 803–805.

Wrightsman, L. S., O'Connor, J., & Baker, N. J. *Cooperation and competition: Readings on mixed-motive games.* Monterey, Calif.: Brooks/Cole, 1972.

Wrong, D. H. The oversocialized conception of man in modern sociology. In N. H. Smelser & W. T. Smelser (Eds.), *Personality and social systems.* New York: Wiley, 1963.

Yang, K.-S., & Yang, P.-H. The effects of anxiety and threat on the learning of balanced and unbalanced social structures. *Journal of Personality and Social Psychology,* 1973, *26,* 201–207.

Yuchtman, E. Reward distribution and work-role attractiveness in the Kibbutz—Reflections on equity theory. *American Sociological Review,* 1972, *37,* 581–595.

Zajonc, R. B. The process of cognitive tuning. *Journal of Abnormal and Social Psychology*, 1960, *61*, 159–167.

Zajonc, R. B. A note on group judgments and group size. *Human Relations*, 1962, *15*, 177–180.

Zajonc, R. B. Social facilitation. *Science*, 1965, *149*, 269–274.

Zajonc, R. B. *Social psychology: An experimental approach.* Monterey, Calif.: Brooks/Cole, 1966.

Zajonc, R. B. Attitudinal effects of mere exposure. *Journal of Personality and Social Psychology Monograph Supplements*, 1968a, *9*(2, Pt. 2), 1–27.

Zajonc, R. B. Cognitive theories in social psychology. In G. Lindzey & E. Aronson (Eds.), *The handbook of social psychology* (2nd ed.), Vol. 1. Reading, Mass.: Addison-Wesley, 1968b. Pp. 320–404.

Zajonc, R. B. *Animal social behavior.* Morristown, N.J.: General Learning Press, 1972.

Zajonc, R. B., & Burnstein, E. The learning of balanced and unbalanced social structures. *Journal of Personality*, 1965a, *33*, 153–163.

Zajonc, R. B., & Burnstein, E. Structural balance, reciprocity, and positivity as sources of cognitive bias. *Journal of Personality*, 1965b, *33*, 570–583.

Zajonc, R. B., & Dorfman, D. D. Perception, drive, and behavior theory. *Psychological Review*, 1964, *71*, 273–290.

Zajonc, R. B., Heingartner, A., & Herman, E. M. Social enhancement and impairment of performance in the cockroach. *Journal of Personality and Social Psychology*, 1969, *13*, 83–92.

Zajonc, R. B., & Sales, S. Social facilitation of dominant and subordinate responses. *Journal of Experimental Social Psychology*, 1966, *2*, 160–168.

Zajonc, R. B., Swap, W., Harrison, A. A., & Roberts, P. Limiting conditions of the exposure effect: Satiation and relativity. *Journal of Personality and Social Psychology*, 1971, *18*, 384–391.

Zajonc, R. B., Wolosin, R. J., & Wolosin, M. A. Group risk taking under various group decision schemes. *Journal of Experimental Social Psychology*, 1972, *8*, 16–30.

Zajonc, R. B., Wolosin, R. J., Wolosin, M., & Sherman, S. J. Individual and group risk taking in a two-choice situation. *Journal of Experimental Social Psychology*, 1968, *4*, 89–106.

Zimbardo, P. The effect of effort and improvisation on self-persuasion produced by role playing. *Journal of Experimental Social Psychology*, 1965, *1*, 103–120.

Zimbardo, P. The human choice: Individuation, reason, and order versus deindividuation, impulse, and chaos. In W. Arnold & M. Levine (Eds.), *Nebraska symposium on motivation, 1969.* Lincoln: University of Nebraska Press, 1970.

Zimbardo, P., Snyder, M., Thomas, J., Gold, A., & Gurwitz, S. Modifying the impact of persuasive communications with external distraction. *Journal of Personality and Social Psychology*, 1970, *16*, 669–680.

Ziv, A., Kruglanski, A. W., & Shulman, S. Children's psychological reactions to wartime stress. *Journal of Personality and Social Psychology*, 1974, *30*, 24–30.

Zubek, J. P. (Ed.). *Sensory deprivation: Fifteen years of research.* New York: Appleton-Century-Crofts, 1969.

Name Index

Abrahams, D., 231, 280, 282
Adair, J. G., 69, 73
Adams, J. S., 165, 504, 505
Adelman, L., 564
Adelson, J., 285
Aderman, D., 217
Adorno, T., 59
Ajzen, I., 193
Akamatsu, T. J., 157
Aldrich, H., 487
Alioto, J. T., 310
Allee, W. C., 441
Allen, H., 324
Allen, J. C., 78
Allen, V. L., 163, 164, 165, 409, 414
Allerton, M. W., 43
Allgeier, A. R., 348
Allport, F. H., 28, 50, 100, 399
Allport, G. W., 3, 11, 27, 29, 51, 99, 105, 122, 192, 562
Altland, R., 290
Altman, D., 334
Altman, I., 7, 348, 354, 355, 356, 427
Alvares, K., 517
Amir, Y., 561
Amoroso, D. M., 253
Anderson, N. H., 121, 122
Andreoli, V., 385
Ansel, M., 331
Archer, D., 349, 354
Ardrey, R., 297, 299
Argyle, M., 341
Argyris, C., 530
Aron, A. P., 279
Aron, R., 576
Aronfreed, J., 169, 170, 171, 172, 315
Aronson, E., 3, 72, 118, 173, 196, 215, 217, 231, 264, 268, 280, 282, 470, 471, 472
Arrowood, A. J., 265
Asch, S., 119, 399, 407, 408, 411, 413, 414, 422
Ashmore, R. D., 203
Ashour, A. S., 517
Austin, J. A., 235
Azrin, N., 306

Back, K., 71, 262, 472, 473
Backman, C. W., 264
Baer, R. S., 329
Baker, N. J., 361, 364, 366
Baldridge, B., 266
Bales, R. F., 390, 391, 392, 393, 395, 396
Ball-Rokeach, S. J., 313
Bamforth, K. W., 501
Bandura, A., 139, 140, 149, 150, 151, 152, 153, 154, 155, 156, 158, 161, 162, 166, 169, 296, 298, 299, 300, 306, 307, 310, 311, 312, 313, 314, 315, 316
Baron, P. H., 457, 458
Baron, R. A., 310, 313, 314
Baron, R. M., 506
Baron, R. S., 236, 457, 458
Barron, J. W., 196
Barry, W. A., 280
Bateson, N., 456
Batson, C. D., 335
Bavelas, A., 393
Baxter, G. W., 364
Bayton, J. A., 549
Beaman, A., 258, 260
Bebout, J., 426, 431, 434, 435
Becker, F., 341
Beckman, R. F., 201
Bem, D., 131, 178, 181, 184, 185, 207, 208, 217, 454, 458
Bem, S., 178, 181, 184, 185, 186
Bennis, W. G., 465
Benoist, F., 547, 548
Berger, D., 381
Berger, S. M., 159, 160
Berkowitz, L., 296, 299, 307, 309, 310, 313, 314, 317, 326, 327, 463, 466, 475
Berlin, I., 21
Berlyne, D. E., 93, 97, 217, 247, 248
Bermann, E., 272
Berne, E., 17
Berry, P. C., 467
Berscheid, E., 101, 262, 266, 272, 281, 282, 283, 376, 380, 504, 506
Bickman, L., 332, 333, 557

657

Biddle, B. J., 16, 17
Billig, M., 547
Birdwhistell, J., 108
Birnbaum, M., 118
Bixenstine, V. E., 268, 365
Blake, R. R., 100, 148, 511, 550
Blanchard, E., 139
Blanchard, F. A., 564
Blane, H. T., 352
Blauner, R., 546, 547
Bless, E., 378, 379
Block, C. H., 467
Bloom, L. M., 42
Bochner, S., 230, 517, 519
Bohn, J., 501
Bolaria, B. S., 500
Bonacich, E., 545
Bonnemains, M. de, 245
Booker, A., 308
Boulanger, G., 245
Bowers, D. G., 520, 528
Braband, J., 333
Braginski, D., 32, 382
Braginski, J. W., 32
Braly, K., 555
Braver, S., 126
Brehm, J. W., 199, 200, 203, 208, 383, 384, 511
Brenner, M., 448
Brewer, M., 38
Brickman, P., 125, 216, 538
Brigham, J., 42, 554, 555
Broadbent, D. E., 103
Brock, T. C., 115, 201
Broll, L., 126
Bronfenbrenner, U., 104, 569
Brooks, J., 527
Brophy, I. N., 561
Broverman, D. M., 179
Broverman, I. K., 179
Brown, R., 165, 218, 456
Brown, R. C., 314
Browning, E. B., 21
Bruel, O., 13
Bruner, J., 90, 91, 100, 120, 220
Bruno, J., 108
Bryan, J. H., 321, 329
Buchanan, W., 267
Buck, R. W., 253, 256, 349
Buckley, W., 487
Bugelski, R., 306
Bunker, A., 4
Burdick, H. A., 215, 216, 248
Burgess, T. D. G., 110
Burke, P. J., 390, 394, 511
Burnes, A. J., 215, 216
Burnstein, E., 216, 459, 460
Buss, A., 308, 406, 407
Buss, E., 308
Byrne, D., 262, 266, 267, 272, 348

Campbell, D. T., 75, 234, 266, 326, 402, 553, 554
Campbell, E. Q., 193
Campbell, J., 425, 434, 467
Cannavale, F. J., 257
Cantril, H., 87, 88
Caplan, N., 31
Carlsmith, J. M., 5, 75, 78, 172, 173, 202, 204, 208
Cartwright, D., 14, 28, 29, 215, 454, 455, 468, 469
Catalan, J., 377, 378
Cates, J. N., 184
Cattell, R. B., 271
Caul, W. F., 349
Cawasjee, S. D., 100
Centers, R., 163, 164
Chafetz, M. E., 352
Chaikin, A. L., 129, 356, 560
Chamberlain, N., 568
Chapanis, A., 346, 347, 351, 485
Chapman, A. J., 441
Chein, I., 549, 552, 554
Chemers, M. M., 517
Chen, S. C., 440
Cheng, J. B., 236
Child, I. L., 181
Christie, R., 380, 381, 382
Cialdini, R., 126, 165, 377, 378, 380, 399
Clark, A. W., 517, 519
Clark, K. B., 549
Clark, M. K., 549
Clark, R. D., 332, 454, 455
Clarkson, F. E., 179
Clausen, G., 321, 332
Clausewitz, K. von, 575
Cline, M., 103, 104
Cline, V. B., 111
Clore, G., 266, 326
Cobbs, P. M., 564
Coch, S., 519
Coffman, T. L., 555
Cohen, A. A., 351
Cohen, A. M., 465
Cohen, A. R., 115, 199, 203, 208, 397, 398
Cohen, J. L., 445
Cohn, W. R., 396, 397
Coles, R., 549
Collins, B. E., 203, 204, 211, 217, 220, 229, 464, 465
Comte, A., 26, 27
Conolley, E., 68, 69, 70, 71, 205, 413
Cook, S., 553, 554, 561, 564
Cook, T. D., 72
Cooper, J., 129, 204, 232, 235, 559
Cope, V., 215
Coser, L. A., 538, 539, 540
Coss, R., 42, 43, 44
Costanzo, P., 49, 50, 51, 52, 410
Cotton, T. S., 467
Cottrell, N. B., 216, 440, 441, 444, 445

Cowan, G., 369, 370
Cowan, P. A., 143
Crandall, R., 97, 98
Crano, W. D., 38, 231
Crawford, A. C., 267
Crisci, R., 229
Criswell, J., 451
Crockett, W. H., 216
Cronbach, L. J., 41, 46, 48
Cross, H. A., 95
Crow, J. W., 105
Crowe, B. J., 517, 519
Crutchfield, R., 408, 409
Culbertson, F., 563
Cyert, R. M., 482, 483, 525

Dabbs, J. M., 236
Damarin, F., 393
Daniels, L., 326
Dannenmaier, W. V., 101
Darby, B. L., 377, 378, 380
Darley, J., 3, 66, 67, 68, 69, 70, 232, 239, 254, 320, 331, 332, 335
Darley, S. A., 239
Davis, E. E., 269
Davis, J. D., 357
Davis, J. H., 445
Davis, K. E., 124, 128, 129, 130, 131, 272, 280, 285, 286
Davison, L., 159
Davitz, J. R., 251, 253, 254, 309, 352, 448
Davitz, L. J., 352
Day, R., 512
Dean, J., 341
Dean, R. B., 235
Deaux, K., 119, 126, 127, 130, 323
Degnore, R., 114
DeLamater, J., 289, 290
Delin, P. S., 101, 111
DeNike, L. D., 166, 167
Derlega, V. J., 356, 560
Dermer, M., 281
Deutsch, M., 366, 368, 372, 399, 411, 412
Devoe, S., 349
Diamond, S. G., 344
Dickoff, H., 376
Dickson, W., 29, 466, 486
Diener, E., 257, 258, 260
DiMatteo, M. R., 349, 354
Dineen, J., 257, 258, 260
Dion, K., 281
Doan, B. K., 247
Dollard, J., 140, 141, 144, 146, 147, 149, 152, 162, 166, 167, 301, 307
Doob, A., 75, 76, 77, 78, 79, 302, 305, 306
Doob, L., 301
Dorfman, D. D., 97, 100, 101
Dorris, J. W., 369
Douglas, R. L., 368, 369

Douvan, E., 285
Driscoll, R., 285, 286
Duck, D., 160
Duncan, B. L., 205
Duncan, S., 349
Dunnette, M. D., 425, 434, 467, 501, 532
Durkheim, E., 27, 247
Dutton, D. G., 265, 279, 558
Duval, S., 134

Egan, G., 425, 428, 429
Eiffler, D., 181
Eisner, W., 4
Ekehammar, B., 12
Ekman, P., 349, 350, 351, 353
Ellertson, N., 466, 474
Ellsworth, P., 5, 349, 350
Elms, A. C., 31, 59, 200, 202, 203, 206, 217, 234, 237, 238, 239, 246, 299, 471
Emrich, D., 275
Emswiller, T., 126, 127, 130, 323
Endler, N. S., 409, 410
Endresen, K., 257, 258, 260
Epley, S. W., 250, 251, 253, 254
Epstein, Y., 368
Eron, L. D., 312
Ettinger, R. F., 409
Etzioni, A., 541, 567, 569, 575, 577, 578, 579
Eustis, A. C., 375
Evans, N. G., 500
Evans, R. I., 268
Evenbeck, S., 399
Exline, R. V., 381

Fadem, J. A., 506
Fane, C., 162
Faust, W. L., 452
Feld, S., 495
Feldman, R., 323
Feldman, S., 117, 118
Feldman-Summers, S., 183, 184
Felipe-Russo, N., 342, 343
Fell, D., 331
Ferguson, G. A., 58
Fernandez, L. E., 313
Feshbach, S., 313
Festinger, L., 195, 202, 208, 231, 236, 248, 249, 257, 262, 472
Fidell, L., 184
Fiedler, F. E., 515, 516, 517, 518
Finck, C., 15, 331
Firestone, I. J., 113, 114, 256, 369, 370
Fisch, E., 330
Fishbein, M., 193
Fisher, E., 181
Fiske, D., 41, 46
Fitch, H. G., 196
Flament, C., 408
Flanders, J. P., 456

Floyd, J., 118
Fode, K., 74
Folger, R., 385
Forster, E. M., 131
Forward, J., 547
Fox, D., 448
Fraser, S., 257, 258, 260, 377
Freedman, J., 76, 77, 377, 378, 379
French, J. R. P., 519
Frenkel-Brunswik, E., 59
Fried, S. B., 78
Friesen, W., 349, 350, 351, 353
Frieze, I., 125
Frijda, N., 108
Fromkin, H., 115

Gaddis, T. E., 295
Gaertner, S. L., 557
Gahagan, J., 577
Gallo, P., 360, 361, 363, 366, 368
Gallwey, M. O., 104
Gardin, H., 369, 370
Garland, H., 505
Gates, M. G., 441
Geen, R., 308, 309, 314, 315
Geis, F. L., 380, 381, 382, 393
Geller, S. H., 409
Gerard, H. B., 68, 69, 70, 71, 255, 399, 400,
    411, 412, 413, 414, 471, 547
Gergen, K. J., 12, 24, 129, 321, 371, 372, 375
Gergen, M. M., 12, 24, 321
Gerst, M. S., 153
Ghiselli, E. E., 46
Gibb, J. R., 427, 431, 434
Gilbert, G. M., 555
Gilfallan, D. P., 402
Gillig, P. M., 231
Gilliland, A. R., 95
Gillis, J. S., 365
Gilmore, J. B., 206
Gitter, A. G., 73
Glaser, B. G., 323
Glass, D. C., 252, 445
Godfrey, B. W., 325
Goethals, G. R., 125, 207, 234
Goffman, E., 16, 17, 279
Goldberg, P., 182
Goldstein, M., 269
Goodman, C. D., 100
Goodstadt, B. E., 73
Goranson, R., 327
Gordon, B., 426, 431, 435
Gordon, E. M., 356
Gordon, K., 448
Gore, W. V., 445
Gouaux, C., 267
Graen, G., 517
Grant, G., 549
Grant, L. D., 467

Graves, W., 268
Green, D., 209
Green, L. B., 290
Greenbaum, C. W., 414
Greenberg, M. S., 327
Greene, D., 497
Greenfield, J., 108
Greenspoon, J., 165, 167
Greenwald, A., 231
Gregory, D., 466, 474
Grider, G., 417
Griffitt, W., 267
Gross, A. E., 302, 306, 393, 412
Grusec, J. L., 6, 153
Guest, H., 501
Gumpert, P., 368, 381
Gumpper, D. C., 78
Gunn, S. P., 42
Gurin, G., 495
Gutman, G. M., 216
Guydosh, R. M., 247

Hackman, R., 496, 520
Hake, D. F., 306
HAL, 346, 347
Halcomb, C. G., 95
Hall, E., 348
Hall, V., 95
Halpin, A. W., 511
Hamblin, R., 512
Hamilton, D. L., 167
Hanratty, M., 309, 313
Hanson, L. R., 118
Harary, F. S., 215
Harburg, E., 216
Harding, J., 104, 549, 552, 554, 562
Hardyk, J. A., 268
Hare, H. P., 395, 396
Hare, N., 539
Harris, M. B., 321
Harris, M. S., 356
Harris, T. M., 381
Harrison, A. A., 93, 94, 97, 98, 114, 362, 363, 366
Harrison, R., 351
Harshberger, D., 464
Hart, H., 377
Hartshorne, H., 12
Harvey, O. J., 8, 542
Hastorf, A. H., 87, 88, 121, 393
Hawkins, G., 268
Hayes, D. P., 352
Heider, F., 212, 214
Heingartner, A., 442, 445
Heller, J. F., 235
Helmreich, R., 204
Henchy, T., 445
Henderson, J. E., 232
Hendrick, C., 38, 268, 273
Henson, A., 5

Herman, E., 442, 445
Herman, P., 399
Heron, W., 247
Herzberg, F., 499, 500
Hickey, C. B., 381
Higbee, K. L., 238
Higgins, G. W., 501
Higgs, W. J., 442
Hildum, D. C., 165
Hill, W. A., 517
Hill, W. F., 251, 253
Hillery, J. M., 442, 443
Hines, P., 93, 94
Hingston, R. W. G., 246, 296
Hitler, A., 116, 567, 568, 570, 573
Hodges, B. H., 121, 122
Hoffman, D., 165
Hoffman, M. L., 6
Hogrefe, R., 562
Hokada, E., 181
Hollander, E., 409, 410, 411
Hollander, S. W., 235
Holmes, J. G., 71, 204, 205
Holmes, L., 330
Homans, G., 173, 466, 486
Hood, T., 71
Hood, W. R., 8, 413, 542
Hook, E. B., 300
Horai, J., 577
Horn, C., 216
Horn, N., 322
Hornbeck, F. W., 203
Hornstein, H., 330
Horowitz, E. L., 561
Horst, L., 529, 530
Horwitz, M., 547, 548
Hovland, C. I., 192, 229, 231, 306
Howell, F. C., 26, 246
Howes, D. H., 91, 103
Hoyt, M. F., 204, 547
Hraba, J., 549
Huang, L. C., 321, 322
Huesmann, L. R., 312
Hull, C., 141, 144, 148, 442
Hunt, P. J., 442, 443
Hurwitz, J. I., 396, 397
Huston, T., 152, 282
Hutchinson, R. R., 306
Hyman, H. H., 561
Hymovitch, B., 396, 397

Inkster, J. A., 199
Insko, C. A., 165, 166, 230, 266, 269, 281, 455
Isen, A., 322, 323

Jaastad, L., 467
Jackson, D. N., 421
Jacobs, L. S., 43
Jacobs, P. I., 121

Jacobs, R. C., 402
Jacobs, T. O., 516
Jacobsen, L., 560
Jahoda, M., 420
Janis, I., 203, 236, 238, 239, 473, 475
Jeffrey, R. W., 154
Jellison, J., 126, 230
Johnson, D. A., 556
Johnson, D. W., 363
Johnson, H., 410
Johnson, L. B., 475
Johnson, R. C., 103
Jones, E. E., 42, 124, 125, 128, 129, 130, 131, 134, 204, 234, 356, 374, 375, 400
Jones, R. A., 38, 208, 235, 375
Jones, S., 240
Jordan, N., 216
Jorgensen, B. W., 71
Jorgensen, C. I., 560
Joseph, K. B., 442
Jourard, S., 357

Kagan, N., 181, 352
Kahn, A., 259, 327, 328, 547, 548
Kahn, H., 573, 574, 575
Kahn, R., 485, 487, 489, 490, 493, 495, 497, 502, 503, 508, 509, 510, 512, 516, 523, 528, 529
Kanfer, F. H., 165, 167
Kanouse, D., 118
Kaplan, H. R., 500
Kaplan, K. J., 113, 114, 256, 369, 370, 500
Karaz, V., 125
Karlins, M., 555
Kassarjian, H., 101
Kassinove, H., 229
Katz, Daniel, 63, 220-223, 225, 485, 487, 489, 490, 493, 495, 497, 508, 509, 510, 512, 516, 523, 528, 529, 552, 563
Katz, David, 555
Kazantzakis, N., 537
Kazdin, A. E., 321, 322
Keasey, C. B., 232
Keasey, M., 232
Keating, J. P., 412
Kelley, H. H., 20, 124, 130, 131, 173, 174, 175, 176, 177, 359, 363, 397, 398, 411, 412, 469
Kelman, H., 193, 194, 220, 223, 224, 225, 226, 563
Kennedy, E. M., 217
Kennedy, J. F., 348, 404, 475, 578, 579
Kepka, E. J., 125
Kepner, C. R., 313
Kerckhoff, A., 272, 280
Kessler, J. J., 505
Khrushchev, N., 578, 579
Kiesler, C. A., 208, 211, 217, 220, 229
Kiesler, S., 182, 183, 184
Kilham, W., 418
Kinch, J., 18
King, N., 500

Kipnis, D., 375
Kite, W. R., 393
Kleinke, C. L., 376
Klugman, S. F., 448, 449
Knight, H. C., 447
Knowles, E. S., 397
Knowles, J. P., 165
Knox, R. E., 199, 216, 368, 369
Koch, S., 431
Koeske, G., 231
Kogan, N., 121, 454, 458
Kohl, J., 377
Koivumaki, J. H., 349, 354
Konečni, V., 305, 306, 332, 379
Koplan, C. A., 506
Kothandapani, V., 193
Krasner, L., 165
Krauss, R., 366
Kravitz, J., 93
Krebs, D., 321
Krishner, H. P., 239
Kruglanski, A., 71, 72, 540
Krugman, H. E., 95
Krupat, E., 381
Ktsanes, T., 271, 272
Ktsanes, V., 271, 272
Kukla, A., 125
Kuo, Z. Y., 299
Kupferberg, H., 320
Kuriloff, A. H., 502
Kutner, B., 549, 552, 554

Ladd, E. C., 104
Lage, E., 421, 422
Laird, J. D., 131
Lake, R. A., 558
Lamb, J. W., 411
Lambert, B. G., 290
Lambert, P., 283
Lamberth, J., 267
Lamm, H., 233, 459
Landauer, T., 75, 76, 77, 78, 79
Landers, D. M., 442, 445
Landy, D., 112
LaPiere, R. T., 193
Larson, L. L., 517, 518
Latané, B., 3, 252, 320, 331, 332
Lave, L. B., 372
Lawler, E. E., 493, 495, 496, 498, 502, 503, 506, 515, 520
Layton, B. D., 281
Lazarsfeld, P., 563
Lazarus, R., 159
Leavitt, H. J., 464
LeBon, G., 257
Lefkowitz, M., 148, 312
LePage, A., 307
Lepper, M. R., 173, 497
Lerner, L., 157

Lerner, M. J., 270, 325, 379
Leventhal, H., 117, 240
Levin, E. M., 181
Levin, P. F., 322, 323
Levine, J. M., 414
Levine, M., 334
Levinger, G., 456
Levinson, D., 59
Levy, P., 331
Levy, S. K., 399
Lewin, K., 29, 31, 469, 518, 519
Lewis, M., 179, 180
Lewis, S. K., 126, 377, 378
Lieberman, M. A., 429, 431, 432, 434, 435
Lieberman, S., 404
Liebert, R., 38, 61, 310, 313, 314
Lien, D., 332
Lightstone, J., 412
Likert, R., 469, 493, 513, 514, 515, 519, 523, 524, 525
Linder, D., 204, 208, 268
Linder, R., 122
Lindsay, J. S. B., 15
Lindskold, S., 577
Lindzey, G., 3, 99, 266, 272
Lipetz, M., 286
Lippitt, R., 29, 469, 518, 530
Lipset, S. M., 104
Lockard, R. B., 297, 299
Lombardo, J. P., 267
London, H., 230
London, O., 267
Long, J. O., 295
Lopes, L. L., 122
Lord, W., 439
Lorenz, K., 251, 297, 298, 299
Lorge, I., 91, 448
Lott, A. J., 117, 409, 414, 468, 472, 473, 474
Lott, B., 117, 468, 472, 473, 474
Lott, D. F., 349
Lowe, C. A., 325
Lublin, S. C., 257
Luce, R. D., 360
Lumsdaine, A., 231
Lundgren, D., 331
Lynn, D. B., 180, 181, 185
Lyons, J., 283

Macauley, J. R., 330
Maccoby, N., 236
MacDonald, A. P., 253
MacNeil, M. K., 402
Maehr, M. L., 560
Malof, M., 409, 414
Malpass, R. S., 93
Mann, J. H., 561
Mann, L., 99, 418
March, J. G., 484
Marino, C. J., 409

Marlatt, G. A., 165, 356
Marrow, A. J., 520
Martella, J. A., 517
Martens, R., 442, 445
Martin, J. B., 247
Marwell, G., 505
Marx, K., 59, 60
Mascaro, G. F., 268
Maslow, A., 498
Mason, D. J., 251, 253, 254
Mason, H. N., 330
Mateljan, P. L., 556
Mathes, E. W., 259
Mathewson, G. C., 472
Matter, W. W., 95
Matthews, G., 379
Mausner, B., 499, 500
May, M., 12
Mayfield, E. C., 117
Mazis, M., 115, 383
McArthur, L. A., 125
McBride, D., 466, 474
McCain, G., 22, 49, 74
McCandless, B., 172, 181
McClelland, D., 61
McClintock, C. G., 222, 360, 361, 362, 365, 366,
    368, 371, 563
McConnell, H. K., 208
McCrimmon, K. R., 482, 483, 525
McDavid, J., 411, 412
McDonald, F. J., 154, 155, 156, 169
McDougall, W., 27, 28
McEvoy, J. E., 561, 563
McGinnies, E., 100, 102, 103
McGrath, J. E., 331
McGraw, D., 266
McGregor, D., 494, 498, 499, 500
McGuire, D., 157
McGuire, W., 31, 32, 62, 80, 192, 231, 233, 237
McNeel, S., 365, 368
McNeil, E. B., 300
Mead, M., 179
Meehl, P., 48
Mehrabian, A., 340, 344, 345, 346, 348, 353, 354
Meichenbaum, D. H., 152
Meltzer, L., 352
Menges, R. J., 83
Menlove, F. L., 153
Menninger, K., 295
Merton, R. K., 317, 485
Messick, S., 421
Meter, K., 12, 321
Mettee, D., 270
Meyer, M., 95
Miles, M., 429, 431, 432, 434, 435
Milgram, S., 333, 334, 399, 415, 416, 417, 418,
    419, 420
Miller, A., 561, 563
Miller, D. R., 17, 272, 406

Miller, J. G., 487, 526
Miller, Neal, 140, 141, 144, 146, 147, 149, 152,
    162, 166, 167, 301, 306, 307
Miller, Norman, 112, 211, 217, 220, 229, 234,
    236, 266
Miller, R. E., 349
Mills, J., 112, 208, 249, 264, 470, 471, 472
Milmoe, S., 352
Minard, R. D., 562
Minh, H. C., 568
Mintz, P. M., 249
Mirels, H., 112, 264
Mischel, W., 11, 12, 161, 162
Montagu, A., 299
Mooney, C. M., 481
Moore, H. T., 95
Moore, L. M., 506
Moore, M., 95, 113, 114, 115, 125
Mordkoff, A. M., 159
Morgan, W. J., 462
Morissette, J., 215
Morris, E. W., 313
Morris, W. C., 529, 530
Morris, W. N., 352, 353
Morrison, B. J., 251, 253
Moscovici, S., 421
Moseley, L., 116
Mouse, M., 160
Mouton, J. S., 148, 511, 550
Mowrer, O. H., 301
Mull, H., 95
Murakawa, N., 267
Murray, H. A., 501
Murstein, B., 270, 273, 282
Mussen, P., 179, 180
Myers, A., 470
Mynatt, C. R., 408
Myrdal, G., 22

Nadien, M., 334
Naffrechoux, M., 421, 422
Nathanson, C. A., 493
Natziuk, T., 409
Neale, J. M., 38, 61
Nelson, D., 266, 267
Nelson, S. D., 32, 297, 299
Nemeth, C., 421, 422
Nesselroade, J. R., 271
Newberry, B. H., 83
Newcomb, T. M., 29, 214, 215, 216, 257, 265,
    404, 405
Newtson, D., 409
Niles, P., 239, 240
Nisbett, R., 131, 133
Nixon, R. M., 404
Noel, R. C., 380
Norman, W. T., 121
Nosanchuk, T. A., 412
Novak, D., 270

Novey, M. S., 352
Nuttin, J., 365

O'Connell, E., 112, 266
O'Connor, J., 361, 364, 366
Odbert, H., 11, 122
Okun, M., 445
O'Leary, V., 184
O'Neal, E. C., 308, 309
Oosterbaan, H., 547, 548
Orne, M., 69, 72
Orris, J. B., 517
Orwell, G., 415
Osborn, A. F., 466
Osgood, C. E., 209, 211, 217, 575, 576, 577, 578
Oskamp, S., 110, 365, 370, 570
Ostrom, T., 42
Owen, D. R., 300

Page, M. M., 166, 167, 168
Page, R., 555
Pallak, M. S., 235
Palmer, J., 267
Panzram, C., 295
Park, R. P., 541
Parke, R. D., 253, 256
Passini, F., 121
Pepitone, A., 257, 317
Perlman, D., 110, 125, 365, 370
Perrow, C., 508
Pessin, J., 441
Peterson, R. C., 563
Pettigrew, T. F., 561, 563
Pheterson, G. I., 182, 183
Piaget, J., 154
Picek, J. S., 216, 235
Pichevin, M. F., 460
Piliavin, I., 323, 324, 329
Piliavin, J., 283, 284, 323, 324, 329
Pilisuk, M., 577
Placencia, P., 559
Plato, 192
Pliner, P., 377
Pollock, A. B., 501
Pomazal, R. J., 194, 326
Porter, L. W., 503
Porter, R. J., 556
Portnoy, N. W., 406, 407
Postman, L., 90, 91, 100
Potash, H. M., 365
Potter, D. A., 111
Potter, E. H., 181
Prasad, A., 267
Prasad, M., 267
Price, K. O., 216
Priest, R. F., 262, 264
Proshansky, H., 549, 552, 554
Pruitt, D., 371, 372, 454, 455, 456

Puckett, E. S., 497
Pugh, R. W., 549, 550

Quay, H., 165

Rabbie, J., 255, 547, 548
Raiffa, H., 360
Ramirez, M., 267
Rasmussen, E. E., 251
Raven, B., 464, 465
Ray, A. A., 133
Reber, A., 169
Reddy, W. B., 432
Reed, L., 125
Reeves, E. T., 446
Regan, D., 236, 379, 384
Rest, S., 125
Richards, J. M., 103, 104
Rickles, D., 313
Riley, M., 396, 397
Riley, R. W., 396, 397
Rim, Y., 381
Ring, K., 31
Ripley, R. L., 162
Riskind, J., 126
Ritter, B., 139
Rittle, R. H., 444
Roberts, P., 97
Rock, L., 125
Rodin, J., 323, 324, 329, 331
Roethlisberger, F., 29, 466, 486
Rogers, C., 432
Rogers, P. L., 349, 354
Rogers, W., 261
Rokeach, M., 268
Roper, G., 457, 458
Rosen, I. C., 563
Rosenbaum, R. M., 125
Rosenbaum, W. B., 505
Rosenberg, M., 192, 203
Rosenberg, S., 121
Rosenhan, D. L., 6, 169, 322
Rosenkrantz, P. S., 179
Rosenthal, R. L., 69, 71, 74, 349, 352, 354, 560
Rosnow, R., 69, 71, 73
Ross, A. S., 333
Ross, C., 181
Ross, D., 152, 311
Ross, E. A., 27
Ross, M., 209
Ross, S., 152, 311, 320
Rossi, A., 184
Rothschild, B. F., 290
Rottman, L., 280, 282
Rowland, K. M., 517, 518
Rubin, Z., 266, 276, 277, 278, 284
Rubovits, P. C., 560
Ruh, R., 319, 320, 519

Rump, E. E., 101, 111
Russell, J. C., 256

Saari, D., 377
Saegert, S., 97, 110
Saks, M. J., 412
Sales, S. M., 59, 60, 91, 110, 247, 248, 443, 444
Sanford, R. N., 59
Sarbin, T. R., 163, 164, 165
Sarnoff, I., 256, 563
Sasfy, J., 445
Sashkin, M., 529, 530
Savicki, V., 356
Savin, V. J., 349
Sawyer, J., 262, 264
Scanlon, J. N., 497
Scarr, H. A., 257
Schachter, B., 73
Schachter, S., 54, 67, 131, 132, 248, 249, 252,
    253, 254, 255, 262, 279, 466, 472, 473,
    474, 475
Schaps, E., 326, 327
Scheflen, K. D., 496
Schein, E. H., 431
Schelling, T. C., 572, 573, 575
Schlenker, B., 25
Schmidt, L., 283, 284
Schmidt, M. J., 412
Schmitt, D. R., 505
Schneider, D. J., 121, 375, 456
Schopler, J., 230, 266, 269, 455
Schulte, R., 91
Schultz, D., 151
Schumsky, D. A., 167
Schwartz, L., 75
Schwartz, S., 320, 321, 332
Scontrino, M. F., 519
Scott, J. F., 288
Scott, J. P., 246
Scott, T. H., 247
Scott, W. A., 203
Sears, R. R., 301, 306
Seashore, S., 474, 520, 528
Sechrest, L., 75
Secord, P. F., 264
Sedlak, A., 121
Segal, G., 22, 49, 74
Segal, M. W., 263
Sekerak, G. J., 444
Selznik, P., 509
Sensenig, J., 384
Seyfried, B. A., 273
Shakespeare, W., 17
Shaver, K. G., 125
Shaw, M. E., 49, 50, 52, 463, 465, 467
Sheatsley, P. B., 561
Sheffield, F., 231
Shepard, H. A., 550

Sherif, C., 8, 542, 550
Sherif, M., 8, 29, 399, 401, 402, 413, 542, 544,
    547, 550, 551, 562, 569
Sherman, S. J., 204, 216, 408, 455
Sherwood, J. J., 196
Shiffrin, R., 216
Shirer, W., 245
Short, J. G., 160
Shostrom, E., 433
Shulman, R. F., 209
Shulman, S., 540
Siegal, A. E., 405, 406
Siegal, A. L., 519
Siegel, S., 405, 406
Sigall, H., 42, 72, 112, 264, 555
Sigler, E., 560
Silver, M. J., 74
Silverman, B. I., 269
Silverman, I., 217
Simmel, G., 541
Simmonds, D. W., 157
Simmons, C. H., 325, 379
Simon, H. A., 484
Simons, L. S., 308
Simpson, G. E., 545
Singer, D. L., 240
Singer, J. E., 131, 132, 257, 382
Singer, R., 313
Sistrunk, F., 411, 412
Skinner, A. E. G., 357
Skolnick, P., 265, 577
Skousen, W. C., 431
Skrzypek, G. J., 517
Slater, P., 390, 391, 392, 393
Smith, E. E., 232
Smith, G. F., 97
Smith, M. B., 220, 268
Smith, P. W., 268
Smith, R. B., 314
Smith, R. E., 332
Smoke, W., 450, 451
Smythe, L., 332
Snyderman, B., 499, 500
Solomon, H., 451
Solomon, L., 425
Solomon, R. L., 91, 103
Sommer, R., 340, 341, 342, 343, 344, 345,
    348, 349
Sosis, R. H., 134
Sparling, S., 379
Spector, A. J., 504
Speisman, J. C., 159
Spielberger, C. D., 166
Stagner, R., 537
Stahelski, A. J., 363
Staneski, R. A., 376
Stang, D., 97, 98, 393, 409, 410
Staub, E., 329

Stein, D. D., 268
Stein, R. T., 393
Steiner, I. D., 30, 31, 410
Steinzor, B., 396
Stephan, W., 101
Stoner, J. A. F., 453, 454
Stonner, D., 314, 315
Storm, T. F., 216
Strand, S., 362, 366
Strauss, A., 323
Stricker, L. J., 121, 421
Strickland, L. H., 204, 205, 513
Strodtbeck, F. L., 393
Stroebe, W., 281
Stumphauzer, J. S., 151, 169
Suls, J. M., 73
Sulzer, J. L., 309
Super, D. E., 501
Suppes, P., 451
Suttle, J. L., 498
Swap, W., 97, 101
Swingle, P., 365

Taguiri, R., 120
Tajfel, H., 100, 408, 547
Tannenbaum, A., 484, 485
Tannenbaum, P. H., 209, 210, 211, 217
Tausky, C., 500
Taylor, A. J. P., 567
Taylor, D. A., 7, 348, 354, 355, 356, 427, 445
Taylor, D. W., 467
Taylor, F. W., 484
Taylor, K. F., 99
Taylor, S., 270
Tedeschi, J. T., 314, 577
Teichman, Y., 255
Terhune, K. W., 364
Terwilliger, R. F., 238
Test, M. A., 329
Thalhofer, N. N., 326
Tharp, R. G., 272
Thelen, M. H., 157
Thibaut, J., 20, 173, 174, 175, 176, 177, 359,
     381, 412, 451, 469
Thiel, D. L., 281
Thistlethwaite, D. L., 456
Thomas, E., 15, 16, 17
Thompson, V. D., 281
Thomson, C. W., 103
Thorndike, E. L., 91
Throm, E. L., 440
Thumin, F. J., 101
Thurstone, L. L., 563
Tice, T., 327, 328
Tobin, T. A., 330
Toby, J., 396, 397
Toch, H. H., 91, 316
Toffler, A., 426, 531, 532

Tom, S., 75, 76, 77, 78, 79
Toman, W., 273, 274, 280
Tomkins, S., 349
Torok, T., 42
Touhey, J., 266
Travis, L. E., 441
Traylor, G., 469
Triplett, N., 27, 440
Trist, E. L., 501
Trope, Y., 459
Tuddenham, R. C., 408, 409
Turner, C. W., 308
Twedt, H., 112

Valins, S., 131, 132, 133
Vanderplass, J. M., 100
Vanderveer, R., 375
VanHoose, T., 72
Venn, J. R., 160
Vernon, P. E., 99
Veroff, J., 495
Vilenna, J., 334
Vinacke, W. E., 361, 364, 366
Vincent, J. E., 377, 378, 380
Vinokur, A., 459, 460
Visser, L., 547, 548
Vogel, S. R., 179
Vroom, V., 467, 492, 493, 495, 505, 506, 519

Wachtler, H., 421, 422
Wack, D. L., 444
Wager, L. W., 524
Wagner, C., 330
Wagner, R. V., 273
Walder, D. O., 312
Walker, C. R., 501
Walkley, R. P., 561
Wallach, N., 454, 458
Wallington, S. A., 378, 379, 380
Walster, E., 101, 231, 262, 266, 272, 278, 279,
     280, 281, 282, 283, 284, 376, 380, 504, 506
Walster, G. W., 282, 283, 284, 504, 506
Walters, G., 555
Walters, R. H., 143, 253, 307, 310, 312
Ward, L. M., 125
Washington, G., 128
Watson, J., 530
Wattenberg, B., 186, 191
Weaver, P., 376
Webb, E., 75
Weber, M., 485
Weber, S. J., 72
Weick, K. E., 402
Weigl, R. H., 564
Weiner, B., 125
Weiss, J. H., 105, 106
Weiss, R. F., 267
Weiss, R. L., 157

Weiss, W., 563
Weitzman, L., 181
Westford, K., 257, 258, 260
Westley, B., 530
Wheeler, D., 377, 378
Wheeler, L., 330
White, A. M., 167
White, B., 8, 542
White, G. M., 157–158
White, H. A., 167
White, R. K., 29, 469, 570
White, R. W., 220
Whitney, R. E., 203
Whyte, R. F., 29
Wichman, H., 369
Wicker, A. W., 194
Wicklund, R. A., 134
Wiener, M., 349
Wiener, Y., 505
Wiggily, U., 574
Wilhelmy, R., 205, 413
Wilkening, H. E., 56
Willems, E. P., 454
Willerman, B., 118
Williams, J., 547
Williams, M., 379
Williams, R. M., 561
Willis, R. H., 409, 411, 421
Willits, J. E., 323
Wilner, D. M., 561
Wilson, E. O., 296, 298
Wilson, K. V., 365
Wilson, P. R., 101
Winch, R. F., 271, 272, 274

Wishner, J., 119, 120
Wolf, I., 352
Wolfe, L. J., 393
Wolkon, G. H., 465
Wolosin, M., 455
Wolosin, R., 408, 455
Wood, L., 305, 306
Woodmansee, J. J., 553, 554
Worchel, P., 304, 305, 306
Worchel, S., 383, 385
Word, C., 332, 559
Wright, O., 439
Wright, P. H., 267
Wright, W., 439
Wrightsman, L. S., 217, 252, 253, 361, 364,
    366, 420
Wrong, D. H., 301

Yalom, I. D., 429, 431, 432, 434, 435
Yang, K.-S., 216
Yang, P.-H., 216
Yinger, J. M., 545
Young, T. F., 506
Yuchtman, E., 505

Zajonc, R. B., 5, 26, 27, 50, 91, 95, 96, 97, 98,
    100, 101, 103, 110, 115, 162, 163, 211, 216,
    366, 440, 441, 443, 444, 445, 448, 450,
    451, 455
Zander, A., 14, 28, 29, 396, 397
Zanna, M. A., 208, 559
Zimbardo, P., 203, 236, 256, 257, 258, 260, 261
Ziv, A., 540
Zubek, J. P., 247

Subject Index

ABX, 214–217
Achievement, 61–62
Acquiescence, 41
Action conformity, 415–420
Action-research model, 530
Adaptive inferiority, 549
Adaptive systems, 489–491
Adhocracy, 532
Adjustive attitudes, 221
Adolescence, 181–182
Affiliation, 245–261
  anxiety and, 255–256
  birth order and, 252–253
  fear and, 250–256
  motives for, 246–251
Agentic shift, 419–420
Agentic state, 419–420
Aggression, 25, 172, 259–261, 295–319, 535–580
  biological bases for, 295–301
  frustration and, 301–310
  intergroup, 535–580
  social learning and, 260, 310–317
Androgyny, 186
Anticipated interaction distance, 112
Anticonformity, 421
Anxiety, 255–266
Arousal, 43, 279–280, 306–310, 369
AR scale, 320–321
Assimilation effects, 111–112
Attitudes, 182–185, 191–240, 552–565
  adjustive, 221
  cognitive-consistency theories of, 195–218
  compliance-based, 223
  components of, 192–193
  functional theories of, 220–228, 563
  identification-based, 224
  internalization-based, 224–225
  knowledge, 223
  prejudicial, 182–185, 552–565
  value-expressive, 222
Attitudes and behavior, 193–194
Attraction, 24, 25, 245–291
Attribution, 116, 122–135, 173, 183–184, 207–209, 296, 377, 378

Attribution (*continued*)
  of abilities, 125–127
  of motives, 127–129
  self-, 131–133, 173, 207–209, 377
Audience effects, 440–446
Authoritarianism, 59–60
Autocratic leadership, 518–520
Autonomous state, 419–420
Averaging model, 121

Balance theory, 212–217, 265
Behaviorism, 427
Belief incongruence, 268–269
Biased scanning, 206–208
Binocular rivalry, 91
Birth order, 252–253
Bogus pipeline, 42, 555–556
Brainstorming, 466–468
Bullies, 200-pound, 304
Bureaucracy, 485–486
Bystander effects, 331–333

Catharsis, 303–305, 306, 312, 314, 315
Causality, 61
Childhood, 179–181
Classical conditioning, 158–160, 254
  observational, 158–160
Coaction, 344, 440–446
Coding systems, 40, 42–44, 390–395
  Bales', 390–395
  Coss', 42–44
Cognitive clarity, 248
Cognitive consistency, 195–218
Cognitive tuning, 115
Cohesiveness, 48, 468, 469–472, 540–543
  antecedents of, 469–472
  dissonance and, 470–472
  exchange theory and, 469–470
  performance and, 468, 472–476
Common sense, 23–24
Communication, 340–359, 369–371, 390–398, 463–465, 523–525, 578
  cooperation and, 369–371
  flow, in organizations, 523–525

Communication (*continued*)
  influence and, 392–395
  nets, 463–465
  nonverbal, 345–354
Comparison level, 176–177
Competence hierarchies, 146–148
Competition, 9, 344, 360–373, 470, 571–575
Complementarity, 270–273
Completion principle, 270–271
Compliance-based attitudes, 223
Conflict, 8–9, 25, 172, 259–261, 295–319,
    360–373, 535–580
Conformity, 25, 66–69, 399–423, 465–468,
    472–476
  action, 415–420
  anonymity and, 412–413
  cohesiveness and, 472–476
  competence and, 409
  fear and, 66–70
  group performance and, 465–468, 472–576
  nonconformity and, 420–423
  personality and, 409–410
  problem solving and, 472–476
  properties of the group and, 413–414
  properties of the individual and, 409–410
  properties of the task and, 411–413
  sex and, 411–412
  unanimity and, 410–411
Congruity theory, 209–212, 398
Conscience, 168–173
Conservative shift, 454–460
Construct validity, 48
Content validity, 48
Contingency tables, 54–56
Contingency theory, 515–518
Contrast effects, 107–108, 111–112
Cooperation, 8, 309, 344, 359–373, 470, 535–580
  communication and, 369–371
  group atmosphere and, 371
  intergroup, 535–580
  other person and, 364–368
  payoff values and, 368–369
  situational factors and, 368–371
Copying, 145
Correlations, 53–62
Counterattitudinal role playing, 202–207, 563
Credibility, 229–231
Criterion measures, 48

Deception, 80–83
Decision making, individual versus group,
    446–460
Defensive avoidance, 238–240
Deindividuation, 257–261
  anonymity and, 257–259
  diffusion of responsibility and, 259
Delay of gratification, 151–152
Demand characteristics, 72–73

Democratic leadership, 518–520
Deterrence strategies, 572–575
Diffusion of responsibility, 257–258, 458
Disarmament, 571–580
Discounting principle, 129, 513
Discrepancy theory, 504
Discriminatory behavior, 184–186, 556–565
Disinhibition effects, 152
Displacement, 303–305
Display rules, 350–351
Dispositional inferences, 123–125
Dispositional variables, 10–13
Dissonance, 75–78, 195–212, 232–233, 264, 286,
    470–472, 505, 540
  cohesiveness and, 470–472
  forced compliance and, 202–207
  free choice and, 198–201
  self-perception and, 207–208
Distraction and persuasion, 235–236
Division of labor, 247
Door-in-the-face hypothesis, 377–378
Duplication theorem, 273–274
Dyads, 6–8, 245–291, 337–385
  attraction in, 245–291
  cooperation in, 359–373
  interaction in, 337–385

Effect dependence, 400, 401
Ego-defensive attitudes, 221
Emotions, 108–109, 349–351
Empiricism, 38–39
Encounter groups, 425–436
  benefits of, 434–436
  culture of, 427–428
  leadership in, 429–431
  norms of, 428–429
  origins of, 426–427
  risks in, 431–434
Endogamy, 289–290
Environments, 340–345
  sociofugal, 340–342
  sociopetal, 342–344
Equity, 504–506
Escalation ladder, 574–575
ESP, 65
Ethics, 42, 78, 80–83
Ethnic groups, 551–565
Ethology, 297–300
Evaluation apprehension, 444–446
Evoking stimuli, 350–351
Evolution, 297–300, 419–420
Exchange theory, 173–177, 263–264, 265, 269,
    284, 355–356, 359–373, 469–470
Exogamy, 289–290
Expectancies, 91–92, 559–560
Experimental games, 359–373
Experimental method, 63–80
Experimenter bias, 73–74

Exploitative relationships, 546–547
Extinction, 143–144
Extremity shifts, 454–460
Extrinsic rewards, 494–498

Face validity, 47
Facilitation effects, 312–314
Faking, 41
Familiarity, 92–98, 262–264, 561–563
Familiarization theory, 456, 459
Fate control, 176–177
Fear, 66–69, 237–246, 250–256
  affiliation and, 250–256
  anxiety and, 255–256
  attitude change and, 245–246
  conformity and, 66–70
Feedback, 429
Field research, 75–79
Foot-in-the-door hypothesis, 377
Forced compliance, 201–207
Forewarning effects, 235
Frustration, 301–310
  aggression and, 301, 310
  arbitrary versus nonarbitrary, 304–305
Functional theories of attitudes, 220–228, 563
Future Shock, 531–532

Ghettos, 546–547
Graduation speeches, 191–192
Grasshoppers, 232–233
GRIT, 567–579
Group, 4, 6–9, 13–19, 28, 29–31, 64, 337–580
  atmosphere, 370–371
  climate, 518–520
  decisions, 446–460
  dynamics, 14, 29–31, 337–386, 387–435,
    437–477, 486–487, 511–518
  encounter, 425–436
  mind, 28
  norms, 401–407, 428–429
  performance, and problem solving, 437–477,
    518–520
  reference, 405–407
Groupthink, 475–476
Guidance, 157–158
Guilt, 322, 378–380

Hedonic relevance, 130
Helping behavior, 6, 12, 24–25, 319–336,
    457–458, 557
  helper and, 24–25, 320–323
  situation and, 24–25, 328–335
  victim and, 323–328, 557
Hierarchy of needs, 498–500
Hullian learning theory, 141–144, 148
Humanistic psychology, 427
Humanizing jobs, 502–503
Human-relations perspective, 486–487
Hypothetical construct, 48

Ideal type, 99–100
Identification, 185–186, 224
Identification-based attitudes, 224
Implicit theories of personality, 120–121
Impression formation, 116–123
Incentive theory, 202
Independence, 421
Informational social influence, 400–401, 409–411
Information dependence, 400, 401, 409–411
Information-exchange theory, 458–460
Ingratiation, 374–377, 397, 398
Inhibition effects, 151–152
Inoculation theory, 237
Input overload, 334, 525–526
Instincts, 27–28, 297–300
Interaction Process Analysis, 390–395
Intergroup relations, 8–9, 371–372, 535–580
  ethnic groups and, 551–565
  national groups and, 566–580
Internal colonialism, 546–547
Internalization-based attitudes, 224–225
International relations, 567–580
Interpersonal attraction, 24, 25, 245–291
Interpersonal influence, 373–385
Interpersonal simulations, 208
Interracial-contact hypothesis, 24,
    561–563
Intervention model, 530
Intrinsic rewards, 498–503
Intrusion, 43, 63, 342, 343
Invasion of privacy, 80–81

Job expansion, 502–503
Joint gain, 361–362, 538
Just-world hypothesis, 325, 379

Kinesic communication, 347–351
Knowledge-based attitudes, 223

Laboratory-training groups, 425–436
Laissez-faire leadership, 518–520
Leadership, 29, 390–395, 428–431, 508–520
  behavioral dimensions of, 515
  climates, 29, 518–520
  contingency model of, 515–518
  encounter group, 429–431
  participative, 518–520
  performance and, 511–518
  satisfaction and, 511–518
  socioemotional, 393–395, 511
  task, 393–395, 511
Liking, 24, 94–98, 109–111, 214–217, 261–275,
    561–563
  complementarity and, 270–273
  contact and, 24, 94–98, 109–111, 264, 561–563
  similarity and, 214–217, 262–264, 268–269
Linking pins, 523–525
Love, 275–291
Love scale, 276–278

Machiavellianism, 380–382
Managerial systems, 489–491
Markers, 341–342
Matched-dependent behavior, 144–145
Maximization dynamic, 491
Maximizing Difference Game, 361–373
Mere exposure, 94–98, 109–111, 263, 561–563
Mere presence, 444–446
Methods, 37–84
    correlational, 53–62
    experimental, 63–79
    field, 75–79
    laboratory, 63–74
Microcultures, 401–402
Midrange theories, 51
Minority influence, 421–423
Mirror-image phenomenon, 569–571
Modeling, 25–26, 139–140, 149–158, 260–261,
        310–317, 329–330, 371, 430, 440
    aggression and, 260, 310–317
    deindividuation and, 260–261
    helping behavior and, 329–330
    live and symbolic, 149–150
    process of, 149–158
Models of organizational change, 529–530
Motivation, 98, 103, 492–506
    extrinsic and intrinsic, 495–503
    perception and, 98–103
    social comparison and, 503–506

Need achievement, 364
Need hierarchy, 498–500
Negative-state relief hypothesis, 380
Negativity in evaluations, 117–118
Nets, 463–465
Nonarbitrary frustrations, 304–305
Nonconformity, 420–423
Nonreactive measures, 75
Nonverbal communication, 234, 345–354, 369
    kinesic, 349–351
    paralinguistic, 351–353
    proxemic, 348–349
Normative social influence, 400, 401, 409–411
Norms, 327, 365, 401–407, 428–429, 552–554
No-trial learning, 153
NOW, 184

Obedience, 415–420
    antecedents of, 416–419
    evolution and, 419–420
Obesity, 54
Observation, 38–51
    qualities of good, 46–49
    scientific, 38–39
    theory and, 49–51
Observational learning, 140–161, 178–186,
        310–317
One-sided presentations, 237
Open-systems theory, 487–491, 521–532

Optimal arousal, 248
Order of presentation, 234
Organizations, 14–16, 18–19, 29, 478–533
    adaptation and change, 521–532
    communication within, 523–525
    conflict within, 522–525
    development of, 490–491
    motivation in, 492–496
    perspectives on, 484–491
Own gain, 361–362, 538
Own-group bias, 543–544, 547–550, 569–571

Paralinguistic communication, 347, 351–353
Parental Interference Scale, 286
Participative decision making, 518–520
Passion, 278–280
Peer groups, 287
Perception, 85–135
    accuracy, 103–106
    expectancy and, 91–92
    motivation and, 98–103
    perceiver variables and, 89–107
    person, 87–89, 102–135
    selective, 99
    situational variables and, 107–116
    social, 87–135
    target and, 123–135
    thing versus person, 88–89
Perceptual accentuation, 100–102
Perceptual defense, 102–103
Personalism, 130
Personality, 5–6, 11, 120–121, 320–321, 362–364,
        409–410
    conformity and, 409–410
    helping behavior and, 12, 321–322
    implicit theories of, 120–121
Personal space, 340–345
Persuasive communications, 228–240
Physical attractiveness, 280–282
Planned-change model, 530
Playing hard to get, 282–283
PONS, 354
Postdecisional dissonance, 198–201
Prediction, 21, 24–26, 53–62
Prejudice, 182–185, 268–269, 287–289, 552–565
    dimensions of, 553–554
    discrimination and, 556–560
    reduction of, 560–565
    stereotypes and, 554–555
Primacy effects, 234
Primary relationships, 18
Prisoner's Dilemma Game, 360–373
Propinquity, 262–264
Psychoanalysis, 427

Race relations, 182–185, 268–269, 549–565
Reactance, 286, 383–385, 511
Recency effects, 234
Reciprocity, 264–265, 327–328

Reference groups, 405–407
Reinforcement, 141–148, 154–157, 162–177,
    314–315
  aggression and, 314–315
  interaction and, 173–177
  performance and, 154–156
Relative gain, 361–362, 538
Releasers, 298
Reliability, 46–47, 277–278
Replication, 49
Research-development-and-diffusion model, 529
Response-facilitation effects, 150
Response sets, 41
Reverse discrimination, 558
Risk-taking, 452–460
Risky shift, 452–460
Roles, 16–18, 178–186, 273, 483
Romeo and Juliet effect, 285–286

Same behavior, 144
Scanlon plan, 497–498
Science, 20–26, 38
Scientific management, 484–485
Secondary relationships, 18
Selective perception, 99
Self-control, 168–173
Self-disclosure, 7, 356–357, 374–375, 428
Self-fulfilling prophecy, 559–560
Self-perception, 131–133, 173, 207–209, 377, 497
Self-report measures, 40–43
Sensitivity groups, 425–436
Sensitivity to individual differences, 104–105
Sensitivity to the generalized other, 104
Sensory deprivation, 247
Sex, 101, 178–186, 278–280, 411–412
Shaping, 148
Signal conformity, 415
Similarity and liking, 214–217, 262–264,
    268–269
Simple sovereign theories, 51
Situational variables, 10–13
Sleeper effects, 231
Snake phobia, 133-134, 139-140
Social-comparison theory, 248–250, 252,
    254–255, 269, 503–506
Social control, 169
Social desirability, 41
Social differentiation, 390–395
Social distance, 340–344, 348
Social facilitation, 50, 439, 440–446
  evaluation apprehension and, 444–446
  mere presence and, 444–446
Social-interaction-and-diffusion model, 529–530
Social learning, 139–186, 260–261, 310–317,
    329–330, 371, 430, 440
Social motives, 361–362, 538
Social norms, 327, 365, 401–407, 428–429,
    552–554
Social penetration, 354–358

Social perception, 84–135
Social psychology, 1–581
  core concerns, 4–9
  definition, 3
  field of, 1–32
  history of, 26–31
  methods of, 37–84
  science and, 20–26
  scope of, 3–4
Social reinforcement, 141–148, 154–157, 162–177,
    314–315
Socioemotional activity, 391, 513–516
Socioemotional leadership, 393–395
Sociofugal space, 340–342
Sociopetal space, 340, 342–344
Sororities, 288
Source characteristics, 229–233
Statisticized groups, 447–449
Status, 396–398, 502
Stereotypes, 179, 554–556
Stingy shift, 457–458
Study of values, 99
Styx, river, 131
Subsystems, 489–491
Summation model, 121–122
Superordinate goals, 544, 550
Systems theory, 487–491, 521–532

Task activity, 391, 513–516
Task leader, 393–395
Territorial defense, 341
T-groups, 425–436
Theory, 49–52
Theory X, 499–500
Theory Y, 499–500
Threat, 366–368, 571–575
Traits, 11–13, 119–120
Trucking Game, 366–368
Two-sided presentations, 237

Unilateral disarmament, 575–580
Urban life, 333–335

Validity, 48, 277–278, 371–372
Value-expressive attitudes, 222
Value theory, 456–458, 460
Variables, 63, 67, 70
Verbal conditioning, 162–168
Veridicality, 89–90

War, 538–542, 567–580
Warm-glow hypothesis, 323
Weapons, effects of, 307–308
Women's Lib, 179, 184
Work modules, 502–503

XYY genotype, 300–301

Yo-yos, 201